Annotated Teacher's Edition

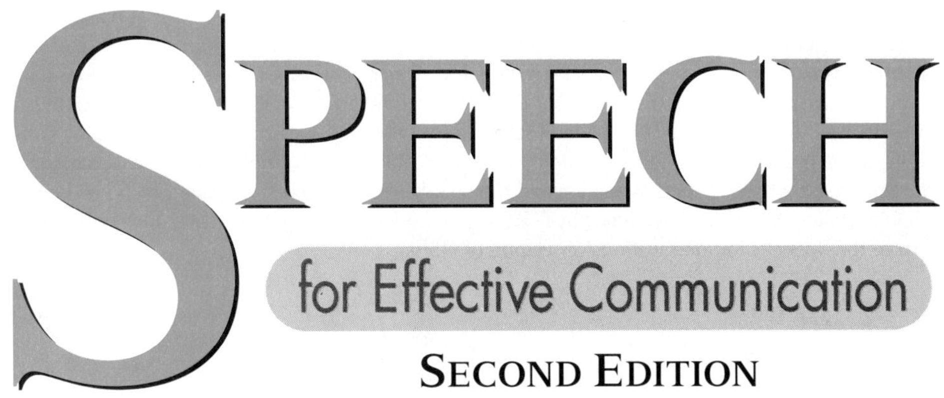

SECOND EDITION

Rudolph F. Verderber

HOLT, RINEHART AND WINSTON
Austin • New York • Orlando • Chicago • Atlanta • San Francisco • Boston • Dallas • Toronto • London

ABOUT THE AUTHOR

Rudolph F. Verderber (Ph.D. University of Missouri) is a Professor and former Head of the Department of Communication at the University of Cincinnati. During his career he has taught speech courses at both the college and high school levels. In addition, he consults with high school teachers and gives workshops for teachers and private organizations. He has served as parliamentarian for state and regional meetings of several national organizations and as Director of Forensics at the University of Cincinnati. He also has experience acting in theater productions. His publications include numerous articles; a manual on debate for high school and college courses; and three best-selling college texts covering public speaking, interpersonal communication, and general speech communication skills. Professor Verderber is a member of the Speech Communication Association and the Central States Speech Association and is the recipient of the prestigious Dolly Cohen Award for Excellence in Teaching at the University of Cincinnati and the Distinguished Service Award from the Speech Communication Association of Ohio.

CRITICAL READERS

Grateful acknowledgement is made to the following critical readers who have reviewed pre-publication materials for this book.

Suzanne Byrom
Barboursville High School
Barboursville, West Virginia

Willie Mae Crews
Brimingham Public Schools
Birmingham, Alabama

Gretchen Polnac
Reagan High School
Austin, Texas

Debarah K. Shoultz
Columbus North High School
Columbus, Indiana

Alease Sims
Jefferson County School District
Birmingham, Alabama

John R. Williamson
Johnson Central High School
Paintsville, Kentucky

PHOTO CREDITS Abbreviations used: (t) top, (c) center, (b) bottom, (l) left, (r) right, (bkgrd) background, (frgrd) foreground.

ATE TABLE OF CONTENTS: Page T4(r), Bob Daemmrich/Image Works; T5(t), Steve Satushek/The Image Bank; T5(l), David Young-Wolff/PhotoEdit; T5(r) Steve Dunwell/Image Bank; T6(t), James Sugar/Black Star; T6(b), HRW Photo by Michelle Bridwell; T7(r), David Young-Wolff/PhotoEdit; T8(t), HRW Photo by Michelle Bridwell; T8(b), Comstock; T9(t), Jeffrey Sylvester/FPG International; T10(t), David R. Frazier Photolibrary; T10(b), David Young-Wolff/PhotoEdit; T11(b), Ellis Herwig/Picture Cube; T12(t), HRW Photo by Eric Beggs; T12(b), Robert Daemmrich/Stock Boston; T13(r), HRW Photo by Michelle Bridwell; T14(l), HRW Photo by Russell Dian; T14(r), Bob Daemmrich/Stock Boston; T15(t), Mike Wilson/FPG International; T15(b), Comstock; T16(r), Rick Freedman/Black Star; T17(l) FPG International; T17(r), mga/Photri; T19(t), Garry Gay/The Image Bank; T20(r), HRW Photo by Michelle Bridwell; T20(b), Paul Light/Lightwave; T21, Candace Cochrane/Positive Images; T22, HRW Photo by Matt Meadows; T24, HRW Photo by John Langford; T30(tl), HRW Photo by Lisa Davis; T30(b), FPG International; T31(c), Tony Freeman/PhotoEdit; T31(inset), HRW Photo by Michelle Bridwell.

ILLUSTRATION CREDITS Jane Thurmond: T4, T7, T8, T9, T11, T12, T14, T15, T16, T18, T19, T20, T30, and T31.

Printed in the United States of America

ISBN 0-03-097526-3

2 3 4 5 6 7 8 9 071 98 97 96 95 94

CONTENTS IN BRIEF

CONTENTS

UNIT 1: The Communication Process

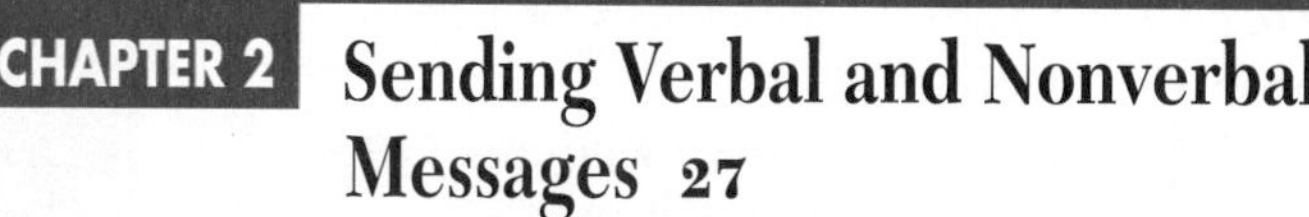

ISU

CHAPTER 4 Listening and Evaluating 81

UNIT 2: Interpersonal Relationships

CHAPTER 5 Analyzing Yourself as a Communicator 109

CHAPTER 6 Communicating Person to Person 139

CHAPTER 7 Speaking Informally 159

CHAPTER 8 Interviewing 187

UNIT 3: Public Speaking

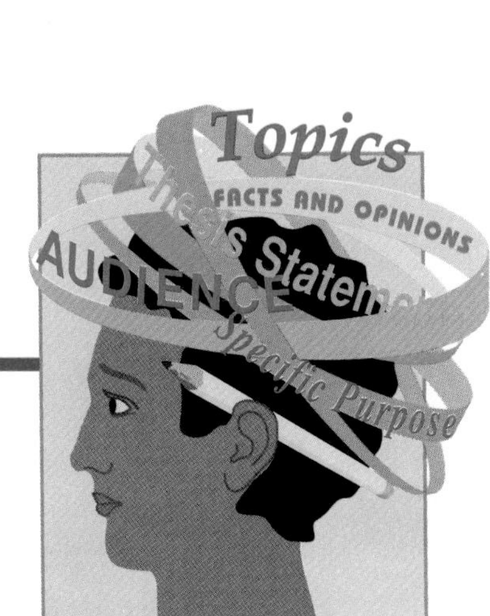

CHAPTER 9 Getting Ready 215

CHAPTER 10 Gathering Information 241

UNIT 4: Speaking for a Purpose

CHAPTER 16 Speaking for a Special Occasion 417

UNIT 5: Democratic Processes

CHAPTER 17 Group Discussion 449

UNIT 6: Performing Arts

CHAPTER 20 Oral Interpretation 553

CHAPTER 21 Theater 589

CHAPTER 22 Radio and Television 629

Appendix of Speeches

A Letter to the Teacher from the Author

by Rudy Verderber

Professor of Communication, University of Cincinnati

The goal of this second edition of *Speech for Effective Communication* is to provide a clear explanation of speech principles in a manner that enables the student to understand and apply them. To accomplish this goal, we have prepared a book that enables you to address the needs of your students regardless of their interests, abilities, or grade levels and to provide adequate content coverage no matter which aspects of speech you wish to highlight.

PUPIL'S EDITION

For those of you using this textbook for the first time, let me explain the rationale for the sequence of ideas addressed in the text.

Unit 1 The Communication Process provides students with a general introduction to the basic concepts used in discussing communication. Chapter 1 explains the interrelated elements of the communication process. Chapter 2 analyzes the role of both verbal and nonverbal messages in effective communication. Chapter 3 explains how the voice is produced and suggests ways to improve vocal production. Chapter 4 covers effective listening skills, critical-listening skills, and strategies for evaluating speeches.

Unit 2 Interpersonal Relationships focuses on communication skills and strategies at various levels of personal and social interaction. Chapter 5 helps students concentrate on assessing their own strengths and weaknesses as communicators and provides techniques to improve effectiveness in communicating. Chapter 6 analyzes the growth and development of a variety of types of personal and social relationships. Chapter 7 discusses practical communication skills (such as making announcements or making and receiving business and social telephone calls) and social communication skills (such as making social introductions or using good conversational skills). Chapter 8 examines interviewing, both for those who are being interviewed (such as for a job or college) and for those who are conducting an interview.

Unit 3 Public Speaking provides students with specific skills and strategies that apply to the planning, preparation, rehearsal, and presentation stages of any type of speech. Chapter 9 gives step-by-step information to help students think of ideas for speech topics, limit a topic to a manageable size, identify the general and the specific purposes for the speech, write a thesis statement, and identify the types of supporting information needed to support the thesis. Chapter 10 provides a guide for using a variety of resource materials to find supporting information for a speech. Chapter 11 helps students to prepare their speeches by providing suggestions for writing introductions, outlines, and conclusions and then by helping students to prepare speech notes for rehearsing and polishing their speeches. Chapter 12 explains and illustrates effective language choices. Chapter 13 helps students as they actually present their speeches. It gives suggestions for handling stage fright, maintaining eye contact, using nonverbal communication, developing appropriate timing, and responding to audience feedback and unexpected events during a speech. The chapter also contains useful tips for student speakers about practicing speaking skills and using audiovisual materials, lecterns, and microphones.

Unit 4 **Speaking for a Purpose** gives practical suggestions that help students to plan, to prepare, and to present speeches for a variety of purposes in a variety of speaking situations. Chapter 14 gives specific suggestions that students can apply when they are preparing an informative speech. Chapter 15 provides a guide to planning and preparing a persuasive speech. Chapter 16 gives specific suggestions that help students prepare speeches for special occasions.

Unit 5 **Democratic Processes** introduces and explains types of speaking situations that are important to the free exchange of ideas that contribute to a strong democracy. Chapter 17 presents suggestions and guidelines for effective group discussions. Chapter 18 provides a general introduction to debate formats and techniques used in formal argumentation. Chapter 19 furnishes a guide to principles of parliamentary procedure.

Unit 6 **Performing Arts** provides information about skills and techniques for speaking in performance situations. Chapter 20 explains the techniques needed in oral interpretation of literary works. Chapter 21 provides information on many different types of stagecraft, including acting skills for formal as well as informal productions. Chapter 22 provides up-to-date information about techniques and terminology used in the broadcast media and gives step-by-step information to help students produce several types of media productions.

Pedagogical Features

Many of you who are familiar with the first edition of this textbook have expressed your appreciation of a number of pedagogically important features such as objectives, emphasis of key terms, activities, profiles in communication, end-of-chapter summaries, and real-life speaking situations. In addition, you will find several new features that we believe make this textbook unique.

Graphic Displays

This edition contains numerous charts, diagrams, and graphics that make concepts more accessible to students with a diversity of learning styles and ability levels.

Specific Examples

Instructional material in this edition is frequently accompanied by clearly labeled specific examples that the student can readily understand and relate to.

Writing Style

This edition features a student-friendly writing style that enables students to quickly identify key ideas, to understand and master the skills and strategies required in communicating effectively, and to evaluate their own as well as other students' performance in common speaking situations.

TEACHER'S EDITION

The *Annotated Teacher's Edition* is designed to provide valuable suggestions and ideas that you may want to include in your daily lesson plans. We are aware that the words *overworked teacher* are redundant, particularly in describing teachers of speech classes. With the variety of preparations necessary during the day, all of us need all the timesavers we can find.

How the Teacher's Edition Helps

This teacher's edition provides you with a wide variety of teaching materials and a variety of teaching methods that you can use or adapt to fit your own and your students' particular needs in the speech classroom. The teacher's edition contains top-margin and side-column features that will help you to

- develop your overall lesson plan
- develop teaching methods that meet individual needs of students
- develop cooperative learning
- stimulate critical thinking
- integrate the language arts
- make connections to situations and events outside the classroom

Even teachers with a secret stash of materials accumulated through the years may yearn for new ideas that they can put to use in their classrooms. In this *Annotated Teacher's Edition,* you are likely to find a new, stimulating idea for nearly every lesson that you plan.

Teacher to Teacher

by Marilyn Swinton

Dr. Swinton is a teacher educator at Southwest Texas State University. She has served as President of the Texas Speech Communication Association.

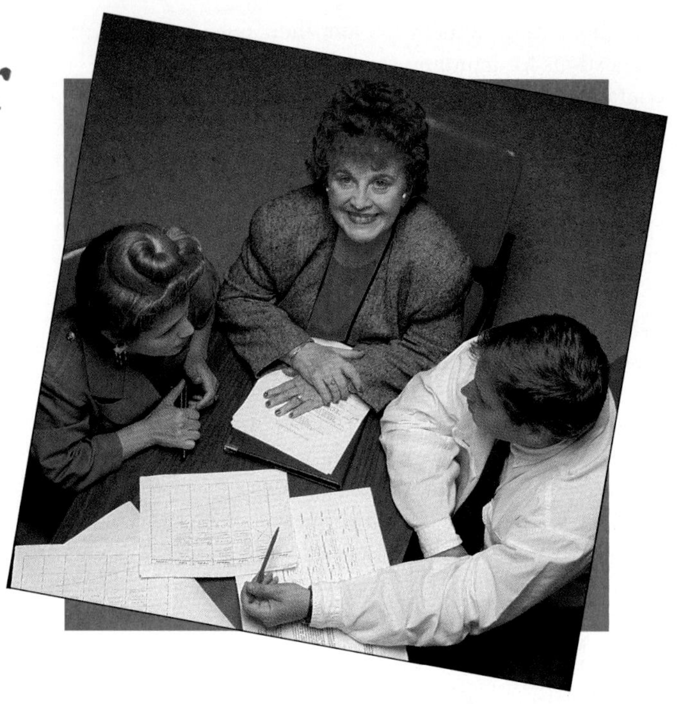

Teaching communication skills is always a challenge—and a privilege! Helping students learn the techniques, concepts, and rewards of effective speaking is especially fulfilling to those of us who have selected speech communication education as a career. As enablers who help our students to practice the interactive process of communication and to discover strategies they need to succeed in our fast-paced society, we try to encourage, instruct, and effect desirable changes in each student's behavior, attitude, and understanding. By teaching our students to become more successful communicators, we help them develop more positive self-concepts and reach their highest goals.

SELF-CONCEPT DEVELOPMENT

Self-concept development is crucial for our students. An impressive body of research now supports what we teachers have long known: Students learn better when they aren't crippled by the limitations of negative self-concepts. And as teachers have also long known, the role of the classroom teacher is a very important factor in the formation and modification of a young person's self-concept.

In our daily contact with students, we are in a strategic position to have an impact on the students' pictures of themselves. Students' perception of the teacher's feeling toward them correlates both positively and significantly with self-perception. Research has found that the more positive a student's perception of the teacher's feelings, the better the student is able to achieve.

Speech communication helps students in many ways:

1. It is a discipline that requires students to be active participants in class, in contrast to other classes that relegate to students only the passive roles of silent note-takers and multiple-choice test-takers.
2. It forces students to overcome anxiety about speaking in front of a group and thereby to gain a sense of accomplishment and of control by conquering their fears.
3. It teaches students that there is a discrete set of skills and strategies that can be learned and practiced that will improve their abilities to communicate in a wide variety of situations.

Communication skills are the key factors in helping to develop positive self-concepts in our students. When we share with them our knowledge of speech content matter and the application of this knowledge in across-the-curriculum activities, we offer students the necessary tools with which to succeed in the complex world, a world built on relationships that start with ourselves and reach out to a multitude of others.

COMMUNICATING AND RELATING

Although much educational emphasis has always been placed on the traditional three R's of "reading, 'riting, and 'rithmetic," we speech communication educators on all levels know the importance of instructing our students in the fourth basic skill: relating.

In our diverse, divisive, and divergent society, all of us must constantly relate to ourselves and to others as we share information, opinions, and feelings in many contexts:

1. **Intrapersonal:** our relationship to ourselves. Analyzing our self-esteem and confidence level is important to the way we see ourselves as communicators.
2. **Dyadic:** our relationships to significant others on a one-on-one level. Many psychologists see these relationships as the glue that holds society together.
3. **Interpersonal:** our relating to others on a social level. Speaking and listening skills are crucial to our personal interactions with others.
4. **Small group interactions:** our relationships to others in a task-centered environment. The ability to think critically and participate in decision making often has a direct effect on success in the workplace.
5. **Public relations:** our relationship to others in one-to-many situations. In real-life situations, many opportunities occur that require an individual speaker to present valuable information, persuasive arguments, and entertaining ideas to a large group of listeners.

As speech communication teachers, we are able to help our students develop these relational skills. Success will help students to see speech communication from a personal and practical perspective.

As young adults, our students also need effective speech communication skills to enable them to participate as citizens of a free and democratic society. They will face making ethical decisions that require communication competence; the ability to make such decisions will help students to prosper in this increasingly complex world. As their instructors, we affect the future of our students and our country as their generation assumes leadership roles.

POSITIVE CLASSROOM CLIMATE

An important factor in achieving these goals is the creation of a positive classroom climate in which all students feel respected for the unique individuals they are and feel that their contributions are valued and accepted. The daily give-and-take between students and teacher and between individual students is not only an example but also a reinforcement of the skills taught in the speech communication course. Therefore, as students communicate, a positive, supportive atmosphere will encourage them to learn.

As you guide your students in learning effective speech communication skills, this *Annotated Teacher's Edition* will provide you with conceptual tools and helpful suggestions to assist you in your instructional planning and presentations.

The *Annotated Teacher's Edition* provides point-of-use information that will assist you in a variety of ways:

1. Teaching notes offer comments and suggestions on the value of specific units to your students.
2. Clearly identified objectives focus on what the students should know and what they should be able to do at the end of the each unit.
3. Instructional strategies offer suggestions on how to use the chapter activities, skill sheets, audiotapes, transparencies, and other materials to engage student interest in chapter content, to develop and extend the material, and to evaluate students' mastery of the objectives in the unit.
4. Suggestions and materials for evaluation help you assess whether students have achieved the desired competencies and outcomes in the stated objectives.
5. Evaluations of exercises and activities and portfolio assessment help students assess their own levels of accomplishment and encourage continuous improvement.

With these materials and with your contribution, you can make your speech communication class the most important course your students will ever take.

About the Program

Speech for Effective Communication is a comprehensive communication program covering all aspects of the speech curriculum. A wealth of activities and features keeps students focused on real-life situations that demand effective communication. *Speech for Effective Communication* gives students the skills they need for communicating in daily life, including strategies used for public speaking, group discussion, debate, parliamentary procedure, and the performing arts. The program offers a "how-to" approach that helps build students' self-confidence while strengthening students' abilities to communicate in a variety of situations.

The Pupil's Edition

ORGANIZATION

The textbook is divided into six units that contain a total of twenty-two chapters:

Unit 1 The Communication Process
Unit 2 Interpersonal Relationships
Unit 3 Public Speaking
Unit 4 Speaking for a Purpose
Unit 5 Democratic Processes
Unit 6 Performing Arts

Each chapter of *Speech for Effective Communication* provides a number of special features designed to aid the student in mastering the concepts presented:

Objectives. The main skills that students are to master are clearly listed at the beginning of each chapter.

How to. Each chapter contains "How to" features that present concise applications to practical situations of the basic concepts presented in the chapter.

Illustrations. Charts, diagrams, photographs, and other visual materials are used extensively in each chapter to help clarify terms, concepts, and skills.

Examples. Throughout each lesson, numerous models and examples demonstrate both correct and faulty applications of the skills and concepts being presented.

Activities. Every main section of each chapter contains at least one activity that gives students a hands-on opportunity to apply the concepts they have learned. Additional activities that emphasize key skills are provided within some lessons and at the end of every chapter.

Communication Journal. Every chapter contains at least one activity feature that suggests a specific entry for students' communication journals. These features encourage students to note brainstorming ideas, to explore their feelings about particular issues, and to record their insights and analyses so that students will be able to use the entries as a personal resource during the speech course.

Guidelines. Each chapter contains helpful, concise evaluation guidelines to help students measure their own effectiveness and the effectiveness of others in all aspects of speaking.

Profiles in Communication. To help students recognize how communication skills play a vital part in everyday life, each chapter includes a full-page feature about a person whose work requires the communication skills covered in that chapter. An activity is provided so that students may practice related skills.

End-of-Chapter Questions. Review and discussion questions that can be used to check understanding are provided.

Real-Life Speaking Situations. On the last page of every chapter, a pair of activities is provided to give students practice in using communication skills in a real-world personal situation as well as in an occupational context.

Model Speeches. Thirteen complete speeches furnish examples for students of a variety of types of speeches.

Glossary. All of the vocabulary words covered in the chapters are listed alphabetically and defined.

Index. To help students locate information quickly, a complete index is provided.

The Annotated Teacher's Edition

CONTENTS

The *Annotated Teacher's Edition* (ATE) of *Speech for Effective Communication* includes all of the Pupil's Edition pages, slightly reduced in size to create top and side margins. The *Annotated Teacher's Edition* is organized into three parts—Chapter Opening, Teaching Text, and Side-Column Features. In addition, the models in the **Appendix of Speeches** are annotated.

CHAPTER PLANNING

The Chapter Opening pages contain a complete listing of all materials in the *Teacher's Resource Binder* and the *Audiovisual Resource Binder* for each chapter. These materials are also identified at their point of use in the chapter. A Bibliography of Additional Materials provides a listing of Professional Readings and Audiovisual Materials. Chapter Overview and Introducing the Chapter features help set the stage for teaching the chapter.

LESSON DEVELOPMENT

The *Annotated Teacher's Edition* separates essential lesson material from the optional suggestions for reinforcement.

Lesson Organization

The *Annotated Teacher's Edition* divides each chapter into two or three segments that may be taught as individual lessons or adapted for use by the teacher as he or she sees fit. The core steps of the lesson are placed at the top of the *Annotated Teacher's Edition* page above the reduced student's page as follows: Objectives, Motivation, Teaching the Lesson, Assessment, Reteaching, Extension, Enrichment, Closure.

Side-Column Features

Additional features in the side columns of the *Annotated Teacher's Edition* suggest ways in which teachers can vary each lesson to meet the needs of students whose ability levels and learning styles may vary greatly.

Meeting Individual Needs helps students with special needs, students with different learning styles, students with limited English proficiency, and less prepared students who may need extra help. Suggestions for challenging gifted students are also provided.

Cooperative Learning suggests opportunities for students to work together to solve problems or to complete tasks.

Critical Thinking provides an opportunity for students to apply higher-level thinking skills to concepts presented in the Pupil's Edition.

Integrating the Language Arts provides strategies for connecting reading, writing, listening, and other language-arts skills to speech.

Making Connections provides strategies to relate speech to other aspects of the curriculum and to situations and events outside the classroom.

Common Error describes a problem that students commonly encounter and offers a solution to that problem.

Writing to Learn encourages students to use the writing process to clarify, explore, and identify ideas.

Additional Activity provides high-interest supplemental activities.

Teaching Note gives the teacher additional information related to the lesson.

Building a Portfolio gives suggestions for material that may be appropriate for students' portfolios.

Answers or Guidelines for questions or activities in the Pupil's Edition complete the list of helpful side-column features.

SPEECH ANNOTATIONS

Each speech in the **Appendix of Speeches** is annotated to aid the teacher in explaining the structure of the various types of speeches.

Teacher's Support Materials

TEACHER'S RESOURCE BINDER

The *Teacher's Resource Binder* is organized by chapters with numbered tabs for each chapter.

Each chapter contains several Skills for Success worksheets, a Vocabulary practice sheet, and a Chapter Test/Answer Key. The contents of each chapter in the *Teacher's Resource Binder* is listed in the *Annotated Teacher's Edition* at the beginning of each chapter and at each item's point of use in the chapter.

In addition, the *Teacher's Resource Binder* contains five additional tabbed sections with supplemental materials as follows:

Portfolio Assessment
Theater
Oral Interpretation
Competition
Debate

VIDEOTAPE WITH TEACHING NOTES

Speaking Out: Evaluating Speeches and Oral Interpretation contains student performances of three model speeches and one oral interpretation. Each presentation is followed by a point-by-point evaluation. The speeches represent the three types that are discussed in the textbook: Informative, Persuasive, and Special Occasion. The oral interpretation is of a poem.

AUDIOVISUAL RESOURCE BINDER

The *Audiovisual Resource Binder* has two components: Audiotapes with Teaching Notes and Instructional Transparencies with Worksheets and Teaching Notes. Materials from the *Audiovisual Resource Binder* are identified at the beginning of each chapter in the *Annotated Teacher's Edition* and are identified again at their point of use in that chapter.

Instructional Transparencies

At least one transparency is provided for each chapter in the textbook. Each transparency is followed by a worksheet and teaching notes for that transparency.

Audiocassettes with Teaching Notes

Audiotape 1 contains ten audio lessons keyed to lessons in the textbook. The audio lessons have been designed to clarify portions of the material in the textbook by permitting students to hear actual spoken models and examples. Nine model oral-interpretation selections are also included on this cassette.

Audiotape 2 contains recordings of the thirteen model speeches that are printed in the **Appendix of Speeches** in the textbook.

Chart of Alternative Courses of Study

To help you in planning how you will use *Speech for Effective Communication* in your course, the following chart displays optional plans for a 36-week course and for three different 18-week courses. While you may choose to follow any of these plans, you will probably want to tailor your coverage of the text to suit the special needs and requirements of your particular course. The chapters in *Speech for Effective Communication* have been carefully designed to be interrelated, yet independent, to give you a full range of speech communication topics from which to formulate your students' course of study.

			36-WEEK COURSE	18-WEEK COURSE A	18-WEEK COURSE B	18-WEEK COURSE C
UNIT 1	1	Understanding Communication	1	1	1	1
	2	Sending Verbal and Nonverbal Messages	2	2	1	1
	3	Using Your Voice	1	1/2	0	0
	4	Listening and Evaluating	2	1/2	2	1
UNIT 2	5	Analyzing Yourself as a Communicator	1	1/2	1/2	1/2
	6	Communicating Person to Person	1	1/2	1/2	1/2
	7	Speaking Informally	1	1/2	1/2	0
	8	Interviewing	1	1/2	1/2	0
UNIT 3	9	Getting Ready	1	1	1/2	1/2
	10	Gathering Information	2	1	1/2	1/2
	11	Preparing Your Speech	2	1	1	1
	12	Using Effective Language	1	*Refer back to study of Chapter 2*		
	13	Presenting Your Speech	2	2	1	1
UNIT 4	14	Speaking to Inform	2	2	2	1
	15	Speaking to Persuade	2	2	2	2
	16	Speaking for a Special Occasion	2	2	2	1
UNIT 5	17	Group Discussion	2	1	1 1/2	2
	18	Debate	2	0	0	1
	19	Parliamentary Procedure	2	0	1 1/2	1
UNIT 6	20	Oral Interpretation	2	0	0	1
	21	Theater	2	0	0	1
	22	Radio and Television	2	0	0	1

The suggestions above offer four different long-range plans for covering the material in *Speech for Effective Communication.* The number in each box gives the number of weeks spent on each lesson.

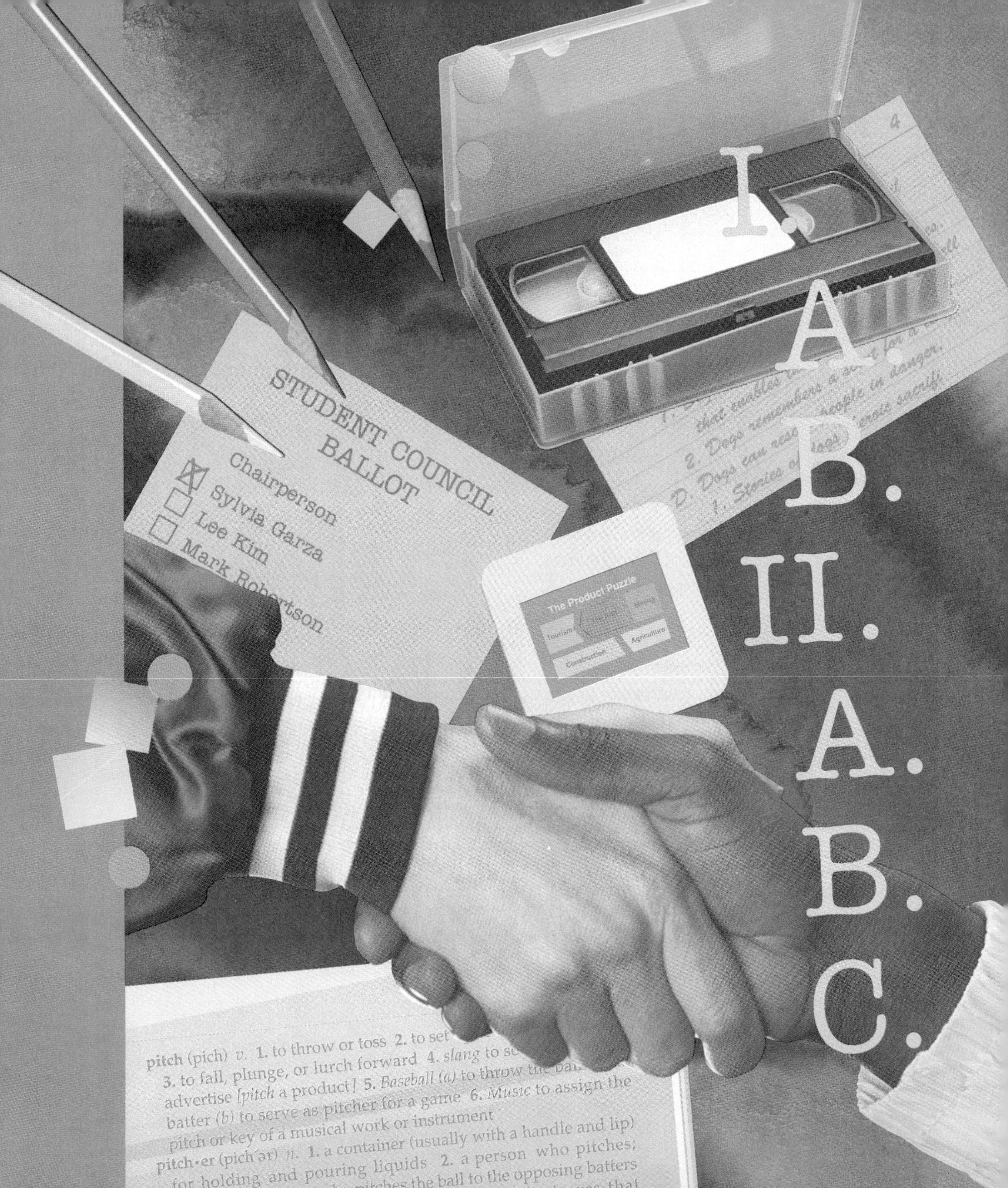
STUDENT COUNCIL
BALLOT
Chairperson
Sylvia Garza
Lee Kim
Mark Robertson
2. Dogs remember
D. Dogs can
1. Stories of dogs
The Product Puzzle
Tourism
The Arts
Mining
Agriculture
Construction
I.
A.
B.
II.
A.
B.
C.
pitch (pich) v. 1. to throw or toss 2. to set
3. to fall, plunge, or lurch forward 4. slang to
advertise [pitch a product] 5. Baseball (a) to throw the
batter (b) to serve as pitcher for a game 6. Music to assign the
pitch or key of a musical work or instrument
pitch·er (pich′ər) n. 1. a container (usually with a handle and lip)
for holding and pouring liquids 2. a person who pitches;
who pitches the ball to the opposing batters

Destinations
Pacific Rim
North America
Europe
Australia
2. Dogs will show where the noise is
coming from.
B. Dogs will intervene when their masters
are attacked.
STOP/EJECT
PLAY
RECORD
Social Security Number
Name
Address
Planning a Budget
Band
Hall Rental
Invitations
Food
A. Food
B. Shelter
C. Water
D. Clothing
B. Safety
MONDAY
TUESDAY
WEDNESDAY
Martin Luther King, Jr. Day
8:00
8:15
8:30
8:45
9:00
Interview—

SPEECH for Effective Communication

SECOND EDITION

Rudolph F. Verderber

HOLT, RINEHART AND WINSTON
Austin • New York • Orlando • Chicago • Atlanta • San Francisco • Boston • Dallas • Toronto • London

Rudolph F. Verderber (Ph.D. University of Missouri) is a professor and former Head of the Department of Communication at the University of Cincinnati. During his career he has taught speech courses at both the college and high school levels. In addition, he consults with high school teachers and gives workshops for teachers and private organizations. He has served as parliamentarian for state and regional meetings of several national organizations and as Director of Forensics at the University of Cincinnati. He also has experience acting in theater productions. His publications include numerous articles; a manual on debate for high school and college courses; and three best-selling college texts covering public speaking, interpersonal communication, and general speech communication skills. Professor Verderber is a member of the Speech Communication Association and the Central States Speech Association and is the recipient of the prestigious Dolly Cohen Award for Excellence in Teaching at the University of Cincinnati and the Distinguished Service Award from the Speech Communication Association of Ohio.

CRITICAL READERS

Grateful acknowledgment is made to the following critical readers who have reviewed pre-publication materials for this book:

Suzanne H. Byrom
Barboursville High School
Barboursville, West Virginia

Pamela Cockcroft
Paris High School
Paris, Illinois

Willie Mae Crews
Birmingham Public Schools
Birmingham, Alabama

Kathleen L. Kinney
West High School
Salt Lake City, Utah

Sandra B. Linn
Huntington East High School
Huntington, West Virginia

Gretchen Polnac
Reagan High School
Austin, Texas

Susan Pundzak
North High School
Des Moines, Iowa

Debarah K. Shoultz
Columbus North High School
Columbus, Indiana

Alease Sims
Jefferson County School District
Birmingham, Alabama

Nancy Sprowls
Brunswick High School
Brunswick, Ohio

Craig R. Streff
Wauwatosa East High School
Wauwatosa, Wisconsin

Acknowledgments: See pages 710–712, which are an extension of the copyright page.

Printed in the United States of America

ISBN 0–03–097525–5

3 4 5 6 069 98 97 96 95 94

FOR YOUR STUDENTS: A LETTER FROM THE AUTHOR

Over the years that I have been teaching speech communication, I have thought not only about how people become better speakers but also why people might want or need to improve their speech skills. I have come up with at least four reasons: to become better citizens, to become more successful, to protect themselves, and to have more fun.

To become better citizens, people who live in a democracy have a responsibility to participate in their government. This means discussing issues with other people, listening to speeches and debates, stating opinions, and taking stands on issues. Studying and practicing speech communication skills help citizens to fulfill these responsibilities and to take an active role in the democratic process.

Personal success is just as important as good citizenship. Being able to communicate well gives people control over their own lives. At times, you may have wondered what to say or do to make friends, to get a job, or to let your parents and teachers know how you feel. By studying speech, you can learn how to talk to people more easily, how to make a good impression in a job interview, and how to express your feelings more clearly.

Learning good communication skills also helps you protect yourself against propaganda that seeks to influence your thoughts and behavior. By applying critical-listening skills, you can judge whether statements and ideas are true, sensible, and worthwhile, and you can defend yourself against those that are not.

Finally, the fourth reason for studying speech communication is to have more fun. Good speech skills can lead you to enjoyable activities such as acting in skits and dramas, reading aloud to your friends and classmates, and appearing on radio or television programs.

As you proceed through this course, keep in mind that speech communication is made up of a set of skills that are learned and that can be changed or polished. The purpose of this book is to help you do just that.

Rudolph F. Verderber

Unit 1 • The Communication Process

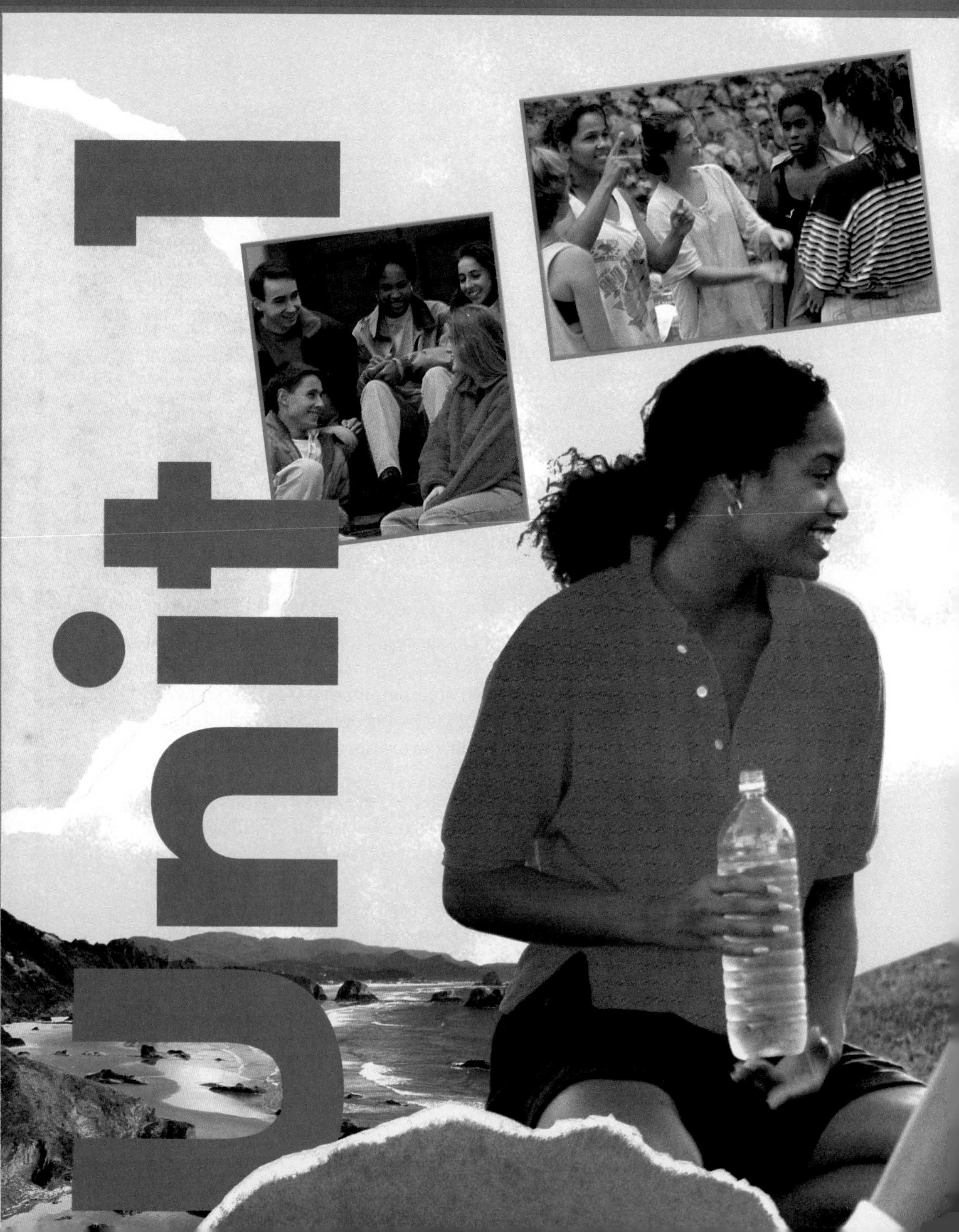

The Communication Process

Chapter 1
Understanding Communication
pp. 2–25

Chapter Overview

This chapter gives an overview of the process of communication. The chapter begins by defining *communication* and by describing the relationships of the elements of communication. The chapter explains that communication helps people to make informed decisions and to meet social needs. Different settings for communication are categorized as informal and formal.

Teacher's Resource Binder

The following materials are identified at their point of use in this chapter:

- Skills for Success
  1. *Sending and Receiving Messages*
  2. *Communicating in Formal Settings*
  3. *Finding Good Ideas to Talk About*
  4. *Dealing with Interference*
- Chapter 1 Vocabulary
- Chapter 1 Test/Answer Key

AV ➤ Audiovisual Resource Binder

The following materials are identified at their point of use in this chapter:

- Transparency 1
  The Elements of Communication
- Transparency 2
  Finding Ideas for Speeches

Finally, the chapter lists the interrelated steps of the communication process and describes how the steps can vary. The steps examined are finding ideas, adapting to an audience, encoding and decoding information, interpreting feedback, and dealing with interference.

Introducing the Chapter

The information in **Chapter 1** is the foundation for the material in subsequent chapters in **Speech for Effective Communication**. Tell students that this chapter should help them to recognize their roles in the communication process. Students will also begin to assess their personal strengths and weaknesses as communicators.

CHAPTER 1

Understanding Communication

OBJECTIVES

After studying this chapter, you should be able to

1. Identify and define the elements of communication.
2. Identify how and why communication skills are important in your own life.
3. Tell the difference between verbal communication and nonverbal communication.
4. Identify and describe various kinds of formal and informal communication settings.
5. List and explain the interrelated steps of the communication process.
6. Explain the qualities that make someone an effective communicator.

What Is Communication?

You communicate every day, and if you are like most people, you take the process of communication for granted. However, to communicate more effectively, you need to take a closer look at how the communication process works.

Communication is the process of sharing information by using symbols to send and receive messages. You communicate when you share thoughts, ideas, and feelings with others. Using a variety of symbols, you probably send messages and receive messages from others, beginning the moment you wake up in the morning and continuing until the moment you fall asleep at night.

Although it is possible to communicate with yourself (see intrapersonal communication, Chapter 5), the type of communication you will primarily study in this book is **interpersonal communication**—communication between two or more people.

Bibliography of Additional Materials

Professional Readings

- Barnouw, Eric, ed. ***International Encyclopedia of Communications.*** New York: Oxford University Press.
- Benson, Thomas W. ***Speech Communication in the 20th Century.*** Carbondale, IL: Southern Illinois University Press.
- Shannon, Claude E., and Warren Weaver. ***The Mathematical Theory of Communication.*** Urbana, IL: University of Illinois Press.

Audiovisuals

- ***American Tongues***—Center for New American Media, New York, NY (videocassette, 56 min.)
- ***The Communications Revolution Series***—Coronet/MTI Film & Video, Deerfield, IL (three videocassettes, 20 min. each)
- ***Destination: Communications***—Coronet/MTI Film & Video, Deerfield, IL (videocassette, 20 min.)
- ***The Eloquent Americans***—Nebraska ETV Council for Higher Education, Lincoln, NE (videocassette, 30 min.)

Segment 1 *pp. 4–12*

- **Sending and Receiving Messages**
- **Using Communication**
- **Considering Different Settings**

Performance Objectives

- To communicate by using verbal and nonverbal messages
- To list instances of using informal communication
- To list instances of using communication skills to convey messages successfully
- To analyze successful communication

MEETING INDIVIDUAL NEEDS

An Alternative Approach

Challenge students who exhibit interest in developing communication models. Have the students design their own models—either general ones that apply to any interpersonal communication or specific ones that apply to particular situations such as a coach giving a pregame pep talk to a team. These models can be elaborate and three-dimensional, or they can be simple. Ask students to present their models to the class and to explain the designs.

Teacher's Resource Binder

Skills for Success 1
Sending and Receiving Messages

Sending and Receiving Messages

Communication between people always involves sending and receiving a message. A **message** consists of the ideas and the feelings that make up the content of communication. The person who sends the message is called the **sender.** The person who receives the message is called the **receiver.**

To be effective, communication must also include **feedback**—a return message. Notice in the diagram below that the sender and receiver exchange roles, depending on whether the message is being transmitted or feedback is being returned.

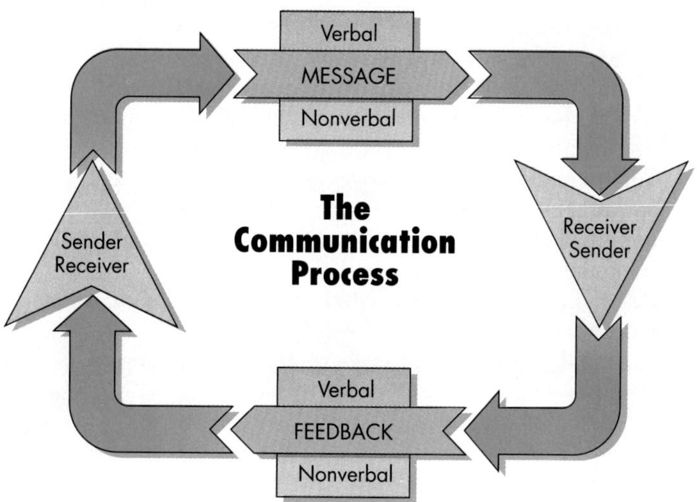

Messages are carried by verbal and nonverbal symbols. **Verbal symbols** are words; **nonverbal symbols** include gestures, facial expressions, and sounds such as laughter, clapping, hissing, and whistling.

All messages are transmitted through **channels,** the means for sending communication. If you use verbal symbols to send a spoken message, the channel is sound waves. If you use nonverbal symbols to send a message, the channel can be sound waves, light waves, or the sense of touch.

To gain a better understanding of the communication process, read the following conversation between Rosalie and her friend Juan about their math assignment. Pay close attention to the verbal as well as the nonverbal portions of the conversation. You will see how the elements of the process work together to create effective communication.

- To list instances of using formal communication
- To identify the elements of communication in specific situations

MOTIVATION

Pause as you read the following list and have students remember these situations: the last heated arguments they had, the best compliments they ever received, the best persuasive techniques they used on their parents, and the last reports they presented to their classmates. Ask students how these occasions made them feel. You may want to list on the chalkboard the responses,

Wrinkling his forehead, Juan worriedly asks, "Rosalie, are we supposed to do *all* of the problems in Part A in the math chapter?"

Calmly placing her hand on Juan's shoulder, Rosalie replies, "No, just the odd-numbered ones." Juan shoots his fist into the air, smiles, and walks toward the bus stop.

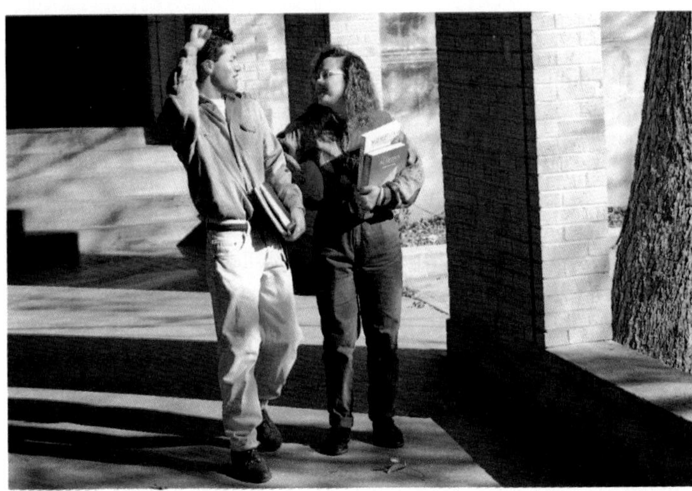

The short exchange between Rosalie and Juan shows how the communication process works. First, as the *sender,* Juan uses *verbal and nonverbal symbols* to send his *message* to Rosalie, the *receiver.* The symbols Juan uses are words, facial expressions, and tone of voice. With these symbols, he communicates his message of nervous uncertainty to Rosalie. Because Juan uses both verbal and nonverbal symbols, the message travels through two *channels:* sound waves that can be heard and light waves that can be seen. After Rosalie receives Juan's message, she gives him her response, or *feedback.* To do so, she must exchange communication roles with Juan.

In the second phase, Rosalie becomes the sender. Like Juan, Rosalie uses both verbal and nonverbal symbols to send her message. The symbols she uses are words, tone of voice, and touch. With these symbols, she communicates her message of calm reassurance to Juan. Her symbols also travel through channels: sound waves and the sense of touch. After Juan receives Rosalie's message, he gives her nonverbal feedback in the form of a gesture and a facial expression.

The chart on the following page summarizes the key elements in the communication process.

CRITICAL THINKING

Analysis and Synthesis

Ask students to write short dialogues similar to the exchange between Rosalie and Juan. Have the students include words that show facial expression, tone of voice, and body movement as communication symbols.

Then have students identify elements in their dialogues by using **The Elements of Communication** chart on p. 6 as a model.

INTEGRATING THE LANGUAGE ARTS

Literature Link

Point out that while the dialogue in novels and stories is obviously verbal communication, authors use description to convey their characters' nonverbal messages. Have students find examples in their literature textbooks or in other books in which authors convey the gestures, tone of voice, facial expressions, and so on, of their characters. Have students work in groups of four or five to read aloud the passages they find and to analyze the impact of the nonverbal messages.

which will probably range from furious to ecstatic. Tell students that they can learn to control such communication situations and to experience feelings that are more positive by improving their communication skills.

Teaching the Lesson

Explain to students that their task in the first segment of this chapter is to analyze communication—to take a new look at something familiar. To model communication, you may want to have two students act out the scene between Rosalie and Juan on p. 5. Then discuss **The Elements of Communication** chart, which analyzes Rosalie and Juan's conversation.

The Elements of Communication

Elements	Definitions	Examples
Senders and Receivers	A person who sends a message is called the sender. A person who receives a message is called the receiver.	When Juan asked Rosalie about the assignment, he *sent* a message. Rosalie *received* the message and *sent* another message *(feedback)* to Juan. They alternated roles as sender and receiver.
Messages	Messages are the ideas and feelings that make up the content of communication.	Juan sent a message to Rosalie, which expressed his feeling of concern about the math assignment.
Verbal and Nonverbal Symbols	Verbal symbols are words. Nonverbal symbols (such as gestures, tone of voice, and facial expressions) are messages sent without words.	Rosalie used verbal symbols when she told Juan the correct assignment. She used a nonverbal symbol when she placed her hand on his shoulder.
Channels	Channels are the sound waves, light waves, and sense of touch by which messages are sent.	Juan's words and tone of voice traveled by means of sound waves. His gestures traveled by means of light waves. Rosalie's feeling of reassurance traveled by means of sense of touch.
Feedback	Feedback consists of the verbal and nonverbal responses to messages.	After Rosalie received Juan's message, she gave him both verbal and nonverbal feedback. After Rosalie told Juan the correct assignment, he sent feedback that showed his relief; he shot his fist into the air and smiled.

AV ***Audiovisual Resource Binder***

Transparency 1
The Elements of Communication

To provide guided practice for sending nonverbal messages, you and a volunteer could act out the convenience store scenario in **Activity 1.** Then have students work in pairs to create original scenes as independent practice.

As you discuss **Considering Different Settings,** which starts on p. 9, you will probably find that most students are familiar with informal settings. However, you may want to spend more time discussing the formal settings. For guided practice, have students discuss any experiences they have had participating in the six formal settings. Then assign **Activity 2** on p. 12 as independent practice.

On p. 9, students are introduced to communication journals. At this point, you may want to explain the way you will use and evaluate journals and to tell students what form of journal you will require.

ACTIVITY 1

Sending Nonverbal Messages

Work with a partner to determine a situation in which you must communicate nonverbally. For example, imagine that you and your partner work part-time in a convenience store. Unknown to your co-worker, your boss has confided in you that she has grown tired of granting favors to her employees. Just as your boss joins you and your co-worker behind the counter, your co-worker whispers to you that he plans to ask for the afternoon off. How would you communicate to him nonverbally that his request is not a good idea? With your partner, make a list of the different ways that you could convey the message. Choose the method that seems the most effective, and practice the scene. Then present it to other members of the class.

Using Communication

Whether you are passing time with friends, participating in class, helping your brother make dinner, or applying for a job, nearly everything you do involves communication. Communicating with others helps you to satisfy your social needs and to make decisions.

Meeting Social Needs

All human beings have social needs. We need to love and to be loved, to show feelings, and to interact with others. Through communication, we fulfill these needs.

ONGOING ASSESSMENT

Activity 1

Students who choose to act out the scene in the textbook might list the following methods of nonverbal communication: secretly nudging the co-worker to get his attention and then shaking your head to communicate to him not to ask for the afternoon off. If students choose different situations, you may want to have the class try to guess the nonverbal messages that are being sent.

WRITING TO LEARN

Have students freewrite for five minutes about their personal methods of communication. Do they smile at or speak to strangers? Do they feel comfortable speaking in front of large groups? Are they good listeners? Do they talk for hours on the telephone?

After the five minutes of freewriting, encourage students to reread what they have written and to compose one or two summarizing statements about themselves as communicators.

Assessment

You can evaluate understanding of nonverbal messages by observing students' performances for **Activity 1.** By checking the entries in students' communication journals and the answers for **Activity 2,** you can assess each student's understanding of the communication process in informal and formal settings.

Reteaching

If students are having difficulty translating verbal messages into nonverbal messages (as required in **Activity 1**), you could have them complete the following activity:

Divide the class into groups of three and give each group member a different list of possible verbal messages such as "I don't know," "definitely not," "keep away," and "I understand."

Common Error

Problem. Students often underestimate the influence of friends and acquaintances on their decision-making processes.

Solution. Suggest that each student analyze the part that others play in his or her decision-making process. With a specific decision in mind, each student might list each person he or she consulted concerning the decision and note what each person said. Then ask students to consider how much influence each person had on their final decisions.

Communicating helps people to feel good about themselves and about their world. Even greeting strangers on the street can give you pleasure and make you feel like you are a part of the world around you. Communication promotes social cohesion and bonding.

Through words and gestures people communicate that they care about each other. A simple "hello" or "what's happening?" can improve your spirits and give your day a cheerful lift.

Communicating also helps people build and maintain satisfying relationships. When you first meet people, you communicate to find out whether you like the same food, listen to the same music, share political beliefs, and have similar hobbies. If you find that you have much in common and that you enjoy each other's company, you become friends. As you continue to communicate, you deepen or maintain your relationships and often establish lasting friendships.

Making Decisions

Every day you must make personal decisions. Making many of these decisions involves communicating with others. By talking with other people, you can get information, exchange ideas and feelings, and ultimately decide what actions to take. For example, you might talk with your next-door neighbor about her college experience when you make decisions about your future education. In this conversation you would use communication to help you make a thoughtful and informed decision.

Communicating with others often involves influencing the decisions they make. For example, you might talk to your supervisor about rescheduling your weekend shift because you have tickets to a concert on Saturday night. In this conversation, you would use communication to help you influence the decision making of another person.

Have each member take turns sending the messages nonverbally to the other group members, who will try to guess each message. Circulate among the groups and offer assistance as needed.

See p. 11 for **EXTENSION, ENRICHMENT,** and **CLOSURE.**

Considering Different Settings

A large percentage of your waking hours is spent communicating. This communication takes place in both formal settings and informal settings.

Communicating in Informal Settings

Most of your communication occurs in **informal settings,** which are casual, unstructured situations. [Informal communication is explored in detail in Chapter 7.] In informal settings, communication is usually spontaneous: You think about what to say as you go along, and then you say it. For example, every day you probably take part in informal communication situations, such as

- talking with family and friends
- introducing people
- giving instructions
- talking on the telephone
- giving and receiving information in class
- asking for directions

COMMUNICATION JOURNAL

In your speech class, one of your goals will be to become aware of yourself as a communicator. One way to do this is to keep a communication journal. Start by recording some instances in which you used communication skills in the ordinary, informal settings that you find in daily life—visiting friends, attending classes, shopping, spending time with your family, walking through your neighborhood. Also record instances in which your communication skills helped you to successfully convey messages. As you jot down these experiences, list one or two reasons why you know that you communicated successfully.

Communicating in Formal Settings

Formal settings are situations that you can prepare for ahead of time. Although much less of your everyday communication may take place in formal settings, these situations allow you to affect the ideas and feelings of people in important positions. The situations described on the following pages are examples of formal settings for speech communication.

CRITICAL THINKING

Analysis

Work with students to brainstorm a list of jobs that are held by teenagers in the community. Have each student speak informally outside of class with an employed teenager regarding the role of communication in his or her job. Suggest that students ask the following questions: Must the teenager communicate regularly with the boss? with other employees? with the public? by phone? Tell students to determine the importance of communication in their subjects' work and to summarize their conclusions in their communication journals.

TEACHER'S RESOURCE BINDER

Skills for Success 2
Communicating in Formal Settings

Cooperative Learning

You may want to divide the class into groups of four to practice group discussion. Have each group member watch or listen to the news on the same night. Group members should plan to watch different television networks or to listen to different radio stations. They should note the events featured, the importance given to each event, and the main content of the stories.

On the following day, have the group members report their findings and compare the various news programs. Did the programs have the same lead stories and the same set of stories? Did each newscaster give particular emphasis to one story? Ask a volunteer from each group to present a summary of findings to the class.

Job and College Interviews. An **interview** is a form of communication in which people ask and answer questions. Interviewing is usually a one-on-one form of communication. In a job interview, you may sit with a potential employer and ask and answer questions about your work skills, your ability to get along with others, the responsibilities of the job, and the salary. In a college interview, you may sit with the dean of admissions, who tells you about the college, asks you about your goals and interests, and answers questions about the school's facilities and requirements.

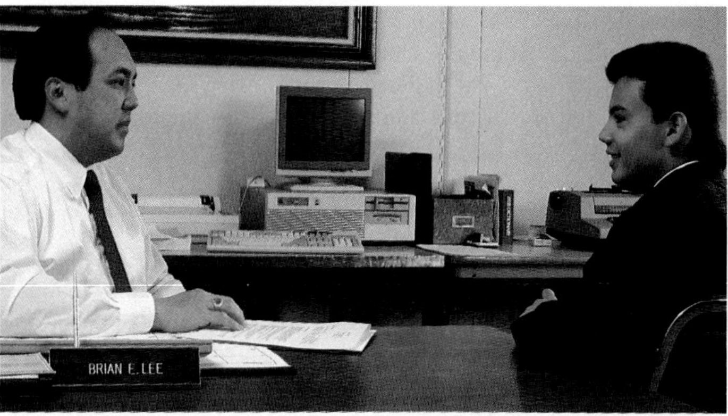

Group Discussions. A **group discussion** is a face-to-face meeting among a small number of people who convey information, express their views, and reach conclusions about particular issues. The more effectively you and the other group members communicate with each other, the more informed your decisions will be. [See Chapter 17 for more about formal methods of problem solving and decision making.]

Extension

You may want to have students make charts to explore the various types of nonverbal symbols. Suggest that students use two columns with the headings "Nonverbal Symbol" and "Meaning." For example, they might list *crossing arms on chest* to mean "reluctance, uncertainty." Remind students to include gestures, facial expressions, body language, and sounds.

Public Speaking. In **public speaking,** one person addresses an **audience**—the listeners or spectators attending a presentation or a performance—to inform, persuade, or entertain them. In this book, you will learn how to prepare and deliver effective speeches. Most people find speaking in public more difficult than speaking in informal situations or in small groups. Yet public speaking is very important. Many key decisions in our society are made on the basis of what we learn from, and how we are influenced by, public speakers.

Debate and Parliamentary Procedure. **Debate** is a formal communication situation in which speakers take opposing sides on an issue and try to prove or disprove a statement about that issue. **Parliamentary procedure** is a set of rules used to conduct orderly meetings. Precise and convincing communication is essential in debating and in conducting meetings that follow parliamentary procedure.

Interpretive Situations. **Oral reading** is a performing art in which literature is read aloud and interpreted for an audience. **Drama** is a performing art in which the characters in a play are interpreted and

ENRICHMENT

Some students rebel against formal speech in any setting. Get them to examine their opinions by having them debate the following resolution: *Resolved,* That formal speech should be used in the classroom.

CLOSURE

Ask students to summarize their understanding of the communication process. Have them recall settings for formal and informal communication.

MAKING CONNECTIONS

Mass Media

To emphasize the role of electronic communication in students' lives, have students keep records in their communication journals of one week's experiences with television, video, and radio programs. Ask students to reflect on the messages they receive and to make notes beside their entries. At the end of the week, you may want to have the class use the data to make generalizations about the use and impact of electronic communication.

ONGOING ASSESSMENT

Activity 2

Students' answers will vary but should show that students have adequately explored their participation in formal speaking situations, including their participation as listeners. Because some students might have limited access to formal communication settings, you could allow students to focus on electronic communication for examples of formal speaking situations.

presented by actors on a stage. To present a powerful oral reading or a dramatic performance, you need to give clear and effective verbal and nonverbal messages to your audience.

Electronic Communication. **Electronic communication** includes radio, television, and video, three of the most common and influential means of mass communication. [Some of the skills specifically related to radio and television performance are covered in Chapter 22.] Electronic communication provides opportunities for reaching an audience of thousands or even millions at one time.

ACTIVITY 2 Analyzing Formal Communication Situations

Identify two formal communication situations that you take part in during an average week. Remember that you can participate in these situations as a listener or as a speaker. For each situation, identify the elements of communication that seem most important when sending and receiving information. [Review the chart on page 6.] Share your findings with your classmates.

Segment 2 *pp. 13–19*

• Developing the Communication Process

• Communicating Effectively

PERFORMANCE OBJECTIVES

- To analyze nonverbal feedback
- To identify and act out situations dealing with interference
- To evaluate efforts at dealing with interference

Developing the Communication Process

The communication process consists of a series of several interrelated steps:

- You find ideas to speak about.
- You adapt your message to the needs of your audience.
- You determine how to present your ideas in the most effective way.
- You interpret audience feedback.
- You deal with verbal and nonverbal interference.

The progression of these steps can vary according to the people involved, the setting, and other circumstances. To some extent, these steps come into play in all communication situations, whether you are talking with one person, participating in a group discussion, or speaking before a large audience.

Finding Ideas

Finding good ideas to talk about is one key to effective speaking. This step is especially important for occasions such as group discussions and public speaking. When you choose ideas, you will need to consider factors such as your audience, the setting, and the time allotted for your presentation.

You can find many interesting ideas for formal and informal speaking situations by

- examining your own experience
- looking at the lives of the people around you
- watching television shows or movies
- reading newspaper or magazine articles

You can find ideas anywhere, any time. Always be open to new ideas. Jot them down in your journal or make notes on scratch paper.

MEETING INDIVIDUAL NEEDS

An Alternative Approach

Because some students have difficulty finding interesting topics or ideas for speeches, you may want to have them begin ongoing topic lists in their communication journals. Give students categories such as food, clothing, sports, and music. Have each student focus on listing three or four specific, concrete words related to each category. Remind students that common, everyday items such as calendars, zippers, cutlery, or chewing gum can be interesting topics for speeches.

TEACHER'S RESOURCE BINDER

Skills for Success 3
Finding Good Ideas to Talk About

Audiovisual Resource Binder

Transparency 2
Finding Ideas for Speeches

Motivation

To emphasize the importance of audience, address your students as if they were preschoolers. Speak in simple sentences, use exaggerated facial expressions, and wear a big smile. For example, you might say, "Hello, boys and girls. Today I'm going to share a poem with you." Then recite a simple nursery rhyme. Afterward, ask students to discuss their reactions.

Teaching the Lesson

As students develop and give speeches throughout the year, they will become more familiar with the interrelated steps of the communication process listed on p. 13. Discussing each step as it is presented on pp. 13–18 should give students an overview of the communication process.

For guided practice in preparation for **Activity 3** on p. 17, you may want to have students

Cooperative Learning

Have students work in groups of three to create descriptions of audiences they would like to speak to and explanations of why they would choose those audiences. Have them consider audience variables—individual, cultural, and sociological characteristics. Then ask students to decide on topics appropriate for their audiences and to write synopses of the ideas, vocabulary, and techniques they would use in their speeches.

Adapting to Your Audience

To communicate effectively, you must adapt to the needs of your audience. Adapting to your audience involves learning something about the people you address. In some formal situations you can learn about your audience before you prepare your speech. However, in many formal and informal settings, you learn about your audience while you communicate with them.

Being aware of cultural, sociological, and individual information about your audience will help you to present thoughts and ideas effectively. These factors will help you to anticipate your audience's response, interpret feedback, and respond to your audience appropriately.

Individual Characteristics. When you examine your audience's **individual characteristics,** you look at such things as a person's personality, interests, and aspirations. These items help you to predict how an individual will respond to certain information. The individual level is particularly important to consider in everyday conversation.

EXAMPLE: If you are speaking to a classmate who is the photographer for the school newspaper, you can assume that she'll understand an anecdote about a single-lens reflex. However, if you want to tell the same story to someone who knows nothing about photography, you may have to begin by explaining that a single-lens reflex is a type of camera.

Cultural Characteristics. When you examine your audience's **cultural characteristics,** you look at such things as age, religion, and national and ethnic background. This helps you to focus your presentation in such a way that your audience will understand and respond favorably to your message.

EXAMPLE: When Robin presented a speech to the prom committee, she knew that several members in the group had recently immigrated from Korea and the Philippines, where proms are not a part of high school culture. Before she discussed the prom theme, she explained its importance and gave examples of prom themes used in previous years.

Sociological Characteristics. When you examine your audience's **sociological characteristics,** you look at elements such as their affiliations, their educational backgrounds, and their occupations. Based on what you discover, you can formulate some general ideas about your listeners.

EXAMPLE: When Tony prepared a speech about the powwow at the Taos Pueblo, he knew he would be addressing a group of craftspeople. For this reason he focused his presentation on the discuss various nonverbal messages that they have given and received. Then have students work independently to draw their cartoons.

As guided practice for **Activity 4** on p. 18, you could have students offer suggestions of how to deal with the interference presented in the examples on pp. 17–18. Then assign **Activity 4** as independent practice.

ASSESSMENT

You could check the cartoons from **Activity 3** to assess students' understanding of nonverbal messages. As students do **Activity 4,** you could move about the classroom to observe their performances and to listen to their evaluations.

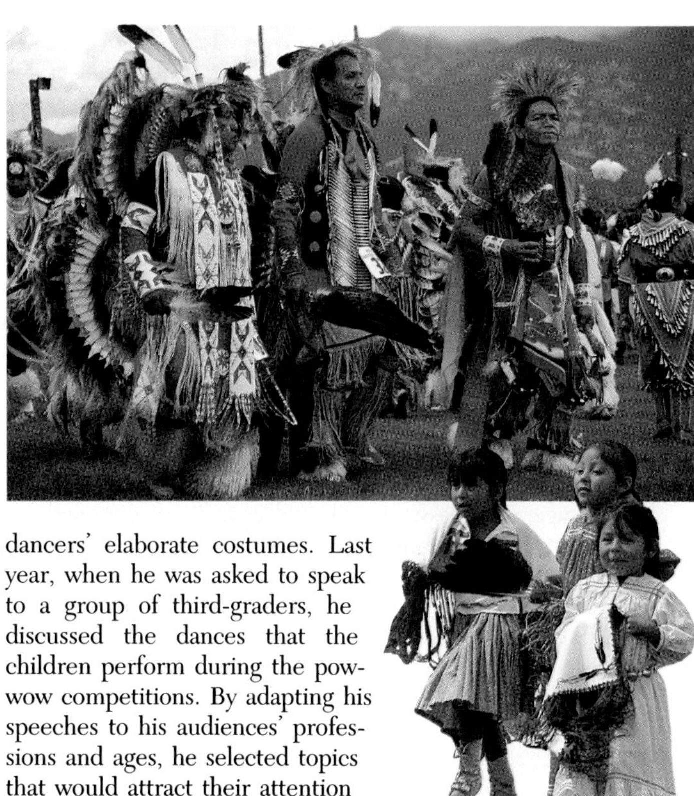

dancers' elaborate costumes. Last year, when he was asked to speak to a group of third-graders, he discussed the dances that the children perform during the pow-wow competitions. By adapting his speeches to his audiences' professions and ages, he selected topics that would attract their attention and hold their interest.

Encoding and Decoding Information

To communicate successfully, you must decide how to send and interpret messages. This process involves encoding and decoding information.

Encoding. The process of turning ideas and feelings into verbal and nonverbal symbols is called **encoding.** In a formal situation, you take time to plan how you want to state a certain idea. For a speech, you may even try two or three ways of stating an idea before you select the best way to present it to a particular audience. Informal speaking is quite different. In informal conversations, the encoding process is nearly instantaneous.

EXAMPLE: If you want salt on your tomatoes, you ask the person next to you to pass the saltshaker. You don't stop and think, "How can I get someone to move the salt closer to me?" You automatically encode your needs into words.

RETEACHING

If students are having difficulty analyzing nonverbal feedback, show them a clip from a movie or a television show in which several people interact. Discuss with students how the gestures, facial expressions, and tone of voice of each character convey messages. Help students determine why nonverbal messages might be misinterpreted.

See p. 18 for **EXTENSION, ENRICHMENT,** and **CLOSURE.**

INTEGRATING THE LANGUAGE ARTS

Literature Link

Challenge students to find examples in literature or in cartoons of failures in communication. The problem for each example could be that the encoding was not suited to the receiver or that the decoding was not accurate. Have students work in groups of four or five to read and analyze their passages or cartoons and to identify what went wrong.

Encoding is not just a matter of verbal communication. At the same time that you verbalize, you almost always send nonverbal messages that affect the receiver's response. The various ways that are possible to combine verbal and nonverbal symbols are almost limitless.

Decoding. For communication to be complete, a receiver must decode a message. **Decoding** is finding the meaning of verbal and nonverbal symbols.

In conversation, the decoding process is usually instantaneous. A split second after you ask for the salt, someone is likely to pass it to you. However, in formal and some informal situations, the receiver may need to translate messages into meanings that make sense in their given context.

> **EXAMPLE:** If you just left a chemistry lab, you may decide to say, "Sylvia, please pass the sodium chloride." Upon receiving this message, your classmate may look at you with a puzzled expression and say, "The *what?*" A few seconds later, she may answer, "Oh, the sodium chloride—the salt—sure." Sylvia, your receiver, would have completed the decoding process, having translated the chemical name for salt from a meaning that made sense in the chemistry lab into a meaning that made sense in the lunchroom.

To a large extent, the words and nonverbal symbols you use in communication depend on your understanding of the needs and abilities of your audience. To encode and decode messages clearly, you will want to consider the individual, cultural, and sociological characteristics of your receiver or sender.

Interpreting Feedback

In conversation we expect others to talk with us. In other words, we expect people to respond to our messages with feedback that expresses what they think, feel, and observe. In public situations, audience responses are generally nonverbal. People clap to show approval, yawn to show boredom, and sometimes actually stand up and leave the room to show disapproval.

In both formal and informal settings, the more you know about your audience, the better able you will be to recognize and interpret the verbal or nonverbal feedback you receive.

Analyzing Nonverbal Feedback

Think of three nonverbal messages that you received today. Then draw cartoons that illustrate each one. Beneath each cartoon, jot down a caption that explains the nonverbal message. For example, you might draw a shopper waving at you as he scurries in front of your car to get to the store. Beneath the drawing, you could write, "A shopper waves to tell me that he appreciates my stopping to let him cross the street." When you complete your cartoons, share them with your classmates.

Dealing with Interference

Interference is anything that gets in the way of clear communication. In formal and informal situations, three common types of interference are *physical noise, psychological noise,* and *semantic noise.*

Physical Noise. **Physical noise** consists of any sound that prevents a person from being heard. Physical noise interferes with a speaker's ability to send messages and with an audience's ability to receive them.

> **EXAMPLE:** When you are giving a speech or acting in a play, people in the audience might interfere with whispers or cheers. Or you could be in the midst of a conversation on a crowded street, and passing cars might make it difficult for you to hear your friend's comments.

Psychological Noise. The thoughts and feelings that distract people from listening to what is said are called **psychological noise.** Psychological noise interferes with the audience's concentration and ability to hear a speaker's presentation.

MEETING **INDIVIDUAL** NEEDS

Linguistically Diverse Students

The text refers to different ways in which audiences respond (nonverbally) in public situations. Invite linguistically diverse students to share information about the ways audiences respond in the students' native cultures. By sharing this information, linguistically diverse students broaden the perspectives of their classmates. When you as the teacher show genuine interest in the behavioral norms of other cultures, you set an invaluable example by encouraging respect for cultural diversity.

Activity 3

Cartoons should reflect students' comprehension of nonverbal communication. Emphasize that the quality of the artwork will not be assessed.

TEACHER'S RESOURCE BINDER

Skills for Success 4
Dealing with Interference

Extension

Have students create their own scenarios for speech occasions. Their task is to analyze audiences, settings, and times and then to determine appropriate topics.

Students with Special Needs

Students with behavioral problems often do not know how to handle unforeseen situations such as those involving interference. For example, aggressive students may react in a hostile manner and passive students may try to ignore the problematic situations altogether. Therefore, **Activity 4** should benefit students. Have students act out both appropriate and inappropriate responses so that they gain awareness of the differences. Provide positive feedback.

Activity 4

1. physical
2. psychological
3. physical
4. physical
5. semantic

You will probably want each group to report to the class the most successful methods for dealing with the five situations.

EXAMPLE: Members of an audience may not pay attention to a speaker because they are absorbed in their own thoughts. One person may be thinking about an idea for a poem, while another is worried about how much homework she has to do, and a third is dreaming of his date for Friday night.

Semantic Noise. The interference caused by words that trigger strong negative feelings against the speaker or the content of the speech is called **semantic noise.** Semantic noise leads to misunderstanding, as well as unpleasant and distracting nonverbal feedback from the audience.

EXAMPLE: An audience of classmates might agree with you if you called your town "a dreary place." However, they might stop listening to you if you began calling the town "a dump."

Dealing with Interference

With three or four classmates, read the following situations and identify the type of interference represented. Decide how you would deal with the interference if you were the speaker. Then take turns being the speaker, and act out each situation. After the performances, discuss whether your attempts to deal with the interference were successful.

1. You and a friend are discussing a problem. Three people at the other side of the room begin to talk so loudly that you cannot concentrate on what your friend is saying.
2. You are leading a group discussion. One of your group members is staring out the window, and another is doodling.
3. You are giving a report to your history class. The lights are making a very loud buzzing noise.
4. You are acting in a play. Suddenly a storm strikes, and thunder drowns out your words.
5. You are giving a speech to an audience of city council members. You mention the recreation center's "stupid, boring weekend dances," and a buzz goes up from the audience.

Communicating Effectively

In this chapter you have looked at the key elements, functions, and steps of the communication process. The guidelines on the next page provide suggestions that will help you to become a more effective communicator.

Enrichment

Have students conduct surveys to identify methods of dealing with interference. Have them ask other teachers, administrators, ministers or rabbis, and so on, to describe techniques for dealing with interference.

Closure

Ask students to name the five interrelated steps in the communication process. You could list the steps on the chalkboard as students name them.

HOW TO *Be an Effective Communicator*

1. **Care about your communication success.** Most of your communication has a purpose or goal. Whether that purpose is to transmit information, to change people's minds, or to greet a friend, your effectiveness will depend on others' believing that you really care about them and that you care about what you are saying to them.
2. **Know what you are talking about.** People are likely to pay attention to someone who has the facts, who is knowledgeable about the given subject, and who clearly understands the situation. To grab your audience's attention and to convey the importance of your topic and your opinions, express your ideas and opinions with wisdom and authority.
3. **Be organized.** When people cannot follow what a speaker says, they lose interest and patience quickly. By organizing your ideas, you allow your audience to understand, quickly and easily, the information that you communicate.
4. **Use language well.** People enjoy listening to a speaker who has a skillful command of language. To communicate effectively, choose your words carefully and put them together in a lively and powerful manner.
5. **Use effective nonverbal signals.** The more effectively you use nonverbal behavior, the more powerful your presentation will be. Your use of gestures, facial expressions, body movement, and tone of voice will reinforce your communications.
6. **Listen carefully.** Sometimes the best communicators are those who are good listeners. By listening carefully, you can learn more and therefore respond appropriately to your audience. Effective listening will enable you to identify when your audience is not receiving your message. It will also help you to determine better ways to communicate your message to your audience.

Teaching Note

You may want to add an element—silence—to the fifth point under **How to Be an Effective Communicator**. Model using silence for effect, and then tell students that deliberately using silence can add either emphasis or an element of drama or mystery.

GUIDELINES *for Effective Communicating*

- Do I care about the success of my communication?
- Do I know what I am talking about?
- Are my thoughts well organized?
- Have I selected my words carefully?
- Do I use effective nonverbal signals?
- Do I listen carefully to others?

Building a Portfolio

Suggest that students rate themselves on a scale of one to ten on each point listed in **Guidelines for Effective Communicating**. Have students include their rating scales in their speech portfolios. Then, periodically throughout the year, suggest that they rate themselves again and that they compare the new ratings with their original scores.

◆ Profiles in Communication

Performance Objective

- To write and act out a dialogue

Teaching the Feature

Before students read the information about March Fong Eu, you may want to ask them what they know about the office of Secretary of State. What duties does it entail? What kinds of communication skills are needed to fill the position successfully? Then ask students to read the profile about Dr. Eu to see if their predictions were on target.

Activity Note

Before students can write their dialogues, they will have to decide on certain information such as the location of the tourist information center, the number of family members, and the approximate amount of money the family wants to spend. You may want to have the class develop a rating scale to use when evaluating the performances of the dialogues.

PROFILES IN COMMUNICATION

March Fong Eu

Every day, March Fong Eu's job as California's Secretary of State depends on speech communication skills: She speaks to others constantly—on the telephone, across her desk, around the conference table, and from the podium. Obviously, she communicates well—she was recently elected to her fifth term in that office. She was first elected Secretary of State in 1974 by a record-setting three million votes, the most votes ever received in California for a statewide constitutional office. Ever since then, she has regularly been the highest vote-getter in a contested race in her state.

Dr. Eu, a doctor of education, was the first woman and the first Asian American to become a member of the Alameda County Board of Education; and soon thereafter, in 1966, she became the first Asian American woman to be elected to the California State Legislature. After serving four terms in the legislature, with more than four hundred bills to her credit, she was elected Secretary of State.

The office of Secretary of State involves different responsibilities in different states. In California, the Secretary of State serves as the chief elections officer, regulates notaries public, heads the California State Archives, promotes overseas trade, and supervises the filing of corporations that want to do business in California. Over the past nineteen years, Dr. Eu has reorganized, computerized, and revitalized the Office of the Secretary of State. To accomplish these tasks, Dr. Eu must use effective communication skills.

ACTIVITY

Any job that involves public relations requires good communication skills. Imagine that you have a part-time job at a tourist information center. A family asks you to recommend a good restaurant. You can tell that they have been driving all day, and they are obviously tired. Write a dialogue with detailed stage directions for yourself to show how you will respond to their request. With a classmate or two, role-play your scene for the class. You may improvise some, but remember that your main purpose is to be a helpful and friendly communicator.

S☆U☆M☆M☆A☆R☆Y

UNDERSTANDING COMMUNICATION means being aware of elements in the process by which you share thoughts, ideas, and feelings with others.

- **Send and receive messages** by using symbols to create messages. Messages, which may be made up of verbal or nonverbal symbols, are transmitted through channels. The communication process involves continuous interchange, starting with a sender who communicates a message to a receiver. The receiver responds by sending feedback.
- **Use communication** as an important part of almost every activity of your daily life. Communication is used by most people to help them meet social needs and to help them make decisions.
- **Consider different settings** that may affect the process of communicating. Communication in informal settings is usually casual and unstructured; communication in formal settings is usually planned in advance.
- **Develop the communication process** in your own speaking as you increase your speaking skills. Begin with an idea; adapt your idea to suit the characteristics of your audience; communicate your idea to others by encoding and decoding information; then interpret and respond to your audience's feedback. Deal appropriately with interference.
- **Communicate effectively** by caring about how well you communicate to others, and by knowing your subject, organizing your ideas, using language well, using effective nonverbal behavior, and being a good listener.

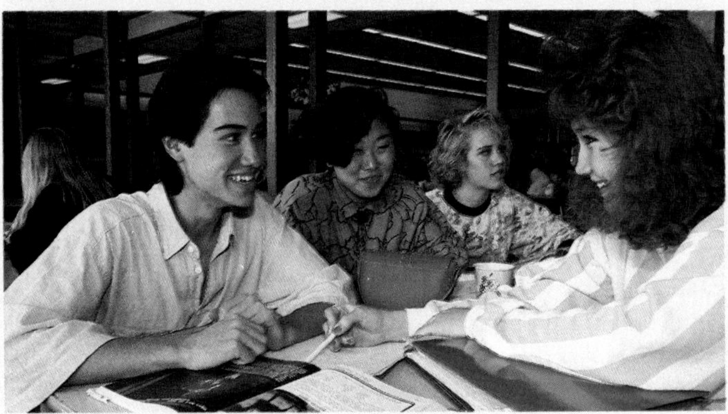

CHAPTER **1**

Vocabulary

Look through this chapter to find the meaning of each of the following words. Write each term and its meaning in your communication journal.

audience, *p. 11*
channels, *p. 4*
communication, *p. 3*
cultural characteristics, *p. 14*
debate, *p. 11*
decoding, *p. 16*
drama, *p. 11*
electronic communication, *p. 12*
encoding, *p. 15*
feedback, *p. 4*
formal settings, *p. 9*
group discussion, *p. 10*
individual characteristics, *p. 14*
informal settings, *p. 9*
interference, *p. 17*
interpersonal communication, *p. 3*
interview, *p. 10*
message, *p. 4*
nonverbal symbols, *p. 4*
oral reading, *p. 11*
parliamentary procedure, *p. 11*
physical noise, *p. 17*
psychological noise, *p. 17*
public speaking, *p. 11*
receiver, *p. 4*
semantic noise, *p. 18*
sender, *p. 4*
sociological characteristics, *p. 14*
verbal symbols, *p. 4*

TEACHER'S RESOURCE BINDER

- Chapter 1 Vocabulary

REVIEW QUESTIONS

Answers

1. the process of sharing information by using symbols to send and receive messages
2. sender, receiver, feedback, verbal and nonverbal symbols, and channels
3. Nonverbal communication does not use words.
4. sound waves, light waves, or the sense of touch
5. lets the sender know how the message is being received
6. job and college interviews, group discussions, public speaking, debates, interpretive situations, and electronic communication
7. Adapt the message to the audience, present ideas effectively, interpret feedback, and deal with interference.
8. so as to be able to anticipate audience's response, interpret feedback, and respond appropriately; information about cultural, sociological,

DISCUSSION QUESTIONS

Guidelines for Assessment

Student responses may vary.

1. Discussion should focus on tone of voice. A joyful tone would suggest a high grade. A sarcastic tone would indicate a low grade.
2. People often send and receive unintended messages through body language, facial expression, language, tone of voice, and personal appearance.
3. For the audience with shared political views, the speaker is apt to stress their shared common bond and goals. For the audience of political opponents, the speaker must guard carefully against provoking semantic and psychological interference.
4. One thing someone says or does can clarify previous words or actions. In the encoding process, speakers should strive for words and gestures that help to clarify the message. Such words and gestures facilitate the decoding process.
5. Students should recognize that although each role requires specific talents, the following communication skills would be helpful in all of the roles mentioned: adapting to one's audience, interpreting feedback, dealing with interference, using language well, using effective nonverbal signals, and listening carefully.

Review Questions

1. What is meant by the term *communication*?
2. The communication process involves six key elements. One of these is the *message.* What are the other five?
3. How does nonverbal communication differ from verbal communication?
4. To a large extent, verbal messages are sent through the air by sound waves. What channel or channels are used to send nonverbal messages?
5. Imagine that two people are having a conversation. What role does *feedback* play in ensuring that effective communication takes place?
6. What are some of the settings in which formal communication takes place?
7. Regardless of the type of communication, a speaker must always *find ideas* to communicate. What are the other steps of the communication process?
8. Why is it important to have information about an audience? What three kinds of information is it important to have?
9. What is interference? What are the three types of interference?
10. What are the six characteristics of an effective communicator?

Discussion Questions

1. Your friend Jan says, "Getting that grade on my project really made my day!" What she means depends not only on her words but also on the way she says those words. Discuss how a listener could interpret Jan's words depending on *how* Jan says them.
2. Discuss the meaning of the following statement: Human beings are always communicating, whether they are conscious of it or not. Do you agree or disagree with this statement?
3. You are to give a speech in support of a political candidate. Discuss the ways in which your knowledge of your audience would affect what you would say and how you would say it. For example, how would a speech given to a group belonging to the same political party as your candidate differ from a speech given to a group that belongs to another political party?
4. Ralph Waldo Emerson once wrote: "All persons are puzzles until at last we find in some word or act the key to the man, to the woman; straightway all their past words and actions lie in light before us." First, discuss the meaning of this quotation. Then, discuss how this quotation relates to the encoding-decoding process.
5. Many wonderful opportunities await you in the near future. You are likely to play the role of college student, employee, boss, and possibly mother or father. Discuss how communication skills will help you to make the most of these roles.

and individual characteristics of the audience

9. anything that gets in the way of clear communication; physical, psychological, and semantic noise
10. cares about communication success, knows the subject, is organized, uses language well, uses effective nonverbal signals, and listens carefully

ACTIVITIES

1. **Identifying Occupational Uses of Communication Skills.** Conduct a survey to find out your classmates' future plans. Then list the occupations that they intend to pursue. Under each occupation, jot down how communication skills will be an effective tool for advancement. For example, a nurse would need good communication skills to understand patients' needs and to tell them about proposed methods of treatment. When you complete your list, share it with your classmates.

2. **Interpreting Nonverbal Communication in Television Programs.**
   - **A.** Watch a television talk show. Make a list of the ways in which people communicate nonverbally during one conversation. Share your list with your classmates.
   - **B.** Watch a television program with the sound off. How much of the story are you able to follow? What nonverbal symbols help you to follow this much of the story? Share your findings with your classmates.
   - **C.** A television advertiser has only fifteen to thirty seconds to communicate a message. Therefore, every second has to count. Watch several television advertisements. How does the level of nonverbal communication in the advertisements compare with that in regular programming? Are there more or fewer gestures and facial expressions? How forceful or dramatic are these gestures and expressions? Share your comparison with your classmates.

3. **Analyzing an Audience.** Look closely at the people in the following photographs. What, if anything, can you tell about their individual, cultural, and sociological characteristics? With a small group of your classmates, list ways in which you as a speaker might adapt a message to each of these audiences.

ACTIVITIES

Guidelines for Assessment

1. Responses should indicate students' understanding of the importance of communication in many types of work.
2. A. Lists should show students' mastery of the concept of nonverbal communication.
   B. Students will likely find that they can understand much of the action without the sound.
   C. Students will probably discover that nonverbal communication is more emphatic in advertisements.
3. Ask students to explain the clues they used from the photographs to help them to adapt a message to each of the audiences.

Summative Evaluation

Your **Teacher's Resource Binder** contains a reproducible **Chapter 1 Test** that may be used to assess students' mastery of the concepts presented in this chapter.

Portfolio Assessment

For future reference and evaluation you may want to have students keep in their portfolios any skill sheets or evaluation forms that you have used with this chapter along with any other recorded or written materials that students have created.

4. Analyses should reflect students' comprehension of the communication process.

5. If a speaker is unavailable, refer students to an encyclopedia or to other reference books that illustrate the alphabet of sign language. Students might be willing to demonstrate their findings to the class.

6. Goal lists should indicate students' awareness of achievement needs. Suggest that students add their lists to their speech portfolios for future reference.

7. Diagrams and summaries should reflect an understanding of the communication process.

8. A. Students should explain the uniqueness of the feedback given by each receiver of the message.

B. Students' verbal and nonverbal feedback should express what students think, feel, and observe.

9. The symbols mean "OK"; "right turn"; "No left turn"; and "We're number one." You can assess students' symbols by the partners' ease in decoding.

4. Creating and Analyzing a Dialogue. Working with a partner, write a brief dialogue. Your dialogue might be humorous or serious, informative or persuasive. Using a chart like the one on page 6, analyze the key elements of your dialogue. Examine the changing roles of the sender and the receiver, and practice encoding and decoding nonverbal symbols.

5. Learning About Manual Communication. Interview, or if possible invite to your class, a person skilled in sign language. A speech pathologist or a sign language instructor from a local university or community college would likely be willing to demonstrate and explain sign language and to teach you some common signs.

6. Identifying Learning Goals in a Speech Class. With a group of four or five classmates, develop a list of goals that you hope to achieve this year. Then discuss what you expect to learn from pursuing these goals. After fifteen minutes, share your list with the class.

7. Diagraming Messages. Review the diagram of the communication process on page 4. Then, using this format, diagram four messages that you sent or received today. In the diagrams, identify the sender and the receiver. Write brief summaries of the messages and feedback.

8. Analyzing Feedback.

A. Prepare a short message. Deliver exactly the same message to five different people. Then tell your class how the feedback you received differed from person to person.

B. In addition to acting as a sender of messages, you also act as a receiver. Report to your class on the feedback you gave to five different messages today.

9. Inventing Nonverbal Symbols. The following illustrations show some common nonverbal symbols. Do you know what each of these symbols means?

Now, invent five nonverbal symbols of your own. These symbols can include gestures, pictures, and colors. When you have finished, take turns showing or demonstrating your symbols to a partner. How effective are your symbols? Is your partner able to decode them correctly?

◆ Real-Life Speaking Situations

Performance Objectives

- To write an acceptance speech for a prize
- To practice and present an acceptance speech
- To write and present a scenario of what a police officer would say in two different public-speaking situations

REAL LIFE Speaking Situations

1 Throughout your life, your abilities and interests, and sometimes even blind luck, will make you eligible to win awards and prizes. Winners are often requested to speak publicly about how they won, their feelings about winning, or the field in which they won. People enjoy hearing what winners have to say about their accomplishments and their prizes or awards.

Picture yourself in such a situation. You have just won an important prize: first place in a writing contest, a blue ribbon in a photography contest, a silver ten-speed in a bicycle race, a trophy for a school gymnastics tournament, or an all-expense-paid trip in a school raffle. Or, you may be the winner in some other situation involving one of your personal skills or a game of chance.

Write a one- or two-page acceptance speech in which you describe the prize, the events that led to it, and how it felt to win. Be sure your speech answers the following three questions: What did you win? How did you win? What did you think about when you won? When you finish, practice your speech aloud and then present it to your classmates. Ask your classmates for feedback after you speak.

2 Police officers need to call on their public-speaking skills many times a day. They speak to the public in many diverse situations, such as when issuing speeding tickets, addressing groups such as service clubs, making public service announcements on television or radio, giving advice and directions, or comforting injured people. Perhaps you have had a police officer speak to one of your classes in school or at a meeting of a club or organization you belong to.

Imagine that you are a police officer. In one or two pages, write a description of what you would say in two public-speaking situations. For instance, you can describe a scenario in which you are arresting a drug dealer, speaking to children in an elementary school, or giving directions to a man on his way to the hospital. Or you can describe a scenario in which you are giving a traffic update on the radio, or discussing wearing seatbelts on television.

As you relate the two experiences, note the differences in your word choice, in your tone of voice, and in other nonverbal behavior that you use in the two situations. Then, read the two scenarios aloud.

Assessment Guidelines

1. Each speech should describe the prize, the events that led to it, and how it felt to win. The speech should be suitable for the audience.
2. The scenarios should reflect appropriate language and nonverbal messages for the two situations.

Chapter 2

Sending Verbal and Nonverbal Messages

pp. 26–51

Chapter Overview

This chapter explains the differences between verbal and nonverbal messages. The first segment begins by discussing the verbal language system. After defining *language* as "a system of symbols that follows rules and conventions," the chapter analyzes how language is acquired. It emphasizes the ways that language changes; then it explains the importance of understanding

Teacher's Resource Binder

The following materials are identified at their point of use in this chapter:

- Skills for Success
  1. *Denotation and Connotation*
  2. *Adapting Language to Specific Situations*
  3. *Communicating with Body Language*
  4. *A Message About Me*
- Chapter 2 Vocabulary
- Chapter 2 Test/Answer Key

AV Audiovisual Resource Binder

The following materials are identified at their point of use in this chapter:

- Transparency 3
  Interaction of Verbal and Nonverbal Language
- Transparency 4
  Our Changing Language
- Transparency 5
  Guidelines for Verbal and Nonverbal Communication
- Audiotape 1, Lesson 1
  Nonverbal Communication

shades of meaning. The segment concludes with a discussion of adapting language to specific situations.

The second segment is concerned with nonverbal communication. After discussing the elements of body language, the segment addresses the issue of personal appearance. It concludes with discussions of paralanguage and of environment.

Introducing the Chapter

Write a sentence on the chalkboard and then speak the sentence while sending a nonverbal cue. Discuss the interaction of the verbal and nonverbal messages. Did the nonverbal message complement, emphasize, or contradict the verbal message? Explain to students that this chapter will explore the effects and describe the methods of verbal and nonverbal messages.

CHAPTER 2

Sending Verbal and Nonverbal Messages

OBJECTIVES

After studying this chapter, you should be able to

1. Explain the differences between verbal and nonverbal language.
2. Identify and explain five characteristics of verbal language.
3. Define *denotation* and *connotation* and explain how they affect communication.
4. Explain the appropriate use of standard American English, jargon, slang, and dialect.
5. Explain how body language, appearance, paralanguage, and environment affect communication.

What Are Messages?

Messages are ideas and feelings that people send or receive when they communicate. People use words to send messages back and forth, but verbal language is not the only way to communicate. When you speak, for example, your listener gets messages not only from what you say but also from how you look and act.

How important is this nonverbal language? In your everyday communication, 50 to 90 percent of the messages you send are nonverbal. Sometimes, however, the verbal and nonverbal messages contradict each other and create confusion.

In this chapter, you will study the relationship between verbal and nonverbal messages and will explore some of the ways that this relationship affects communication.

Bibliography of Additional Materials

Professional Readings

- Bremmer, Jay, and Herman Roodenburg. ***A Cultural History of Gesture.*** Ithaca, NY: Cornell University Press.
- Condon, John C., and Faithi S. Yousef. ***An Introduction to Intercultural Communication.*** New York: Macmillan Publishing Co., Inc.
- Knapp, Mark, and Judy Hall. ***Nonverbal Communication in Human Interaction.*** Fort Worth: Harcourt Brace Jovanovich.

Audiovisuals

- ***Communication by Voice and Action***—Coronet/MTI Film & Video, Deerfield, IL (videocassette, 14 min.)
- ***Effective Communication Skills, Program 13: Nonverbal Communication: Eye Contact and Kinesics***—Wisconsin Foundation for Vocational, Technical, and Adult Education, Middleton, WI (videocassette, 28 min.)
- ***Japanese Nonverbal Communication***—Indiana University Audio-Visual Center, Bloomington, IN (videocassette, 20 min.)

Segment 1 pp. 28–35

- **Comparing Verbal Language and Nonverbal Language**
- **Understanding Verbal Language**

PERFORMANCE OBJECTIVES

- To use nonverbal messages to convey meaning
- To find the current meanings and the earliest meanings of words
- To identify positive and negative connotations in advertising
- To analyze contemporary slang and slang from the past

MEETING INDIVIDUAL NEEDS

Cultural Diversity

ESL students may have few opportunities to discuss their own cultures. If you have students from other countries in your classroom, you might have them give examples of nonverbal cues in their native cultures. Sharing and contrasting cultural behaviors can promote appreciation and respect for diversity among students.

ONGOING ASSESSMENT

Activity 1

Students can use the nonverbal cues listed in the **Interaction of Verbal and Nonverbal Language** chart as a guide for this activity. Students' nonverbal messages should be clear enough to allow the partners to identify the meanings being communicated.

***AV* Audiovisual Resource Binder**

Transparency 3
Interaction of Verbal and Nonverbal Language

Comparing Verbal Language and Nonverbal Language

People send and receive messages by using verbal and nonverbal language. **Verbal language** is a system of spoken and written words. **Nonverbal language** is communication without words. Body language, appearance, and the sound of the voice are the **cues,** or signals, of nonverbal communication. Nonverbal language serves four functions:

- to complement (agree with) verbal messages
- to emphasize verbal messages
- to replace verbal messages
- to contradict verbal messages

Interaction of Verbal and Nonverbal Language

Verbal Message	Nonverbal Cues	Function
"That's hilarious."	smiling, laughing	complements verbal message
"Do it now!"	pounding on desk	emphasizes verbal message
No verbal answer (in response to the question "Did you get tickets?")	nodding or shaking your head	replaces verbal message
"Great haircut you got there."	spoken in an unfriendly tone of voice	contradicts verbal message

ACTIVITY 1 Exploring the Effects of Verbal and Nonverbal Messages

Think of a short verbal message to send to a partner. For example, "I've got to leave now," "Where did you get that sweater?" or "Please don't say that." Express the same message verbally three times. However, each time you repeat the words, change your nonverbal message to convey a different meaning.

- To observe speakers and to take notes about effective speaking methods for a communication journal

Motivation

Write "Words do not have meaning; people do" on the chalkboard before students arrive. When class begins, ask a volunteer to paraphrase the statement. Guide students to realize that people attach meaning to words. Point out that the ways people attach meaning to words will be addressed in this segment.

Understanding Verbal Language

Analyzing Language

Verbal language is a system of sounds and symbols used to communicate ideas and feelings. Verbal language has five important features:

1. **Language Is a System.** A **system** is a group of elements that work together. A language system consists of three subsystems—sounds, words, and the way these sounds and words are arranged. All three must be blended together to make a language.

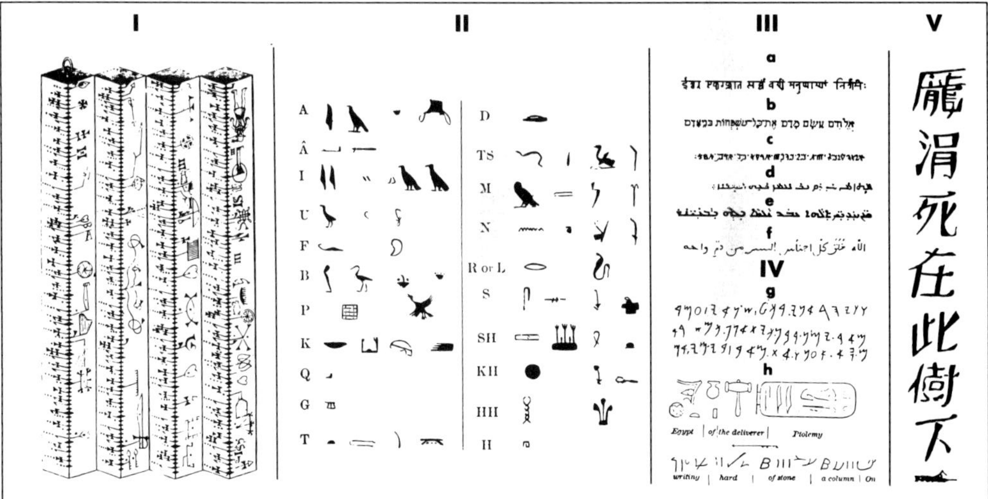

I. Clog Almanac
II. Egyptian Hieroglyphic Letters
III. Phonetic Languages of Asia
a. Sanskrit
b. Hebrew
c. Samaritan
d. Syriac
e. Syrio-Chaldaic
f. Arabic
IV. Phoenician and Egyptian Writing
g. Moabite Stone
h. Rosetta Stone
V. Chinese Ideographic Writing

2. **Language Is Symbolic.** A **symbol** is something that stands for something else. Words are symbols for ideas, actions, objects, and feelings. For example, *car* is a word that stands for something you drive. The word *car,* of course, is not the object. It represents the object.
3. **Language Is Conventional.** **Conventional** means "accepted by a large number of people." Speakers of English have accepted the word *pen* or *pencil* to stand for a particular object that you write with. If you call a pen a *gork,* other people will not know what you are talking about. Words in a language communicate meaning because the large numbers of people who use that language recognize specific meanings for specific words.
4. **Language Is Learned.** Children learn the language of their culture. The process of learning language follows general principles.

Additional Activity

Survey students to find out the names they use for their grandparents. Make a list of these names on the chalkboard and elicit stories of how the names came into existence. In many cases these names reflect children's incomplete mastery of the sound system of English. The names stick because adults consider them cute.

TEACHING THE LESSON

You could introduce the interaction of verbal and nonverbal language by reading through the **Interaction of Verbal and Nonverbal Language** chart on p. 28 with students and discussing the examples and functions of nonverbal language. Have volunteers demonstrate how to communicate nonverbal messages by acting out the examples from the chart or by developing examples of their own. You might demonstrate an original message before you assign **Activity 1**.

Have students read **Understanding Verbal Language** on pp. 29–35 as homework so that you can have a class discussion the following day. When you examine **Analyzing Language** on pp. 29–31, review the features of language and emphasize how language is developed. Use the **Common Ways That Language Changes** chart on this page to discuss ways that language changes

An Alternative Approach

Some of your students may be parents of young children, and these students' parental responsibilities place them at risk of dropping out of school. You may be able to encourage students and help turn a risk factor into something positive by having students report to the class on the language-learning processes of their children. This activity should be entirely voluntary and should be done only by those student parents who feel comfortable with it.

COOPERATIVE LEARNING

Let students work in groups of four to come up with examples of words that are acronyms (*scuba* for *self-contained underwater breathing apparatus*) and clipped forms (*gym* for *gymnasium*). Ask each student to initial his or her contribution to the group effort. After ten minutes of group work, let each group share its list with the class.

 **Audiovisual Resource Binder**

Transparency 4
Our Changing Language

- Children learn symbolic meanings first. For example, children quickly learn short words like *yes* and *no.* In addition, children learn specific words like *mama, daddy,* and *milk* before learning general words like *parents* and *food* or abstract words like *love* and *hunger.*
- Once children learn a rule of language, they often **generalize** that rule, applying it to all cases, including some to which the rule does not apply. For example, after learning to form the past tense by adding *–ed* to verbs, children often add *–ed* to all verbs. They will say, "She drinked her milk."
- Children understand more symbols than they use. For example, hearing the sentence "Paul was *imbued* with the qualities of goodness and kindness," a child might know that *imbued* means "filled." However, the child might not feel comfortable using the word *imbued.*

5. Language Changes. The English language is constantly changing. The meanings of words change, new meanings are given to words, and new words are added. However, these changes usually occur slowly enough so that most speakers of the language can adapt to the changes as they occur. Building a broad, effective vocabulary is important, because the more words you know and use, the better you will be at communicating both spoken and written messages.

Common Ways That Language Changes

Sources of Change	Examples
Words come from other languages.	Spanish: *canyon, tornado* Native American: *raccoon, persimmon* Chinese: *typhoon, ketchup*
Whole words are put together to create new meanings.	*busybody, downfall, lifesaving, videotape, skateboard*
Words are blended to create new meanings.	*smoke + fog = smog* *motor + hotel = motel*
New words are needed for new objects and ideas.	*microchip, artificial intelligence, ethanol, laser, killer bees*
Meanings of words change.	meanings of *nice* over six hundred years: "foolish," "strange," "lazy," "modest," "precise," "dainty," and "pleasant"

over time. Before assigning **Activity 2,** select one of the words in the activity, discuss with students the word's connotations, and then have students look up the word in both dictionaries.

Discuss the examples of denotation and connotation and the ways that language gains positive or negative connotations. As guided practice for **Activity 3** on p. 32, you might videotape a television commercial for class viewing and model for students the analysis of words for positive and negative meanings. Assign **Activity 3** as independent practice.

To prepare students for **Activity 4,** analyze the **Sublanguages** chart on p. 34 and discuss some current slang expressions or jargon phrases students are familiar with. You might discuss some of your favorite slang phrases that have faded from popularity or that are indicative of past fads before asking students to collect slang expressions for **Activity 4**.

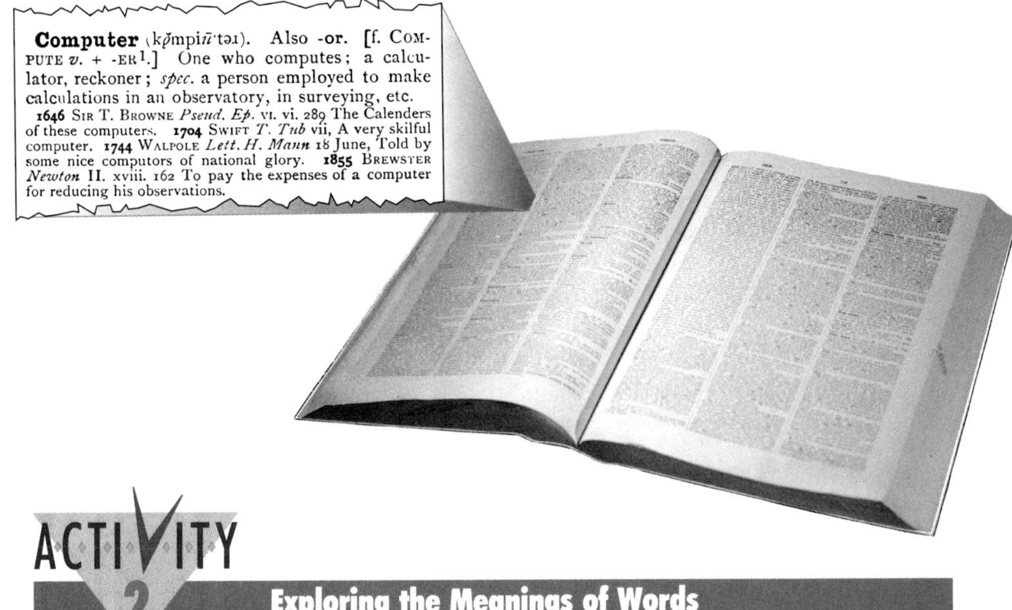

Computer (kǒmpiū·təɹ). Also **-or.** [f. COMPUTE *v.* + -ER[1].] One who computes; a calculator, reckoner; *spec.* a person employed to make calculations in an observatory, in surveying, etc. **1646** SIR T. BROWNE *Pseud. Ep.* VI. vi. 289 The Calenders of these computers. **1704** SWIFT *T. Tub* vii, A very skilful computer. **1744** WALPOLE *Lett. H. Mann* 18 June, Told by some nice computors of national glory. **1855** BREWSTER *Newton* II. xviii. 162 To pay the expenses of a computer for reducing his observations.

ACTIVITY 2

Exploring the Meanings of Words

In a group with two or three other students, choose one of the following words. Discuss what you think the word means until your group can agree on a definition. Then check your definition in the dictionary you regularly use. Finally, consult the *Oxford English Dictionary* to find the earliest meaning of the word. Share your group's findings with the rest of the class.

amuse	fond	hobby	October	stew
bread	forlorn	nice	silly	temper

Understanding Shades of Meaning

To communicate well, you need to keep in mind that words may have a variety of meanings, some of which are not immediately apparent. These hidden meanings of words may have a great effect on your ability to convey the message you intend. Meaning is communicated through both a word's denotation and its connotation.

Denotation. The **denotation** of a word is its dictionary meaning. The same word may have several different denotations.

EXAMPLE: One denotation for the word *quarter* is "one fourth of a unit of measure, such as a dollar." Another denotation for *quarter* is "an area or section of a city." Still another denotation of *quarter* is "the compassionate treatment given to an enemy who surrenders."

ONGOING ASSESSMENT

Activity 2

Answers may vary according to the dictionary used. These definitions are taken from *Webster's New World Dictionary, Third College Edition* and the *Oxford English Dictionary:*

amuse: to entertain
earliest: to delude, cheat, or deceive
bread: baked food made from a leavened, kneaded dough
earliest: a bit, piece, morsel (of food)
fond: affectionate, loving
earliest: infatuated, foolish, silly
forlorn: deserted, miserable
earliest: morally lost or depraved
hobby: something one likes to do or study in spare time
earliest: a small or middle-sized horse; a pony
nice: pleasing; agreeable
earliest: foolish or stupid
October: tenth month of the year
earliest: eighth month of the year
silly: showing little sense or judgment; foolish; absurd
earliest: deserving of pity
stew: to cook by simmering or boiling slowly for a long time; food so cooked
earliest: a vessel for boiling such as a cauldron
temper: frame of mind; disposition; mood
earliest: to bring to a proper condition by mingling with something else

Assessment

Performances on the activities should provide information about how well students have met the objectives of the segment. In addition, you can assess students' mastery of the first and third objectives by observing how students employ nonverbal communication and connotations of words in speeches they give throughout the term.

Reteaching

You can reteach the first objective by asking a student to pantomime a simple statement such as "I'm hungry." As the student communicates the information nonverbally, ask the others to write down what they think the student is "saying." Then analyze how the nonverbal actions indicate the meaning of the message.

Meeting Individual Needs

Students with Special Needs

Students with learning disabilities may have trouble holding information from television or radio commercials in their minds long enough to work with it. You could adapt **Activity 3** to allow students to work with print advertising.

Ongoing Assessment

Activity 3

To help students get started, suggest that they each find at least one commercial that compares a product or a service to a competitor's product or service. Ask if students can name any examples. Students may need to preview several advertisements before they select three that are appropriate. You may want to have students share their findings in small groups. Then you could compile a master list of words from all the advertisements.

Teacher's Resource Binder

Skills for Success 1
Denotation and Connotation

Connotation. The **connotation** of a word is its hidden meaning, the often powerful feelings and associations that the word arouses. The feelings that you have about a word may depend on the experiences you have had.

EXAMPLE: If you have had pleasant experiences with dogs, the word *dog* may give you feelings of love, warmth, and security. If a dog has chased you or bitten you, however, the word *dog* might give you feelings of fear and hostility.

Good communicators choose words that lead an audience to make certain associations. Advertisers, for instance, sell their products with words that are likely to have positive connotations. You can make the connotations of words work for you by becoming sensitive to the reactions words arouse.

EXAMPLES:

1. Positive connotation: handsome, natural, healthy
2. Negative connotation: rat, pain, decay, foul
3. Neutral connotation: table, number, paragraph, exterior

PEANUTS reprinted by permission of UFS, Inc.

Activity 3: Identifying Positive and Negative Connotations in Advertising

Tape-record and listen to three different commercials from television or from the radio. On a sheet of paper, make two lists for each commercial. In one list, write the words that the advertisers have used to arouse the audience's positive feelings toward the products or services. In the other list, note any words the advertisers have used to arouse their listeners' negative feelings toward competitors' products or services or toward consequences that may follow from a listener's failure to use whatever the advertisers are promoting. Share your findings with your classmates.

To illustrate the language changes specified in the second objective, find in the *Oxford English Dictionary* a word that has undergone significant change in meaning through the centuries. Ask students to give its present meaning and then to read the meanings the word has had at various times. Discuss why these changes may have occurred.

To reteach the concept of positive and negative connotations, ask students to rewrite magazine ads to replace the key words with synonyms. Discuss whether the ads are as appealing with the new words as they were with the original words. Finally, demonstrate how slang changes by bringing a slang dictionary to class and having students look up slang terms in current use. In many cases, slang terms will have undergone considerable change in meaning.

Adapting Language to Specific Situations

Speakers adapt their language to fit the situation, or setting. You probably would speak one way to the person who interviews you for a job, and another way to your friends at a basketball game. In formal situations you would use standard American English. However, in informal situations, you might relax the rules and conventions.

Standard American English. **Standard American English** is language that follows the rules and guidelines found in grammar and composition books. These rules and guidelines cover topics such as agreement of subject and verb, correct use of tenses, and avoidance of double negatives. Because standard American English is widely used and accepted, it allows people from many different regions and cultures to communicate clearly with one another. [For more about the use of standard American English, see pages 289–299.]

Jargon, Slang, and Dialect. Jargon, slang, and dialect are all sublanguages. A **sublanguage** is a subsystem of an established language. **Jargon** is the specialized vocabulary that is understood by people in a particular group or field. **Slang** consists of recently coined words or old words used in new ways. As a sublanguage that is usually limited to a particular time period, slang starts within a group—such as teenagers or rock musicians. It often spreads quickly to the general population and just as quickly begins to sound old and dated. A **dialect** is a regional or cultural variety of language differing from standard American English in pronunciation, grammar, or word choice.

MEETING **INDIVIDUAL** NEEDS

An Alternative Approach

In the mid-1970s, the National Council of Teachers of English issued a policy statement questioning the validity of standard American English. Invite students who are specially interested in language to research the controversy this action sparked and to report on their findings to the class. One place to begin this research is the article "Students' Right to Their Own Language," which is in the February 1975 issue of *College English*.

Linguistically Diverse Students

You may have some students who speak dialects of American English and some who speak other languages. You can help both groups by emphasizing that nearly all languages have dialects; that dialects are normal; and that many languages, including English, French, and Spanish, have standard forms for writing and speaking so that people who do not speak the same dialect can understand each other.

TEACHER'S RESOURCE BINDER

Skills for Success 2
Adapting Language to Specific Situations

Extension

In publications that have opposing philosophies (such as liberal and conservative), find two different descriptions of the same event. Ask each student to read both descriptions and to make a list of words from each article that seems to support the philosophy of the publication. Discuss how the connotations of these words support the position of each writer.

Enrichment

Invite a teacher of hearing-impaired students, an audiologist, or a speech pathologist to class to discuss the language-acquisition processes of deaf children. Ask the guest to demonstrate sign language as well.

Another enrichment activity is to show the film version of *The Miracle Worker*. Ask students to pay particular attention to Helen Keller's difficulty

Integrating the Language Arts

Dictionary Link

Have students look up *dialect* in a dictionary to find the word's etymology [from the Greek *dia-* for "between" and *legein* for "talk"] Ask each student to write for his or her communication journal a paragraph explaining how the etymology of the word is related to its present meaning.

Usage Link

To illustrate how slang changes, bring one or two slang dictionaries to class and let students examine them. Ask students to find slang terms that have changed in meaning over time and to ask each other to guess the terms' older meanings.

Ongoing Assessment

Activity 4

Lists of expressions will vary from group to group. The test of whether an expression is in current use should be whether other members of the class agree that it is. As an alternative to having students ask parents and grandparents for slang expressions, allow students to use slang dictionaries that give dates indicating when the slang expressions were popular.

Sublanguages

Type	Examples	Appropriate Use	Inappropriate Use
Jargon	• television: *sound bite, anchor, talking head* • football: *punt, nose guard, goal*	when speaking to people in a particular group or field that uses that jargon	when speaking outside the particular group that uses that jargon
Slang	• newly coined words: *nerd, hassle, bummer* • old words used in new ways: *awesome, hot, cool, dude*	when speaking in informal situations	when speaking for formal occasions
Dialect	• pronunciation: *greassy/greazy* or *hog/hawg* • grammar: *you/youse/ you'uns/y'all* or "He don't care." • word choice: *pail/bucket* or *flapjack/pancake*	when communicating with others who use that dialect	when speaking for formal occasions

ACTIVITY 4 — Analyzing Slang

Working in a small group, draw up a list of ten slang expressions that you hear at your school. Then ask your parents or grandparents for five slang expressions that they used when they were in school. Share your group's findings with the class. Then, working with the whole class, compile two new lists, one of common slang expressions popular today and one of common slang expressions from the past. What expressions appear on both lists? What conclusions about the times can you draw from these lists?

Sharing Language with Your Audience. Language is a powerful tool. In choosing what to say and how to say it, concentrate on the expectations and limitations of your audience. The less well you know people, the more important your words become in establishing shared meanings and understanding. Learn to use language carefully to improve your effectiveness as a speaker.

with learning language and to the part that nonverbal communication played in her life.

CLOSURE

Ask students to look through the segment and to make lists of the important terms that are discussed. Make a master list of these terms on the chalkboard, and ask students to explain each term. Allow students to use their textbooks for reference.

HOW TO Use Language to Present the Best Possible You

1. **Use words carefully.** If you are not sure of the meaning of a word, look it up in a dictionary before you use the word in speaking or writing.
2. **Understand the connotations of words.** Know not only what a word means, but also what it suggests—the feelings and associations it arouses. Use words that will get the reactions you want from your listeners.
3. **Use language that is appropriate to the communication setting.** Know and respond to the expectations of your audience. In formal settings, use standard American English. In professional or occupational settings, you may use jargon when your listeners understand it. In informal settings, slang and dialect may be more appropriate than standard American English.
4. **Improve your language.** Use your ears and eyes to study the way effective speakers and writers communicate. Listen carefully, read as much as you can, and write!

Set aside several pages in your journal to take notes about the methods effective speakers use. Whenever a guest speaker, a newscaster on television, a teacher, or a friend impresses you with his or her speaking ability, try to determine why the speech is effective. Is it the speaker's delivery? the choice of words? the body language?

INTEGRATING THE LANGUAGE ARTS

Dictionary Link

College dictionaries often mark slang terms with special symbols. Ask your students to look in the front or back matter of their dictionaries to identify the symbol or word the dictionaries use to indicate slang. Then ask students to flip through the dictionaries to locate terms marked with the symbol or word. Have each student note at least three slang terms to share with the class. Remind students that words must be appropriate for the classroom.

WRITING TO LEARN

Ask students to use their communication journals to describe times they've judged other people based on the people's use of language. Were the reactions positive or negative? Why? Mention that a verbal exchange need not have been lengthy to have sent a message about the sender to the receiver.

• Understanding Nonverbal Language

Performance Objectives

- To express emotions through body language
- To analyze pictures for nonverbal cues about appearance
- To use paralanguage to communicate different meanings in a dialogue

MEETING INDIVIDUAL NEEDS

Learning Styles

Kinetic Learners. Students with a keen sense of body movement may recognize the effectiveness of aspects of nonverbal communication more readily than other students do. Encourage students who learn best through movement to participate actively in class discussions of the material in this segment and to share their insights with the class.

Understanding Nonverbal Language

Nonverbal language uses all the elements of communication except words. Instead, a person using nonverbal language conveys messages through signals called cues—body language, appearance, and vocal sounds. Other people interpret these signals as indicating particular meanings. Since nonverbal messages often accompany verbal messages, they tend to have one of the following effects on the verbal message: They may complement or reinforce the verbal message, they may emphasize it, they may contradict it, or they may completely replace a verbal message.

> EXAMPLE: You are reading and your brother leans over, pulls down the book and asks, "Did you get the tickets yet?" In response, you slowly squint one eye at him, then nod your head and raise your book to continue reading. Your brother could probably interpret the meaning of your nonverbal message: "Of course, I got the tickets. Don't bother me with silly questions while I'm busy reading."

If a nonverbal message is interpreted incorrectly, however, an inappropriate response may result. For this reason, people often do a **perception check,** a verbal response stating one person's understanding of someone else's nonverbal behavior.

> EXAMPLE: Lucia asks Tyrone if he liked the game. Tyrone looks upward briefly, then glances at Lucia and says, "Right." Lucia does a perception check. She says, "It looks as though you really mean that the game was awful. What happened?"

Analyzing Body Language

Body language is the use of facial expressions, eye contact, gestures, posture, and movement to communicate.

- **Facial expressions.** People are capable of making many facial expressions that can have a variety of meanings. People also use **masking** (adopting facial expressions normally associated with one feeling to disguise other, true feelings—smiling to hide pain, for example).
- **Eye contact.** In American society, a speaker and a listener generally look each other in the eye during much of a conversation. Eye contact is usually interpreted as a sign of honesty and straightforwardness. However, staring directly at a person too long is considered impolite.
- **Gestures.** Gestures are the movements people make with their arms, hands, and fingers.

- To analyze the color, lighting, sound, and space of three different communication environments
- To describe two social situations with different space requirements

Motivation

Consider beginning the class period by using nonverbal signals instead of your usual verbal greeting to students. For example, simply look at the students and use your eyes and facial expressions to tell them you are ready to begin. When you have their attention, hold up your textbook opened to the page you want them to find and signal for them to open their books to the same

- **Posture.** Posture is body position. The way you hold your body when you walk and the way you sit on a chair tell others a great deal about you.
- **Movement.** Movement is simply the way a person moves. The way you walk, stand, sit, and perform other actions creates an impression on others and is interpreted as having meaning.

Body language can sometimes express a message clearly without the need for words.

Communicating with Body Language

Type	Examples or Meanings	Functions
Facial expression	winking; making eye contact; raising an eyebrow; smiling; frowning; sneering	• can help to show a person's feelings, either as a substitute for or as a reinforcement of a verbal message • can emphasize or contradict verbal language
Eye contact	looking the other person in the eye while speaking or listening	• can indicate honesty, sincerity • can demonstrate the intensity of interest that the speaker or listener feels about the communication between them
Gestures	nodding for "yes"; shrugging the shoulders for "I don't know"; pointing with index finger; gesturing to show size, shape, or length	• can replace words in certain messages • can emphasize meaning of verbal language • can add to meaning when a speaker gives descriptions
Posture	standing tall and sure; slumping in a chair	• can convey attitude, such as confidence and poise or dejection and weariness
Movement	walking with a quick, lively step; dragging feet reluctantly	• can enhance the impression you want to make or the message you intend to convey

Critical Thinking

Synthesis

Show without sound a videotape of people talking. Have students work in small groups to write brief dialogues based on what they think the people on the tape are saying. Have each group act out its dialogue for the class.

Making Connections

Mass Media

Show without sound a videotape of a television talk show that involves the expression of strong emotion. Ask students to catalogue the facial expressions and gestures the people use. Then have students decide, based on body language, how they think the people conversing feel about one another. Finally, play the tape with sound to let students check their impressions.

Teacher's Resource Binder

Skills for Success 3
Communicating with Body Language

page. Hold up a pen and a notebook and indicate that students should take out note-taking equipment. Answer any questions by nodding or shaking your head. Finally, talk to students about what you've been doing and why you've been doing it: to introduce nonverbal communication.

TEACHING THE LESSON

Have students read **Understanding Nonverbal Language** on pp. 36–45 for homework so that you can spend class time discussing the examples given and any additional examples you feel are necessary for understanding. As you discuss the **Communicating with Body Language** chart on p. 37, demonstrate the types of expressions shown and have students comment on the uses of

ONGOING ASSESSMENT

Activity 5

You may want to emphasize that students should act out situations without giving verbal cues to their emotions. If performance anxiety is a problem for some students, you could suggest that they stand still, take a couple of deep breaths, and focus on visualizing the situations before they begin acting out their scenes. You may want to circulate around the room to give support and to monitor students' participation.

CRITICAL THINKING

Analysis

Lead students in a discussion of the styles and brands of clothing popular in your school. After you have listed on the chalkboard the popular clothing, ask students "What social functions do styles of clothing serve in this school?" [Answers will vary. In most cases, styles of clothing serve to identify people as members of particular groups, but they also announce a person's economic status, reflect personal attitudes and choices, and indicate individuality.]

ACTIVITY 5 Using Body Language to Express Emotion

Work in a group of five or six students. Have each person act out a situation in which he or she uses body language to express a strong emotion. The situation could be stubbing a toe, dropping car keys into a sewer, finding a dollar on the ground, bringing home good (or bad) grades, or winning a prize. Write down the body language that each student uses to present the situation and to show emotions. After everyone has had a turn, discuss the different types of body language each group member used.

Evaluating the Message Your Appearance Sends

As you get to know people better and they get to know you, appearance becomes less important in making judgments. Nevertheless, first impressions count. A major part of a first impression is created by appearance.

1. Appearance can be interpreted by others as a clue to your interests.

EXAMPLES: If you wear a business suit and carry a briefcase, people will assume you spend time in a business environment. If you wear jogging shorts and running shoes, people will assume you are interested in running.

2. Appearance can be interpreted as expressing a person's attitude toward another person, especially when a specific kind of attire is expected.

EXAMPLE: Juliana asks her friend Dan to join her family for dinner at one of the town's better restaurants. Although Juliana does not say anything to Dan, she expects him to dress formally.

body language. This classwork should prepare students to complete **Activity 5** in groups as independent practice. Allow class time for discussion after students act out their situations.

Discuss appearance by reading the examples aloud with students and then by inviting comments. You might use photographs to enhance your discussion and to prepare students for analyzing the appearances of people in pictures in **Activity 6**. Assign **Activity 6** as independent practice.

You could have a volunteer read aloud **Analyzing Paralanguage** on p. 40 and have students demonstrate types of paralanguage. Prepare students for **Activity 7** either by modeling a brief conversation with a student or by acting out both roles yourself. Encourage students to think of cues they can use to dramatize

If Dan shows up in cutoffs and a T-shirt, she may feel hurt, assuming from his informal attire that he thinks meeting her family is unimportant.

3. Appearance can be interpreted as a sign of a person's self-regard.

EXAMPLE: If your clothing consistently looks messy, wrinkled, or soiled, people may interpret your lack of grooming as a sign that you do not think very highly of yourself. If you are well groomed, people may assume you have a good opinion of yourself.

In deciding how you want to look, first consider the impression you want to make, the image you want to project. Second, consider the expectations of others. Then groom yourself and select clothing that projects the image you want to convey to others.

ACTIVITY 6 Analyzing Pictures for Nonverbal Cues

Find a magazine article or an advertisement that features a photograph of one person, and bring it to class. Work with a group of five or six classmates, studying—without discussing—the photographs that everyone in the group brought. Silently, jot down three to five adjectives for each photograph, such as *lively, warm,* and *sympathetic,* that you associate with the person in each photograph. Then compare your lists of adjectives with those compiled by other members of the group. Discuss why each of you selected your particular adjectives. Are there any major differences among the descriptions?

MEETING INDIVIDUAL NEEDS

An Alternative Approach

Ask students who are interested in the effect that appearance can make to read portions of John T. Molloy's *Dress for Success* and to report to the class on what they learn. Other books that students can investigate and report on are Carole Jackson's *Color Me Beautiful* and *Color for Men.*

ONGOING ASSESSMENT

Activity 6

In selecting adjectives to fit pictures, students should consider the full range of body-language and appearance factors that contribute to the total look of the person in the picture. If the picture is from an advertisement, you could ask students to consider whether the picture is appropriate for the product the ad is selling.

their dialogues. Then assign **Activity 7** as independent practice.

When you discuss environmental factors, you might want to arrange to demonstrate the effect of several factors. For example, you could change the lighting in the classroom, play a variety of music or sound tapes, and discuss color and its effects. If possible, you could graphically demonstrate the effects of color by borrowing a light and different-colored gels from the drama department and having students observe their reactions to the different colors. To discuss the consequences of space on communication, have students work with partners to try standing at varying distances from one another. Have them notice their levels of comfort and discomfort with the different distances. These exercises and demonstrations should prepare students to complete **Activity 8** as independent practice.

Analyzing Paralanguage

To emphasize the importance of paralanguage, write on the chalkboard several commonly used phrases such as "I can't believe it!" and "Who said that?" Regional phrases are also appropriate for this activity. Ask volunteers to read each phrase with different vocal tones and inflections to illustrate different meanings. Ask students to identify the specific nonverbal aspects of each reading that communicated meaning.

Additional Activity

To help make students aware of extraneous sounds, ask them to listen to an extemporaneous speech and to count the number of extraneous sounds and words the speaker uses. Then ask students to discuss the effect these sounds and words have on the presentation.

AV *Audiovisual Resource Binder*

Audiotape 1, Lesson 1
Nonverbal Communication

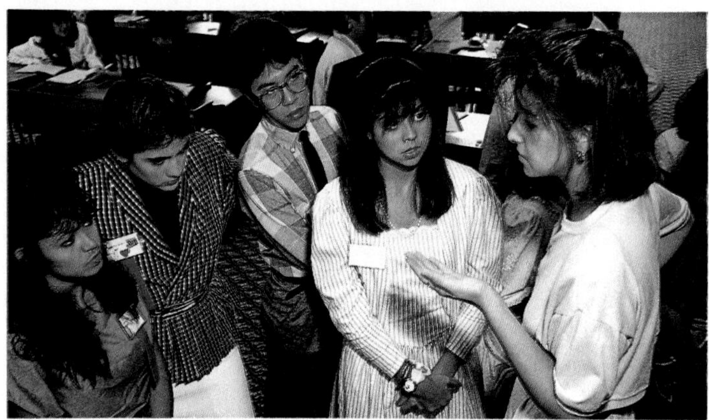

Analyzing Paralanguage

Paralanguage is a type of nonverbal communication that involves using voice variation and extraneous words and sounds to communicate. Although paralanguage may involve making sounds, these sounds are simply used to fill a pause. The three types of paralanguage are shown in the sound of a speaker's voice, the speaker's use of pauses, and the speaker's use of extraneous sounds.

The sound of a person's voice is one aspect of paralanguage. Your voice can be as flexible as any musical instrument. Your voice can

- go up and down in scale (pitch)
- be loud or soft (volume)
- say words quickly or slowly (rate)
- take on different tones or qualities to express various emotions (quality or tone of voice)

A second aspect of paralanguage is a speaker's use of pauses. You can use pauses to indicate uncertainty or to create suspense, or you can pause to add emphasis. For example, a speaker might use a pause to add emphasis or create suspense in saying, "The winner of the scholarship is (pause) Vincente Martinez."

A third aspect of paralanguage is the use of extraneous words and sounds in spoken communication. Some of the words and sounds most commonly used are "uh," "well uh," "um," and "you know." Even though some of these are words, they are considered to be vocalized pauses because they contribute no information to the verbal message into which they are inserted by a speaker. For example, if you say, "Well uh, I think I'm unhappy about my term paper grade," you are using *well* simply to introduce what you are going to say.

Activities 5–8 should give students adequate independent practice for the objectives in the segment. Refer students to this chapter when their messages are one-dimensional and need nonverbal language cues to become livelier and more expressive.

ASSESSMENT

You can assess mastery of the objectives by evaluating students' performances on **Activities 5–8.** In addition, you can assess understanding of body language, appearance, and paralanguage through informal observation of students' discussions and speeches.

ACTIVITY 7
Using Paralanguage to Communicate Meaning

Dramatize the following brief dialogue in three ways. First, add paralanguage cues to the dialogue to show that the two people speaking really like each other. Second, use another set of paralanguage cues to indicate that the two people are not particularly interested in each other but are just being polite. Finally, use paralanguage cues to show that the two people do not like each other at all. After the dramatizations are completed, discuss how paralanguage affected the message in each situation.

"How are you?"
"Great. How about yourself?"
"Just fine."
"I've got to be going now."
"I'll catch you later."

Identifying How Environment Affects Communication

Your **environment** includes all features of the immediate surroundings. Features of the environment are counted as nonverbal communication because they can affect your behavior and mood as well as that of your audience.

When you think of nonverbal communication, you may not think immediately about the effect of the environment, but features of the environment can send important messages. These features may include

- color
- lighting
- sound
- space

ONGOING ASSESSMENT

Activity 7

To save time, you may want to handle this activity as a cooperative-learning activity with groups of six students. Within each group, students can act out the dialogue in pairs. If you do this activity with the whole class, you can let a different pair of students act out each of the three ways of presenting the dialogue. The discussion of paralanguage should focus on the use of vocal sounds, pauses, and extraneous sounds.

RETEACHING

To reteach concepts of nonverbal communication, show without sound a videotape of people in conversation. Ask students to give their impressions of the emotions the people are conveying. Analyze with students the factors of body language and appearance that contributed to their impressions. Then show the tape again with sound and have students compare their first impressions with the impressions they form when they see the tape with sound.

To reteach concepts of paralanguage, make up some nonsense sentences that employ vocal sounds, pauses, and extraneous sounds; then read the sentences to the class. Ask students to give their impressions of how you felt about what you read; then discuss factors that contributed to these impressions. Demonstrate the importance of space by purposely violating the space rules

MAKING CONNECTIONS

Mass Media

Show a videotape of clips of television soap operas and ask students to pay close attention to the lighting and the sound. Then discuss these questions: How do lighting and sound change from scene to scene? What effect do these changes have on the mood?

Color. People often respond to the subtle effects of color in their surroundings. Some colors, such as reds, yellows, and oranges, have a stimulating effect. To many people, these colors seem warm, full of vitality, and exciting. Other people see blues, greens, and beiges as cool, peaceful, or neutral. In general, black and brown seem mysterious and sophisticated, while white seems innocent and childlike.

Lighting. Lighting can affect an audience's behavior and mood in various ways. Low lighting tends to create a relaxed, quiet atmosphere in which people want to linger. Bright lighting stimulates conversation and interaction, while extremely bright lighting may cause fatigue.

Sound. Sound often complements lighting. In a dimly lit restaurant, you expect soft music. In a brightly lit restaurant, you expect somewhat louder music. However, loud or continuous noises are almost always distracting. A lawn mower outside, a jet overhead, a noisy air conditioner, or a faulty fluorescent light buzzing makes communication difficult.

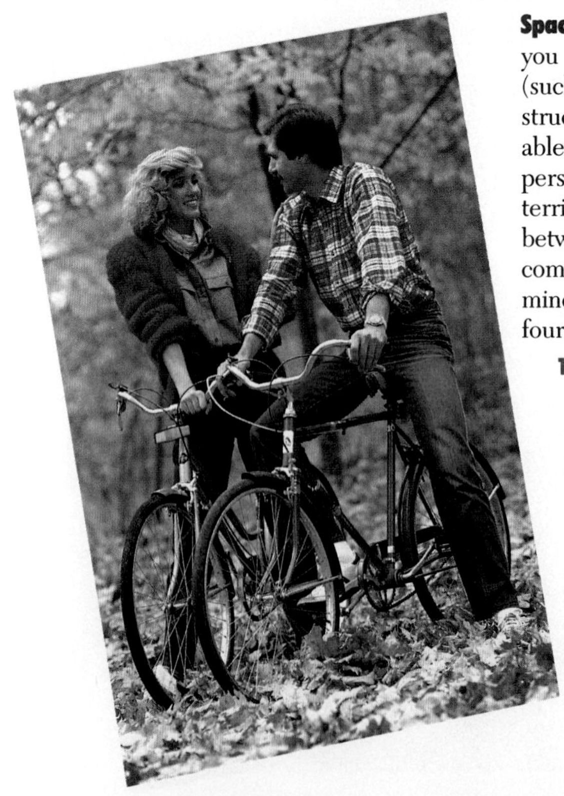

Space. Strictly defined, the space around you may include large, permanent elements (such as various kinds of buildings), smaller structures (such as rooms and walls), movable elements (such as furniture), and the personal spaces that people regard as their territory. Generally, the amount of space between you and your audience affects your communication. Researchers have determined that most people function with at least four different distances.

1. Your **intimate space** consists of up to eighteen inches between you and other people. It is the distance at which you feel comfortable communicating with family members and close friends. Violation of intimate space by strangers causes friction. Most people will back away from others who get within the eighteen-inch range if they are not close friends or relatives. To some extent, the boundary of intimate space is dictated by custom. In other countries it may be less or more than it is in the United States.

when talking to students. Ask them to say how this made them feel, and ask them to draw conclusions about the importance of space as a factor in communication.

2. Your **personal space** consists of a distance ranging from eighteen inches to four feet between you and other people. It is the distance at which you conduct most conversations with acquaintances. You want people to be close enough so that you can hear and see each other easily, but not so close that either of you feels uncomfortable.

3. Your **social space** consists of a distance from four to twelve feet between you and other people. It is the distance at which you carry on interviews and other formal kinds of conversations.

ADDITIONAL ACTIVITY

You can demonstrate the importance of space by changing the distance between you and the class as you speak. Start at the front of the room or at your usual speaking place. Then walk to the middle of the classroom as you continue talking. Finally, walk up to individual students and look at them as though you were addressing them individually. When you've done this several times, ask for students' reactions.

Extension

Show videotapes of both nationally distributed and locally made television commercials. Ask students to analyze the actors' body language, appearance, and paralanguage. Also have students consider the environment of each commercial. Then ask students to rate the overall effectiveness of each commercial. Lead a class discussion about the extent to which the nonverbal factors contribute to the relative effectiveness of commercials.

Ongoing Assessment

Activity 8

In their responses, students should note such factors as the degree of intimacy or formality in each environment. They should make an effort to link these factors to the color, lighting, sound, and space of each environment.

4. Your **public space** consists of the area beyond twelve feet between you and others. It is the distance at which you expect such types of communication as public speeches and oral readings to take place.

Analyzing an Environment

Select three communication environments—for example, a classroom, a sitting area in your home, and a public meeting room. Describe the color, lighting, sound, and space in each environment. How do these features contribute to or detract from the communication setting? How do these features differ from one environment to another? Compare your findings with those of your classmates.

HOW TO *Use Nonverbal Communication Effectively*

1. **Use body language that supplements what you want to say.** Consider your facial expressions, eye contact, gestures, posture, and movements. Change any that contradict your verbal message.
2. **Make sure your appearance is in keeping with what you want to accomplish.** Consider the image you wish to project. How does it relate to your listeners' expectations and to the demands of the situation?
3. **Make sure that the sound of your voice is in keeping with your message.** Learn to control the pitch, volume, rate, and quality of your voice. Pay attention to your use of pauses and extraneous sounds and words.
4. **If possible, create an environment that is suitable for the kind of communication you want.** Use color, lighting, sound, and space to accomplish your purpose.

Think of situations in which people gather together to talk. Describe briefly a situation in which people would feel comfortable talking at an intimate distance. Then briefly describe a situation in which the participants would feel more comfortable conversing at a personal distance.

Teacher's Resource Binder

Skills for Success 4
A Message About Me

ENRICHMENT

To enrich your students' understanding of nonverbal communication, let students play a few rounds of charades. You might want to divide the class into teams of five or six for this activity so everyone has a chance to participate.

CLOSURE

Review the ideas presented in the segment by calling on students to explain and to demonstrate the major concepts of body language, appearance, paralanguage, and environment.

WRITING TO LEARN

Have students review the second part of the chapter to determine the aspects of nonverbal language that they feel most comfortable with. Have each student describe in a journal entry the body language, image, and environment that make him or her feel most comfortable in speaking. Have students write about ways they can control these factors and ways they might stretch their levels of comfort to include wider ranges of language behaviors.

GUIDELINES

for Effective Verbal and Nonverbal Communication

- Do I understand the denotations and connotations of the words I use?
- Do I use standard American English when appropriate?
- Do I use jargon, slang, and dialect only in appropriate settings?
- Does my body language complement my verbal message?
- Does my appearance project the image I wish to create?
- Is the sound of my voice in keeping with my verbal message?
- Do I consider how my environment affects my communication?
- Am I aware of what my verbal language and nonverbal language tell others about me?
- Am I working to improve my verbal and nonverbal messages?

BUILDING A PORTFOLIO

Have students write responses to the questions in **Guidelines for Effective Verbal and Nonverbal Communication.** Students could keep their responses in their assessment portfolios and check later in the term to see if their levels of mastery have increased.

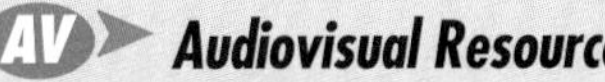

Audiovisual Resource Binder

Transparency 5
Guidelines for Verbal and Nonverbal Communication

◆ Profiles in Communication

Performance Objectives

- To examine, categorize, and record the ways people use nonverbal signals
- To share findings in a class discussion

Teaching the Feature

Have students read the profile of interpreter Kay Trowbridge. If some of your students know ASL, ask them to demonstrate to the class how the different elements of ASL work to transmit communication. If there are no such students in the class, you might want to show students a videotape on ASL or to bring to class a guest speaker who could demonstrate signing.

Activity Note

To begin the activity, have a volunteer draw on the chalkboard a model of the chart and have students use this model to set up their charts in class. Students should gather data in class and as independent practice at home and in other classes.

You may want to divide the class into groups of three or four to discuss findings. Have a spokesperson for each group report to the class the group's most interesting conclusions and observations.

PROFILES IN COMMUNICATION

Kay N. Trowbridge

Kay Trowbridge, an interpreter at the Texas School for the Deaf, facilitates communication between users of different languages. In her case, the two languages are English and American Sign Language (ASL). "ASL isn't just English translated word-for-word into gestures," she explains. "It's a very different language, with its own grammar, sentence structure, and idiomatic expressions. ASL is unique since it is a visual, gestural, and spatial language which is closely tied to Deaf culture."

ASL's vocabulary includes thousands of signs, which may involve a combination of mime, facial expressions, eye movement, and body language. "These elements are an integral part of ASL," she adds. "If you miss a facial expression, you might misinterpret a concept that's essential to the meaning of the sentence. Signing faster or slower, harder or softer in conjunction with facial expressions represents voice inflection." ASL, she believes, can express nuances equaling that of any spoken language.

Ms. Trowbridge works with deaf children in public schools, attending their classes and interpreting for them, their teachers, and their classmates. The most rewarding aspect of her job, she says, is enabling deaf and hearing people to bridge the gap between each other's cultures and perspectives.

ACTIVITY

Spend a day recording the ways people use nonverbal signals. Make a chart with four columns (one for each function of nonverbal communication) and three rows (for facial expressions, gestures, and posture). As you notice people's body language, decide which row each signal belongs in. Then decide which column best describes the purpose of that expression, gesture, or posture. Compare your findings with those of your classmates. Discuss the most and least frequently used types of body language. Also note the most common and least common functions of nonverbal signals. Then try to reach a consensus about how expressive people are when they speak. Do you agree that people could be more open with their feelings in conversation? Why or why not?

S·U·M·M·A·R·Y

SENDING VERBAL AND NONVERBAL MESSAGES involves both verbal and nonverbal language. Verbal language uses spoken and written words; nonverbal language uses cues that communicate ideas and feelings without using words. When you communicate, your verbal language and your nonverbal language work together to reveal a great deal about you.

- **Understand verbal language** as a system of sounds and symbols. Verbal language relies on learned conventions that are slowly, but constantly, changing.
- **Understand shades of meaning** of words. A word's meanings may include a variety of denotations or connotations. Denotations are the dictionary definitions of a word, and connotations are the positive, negative, or neutral associations and feelings the word arouses. Verbal language adapts to suit the communication situation. Depending on the circumstances, a speaker can usually use standard American English. In specific instances, a speaker may use jargon, slang, or dialect to communicate.
- **Understand nonverbal language** as a system that uses all the elements of communication except words. Nonverbal communication serves four main functions: to complement, to emphasize, to contradict, and to replace verbal messages. Nonverbal communication involves body language, appearance, the sound of the speaker's voice, and environmental features.

CHAPTER 2

Vocabulary

Look back through this chapter to find the meaning of each of the following terms. Write each term and its meaning in your communication journal.

body language, *p. 36*
connotation, *p. 32*
conventional, *p. 29*
cues, *p. 28*
denotation, *p. 31*
dialect, *p. 33*
environment, *p. 41*
generalize, *p. 30*
intimate space, *p. 42*
jargon, *p. 33*
masking, *p. 36*
messages, *p. 27*
nonverbal language, *p. 28*
paralanguage, *p. 40*
perception check, *p. 36*
personal space, *p. 43*
public space, *p. 44*
slang, *p. 33*
social space, *p. 43*
standard American English, *p. 33*
sublanguage, *p. 33*
symbol, *p. 29*
system, *p. 29*
verbal language, *p. 28*

TEACHER'S RESOURCE BINDER

- Chapter 2 Vocabulary

Review Questions

Answers

1. to complement, emphasize, replace, and contradict verbal messages
2. Verbal language is a system of sounds and symbols used to communicate ideas and feelings. Verbal language is a system; it's symbolic; it's conventional; it's learned; and it changes.
3. Such learning involves generalizing rules once they are learned. Most people can understand more words than they can comfortably use.
4. through the processes of borrowing words from other languages, putting words together to create new meanings, creating new words to describe new objects and ideas, and permitting meanings to change over time
5. The denotation of a word is its dictionary meaning. The connotation is the feelings and associations the word arouses.

Discussion Questions

Guidelines for Assessment

Student responses may vary.

1. Some students will use a logical approach and others will act intuitively. Have students explain their naming processes.
2. Sandburg's image of slang is one of tough, hard-working, unrefined language that gets the job done. Students should include explanations for the reactions.
3. To encourage people to talk and to show that you are listening, use direct and steady eye contact. To show that you would like a conversation to end, use shifty or occasional eye contact, look at a wristwatch, or gaze out a window.
4. Nordell is mimicking the tendency of modern speakers to include pauses and extraneous words like *like* and *right* in their informal conversations.
5. Have students share their ways of expressing emotions. The nonverbal signals students might use will vary according to individual, social, and cultural differences. Encourage students who are from or who are familiar with different cultures to share their knowledge about the ways that emotions are expressed culturally with different nonverbal signs. Help students recognize the variety of individual and group differences in expressing emotions nonverbally.

CHAPTER 2

Review Questions

1. What are the functions of nonverbal communication?
2. Define *verbal language* and list five important features of it.
3. One principle of language learning is that such learning proceeds from simple to complex. What are two other principles of learning language?
4. List four ways in which the English language changes.
5. What is the difference between the denotation and the connotation of a word?
6. Why is it important to communication to establish a common language such as standard American English? When is it appropriate to use nonstandard English?
7. How can you improve your use of language?
8. One way that body language communicates is through gestures. What are four other ways that body language communicates messages?
9. What is paralanguage?
10. Social space is one type of distance between people who are talking to each other. What are three other types of space, or distance, that affect communication?

Discussion Questions

1. You have discovered an object for which there is no name. What will you call it? Will the name you choose describe what the object does, tell what it is made of, or perhaps, show the object's similarity to something else? Discuss how the name you give the object would become part of the language.
2. In a *New York Times* interview, Carl Sandburg once called slang "language that rolls up its sleeves, spits on its hands, and goes to work." What do you think Sandburg meant by this description? Do you agree or disagree with Sandburg's statement? Discuss your reactions to slang.
3. Eye contact is an important part of conversation. Discuss how you can use eye contact to (a) encourage people to talk, (b) show that you are listening, and (c) show that you would like the conversation to end.
4. Roderick Nordell once wrote, "If only everyone talked the way we do in my household. I mean . . . if only everyone . . . like . . . talked . . . you know . . . the way we do . . . right? It would be so much . . . like . . . easier to . . . you know . . . understand . . . right?" What characteristic of modern speech is Nordell making fun of? How does this characteristic of modern speech affect our communication?
5. Discuss the kinds of nonverbal communication you would use to show each of the following emotions: anger, interest, surprise, self-confidence, happiness, and boredom. Then discuss whether you think people from different cultures use basically the same nonverbal cues to express these feelings.

6. to allow people from many different regions and cultures to communicate clearly with one another; in most informal situations
7. by using your ears and eyes to study the ways effective speakers and writers communicate, by listening carefully, by reading as much as you can, and by writing
8. facial expressions, eye contact, posture, and movement
9. Paralanguage involves using voice variations and non-word sounds to communicate nonverbally. Its elements are the use of vocal sounds, pauses, and extraneous sounds.
10. intimate space, personal space, and public space

ACTIVITIES

1. **Analyzing the Meanings of Words.** List the five words you use most frequently to show your approval of something or someone. First, write the meanings you intend the words to have. Then look up the meaning of each word in a dictionary. Do the words mean what you thought they meant? How many of the words are dialect or slang? Share your findings with your classmates.
2. **Defining Language.** Many writers have tried to define *language.* Use quotation books such as Bartlett's *Familiar Quotations* to compile a list of five quotations about language that you especially like. Share your list with your classmates.
3. **Using Pantomime to Communicate Nonverbal Messages.** Pantomime is a way of sending messages nonverbally. Use pantomime to convey one of the following messages or another message that you choose.
   a. I'm really glad to see you.
   b. Which way should we go?
   c. Don't tell me any more!
   d. What did he say?
   e. That's a great idea!
4. **Adjusting Language to Suit Different Audiences.** Identify two different communication settings, such as talking with your friends and visiting with your grandparents. Plan to present the same information in each setting: that you have been offered a scholarship to your first-choice college or university. How do you alter your verbal and nonverbal language from one communication setting to the next?
5. **Analyzing Problems in Communication.** Being in certain situations can make it difficult for you to communicate clearly. Look at each of the situations shown in the photos on this page. What elements of the situation would likely interfere with communication? What could a speaker do to compensate for such interference? What could a listener do?

6. **Analyzing Nonverbal Communication in Silent Movies.** Watch a silent movie such as Charlie Chaplin's *The Gold Rush* or Mel Brooks's *Silent Movie.* Or, simply

ACTIVITIES

Guidelines for Assessment

You may want to assign only one of these activities to each student or let students choose the ones they wish to do.

1. Words and meanings will vary. Remind students to check the front or back matter of their dictionaries to find the symbol or word used to indicate slang terms so the students will know which of their favorite words are slang.
2. Answers will vary. The quotations should deal with language in general and not with particular words.
3. Students should be given an opportunity to rehearse the pantomimes before presenting them to the class.
4. Students probably speak more formally with their grandparents than with their friends.
5. (top) Noise and lack of privacy would interfere. The speaker and listener could move closer together. (middle) There are no nonverbal cues in phone conversations. The speaker can be precise. The listener can ask the speaker for clarification.
   (bottom) The phone conversation is entirely verbal, while communication with the child relies heavily on nonverbal cues, and the child can't be expected to understand the need for silence. The speaker and listener can both expect and be patient with interruptions from the child.
6. See next page.

Summative Evaluation

Your **Teacher's Resource Binder** contains a reproducible **Chapter 2 Test** that may be used to assess students' mastery of the concepts presented in this chapter.

Portfolio Assessment

For future reference and evaluation you may want to have students keep in their portfolios any skill sheets or evaluation forms that you have used with this chapter along with any other recorded or written materials that students have created.

6. You might want to have students present their gestures in small groups. You could also have students comment on whether or not the gestures from the movies are comfortable for them to use.

7. The oral reports should focus on information about nonverbal factors as they influence the effectiveness of a speaker or as those factors influence the ability of the audience to understand the speaker's message.

8. Students should select brief messages. You may want to group student pairs so that each pair presents its "dialogue" to one or two other pairs rather than to the whole class.

9. If possible, make the taping unobtrusive so that students won't feel self-conscious and exaggerate their nonverbal language. This activity can help students identify aspects of their communication they would like to improve.

10. Although the activity asks students to use photographs, they might want to view clips from videotapes of Olmos's performances in these two movies and then discuss more completely the actor's appearance and use of body language.

turn down the volume on a regular movie. How do performers in the movie communicate? Which gestures seem to be more effective? Present five of these gestures to your class and describe how the gestures were used in the movie. Discuss how such gestures are used in normal speech.

7. **Giving an Oral Report on Nonverbal Factors Affecting Communication.** Many self-help books tell people how to dress, use body language, or design an environment to achieve power or success. Read one of these books, such as John T. Molloy's *Dress for Success* or Jill Briscoe's *Body Language,* and present an oral report about it.

8. **Communicating by Using Paralanguage.** Working with a partner, choose an animal whose sounds you will use to communicate. For example, you might decide to meow, hiss, and purr like a cat. Make up a brief message; then try to communicate this message using only paralanguage and the animal sounds you chose. Wherever appropriate, use animal gestures to reinforce the message. See if your classmates can guess what message you and your partner are expressing.

9. **Analyzing Verbal and Nonverbal Language.** Record a conversation between yourself and a partner. (Ask a classmate to make a videotape of the conversation if you have access to a video camera.) The conversation may be about a subject such as sports, music, movies, food, computers, or cars—any subject that interests both of you. After you've recorded the conversation, play it back. Analyze and evaluate the verbal and nonverbal language you hear and see on the tape.

10. **Using Nonverbal Communication in Drama.** Examine the three photographs of Edward James Olmos shown on this page. The first picture shows Olmos in everyday life. The second shows him portraying a role in the movie *Blade Runner.* The third shows Olmos as he appeared in the movie *Stand and Deliver.* Discuss the ways in which Olmos "creates new characters" by changing his appearance and body language.

◆ Real-Life Speaking Situations

Performance Objectives

- To identify situations in which spoken language is not helpful to communication
- To prepare and deliver a speech explaining the use of nonverbal cues in two different communication situations
- To act out nonverbal messages
- To prepare and deliver a dialogue in which an employee asks a boss for a raise

REAL LIFE Speaking Situations

1 Many people secretly—or not so secretly—believe that they can talk their way out of almost anything. Sometimes, however, talking does not work. Language itself can be a barrier. At such times, people need patience and a little creativity.

For example, in communicating with someone who speaks only a little English, verbal communication is often much less effective than nonverbal communication. If, for instance, you were giving directions, you would likely find it more effective to point or to draw a simple map than to use abstract words like *north, left,* or *block.*

What other situations can you imagine in which spoken language is either a barrier or of little help in communicating? Identify two situations in which verbal communication creates problems. How could you use nonverbal language to communicate your message in each situation? What type of nonverbal cues could be the most effective? Prepare a short speech explaining how you would use nonverbal cues to communicate in the two situations. Also be ready to discuss your choice of cues and to act out your nonverbal messages for the class.

2 Eventually, in any field of work you choose, there will come a time when you want a raise in salary. To get your raise, you will likely have to ask for it, and when you approach your supervisor, manager, or director, you will want to exhibit your best qualities.

You have a job and have decided to ask for a raise. (If you do not have a job, imagine that you have your ideal job and that it is time to ask for a raise.) Why do you deserve the raise? Can you state your reasons clearly and convincingly? What are some different approaches that you might use to present your request? Which of these approaches do you think will work best with your boss?

Working with a partner, prepare a dialogue. Take turns having the person playing the employee ask the other person, playing the boss, for a raise. As the employee asking for the raise, you should explain why you deserve the increase in pay. Tailor your request—which should be brief and positive in tone—to suit your audience. Now trade places and repeat the dialogue. Be prepared to act out your dialogue for the class.

Assessment Guidelines

1. You might want to brainstorm with students before they begin this exercise so they have several good ideas about situations in which spoken language is ineffective. Have them give their short presentations using nonverbal messages as part of their deliveries.
2. Students should decide on the attitudes they want to take as they make their requests. The words they choose and the nonverbal cues they employ should fit their attitudes. Students should practice the dialogues before presenting them to the class.

Chapter 3
Using Your Voice
pp. 52–79

Chapter Overview

This chapter explains voice production and voice effectiveness. The first segment suggests proper breathing techniques and familiarizes students with the International Phonetic Alphabet. The second segment covers common difficulties in vocalization and articulation. Finally, the chapter presents guidelines for vocalizing.

Teacher's Resource Binder

The following materials are identified at their point of use in this chapter:

- Skills for Success
  1 *Improving Breath Control and Vocal Resonance*
  2 *Using the International Phonetic Alphabet*
  3 *Improving Vocalization*
  4 *Correcting Articulation Problems*
- Chapter 3 Vocabulary
- Chapter 3 Test/Answer Key

AV *Audiovisual Resource Binder*

The following materials are identified at their point of use in this chapter:

- Transparency 6
  Guidelines for Vocalizing
- Audiotape 1, Lesson 2
  The Vocalization Process
- Audiotape 1, Lesson 3
  Problems in Articulation

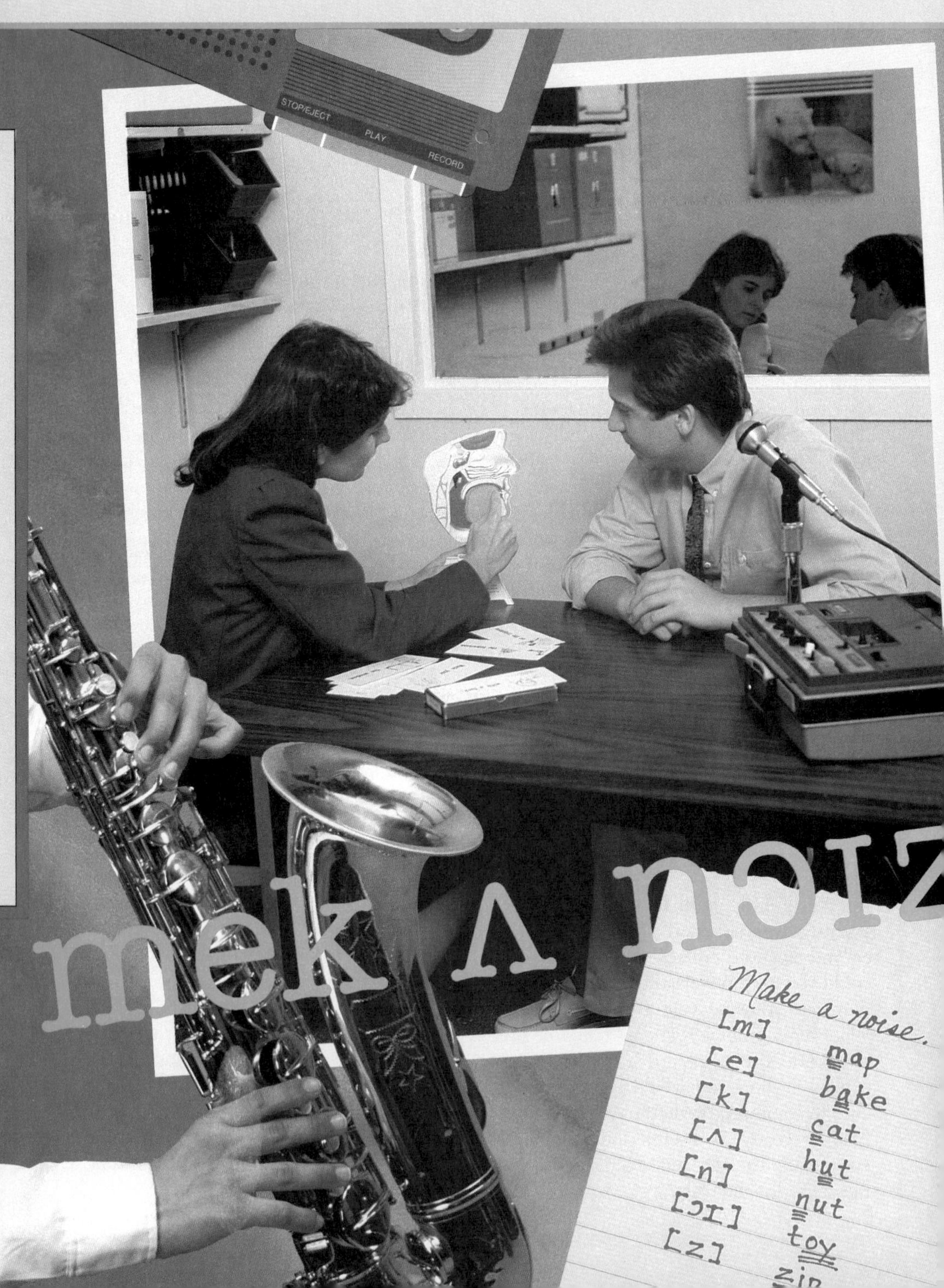

INTRODUCING THE CHAPTER

The prospect of delivering a speech before a crowd may well instill fear in the hearts of many of your students. Tell students that a clear understanding of how voice is generated, resonated, and articulated will give them a new tool to use in dealing with such nervousness. In addition, this chapter will help students to refine their speaking skills by addressing such potential problems as incorrect articulation, poor volume, and unpleasant vocal quality.

CHAPTER 3

Using Your Voice

OBJECTIVES

After studying this chapter, you should be able to

1. Explain how sound is generated.
2. Define *resonance* and identify each of the major resonators of voice.
3. Define *articulation* and identify each of the major articulators of sound.
4. Identify and define each of the key characteristics of vocalization.
5. List the four major aspects of vocalization that affect how you sound to others.
6. List four common articulation problems.

How Your Voice Is Produced

Speaking is our ability to form sounds and to use them to communicate abstract ideas and feelings. We do not have a specialized speech system in the same way that we have a digestive system or a respiratory system. The human voice is generated and shaped by parts of the body that have primary functions other than producing speech. The lungs are primarily for breathing, while the various parts of the mouth and throat are primarily for chewing and swallowing food.

To produce speech, the lungs, the mouth, and the throat and other parts of the body coordinate to

- *generate* sound
- *resonate* sound
- *articulate* sound

In this chapter you will learn how your voice is produced and how to best use your voice.

Bibliography of Additional Materials

➡ PROFESSIONAL READINGS

- Tanner, Fran Averett. ***Creative Communication.*** Topeka, KS: Clark Publishing.
- Utterback, Ann S. ***Improving Your Speaking Voice.*** Washington, D.C.: Transemantics.

➡ AUDIOVISUALS

- ***Chris and Carole Beatty: The Vocal Coach***—Sparrow/Star Song Distribution, Chatsworth, CA (videocassette, 60 min.)
- ***Examination of the Oral Mechanism***—University of Iowa, Iowa City, IA (videocassette, 26 min.)
- ***Speak for Yourself: A Dynamic Vocal Workout***—First Light Video Publishing, Los Angeles, CA (videocassette, 26 min.)
- ***Theatre Fundamentals: Breath of Performance***—Indiana University Audio-Visual Center, Bloomington, IN (videocassette, 14 min.)
- ***Voice in Exile***—Barr Films, Pasadena, CA (videocassette, 29 min.)

Segment 1 *pp. 54–62*

- **Identifying the Generators of Sound**
- **Understanding the Resonators**
- **Identifying the Articulators of Sound**

Performance Objectives

- To practice proper breathing techniques
- To experiment with sound production
- To use the International Phonetic Alphabet to decipher statements

Making Connections

Technology

Discussing sound generation offers an excellent opportunity to introduce students to current research in the science of voice production. Researchers and speech pathologists use computers to analyze the voice and to produce spectrograms, graphic representations of vocal characteristics. You may want to invite a speech pathologist specializing in voice disorders to bring a voice analyzer to class and to demonstrate how it works. A voice analyzer can identify such potential problems as breathiness, harshness, and inappropriate pitch or loudness.

Identifying the Generators of Sound

Respiration is the main function of the breathing structure, but it is not the only function. This structure also helps you generate, or produce, sounds for speech.

The primary generators of sound are the **vocal folds** (commonly known as the **vocal cords**), which are the muscles that make up the larynx. Sound is generated by pushing out air in such a way that the vocal folds vibrate. To understand this process better, look at the following illustration. Notice that many body parts must coordinate, or work together, to produce sound.

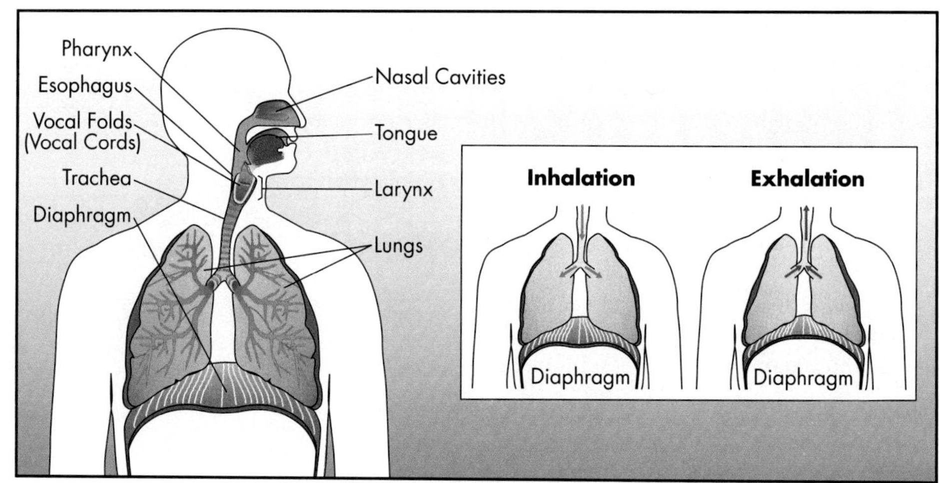

The diagram at the left shows the parts of the body that play a part in generating speech. The diagram at the right illustrates how the diaphragm contracts for inhalation and relaxes for exhalation.

The Respiration Cycle

The respiration cycle consists of inhalation and exhalation, the drawing in and breathing out of air from the lungs. This cycle begins with contraction of the **diaphragm,** a dome-shaped muscle at the base of the lungs. The cycle ends when the diaphragm relaxes. Another cycle begins again almost immediately with the next contraction, and thus the cycles continue. [See the illustration above.]

Inhalation. As the diaphragm contracts, air is drawn in through the mouth or nose and down the throat. In the throat, the air passes through the **larynx** (what most people call the voice box) and the **trachea** (what most people call the windpipe), and then is drawn into the lungs.

Motivation

You may want to begin the lesson by asking students to name the parts of the body that they believe produce voice and shape it into recognizable speech. After the students have generated a list, refer them to the illustration on p. 54—they are likely to be surprised by the many structures that contribute to voice production.

Teaching the Lesson

After students have read **The Respiration Cycle,** you might group students in pairs and have them observe each other's resting respiration. Next, have them observe each other's breathing patterns while speaking. Ask them to jot down notes about how respiration for speech differs from resting respiration. Then introduce **Activity 1** on p. 56; take this opportunity to tell students that

Exhalation. As the diaphragm relaxes, the air in the lungs is pushed back up through the trachea and larynx, through the throat, and out through the mouth or nose. Since the same upper passageway is used for air, food, and drink, a valve in the larynx must open and close to make sure that food and drink go one way while air goes another.

During quiet breathing, the vocal folds remain open so that air can move freely in and out of the lungs. When you eat or drink, the vocal folds protect you from choking by closing off the trachea.

Using Respiration for Speaking

When you speak, you make slight changes in regular breathing to generate sound.

1. You send a burst of air from the lungs up to the larynx to set the vocal folds into vibration. You can feel this vibration if you place your hand lightly on your throat while saying "ah." Because you must be able to sustain this vibration in the larynx to speak clearly and completely, you make two adaptations to your normal breathing pattern:
   - You inhale more swiftly and more deeply than you do during normal breathing.
   - You prolong the airflow as you exhale.

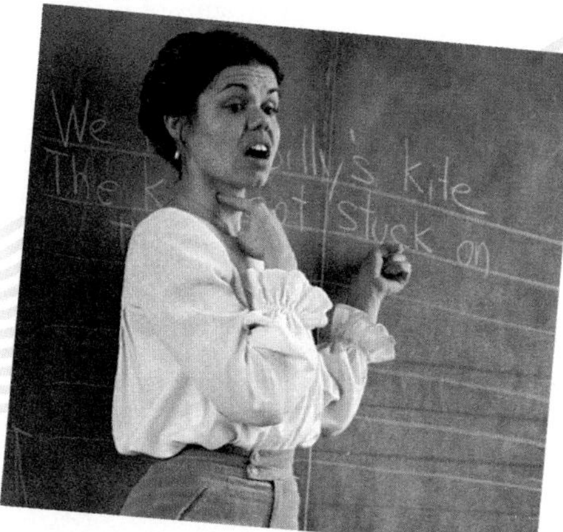

2. Muscles in the chest wall contract to counteract the force of the relaxing diaphragm as you exhale so that all your air does not escape at once. When you are about to run out of air, another set of muscles begins to contract, forcing a bit more air from your lungs and allowing you to sustain speech. When speaking, you learn to control the amount of air you take in, or else you find yourself "gulping air," or taking in large quantities of air quickly, in order to finish sentences.

OOPS Common Error

Problem. Beginning public speakers tend to breathe too shallowly or too quickly during speeches. This kind of breathing leads to a decrease in the oxygen available to the brain and in the amount of air available to support speech and ensure adequate volume.

Solution. Have your class practice diaphragmatic breathing. Emphasize to students that increased pressure from the stomach and lower chest muscles projects the voice.

Teacher's Resource Binder

Skills for Success 1
Improving Breath Control and Vocal Resonance

many professional performers use such breathing exercises to control stage fright.

As you move to **Understanding the Resonators**, you could show the class a videotape, if available, of vocal fold vibration. Such a video should help students to envision clearly the manner in which phonation is achieved. Explain to students that the buzzing sound that occurs when the vocal folds vibrate is not anything like speech and must be shaped by the resonators to be recognizable as speech. Then introduce **Activity 2** on p. 59. You might demonstrate this experiment before the class and solicit students' interpretations of what they have observed.

After discussing **Identifying the Articulators of Sound** on pp. 59–61, you may want to help students use the **International Phonetic Alphabet** chart on p. 60 to write their names. Then assign **Activity 3** on p. 62 as independent practice. In addition, you might assign **Review Questions**

Ongoing Assessment

Activity 1

You may want to have students jot down what they learned about proper breathing as they practiced this activity. Then you can assess their observations.

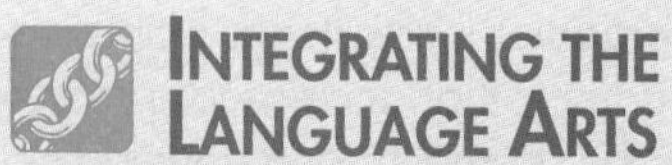

Integrating the Language Arts

Listening Link

Have students listen to the voices of actors, singers, and others who are recognized for the resonance of their voices. For example, you might show clips of Yul Brenner in *The King and I* and clips of James Earl Jones in *Field of Dreams* or *Star Wars* (as the voice of Darth Vader). Discuss with students the anatomical characteristics that lend resonance to these performers' voices (size and shape of throat, nose, and mouth) and how these actors may have further developed their voices through proper use.

Activity 1

Practicing Proper Breathing

For speaking, you need to regulate your airflow so that you do not run out of air in the middle of a sentence. Practice proper breathing by placing the open palms of your hands tightly against your lower front ribs. Inhale slowly and deeply through your mouth and your nose. Notice how your lower ribs push against your hands as you inhale. Hold your breath for the count of five and then say a long, continuous "oooh" as you exhale slowly. Practice this procedure until you are able to control the rate at which you exhale.

Understanding the Resonators

Before sound produced by exhaling air can be speech, it must be given **resonance,** or reinforcement produced by vibration. The **resonators** of sound for speech are

- the bones in the chest, neck, and head
- the cavities of the throat, nose, and mouth

These two groups of resonators amplify sound in different ways.

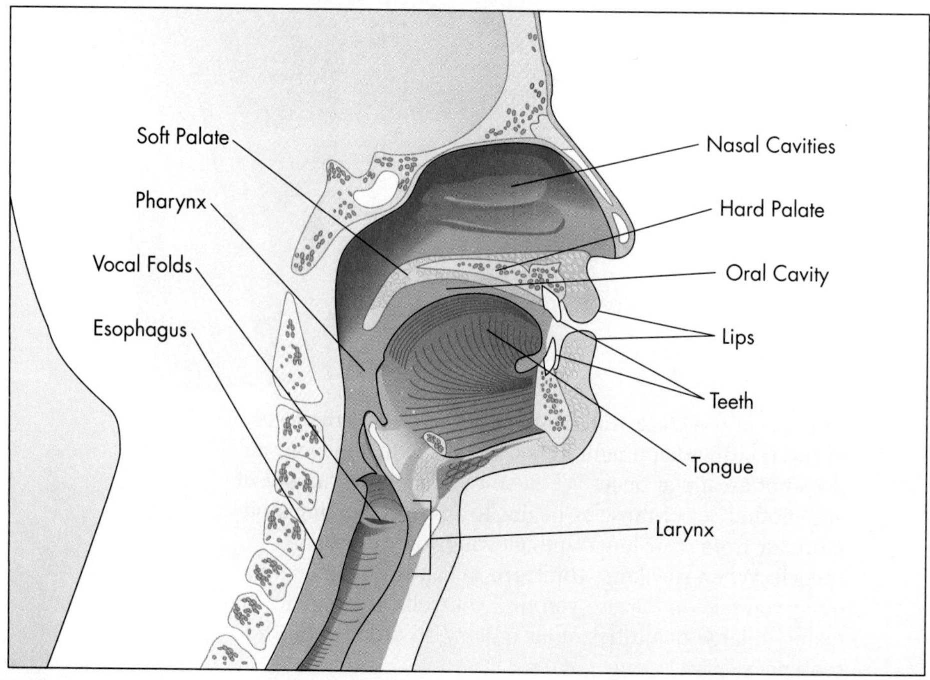

1–5 on p. 76 as homework to provide students with an opportunity to review the information covered in this segment.

Assessment

You can assess understanding of breath control and sound production by observing students' performances on **Activities 1** and **2.** Evaluate students' understanding of the International Phonetic Alphabet by checking answers to **Activity 3.**

Bones resonate by picking up vibrations of sound. To discover how bone resonance works, try a few simple experiments. As you follow these instructions, remember to keep your throat, jaws, lips, and tongue relaxed.

1. With your lips barely touching, hum *m-m-m-m-m-m-m-m.* Feel how this sound vibrates in the bones of your head.
2. Touching the bridge of your nose, hum *ng-ng-ng-ng-ng.* You can feel the resonance of these sounds as you pronounce them.

Most resonance occurs in the cavities of the throat, nose, and mouth. A **cavity** is a partially enclosed area. Every cavity has a natural range of sounds it reinforces, depending on

- the cavity's size
- the cavity's shape
- the texture of the material forming the cavity
- the size of the opening into the cavity

Ordinarily, the larger the cavity, the lower the sounds that it resonates; similarly, the smaller the cavity, the higher the sounds it resonates. To remember this, think of cavity resonance in terms of musical instruments. The tuba—a wind instrument with a large cavity and opening—resonates the deepest sounds. In contrast, the piccolo—one of the smallest of the wind instruments—resonates the highest sounds. Remember that the texture of the walls of the cavity also affects sound. For example, the sound of a metal clarinet differs from that of a wooden clarinet.

Reteaching

Some students might have difficulty using the International Phonetic Alphabet. After reviewing the chart on p. 60, you could write a phonetic spelling on the chalkboard and offer three choices of deciphered words. For example, write *cʊd* and offer *cold, called,* and *could* as choices. Help students to determine the correct answer [could]. Continue the same process with different spellings and choices until students seem more comfortable with the International Phonetic Alphabet.

The Throat

Resonance begins in the throat, or **pharyngeal cavity.** Because this cavity is very flexible and differs in size and wall thickness from person to person, each individual has a distinct resonance or vocal quality. In addition, you have a great amount of control over how you use your throat to create sound.

EXAMPLE: When your throat is tense, it resonates high pitches, and your voice is likely to sound harsh. When your throat is relaxed, it resonates lower pitches, and your voice will usually sound mellow. When you tense your throat, it resonates high pitches—metallic sounds. However, when you relax your throat, it resonates lower pitches—deep, rich, mellow sounds.

The Nose

The nose, or **nasal cavity,** has a direct effect on the three nasal sounds that you make:

- the [m] as in *make*
- the [n] as in *now*
- the [ŋ] as in *sing*

When you produce each of these sounds, your teeth and tongue block the passage of air, forcing the sound to come out of your nose. To some extent, the nasal cavity affects the sound of all speech.

EXAMPLE: When people talk with their mouths partly closed, the nose resonates all their vowel sounds, and their speech has a twangy quality. In contrast, when someone has a cold, the nasal passages get blocked and the nose gives little resonance, even to the [m], [n], and [ŋ] sounds. As a result, that person's speech has a dull or muffled quality.

The Mouth

Of all the resonators, the mouth, or **oral cavity,** is the easiest to alter. You can change the size of the cavity and the shape of its opening by moving your tongue, lips, and jaw.

EXAMPLE: You form various vowel sounds by changing the size of your oral cavity. You keep your tongue back and your mouth open wide to form the *o* in *hot,* while your tongue is forward and your mouth is more nearly closed to form the *ee* in *meet.*

[For more on the function of the throat, the nose, and the mouth, see the discussion of vocal quality on pages 67–69.]

See p. 60 for **EXTENSION, ENRICHMENT,** and **CLOSURE.**

ACTIVITY 2

Experimenting with Sound Production

To experiment with sound production, take a large rubber band (the kind sometimes used to bind daily newspapers or bundles of papers). Loop the band over your hands and stretch it as far as it will go without danger of breaking. While it is stretched tight, pluck the band with your thumb. Describe the sound.

Now move your hands closer together to loosen the band. Pluck it again. Compare the sound of the tightly stretched band to that of the looser band. What does this experiment show you about sound production? How do your findings relate to the process of producing human speech?

Identifying the Articulators of Sound

Articulation is the shaping of speech sounds into recognizable oral symbols that go together to make up a word. Many communication problems are caused by poor articulation.

The major articulators of sound are in the mouth:

- the tongue
- the hard and soft palates
- the teeth
- the lips

Vowel sounds are formed by changing the size of the oral cavity and the shape of the opening. Consonant sounds are formed in three ways: by moving the tongue to various parts of the mouth; by pointing, arching, or flattening the tongue; and by moving and shaping the lips.

EXAMPLE: While saying "ah," raise the tip of your tongue so that it touches the edge of the gum behind the two upper-front teeth. Notice that the sound changes from "ah" to [l]. Now while saying "ah," bring your upper and lower lips together. Notice that the sound changes from "ah" to [m].

The Sounds of English

A speaker who produces clear consonants and distinct vowels is said to have good articulation. If the speaker combines precisely articulated sounds into distinct words, then the speaker is said to have good **pronunciation.** If you have ever had difficulty understanding the speech of someone from another region of America or from another English-speaking country, you are already aware of the importance of clear pronunciation.

Activity 2

Students should say that the tighter rubber band will resonate at a higher frequency than the more loosely stretched rubber band. From their findings, they should deduce that a tight, tense vocal tract will lead to a higher, tinny vocal quality and that a more relaxed vocal tract will produce a richer, fuller voice.

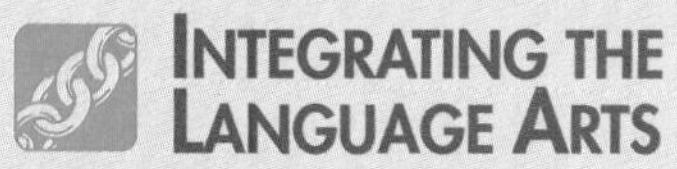

Literature Link

You may want to assign students to find examples of dialect in such books as *Huckleberry Finn, The Color Purple,* and *The Red Badge of Courage.* Have students discuss how the authors have their characters use atypical pronunciations of English words to achieve desired effects. Emphasize to students that incorrect pronunciation is at times appropriate as in informal situations in which pronunciation is consistent with the dialect or in literature when it helps shape and define characters. However, in a more formal setting, such as the delivery of a speech, standard American English pronunciation is generally preferred.

EXTENSION

Ask a local news announcer to visit your class to explain how he or she uses the concepts discussed in this segment for effective public speaking. Students are likely to learn techniques for proper breathing, relaxation, projection, and enunciation that they can apply to their own public speaking.

ADDITIONAL ACTIVITY

You may want to give students additional practice in using the International Phonetic Alphabet. Ask each student to write down a list of ten words and to underline each letter or letter combination that has a symbol in the IPA. Then ask students to exchange lists with partners and to write the symbol that represents each underlined sound. For example, if the letters *oo* are underlined in the word *moon,* a student would write [u]. Then students can return the lists to their partners for checking.

TEACHER'S RESOURCE BINDER

Skills for Success 2
Using the International Phonetic Alphabet

Audiovisual Resource Binder

Audiotape 1, Lesson 2
The Vocalization Process

While the English alphabet has only twenty-six letters, the English language uses forty-five different sounds: twenty-five consonant sounds and twenty vowel sounds. Frequently, the same letter is used to represent different sounds. For instance, *c* is pronounced [k] in *cattle* and [s] in *exercise.*

A more effective system for symbolizing sound is the International Phonetic Alphabet (IPA). In this system, each of the forty-five sounds in English has its own individual symbol. Familiarity with this system, shown in the chart, is important for anyone trying to talk about or write about sound.

As you review this chart, keep in mind the following points.

1. Each IPA symbol represents only one unit of sound.
2. When a sound is shown in a sentence, it is placed within brackets. For instance, the sound [d] is one sound.
3. A consonant sound is pronounced by itself, without an accompanying vowel sound. For instance, usually when you are asked to give the sound for the letter *d,* you say "dee." However, "dee" is two sounds—a [d] and an [i]. (The IPA symbol [i] is the same sound that is represented by the letters *ee.*) The actual pronunciation of the sound produced by the letter *d* is simply [d].

International Phonetic Alphabet (IPA) Symbols Frequently Used in Speech

CONSONANTS							
[b]	*b*oy	[p]	*p*ie	[d]	*d*ot	[t]	*t*ap
[g]	*g*ot	[k]	*c*at	[v]	*v*ain	[f]	*f*ar
[ð]	*th*en	[θ]	*th*in	[z]	*z*ip	[s]	*s*at
[ʒ]	lei*s*ure	[ʃ]	*sh*ow	[dʒ]	*j*et	[tʃ]	*ch*in
[h]	*h*ot	[m]	*m*ap	[n]	*n*ow	[ŋ]	ri*ng*
[l]	*l*it	[r]	*r*id	[j]	*y*et	[hw]	*wh*y
						[w]	*w*it
VOWELS							
[i]	m*e*	[ɪ]	*i*t	[e]	b*a*ke	[ɛ]	p*e*t
[æ]	b*a*ck	[a]	b*o*ther	[ɔ]	c*augh*t	[o]	g*o*
[ʊ]	t*oo*k	[u]	s*oo*n	[ʌ]	h*u*t	[ə]	*a*bove
[ɝ]	b*ir*d	[ɚ]	nev*er*				
DIPHTHONGS							
[aɪ]	r*i*de	[aʊ]	c*ow*	[ɔɪ]	t*oy*	[ju]	c*u*te
[eɪ]	m*ay*	[oʊ]	h*oe*				

Enrichment

Proper breathing is an important aspect of relaxation techniques such as yoga. Ask students to investigate breathing exercises used for meditation or relaxation and to report their findings to the rest of the class. Encourage demonstrations of the breathing exercises.

Closure

Ask volunteers to explain the slight changes that individuals make in regular breathing to generate sound. Then ask volunteers to explain what happens to the voice in the following situations: tensing the throat, relaxing the throat, and talking with the mouth closed.

The caveman's statement is humorously ungrammatical: "If we want to talk really good, we'll have to invent vowels." The caveman's point, however, is a good one. The consonant sounds of English are fairly predictable, while the vowel sounds differ widely, depending on how they are combined in a word, how stress is placed on various syllables of the word, and how individual speakers pronounce certain sounds.

Classification of Sounds

Sounds are either voiced or voiceless. **Voiced** means that the vocal folds are vibrating when the sound is being made. **Voiceless** means that the vocal folds are held open so that air breathed out does not vibrate them.

EXAMPLE: First, say the word *view.* Notice that [v] is made by placing the lower lip against the inside of the upper front teeth. Now say the word *few.* Notice that the placement of your lip and teeth for [f] is exactly the same as for [v]. The difference is that the [v] sound is voiced, while the [f] sound is voiceless. (Place two fingers on your Adam's apple, and alternate saying *view* and *few.* When you say the [v] sound, you should feel a vibration. However, when you say the [f] sound, you should not feel any vibration.)

Consonant sounds can be further divided into four separate sound groups.

1. The **plosives** form a small explosion when you say them. The sounds [p] and [b], [t] and [d], and [k] and [g] are all plosives.
2. The **fricatives** make a frictionlike noise as they are spoken. The fricatives are [f] and [v], [θ] and [ð], [s] and [z], [ʃ] and [ʒ], and [j].
3. The **nasals** are sounds that are resonated in the nasal cavity. The nasals are: [m], [n], and [ŋ].
4. The **glides** are sounds that result from the gliding movement of the articulators. The sounds [l], [r], [w], [hw] and [j] are glides.

Segment 2 *pp. 62–73*

- **Improving Vocalization**
- **Correcting Articulation Problems**
- **Sending Effective Vocal Messages**

Performance Objectives

- To demonstrate how pitch affects meaning
- To experiment with volume
- To measure and compare speaking rate in conversation and in reading aloud
- To analyze speakers' voices for pleasant and irritating qualities
- To identify and correct errors in articulation

Ongoing Assessment

Activity 3

1. Why me?
2. Who took the ball?
3. I love pizza.
4. Give me a chance.
5. I just ate.

Making Connections

Mass Media

You may want to bring to class a videotape of a television talk show with audience participation and one of a more staid broadcast such as the evening news. Have students compare each announcer's use of pitch and volume to achieve a desired tone and to elicit the desired audience response. Ask students which style they prefer and why.

Teacher's Resource Binder

Skills for Success 3
Improving Vocalization

Activity 3 — Using the International Phonetic Alphabet

Using the International Phonetic Alphabet (IPA) shown on page 60, decipher each of the following statements.

1. hwaɪ mi?
2. hu tʊk ðə bɔl?
3. aɪ lʌv pitsə.
4. gɪv mi ə tʃæns.
5. aɪ dʒʌst eɪt.

Improving Vocalization

There are four aspects, or characteristics, of vocalization that affect how you sound to others: pitch, volume, rate, and quality. In this section, you will look at these aspects and at some of the problems that speakers have with them. Fortunately, there are ways to correct these problems.

Pitch

Pitch is the highness or lowness of the sound you make. Vocal pitch varies from person to person, depending on individual differences in vocal structure. To understand pitch, think of the strings of a guitar or a violin. The longer, thicker, or looser the string, the lower the pitch. The shorter, thinner, or tighter the string, the higher the pitch. Several factors are included in evaluating pitch: key, melody, range, and inflection.

Key is the average pitch at which you speak.

Common Problem: Speaking in too high or too low a key can be a problem because it can strain your voice or cause it to sound unpleasant.

Solution: Find your **optimum pitch**—the pitch at which you speak with the least strain and with the very best resonance. Your optimum pitch will probably be about four notes above the lowest note at which you can speak comfortably.

MOTIVATION

As you read aloud the following passage, try speaking in a very loud voice, at an exceptionally fast pace, or in a monotone. Ask students to listen for problems in vocalization and articulation.

"Could you aks the photographer to bring an extra roll of filum to tonight's athaletic event? Also, member to tell'um that we perfer action shots, especially of da childern on da sidelines."

Tell students that this segment covers problems in vocalization and articulation.

Melody refers to the variations in pitch that help to give expression to a person's voice.

COMMON PROBLEM: A **monotone** is a melody pattern that consists of only one tone. No one actually talks in a true monotone, with every word spoken at exactly the same pitch. However, many people approach a monotone when they are giving a speech or reading out loud.

SOLUTION: When you speak, you should try to vary your melody to help give meaning to what you are saying—to make your voice expressive.

Range is the spread between the lowest and the highest notes you can speak comfortably. The greater your range, the more flexible your voice.

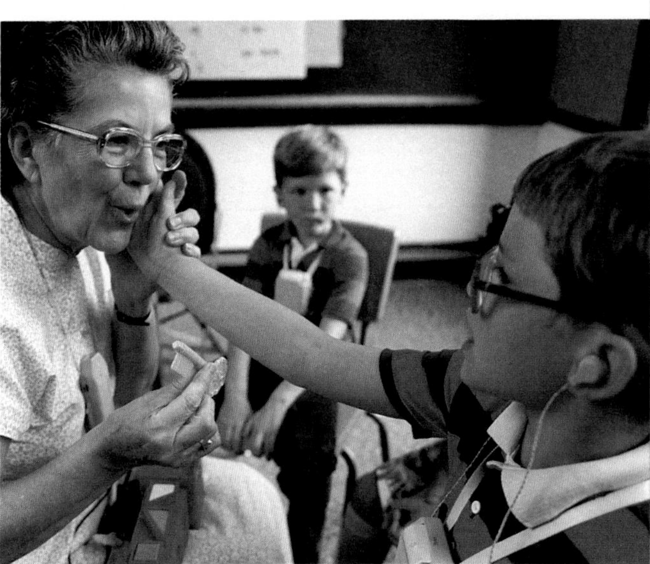

COMMON PROBLEM: If your voice is limited to a range of three notes or fewer, it will sound monotonous.

SOLUTION: Practice extending your vocal range until you can cover ten tones. Having a greater vocal range will allow you more room for variation in your pitch and will therefore enable your voice to be more expressive.

Inflection is the upward or downward glide of your pitch as you speak. By altering your voice upward or downward, you express shades of meaning.

1. Rising inflections are generally used in communicating doubt, uncertainty, indecision, questioning, surprise, or an unfinished thought.

   EXAMPLE: If you glide your voice upward on the word *home* in the following sentence, the upward glide indicates uncertainty: *Are you going home?*

2. Falling inflections are generally used in communicating certainty, finality, or a completed thought.

   EXAMPLE: If you glide your voice downward on the word *home* in the next sentence, the downward glide indicates certainty: *I'm going home.*

MEETING **INDIVIDUAL** NEEDS

An Alternative Approach

Students who readily understand the importance of vocal quality may be willing to experiment more with their own voices as instruments of sound. You may wish to select poetry and prose passages for these students to read aloud to achieve variety in vocal characteristics such as pitch, rate, and volume.

COOPERATIVE LEARNING

Have students work in pairs or small groups to go through the **Common Problem** and **Solution** scenarios on pp. 62–65. Tell students to simulate each erroneous vocal pattern presented and then to correct it. Have each group write down its reactions to the erroneous vocal patterns. Ask the groups how they would feel if they had to listen to this type of speech for a full class period or throughout a politician's speech.

TEACHING THE LESSON

You may want to explain to students that improving vocalization and articulation can greatly improve their speaking ability. Students are most likely to be interested in the material when they see how it relates to them personally. You will probably want to offer opportunities for students to practice vocalization and articulation as they read and discuss the material.

As guided practice for **Activity 4,** you could read aloud the following sentence several times: "You will eat in the cafeteria." Each time, change the pitch to give the sentence a different sound and meaning. Then assign **Activity 4** as independent practice.

Discussion of pitch, volume, and rate naturally leads to consideration of voice production in stressful circumstances. Tell students that these three characteristics are the aspects of voice most

MAKING CONNECTIONS

Technology

If available, a computerized voice analyzer could help to give students a better understanding of pitch as they complete **Activity 4.** The voice analyzer will provide students with a graphic representation of pitch changes and will help students to differentiate between changes in pitch and changes in volume for emphasis.

For example, as students repeat the sentence emphasizing that Tom took the book, the spectrogram will show a rise in pitch on the emphasized word, *Tom.* Explain that this word was not necessarily produced more loudly than the other words in the sentence but was emphasized by a rise in pitch.

ONGOING ASSESSMENT

Activity 4

To assess comprehension, you could circulate among the groups as they experiment with changing pitch to give the sentence different sounds and meanings. You may want to have representatives from each group briefly share their findings.

3. A **circumflex** is an up-and-down inflection.

   EXAMPLE: Suppose someone asks you what you are doing tomorrow, and you respond, "Tomorrow? Hmm, I'm not surc." As you say the word *tomorrow,* it is likely that your voice will glide up and down the scale.

4. While inflections are gradual upward or downward glides, a **step** is an abrupt change in pitch. By abruptly changing your pitch, you emphasize a word in a sentence.

   EXAMPLE: Suppose a friend demands that you drop what you are doing and go with him. If you reply "I can't go," most likely you will abruptly change your pitch to emphasize the word *can't*:

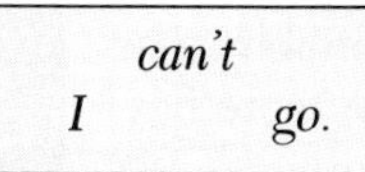

Hi & Lois by Dik Browne. Reprinted with special permission of King Features Syndicate, Inc.

ACTIVITY 4 Evaluating Vocal Pitch

Experiment with two classmates to demonstrate how pitch affects meaning. Use the sentence *Tom is the one who took the book.* Have every speaker read the sentence, changing pitch to give the sentence a different sound and meaning.

Begin by having the first speaker say the sentence in a monotone, expressing every word on the same pitch. Have the second speaker say the sentence in a way that emphasizes that it was Tom, not someone else, who took the book. Have a third speaker say the same sentence, this time emphasizing that it was the book Tom took, not a pencil.

Discuss in the group how each speaker used pitch to change the meaning of the sentence. You might experiment further to see how many other ways you could change pitch to give this sentence other meanings.

likely to be affected when the speaker is nervous or tense. Pitch is likely to rise, volume may increase or decrease, and rate is likely to be excessive. **Activity 5** on p. 66 and **Activity 6** on p. 67 should help to heighten students' awareness of these aspects of speech. Because both activities deal with personal experiments, students should need little guidance.

Next, briefly consider vocal quality. Students who demonstrate significant difficulties in this area (harsh or hoarse voice, for example) probably already have been identified to receive specialized speech-therapy services. The purpose is to help students identify any unusual habits that may be interfering with the development of their best speaking voices.

Finally, consider articulation problems. This section can be challenging to teach if many of your students do not speak standard American English. Having students complete **Activity 7** on

Volume

Volume, or loudness, is the intensity of sound. Volume depends on the force exerted to produce the speech tone. To increase loudness, you have to increase the pressure behind the column of air being forced up from the lungs through the vocal folds. The louder you want to talk, the more pressure you need.

COMMON PROBLEM: Some people talk too loudly or too softly and do not realize that their volume is a problem. They have become so used to the way they talk that it sounds just right to them.

SOLUTION: To identify this problem in your own speech, ask a friend to alert you whenever you speak too loudly or too softly.

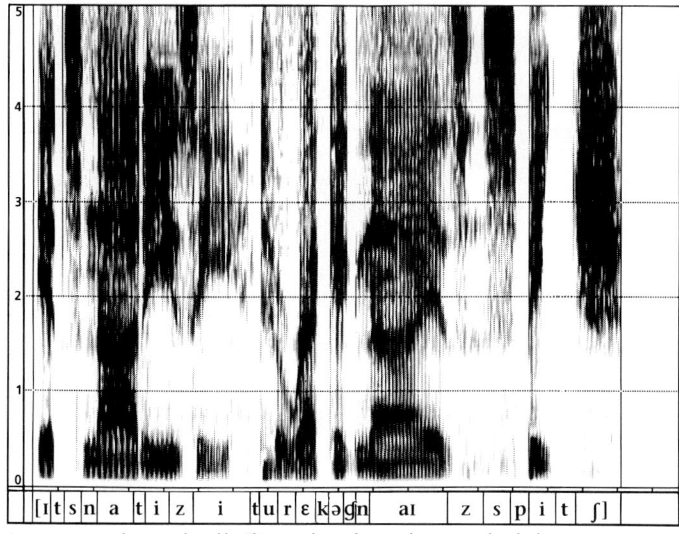

A *spectrogram* makes speech visible. This one shows the sound waves produced when a person says, "It's not easy to recognize speech."

To talk loudly, you must exert pressure. This pressure should come from muscles in the stomach area or the lower chest, not from the neck or upper chest. If that pressure comes from muscles in your neck or upper chest, you will sound louder, but your voice will have an unpleasant, harsh, metallic sound.

By getting pressure from the right place—the stomach and lower chest—you can talk loud for quite a while without getting tired or hoarse. However, if you get pressure from the wrong place—the neck and upper chest—your throat will soon hurt, you will grow tired, and you will probably become hoarse.

MEETING **INDIVIDUAL** NEEDS

Students with Special Needs

When students with behavior disorders become excited or upset, they often have difficulty using proper pitch, volume, and rate. This behavior frequently disrupts the class and creates confrontations with other students.

On such occasions, you could suggest that students implement one or more of the following relaxation techniques:

1. breathing deeply
2. counting to ten
3. taking time out in private (Designate places the students may go to calm down.)
4. listening to soft music

p. 72 in class will allow you to determine which students are having trouble with articulation.

ASSESSMENT

You can assess mastery of the concepts covered in this segment by observing students' performances on **Activities 4–7**. The ultimate display of mastery, of course, is using the voice effectively when speaking to an audience. You could ask each student to present a three- to five-minute speech on a topic of his or her choice. Emphasize that presentation, not content, will be graded.

WRITING TO LEARN

As students progress through this chapter, they will evaluate various aspects of using their voices. Suggest that they document what they have learned about their speaking abilities. If students have encountered problems, suggest that they write strategies to combat their problems.

You may want to ask students to include these written evaluations in their assessment portfolios. They can reassess their vocalization and articulation at various times throughout the school year and compare results.

ONGOING ASSESSMENT

Activity 5

Have students practice the vocalization technique described in **Activity 5** several times so that you can move around the room and observe each student. You may want to demonstrate the technique to students who appear to be having difficulties.

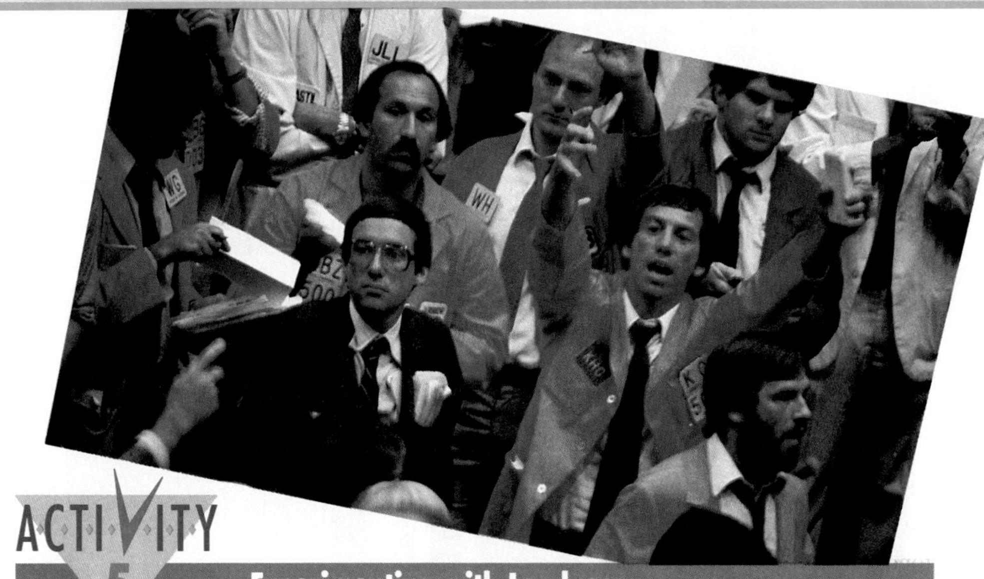

ACTIVITY 5 Experimenting with Loudness

You will be able to speak more effectively and efficiently if you learn to use the correct muscles to increase volume. Place your hands around your waist like a belt. In a normal voice say, "Get over here as fast as you can." You will probably feel light pressure at your waist. Now say the same sentence very loudly. On at least three of the words, you should feel a sharp tensing of the stomach muscles. If you do, you are getting pressure from the right place. To identify power from the wrong source, again say the sentence very loudly. This time, though, wrap your arms tightly around your waist to prevent use of your stomach muscles. You should feel tension in your throat and should notice that your voice takes on an unpleasant, harsh quality.

Rate

Rate is the speed at which you talk. Normal speed is from about 120 to about 160 words per minute. Rate is influenced by a number of factors, including the emotional content of the message.

> EXAMPLE: When you read aloud, you are likely to go much faster than when you talk with a friend. If what you read is simple material, your speech may get to a rate of 180 words per minute. Also, your rate of speech will be affected by the emotion or mood of the passage you are reading.

Changes in rate are normal—in fact, they are necessary. Like changes in pitch, they help communicate the shades of meaning that you wish to convey to your listeners.

Reteaching

You may want to recruit articulate students to tutor those who, after having worked through this segment, can identify in themselves specific speech problems. If this strategy is not workable, you could schedule brief conferences with students to offer individualized instruction.

See p. 71 for **EXTENSION, ENRICHMENT,** and **CLOSURE.**

ACTIVITY 6

Timing Your Rate of Speech

Measure and compare your speaking rates in conversation and in reading aloud. (You need to measure both because these rates differ.) First, with the permission of the person you are speaking to, tape-record a conversation. Next, record a few minutes of oral reading—perhaps an article in the newspaper or a passage of average difficulty from a book. Then, using a timer or a watch, listen to the tape and count the number of words you spoke or read in one minute. If your average rate of conversational speech is outside the normal range (120 to 160 words per minute), you can make a conscious effort to slow down or to speed up.

Quality

Quality is the tone of your voice. Your personal vocal quality is the tone that makes your voice identifiable as yours. Sometimes, a speaker's unpleasant vocal quality is caused by a physical problem or impairment. However, some people develop unpleasant qualities that can and should be changed. The most common quality problems are nasality, breathiness, hoarseness, and harshness.

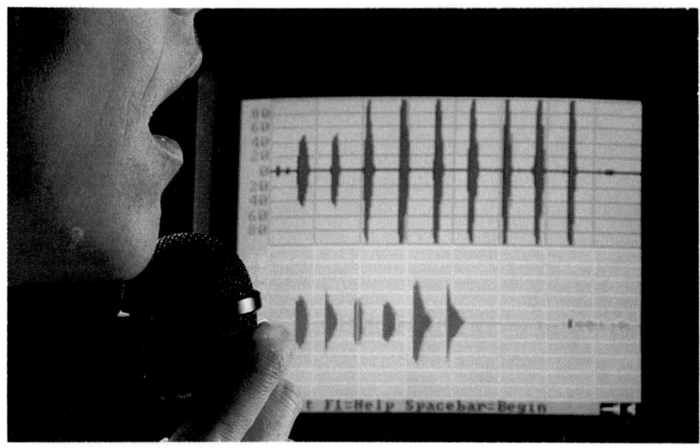

1. **Nasality** is characterized by too much nasal resonance of all vocal sounds. It is caused by incomplete closure of the passage between the oral cavity and the nasal cavity. Nasal resonance itself is not wrong. The three sounds [m], [n], and [ŋ] are supposed to be nasal. In addition, most people have a touch of nasal resonance in normal conversation. The problem arises when the nasal resonance is so pronounced that the voice sounds whiny or tinny.

Ongoing Assessment

Activity 6

You may want to have students write down their findings about their speaking rates in conversation and in reading aloud. Do their speaking rates fall inside or outside the normal range? If they fall outside the range, have students suggest possible reasons, and ask them to propose possible solutions. Then you can collect their analyses for assessment purposes.

Cooperative Learning

You may want to select a book from your students' current reading list and have students work in small groups to recreate sections of dialogue. Have each group present its dialogue to the class. Then ask the class to discuss which vocal characteristics the presenters used to bring their characters to life. How did the voices they used contribute to the development of each character?

Making Connections

Drama

You may want to invite a speaker from your school's drama department to discuss with the class the importance of pitch, volume, rate, quality, and articulation in dramatic performances. The speaker should emphasize to students that these vocal variations give voice its "ear appeal"; that is, they make it pleasant to hear. You might also ask students to speculate why futuristic TV shows and movies such as *Star Trek: The Next Generation* and *2001: A Space Odyssey* have computers with soothing voices. How does a pleasant voice enhance and invite interaction?

Example: To hear how a truly nasal voice sounds, try talking "through your nose." Raise the back of your tongue toward the roof of your mouth so that the mouth is blocked and that sound is directed into the nasal cavity. Now speak. Notice how unpleasant the sound is. While you are speaking, lower the back of your tongue so that sound is sent to the mouth. Notice how your voice changes.

2. **Breathiness** results from too much unvoiced air escaping through the vocal folds as a person is speaking. It is caused by failure to bring the vocal folds close enough together. One cause of breathiness is habit: People may prefer breathy speaking because it takes less energy. Another is the development of growths on the vocal folds themselves. These growths prevent the folds from coming together smoothly.

A breathy quality may be fine if you wish to sound that way. Some people even associate breathiness with softness or warmth. However, if your voice is too breathy, your listeners may be distracted by the quality of your voice and not be attentive to your message. If you have a problem with breathiness, you may want to consult a speech therapist to find out its cause. If the cause is simple laziness, you can correct it by doing vocal exercises.

Film actress Marilyn Monroe was famous for the breathiness of her voice.

3. **Harshness** is characterized by an unpleasant, grating sound that may also be hard or metallic. Harshness is caused by speaking with too much tension in the larynx area. People who wrestle, play football, or engage in other activities that demand strong neck muscles may tend to keep their neck muscles tense all the time. A harsh voice is sometimes caused by a speaker's attempt to talk at a pitch that is too high or too low. The cure for harshness is to relax the neck muscles.

Example: To hear what harshness sounds like, tense your neck muscles as much as you can. Then try to talk for two minutes. Notice what happens to the sound of your voice after just two minutes.

4. Hoarseness is characterized by a thickness of sound or a muffled or rasping sound. Like harshness, hoarseness is caused by speaking with excessive tension in the larynx area. Although a physical problem may lead to hoarseness, in many cases hoarseness is brought on by poor speech habits.

EXAMPLE: People often abuse their voices by yelling at athletic events or by screaming at rock concerts. The kind of hoarseness that results from this abuse is usually temporary and can be cured by resting the vocal folds.

As you go about your daily routine, make notes in your communication journal about speakers you encounter who have especially good voices to listen to and those whose voices are somehow unpleasant to listen to. Write down your ideas about what makes one speaker's voice pleasing and another's irritating.

MEETING INDIVIDUAL NEEDS

An Alternative Approach

Students who have difficulty with expressing their ideas in writing might benefit from an opportunity to use tape recorders for the **Communication Journal** assignment. Rather than have students make notes in their communication journals, have them develop audio journals in which they record the speeches of their favorite speakers. Have students provide commentaries to explain what makes these individuals' speeches pleasant to listen to. Similarly, ask students to record unpleasant speech samples and to explain the reasons for their choices. Remind students to get permission before they tape speakers.

MEETING INDIVIDUAL NEEDS

Linguistically Diverse Students

Students whose speech patterns are heavily dialectical may be disinclined to correct articulation problems that they do not perceive to be errors. One way to approach this situation is to invite to class a local media personality who has come from a similar communication background. Ask this individual to describe to students how he or she changed speaking patterns to adopt the standard American English pronunciations of words and how this effort was helpful in his or her career development. You may also want to ask the visitor to share situations in which dialect might be more appropriate than standard American English.

USING THE CHARTS

You might ask volunteers to compose sentences with examples of the problems in the charts on pp. 70–72 and then to say sentences with the correct articulation. For example, a student might say, "I drank da milk; I drank the milk." Have the speaker emphasize the example word in each sentence. Hearing the words articulated in sentences should be particularly helpful for auditory learners.

Correcting Articulation Problems

To communicate effectively, you must speak so that people in your audience can understand your message clearly and easily. Once a speaker has discovered one of the common articulation problems, he or she can usually remedy the difficulty with practice.

Substituting One Sound for Another

Substituting some sounds for others may not prevent your speech from being understood, particularly among family, friends, and neighbors. These sound substitutions may, however, diminish your effectiveness when you are communicating to some listeners.

Common Substitution Problems

Substitutions	Examples
[d] for [ð]	**da** for **the, radder** for **rather, dose** for **those**
[t] for [θ]	**tink** for **think, anyting** for **anything, bot** for **both**
[ks] for [s]	**excape** for **escape, expecially** for **especially**
[f] for [θ]	**bref** for **breath, bof** for **both, arifmatic** for **arithmatic**
[n] for [ŋ]	**doin** for **doing, growin** for **growing, bein** for **being**
[t] for [d]	**coutn't** for **couldn't, woutn't** for **wouldn't**
[ɪ] for [ʌ]	**jist** for **just**
[ɪ] for [ɛ]	**git** for **get, pin** for **pen**

EXTENSION

Assign students to attend political speeches or other occasions in your community in which the presentations are likely to be emotionally charged. Have students take notes about how the speakers use good vocal qualities to effectively relay their messages. Be sure students comment on the speakers' use of pitch, loudness, rate, quality, and articulation. Have students report their findings to the class.

Leaving Out a Sound (Omission)

Leaving out, or omitting, sounds is a kind of shortcutting. Although some shortcutting is normal when speaking, excessive shortcutting is considered an articulation problem.

Common Omission Problems

Omissions	Examples
dropping [d]	**wount** for **wouldn't, frien** for **friend, gole** for **gold**
dropping [t]	**mos** for **most, jus** for **just, kep** for **kept, bes** for **best**
dropping [l]	**hep** for **help, sef** for **self, woff** for **wolf, sauve** for **solve**
dropping initial [h] after other words	**see'um** for **see him, gave'er** for **gave her**
dropping [ə] along with a consonant sound	**probly** for **probably, member** for **remember, awmobile** for **automobile**

Adding an Extra Sound

Sometimes the problem of adding a sound stems from pronouncing a letter that should be silent. Sometimes it is the result of adding a sound to make a word easier to say.

Common Problems with Adding Sounds

Additions	Examples
adding [t] in words where *t* is silent	**soften** for **sofen, hasten** for **hasen**
adding [ə]	**filum** for **film, athaletic** for **athletic, childaren** for **children**
adding [r] to ends of words	**idear** for **idea, drawr** for **draw**
adding a sound to the beginning of a word	**ahold** for **hold, especial** for **special, ascared** for **scared**

TEACHER'S RESOURCE BINDER

Skills for Success 4
Correcting Articulation Problems

Audiotape 1, Lesson 3
Problems in Articulation

Enrichment

If your students have read *To Kill a Mockingbird,* you could have them view clips of the movie in class to identify the vocal qualities used by the actors to portray each of the main characters. Ask students to compare the smooth, resonant voice and precise articulation of Atticus Finch to the harsh voice of Bob Ewell. Have students describe how voice is used to develop the characters' personalities. Would the characters have been as effective if their voices had been different?

Transposing Sounds

Transposing sounds refers to the switching, or reversing, of the order in which sounds are spoken.

Common Problems with Transposing Sounds

Transpositions	Examples
[ks] for [sk]	**aks** for **ask**
[ɚd] for [rɛd]	**hunderd** for **hundred**
[pɚ] for [pri]	**perscribe** for **prescribe, perfer** for **prefer**
[ɚn] for [rɛn] or [rɛn] for [ɚn]	**childern** for **children, modren** for **modern**

Ongoing Assessment

Activity 7

For **Activity 7,** you may want to have each student write a brief, personal assessment of his or her articulation capabilities. Then you can review the assessments.

Timesaver

You may want to have students work in groups of three or four to complete **Activity 7**. Have a student recorder in each group keep track of the words that each student has trouble with. You can quickly assess students' articulation problems by reviewing the recorders' notes.

Correcting Articulation Problems

Identify any problems you have with substituting, omitting, adding, or transposing sounds. To do this, read aloud the words used as examples in the four parts of this section. Practice the correct pronunciations. After you have pronounced the sounds correctly for a while, they will become a natural part of your speech.

Sending Effective Vocal Messages

1. **Breathe properly.** Proper breathing gives you the air necessary to generate speech: It also allows you to talk without excessive strain on your neck and chest muscles.
2. **Resonate sounds effectively.** Proper use of the throat, the nose, and the mouth helps you to shape the vowel sounds necessary for clear speech. It also produces a strong, rich vocal tone free of excessive breathiness, nasality, harshness, or hoarseness.
3. **Articulate clearly.** Good articulation enables you to deliver your words clearly so that your listeners can understand you.
4. **Use vocal variety and appropriate emphasis.** Vocal variation and emphasis allows you to give the precise meaning you intend to your words and sentences. Moreover, your use of proper pitch, loudness, and rate makes your voice expressive and pleasant.

Closure

Ask students to explain how vocalization and articulation problems might affect an audience. Ask students to identify in particular those characteristics of speech that are most annoying to them. Emphasize again that while the content of a speaker's message may be well thought out and even interesting to the audience, listeners will not pay attention for long if the presentation is annoying.

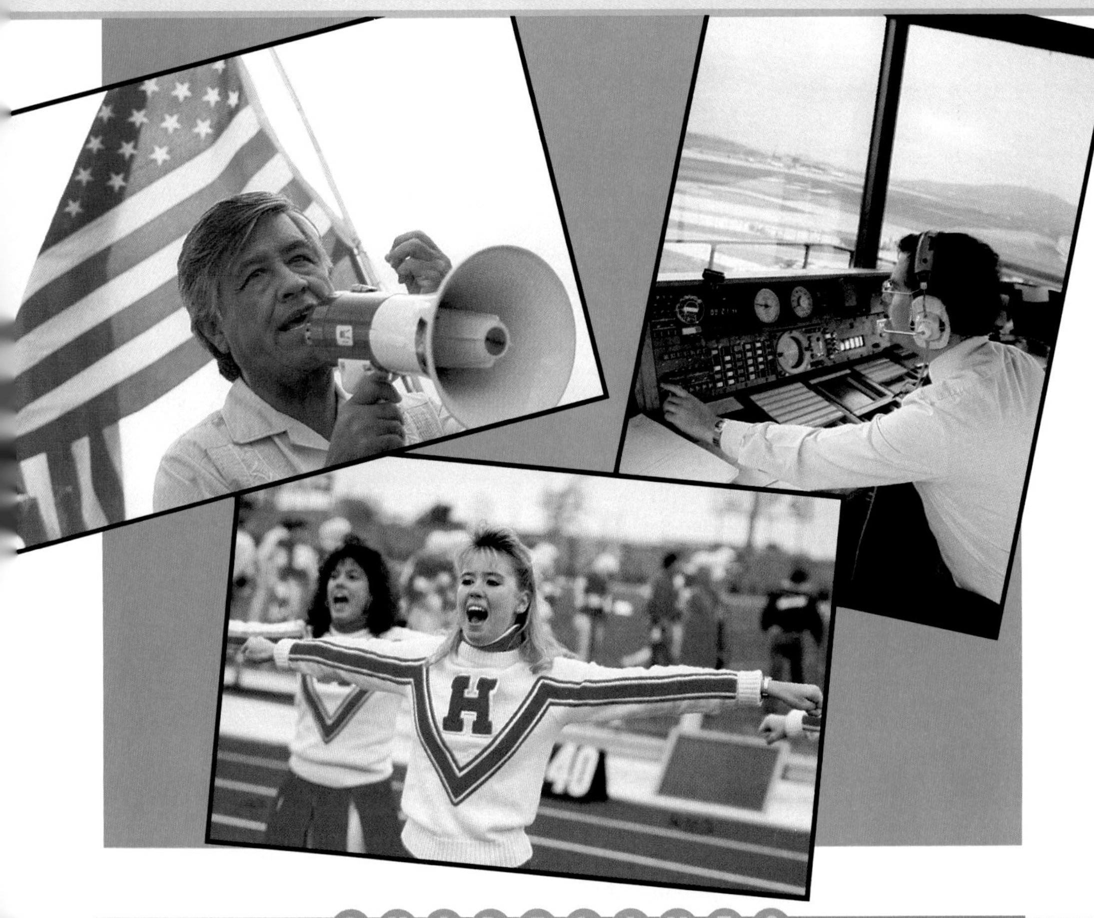

GUIDELINES for Vocalizing

- Do I breathe properly?
- Do I get power for speech from the proper sources?
- Do I resonate my sounds effectively; in other words, are the sounds I produce loud and full?
- Do I speak in a key that is at my optimum pitch?
- Do I use inflections and steps to produce vocal variation and emphasis?
- Do I speak slowly enough to be understood yet fast enough to be interesting?
- Is my voice free of breathiness, nasality, harshness, and hoarseness?
- Is my speech free of substitutions, omissions, extra sounds, and transpositions?

Building a Portfolio

You could suggest that students use the **Guidelines for Vocalizing** to evaluate presentations they give to the class. Have them store their evaluations in their speech portfolios.

At a later date, ask students to repeat the evaluation process and to compare their findings. Have their presentations improved? Are there any areas on which they should continue to concentrate?

AV ➤ *Audiovisual Resource Binder*

Transparency 6
Guidelines for Vocalizing

◆ Profiles in Communication

Performance Objectives

- To analyze vocalization of a computerized vocal message
- To share the analysis with the rest of the class

Teaching the Feature

You may want to have students read the profile of Ann Hillis. Then ask students to list the communication skills that they think are most important in Ms. Hillis's profession. Because such a list is not presented in the text, students will have to devise one. [They might include the following skills: adeptness with nonverbal clues—gestures, facial expressions, voice inflection, and eye contact; the ability to listen well; and the ability to adapt language to specific audiences.]

Activity Note

Have students read the **Activity**. Check to see if there are any questions. Because some students might not have access to computerized voices, you may want to have one available on tape. To prepare students for writing analyses, you may want to work with the class to list the guidelines that the chapter gives for good vocalization.

In their analyses, students should discuss pitch (key, melody, range, and inflection), volume, rate, quality, and articulation.

PROFILES IN COMMUNICATION

Ann M. Hillis

As a speech pathologist in a medical center, Ann Hillis helps patients who have impaired language abilities. Many of the vocalization problems that she diagnoses and treats have a physical source. For example, a patient may have difficulty articulating sounds because of weakened muscles in the mouth. Another patient may have an undesirable voice quality due to damaged vocal folds.

Whenever Ms. Hillis is planning the treatment of a patient, she always carefully emphasizes that she, the patient, and the patient's family need to communicate clearly with one another about their goals. "Being a good listener—tapping into what is important to my patient—is essential to successful rehabilitation," Ms. Hillis states.

Ms. Hillis always tries to model effective communication skills, especially clear articulation and enunciation. Although modeling alone cannot correct her patients' speech disorders, it provides one more strategy Ms. Hillis can use to help her patients learn the speech patterns they need to develop.

Dedicated to helping her patients, she feels deep satisfaction in their triumphs. When progress is slow, she encourages her patients to meet the challenge of making steady gains in improving their language and vocalization skills.

ACTIVITY

Practice analyzing vocalization by listening to a computerized vocal message. For example, you might analyze the voice that calls out prices at a supermarket checkout or the electronic voice of a talking doll or a video game. As a basis for your analysis, consider the guidelines for good vocalization given in this chapter. What characteristics make the electronic voice sound unnatural? What changes could be made to make it sound more human? Share your ideas with your classmates.

S☆U☆M☆M☆A☆R☆Y

USING YOUR VOICE means that you must coordinate parts of your body to generate sound, to resonate sound, and to articulate sound.

- **Generating sound** is primarily a function of the vocal folds (vocal cords)—the muscles of the larynx that vibrate when they are drawn close together.
- **Resonating sound** is effected by the bones in the chest, neck, and head and the cavities of the throat, the nose, and the mouth. These groups of resonators amplify sound.
- **Articulation** is the shaping of the speech sounds into recognizable oral symbols that go together to make a word.
- **Vocalization** has many characteristics: *pitch* (the highness or lowness of sound), *volume* (the force exerted to produce speech tones), *rate* (the speed at which a person speaks—normally from 120 to 160 words per minute), and *quality* (the tone of voice).
- **Articulation problems** make it difficult for a speaker to be understood clearly and easily. The four most common articulation problems are sound substitutions, omissions, additions, and transpositions.
- **Vocalizing effectively** requires breathing properly, using resonators effectively, articulating clearly, and using variety and emphasis.

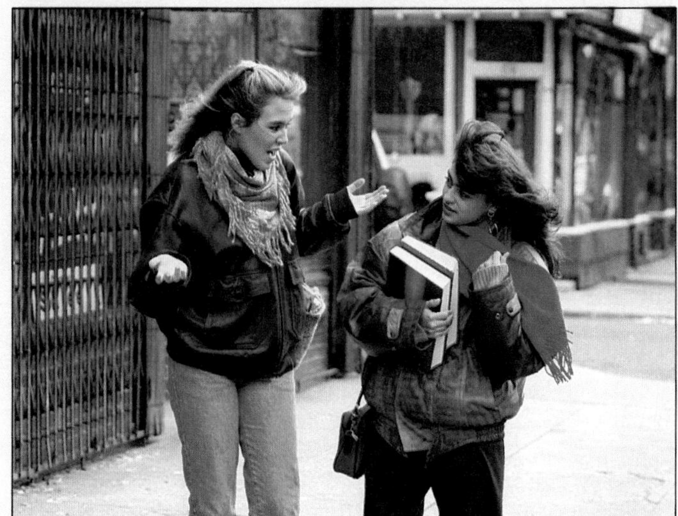

CHAPTER 3

Vocabulary

Look back through this chapter and find the meaning for each of the following terms. Write each term and its meaning in your communication journal.

articulation, *p. 59*
breathiness, *p. 68*
cavity, *p. 57*
circumflex, *p. 64*
diaphragm, *p. 54*
fricatives, *p. 61*
glides, *p. 61*
harshness, *p. 68*
hoarseness, *p. 69*
inflection, *p. 63*
key, *p. 62*
larynx, *p. 54*
melody, *p. 63*
monotone, *p. 63*
nasal cavity, *p. 58*
nasality, *p. 67*
nasals, *p. 61*
optimum pitch, *p. 62*
oral cavity, *p. 58*
pharyngeal cavity, *p. 58*
pitch, *p. 62*
plosives, *p. 61*
pronunciation, *p. 59*
quality, *p. 67*
range, *p. 63*
rate, *p. 66*
resonance, *p. 56*
resonators, *p. 56*
step, *p. 64*
trachea, *p. 54*
vocal folds (vocal cords), *p. 54*
voiced, *p. 61*
voiceless, *p. 61*
volume (loudness), *p. 65*

TEACHER'S RESOURCE BINDER

- Chapter 3 Vocabulary

Review Questions

Answers

1. During speech, a person inhales more swiftly and more deeply than during normal breathing and uses the muscles of the chest and stomach to prolong air flow.
2. Resonance is reinforcement produced by vibration. Bones resonate by picking up vibrations of sound. Every cavity has a natural range of sounds it reinforces, depending on its size, shape, and texture and on the size of its opening.
3. When the pharyngeal cavity (throat) is tense, pitch is high and harsh; when it is relaxed, pitch is low and mellow. Although the nasal cavity (nose) affects the sound of all speech, it has a direct effect on the sounds [m], [n], and [ŋ]. Various vowel sounds can be made by changing the size of the oral cavity (mouth) and the shape of its opening.

Discussion Questions

Guidelines for Assessment

Student responses may vary.

1. Various aspects of pitch—melody, range, and inflection—affect expressiveness and can be used for emphasis. Rate can be increased to show excitement or to address an audience familiar with the topic. Similarly, a volume increase shows excitement or enthusiasm, and a volume decrease sets a more serious tone.
2. After the speaker identifies the specific problem(s), he or she might use flashcards to learn the correct pronunciations of the mispronounced words, correctly say the words into a tape recorder and listen to the pronunciation, listen to a partner pronounce the words correctly, or repeatedly say sentences using the correct pronunciation of problematic words.
3. Speaking too loudly can give the voice an unpleasant, metallic, harsh sound if the pressure comes from muscles in the neck or upper chest. Speakers should be sure to breathe deeply by extending the abdomen as well as the lungs. Pressure should come from the muscles in the stomach area or the lower chest.
4. Encourage students to consider how these individuals use pitch, loudness, rate, and quality to enhance their messages.

Review Questions

1. What is the basic difference between the breathing process used in regular breathing and the breathing process used by a person who is speaking?
2. Define *resonance* and explain how bone resonance differs from cavity resonance.
3. Identify the three major cavity resonators and explain how each one affects the sound of the voice.
4. What are the major articulators of sound that are located in the mouth?
5. Why is the International Phonetic Alphabet more effective in symbolizing sound and in studying speech and speech problems than the regular alphabet?
6. What is the difference between pitch and volume as aspects of vocalization?
7. What common problems do speakers have in controlling volume, or loudness?
8. What are the four major vocalization problems that relate to the quality, or tone, of the voice?
9. What are the four major articulation problems that can be remedied with practice?
10. What is the difference between nasal resonance and nasality?

Discussion Questions

1. Discuss how learning to control pitch, rate, and volume can contribute to the expressiveness of your voice. How can these aspects of your voice be used to emphasize key ideas?
2. Identify ways that a speaker might remedy any of the four articulation problems discussed on pages 70–72—substituting, omitting, adding, or transposing sounds. What particular methods might help to correct these problems?
3. Suppose you are giving a speech in a large room with no public address system. To be heard by everyone in the room, you have to use a loud voice to deliver the speech. Discuss the specific vocalization problems this situation presents. Then discuss the ways in which you can assure yourself that you are generating loudness from the proper source.
4. Consider a wide range of people in the public eye—such as politicians, performers, and newscasters. Do you think that having effective voices is particularly useful for these people? Why or why not? Which of these people in the public eye have particularly effective voices? What makes their voices so effective?
5. The movie *My Fair Lady* is based on Bernard Shaw's play *Pygmalion*. In the play, Professor Higgins claims that he can pass off a flower peddler as a cultured person simply by teaching her how to speak properly. Discuss with your class whether or not such a feat is possible.

4. The articulators are the tongue, teeth, lips, and hard and soft palates.
5. The IPA has one symbol for each of the forty-five sounds of the English language.
6. Pitch is the highness or lowness of sound; volume is the intensity of sound.
7. Problems include speaking too loudly or too softly and exerting pressure from the muscles of the throat and upper chest to increase volume.
8. nasality, breathiness, hoarseness, and harshness
9. substitution, omission, addition, and transposition
10. Nasal resonance is normal and necessary for some sounds, primarily [m], [n], and [ŋ]. Nasality is the whiny or tinny quality of speech that occurs when too much air escapes through the nose.

ACTIVITIES

CHAPTER 3

1. Practicing Breath Control. Refer to the picture below as you practice the following breath control technique.

a. With your open palms against your ribs, inhale quickly through your mouth, purse your lips, and blow a steady, forceful stream of air, as if you were trying to blow out a candle some distance from you.

b. Continue blowing until most of your breath is exhausted.

c. Feel the inward movement of the abdominal wall and the gradual lowering of the ribs.

d. Try this also with an actual candle in front of you, this time blowing evenly, with little force, so that the flame merely bends steadily away from you but does not go out and does not waver.

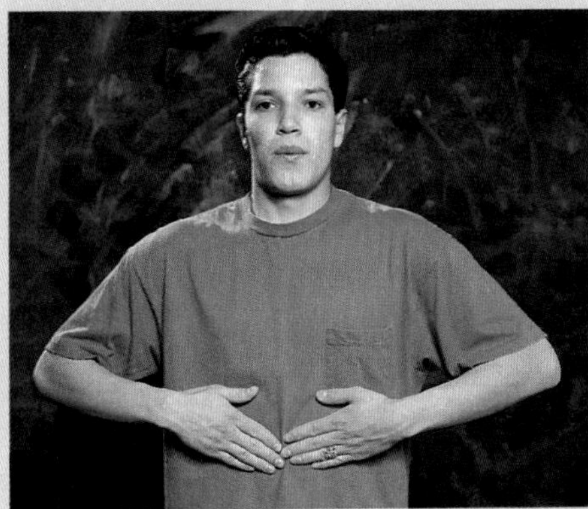

2. Practicing Vowel Sounds. The formation of vowel sounds is dependent on how the mouth opening is formed. Say "ah," "aw," "o," "oo," and "ee." Note how your mouth moves from open to closed. Now say the following words separately: *cow, taught, nose, who,* and *me.* Note the opening of your mouth and the changes in that opening as you go through all the words.

3. Experimenting with Resonance.

A. Look at the following illustration of bottles filled with liquid. Describe what you think would be the differences in the sound each bottle would make if you blew into each of the bottles in turn to make a musical sound.

B. To perform an actual experiment with cavity resonance, find four 12- or 16-ounce glass bottles similar to the ones shown. Fill each with a different amount of water. Now stretch a thick rubber band between your two hands until it is tight. Hold the rubber band about one inch above one of the bottle openings and then pluck it with your thumb. Repeat this procedure for each of the bottles. In which case was the sound the loudest or fullest? In which case was it the weakest?

C. Next, experiment with different degrees of tightness. While plucking the rubber band, move your hands closer together and then farther apart. When you stretch the rubber band very tight, which bottle now resonates the sound—the one with the most or the one with the least water? Explain your observation about how cavity size affects sound production to your class.

5. Have students consider the following points during this discussion: Is it possible to completely change one's customary pronunciation? If it is possible, how much would other people's view of that person change? What other characteristics besides good articulation indicate a cultured upbringing?

ACTIVITIES

Guidelines for Assessment

1. You may want to have students write brief descriptions of what they learned in this activity about breath control.
2. Inform students that vowels allow the voice to carry. While most consonant sounds are staccato, or brief in their pronunciation, the vowels are extended and form the nuclei of most words.
3. A. Students will discover that the more water, the higher the sound.
   B. Students should discover that the larger the cavity, the louder and fuller the resonance.
   C. A tighter rubber band will vibrate at a higher frequency.

Summative Evaluation

Your **Teacher's Resource Binder** contains a reproducible **Chapter 3 Test** that may be used to assess students' mastery of the concepts presented in this chapter.

Portfolio Assessment

For future reference and evaluation you may want to have students keep in their portfolios any skill sheets or evaluation forms that you have used with this chapter along with any other recorded or written materials that students have created.

4. You may want to have students record their findings about relaxing the throat to gain resonance.

5. You may want to allow students to work in pairs to listen to each other's pronunciations. You could circulate among the pairs as they recite.

6. a. roas—omission; sammich—substitution
b. athaletic—extra sound
c. bout—omission
d. aksed—transposed sound
e. drawring—extra sound
f. jist—substitution; dose—substitution
g. liberry—omission
h. ascared—extra sound
i. Bof—substitution; dese—substitution; fixin—substitution
j. favrite—omission; preformer—transposed sound; line—omission

CHAPTER 3

4. Relaxing the Throat to Gain Resonance. The throat works best as a resonator when it is open and relaxed. To open and relax your throat, begin by yawning. Feel the tongue as it is lowered in the back. Your throat is now open. With the aid of a mirror, explore as much as you can see of your mouth and throat during this exercise. Note the position of the tongue when the throat opens. Then with your throat open, read the following phrases aloud to hear how opening your throat affects the sound of your voice.

Who are you?
Over the rolling waters go
Up, up, and away
Our other operator

5. Practicing Pronunciation and Articulation. Say each of the following lines aloud three times in succession. Try to pronounce each word as carefully as you can.

a. The sea ceaseth and it sufficeth us.
b. The sixth sheik's sixth sheep is sick.
c. She sells seashells by the seashore.
d. The pitcher chided the churlish catcher for changing his signals.
e. Ruby rented rubber baby-buggy bumpers.
f. Three sixths equals six twelfths.
g. Theosphilus Thistle, the successful thistle sifter, in shifting a sieve full of unsifted thistles, thrust three thousand thistles through the thick of his thumb.
h. A tree toad loved a she toad that lived up in a tree.
He was a three-toed tree toad, but a two-toed toad was she.
The three-toed tree toad tried to win the she toad's friendly nod,
For the three-toed tree toad loved the ground
That the two-toed tree toad trod.
i. How much wood could a woodchuck chuck if a woodchuck could chuck wood? A woodchuck couldn't chuck but a chopped-up chunk if a woodchuck could chuck wood.
j. Peter Piper picked a peck of pickled peppers. If Peter Piper picked a peck of pickled peppers, where is the peck of pickled peppers Peter Piper picked?

6. Identifying Articulation Problems. Read each of the following sentences aloud. Then identify each word or word part that contains an articulation problem. Label each problem as a substitution, an omission, an extra sound, or a transposed sound.

a. I think I'll order the roas beef sammich.
b. Janine got an athaletic scholarship to the state university.
c. I'm bout at the end of my rope.
d. Larry aksed her to dance.
e. A scale drawring of the project is available on request.
f. Grandpa jist planted dose rose bushes.
g. This book is due back in the liberry on November 12.
h. My dog Ruffles is ascared of thunder.
i. Bof of dese typewriters need fixin.
j. My favrite circus preformer is the fearless line tamer.

◆ Real-Life Speaking Situations

PERFORMANCE OBJECTIVES

- To adapt messages to suit different target audiences
- To present a scenario in class to demonstrate how messages vary based on audience
- To select a message, a medium, and a target audience and to adapt the message accordingly
- To present an announcement in class

REAL LIFE Speaking Situations

1 Dealing successfully with different people and situations requires different methods of communication. You need to be flexible to switch roles and to change your manner of speaking to suit various circumstances. How do you act and speak at school? at work? at home? at a party? In each case, you probably know how to adapt yourself to meet the expectations of others. Sometimes, however, you have to adapt quickly to unexpected or changing circumstances.

Your car has been rear-ended at a stoplight. As you climb out of your car to check the damage, you see a huge man, yelling angrily, leave his car and stomp down the lane toward you. How would you address this irate driver?

A few minutes later, a police officer arrives on the scene to investigate the accident. How would you address the officer? How would you approach witnesses to get their statements? Outline a short scenario indicating how you would use communication skills to deal with these different people.

Be prepared to present your scenario in class and to discuss how and why you might vary your communication to meet each situation.

2 In most communities people share information in a number of different ways—through public addresses, through radio and television announcements, through all sorts of printed matter, and through various other means. To relay this information, most journalists and others involved in public communication must master different forms of language.

You are working for a company that needs to make a public announcement about a new development or product. You have been called upon to deliver the announcement in short public addresses to business and service groups and on television and radio.

First, identify an imaginary development in a field in which you have had some experience—perhaps mechanics, food preparation, computers, or child care. Next, define your audience. Choose a specific group and a specific radio station or television channel. Tailor your announcements to suit these audiences. Finally, prepare your announcements and present one or both of them in class. Ask for feedback on the effectiveness and clarity of your presentation.

ASSESSMENT GUIDELINES

1. Students will probably say that they would attempt to be calming in speaking with the irate driver, respectful and cooperative with the police officer, and polite to the witnesses. They might note any changes in loudness, tone, and rate as they address these different audiences.
2. Students' target audiences will vary in gender, age, and other characteristics. Be sure students tailor their messages to appeal to their audiences. Students should note that if their announcements are designed for radio instead of television broadcast, then they should include more description of visual and tactile characteristics.

Chapter 4

Listening and Evaluating

pp. 80–105

Chapter Overview

This chapter presents skills that students can use to become better listeners. The first segment identifies factors that affect listening. Then it provides techniques for critical listening and techniques for active listening. The second segment presents five logical fallacies, discusses seven propaganda techniques, and concludes with a brief discussion of evaluating speeches.

Teacher's Resource Binder

The following materials are identified at their point of use in this chapter:

- Skills for Success
  1 *Analyzing Your Listening Skills*
  2 *Listening Critically*
  3 *Evaluating a Speaker's Reasoning*
  4 *Analyzing Propaganda Techniques*
- Chapter 4 Vocabulary
- Chapter 4 Test/Answer Key

AV ➤ Audiovisual Resource Binder

The following materials are identified at their point of use in this chapter:

- Transparency 7
  Listening Actively
- Transparency 8
  Critiquing a Speech
- Audiotape 1, Lesson 4
  Listening
- Audiotape 1, Lesson 5
  Conversation

INTRODUCING THE CHAPTER

Most people spend a great deal of time listening to people talk, and an increasing number of people receive most or all of the news of the day by listening. In addition, people need keen listening skills to avoid being taken in by some of the false and misleading claims of advertising. Point out to students that listening skills involve more than just hearing messages and that these skills can be learned. Whether as students listening to lectures and class discussions, as citizens hearing the news or discussions of public affairs on radio and TV, or as consumers trying to get the most for their money, people need to develop good listening skills as a matter of survival.

C H A P T E R

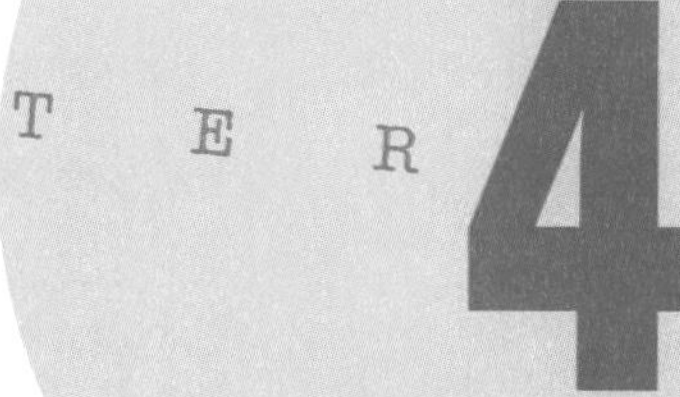

Listening and Evaluating

OBJECTIVES

After studying this chapter, you should be able to

1. Name and analyze factors that affect listening.
2. Identify skills for critical and active listening.
3. List and explain five types of faulty reasoning.
4. Explain what is meant by propaganda.
5. Identify the most commonly used propaganda techniques.
6. Evaluate a speech with an oral critique and a written critique.

What Makes a Good Listener?

How often has a friend, a relative, or a teacher accused you of not listening? You were obviously within earshot, and you heard what had been said. But hearing and listening are different. **Hearing** means being able to detect sounds. **Listening** means getting meaning from sounds that are heard. Listening seems to be such an easy thing to do, but good listening can be one of the most difficult of all communication skills to master.

What does being a good listener mean? If you try to pinpoint examples of good listening or of people you admire as being good listeners, you begin to see that listening is a valuable skill. Good listeners are attentive and receptive. They actively seek out information, evaluate what they hear, and respond to it.

Effective listening requires concentration and effort. The rewards are worth the effort; as a good listener, you can

- develop your interpersonal skills
- discover unexpected insights
- increase your knowledge and your ability to evaluate
- improve your performance in school and at work

Bibliography of Additional Materials

➥ PROFESSIONAL READINGS

- Bronwell, Judi, ed. ***Multiple Perspectives: Proceedings of the Cornell Conference on Listening.*** Ithaca, NY: Cornell University.
- Friedman, Paul. ***Listening Processes: Attention, Understanding, Evaluation.*** Washington, D.C.: National Education Association.

➥ AUDIOVISUALS

- ***Effective Communication Skills, Program 20: Effective Listening***—Wisconsin Foundation for Vocational, Technical, and Adult Education, Middleton, WI (videocassette, 28 min.)
- ***Effective Communication Skills, Program 21: Critical Listening***—Wisconsin Foundation for Vocational, Technical, and Adult Education, Middleton, WI (videocassette, 28 min.)
- ***You're Not Listening***—Barr Films, Pasadena, CA (videocassette, 21 min.)

Segment 1 *pp. 82–89*

- **Analyzing Factors That Affect Listening**
- **Listening Critically**
- **Listening Actively**

Performance Objectives

- To analyze personal listening habits
- To use critical-listening skills
- To analyze personal active-listening techniques

Cooperative Learning

To help students focus on effective listening strategies, have students work in groups of three. Ask each group to describe what they do when they really want to listen. Encourage them to list as many techniques as possible. Then let groups share their strategies with the rest of the class. You may want to make a class list of the more ingenious strategies; then, as you work through the information in the textbook on critical-listening skills and active-listening skills, students can add to the list.

Teacher's Resource Binder

Skills for Success 1
Analyzing Your Listening Skills

Analyzing Factors That Affect Listening

Your ability to listen depends on many factors. Recognizing these factors, or conditions, is a first step toward becoming a good listener. Each factor is a potential obstacle to good listening. However, you can learn how to control each one and how to make it work to your advantage.

Your Physical and Mental State

Attentive listening requires energy and focus. Your energy level can be affected if you are tired or hungry. For example, your ability to focus is lessened if you are distracted by thoughts about personal problems, your plans for the upcoming weekend, or other issues.

The Speaker

Some people base their willingness to listen on how well they respond to the personality of the speaker. Personality involves a person's traits, attitudes, and habits. Some people attract us; some people annoy us. In listening, personal biases may apply not just to a topic but also to the person speaking. It is true that good listeners prefer to hear dynamic speakers. But you may miss some real enrichment or entertainment if you respond only to a speaker's personality and characteristics or to the manner of delivery.

MOTIVATION

You may want to ask volunteers to share with the class situations in which their failure to listen carefully caused problems. Point out to students that listening was the first verbal behavior they engaged in when they were babies and that they probably spend more time listening than they do speaking, reading, or writing. Remind them that as their own examples illustrate, failing to listen carefully can often create problems. Tell students that the information in this segment should help them to develop better listening skills.

Your Prejudices

A **prejudice** is a "prejudgment," or bias: a belief you have already formed that may not be grounded in facts. It is natural to have opinions about ideas, events, and issues. Sometimes, though, you might block real listening by starting out with fixed ideas of what is right or wrong, interesting or boring. Recognizing the effects of your prejudices can help you become a better listener.

The Environment

The physical setting affects how well you can listen. Are you at a cookout near a lake? Are you in an air-conditioned car on a freeway? Are you in a crowded and overheated auditorium? Are you in a telephone booth at a busy intersection on a cold and windy day?

Listeners constantly have to confront a number of environmental factors such as temperature, light, noise, space and seating, and other people. Good listeners try to overcome the effects of a poor listening environment. For example, despite irritating noise, a good listener may simply concentrate harder to tune out background distractions.

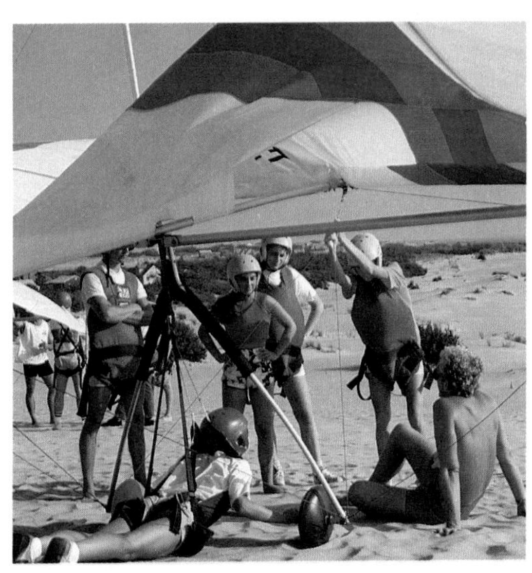

HOW TO Control Factors That Affect Listening

1. **Be energetic and focused.** Whenever you must be prepared to listen well (for example, in an important review class or in an interview), eat and sleep well beforehand. As you listen, push aside distracting thoughts, plans, or worries.
2. **Focus on the message.** Listen to what is being said. Try to overlook distracting mannerisms that the speaker may have or annoying qualities of the speaker's voice.
3. **Keep an open mind.** Don't shut out any topic or viewpoint. Be ready to learn something new or to deepen your appreciation of your own position.
4. **Do what you can to adjust the physical environment.** When you can, choose your position in the room. Adjust the temperature and lighting, if this is possible. Block out noises or other interference as much as you can.

WRITING TO LEARN

Ask students to study the four points under **How to Control Factors That Affect Listening** and to pick out the one factor that causes them the most trouble. Then ask them each to write a personal plan of action for controlling that factor. Have volunteers share their plans with the class, and encourage others to add ideas to their plans if the ideas apply.

BUILDING A PORTFOLIO

You may want to have students include in their portfolios their action plans from **Writing to Learn** above. Have them review their plans periodically throughout the course so they can assess their progress and modify the plans if needed.

Teaching the Lesson

The material in this segment may not be new for students, but students can benefit from reviewing it and from practicing the skills and strategies it discusses. At the start of the segment, you may want to tell students that you plan to encourage good listening by giving directions and making comments to the class only once. You can reassure students that you will answer specific questions about what you say, but warn them that you will not routinely repeat yourself. You can monitor the students' progress in becoming better listeners by noting whether the number of questions diminishes after a few days.

As guided practice for **Activity 1,** you could identify and analyze a personal listening situation. To provide guided practice for **Activity 2** on p. 87, you may want to act out the assignment with a student volunteer. To guide students

Ongoing Assessment

Activity 1

If students claim to have listened attentively, they should indicate the factors that helped them to listen. If they had trouble listening, they should indicate why. You can evaluate students' work by determining how well the students employed, or tried to employ, the factors that affect listening listed in the "**How to**" chart on p. 83.

Additional Activity

To give students additional practice in listening critically, you may want to play a tape-recorded message such as a newscast or an oral reading you have prepared. Then ask five or six recall questions and let students respond orally or in writing. You can repeat this activity every few days throughout the term to encourage students to practice listening skills.

Teacher's Resource Binder

Skills for Success 2
Listening Critically

AV Audiovisual Resource Binder

Audiotape 1, Lesson 4
Listening

ACTIVITY 1

Analyzing Your Listening Habits

Over the next two days, identify five listening situations and determine whether or not you listened attentively in each situation. If so, what factors helped you to listen so well? If you had trouble listening, what factors hindered you? Were you able to overcome these factors? How? Share your findings.

Listening Critically

Critical listening means not only comprehending what is being said but also testing the strength of the ideas. Critical listeners are active, not passive.

Identifying the Speaker's Goal

Good listeners are careful to identify a speaker's specific goal so that they can examine how effectively the speaker achieves that goal. A speaker's **goal** is the purpose he or she has for giving a speech. A speaker has both a general goal and a specific goal.

EXAMPLES: A speaker whose general goal is to amuse an audience might have the specific goal of telling about being a department-store Santa Claus. A speaker whose general goal is to influence others' beliefs might have the specific goal of convincing listeners of the benefit of using solar energy. A speaker who wants to inform his or her audience might explain a geometry theorem.

Sometimes, you will hear the speaker state a goal at the very beginning of the speech. At other times, you will notice that a speaker builds toward the goal and states it only at the conclusion.

Identifying Main Ideas

Main ideas are the speaker's most important points. When speakers imply their main ideas or refer to them vaguely, you will have to analyze the information to identify what you believe are the main ideas. However, some speakers state their main ideas quite clearly—often in the introduction or the conclusion.

EXAMPLE: To conclude, the arguments for solar energy are irrefutable: It is clean, practical, inexpensive, and inexhaustible.

Listen for two techniques, or devices, that speakers use to alert their listeners to main ideas. A speaker may use **repetition,** or repeat a certain word, phrase, or sentence each time a new point is through **Activity 3** on p. 89, play a taped speech and have students work together to list the active-listening techniques they used. Then assign the three activities for independent practice.

Assessment

You could evaluate students' listening habits and students' understanding of critical-listening skills by circulating throughout the room as students complete **Activities 1** and **2.** Post-activity discussion of students' findings could also help in your assessment. Checking the summaries from **Activity 3** could help you to assess students' active-listening skills.

raised. Some speakers rely on **signal words,** words that indicate that a list, contrast, or connection is about to be made.

EXAMPLES:

Repetition: In this election, *we are fighting for* health care. *We are fighting for* new jobs. *We are fighting for* change.

Signal words: *Above all,* we want to vote for change.

Identifying Supporting Details

Supporting details are the examples, facts, statistics, reasons, anecdotes, or expert testimony that a speaker uses to back up main ideas. Identifying supporting details helps you to evaluate whether or not the evidence sufficiently supports the speaker's ideas.

EXAMPLE: To support the main idea that solar energy is inexpensive, the speaker might use the following statistic: Out of a sample of 500 families living in Vermont, those who heated their houses with solar energy spent 50 percent less on heating during one winter than did those who heated their houses with oil.

Using Context Clues

When using words or technical terms that are unfamiliar to an audience, speakers usually provide meaning clues for such terms in the **context,** the surrounding words and sentences. Listen for context clues that a speaker gives you through his or her use of synonyms, comparisons, contrasts, and examples.

EXAMPLES:

Synonyms: The immune system is vigilant in its search for viruses, always watchful for dangerous invaders. (The less familiar word *vigilant* is explained by the more familiar synonym, *watchful.*)

An Alternative Approach

You may want to provide additional written examples of the various types of context clues for students to examine. Go over each example and explain how the context clue helps to define a difficult or unfamiliar word. Then you can read aloud several different examples and help students to identify the context clues.

Reteaching

Divide the segment into sections such as **Analyzing Factors That Affect Listening, Listening Critically,** and **Listening Actively.** Assign each section to two different groups of students of approximately five members each. Each group should prepare a presentation of the material in the section. Each presentation should include a demonstration, an audiovisual aid, and an activity in addition to an oral explanation. Let the two groups that work on the first section give their demonstrations. Then let the rest of the class compare the presentations. Do the same for the other sections.

Comparisons or contrasts: Many invading agents are benign, but the body defends itself anyway. (The contrasting word *but* signals that the body does not need defense from something benign. Using this clue, you can guess that *benign* means "not harmful.")

Examples: Some people experience anaphylaxis from allergies and can break out in hives, go into shock, and stop breathing. (The examples—break out in hives, go into shock, and stop breathing—show that *anaphylaxis* is a technical term for a severe, life-threatening allergic reaction.)

Taking Advantage of Nonverbal Clues

In Chapter 2 you learned the importance of **nonverbal clues** such as

- eye contact
- posture
- paralanguage (voice sound and variations)
- movement and gestures
- facial expression
- silence

Since nonverbal clues provide as much as 85 percent of the social meaning of communication, effective listeners carefully weigh speakers' behavior against their words. For many good listeners, paying attention to nonverbal clues—especially those that emphasize or contradict a speaker's words—is an unconscious part of their behavior. To avoid being misled, be alert to two basic effects of nonverbal clues.

Critical Thinking

Analysis

Ask students to watch a videotape of a speech with the sound turned off. Give the topic of the speech but not the speaker's position on the topic. Ask students to analyze the speaker's nonverbal communication expressed through gestures, facial expressions, posture, and movement. Have students determine the speaker's position based on these behaviors and have them defend their conclusions by citing specific instances of nonverbal communication.

Extension

You may want to prepare three 2-minute tape recordings of people talking about different topics. Place one tape player at the back of the room, one on the right, and one on the left. Play all three tapes at the same time and ask students to answer in writing five questions based on each of the three messages. Go over the answers so students can determine how well they comprehended each of the messages. Then discuss with students whether they concentrated on one message and ignored the others or whether they comprehended bits of each message. You can also discuss any frustration the students felt.

Emphasis. Speakers can emphasize key meanings through changing volume, stressing certain words, and using gestures.

EXAMPLE: Someone has placed a birthday gift on Maria's desk, and LuAnne is asked if she saw Greg and Xavier leave the gift. The suggested meaning of LuAnne's response will change depending on how she stresses different words.

*I didn't **see** Greg and Xavier put anything on your desk.*
*I didn't see **Greg and Xavier** put anything on your desk.*
*I didn't see Greg and Xavier put **anything** on your desk.*

Contradiction. By contradicting what a person says, nonverbal clues are like warning flags. However, contradiction does not always mean "This is a lie—beware!"; it may indicate the speaker's uncertainty, confusion, or hidden motive.

EXAMPLE: A friend announces what would seem like good news by saying, "I finally got the letter. I've been accepted at Morganton." However, his low tone of voice and subdued manner indicate his uncertainty.

Activity 2: Using Critical-Listening Skills

Read an editorial or feature article in your local newspaper. Identify the writer's goal(s), main ideas, and supporting details. Use context clues to determine the meanings of unfamiliar words. Then read your article aloud to a partner while your partner uses critical-listening skills to identify the goal(s), main ideas, supporting details, and context clues. Compare your findings. Then have your partner read his or her article aloud while you practice your critical-listening skills.

Timesaver

You can save time evaluating **Activity 2** by giving all the pairs of students the same two articles to use for the activity. This way you will not have to read and analyze a different article for every student.

Ongoing Assessment

Activity 2

To assess understanding of goals, main ideas, supporting details, and context clues, you could ask students to write down that information for the articles they read aloud. To assess students' critical-listening skills, you could ask students to write brief reports of how accurately they identified the goals, main ideas, supporting details, and context clues in the articles that were read to them.

ENRICHMENT

Your students might enjoy playing a listening game. At the end of a class period, explain that the next day you will expect them to listen carefully for the number of times you say a specific word. (Any word will do as long as it is not so unusual as to attract undue attention.) The next day make a point of using the word a predetermined number of times and ask students to keep a tally of how often you use it.

Listening Actively

Good listeners are active, not passive. They look for meaning, think about what they hear, and respond to it. The following chart lists a number of techniques that you can use to develop your ability to listen actively.

Techniques for Active Listening	
Strategy	**Examples**
Apply what you hear to yourself.	• Relate the information to your personal experience. • Use your own knowledge to understand new information. • Imagine yourself using the information in the future.
Think as you listen.	• Summarize and review throughout the presentation. • Start thinking of questions you want to ask the speaker later. • Predict the speaker's direction, but do not jump to conclusions. • If your prediction about the speaker's meaning is wrong, decide what misled you.
Use associations and mnemonic devices to remember important details.	• Make an **association**—a vivid mental image—that will help you remember. For example, picture the main factors in early U.S. economic development (cotton and transportation) as a locomotive pulling a canal boat carrying a cotton gin. • Use a **mnemonic device**—a rhyme, acronym (word formed from initials), or other wordplay. For example, the acronym *PIE* might help you to remember three speaking purposes: persuade, inform, entertain.
Take notes.	• Do not write every detail or quotation verbatim. Use your own words (paraphrase), and focus on key phrases and topics. • Develop a consistent method you can use every time you take notes. For example, write key ideas on the left and details on the right.
Give the speaker—and yourself—feedback.	• Use body language such as eye contact or a nod to show that you are listening. • Courteously comment or ask questions when the speaker gives you the opportunity to do so. • Always assess your response. Were you impressed, irritated, or neutral? Why?

***AV* Audiovisual Resource Binder**

Transparency 7
Listening Actively

Audiotape 1, Lesson 5
Conversation

Closure

Ask each student to complete the following statement: "One important thing I learned about listening was ____." Then have students take turns reading aloud their statements. To encourage listening, you may want to have each student repeat the previous student's statement before reading the one he or she wrote.

Listening attentively not only shows your regard for others but also improves your ability to understand and respond to the speaker's message.

Activity 3: Analyzing Your Use of Active-Listening Techniques

Choose a situation in which you can practice active listening. You might choose a situation in the classroom, such as a teacher's lecture or a classmate's speech. Use the chart on page 88 to remind you of specific active-listening techniques that you can use to improve your ability to listen effectively. After the lecture or speech, write a brief summary of the techniques for active listening that you used. Were some of these techniques easier for you to use than others? If you neglected certain techniques, determine why. Then share your summary with a partner or with a small group.

SMALL SOCIETY reprinted with special permission of King Features Syndicate, Inc.

Ongoing Assessment

Activity 3

Students should address all of the techniques listed on p. 88, either because the students used the techniques or because they neglected the techniques. The summaries should be concise and should indicate genuine reflection on the task.

Building a Portfolio

You may want to have students include in their portfolios their summaries from **Activity 3**. They can refer to these throughout the term to assess their progress in active listening.

Segment 2 *pp. 90–99*

- Evaluating a Speaker's Reasoning
- Examining Propaganda Techniques
- Listening and Evaluating

PERFORMANCE OBJECTIVES

- To analyze faulty reasoning
- To identify propaganda techniques
- To evaluate the effectiveness of speakers
- To deliver a speech
- To give an oral and a written critique of a speech

INTEGRATING THE LANGUAGE ARTS

Vocabulary Link

You may want to have students look up *logic* in a dictionary to find the word's etymology. What Greek roots does *logic* come from? [*logikos,* of speaking or reasoning; *logos,* a work, a reckoning, or a thought; *legein,* to speak, choose, read] What do the Greek roots suggest about the content of logic? [Logic deals with ways of speaking and reasoning.]

MEETING INDIVIDUAL NEEDS

An Alternative Approach

Students who seem particularly interested in logical fallacies or who are adept at recognizing them may benefit from further exploration of the types of fallacies. You can refer these students to books on logic and to college rhetoric textbooks for additional research. Students can report to the class on their findings. Some of the fallacies that are commonly treated include *post hoc, ad hominem, non sequitur,* either-or, only cause, false authority, and circular reasoning.

Evaluating a Speaker's Reasoning

An important part of being an effective listener is evaluating a speaker's reasoning, or logical thinking. Ask yourself if the speaker is using faulty reasoning. **Faulty reasoning** may sound like a contradiction, but it is all too common. Statements that seem reasonable, even well reasoned, are very often based on mistakes in logic. Good listeners know that even when supporting details are precise and accurate, the conclusions drawn from them may be illogical. They can recognize several types of faulty reasoning.

Hasty Generalizations

Generalizations are general conclusions or opinions drawn from particular observations. Valid generalizations are based on sufficient evidence and carry required qualifying words like *most, some,* and *generally.* **Hasty generalizations** are conclusions or opinions that are drawn from very few observations or that ignore exceptions.

EXAMPLE: Seeing John turn his paper in late today, a classmate might make the hasty generalization that John never turns his work in on time.

ANALYSIS: Today may be the only time John has turned in a paper late. Basing a conclusion on only one observation is faulty reasoning.

Begging the Question

Begging the question means assuming the truth of a statement before it is proven. Listeners must be careful to see that speakers have actually proven what they claim as fact.

EXAMPLE: A speaker says, "With my plan, this country's failed and ineffective health care system can be remedied within a decade."

ANALYSIS: The speaker has given no proof that the country's health care system is an ineffective failure.

Motivation

Ask volunteers to describe a TV commercial that annoys them or that makes them angry and have them explain why. Keep this up until two or three students have identified commercials with offending elements that are either logical fallacies or overt propaganda techniques. Tell students that reasonable people are bothered by faulty reasoning and that this segment explains some of the common errors in reasoning that people use in trying to persuade others. Students' goal should be to learn to recognize faulty reasoning in order to become better listeners.

False Premises

A **premise** is a stated or implied starting point for an argument: It is assumed to be true. A **false premise** is a premise that is untrue or distorted.

EXAMPLE: We're bound to have a winning team this year. Five of our starters are back.

ANALYSIS: This statement is built on the premise that experience ensures skill and success. This is not necessarily true (the five returning players may be mediocre), so you cannot conclude that the team will automatically have a winning season this year.

False Analogies

Analogy is a form of reasoning by comparison. A good analogy draws valid conclusions from items that can be logically compared. A **false analogy** draws invalid conclusions from weak or often far-fetched comparisons.

EXAMPLE: A band member says to a friend, "I wish you'd learn to play the saxophone so you could join the marching band. Since you play the violin so well, I'm sure you could learn the sax easily."

ANALYSIS: The speaker's reasoning is based on a false analogy. Playing a violin well does not ensure that one can also play a saxophone well; both the instruments and the skills needed to play them are very different.

In this illustration, the analogy is based on a comparison of energy sources, or fuels.

Cooperative Learning

You may want to have students work in groups of three to identify and analyze logical fallacies in magazine advertisements and in letters to the editors of newspapers. Tell the students to look for the five fallacies presented in the text, but also encourage them to find other illogical arguments as well. Have the groups report their findings to the rest of the class.

Critical Thinking

Analysis

Ask students to analyze the following statements to identify the logical fallacies they contain:

1. With my plan, the school's unfair rules will be changed. [begging the question]
2. I saw a sixteen-year-old girl run a stop light. You just can't trust teenage drivers. [hasty generalization]
3. Our debate team is bound to win. The coach was a national champion. [false premise]
4. I know you'll like this cake. It cost twenty dollars. [irrelevant evidence]

Teacher's Resource Binder

Skills for Success 3
Evaluating a Speaker's Reasoning

Teaching the Lesson

You may want to have your students read the material on fallacies and propaganda techniques for homework and to spend class time on the activities in the textbook and on those suggested in the side margins. In any case, the more examples you can provide and elicit from students, the more likely your students will understand and remember the information. You may want to point out that the text contains only a brief list of fallacies and propaganda techniques, but by understanding these, students can begin to recognize other cases of faulty reasoning without necessarily having names for the fallacies. You can also point out that some examples of faulty reasoning can be given more than one label, depending on how the listener analyzes them.

MEETING **INDIVIDUAL** NEEDS

Linguistically Diverse Students

Nonnative speakers may have difficulty with **Activity 4,** not because their reasoning is flawed, but because detecting faulty reasoning requires a language facility that they may not have acquired yet. You may want to pair these students with peer tutors who have strong communicative and cognitive skills. Have the students work on the exercise together and allow class time to discuss the results.

Activity 4

Answers may vary. Make sure students' explanations are logical.

1. hasty generalization
2. false analogy
3. begging the question
4. irrelevant evidence
5. false premise

Teacher's Resource Binder

Skills for Success 4
Analyzing Propaganda Techniques

Irrelevant Evidence

Irrelevant evidence is information that has nothing to do with the argument being made. The evidence may sound impressive, but unless it is related to the point at hand, you should ignore it.

EXAMPLE: The merchandise at the Ultra Store is top quality. The manager has clothes shipped in from all over the world.

ANALYSIS: The fact that the clothes come from all over the world is an irrelevant detail that does not support the conclusion that the merchandise is top quality. The manager could be searching worldwide for cheap goods.

Analyzing Faulty Reasoning

With a partner or small group, evaluate each of the following items. Identify the form of faulty reasoning in each one—hasty generalization, begging the question, irrelevant evidence, false premise, or false analogy—and write a brief logical analysis explaining your answer. Be prepared to discuss your answers with the rest of the class.

1. Jackson was the lowest scorer in the game last night. He's simply not a great player and not worth the big money they paid for him.
2. The people claiming doom from the greenhouse effect are like the little boy crying wolf. It hasn't happened, and we shouldn't respond.
3. The nation's food companies are cheating their consumers—every one of us—by raising prices this year. After all, farmers had perfect weather and no shortage of workers.
4. The saleswoman said I looked terrific in the jacket, so I bought it.
5. Look at the year's progress: five new downtown high-rises and not one new park. The manipulation of the city commissioners by real estate developers must be stopped.

Examining Propaganda Techniques

Persuasion is the attempt to convince others to do something or to change a belief of their own free will. [For more information on persuasion and its purposes, see Chapter 15, pages 383–415.] **Propaganda** is persuasion that deliberately discourages people from thinking for themselves. Because its sole purpose is to spread information and claims that further—or destroy—a cause, idea, product, or person, propaganda at its worst relies on one-sided or distorted arguments.

It may be a good idea to handle all of the material in **Listening and Evaluating** in class. You can tell students that they will learn more about analyzing and evaluating speeches in other chapters.

You can offer guided practice for **Activity 4** on p. 92 and **Activity 5** on p. 96 by demonstrating how to do the first item in each. Students can then work on the rest of the items for independent practice.

If students are presenting informative speeches in response to this chapter, you may want to work through **Activity 6** on p. 99 as guided practice in giving oral and written critiques. If you do not plan to have students present speeches at this time, you could work with one of your more adept students to demonstrate **Activity 6**, and then you could assign the activity for independent practice.

Persuasion also relies heavily on emotional appeals, which attempt to sway people through feelings, not logic. Emotional appeals are perfectly acceptable in persuasion; in fact, they are very important. But when emotional appeals ignore logic or reason, they become a propaganda device. A good listener closely examines any persuasive statement to identify propaganda techniques.

Transfer

Transfer is a method that builds a connection between things that are not logically connected. In advertising, this connection is built between a product and a positive value. Good listeners demand that the link between these things be supported by evidence.

EXAMPLE: An advertisement might show a prosperous, happy, loving family drinking a certain brand of milk. The goal of the transfer technique is to get the viewer to associate the brand of milk with prosperity, happiness, and love.

ONE BIG HAPPY by Rick Detorie. By permission of Rick Detorie and Creators Syndicate.

Mass Media

You may want to have students identify TV commercials that employ transfer, bandwagon, and emotional appeal techniques. Lead the class in a discussion of the ethics of using these techniques.

An Alternative Approach

You could challenge interested students to research and report on additional propaganda techniques including glittering generalities, plain folks appeal, and snob appeal.

Assessment

Activities 4 and **5** should help you to assess students' understanding of faulty reasoning and propaganda techniques. If you need additional examples of fallacies and propaganda techniques for assessment or for further practice, these can usually be found in textbooks on composition and rhetoric. Checking oral and written critiques in response to **Activity 6** or in response to actual informative-speech presentations should help you assess students' abilities to evaluate.

Critical Thinking

Synthesis

Ask students to create additional examples for each of the propaganda techniques. Students can work alone or in groups. You can then make a master list of these examples and distribute the list to the class. Students can include the master list of additional examples of propaganda techniques in their communication journals for future reference.

Common Error

Problem. Some people fall victim to the technique of stereotyping because they fail to analyze claims that involve stereotypes.

Solution. Tell students to ask themselves if a statement says or implies that the claim made in the statement fits all members of the group in question. If the statement does say or imply universality for the group, it is probably a stereotype.

Bandwagon

The **bandwagon** technique encourages people to act because everyone else is doing it. Bandwagon attempts to substitute peer or crowd pressure for analysis of an issue or action. Good listeners insist that the speaker give support for the call to action.

EXAMPLE: Someone says that you should vote for a proposal because all your friends are voting for it; however, no one mentions why the proposal is worth supporting.

Name-Calling

Name-calling is labeling intended to arouse powerful negative feelings. Its purpose is to represent a particular person or group as inferior or bad without providing evidence to support the claim. Good listeners look beyond labels and ask for evidence to back up the speaker's position.

EXAMPLE: A speaker might ask you to vote against a candidate because that candidate is "a warmonger," "a tree hugger," "a preppie," or "an egghead."

Card-Stacking

Card-stacking is based on half-truths. It presents only partial information in order to leave an inaccurate impression. All effective speakers emphasize information that supports their viewpoint. Good listeners withhold judgment until they hear the supporting details or the case for the other side.

EXAMPLE: A speaker might refer to a person who has amassed a fortune through intimidation and illegal means as a "good breadwinner." This phrase tells only part of the story since it ignores the negative methods the person used to become a "good breadwinner."

Stereotypes

A **stereotype** is a biased belief about a whole group of people based on insufficient or irrelevant evidence. A stereotype ignores the individual. Good listeners reject stereotypes and demand specific information.

EXAMPLE: A co-worker might say, "Surely you don't plan to discuss the issue with the president of the company! Presidents are too interested in profit and personal gain to care about the problems of a single employee."

RETEACHING

One way to reteach the material on fallacies and propaganda techniques is to find examples of faulty reasoning in advertisements, political speeches, and letters to the editor in newspapers. Bring these to class and discuss why they illustrate faulty reasoning. Then ask students to use their textbooks to locate the terms that best describe the types of faulty reasoning you have discussed.

See p. 98 for **EXTENSION, ENRICHMENT,** and **CLOSURE.**

Loaded Words

Loaded words evoke, or draw out, very strong positive or negative attitudes toward a person, group, or idea. They can be powerful in their ability to create bias, a leaning toward a particular point of view. The "load" they carry is **connotation,** the feelings or associations a word evokes, in addition to its **denotation,** or specific meaning. Good listeners carefully evaluate the connotations and denotations of words. [See Chapter 2 for a detailed explanation of connotation and denotation.]

EXAMPLE: In discussing assertive behavior, Nan describes herself as "confident," Chris as "pushy," and Rita as a "braggart." Although the behavior described is exactly the same, the use of loaded words makes Nan's behavior seem positive, Chris's behavior seem negative, and Rita's behavior seem worst.

Emotional Appeals

Emotional appeals, or statements used to arouse emotional reactions, can be appropriately used in persuasion. However, when emotional appeals distort the truth or provoke irrational desires and fears, they become propaganda techniques. Good listeners respond to emotional appeals but demand support for any conclusion presented.

EXAMPLE: To gain support for the local humane society, a speaker might tell moving stories about the disposal of animals because of limited resources. People who want to help animals would probably respond emotionally to these specific examples.

In this scene from Arthur Miller's play, *Death of a Salesman,* a son (played by Stephen Lang) makes an emotional appeal for understanding to his father, Willy Loman (played by Dustin Hoffman).

ADDITIONAL ACTIVITY

To give students extra practice with recognizing loaded words, ask each student to compile a list of ten loaded words and a neutral synonym for each word. Then have students scramble the order of the neutral synonyms and exchange their lists with partners. The partners should try to match each loaded word with its appropriate synonym. You could circulate throughout the room to offer assistance as needed.

Learning Styles

Visual Learners. You may want to facilitate students' understanding of propaganda techniques by using visual media. Find real-life examples of these techniques in magazine ads, or show videotaped television advertisements. Clearly identify some of the techniques in the ads, and then let students work together to identify others. Providing visual learners the opportunity to grasp concepts first through visual contexts might help them to later identify these same concepts at the aural level.

Ongoing Assessment

Activity 5

Answers may vary.

1. bandwagon
2. stereotype
3. transfer
4. name-calling
5. card-stacking
6. emotional appeal
7. loaded words
8. transfer
9. bandwagon
10. loaded words

ACTIVITY 5 Identifying Propaganda Techniques

Identify each of the following items as an example of one of the propaganda techniques discussed in this chapter. When you complete the items, work with a small group of your classmates to compare your answers. Do you disagree on any items? Be prepared to explain your answers.

1. Folks, the upcoming election is going to be a landslide. Garver is carrying the entire West Side. Here's your chance to support a winner the people really want!
2. Friends, my opponent is a fine woman, but she is over sixty. Can you afford a mayor without youth's vigor—who might tire under the pressure, long hours, and huge workload?
3. Only fashionable, good-looking people buy Goodlook clothing. It's the brand to buy.
4. Wilson must be a gangster; he comes from a family of gangsters. A vote for Wilson will put the criminals in control.
5. They're calling Wilson a mouthpiece of organized crime. But would a criminal treat his family in the loving way Wilson does? He is a devoted husband and father. Vote for Wilson.
6. At night, these refugees go to sleep with no food or shelter. In the morning, they wake up to face another day of hunger. Do not ignore the plight of these helpless people. Send money to feed them now.
7. I might be thin, but Kelly is skinny. And Yolanda looks practically emaciated!
8. I want to tell you what a vote for me means. My roots are in a small, rural town. There the sick were always cared for. There the police were always friends, not adversaries.
9. The whole student council and the Athletes' Forum are going to the school board meeting to protest the dress code. You'll be part of the group that stands up and fights!
10. The all-wheel-drive Lion doesn't just go up hills. It positively leaps. Stubborn and sure-footed, it is king of the mountain. If your dream is to stand alone on the top, get one vehicle only: the Lion.

Listening and Evaluating

As a critical, active listener you are always evaluating what a speaker says and how the speaker says it. After your classmates present speeches, you might be called upon to give an oral or written critique of the speaker's effectiveness. A **critique** is an analysis and evaluation.

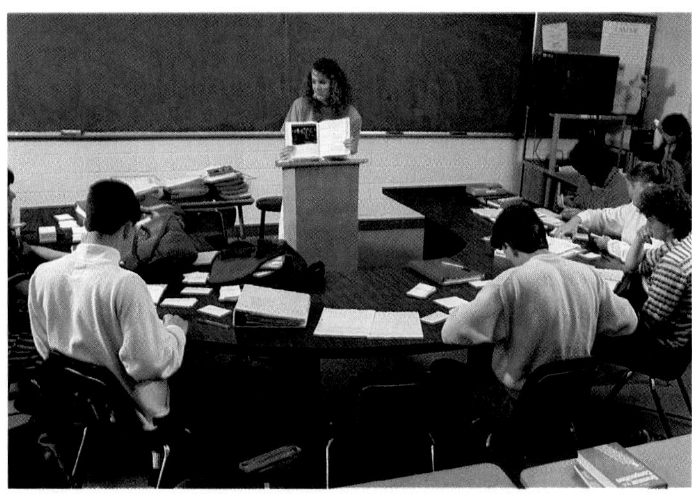

The Oral Critique

Oral critiques—analyses and evaluations given out loud—provide a valuable learning tool because everyone in the class can profit from analyzing the successes and mistakes of others. Remember that the purpose of an oral critique is not to show how wonderful the critic is. It is to help the speaker understand what went right and what went wrong in the speech. In this way, the speaker can try to build on successes and make needed improvements in later speeches.

HOW TO Give an Oral Critique

1. **Give positive feedback.** Remember that everyone needs positive reinforcement. Praise one or two things that the speaker did well in the speech. This positive feedback gives the speaker something to build on in the next speech.
2. **When giving negative feedback, concentrate on only one or two criticisms.** Try to avoid overwhelming the speaker by identifying everything that you think the speaker did wrong.
3. **When making criticisms, mention what the speaker could do to improve.** The speaker will find it helpful to have a suggestion or two to think about.
4. **Be specific.** Mention something in particular that the speaker did well. Once again, the speaker will be able to use this information to make his or her next speech better.

TEACHING NOTE

How to Give an Oral Critique deals with the content of any critique, oral or written. The guidelines provide a basic framework for presenting the results of an analysis of a speech. As such, they should be studied and used in conjunction with **How to Develop a Written Critique** on p. 98.

Extension

Ask students to work in pairs to create print advertisements or scenarios for television commercials employing as many of the logical fallacies and propaganda techniques as possible. Then have each pair exchange their ad with another pair for analysis. Finally, have the pair who wrote the ad or commercial and the pair who analyzed it make a joint presentation to the class on their work.

The Written Critique

A written critique usually takes a more complete and detailed look at a speech than an oral critique does. One good way to develop a written critique is to make a checklist of questions. Group these questions in four sections: organization, content, language, and delivery. The answers to your questions will provide you with specific details for your critique.

HOW TO *Develop a Written Critique*

1. **Think about the organization of the speech.** How well did all the parts of the speech work together? Did the introduction gain the audience's attention and present a clear statement of purpose? Were the key points of the speech well linked and easy to follow? How effective was the conclusion in summarizing the key points and closing the speech on a high point?
2. **Consider the content of the speech.** Think about how easy it was to understand the message of the speech. Was the topic well developed with sufficient details and examples? Was the message of the speech made clear to the specific audience? Do you think the audience will remember the key ideas of the speech? What did the speaker do to help the audience remember the key ideas?
3. **Analyze the language the speaker used.** Did the language help or hinder the audience's understanding of the speech? Did the speaker use words that the audience understood? Did the speaker define any unfamiliar words or technical vocabulary? Were the words of the speech concrete and vivid or vague and empty?
4. **Comment on the delivery the speaker used.** What do you remember about the speaker's appearance, voice, attitude, and mannerisms? How did each of these affect the success of the speech? What could the speaker do differently in his or her next speech?

How would you evaluate the speakers you hear on television programs, on the radio, and in your daily life? Make notes in your communication journal about speakers whom you found to be particularly effective. What did they do to make their speeches memorable? What could they have done differently?

AV ➤ *Audiovisual Resource Binder*

Transparency 8
Critiquing a Speech

Enrichment

You may want to ask a teacher of American history to talk to the class about the use of anti-German and anti-Japanese propaganda in American media during World War II.

Closure

Conduct a review of the fallacies and propaganda techniques by giving the name of one of these and having students cite examples of it from their experiences. You can conclude by having each student write one sentence about the dangers of logical fallacies and propaganda techniques to a free society.

ACTIVITY 6

Giving an Oral and a Written Critique

Look at the speeches that are listed in the *Appendix of Speeches* [pages 658–683]. Choose one of the speeches listed in the *Appendix* and practice evaluations with a partner. Deliver the speech as if you were delivering a speech you had written. Have your partner use the guidelines discussed in this section to give you an oral critique. Practice to improve your delivery, and then give the speech again. Then, your partner should deliver the speech and you should prepare a written critique of the content and delivery.

GUIDELINES for Listening Effectively

- Do I get enough rest and eat properly?
- Do I clear my mind of thoughts and worries that may distract me or affect my ability to concentrate?
- Am I able to overcome a poor listening environment by adjusting it or by ignoring distractions?
- Do I listen even when I am not particularly interested in the topic or disagree with the speaker's position?
- Do I listen to content—what the speaker is saying—rather than focus on a speaker's personality or delivery?
- Do I listen critically by identifying the speaker's goal, the main ideas, and the supporting details of the speech?
- Do I listen actively by thinking as I listen?
- Do I evaluate carefully, keeping alert to faulty reasoning and propaganda techniques?

Ongoing Assessment

Activity 6

Both the oral and written critiques should follow the "**How to**" points listed on pp. 97 and 98.

Building a Portfolio

Guidelines for Listening Effectively can be used by students for self-evaluation. Have students refer to these guidelines from time to time during the term to check themselves on their progress toward becoming better listeners. They can keep their evaluative results in their portfolios.

◆ Profiles in Communication

Performance Objectives

- To list appropriate listening strategies and questioning techniques for a specific situation
- To present a question-and-answer session

Teaching the Feature

Before students read about Dr. Manuel Galceran, you may want to ask volunteers to discuss the importance of communication skills in the practice of medicine. After students read the profile, you could focus your discussion on the importance of good listening skills.

Activity Note

Before students make lists of questions, suggest that they choose specific classes and specific homework assignments. As they make their lists, students will have to employ critical-listening skills to gain the necessary information from the students needing help. You will probably want to consider the feedback of classmates when you assess students' performances.

PROFILES IN COMMUNICATION

"Listening is vital in the practice of medicine," says Dr. Manuel Galceran, a busy family physician. "It is part of observation, and it can help in making a diagnosis." The importance of good listening was emphasized throughout Dr. Galceran's medical training. Not just the patient's words, but also his or her tone of voice, facial expressions, posture, body movement, and gestures, contribute information that helps lead to a diagnosis.

Teenagers, observes Dr. Galceran, can present special listening challenges. "It can be harder to get teens to open up because they often try to play down their problems." Dr. Galceran draws young patients out through careful questioning, noticing both what they do say and what they don't say.

If a question seems sensitive or receives no response, Dr. Galceran often rephrases it or returns to it later. To keep from leading patients into describing symptoms incorrectly, Dr. Galceran avoids asking yes or no questions. Instead, he may offer the patient options—for example, "Is the pain burning or sharp?"

Dr. Galceran also believes that nonverbal behavior is extremely important. He lets the patient know he is interested by making eye contact, not rushing or fidgeting, taking notes, and staying on the subject.

Dr. Galceran uses his communication skills daily. He feels that "one cannot be a good speaker without being a good listener."

ACTIVITY

In one of your classes a classmate asks you for help with a homework assignment. Your classmate seems to understand the subject, but is having trouble completing the assignment. Make a list of questions you would use to determine what part of the assignment your classmate needs to understand. Have a partner play the role of the confused classmate, and then present the question-and-answer session to the class. Ask for feedback about how effectively you helped your classmate.

S·U·M·M·A·R·Y

LISTENING AND EVALUATING are essential skills for communication. An effective listener is attentive and receptive, actively seeks out meaning, evaluates what is said, and responds to it. Becoming an effective listener includes the following steps:

- **Analyze factors that affect listening.** These include your physical and mental state, your prejudices, the speaker's personality and delivery, and the general environment.
- **Recognize and learn to overcome obstacles** to listening.
- **Listen critically** by identifying the speaker's goal, main ideas, and supporting details; by using context clues; and by taking advantage of nonverbal clues.
- **Listen actively** by applying what you hear to yourself, by thinking ahead, by using associations and mnemonic devices to remember important details, by taking notes, and by giving the speaker and yourself feedback.
- **Recognize faulty reasoning,** including hasty generalizations, begging the question, using irrelevant evidence, reasoning from false premises, and using false analogies.
- **Identify propaganda techniques** such as transfer, bandwagon, name-calling, card-stacking, stereotypes, loaded words, and emotional appeals.
- **Give oral critiques and written critiques** of speeches by using guidelines.

CHAPTER 4

Vocabulary

Look back through this chapter to find the meaning of each of the following terms. Write each term and its meaning in your communication journal.

analogy, ***p. 91***
association, ***p. 88***
bandwagon, ***p. 94***
begging the question, ***p. 90***
card-stacking, ***p. 94***
connotation, ***p. 95***
context, ***p. 85***
critical listening, ***p. 84***
critique, ***p. 96***
denotation, ***p. 95***
emotional appeals, ***p. 95***
false analogy, ***p. 91***
false premise, ***p. 91***
faulty reasoning, ***p. 90***
generalizations, ***p. 90***
goal, ***p. 84***
hasty generalizations, ***p. 90***
hearing, ***p. 81***
irrelevant evidence, ***p. 92***
listening, ***p. 81***
loaded words, ***p. 95***
main ideas, ***p. 84***
mnemonic device, ***p. 88***
name-calling, ***p. 94***
nonverbal clues, ***p. 86***
persuasion, ***p. 92***
prejudice, ***p. 83***
premise, ***p. 91***
propaganda, ***p. 92***
repetition, ***p. 84***
signal words, ***p. 85***
stereotype, ***p. 94***
supporting details, ***p. 85***
transfer, ***p. 93***

TEACHER'S RESOURCE BINDER

- Chapter 4 Vocabulary

Review Questions

Answers

1. *Hearing* means "detecting sounds"; *listening* means "getting meaning from sounds and nonverbal signals."
2. develop interpersonal skills, discover unexpected insights, increase knowledge and evaluative ability, and improve performance in school and at work
3. your physical and mental state—be energetic and focused; the speaker—focus on the message; your prejudices—keep an open mind; the environment—adjust the physical environment
4. Identify the speaker's goal; identify main ideas; identify supporting details; use context clues; and take advantage of nonverbal clues.
5. They can emphasize or contradict the message.
6. Answers will vary. See the chart on p. 88 for a complete list of techniques.

Discussion Questions

Guidelines for Assessment

Student responses may vary.

1. Average listening involves hearing a message and attaching meaning to it; active, critical listening means also evaluating the message's meaning and responding to it.
2. Obstacles include lack of food or rest, lack of interest in the material, the personality or mannerisms of the teacher, desire to impress or attract a classmate, and the presence of uncomfortable environmental conditions. The student can overcome these obstacles by eating a good breakfast and lunch, getting enough sleep at night, keeping his or her mind on track by taking notes, and politely requesting a change in environmental conditions.
3. The quotation suggests that two ears and one mouth provide more listening power than speaking power.
4. Critical listeners question and evaluate as they listen. Lowell's mention of "wise skepticism" could refer to the doubting and questioning of a critical listener. The use of "wise" shows that Lowell probably does not advocate a refusal to accept reasonable arguments or proofs.
5. One should carefully analyze a speaker's words and not be swayed by an argument that only sounds good. Careful analysis will help a listener to identify propaganda, persuasion that deliberately discourages people from thinking for themselves.

CHAPTER **4**

Review Questions

1. How is listening different from hearing?
2. What are four reasons for developing good listening skills?
3. There are four obstacles to effective listening. List all four obstacles and give one possible way to overcome each obstacle you named.
4. List and explain the five strategies that enable a critical listener to test the strength of the ideas he or she hears.
5. One aspect of critical listening is being able to understand nonverbal clues. In what two important ways can nonverbal clues affect the meaning of a message?
6. Two active-listening techniques are to think ahead and to give the speaker feedback. What is one way you can use each of these techniques?
7. Name and explain five types of faulty reasoning.
8. Define the propaganda technique called card-stacking.
9. What are three other propaganda techniques?
10. List the four guidelines for giving an oral critique.

Discussion Questions

1. Discuss the difference between average listening and active, critical listening.
2. Imagine that you are in a class that is reviewing information for a test. Discuss some specific obstacles that might interfere with good listening. Then discuss specific behaviors that can help you to overcome these obstacles.
3. Some feel that one of the major problems people face is the inability to listen to each other—to give each other a fair hearing. The Greek philosopher Zeno of Citium wrote, "The reason why we have two ears and only one mouth is that we may listen the more and talk the less." Discuss the meaning of Zeno's words and explain whether or not you agree with him.
4. James Russell Lowell—an American diplomat, essay-writer, poet, and editor—once wrote, "A wise scepticism is the first attribute of a good critic." Discuss the difference between critical listening and uncritical listening. How does this difference relate to Lowell's statement? Do you think he is advocating a refusal to accept reasonable arguments or proofs? Why or why not?
5. The novelist Joseph Conrad—whose works often deal with how a person's beliefs affect his or her goals and choices in life—wrote, "He who wants to persuade should put his trust not in the right argument, but in the right word. The power of sound has always been greater than the power of sense." Discuss the meaning of Conrad's statement. Then discuss how this quotation relates to the difference between persuasion and propaganda.

7. making hasty generalizations: jumping to conclusions based on insufficient evidence; begging the question: assuming the truth of a statement before it's proven; reasoning from false premises: basing an argument on a stated or implied starting point that isn't true; false analogies: drawing invalid conclusions from weak or far-fetched comparisons; using irrelevant evidence: basing an argument on information that has nothing to do with the argument
8. basing an argument or appeal on half-truths or partial information to create a false impression
9. transfer, bandwagon, name-calling, stereotypes, loaded words, and emotional appeals
10. Give positive feedback; concentrate on only one or two criticisms when giving negative feedback; mention how the speaker can improve; and be specific.

ACTIVITIES

1. **Observing and Analyzing Listening Behavior.** As you talk with people, you are probably conscious of those who really listen and those who do not. The next time you are talking to a group, notice listening behavior. What indicates that a person is listening carefully or is not? What effect does your listeners' attention or inattention have on you as a speaker? Share your findings with your class.

2. **Understanding Propaganda Techniques.** Look closely at the cartoon below. What propaganda technique is Charlie Brown's little sister trying to use on him? What technique does Charlie Brown use in return? Explain which propaganda techniques you think are used and how they are intended to affect the listener. Compare your answers to these questions with your classmates' answers.

3. **Practicing Listening Skills to Gather Information.**
   A. Talk with two people who have lived in your neighborhood or nearby for at least twenty years. Ask them to tell you what the area was like when they first lived there. Make no notes while they talk, but listen attentively. After each session, write down the important facts you remember. Share your findings with your classmates.
   B. Working with a partner, listen to a five-minute segment of a radio news broadcast. Then, write down everything you remember hearing. Compare your notes with your partner's.

4. **Interpreting Nonverbal Clues.**
   A. As you read the items below, try to picture each scene in your mind. Decide whether the nonverbal signals used in each situation serve to emphasize or to contradict the verbal message. Compare your answers with those of your classmates.
      1. Laila has been named valedictorian. On hearing the news, Rhonda, a friend of Laila's, looks away and, in a monotone, mutters, "Congratulations. I'm so happy for you."
      2. Brandon's sister Felicia is competing in her first marathon. As Felicia nears the finish line, Brandon claps, cheers wildly, and yells, "Way to go, Fish-face! You can do it!"
      3. Your new classmate Travis is eating lunch by himself in the cafeteria. You go over to where he is sitting and ask if you may join him. Travis shrugs and says, "Suit yourself," and returns to the book he is reading.
      4. You are worried about your neighbor Mr. Winthrop. Lately, you haven't seen him working in his garden as much as you used to. When you ask him if anything is wrong, he looks thoughtful, slowly shakes his head, and says, "No, nothing. Everything's OK."
      5. Todd is applying for a job at a fast-food restaurant. He has just asked

ACTIVITIES

Guidelines for Assessment

1. You can ususally tell by a person's posture and eye contact whether he or she is listening. Some students may not be affected by nonlisteners; others might suggest such strategies as pausing or speaking loudly to gain the attention of nonlisteners.
2. Because answers may vary, be sure that students support their responses. Students might say that the little sister is stereotyping children to persuade Charlie Brown that she has not intentionally lied. Students might say that Charlie Brown uses the transfer method.
3. A. The notes should contain the main ideas and some supporting details that the speaker used.
   B. Both students should write down the main ideas and some supporting details.
4. A. Ask students to explain their answers.
   1. contradict
   2. emphasize
   3. contradict
   4. contradict
   5. contradict

SUMMATIVE EVALUATION

Your **Teacher's Resource Binder** contains a reproducible **Chapter 4 Test** that may be used to assess students' mastery of the concepts presented in this chapter.

PORTFOLIO ASSESSMENT

For future reference and evaluation you may want to have students keep in their portfolios any skill sheets or evaluation forms that you have used in this chapter along with any other recorded or written materials that students have created.

B. You may want students to write down the revisions for easier assessment.

5. Good memory devices are simple and directly related to the material to be remembered.

6. Students' lists should reflect a variety of propaganda techniques, though not necessarily all seven given in the text. The explanations of the techniques should clearly indicate how the examples distort the truth.

7. A. Answers will vary, but in general, the ways to change behavior should reflect the ideas in the **How to Control Factors That Affect Listening** chart on p. 83.

B. You may want to have students write their responses to these items and to keep the responses in their portfolios for reference and reassessment later in the term.

the manager about opportunities for advancement in the business. After clearing her throat a few times, the manager says, "Well, um, . . . you know . . . with hard work and, um, determination, you just might, ah, work your way up to a job like mine someday."

B. Working with a partner, review the items you found to be contradictory in Part A. Then, try to make the verbal and nonverbal messages agree. Have one partner revise the nonverbal signals to be consistent with the verbal message. Have the other partner revise the verbal messages to be consistent with the nonverbal signals.

5. Identifying Memory Devices and Analyzing Their Usefulness. Make a list of associations and mnemonic devices you use to remember things. For example, some people remember the spelling of *surgeon* because it has two words in it, *surge* and *on.* Make a class list of memory devices. Discuss what makes some of these devices more useful than others and which new ones you will try.

6. Identifying and Evaluating Propaganda Techniques. Spend one week listening and looking for propaganda techniques. Advertisements, commercials, and political speeches are rich sources, but also read newspaper editorials and listen to other speeches, discussions in school or clubs, and television news and talk shows. Record any examples you find of the propaganda techniques on pages 93–95; list, or be ready to explain, their distortions.

7. Identifying Your Negative Listening Habits.

A. The following statements identify negative listening habits. Do any of them represent your behavior? For each one that does, indicate possible ways to change your behavior.

1. I may fall asleep in afternoon lectures.
2. There are some people I just can't listen to, no matter what they say.
3. When I'm interested in a topic or when I really think a speaker is wrong, I keep butting in.
4. When someone's voice irritates me, I stop listening.
5. I get so tense when we talk about tests that my mind races and I miss what's being said.

B. Read the following statements; then indicate whether each statement applies to you often, seldom, or never. Give yourself three points for each *often,* two for each *seldom,* and one for each *never.* If you score ten points or more, you need to work on improving your listening behavior.

1. I do not let a person complete more than a few sentences before I interrupt.
2. I like to finish people's sentences for them.
3. I fiddle with a pen or a pencil or gaze out the window rather than look at the person who is speaking.
4. I do not question a point, ask for examples, or challenge a speaker.
5. I do not try to summarize the key points that a person has made.

◆ Real-Life Speaking Situations

Performance Objectives

- To write and present to the class a dialogue of a discussion between a parent and his or her teenage son or daughter
- To write and present a dialogue between a counselor and a client
- To evaluate dialogues

REAL LIFE Speaking Situations

1 Listening skills are vital in communicating with others. Nowhere is this fact more evident than in communication between parents and their teenage sons and daughters. Teenagers often complain that their parents do not listen to them, and parents commonly have the same complaint about their teenagers. Can teenagers and their parents improve their listening skills and learn to communicate more effectively?

Imagine that you are a parent and that you are in a discussion with your teenage son or daughter about improving his or her performance in school. How can you get your point across without causing a stand-off or a fight? What kinds of questions should you ask? What kinds of statements should you make? How should you respond to the answers and statements that your son or daughter makes? Should you use direct confrontation or an indirect approach? When should you talk and when should you listen?

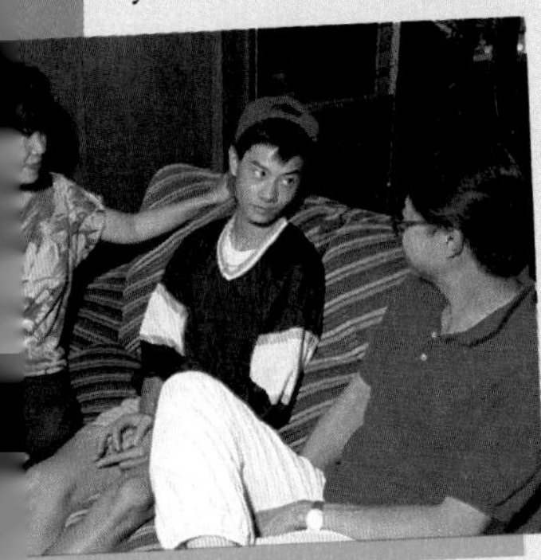

Write a short dialogue of the discussion between you and your teenager. Present your dialogue in class and discuss how listening skills can improve parent-teen communication.

2 Counseling is one occupation in which listening skills are critically important. Counselors must listen carefully to what clients say to help them find the sources of and solutions to their problems.

Imagine that you are a counselor working with a new client. First, write a brief description of the client's appearance and behavior. Then, create a hypothetical counseling situation. Why has this client come to you for counseling? Is he or she feeling depressed? anxious? Is he or she having problems with a girlfriend or a boyfriend? What clues should you listen and watch for to understand the problem?

Finally, write a dialogue of the question-and-answer session between you and your client. Working with a partner, practice the dialogue with you as the counselor and your partner as the client. Rehearse the scene well enough to be able to give a believable representation of a dialogue between a counselor and a client. If you feel comfortable enough with your roles, both counselor and client may improvise from the script.

Present the scene to the class. Ask classmates to evaluate how well you, as the counselor, listened to the client.

Assessment Guidelines

1. Although the parent character should take the lead in each dialogue, both characters should listen to one another and employ the methods in the **Techniques for Active Listening** chart on p. 88. The dialogues should sound natural, and the presentations should be smooth and well rehearsed.
2. The focus of each dialogue should be on the client, who should do most of the talking. The student who acts as the counselor should use the methods from the **Techniques for Active Listening** chart on p. 88 and should emphasize giving the speaker (the client) feedback. The presentations should be natural, smooth, and well rehearsed.

Unit 2 • Interpersonal Relationships

Interpersonal Relationships

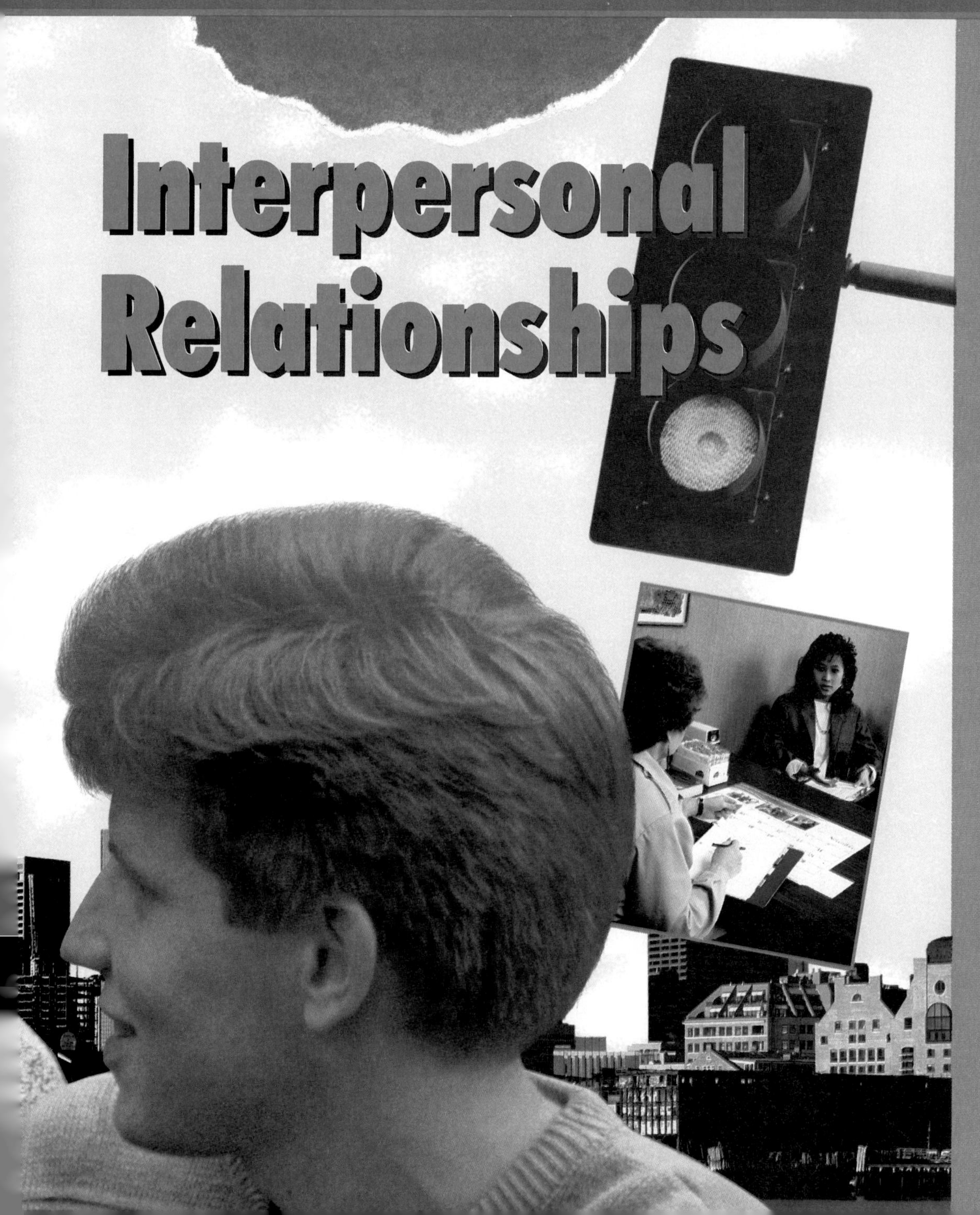

Chapter 5
Analyzing Yourself as a Communicator
pp. 108–137

Chapter Overview

This chapter begins with a discussion of perception and then addresses self-concept and how it affects communication. The second segment considers personal needs and factors that affect interactions with others.

Teacher's Resource Binder

The following materials are identified at their point of use in this chapter:

- Skills for Success
  1. *Analyzing Your Self-Concept*
  2. *Understanding Yourself as a Communicator*
  3. *Assessing Needs*
  4. *Analyzing Interpersonal Situations*
- Chapter 5 Vocabulary
- Chapter 5 Test/Answer Key

AV Audiovisual Resource Binder

The following materials are identified at their point of use in this chapter:

- Transparency 9
  Maslow's Hierarchy of Needs
- Transparency 10
  Setting Goals

INTRODUCING THE CHAPTER

Many adolescents seem worried and confused about who they are and about how other people see them. This chapter provides an opportunity for students to explore their feelings about themselves. Point out that this chapter seems to have little to do with public speaking but that it has everything to do with people as communicators. Some of the insights that students will gain about themselves will be too personal and private to share with others, so inform students that you will respect their privacy. Encourage students to give reflective attention to the ideas they study.

CHAPTER 5

Analyzing Yourself as a Communicator

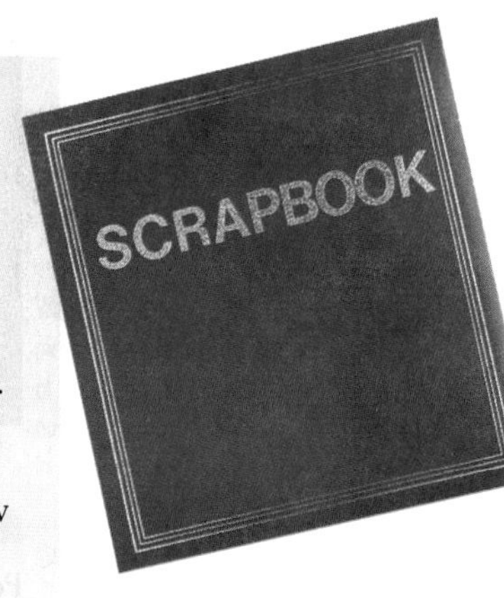

OBJECTIVES

After studying this chapter, you should be able to

1. Define *intrapersonal communication.*
2. Define *perception* and list factors that affect the accuracy of perception.
3. Explain how self-concept affects communication.
4. Explain how interpersonal needs affect behavior and communication, and assess needs to improve communication.
5. Explain how attitudes, goals, and interpersonal roles affect communication.
6. Explain how to make predictions about other people and how to check those predictions.

What Is Intrapersonal Communication?

Although you may think of communication primarily as interpersonal, or taking place between you and others, you probably spend a great deal of time talking with yourself. This "self-talk" is called **intrapersonal communication.**

Intrapersonal communication helps you determine what you think and how you behave. Much of your thought and behavior depends on how you perceive the world around you.

Your perceptions affect the way you feel about yourself, your attitudes toward communicating, and your ability to make predictions about others.

Bibliography of Additional Materials

PROFESSIONAL READINGS

- Griffin, Kim, and Bobby R. Patton. ***Fundamentals of Interpersonal Communication.*** Lanham, MD: University Press of America.
- Hamilton, Cheryl, and Cordell Parker. ***Communicating for Results.*** Belmont, CA: Wadsworth Publishing Company.

AUDIOVISUALS

- ***Communication Breakdown: A Repair Guide***—The Learning Seed, Lake Zurich, IL (videocassette, 22 min.)
- ***Discovering Social Styles***—University Associates, San Diego, CA (videocassette, 30 min.)
- ***Effective Communication Skills, Program 11: The Self Concept***—Wisconsin Foundation for Vocational, Technical, and Adult Education, Middleton, WI (videocassette, 28 min.)
- ***Your Speaking Image, Program 6: Interactions That Count***—Agency for Instructional Technology, Bloomington, IN (videocassette, 30 min.)

Teaching the Lesson

After students have read and discussed the material dealing with perception, you may want to show the class a magazine photograph that is cluttered with people and objects. After fifteen seconds, ask students to write down everything in the picture they remember. Then ask them to group what they remembered into categories. [The categories will vary depending on the photo, but some natural categories should emerge.] Then discuss why someone might notice some things and not notice others. This guided practice should prepare students to complete **Activity 1** independently.

After students have read the information about self-concept beginning on p. 113, you will probably want to model **Activity 2** on p. 117. If you find the activity too personal, you could base it on a literary or media character that your

Writing to Learn

Ask students to freewrite about times when they were disappointed by something they had been looking forward to. Encourage students to analyze how their backgrounds and experiences might have contributed to their disappointments.

Individual Differences in Perception

Perception is affected by individual differences. Each person perceives objects, places, events, and people somewhat differently as a result of individual traits, including physical characteristics, background and experience, selected focus, and current mood and circumstances.

Physical Characteristics. Your perceptions are affected by physical characteristics such as your age, size, health, and gender.

> EXAMPLE: Mike tried to take his five-year-old son Jerry on the Junior Racer, a children's ride in an amusement park. As they approached, Jerry began to cry: "I don't want to go on this ride. It's too big." Mike was about to say, "No, this is a little ride," but when he looked at it through Jerry's eyes, he understood why his son was afraid.

Background and Experience. Your unique background and past experiences also affect your perceptions. Your past experiences differ from the experiences of others, and other people do not necessarily share perceptions that you take for granted.

> EXAMPLE: Two new friends, Laura and Tanya, were trying to decide where to have lunch. Laura had eaten sushi all her life and suggested that Tanya come with her to her favorite Japanese restaurant. "Oh, gross!" replied Tanya. "How could you stand to eat raw fish?" Laura realized that she should not have assumed her new friend would share her opinion and experience of certain kinds of food.

Selected Focus. At any given time, your mind has a focus that affects how you perceive the environment. This selected focus leads you to notice some things and to ignore others.

students are familiar with. Then assign **Activity 2** for independent practice.

Assessment

Because **Activities 1** and **2** are highly subjective, assessing content might be difficult. Therefore, you may want to have students write brief summaries about what they learned about their perceptions and their self-concepts from completing the activities.

Example: In art class Krista is studying fabric design and color. When she stops by a friend's house, she is struck by the unusual geometric patterns in the living room drapes. "Wow," Krista says. "I've been in this house several times and never noticed the design of these drapes."

Current Mood and Circumstances. Immediate circumstances and mood also affect perceptions.

Example: When you are walking downtown, your perceptions will differ dramatically depending on how you are feeling and what you are thinking about. If you are hungry, you will see everything in terms of food. You may walk right by a sale of your favorite running shoes as you look for a restaurant. If you have read about an increase in crime downtown, you may watch the people around you carefully, and tightly clutch the packages you are carrying.

Activity 1 Analyzing Your Perceptions

Take a minute to perceive everything that is around you. Now close your eyes and describe what you saw to a partner. Open your eyes and look again. What did you miss? Can you explain why you selected the items you were able to describe? What caused you to notice these and not other aspects of the environment?

Thinking About Your Self-Concept

How you communicate and how you behave depend a great deal on what you think of yourself. This section discusses the formation of the self-concept, the accuracy of your self-concept, and the relation of self-concept to communication.

Additional Activity

Ask students who participate in activities like marching band, athletics, and theater to share how they perceive their audiences during performances. Ask students to address how their moods and circumstances affect what they notice.

Ongoing Assessment

Activity 1

You may want to have students write their answers to the questions in **Activity 1.** You can focus your assessment on the extent to which students incorporate ideas from the text in their answers to the last two questions.

Reteaching

If students are unable to analyze why they notice some items but not others when they look at a picture or a scene for a brief time, try having them focus on what interests them. Select a picture from a magazine and tell students what the picture deals with without showing it to them. Then ask them to write down everything they know about the subject of the picture and everything they expect to see in the picture. Next, show the picture for a few seconds, and then ask students to list what they saw. Discuss how accurate they were and how their previous knowledge and expectations might have affected their perceptions. Repeat this activity several times, and encourage students to pay closer attention as they look at each picture.

Teaching Note

For some students who hold poor self-concepts and who suffer from low self-esteem, the material in this section may be difficult to deal with. For this reason, you may want to exercise caution in forcing reluctant students to participate in class discussions.

Integrating the Language Arts

Literature Link

If the selection is available, have students read "The Secret Life of Walter Mitty" by James Thurber. Discuss Mitty's self-concept with the class. How does he see himself in real life? [as a bumbling incompetent] How does he see himself in his secret life? [as a hero capable of anything] How does his real life trigger, or cause, his secret life? [Answers will vary. In general, Mitty enters his secret life to escape his real life.]

Teacher's Resource Binder

Skills for Success 1
Analyzing Your Self-Concept

Forming a Self-Concept

Your **self-concept** represents a collection of perceptions about every aspect of your being, including your physical and mental capabilities, your vocational potential, and your communication abilities. The self-concept is formed through what you see and experience, and through what others tell you about yourself.

Observation and Experience. Many of your self-impressions are formed by how you observe yourself. You look at yourself in the mirror and make judgments about your weight, attractiveness, dress, makeup, and hairstyle.

EXAMPLE: Gloria is trying on clothes. What she sees will affect what she thinks about herself. If she likes what she sees, she may say, "This looks great! I can really handle these new styles." If she doesn't like what she sees, she may say, "I've got to cut down on junk food—and it wouldn't hurt to get a little more exercise."

Your impression of yourself is also based on experience. You make judgments about what you are good at and what you like.

EXAMPLE: Since Darnell gets his best grades in French class and sees himself as being able to handle the homework in nearly record time each night, he is likely to say to himself, "I'm really good at foreign language."

In general, the greater the number of positive experiences you have, the more positive your self-concept becomes. Likewise, the greater the number of negative experiences you have, the more negative your self-concept may become.

See p. 116 for **Extension, Enrichment,** and **Closure.**

What Others Tell You. In addition to your own observations and personal experiences, your self-concept is usually affected by what others tell you about yourself.

EXAMPLE: You have just given your interpretation of a character in a play you are studying in English class. One of your classmates says, "I didn't really understand the meaning of the main character's actions in that scene until you explained it—you're really good at analyzing plays."

Positive comments are likely to strengthen your self-concept, especially if you admire and respect the person making the comment about you. You use such comments to confirm, strengthen, or alter your self-concept. The more positive comments you receive about yourself, the more positive your total self-concept usually becomes. You feel better about yourself.

Developing an Accurate Self-Concept

The accuracy of your self-concept depends on the accuracy of your perceptions. Everyone experiences success and failure, and everyone hears praise and blame. If you remember your most successful experiences and positive responses, your self-concept will probably be positive as well. If, however, you perceive and focus on negative experiences and criticism, your perception will be correspondingly negative and your self-concept will be weak. In neither case does the self-concept necessarily conform to reality. Yet in terms of behavior, your *perception* of yourself—what you *think* you are like—will probably have a far greater effect on your behavior than reality is likely to have.

In your communication journal, write down notes expressing your current observations and feelings about your self-concept. You can organize your comments into three categories: "How I see myself," "How others see me," and "How I wish I were." Compare your comments, and note similarities and differences among your three lists. Then write a short statement that summarizes what you have learned about yourself. Because this information is for your own benefit, you do not have to share it with anyone else unless you feel comfortable revealing your personal thoughts and feelings to your classmates.

MEETING INDIVIDUAL NEEDS

An Alternative Approach

Students who do not do well in school often have negative concepts of themselves as learners. You can help improve low self-concepts by calling on these students from time to time to answer questions or to give demonstrations that you are sure they can handle. Then offer specific praise for what the student has said or done.

Cultural Diversity

In some cultures, young people are taught to be close-mouthed, to keep their feelings to themselves. Students from such cultures may have difficulty sharing personal information and may even find it uncomfortable to comment about self-concept in their journals. Therefore, emphasize that no one, not even you as teacher, will be privy to these notes and that the **Communication Journal** activity is optional rather than required.

You can ensure students of their privacy on this activity by having them fold over and staple closed the page or pages in their communication journals they use for this work. You can assess their efforts by simply determining whether or not they did the assignment.

Extension

You may want to have students use the chart in **Activity 2** as a framework for developing descriptions of characters from short stories or from TV shows. First, have students fill out the chart as they think the characters would. Then have each student use the character's point of view to write a brief analysis that explains the ratings. Finally, ask students to share their analyses with the rest of the class.

Self-Concept and Communication

Your self-concept affects many aspects of your life, especially your intrapersonal communication: problem solving and decision making, behavior, and processing of feedback.

Problem Solving and Decision Making. Your self-concept affects the intrapersonal communication you use in problem solving and decision making. When you are thinking, in a sense you are talking to yourself. Faced with a problem or with the need to make a decision, you may be especially conscious of different, and often competing, mental voices.

Example: After a party, Miguel had this intrapersonal conversation: "I think I made a good impression on Suki. I think I'm going to give her a call. Wait, but she also talked with a lot of other people. Yes, but she spent a lot more time with me than with anyone else. But then, that doesn't mean she cares about me personally. She probably won't even remember who I am."

Several of Miguel's thoughts are competing. His self-concept is likely to determine which voice he listens to. If Miguel feels good about himself, he will probably conclude that Suki was sincere, and he will call her.

Behavior. Self-concept also directly affects your behavior. People with strong self-concepts are likely to focus on positive experiences they have had; people with weaker self-concepts are more likely to focus on negative experiences. This intrapersonal communication will actually influence performance.

Example: Anton perceives himself as a good public speaker. Concerning a speech assignment, he thinks, "I've got a lot going for me. I'll do well on this assignment." Because he is confident, he stays relaxed, prepares calmly, and practices the speech. Just as he predicted, he gives a good speech and receives a high grade. Bryan, on the other hand, perceives himself as a poor speaker. He thinks, "I know I'll mess up this speech!" Expecting failure, he cannot concentrate on preparing, he does not take time to practice the speech, and he tells himself constantly that he is going to do poorly. Just as he predicted, he gives a poor speech and receives a low grade.

Teacher's Resource Binder

Skills for Success 2
Understanding Yourself as a Communicator

ENRICHMENT

Invite a counselor, social worker, or other mental-health professional to discuss with the class how he or she assesses clients' self-concepts and what he or she does to help clients improve.

CLOSURE

Ask your students to look back through the segment and to write down the two ideas they considered the most important. Then let volunteers share with the class their ideas and their reasons for choosing these ideas. If important ideas are omitted, you can fill in the gaps.

Processing of Feedback. Self-concept can also affect how you process the feedback you receive. You are likely to choose to listen to messages that reinforce, or strengthen, your self-perception. In effect, you hear only what you want to hear. However, positive feedback can improve your self-concept.

EXAMPLE: Anton thinks he is a good speaker. If he hears one comment praising his information and one criticizing his eye contact, he will listen to the praise and say, "I guess my eye contact wasn't as good as it could have been, but I'll improve that before the next speech."

If Bryan gets the same comments, he will probably process them differently. He will listen to negative comments about his speech and play down or screen out positive comments. Thus, Bryan will say to himself, "I don't know why I got praise for my material. It wasn't that good; anyone could have found out that information. But my poor eye contact really must have ruined the speech. I'll never get any better."

Conducting a Self-Concept Check

For each of the following topics, write down the number that most closely represents your self-evaluation in that area.

Topic	Negative		Neutral	Positive	
1. My appearance	1	2	3	4	5
2. My work habits	1	2	3	4	5
3. My accomplishments	1	2	3	4	5
4. My scholastic abilities	1	2	3	4	5
5. My athletic abilities	1	2	3	4	5
6. My social skills	1	2	3	4	5

For each topic area for which you recorded a *1* or a *2*, write one example to illustrate this evaluation. Then, for each of these statements, write three examples that give a more positive view. Now reconsider your ratings: Is it possible that you were too hard on yourself?

Students with Special Needs

Students with disabilities often have poor self-images and low self-esteem. Therefore, you may want to modify **Activity 2** by asking students to include specific adjectives that define their feelings about themselves. Help students to focus on positive aspects as well as to target behaviors they would like to change. Then assist students in setting realistic goals in changing behaviors.

ONGOING ASSESSMENT

Activity 2

If students prefer to keep the particulars of their self-concept checks private, you may want to have them write a few statements that summarize their findings.

BUILDING A PORTFOLIO

Encourage students to keep their self-concept checks in their portfolios for personal assessment. Later in the term, ask students to complete the checks again and to compare results.

Segment 2 *pp. 118–131*

- **Assessing Needs: Sources of Behavior**
- **Interacting with Others**
- **Making Predictions About Others**

Performance Objectives

- To assess personal roles in a variety of communication situations
- To analyze personal predictions about others

Using the Chart

You can use the chart for a class activity by first discussing the meaning of each term. Then ask students to rank the common social needs as they feel the needs apply to them. Discuss the rankings and allow students to change their minds about their rankings if they want to do so.

Teacher's Resource Binder

Skills for Success 3
Assessing Needs

Assessing Needs: Sources of Behavior

Why did Maria decide to run for student council president? Why did Tyrone elect a course in psychology rather than computer science? Why did Jasmine stay up so late studying? These questions consider **motives,** the sources of behavior. People display very diverse motives as they respond to biological and social needs.

Types of Needs

People have the same biological needs: the needs for food, water, and sleep. But social needs vary on the basis of background and experience.

Interpersonal Needs Theory. Many social scientists have demonstrated that interpersonal needs influence behavior. For instance, William Schutz, a psychologist, lists three basic interpersonal needs that affect behavior:

- the need to give or receive affection from others
- the need to include others or be included in relationships
- the need to control others or relinquish control to them

People also have needs for pleasure, relaxation, and escape. Thus, people communicate with others to have fun, to unwind, and to fill time while avoiding other activities.

Common Social Needs		
achievement	escape	nurturing
affection	inclusion	pleasure
control	independence	relaxation

People's needs differ and change over time. When other people's needs differ significantly from yours and you do not understand that, communication may break down. Moreover, unfulfilled needs can lead to anxiety or unhappiness and may weaken a person's self-concept.

Maslow's Hierarchy of Needs. According to Abraham Maslow, a noted psychologist, behavior is motivated by a **hierarchy of needs,** a ranking of five general categories of needs: physiological, safety, love, esteem, and self-actualization. These needs form a pyramid, with the most basic needs at the bottom of the pyramid. Once the basic, lower-level needs are met, people move to higher levels of need.

MOTIVATION

Ask students to write lists of five things they need in order to be happy. Make sure they understand that these are not necessarily things they do not already have. Collect the papers, choose a few at random, and write the lists on the chalkboard. Go through the items with the class and ask students to evaluate each one to determine whether it is a true need or merely a want. If students seem engaged by this activity, you can then ask them to rank the needs from most to least important.

Explain that this segment will consider some of the basic human needs that psychologists have identified. Unlike things people would like to have but could live without, the kinds of needs the students will be studying are fundamental to happy, productive living.

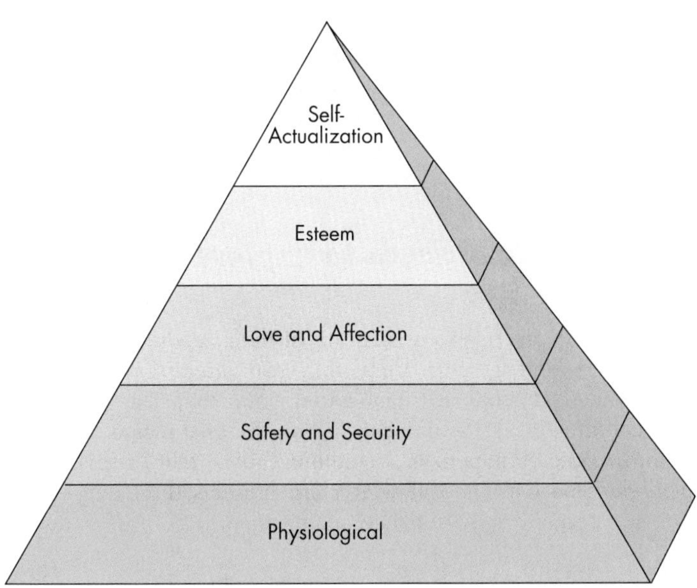

- **Physiological Needs:** The most basic needs are the physiological, or bodily, needs for food, water, and stable body temperature. They form the base of the "needs pyramid." These basic needs must be satisfied before a person can become concerned about needs at higher levels.
- **Safety and Security Needs:** These needs include self-preservation and concern about long-term survival. They motivate people to take care of themselves—for example, to take a course in self-defense. These needs also motivate people to seek stable jobs, to buy insurance, and to save money for the future.
- **Love and Affection Needs:** These needs are met by group and family membership and by the development of friendships. People want to feel as though they have someone to count on, especially when they go through hard times.
- **Esteem Needs:** People need status, recognition, and attention. They can meet these needs by gaining expertise in a particular job or area of study, by sharpening athletic skills, or by purchasing products that will make them feel good and look good in the eyes of their peers.
- **Need for Self-actualization:** The drive a person has to be everything that he or she can be, to take full advantage of his or her talents and abilities, is called **self-actualization.**

Seeing needs as a hierarchy helps to explain behavior. For example, when you are hungry or tired, you may not want to talk

TEACHING NOTE

Some students may think that each of the five components of Maslow's hierarchy of needs must be met in full before moving on to the next level. You may want to explain that physiological needs must be met before the other needs can be considered, but the other four needs can be met simultaneously. For example, people need esteem even if their long-term security needs are not fully met. Explain to students that the hierarchy, after the lowest level, is a logical progression, not necessarily a chronological progression in the ordinary sense.

Audiovisual Resource Binder

Transparency 9

Maslow's Hierarchy of Needs

TEACHING THE LESSON

You may want to tell students that this segment deals with examining how their personal needs, attitudes, and goals affect the ways they interact with and make predictions about others. After students read the information on pp. 118–126, you will probably want to provide guided practice for **Activity 3** on p. 126. You could model the activity by discussing the different roles that you assume in a normal day. Then analyze the roles by addressing the questions in **Activity 3**. With such guidance, students should be ready to complete the activity as independent practice.

In **Making Predictions About Others,** beginning on p. 127, students will see how their self-concepts (which they studied earlier in the chapter) and their first impressions affect how they perceive others. You may want to discuss **How to Check Your Perceptions** on p. 130

with a friend or work on your homework. First you need to meet a basic physiological need. This hierarchy helps you understand other people's motivations as well as your own. For example, if a friend needs esteem, he may seek compliments or praise after doing a job well.

Assessing Your Needs to Improve Communication

Most people are relatively unaware of their needs until they feel something missing; even then, they may attempt to satisfy the wrong need. If people are unable to discover their real needs, they will continue in a state of dissatisfaction. By what means do people improve the intrapersonal communication that assesses and addresses needs? The following chart presents three suggestions for monitoring intrapersonal communication.

HOW TO *Monitor Intrapersonal Communication*

1. **Take time to be alone and to think about yourself.** During your time alone, you can evaluate how well you are meeting your personal goals. If you are not meeting those goals, you have a choice: Work out different methods for achieving your goals, or set more realistic personal goals. Try to determine what you really want to do, both in the short term (for instance, three months from now) and in the long term (perhaps next year). For example, maybe you want to be a lifeguard next summer but are not currently qualified for the job. A short-term goal might be to find out how you can become qualified. A long-term goal might be to learn the necessary skills so that you can apply for a job as a lifeguard.
2. **Conduct a self-concept check.** Discover how you are feeling about yourself. If you find aspects of your self-concept that you wish were different, plan ways of making changes. For instance, if being out of shape is causing a negative self-concept, set a goal of walking for thirty minutes three days a week.
3. **Check your ideas with a close friend, relative, or trusted adult.** Make lists of your strengths and weaknesses, your goals, and your methods of achieving those goals. Then, discuss these lists with someone who can help you check the accuracy of your self-concept. For instance, you may believe that people stay aloof from you because they do not like you. However, as you discuss this idea with the person you trust, your confidant may suggest a reason for people's behavior that you have not considered. For instance, your friend may point out that people seem aloof because they see you as having more self-discipline than they have, which in turn makes them feel uncomfortable.

HOW TO MONITOR INTRAPERSONAL COMMUNICATION

You may want to set aside twenty or thirty minutes of class time for students to review their goals. Students can write their goals in their communication journals and refer to the lists from time to time. The self-concept check referred to in the second item of the guidelines can be found in **Activity 2,** p. 117. Remind students that guidance counselors and other sympathetic adults are available at school to discuss with them the ideas in the third item of the guidelines.

before moving on to **Activity 4** on p. 131. As guided practice for **Activity 4**, you could have the class choose a person with whom everyone is familiar. You might use a film star or a local celebrity. With the class, address the questions in the activity that analyze predictions about the person the students chose. Then assign **Activity 4** as independent practice.

For Better or For Worse® **by Lynn Johnston**

Making Changes in Self-Concept

Even though people are constantly changing physically, they are likely to resist changes in their self-concept. At times, people seem bent on maintaining low impressions of their abilities or performances.

EXAMPLE: In middle school, Josie did not get good grades in math. Later, when Josie took algebra and geometry in high school, she found herself getting above-average grades. However, when a friend asked whether she would take precalculus, Josie said, "No, I've just been lucky—I'm not really very good at math." Josie's self-concept does not reflect her actual ability. Stubbornly maintaining that she cannot do well in math cements artificial limits that may prevent her overall growth.

To make any conscious change in self-concept, you first have to recognize that some kinds of behavior are more likely to get positive responses. Then you need to engage in those kinds of behavior.

As you make positive changes in your self-concept, you are likely to begin getting positive responses from others. If your self-concept tends to be weak, these positive responses may encourage you, proving that it was not *you* that people acted negatively toward, but your former behavior. Keep the following ideas in mind as you consider making changes in your self-concept.

- Ask yourself if you really need to change, or if you are being overly critical of yourself.
- Remember that you cannot change everything and that change takes time.
- Commit yourself to change through self-discipline.
- Seek advice about making changes from parents, friends, teachers, and counselors.

INTEGRATING THE LANGUAGE ARTS

Literature Link

The failure to make changes in self-concept because of an inaccurate self-assessment is dealt with in a number of works of literature. This failure especially surfaces in plays under the theme of illusion versus reality. You may want to have students read a play that deals with this theme and to explore the theme in conjunction with your discussion of **Making Changes in Self-Concept**. Some plays that deal with this theme include *The Glass Menagerie* by Tennessee Williams, *Death of a Salesman* by Arthur Miller, and *Oedipus Rex* by Sophocles.

Assessment

You can assess students' understanding of roles and predictions by checking **Activities 3** and **4.** If you feel the need for further assessment activities, you can show videotapes of people in communication situations and ask students to write analyses of the roles each person plays. Also, you can show a videotape of a brief portion of a TV talk show and ask students to make predictions about the interviewee.

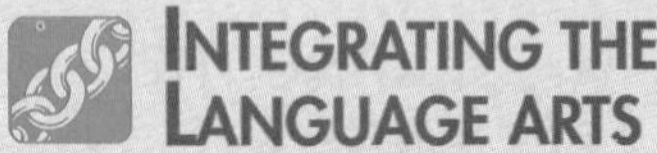

Integrating the Language Arts

Vocabulary Link

Have students look up *introvert* and *extrovert* in a dictionary. Discuss the definitions and ask students to list some of the characteristics that they associate with each type of personality.

Additional Activity

Ask your students to give reasons that some people are shy. Some students may have conquered their shyness in particular situations and may be willing to share with others how they did it.

Interacting with Others

How well you interact with others depends on your attitudes and goals and on your understanding of interpersonal roles.

Examining Attitudes and Goals

When you approach people, what is your attitude toward communication? Are you positive or negative? What are your communication goals?

Attitudes. **Attitudes** are relatively long-lasting organizations of beliefs that cause you to respond in particular ways. Attitudes include positive or negative evaluations or feelings toward objects, people, and events. Your attitude toward communication depends on your personal orientation, your level of shyness, and your sense of control.

- **Personal Orientation:** Your own attitude toward communication is closely related to your self-concept. Some people see themselves as **extroverted,** social individuals who are relationship-oriented and responsive to the needs of others. Extroverted people are likely to look forward to communicating and interacting with people. Other people may see themselves as **introverted,** or withdrawn, individuals who keep more to themselves and who are less responsive to others' needs. Introverted individuals are less likely to look forward to communication. They tend to look for activities that they can do alone.
- **Level of Shyness:** Your attitude toward communication may depend on your level of shyness. Regardless of how extroverted you might be, you are likely to experience

Reteaching

If your students have difficulty analyzing the different roles they project in different communication situations, have volunteers act out situations in which a student must explain to a teacher, a friend, and a parent why he or she missed a deadline on an important assignment. Videotape the scenarios and then play them back for the class. Stop frequently to analyze how the student behaves differently in each situation. Have students use their textbooks to refresh their memories on the factors that affect roles.

To help students with making predictions, show magazine photographs of people who are not celebrities. Ask students to write down what kind of person they think the subject of each picture is. Then discuss with the students their responses and ask what factors influenced their impressions. Have students refer to **Basing** 

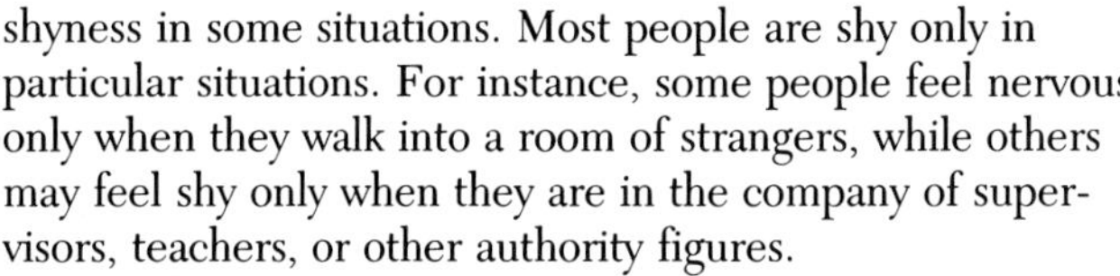

shyness in some situations. Most people are shy only in particular situations. For instance, some people feel nervous only when they walk into a room of strangers, while others may feel shy only when they are in the company of supervisors, teachers, or other authority figures.

- **Sense of Control:** Your attitude toward communication may be based in part on your sense of control—whether you view life and events as being within your control. People who believe that what happens to them is controlled by forces outside of themselves are less likely to have favorable attitudes toward communication. On the other hand, people who believe that nearly every aspect of life is within their control are more likely to have favorable attitudes toward communication. They see themselves as capable of having an effect on their own lives, others' lives, and their environment.

Goals. **Goals** are aims that you hope to achieve or accomplish through communication. Make your goals realistic. Expect to find a summer job as a sales clerk rather than as a sales manager. The better you are at setting and accomplishing realistic goals, the higher your self-esteem will rise. If you have clearly defined goals and if you believe that you have some control over your destiny, then you are more likely to look favorably on communication as a means of achieving your goals.

Calvin and Hobbes by Bill Watterson

Your Commitment to Effective Communication. To begin to improve your communication, you must be committed to communicating well. You must be willing to talk with others in an effort to improve your communication. Most people do not become better communicators without this kind of conscious effort.

Integrating the Language Arts

Literature Link

In discussing the sense of control that helps determine attitudes, students may enjoy reading and discussing Thomas Hardy's short poem "Hap." This poem deals with human helplessness in controlling destiny. Ask students to consider whether the speaker in the poem has an entirely negative outlook.

 ***Audiovisual Resource Binder***

Transparency 10
Setting Goals

Predictions on First Impressions on pp. 128–130 and to the **"How to"** chart on p. 130 to check perceptions as they analyze the factors that influenced their impressions.

See p. 129 for **EXTENSION, ENRICHMENT,** and **CLOSURE.**

An Alternative Approach

Some students may be interested in learning more about the ways that people adapt their language to the various roles they play. You can have these students look up and report to the class on ideas about "style shifting" in speech. One place to begin this research is *Sociolinguistic Patterns* by William Labov (University of Pennsylvania Press).

TEACHER'S RESOURCE BINDER

Skills for Success 4
Analyzing Interpersonal Situations

Analyzing Interpersonal Situations

As you have grown up, you have learned to adapt your behavior to particular interpersonal situations. You have probably developed a public as well as a private self. Your public self is shown through a variety of roles that you choose to play. How successful you are in interpersonal situations depends on how accurately you assess the times and places for playing these different roles.

Your Public and Private Selves. Your **public self** is that part of yourself which you choose to share with everyone. You may show a different public self in different circumstances. For example, you might show yourself to be outgoing, confident, and fun loving; you might show yourself to be thoughtful, caring, and cautious; or you might show yourself to be powerful, in charge, and boisterous. Your public self is thus displayed in the various roles you choose to play.

Your **private self** is that part of yourself which is most true to your self-concept. You may choose to show yourself to be outgoing, confident, and fun loving, when in reality you may be just the opposite. Ordinarily you reveal your private self only to those who are close to you.

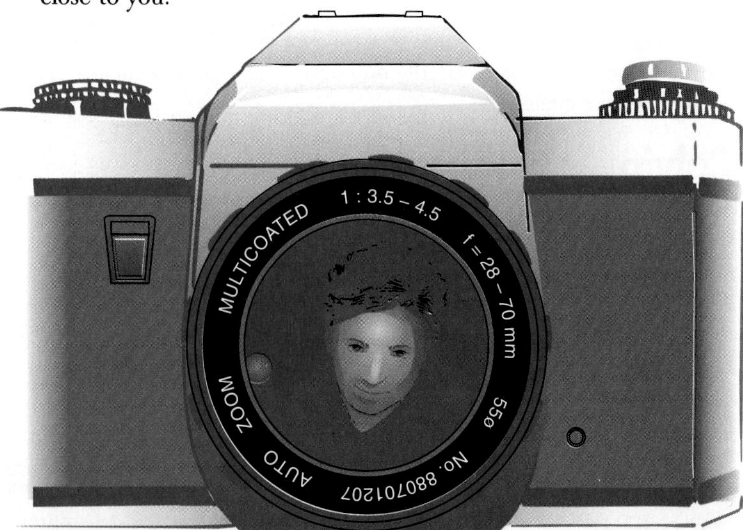

Playing Different Roles in Different Circumstances. In your interactions with others, you display your public self by playing various roles. A **role** is a pattern of behavior that characterizes a person in a given context, or situation. Based on your self-concept, needs, and attitudes, you learn many roles that you can play. With some of these roles you have great success, and these become roles that you enjoy playing. With others, you do not do as well, and so you may stop trying to play them.

EXAMPLE: Whenever Rubén senses tension in his Spanish class, he responds by behaving humorously. The other students laugh, and even the teacher smiles. Since Rubén enjoys this attention, he begins to exhibit similar behavior in similar circumstances. Again, Rubén enjoys the attention it gets him, and the role of class comedian becomes a major part of his public self.

Jason sees the attention Rubén is getting, so he too tries to act up in similar circumstances. However, if the class does not respond as they do for Rubén, Jason is likely to question whether he should continue trying to play the role of comedian. If the class consistently responds in a negative way, Jason will probably stop playing this role.

Assessing the Time and Place to Play a Role. The appropriateness of a role depends on the time and the place. You need to assess when a role you are playing is appropriate.

EXAMPLE: Rubén has learned that he can behave humorously and get positive reinforcement from his friends and classmates. But Rubén must also learn that this role is not always appropriate. When the situation calls for giving information or solving problems and Rubén tries clowning, his behavior is likely to be disruptive and inappropriate. If Rubén's little brother Juan asks for advice and Rubén tells him a joke, Rubén is likely to get a negative response. He must learn that although there may be room for a little humor in certain contexts, this behavior becomes obnoxious when circumstances call for a serious approach.

Good communicators are adept at a variety of roles. Over time, you learn when the various roles you can play are most appropriate for the situation and for the people with whom you are communicating. When you determine what role to play, you will need to consider the compatibility of needs and the best way to arrive at shared goals.

- **Need Compatibilities:** Often, it is important that the roles you play meet others' needs. When you are talking, what you say will be evaluated by others in terms of their needs. When the role you wish to play is not compatible with others' needs, they will probably assess the role you are playing as inappropriate.

EXAMPLE: Gail and George are sharing humorous stories of their work experiences. Marcia gets into the conversation and begins playing the role of advice giver. The other two ignore Marcia's advice and return to their conversation. Because Gail and George are sharing the stories for entertainment, not to get advice, Marcia receives a negative response. The role she is playing is not appropriate to the needs of Gail and George.

- **Shared Goals:** Communication works best when the roles of those involved meet shared goals. Although you may have your own motivation for behaving a certain way at a certain time, the various roles that you play will be considered inappropriate if they do not fit in with the shared goals of your group.

EXAMPLE: A committee is trying to complete the final draft of a proposal that it must finish right away. Andrew decides to take his time and to analyze every statement thoroughly. Although careful examination is often necessary, the current shared goal is for the group to complete the task as quickly as possible. Therefore, Andrew's role of careful analyzer is likely to be seen as inappropriate by other committee members at this time.

ONGOING ASSESSMENT

Activity 3

You may want to shorten the time allowed for this assignment from three to two days or one day, and you may also want to specify how many communication situations students should analyze. The analyses should reflect an awareness of the material in the text.

ACTIVITY 3 Assessing Roles

For three days, record the various communication situations you experience. Describe the roles you chose to project in each. Then write an analysis of these roles and observations. To what extent does your communication behavior differ, and to what extent does it remain the same in different situations? What factors in a situation seem to trigger certain behaviors in you? How satisfied are you with the roles that you displayed in each situation? In which situation were you most pleased? least pleased?

Making Predictions About Others

How well you communicate with others depends at least in part on your ability to make accurate predictions about them. Predictions about others are based on your own self-concept and on your first impressions.

Basing Predictions on the Self-Concept

Your self-concept not only influences your communication behavior but also affects how you perceive others. The specific influence of your self-concept on your understanding of others can be seen in three areas: accuracy, acceptance, and personality.

Accuracy. The more accurate your self-concept, the more accurately you can perceive others. However, if you have difficulty determining your own strengths and weaknesses, you will probably be unable to determine accurately the strengths and weaknesses of others. For example, if Angela fails to see that she tends to be dependent on others, she is not very likely when she meets Mark to see that he is self-centered.

Acceptance. The more you accept yourself, the more likely you are to see others favorably. If you have difficulty liking who you are, you will be less likely to care for others. For example, if Sarah likes herself, she is more likely to see positive qualities in other people.

Personality. Your personal characteristics influence the type of characteristics you are likely to perceive in others. For example, Taneesha is a very caring person. Given her own level of caring, she perceives that the people she meets are caring as well.

ADDITIONAL ACTIVITY

You may want to ask each student to write down three characteristics that are desirable in people who might eventually become friends. Use five sets of characteristics randomly and anonymously drawn from the class and write these on the chalkboard. Lead the class in a discussion about what these characteristics suggest about self-concept.

COOPERATIVE LEARNING

To provide practice for making predictions, divide the class into groups of four and ask one student in each group to read aloud the exposition portion of a short story. After the reading, the students should discuss how they think the main character of the story will act throughout the rest of the story based on their first impressions. The group members should write one- or two-sentence summaries of the predictions they agree on and then finish reading the story to decide if their predictions were accurate.

Basing Predictions on First Impressions

Besides being affected by self-concept, predictions about others are also a result of factors that influence first impressions: physical characteristics, social traits, stereotyping, and emotional states.

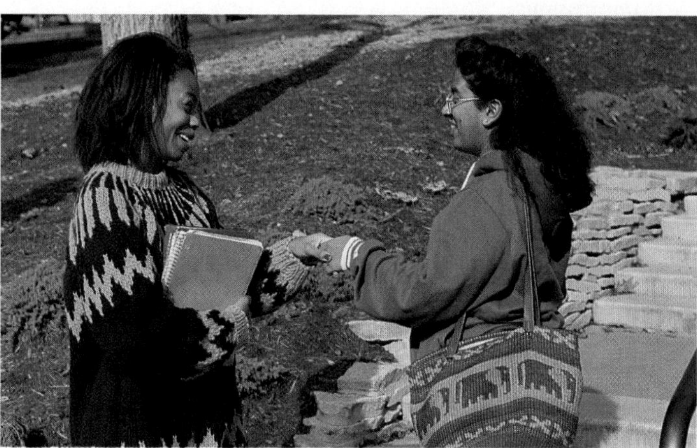

Physical Characteristics. When two people meet, they form first impressions of each other based on physical characteristics. For example, at a party Ken sees an attractive young woman across the room. He taps his friend Dave on the shoulder, points to her, and says, "I've got to meet her." In some cases, merely looking at a photograph may create a strong impression.

Social Traits. First impressions are also made on the basis of perceived social traits. As a result of seeing a single instance of behavior, you may attribute certain traits to people. For example, after a party, Carlos asks Mimi what she thought of Randy. Mimi, who had heard Randy bragging about himself to a group of people, answers, "Randy? He's really self-centered."

Notice that this judgment follows a single episode. Observing a person's behavior in a single situation and basing a judgment on that one situation can lead you to judge a person's other characteristics without further investigation—a tendency known as the **halo effect.**

> **EXAMPLE:** Sonja perceives Francesca as a warm, caring person. Since these characteristics are important to Sonja and are part of her own personality, Francesca has a "halo effect" as far as Sonja is concerned. If a friend accuses Francesca of being aloof, Sonja may rush to Francesca's defense. The halo effect may lead Sonja to assume that Francesca is always friendly.

WRITING TO LEARN

Ask students to freewrite for ten minutes in response to the following statement: "Jokes are responsible for maintaining and spreading many stereotypes." After students have spent time writing, ask them to share their ideas with the class.

Students can include their writing on jokes and stereotypes in their portfolios or in their communication journals. At some point in the future, the ideas they have generated may be useful for speeches.

Extension

You may want to show a videotape of the first scene of the movie *My Fair Lady* to students and ask them to determine their first impressions of Henry Higgins, Colonel Pickering, and Eliza Doolittle. Then discuss the ideas that Higgins asserts regarding language. To what extent does the viewer form impressions of people based on how they talk? Is pronunciation more important than vocabulary? How does grammar influence the viewer? How can one create the impression he or she wants to make by changing his or her speech?

Then you could allow students to view the rest of *My Fair Lady* and discuss with the class the ways in which what people say and how they say it determine who they are.

Cooperative Learning

Ask students to work in groups of four to identify instances of stereotypes in magazine advertisements and TV commercials. Each group should find five stereotypes. Groups can share their findings with other groups or with the whole class.

Stereotyping. **Stereotyping** is assigning characteristics to a person solely on the basis of the person's membership in a certain group. Remember that everyone is a member of some identifiable group. Once you identify a person as a member of a specific group, you must be careful not to judge the individual on the basis of impressions that you associate with the particular group. Remember that each person you meet is a unique individual.

> **EXAMPLE:** When Della is introduced to Carl, a football player, her first impression may be affected by her stereotype of athletes. Because the few athletes she has known didn't do very well in school, Della has always assumed that *all* athletes are poor students. If Della judges Carl on the basis of this stereotype, she may be surprised when she learns that Carl is an honor student.

The problem with stereotypes is that they are often wrong. They can also be terribly hurtful. Stereotypes are oversimplified opinions or uncritical judgments of others formed when people perceive a characteristic in a few members of a group and assume that the characteristic is typical of the entire group. Stereotyping ignores individual differences. In even its mildest form, this particular shortcut will lead to inaccurate predictions about others and thus to ineffective communication.

Emotional States. Your feelings at any given moment also affect your first impressions of others. If you are cheery, your impressions of people are likely to be positive; if you are depressed or angry, your first impressions are likely to be negative.

> **EXAMPLE:** Bonnie is having a great day. Dana introduces her to Marsha, a girl who has just transferred from another school. Since Bonnie feels happy, she is willing to see Marsha in a positive light. Bonnie offers to be a friend, saying, "Transferring to a new school has to be tough; if I can help you with anything, I'll be glad to." Linda, on the other hand, is having a bad day. As Dana introduces her to Marsha, she thinks, "Oh, great. A helpless new kid. I hope Dana doesn't expect me to play nanny and show her around."

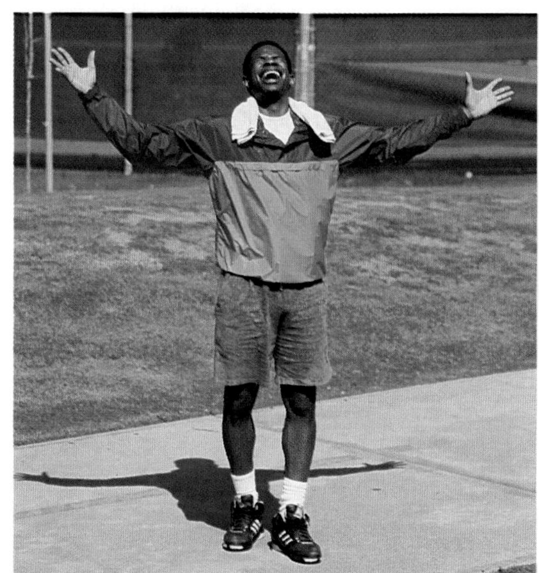

Enrichment

You may want to ask each student to read a biography or an autobiography of someone who interests the student. As students read, ask them to pay attention to the characters' self-concepts. How did the characters feel about themselves? How did others' actions and words affect the characters? Did the characters make changes in their self-concepts? What were their attitudes and goals? How well did the characters interact with others? Were the characters' perceptions realistic?

Then have students report their findings to the rest of the class with special emphasis on how the self-concepts of their characters affected their characters' lives.

How to Check Your Perceptions

You may want to ask students to conduct brief self-assessments of how well they follow each of the suggestions in **How to Check Your Perceptions.** After determining whether students routinely follow the suggestions, you can encourage them to set goals for themselves in areas where they are not satisfied with their performances. Encourage students to write in their communication journals any goals they set and to refer to these goals periodically throughout the term.

Your emotional state may also affect the motives you assign to others' behavior. Besides making judgments about people, you also try to construct reasons about why people behave as they do.

Example: Darlene has agreed to meet Justine right after school. After waiting for half an hour, Darlene begins thinking of reasons why Justine is late. If she is in a good mood, Darlene may decide that Justine's lateness is for a good reason. If she is in a bad mood, Darlene may believe Justine is simply being inconsiderate.

Confirming Perceptions

Because inaccuracies in perception are common and influence how you communicate, improving perceptual accuracy is an important first step in becoming an effective communicator. The following suggestions can help you to construct a more realistic impression of others as well as to assess the soundness of your perceptions.

HOW TO *Check Your Perceptions*

1. **Seek more information to verify perceptions.** If your impression of someone is based on only a few pieces of information, you need to learn more before you act on your conclusions. Remember that your perception is subject to change. You can then collect more information to determine whether your original perception is accurate.
2. **Recognize that even if your original perceptions were accurate, people change over time.** You need to make an effort to observe a person's behavior without bias and be prepared to change your perception when it is appropriate. For example, someone you did not like in elementary school may now be a different kind of person.
3. **Talk with the people about whom you are forming perceptions.** The more information you have to work with, the more likely your perceptions are to be accurate. And the best way to get information about people is to talk with them. If you have perceived someone as self-centered or untrustworthy on the basis of one experience, postpone your judgment until you have a chance to get to know the person.
4. **Check perceptions verbally.** Because your judgments affect your ability to communicate effectively, you should try to confirm your perceptions. A **perception check** is a verbal statement that reflects your understanding of another person's nonverbal cues. [See page 28 of Chapter 2.] You should (1) watch the behavior of the other person, (2) ask yourself, "What does that behavior mean to me?" and (3) put your interpretation of the behavior *into words* to verify whether your perception is accurate.

Closure

Ask a volunteer to explain how someone forms an inaccurate first impression. Then ask students to discuss steps for improving perceptual accuracy.

Activity 4: Analyzing Predictions About Others

Think of a recent situation in which you made a prediction about someone. In a paragraph, analyze your perception of that person and how you developed this impression. What was your perception of the person? How was it affected by your self-concept? How was your perception affected by your first impression? How did you confirm your perception of this person? Do you think your perception—your prediction about this person—was accurate?

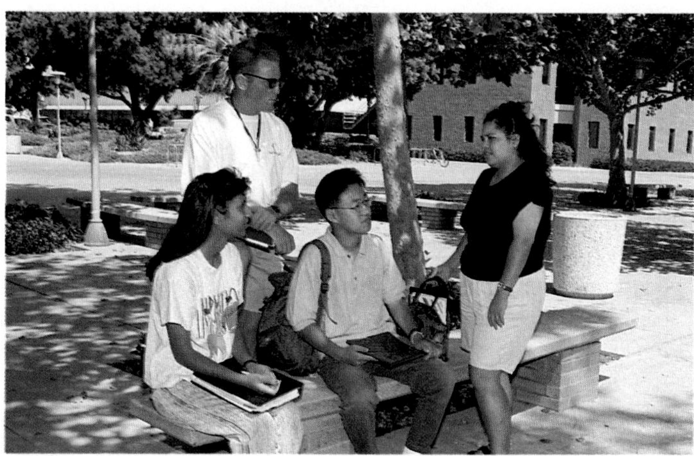

GUIDELINES for Analyzing Yourself as a Communicator

- Do I use intrapersonal communication to assess my perceptions and needs?
- Are my perceptions of myself and others accurate and realistic?
- Am I trying to achieve a positive self-concept?
- Do I have a positive attitude toward interacting with others?
- Have I made a commitment to communicating effectively?
- Am I aware that the roles I adopt must be appropriate to the time and place and to others' needs?
- Do I make accurate predictions about others?
- Do I check my perceptions of others for accuracy?

Ongoing Assessment

Activity 4

Because of the personal nature of some of the questions in this activity, you may want to give completion grades rather than assess the content of students' analyses. If you do decide to evaluate the work, you can base your evaluations on how well students took into consideration the ideas expressed in the segment when analyzing their predictions about others.

Building a Portfolio

You may want to ask students to answer each of the questions in the **Guidelines for Analyzing Yourself as a Communicator**. From time to time during the rest of the term, encourage students to review the questions and their answers to assess whether they are making satisfactory progress in improving their ability to communicate.

◆ Profiles in Communication

Performance Objectives

- To write a paragraph based on a discussion with a partner
- To collaborate with a partner to verify information

Teaching the Feature

Before students read the profile of Carl S. Richie II, you may want to ask them what they think the duties of a Deputy Chief of Staff to the Texas Governor might be. Then have them read the profile to see if their predictions are correct. Discuss with students the communication skills Mr. Richie must have to be successful in his job. Ask students to analyze Mr. Richie's quotations to determine whether he has a positive attitude toward interacting with others.

Activity Note

Ask students to review the **Guidelines for Analyzing Yourself as a Communicator** on p. 131 before they converse with partners. Encourage students to address during their discussions all of the questions in the activity. For assessment purposes, you may want to ask students to write down any comments about their partners' paragraphs. Then you can evaluate both the paragraphs and the comments.

PROFILES IN COMMUNICATION

Carl S. Richie

"In a way, I feel like a Michael Jordan—I'm getting paid to do just what I've always wanted to do—to work in politics," says Carl S. Richie II, Deputy Chief of Staff to Texas Governor Ann W. Richards. Mr. Richie, an attorney, holds a position of great responsibility. He advises Governor Richards on gubernatorial appointments, assists her in developing legislative programs and in getting bills approved by the legislature, and represents the governor at various public events.

During the 1980s, Mr. Richie worked for candidates running for local, state, and national office; then he joined the Richards campaign in 1990. "Politics has taught me to pick and choose my words very carefully," he reflects. "Before I speak, I think about the message I'm trying to communicate. A slip of the tongue can be detrimental when building and nurturing relationships. Also, I always have a purpose for speaking because a person should not talk just to be heard or to get attention."

Mr. Richie's goal in any disagreement is to get his point across in a way that is firm but not offensive. "People react badly to ultimatums," he says. "They're much more willing to work with you when you can show them the rewards of being a team player. Sometimes you can create a win-win situation by persuading an opponent to take a neutral position."

ACTIVITY

Get together with a classmate you don't know very well for a friendly conversation. Ask questions and listen carefully to responses to find out more about the person. Ask your classmate to tell you about what he or she likes to do. What role does your classmate play when he or she is engaged in this activity? How does participation in the activity affect your classmate's self-concept? After the conversation, write a paragraph about what you discussed and share it with your classmate. Does he or she agree with what you have written? If not, or if you left out important information, discuss any ideas you and your classmate have for revising the paragraph.

S•U•M•M•A•R•Y

ANALYZING YOURSELF AS A COMMUNICATOR involves intrapersonal communication. This "self-talk" helps you to determine what you think and how you behave. Much of your thought and behavior depends on how you perceive others and the world around you.

- **Understand perception** as a process of selecting, organizing, and interpreting sensory information. Individual differences in perception occur because of physical characteristics, background and experience, selected focus, and current mood and circumstances.
- **Think about your self-concept,** a collection of perceptions based on your own observations and experience as well as what others tell you about yourself. An accurate self-concept helps you with problem solving and decision making; it also affects your behavior and how you process feedback.
- **Assess needs,** your own as well as others', to evaluate reasons for actions and attitudes in order to improve your ability to communicate.
- **Interact with others** by examining your own attitudes and personal goals and analyzing interpersonal situations in which you wish to communicate.
- **Make predictions** about appropriate communication based on your own self-concept and on your impressions about others. Then check your perceptions for accuracy.

CHAPTER 5

Vocabulary

Look back through this chapter to find the meaning of each of the following terms. Write each term and its meaning in your communication journal.

attitudes, *p. 122*
extroverted, *p. 122*
goals, *p. 123*
halo effect, *p. 128*
hierarchy of needs, *p. 118*
interpretation, *p. 111*
intrapersonal communication, *p. 109*
introverted, *p. 122*
motives, *p. 118*
perception, *p. 110*
perception check, *p. 130*
private self, *p. 124*
public self, *p. 124*
role, *p. 124*
self-actualization, *p. 119*
self-concept, *p. 114*
stereotyping, *p. 129*

TEACHER'S RESOURCE BINDER

- Chapter 5 Vocabulary

Review Questions

Answers

1. "Self-talk"—the talking you do with yourself—helps you determine what you think and how you behave.
2. selection, organization, and interpretation of sensory information
3. physical characteristics, background and experience, selected focus, and current mood and circumstances
4. Your self-concept is a collection of perceptions about every aspect of yourself. It is based on your observation and experience and on what others tell you about yourself.
5. problem solving and decision making, behavior, and the processing of feedback

Discussion Questions

Guidelines for Assessment

Student responses may vary.

1. A positive self-concept makes you a more positive person who is open to ideas and to other people. It affects your communication with others by making you more willing to see other points of view.
2. People who undervalue themselves project poor images to others. The way you think about yourself (intrapersonal communications) affects how you value yourself and project yourself. Thus, thinking about yourself in negative terms causes others to see you negatively.
3. A good judge of character is someone who is able to perceive motives for what is said and done by others. A good judge of character knows that many statements and events can be interpreted in several ways and considers all possible interpretations.
4. Stereotyping is basically assigning a label on the basis of a person's membership in a group without considering whether the label really fits the individual. Deciding whether a label fits requires thinking, and stereotyping eliminates this process.
5. Students should recount personal experiences in which they applied the **"How to"** suggestions on p. 130.

CHAPTER 5

Review Questions

1. Define *intrapersonal communication* and explain how it is useful.
2. *Perception* is the process of giving meaning to information you receive from your senses. What are three aspects of perception?
3. Individuals often differ in the way they perceive people, places, and things. What are four different factors that may affect perceptions?
4. Define the term *self-concept* and explain how a self-concept is formed.
5. What are the three ways that the self-concept affects someone's intrapersonal communication?
6. From lowest to highest, what are the five levels of needs in the hierarchy of needs as defined by Maslow?
7. Identify three ways that you can monitor your intrapersonal communication.
8. What are three factors that may have an effect on your attitude toward communicating?
9. In many cases, predictions we make about others are affected by our own self-concepts, but these perceptions may also be affected by *stereotyping.* What is stereotyping?
10. A good method for determining the accuracy of your evaluations or judgments is to confirm your understanding with a *perception check.* What is a perception check?

Discussion Questions

1. Discuss the importance of developing a positive self-concept. Then discuss the ways that a person's positive self-concept can affect his or her ability to communicate with other people.
2. The English writer William Hazlitt once wrote, "He who undervalues himself is justly undervalued by others." Discuss the meaning of this quotation. Do you agree or disagree? Discuss how this quotation relates to intrapersonal communication.
3. Do you consider yourself a good judge of a person's character? Discuss what you think makes someone a good judge of character. Identify several specific characteristics that you think a good judge of character should have.
4. The journalist John Morley wrote, "Labels are devices for saving talkative persons the trouble of thinking." Discuss the meaning of this statement, and explain how this statement relates to the concept of stereotyping.
5. Discuss at least one recent situation that you were involved in (either as a participant or a witness) in which a perception check helped the people involved in the situation to communicate more effectively.

6. physiological, safety and security, love and affection, esteem, and self-actualization
7. Take time to be alone and to think about yourself; conduct a self-concept check; and discuss yourself and your goals with another.
8. personal orientation, level of shyness, and sense of control
9. assigning characteristics to a person solely on the person's membership in a certain group
10. a verbal statement that reflects your understanding of another person's nonverbal clues

ACTIVITIES

1. **Developing a Self-Logo.** Develop a logo that represents you. A logo is a distinctive trademark. For example, thumb through magazines to examine the logos for car and clothing companies. Your logo should contain a name and some kind of visual element or illustration. Be prepared to give a short explanation of how the logo you have designed features your key characteristics.
2. **Writing a Tribute or Eulogy.** Every newspaper keeps prewritten statements about people in the news so that it will have an article ready if the paper is ever required to print a tribute or a eulogy in the next edition. If a newspaper kept a file about you, what do you think the article would say? Write a two-paragraph statement that you believe captures your personal qualities.
3. **Analyzing Your Strengths and Weaknesses.** For your own information, copy and then complete the following chart. Because this is primarily for you, you do not need to share your analysis with anyone else.

   Contrast your responses in the top and bottom portions of the chart. What have you learned from successful situations that you might use in situations in which you do not handle yourself as well as you would like?
4. **Writing Perception Checks.** For each of the following situations, write a well-phrased perception check—a statement that indicates how you would interpret the emotional state of the person. Then say each statement aloud as if you were speaking to the person described. Does each of your statements sound honest and natural? If not, revise each statement until it does.
   a. Natalie comes rushing into her room, throws her books on the floor, and sits at her desk, holding her head between her hands.
   b. Franco comes home from football practice with a pale face and slumped shoulders.
   c. As you return the sweater you borrowed from Tammy, she stiffens, grabs the sweater, and starts to walk away down the hall.

Situations I do not handle as well as I would like	How I feel in the situation	How I handle the situation	How I might handle the situation with a greater sense of self-worth
Situations I handle well	How I feel in the situation	How I handle the situation	What gives me a sense of self-worth about the way I handle the situation

ACTIVITIES

Guidelines for Assessment

1. Logos will vary and will be limited by students' artistic ability. However, students should explain how the logos feature their key characteristics.
2. Students may be tempted to make up all sorts of accomplishments for themselves. Remind them that they are supposed to describe their personal qualities. The statements should be clear, direct, and accurate. They should deal with physical, intellectual, and social qualities that the students are willing to share with others.
3. This activity need not be assessed except for completion.
4. You may want to let students share their perception checks with partners. Partners could help each other to evaluate the content and tone of the statements. Then have each twosome briefly report its findings to the rest of the class.

Summative Evaluation

Your **Teacher's Resource Binder** contains a reproducible **Chapter 5 Test** that may be used to assess students' mastery of the concepts presented in this chapter.

Portfolio Assessment

For future reference and evaluation you may want to have students keep in their portfolios any skill sheets or evaluation forms that you have used with this chapter along with any other recorded or written materials that students have created.

d. Miss Hicks told you earlier today that you could come in after school this afternoon to talk with her about your college search. When you arrive at her office, she looks up at you, squints her eyes, and frowns.

5. Identifying Occupational Stereotypes. Make a chart like the one below. To complete the chart, picture a person working in each of the occupations listed. As you picture the person, identify descriptive characteristics for each one. Then answer the following questions.

a. What did you use as a basis for filling in the chart?
b. How well do you think your chart would provide you with information about someone introduced to you as having that occupation?
c. How much do you think the information from your chart would influence your attitude toward the person?
d. What have you learned about stereotyping as a result of completing this activity?

5. For assessment purposes, you may want to have students write the answers to the four questions that precede the chart. If time allows, you could let students work in small groups to compare their charts and the answers to their questions.

Occupation	Physical characteristics	Gender	Salary	Education	Leisure activity	Automobile
Television newscaster						
Department store salesperson						
High school teacher						
Doctor						
Automobile mechanic						
Clerical worker						
Construction worker						

◆ Real-Life Speaking Situations

Performance Objectives

- To write a composition identifying a personal hero and the hero's traits
- To analyze personal traits
- To write a composition analyzing the roles played over three days in a variety of situations

REAL LIFE Speaking Situations

1 Your self-concept—that is, what you think of yourself—can be influenced by what you admire in other people. For example, you may have a personal hero, someone who possesses personal traits that you think are important and that you would like to have. You may, for instance, admire the strength and integrity of Superman, the kindness of Mother Teresa, the eloquence of Chief Joseph, the mechanical ability of your next-door neighbor, or your best friend's wit.

In a brief paper, identify a personal hero—perhaps someone you know, a fictional character, a historical figure, or someone in public life—and consider what you might learn from the example set by this person. What admirable traits does this person have? Do you see any of these traits in yourself? Would you like to? How do you think you could build these characteristics in yourself?

Think of at least three ways in which you could begin to incorporate these traits in your everyday behavior. Now, imagine that you have incorporated some of these admirable traits. How would your self-concept be affected?

2 Like most people, you play a variety of roles every day and throughout the week. You are a student, a son or daughter, and a friend. You may also be a brother or sister, an employee, an adviser, an athlete, or a musician. Each of the roles you play is a part of who you are.

For three days, keep track of the roles you play and the situations in which you play them. You may want to keep an hour-by-hour log of your activities, or you may prefer to wait until the end of the day to record your findings in a journal entry. At the end of this observation time, write a brief report analyzing the roles you noticed yourself playing.

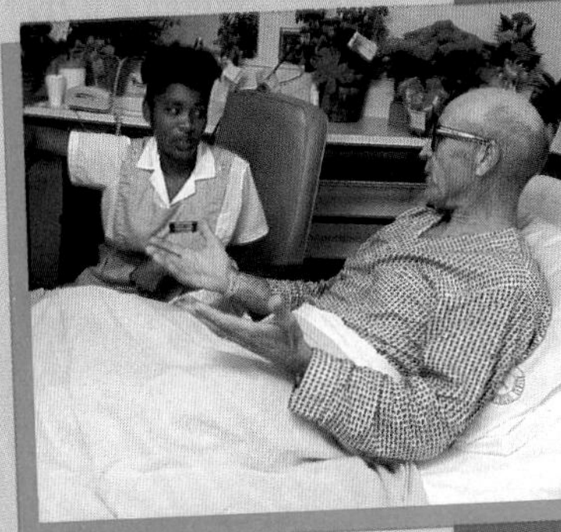

Begin your analysis by noting the type of role, the situation in which you played the role, and the other people who were involved in the situation. Then consider the following questions. What do you notice about how your roles change in different circumstances and with different people? Are you surprised to discover how great a variety of roles you play? In your opinion, would it be possible for a person to play the same role all the time? Would it be at all desirable to do so?

Assessment Guidelines

1. The people students choose as personal heroes do not have to be famous, but the traits students identify should constitute qualities that are generally thought of as heroic. Students should address each of the questions asked in the assignment.
2. To keep this assignment manageable, you can limit students to two or three situations per day or reduce the number of days. The analyses should indicate an understanding of what a role is and how circumstances affect how the students project themselves.

Chapter 6
Communicating Person to Person
pp. 138–157

Chapter Overview

This chapter presents methods for developing good interpersonal communication. It describes relationships' stages of development, and it leads students through steps to help build good relationships. The chapter explains practical skills such as questioning and paraphrasing, and it directs students in sharing their feelings. Finally, the chapter briefly analyzes some assertiveness

Teacher's Resource Binder

The following materials are identified at their point of use in this chapter:

- Skills for Success
  1 *Building Interpersonal Relationships*
  2 *Checking Understanding*
  3 *Communicating and Sharing*
  4 *Handling Constructive Criticism*
- Chapter 6 Vocabulary
- Chapter 6 Test/Answer Key

AV Audiovisual Resource Binder

The following materials are identified at their point of use in this chapter:

- Transparency 11
  Giving and Accepting Criticism
- Audiotape 1, Lesson 9
  Paraphrasing

techniques and summarizes ways to give and receive criticism.

Introducing the Chapter

Although person-to-person communication begins as soon as language is learned, people do not always effectively communicate their ideas and feelings. Explain to students that this chapter will introduce them to techniques that are conducive to effective communication between individuals. Such techniques should help students to develop and to improve relationships.

CHAPTER 6
Communicating Person to Person

OBJECTIVES

After studying this chapter, you should be able to

1. Identify three stages of relationships.
2. Build and maintain a personal relationship.
3. Respond to others with respect and understanding.
4. Communicate thoughts and feelings that are appropriate for your public self and for your private self.
5. Disclose your feelings in a useful manner and assert yourself when you need to do so.
6. Give and receive constructive criticism.

What Is Interpersonal Communication?

Interpersonal communication is the communication that occurs between two or more people, usually people who have a personal relationship. The spectrum of relationships may range from casual acquaintances to close personal friends or family members. The skills of interpersonal communication include

- developing relationships
- responding to others
- communicating thoughts and feelings
- giving and accepting criticism

Some examples of interpersonal communication include a discussion about work responsibilities with a co-worker, a conversation with a classmate about a math test, and a conversation with a close friend about the friend's fear of driving a car.

In this chapter, you will learn what interpersonal communication skills are and how to use them.

Bibliography of Additional Materials

Professional Readings

- Jones, Stanley. ***The Right Touch: Understanding and Using the Language of Physical Contact.*** Annandale, VA: Speech Communication Association.
- Wilmot, W. W. ***Dyadic Communication.*** Reading, MA: Addison-Wesley Publishing Company.

Audiovisuals

- ***Communicating Non-Defensively: Don't Take it Personally***—CRM Films, Carlsbad, CA (videocassette, 22 min.)
- ***Conversation***—Films for the Humanities and Sciences, Princeton, NJ (two filmstrips with audio, 15 min. each)
- ***Level with Me: Honest Communication***—The Learning Seed, Lake Zurich, IL (videocassette, 29 min.)
- ***Manners at Work***—The Learning Seed, Lake Zurich, IL (videocassette, 18 min.)

Segment 1 *pp. 140–145*

• Developing Relationships
• Responding to Others

PERFORMANCE OBJECTIVES

- To classify people as acquaintances, casual friends, or close friends
- To determine topics appropriate for discussion in different types of personal relationships
- To analyze a friendship to determine what factors allowed the relationship to grow

MEETING INDIVIDUAL NEEDS

Linguistically Diverse Students

While many native speakers of English experience apprehension about communicating, this anxiety may be compounded for the non-native speaker. Therefore, strive to create a safe classroom environment in which personal rapport is encouraged among students and in which meaningful topics relating to students' daily lives are discussed. Good strategies to promote meaningful communication are to have students work together frequently in small groups and to target issues around which these students are apt to hold strong opinions or beliefs.

Developing Relationships

Most of us look forward to starting, building, and maintaining good relationships with others. A good relationship involves interactions with another person that are satisfactory to both of you.

Recognizing Stages of Relationships

Acquaintances. People you know and talk with when you happen to meet them are **acquaintances.** Your interactions are casual and limited. You might become acquainted with the people who live down the street or with the people who share some of your activities, but you do not make arrangements to spend time with them.

Friendships. You become friends with some people because you enjoy their company. **Friendships** usually begin casually but grow when you find that you like each other and that the relationship is mutually satisfying. While playing tennis with an acquaintance, you might discover that, in addition to your enjoyment of the game, you share other interests. Once your friendship has taken root, you would deliberately plan to spend time together.

Close Relationships. A **close relationship** is one in which people share their deepest feelings with each other. Such a relationship is built on trust and commitment. Close friends go out of their way to help each other; they are concerned about each other. Although a close relationship can involve a romantic attachment, it need not. Close relationships grow when you share the most critical moments of your life with another person, when you share both your sorrows and your joys.

- To record and critique the responses in a conversation involving differences of opinion
- To practice paraphrasing and questioning while acting out conversations

Motivation

Lead students in a discussion of the kinds of interactions that go on between people. Ask students if they share the same things with their parents that they do with their friends or if they share the same details and emotions with all their friends. What determines what is shared between people? Explain that in this segment students will learn about the stages of relationships

Activity 1

Analyzing Your Personal Relationships

Think about the people you know. Estimate what percentage you would classify as acquaintances, as casual friends, and as close friends. Then make three lists to show what you are likely to talk about with each kind of friend. If you feel comfortable doing so, share your lists with your classmates.

Building Relationships

A good relationship does not just happen; it must be built through the efforts of both people in the relationship.

Approaching Others with Empathy. To create a good relationship, two people must approach each other with **empathy.** Empathizing is "walking in another person's shoes" to understand how that person feels. Since the world you see cannot be exactly the world that someone else sees, being empathetic is not always easy. But when you empathize, others feel that you are trying to understand what happens to them, and they are more likely to trust you.

> **Example:** When Latoya tells Trish of her uneasiness in expressing ideas in class, Trish listens carefully to what Latoya says. Since Trish enjoys talking in class, she tries to put herself in Latoya's shoes—she imagines how she would feel if she were a quieter person who was as anxious about speaking up in front of her classmates as Latoya is.

Sharing Feelings. It takes two people to have a relationship, and each needs to share in making it work. In a good relationship, each person needs to feel that the other person makes an effort to share feelings so that both people feel that the relationship is equally and fairly balanced.

CATHY by Cathy Guisewite

Ongoing Assessment

Activity 1

You might evaluate the lists to see if students are using information about stages of relationships to determine what to talk about with each group of people.

Critical Thinking

Analysis

Ask each student to list five factors that indicate differences that could cause difficulty in empathizing. You might list the following examples on the chalkboard: personality differences, neighborhoods, family customs, talents, and interests. Compile a master list of students' ideas. Then have students suggest ways to overcome each of these differences.

Teacher's Resource Binder

Skills for Success 1
Building Interpersonal Relationships

ASSESSMENT

You could use the activities in this segment to evaluate how well students are using appropriate interpersonal communication skills. In addition, note when students integrate the learning into everyday conversations and classwork.

RETEACHING

Ask students to think of people they would like to get to know better. Have them discuss some of the methods they would use to build friendships with these people. You might also encourage students to act out a few encounters that exemplify the methods.

COOPERATIVE LEARNING

Students may benefit from additional practice in questioning and paraphrasing. Have students form groups of four—two pairs each—to act out methods that check understanding. Each pair could work out a script and perform it for the other pair in the group to evaluate.

TEACHER'S RESOURCE BINDER

Skills for Success 2
Checking Understanding

 ***Audiovisual Resource Binder***

Audiotape 1, Lesson 9
Paraphrasing

Checking Understanding

Effective responses are thoughtful as well as respectful, and these types of responses are dependent upon a clear understanding of what the other person is saying. A **misunderstanding** is a lack of clear communication that may come about if you

- assume, or take for granted, that you know what the other person means
- do not pay close and careful attention to what the other person is saying
- do not take time to make sure that you understand what has been said

Questioning and paraphrasing are two techniques for making sure that you understand.

Questioning to Be Sure. You have been asking questions since you learned to talk. Generally, you ask questions to obtain information or to engage someone in conversation. To communicate effectively person to person, you also ask questions to make sure that you do not misunderstand what the other person is saying. Here are some examples of questions that attempt to clarify.

- "Are you saying that ____?"
- "Do you think that ____?"
- "What did you mean when you said ____?"
- "Would you mind repeating what you just said? I'm not sure I understand."

EXTENSION

You may want to challenge students to determine the role that nonverbal messages play in person-to-person communication. Have students consider how facial expressions, spatial relations, gestures, touch, and voice communicate thoughts and feelings. When students report their findings to the class, they might want to include demonstrations of the nonverbal messages.

CLOSURE

Ask students to list valuable communication skills they have learned from this lesson. Then ask students which of the skills they will try to use in their relationships. Which seem most obvious but may require more work to master? Which seem most unusual in everyday encounters?

Paraphrasing to Understand Meaning. **Paraphrasing** means using your own words to restate what another person has said. By paraphrasing someone's words, you let that person know what you think he or she said. In that way, you give the person a chance to correct you if you are mistaken. You can introduce your paraphrase with comments like these:

- "So, what you're saying is ______."
- "I take it that you believe ______."
- "What I heard you say is ______."

WIZARD OF ID By permission of Johnny Hart and Creators Syndicate, Inc.

ACTIVITY 3 Practicing Questioning and Paraphrasing

Working with a partner, use the following situations as opportunities to practice questioning and paraphrasing. As you each take a part and act out your conversations, try to include other interpersonal communication skills as well—showing empathy, sharing feelings, respecting opinions, taking turns, and using tact.

- It is Friday and Michael is upset because he did not make the basketball team; Jennifer has been looking forward to their date for the Thanksgiving dance all week.
- Margaret is afraid that she will not pass her math course, and she is embarrassed to ask for help; Juana is willing to tutor, but she doesn't know how to approach her friend.
- Melissa wants to try out for the school softball team, but she is afraid that she does not play well enough; Tom would rather have Melissa spend time with him than practice ball.
- John has a part-time job to help save money for college, and he is a little envious of his friend Ian's free time. Ian plans to go to college, but he is really more interested in all of his high school activities than he is in planning for college.

MAKING CONNECTIONS

Art and Design

Have students plan a bulletin board that displays methods for checking understanding. Students might use photographs or sketches of people and then add conversation balloons that illustrate ways to paraphrase and to question.

ONGOING ASSESSMENT

Activity 3

You may want to have each pair rate themselves on how well they show empathy, share feelings, respect opinions, take turns, and use tact. These student ratings can help with your assessment.

Segment 2 *pp. 146–151*

- **Communicating Your Thoughts and Feelings**
- **Giving and Accepting Criticism**

Performance Objectives

- To assess personal emotions and to analyze how well they are communicated to others
- To observe communication behavior and to determine which methods are productive
- To analyze constructive criticism

Meeting Individual Needs

Students with Special Needs

Both learning disabled and emotionally disturbed students may have difficulty making judgments about what is appropriate to share in relationships. Emphasize to students who do not discriminate well in their friendships the "private self" concept. Explain that all relationships do not develop to such a degree that everything can be shared. Privacy about many personal things is necessary, even with friends.

Teacher's Resource Binder

Skills for Success 3
Communicating and Sharing

Communicating Your Thoughts and Feelings

Communication is a two-way street. In addition to responding to what the other person says, you must share things about yourself—your thoughts, your feelings, and your ideas.

Judging What Is Appropriate to Share

Your **private self** is that part of yourself which is most true to your self-concept, while your **public self** is that part of yourself which you choose to share with others. The following suggestions should help you to judge what to share with others.

1. **Increase the level of sharing gradually.** When you first get to know someone, share information about topics that are of general interest—hobbies, sports, and current events. Wait until you have developed an ongoing relationship to talk about your feelings, attitudes, and private thoughts.
2. **Share private information only with someone you trust.** There is some risk involved in telling about yourself, so share your fears, deep feelings, and secrets with those whom you know you can rely on to keep your confidences.
3. **Continue to share only if the other person confides in you.** You may misread someone and tell more about yourself than the other person shares about himself or herself. If that happens, you might want to avoid sharing too much until your friendship has developed into a closer relationship.

MOTIVATION

Ask students if they have ever watched talk shows in which participants aired grievances with one another. Ask students if they think a talk show is the best place to bring up differences of opinion. What things about the discussions were not beneficial to the people in the relationships? Point out in this segment students will learn ways to disclose feelings, make criticisms, and speak up for themselves without harming another person in a relationship.

Disclosing Your Feelings

Even in a close relationship, it is sometimes difficult to handle the sharing of feelings. However, unless you can learn to share feelings with others in a positive way, you will not be able to maintain a relationship of mutual trust.

Avoid Always Withholding Your Feelings. Sometimes it is so uncomfortable to disclose your feelings that you withhold, or keep your feelings inside. Psychologists believe that if people constantly withhold feelings they can develop physical problems such as ulcers, high blood pressure, or even cancer, as well as emotional problems such as sadness, depression, or tension.

Although withholding feelings may be wise in some situations, always doing so can have negative effects on relationships. If you care about someone, make it a point to communicate how you feel about what they say and do.

Avoid Displays of Negative Feelings. People share their feelings not only with words, but also with actions. Cheering at a pep rally, patting a friend on the back, and sharing a hug are all positive displays of emotion. But displays of negative feelings can actually interfere with communication. Slamming a door behind you, sulking, and shouting certainly show feelings, but they don't tell the other person exactly what you are feeling or why. It is much better to describe your feelings than to display them with negative, or aggressive, behavior.

Describe Your Feelings. Instead of withdrawing or displaying your feelings in a negative way, learn how to describe them. When you describe your feelings, try to put your feelings into words in a calm, nonjudgmental way. Describing your feelings in this way will give other people knowledge that will be helpful in future interactions with you.

When you describe your feelings, try to describe, honestly and accurately, what you are experiencing. You may find it easier to be honest if you first accept that it is all right to feel what you are experiencing. To begin with, you may find it easier to describe positive feelings: "I'm so glad you called. I needed to talk to someone." However, as a relationship develops, it becomes important to describe your negative feelings as well. You might begin with something that affects you but not the relationship: "When I stay by myself at night, I really get nervous. Every little noise spooks me."

Then, as you experience success and develop trust in the relationship, learn to describe what bothers you about what the other person has said or done. Describing is especially helpful with

COOPERATIVE LEARNING

Ask students to work in pairs to prepare and present scenarios that demonstrate the sharing of feelings. Encourage students to include both positive and negative interactions. When the audience discusses the presentations, have students note what is destructive about the negative interactions and what is productive about the positive interactions. You could suggest the following scenarios to any pairs who are having difficulty getting started:

1. Joy and Tamara usually study together in the evening, but one night Tamara makes other plans without letting Joy know. Joy is hurt and withdraws.
2. Joel and Taro, who are best friends, both tried out for the basketball team. When the two friends check the coach's posted list of team members, they realize that Taro's name has not been included.

Teaching the Lesson

You may want to direct students to **Judging What Is Appropriate to Share** on p. 146. As you go through the numbered list, you might ask students to think of ways that their friendships exemplify the suggestions.

To help students understand the value of disclosing feelings, you might act out an unresolved conflict with the class by using each of the three listed ways—withholding (perhaps sulking for emphasis), negative displaying (shouting or slamming books), and accurately describing how you feel. Ask students to evaluate the effectiveness of each of these methods. How did each demonstration make them feel? What did they want to do in response? Did they care about your feelings equally with each demonstration? As a follow-up, ask students to complete the **Communication Journal** activity in which they

negative feelings because it gives the other person helpful information. Remember to describe the situation as it affects you and your feelings.

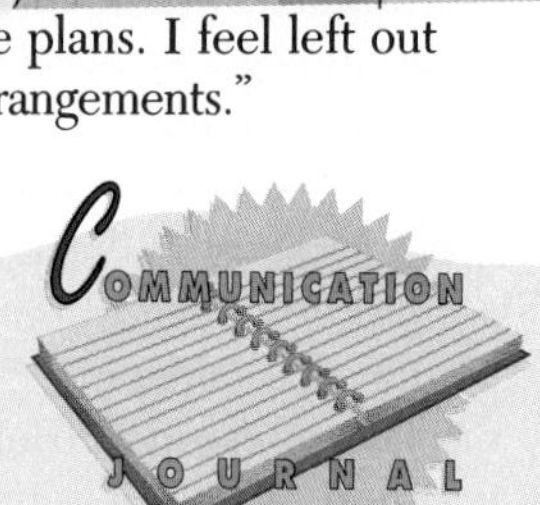

- "When you criticize how I play when I'm trying my hardest, I feel defeated."
- "When you told him about our conversation, I was angry. I didn't want anyone else to know."
- "I waited for your call before I made plans. I feel left out when you don't let me in on your arrangements."

Communication Journal

Think back over the events of the day. Were there any times when you felt particularly happy, angry, disappointed, excited, sad? Jot down a few emotions that you recall. How did you communicate your feelings to others? Write down how you shared the feelings you listed. If you discover that you tended to withhold your feelings or to display them inappropriately, write down what you might have done to describe your emotions positively to someone else.

Critical Thinking

Application

You may want to prepare a list of statements that disclose feelings. Ask students to add assertive statements that propose actions. For example, you might use the following statements. Possible student responses are in brackets.

1. "Having no privacy in the house bothers me. We all deserve space of our own." [Please stay out of my personal things.]
2. "I'm sorry we can't decide this argument now; this shouting upsets me." [I want to stop the quarreling until we both calm down and can resolve our differences.]

Speaking Up for Yourself

Even within caring relationships, people sometimes seem to take advantage of you and to ignore your feelings. It may even seem as if they do not listen to you at all. Sharing your thoughts and feelings under these conditions can be very difficult, but it is sometimes necessary to let another person know exactly what you want.

Psychologists define **assertiveness** as the practice of exercising your personal rights. When you are assertive, you give the reasons why you feel or believe or think as you do and suggest a responsible action from someone in response.

EXAMPLE: "I explained to you that I have homework on weeknights. It frustrates me when you expect long phone conversations. I'd like to limit our weeknight calls to thirty minutes."

evaluate how well they communicate their feelings to others.

After students read **Speaking Up for Yourself,** emphasize why it is necessary to be specific when asserting oneself. Discuss some examples of passive behavior, aggressive behavior, and assertive behavior. Then assign **Activity 4** as independent practice.

Read through **How to Give and Accept Criticism** on p. 150 with the class and discuss both positive and negative examples of each point. Students may recall examples from their own relationships; remind them to talk about behaviors, not people. Then assign **Activity 5** on p. 151 as independent practice in analyzing constructive criticism.

It is often difficult for quiet people who normally keep things to themselves to speak up. Asserting yourself does not mean being aggressive, but it does mean letting someone know what you want.

WHERE I'M COMING FROM **BY BARBARA BRANDON**

HOW TO *Assert Yourself*

1. **Avoid language that can lead to arguments.** Do not threaten or criticize. In fact, do not focus on the other person at all; talk about yourself.
2. **Be specific about what you want.** Sometimes you know someone so well that you think the person can read your mind. However, the only way to make sure that the person knows what you want is to say exactly what it is.
3. **Keep a firm but pleasant tone of voice.** Although it is difficult when you are upset, it is very important to control the tone, pitch, and volume of your voice. If you get off to a bad start, stop for a moment and gain control of yourself.

ACTIVITY 4 Observing Communication Behavior

For two days, observe people communicating. Note situations in which people withhold their feelings or withdraw (passive behavior), display negative feelings (aggressive behavior), or describe their feelings and speak up for themselves (assertive behavior). Which types of behavior seem to be more productive? With a partner, discuss your observations and write a summary of your findings.

ONGOING ASSESSMENT

Activity 4

You may want to require that students observe a set number of situations. Students' summaries should cover the set number of situations and should include each of the suggested types of behavior: passive, aggressive, and assertive.

ASSESSMENT

You could use **Activities 4** and **5** to evaluate how well students understand the concepts in this segment. Because the skills take time to develop and require practice to become natural, note also how well students integrate the learning into class discussions and dialogues.

RETEACHING

Students might be having trouble expressing the ways they feel because their vocabularies are limited. You could brainstorm with the class to list adjectives that describe feelings. The following list will help you to get started: *aggravated, helpless, overwhelmed, powerful, calm, confused, rejected, satisfied,* and *proud.*

MAKING CONNECTIONS

Mass Media

Talk shows often present people with long-term disagreements in forums before TV audiences. Tape portions of one of these programs to share with students in class. Discuss the program in terms of the techniques listed in **How to Give and Accept Criticism.** Have students identify in the programs the techniques that are used and those that are ignored. Then have students discuss how the interactions could have been improved.

CRITICAL THINKING

Analysis

After you analyze the talk show as suggested in the **Making Connections** feature above, discuss with students the effect this type of television programming has on viewers. What is the audience for these programs? Do many people learn ways of relating to one another by watching televised disputes? Are viewers learning effective methods of relating person to person?

Audiovisual Resource Binder

Transparency 11
Giving and Accepting Criticism

Giving and Accepting Criticism

In any friendship or close relationship there may be a need for **constructive criticism,** criticism that is beneficial and helpful rather than disapproving. Since people, at one time or another, all find criticism difficult to accept, it is important to express and receive criticism with discretion and care. The information in the following chart will help you to learn how to give and receive constructive criticism.

Give and Accept Criticism

Giving Criticism

1. **Choose an appropriate time and place.** Try not to criticize someone in front of others. When you discuss a problem, try to choose a time when the other person is relaxed and willing to listen. After you are sure that you have the other person's complete attention, be brief and to the point.
2. **Choose only one or two specific points for criticism.** Do not attempt to recite an entire list of problems. Instead, identify only one, or possibly two, specific actions or statements that you feel need to be changed.
3. **Describe the person's behavior carefully and accurately.** Talk about specific actions, not personality, character, or values. For example, you might say, "I wish you would not interrupt me," rather than "You are the rudest person I know."
4. **Respond to the present, not to the past.** Sometimes it is tempting to bring up unresolved, bad feelings from the past and to rehash old arguments in an attempt to resolve them. However, this is usually not very effective in changing behavior.
5. **Try to include ideas for solutions.** It is usually possible to come up with positive suggestions, and such suggestions show the other person that your intentions are positive.

Accepting Criticism

1. **Think of criticism as an opportunity for improvement.** When you receive a negative review from someone, try to see it as a chance to learn something about your behavior that you did not know before. Constructive criticism is in your best interest.
2. **Make sure that you understand what you hear.** Don't jump to conclusions about what you think someone means. If you are confused, ask for clarification.
3. **Recognize those who use constructive criticism.** Since giving constructive criticism is not easy, thank the people who take the time to do so.

Extension

Invite a psychologist or a specialist in interpersonal communication to visit the class to talk about one of the communication methods discussed in this chapter—speaking assertively, avoiding misunderstandings, describing feelings, or using constructive criticism. Involve students in making arrangements and in following up with courtesies.

Closure

You may want to use the last five questions in **Guidelines for Communicating Person to Person** for students to assess their strengths and weaknesses in communicating interpersonally. Have students determine what improvements they could make. Ask students to predict the difficulties they might have in mastering these techniques.

Activity 5

Analyzing Constructive Criticism

Think about a time when a close friend criticized you for a specific behavior. Analyze the effectiveness of the criticism that you were given by asking yourself the following questions.

1. What specific action, or actions, were criticized? What specific changes were you requested to make in your behavior?
2. Did you accept the criticism constructively? If so, how did you change your behavior? If not, why not?
3. What, if anything, could the person criticizing you have done differently to make the criticism, or the suggestion for change, more constructive?
4. What, if anything, could you have done to make the situation more constructive?

Ongoing Assessment

Activity 5

You may want to ask students to write the answers to the four questions in the activity. Students' answers should reflect an understanding of constructive criticism.

Guidelines

for Communicating Person to Person

- Do I approach others with empathy (understanding their point of view)?
- Are my close relationships built upon shared feelings and trust?
- Do my relationships allow me to grow as a person?
- Do I put the same energy into maintaining relationships that I put into building them?
- Do I treat friends with courtesy, and do I respect their opinions?
- Am I tactful when I disagree with someone?
- In conversations, do I allow the other person equal opportunity to talk?
- Do I use questioning and paraphrasing to make sure that I know what someone means?
- Do I make good judgments about when to share personal information with friends?
- Do I describe my negative feelings rather than acting them out?
- Am I learning to assert myself and speak up for what I want?
- Do I give criticism so that it is received constructively?
- Do I learn from the helpful comments of my friends, even when an opinion is negative?

Teacher's Resource Binder

Skills for Success 4
Handling Constructive Criticism

◆ Profiles in Communication

Performance Objectives

- To suggest effective interpersonal communication methods to resolve an argument between two children
- To write a paragraph describing the recommendations
- To evaluate suggested dispute resolution techniques of classmates

Teaching the Feature

Ask students if they have ever witnessed disagreements between neighbors, relatives, or friends. Explain that some unresolved disagreements end up in increasingly overburdened courtrooms, and that to keep courtrooms free for more severe disagreements involving legalities, the dispute resolution method has evolved. Instead of relying on the law to resolve the disagreements, the method relies on the principles of interpersonal communication. Have students read the profile of Gael Sherman and the mediation profession to determine what skills she needs to perform her job.

Activity Note

Some students may want to include exact dialogues of what they would say in their paragraphs while others may prefer listing the principles they feel would be important. Students should concentrate on resolving the conflict with both children feeling better rather than on assessing blame.

PROFILES IN COMMUNICATION

G Sherman

Have you ever been involved in a dispute and wished there were another person present—someone impartial who could help the two parties communicate? Gael Sherman, a professional mediator, helps resolve many kinds of disagreements. Often the problem is among family members. At other times, the dispute may be with a neighbor, employer, merchant, or civic group.

Never taking sides, Ms. Sherman first creates a safe environment in which her clients can feel free to express their grievances. "I must see that each person states his or her side of the issue clearly and that he or she is clearly heard by the other person," she explains. To do this, she may paraphrase or summarize one person's viewpoint and then ask that person to verify it. Then she asks what the communication meant to the other person. "When each party really understands the other's interest, animosity often falls away," she remarks, "opening the way for a solution that satisfies everyone."

Ms. Sherman gains so much fulfillment from mediating that she volunteers her time at a dispute resolution center. This inexpensive service helps people settle their problems privately instead of through the courts.

ACTIVITY

Although you may not always realize it, opportunities to settle disputes often occur in your daily life, even in circumstances that are not unusual or extraordinary. Imagine you are baby-sitting two young children who get into an argument. In order to settle the dispute, you must listen to each child carefully and determine the nature of the problem. How will you get the children to communicate with you about their own responsibility in the argument? Remember that since children don't always admit things that they feel uncomfortable about, you will need to use extra sensitivity and special questioning tactics. Your main goal is to resolve the disagreement with both children feeling better about it. Write a paragraph describing how you would handle the situation. Get feedback from your classmates on the probable effectiveness of your approach. Are your approaches at all similar?

CHAPTER 6

S•U•M•M•A•R•Y

COMMUNICATING PERSON TO PERSON is sometimes called interpersonal communication. It refers to the communication that occurs between two people who have a personal relationship. Personal relationships range from casual acquaintances to very close friendships or family connections. Good communication skills are important in building and maintaining personal relationships.

- **Develop good relationships** by recognizing the various types of relationships and working to build and maintain them. Approach others with empathy, share your feelings, and establish trust with your friends. Take advantage of good relationships to achieve personal growth.
- **Respond to others with respect.** Treat others with courtesy, respect their opinions, be tactful when disagreeing, and give them a chance to talk during a conversation. To be sure that you know what the other person means, check your perceptions by questioning or paraphrasing what has been said.
- **Communicate your thoughts and feelings** to people with whom you have close relationships, but share only what you feel comfortable sharing. When you disclose your feelings, be careful not to withhold feelings that you need to express. When you have negative feelings toward the other person, describe them rather than acting them out. Be willing to speak up for yourself when you have something to say. Learn to give and receive constructive criticism.

Vocabulary

Look back through this chapter to find the meaning of each of the following terms. Write each term and its meaning in your communication journal.

acquaintances, p. 140
assertiveness, p. 148
close relationship, p. 140
constructive criticism, p. 150
empathy, p. 141
friendships, p. 140
interpersonal communication, p. 139
misunderstanding, p. 144
paraphrasing, p. 145
private self, p. 146
public self, p. 146
respect, p. 143
trust, p. 142

TEACHER'S RESOURCE BINDER

- Chapter 6 Vocabulary

Review Questions

Answers

1. the communication that occurs between two or more people who usually have a personal relationship
2. acquaintances, friendships, and close relationships
3. Approach others with empathy, share feelings, establish trust, and achieve personal growth.
4. Trust reduces risk in relationships and helps relationships to grow.
5. Relationships will not last without additional communication effort.
6. Treat friends with courtesy, respect other people's opinions, be tactful, and respect other people's right to be heard.
7. questioning and paraphrasing
8. Increase sharing gradually, share private information only with someone you trust, and continue to share only when someone confides in you.

Discussion Questions

Guidelines for Assessment

Student responses may vary.

1. You and an acquaintance lack similar interests or values; you do not find qualities in the person that you appreciate; or you just do not enjoy the person's company.
2. Learning to empathize is not easy because no two people see anything in exactly the same way. Age, culture, family life—all past experiences—create differences in opinion. To bring about better understanding in relationships, one might visit in others' homes, talk with others' families, ask questions about others' ideas, show interest in others' activities, and learn what ideals others cherish.
3. Describing your feelings and speaking up for yourself give other people knowledge that will be helpful in their interactions with you. Practicing and using the two methods can help to ensure positive communication.
4. Students might say that La Rochefoucauld was aware that conversations require more than talking; they require careful listening so that responses are tailored to the words that come before. Conversation is not isolated ideas bouncing from person to person.
5. Students will probably say that Dankevich realizes that only with criticism can one learn how to improve behavior. One who is afraid of criticism is probably afraid of growth, "flowering," and change.

CHAPTER 6

Review Questions

1. What is interpersonal communication?
2. What are the three stages of relationships?
3. When you begin friendships, what are two methods that will help you to build good relationships?
4. What is the importance of trust in a relationship?
5. Why is it important to continue good communication skills as a relationship grows?
6. What are four good ways to show respect to another person in a relationship?
7. What are two methods that can help you to determine whether you understand what another person is saying?
8. What are three techniques for determining what is appropriate to share with someone?
9. What are two positive ways to reveal your feelings to someone else? Why are these methods more effective than withholding feelings or acting them out?
10. List three or four good hints for giving and receiving constructive criticism.

Discussion Questions

1. Your relationships grow in intensity as you discover what you have in common with other people. Discuss some indicators that tell you a relationship probably will not grow.
2. With your classmates, discuss why empathizing is not as easy as it may sound. What differences between people make it difficult to understand what it is like to be "in the other person's shoes"? What can someone do to better understand the circumstances of someone else?
3. Unfortunately, many people use ineffective methods to reveal their feelings to others. However, their actions represent learned behavior and, like all behavior, it can change. Discuss why it is important to practice describing your feelings and speaking up for yourself assertively.
4. La Rochefoucauld, a seventeenth-century French writer, once wrote, "To listen closely and reply well is the highest perfection we are able to attain in the art of conversation." Discuss the meaning of this quotation. How does it relate to the ability of a good communicator to respond to another person?
5. Konstantin Dankevich, in *The New York Times* (November 19, 1959), wrote, "Only paper flowers are afraid of the rain. We are not afraid of the noble rain of criticism because with it will flourish the magnificent garden of music." Discuss the meaning of this quotation in reference to constructive criticism.

9. Describing your feelings and speaking up for yourself assertively are positive, effective methods because they are specific. They let someone know what bothers you, why it bothers you, and what to do about it.
10. In giving criticism, choose an appropriate time and place; respond to the action, not the person; describe the person's behavior carefully and accurately; respond to the present, not the past; and include ideas for solutions. In accepting criticism, think of it as being in your best interest, make sure you understand what you hear, and recognize those who use constructive criticism.

ACTIVITIES

1. **Making Up Proverbs.** Proverbs are short statements that record the wisdom of a certain time. "Two wrongs do not make a right" is a proverb that might apply to interpersonal communication. Make up one- or two-sentence proverbs for our time about person-to-person communication. Start by trying to think of clever or ironic insights about interpersonal relationships. Perhaps you have learned something about how people relate to one another that strikes you as amusing. Share your proverbs with your classmates.
2. **Writing Paraphrases.** For each of the following statements, write a paraphrase that shows your understanding of the meaning of the statement.
   a. "I've been playing piano for eight years, and this is the first time anyone has asked me to perform. Even though I've had recitals, they have been small. I don't know whether I'm ready for a large performance yet."
   b. "I asked him if he had had a good time, but all he did was shrug his shoulders. I just can't seem to get him to say anything more. I am really tired of trying to communicate."
   c. "I did want to go to that party, but since I didn't get an invitation until just a day before, I decided to stay home. I think she must have found out I was bothered, so she sent me the invitation."
   d. "The car is not running right. It doesn't have any pep, and it keeps stalling at lights. People behind me honk and act irritated at me. I am afraid it wasn't a very good buy. It really bugs me."
   e. "Ever since we moved to our new house, my dog and cat fight all the time. Mom says one of them may have to go. I don't understand their behavior, and I don't know what to do."
3. **Describing Feelings.**
   A. Practice describing feelings by acting out with your classmates one of the situations shown below or a specific situation of your own choosing. Positive reactions are easier to act out, but you can handle the negative ones by describing how you feel about the situation.

   B. Imagine that you find yourself in each of the situations described in the following scenes. Describe what your feelings might be, whether positive or negative, about the situation.
   1. Someone you don't know very well takes the time to help you with some math problems that stump you. With this help you later get a better test grade than you have ever gotten.

ACTIVITIES

Guidelines for Assessment

1. Students' proverbs should be short, should reflect the wisdom of the time, and should pertain to person-to-person communication.
2. Answers will vary. Here are some possibilities:
   a. Even though you've had several years of practice and performed before a few small groups, you're hesitant to give performances before large groups.
   b. You're weary of trying to communicate with him when he won't tell you how he feels about things.
   c. You stayed away from the party because you felt slighted that you weren't invited until the last minute.
   d. You're feeling irritated that you bought the car and think it may have been a bad idea. Its failures are causing traffic problems in addition to upsetting you.
   e. You're confused by your dog's and cat's behavior, and you're afraid that your mom's anger will lead to losing one of your pets.
3. A. In acting out the scenarios, students should use appropriate language to describe their feelings in a calm, nonjudgmental way.
   B. Students might include the following feelings in their descriptions:
   1. grateful to the helper, confident in the subject, and elated with the good grade

SUMMATIVE EVALUATION

Your **Teacher's Resource Binder** contains a reproducible **Chapter 6 Test** that may be used to assess students' mastery of the concepts presented in this chapter.

PORTFOLIO ASSESSMENT

For future reference and evaluation you may want to have students keep in their portfolios any skill sheets or evaluation forms that you have used with this chapter along with any other recorded or written materials that students have created.

2. pleased by your dad's appearance and disappointed at your loss
3. hesitant to become frightened, embarrassed by your fears, and resentful toward your baby-sitting commitment
4. grateful that your friends included you, apprehensive about the danger, and embarrassed by your lack of skill
5. disappointed with the situation, irritated with your date, and anxious for a better explanation
6. betrayed by your friend, sorry that your actions may hurt another, and embarrassed to face the person who confided in you

4. Encourage students to organize their responses to include answers to three questions: What's the problem? Why does it bother me? What do I want to be done about it?

5. You could use the **"How to"** chart on p. 150 as a checklist to evaluate students' dialogues.

2. Your dad travels for business and doesn't get to come to many of your games. However, he makes the last game of the season, and the team loses.
3. Your friend asks you to go to the haunted house and midnight horror movie on Halloween night. You are baby-sitting later that weekend and know that you might spend the night in fear if you spend Halloween night having scary experiences.
4. Several friends ask you to go on a raft trip down a nearby river after a heavy rainfall. You are not a very strong swimmer, and you know that the current will be strong.
5. You've been looking forward to going to the Winter Carnival at school. You even bought a new outfit and got someone you work with to trade nights. Your date calls you the day before and says, "I'm sorry, I'm not going to be able to make it. I hope you're not mad. Maybe we can go to the dance next weekend."
6. You discover that several people know a secret that you had told a friend in confidence. It affects not only you, since it involves a comment you made about someone else.

4. Asserting Yourself. Now that you have practiced describing how you feel, add another dimension. In these situations, show how you want to be treated. Do not yell—describe what you want. First, tell what bothers you. Then describe how you feel about it. Finally, tell how you want the other person to act.

a. You plan to have a few friends over for a cookout. You do not have a lot of money for food, so you limit the invitations to a few close friends. However, one of your friends brings along an extra crowd of people who turn out to be hungry, rowdy, and rude. What do you tell your friend?

b. You come home late from school after practice. You are tired, hungry, dirty, and impatient to get to the movies. The dinner that your mother saved for you was given to the dog; someone is in the bath; and you discover that your sibling has borrowed the sweater you wanted to wear. (Hint: Keep your response specific to the action that you can do something about.)

c. You and a friend have made plans to go skating on Sunday afternoon. At the last minute, your mother decides to go visit a friend of hers that you know and wants you to go with her.

5. Criticizing Constructively. The following situations call for constructive criticism. For each situation, write out a dialogue expressing constructive criticism. Share your wording with a small group of classmates in a discussion.

a. You ride to school in a car pool. On the days your friend drives, you are usually late getting to school.

b. A good friend says "like" in every sentence and uses other expressions that you think are immature. It bothers you, and you are aware that other people make fun of it.

c. A friend of yours borrows some tapes and CDs from several friends and forgets to return them. The friends complain to you.

◆ Real-Life Speaking Situations

PERFORMANCE OBJECTIVES

- To plan and present a speech that teaches the techniques of positive response and constructive criticism
- To design a visual to use with a presentation
- To act out a conversation illustrating effective communication techniques
- To critique classmates' presentations
- To write a script for a conversation that addresses a living-arrangement disagreement
- To read the script to classmates and to respond to comments
- To evaluate classmates' scripts for effective use of communication techniques

REAL LIFE Speaking Situations

1 Corporations sometimes hire professional communications experts to come into their places of business to train their employees in interpersonal communication. These corporations understand that the ability of their employees to communicate effectively with customers is directly related to the employees' successful use of interpersonal communication skills.

You and your partner are two professional communications experts, and you have been hired by a major corporation to train its employees. You have been asked to make a presentation that teaches the techniques of positive response and constructive criticism. You will begin your training session with a five-minute speech in which you provide an overview of these communications techniques.

Your speech should include at least one visual. After the speech, you and your partner will act out a three- to five-minute conversation illustrating one or more of the techniques you identified in your speech.

Give the speech and act out the conversation before your classmates. Ask for a critique of your work. Then have your partner do the same.

2 You have been out of school for one year, and you are sharing an apartment with your brother or sister to save on expenses. The two of you get along together, but living together as roommates has highlighted some of the differences between you.

A problem that has been bothering you for some time has driven you beyond your limit of tolerance. You cannot stand dirt or messiness, but your "roommate" seems to be oblivious to it. Your brother or sister leaves dirty dishes in the sink, newspapers on the sofa, damp towels on the bathroom door, and articles of clothing scattered around the living room.

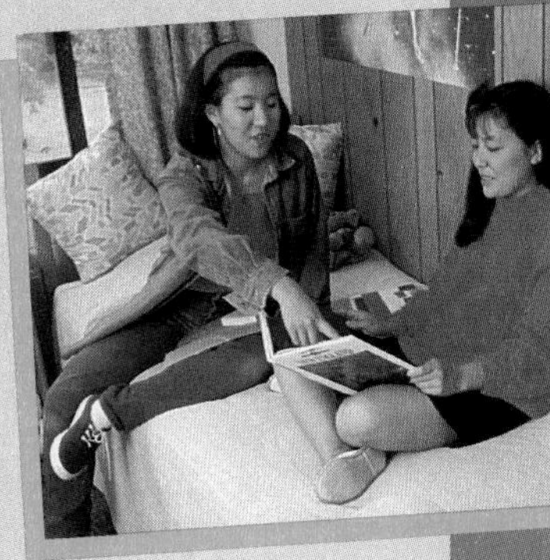

How can you work out this problem and still get along well? How do you bring up the topic without creating a problem in the relationship? Write a script for a five- to ten-minute conversation in which you attempt to work out this problem. Then ask a classmate to read one part of the dialogue while you read the other. Read the prepared script for your entire class, and ask your classmates for comments on how effectively you gave your criticism and, in general, on the success of the communications techniques you used.

ASSESSMENT GUIDELINES

1. You might want to use the **Evaluation Checklist** on p. 375 (or a modified version) to assess students' speeches. Students should be aware in advance of the criteria on which they will be evaluated. Students' visuals should effectively create interest, explain, or give examples. Students' conversations should focus on one or more techniques of positive response and constructive criticism.
2. Students' scripts should reflect an understanding of effective communication. You will probably want to consider in your evaluations students' comments about the dialogues.

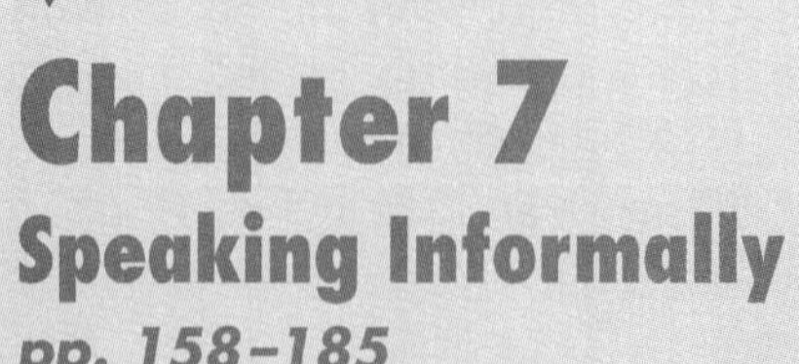

Chapter 7
Speaking Informally
pp. 158–185

Chapter Overview

This chapter presents guidelines and activities for speaking informally for both practical and social purposes.

The chapter begins with guidelines for the practical skills of giving and receiving directions. Next, the chapter presents information on making and receiving social and business telephone calls. Also addressed are how to use answering

Teacher's Resource Binder

The following materials are identified at their point of use in this chapter:

- Skills for Success
  1 *Giving Directions Clearly*
  2 *Answering a Business Telephone*
  3 *Making Introductions*
  4 *Identifying Open and Closed Questions*
- Chapter 7 Vocabulary
- Chapter 7 Test/Answer Key

AV ➤ Audiovisual Resource Binder

The following materials are identified at their point of use in this chapter:

- Transparency 12
  Giving and Receiving Directions
- Transparency 13
  Strategies for Conversing
- Audiotape 1, Lesson 5
  Conversation
- Audiotape 1, Lesson 9
  Paraphrasing

machines and how to relay messages. The segment concludes with guidelines for making announcements.

The second segment considers speaking for social purposes. After discussing how to make and respond to introductions, the segment deals with specific strategies for improving conversational skills, including using feedback to solve problems.

Introducing the Chapter

This chapter teaches social skills that students will use for the rest of their lives. Remind students that employers and other adults expect people to communicate skillfully in social and business situations. Point out that once they master these skills, students will feel more comfortable with informal speaking situations.

CHAPTER 7

Speaking Informally

OBJECTIVES

After studying this chapter, you should be able to

1. Give clear directions and understand directions that you receive from others.
2. Use the telephone effectively for social and business purposes.
3. Make effective announcements.
4. Introduce people to each other.
5. Identify qualities of a good conversationalist.
6. Start and carry on interesting conversations.
7. Use constructive feedback to solve problems and to settle disagreements.

What Is Informal Communication?

Informal communication involves giving and receiving messages in casual, person-to-person interactions, rather than in structured situations such as formal speeches and debates. Two broad types of informal communication are

- **practical communication,** which is useful, direct, and goal oriented
- **social communication,** which is friendly, cordial, and enjoyable

Examples of practical communication are a phone call to a video store to find out whether a movie you want to rent is available and an announcement over the school's public-address system of a change in schedule for a school club's meeting. An example of social communication is a conversation in the school cafeteria about what took place at the class picnic the previous Saturday.

In this chapter, you will learn skills that will improve your ability to communicate practically and socially.

Bibliography of Additional Materials

Professional Readings

- Egan, Gerard. ***Interpersonal Living: A Skills-Contract Approach to Human Relations Training in Groups.*** Pacific Grove, CA: Brooks/Cole Publishing Company.
- Eldon, Freda S. ***Let's Talk: An Introduction to Interpersonal Communication.*** Needham, MA: Ginn Press.

Audiovisuals

- ***Effective Communication: Better Choice of Words***—Coronet/MTI Film & Video, Deerfield, IL (videocassette, 10 min.)
- ***Effective Telephone Calling***—Britannica Films, Chicago, IL (videocassette, 12 min.)
- ***Let's Start at the Very Beginning***—AIMS Media, Chatsworth, CA (videocassette, 6 min.)
- ***You Can Speak Well***—Resources for Education and Management, Decatur, GA (videocassette, 13 min.)

Segment 1 pp. 160–169

- Speaking for Practical Purposes

Performance Objectives

- To act out situations that involve giving and receiving directions
- To act out situations that involve social telephone calls
- To act out situations that involve business telephone calls
- To solve problems that involve giving messages and making announcements

Critical Thinking

Synthesis

To have students practice giving directions in logical steps, write simple directions from the classroom to places on campus with which students are familiar. Scramble the directions and ask students to rearrange them in logical order.

Teacher's Resource Binder

Skills for Success 1
Giving Directions Clearly

Audiovisual Resource Binder

Transparency 12
Giving and Receiving Directions

Speaking for Practical Purposes

Giving and Receiving Directions

Directions are instructions for finding a particular place. [See Chapter 14 for information about instructions for carrying out a process.]

Giving Directions. When someone needs directions for finding a particular place, your ability to provide clear and accurate information is crucial. To ensure clarity and accuracy, follow these suggestions.

1. *Give directions fluently.* Before you give directions, think through what you want to say. You will be more likely to get through the steps without hesitating or confusing your listener if you are clear in your mind about the best route to take.
2. *Select the simplest route.* Give directions for the easiest way to get to a place for someone who is not familiar with the area. You may know shortcuts, but shortcuts often involve unmarked streets or roads that are difficult to find.
3. *Give directions in a series of logical steps.* The person asking for directions needs to know what to do first, what to do second, and so on.
4. *Use visual terms when possible.* Directions such as *go right* and *turn left* are easier for most people to follow than *turn north* or *go south.* Any landmark that you mention should stand out from its surroundings.
5. *Consider drawing a map.* Unless the directions are extremely simple, you may want to draw a map. A good map includes only those details that the person needs in order to find the way.
6. *Repeat directions, if necessary.* If your instructions are at all complicated, repeat them, using language as close to your original wording as possible. In addition, have the person confirm his or her understanding by repeating the directions to you.

Receiving Directions. When you are asking for directions, you can use the following guidelines to ensure that you receive the information you need.

1. *Ask for directions clearly.* Frame your request so that your listener will understand what you want to know. Be specific. For example, instead of saying, "I'm looking for Computer House," you might say, "I'm looking for a store called Computer House on Adams Avenue. Can you tell me how to get there?"
2. *Listen carefully.* Make sure that you have understood all the steps. If you have a pencil and paper, take notes. Be patient; the person giving you directions is trying to be helpful.

MOTIVATION

Several days before beginning this segment, ask two of the better actors in the class to read the material on pp. 162–163 on using the telephone for social calls and to prepare a skit in which a caller is very inept at telephone etiquette. Emphasize that the skit should be as humorous as possible.

Have the students present their skit to the class. After the skit, ask volunteers to comment on some of the problems the caller had. Point out that this segment of the chapter will deal with telephone skills. Ask students to pay particular attention to the material to find ways of helping the caller in the skit improve communication and social skills.

3. *Repeat the directions.* To ensure that you have understood, repeat the directions out loud so that the person who gave them can double-check their accuracy.
4. *Thank the person.* Always thank people who try to help you, even if they give confusing directions. If some of the directions were not clear enough to follow, go part of the way and then ask someone else for further directions.

ACTIVITY 1 Giving and Receiving Directions

Work with a partner to act out one of the following situations. Choose the situation that you like best and, after practicing, act it out for your classmates. Then listen to your classmates' feedback about the effectiveness of your directions.

1. This is your first day at school. You need to find your way to the lunchroom. Ask for directions from your partner.
2. In your math class, you strike up a conversation with the person sitting behind you, and you invite this person to come to your house after school. Give directions for how to get to your home from the school.
3. Your class is planning a picnic. You have been put in charge of arranging the location. Select a specific location, such as a lakefront picnic area or a hillside park, and give directions to your classmates to guide them to this location.
4. The school chorus is putting on a concert at a local elementary school on an upcoming Saturday afternoon. Another member of the chorus has asked you for directions to get from your school to the elementary school where the concert is to be held. Give the requested directions to your classmate.

Maps like the one shown here are designed to be used by people who have visual impairments.

MEETING INDIVIDUAL NEEDS

Learning Styles

Visual, Kinetic, and Tactile Learners. Students who have difficulty with the auditory learning mode may need help with remembering verbal directions. To help students develop strategies to increase their auditory memories, ask them to brainstorm for ideas they can use to remember oral directions. Make a list of these strategies and have students practice using them individually or in small groups.

ONGOING ASSESSMENT

Activity 1

Students should be able to use simple dialogue to act out these situations. Students can draw maps to illustrate the directions. The evaluation emphasis might be on students' ability to show the most direct route in logical steps.

TIMESAVER

You can save time on **Activities 1–3** by having students act out the situations in front of small groups instead of the whole class. You can have students write self-assessments based on the comments of their groups; use these to determine whether students need reteaching.

Teaching the Lesson

You may want to spend as many as four days on this segment, with one day each spent on directions, social telephone calls, business telephone calls, and announcements.

Since the segment contains rather detailed guidelines, you might have students read the material aloud in class so you can stop the reading when necessary to explain points in more detail, to give and to elicit examples, and to show the relationships between ideas.

All of the activities involve cooperative learning, so you might let students work on them during the last part of the class period. To prepare students for **Activities 1–4,** demonstrate how you would act out or respond to one of the items in each activity. Use student volunteers as your partners. Have the class make suggestions to improve your performance. Allow students to

Writing to Learn

Ask students to freewrite on what their lives would be like if the telephone had never been invented. Ask them to consider how they would conduct social and business affairs without the telephone. If you have students who live in households without phones, these students might write about how having telephones would change their lives.

An Alternative Approach

Ask interested students to report to the class on how telephones have been modified for people who have hearing impairments.

Speaking on the Telephone

Although you have probably been using the telephone since early childhood, you can always practice and improve your telephone skills.

Making a Social Call. A **social call** is a telephone call made for personal reasons—to talk with family members, friends, or social acquaintances.

1. *Call at appropriate times.* Unless your call is urgent, make it at a time that is convenient for the other person. In most cases, avoid making calls early in the morning, late at night, or at mealtimes. Be aware of time zones across the country. If you place a 9:00 A.M. call from Massachusetts, it may wake up your cousin in California. It is also always polite to ask, "Are you in the middle of something?" or "Can you talk now?"
2. *Dial correctly.* Check the number you are calling and be sure to touch or dial carefully. If you do not recognize the voice that answers the phone, give the number you are calling and ask if you have reached it. If you have made a mistake, apologize for the inconvenience.
3. *Allow time for someone to answer the phone.* You should probably let the phone ring at least six to ten times. Six rings gives the person only about eighteen seconds to reach the phone.

"Reprinted with special permission of North America Syndicate"

4. *Identify yourself and state your purpose.* When someone answers the telephone, say who you are and ask for the person you wish to speak to. You cannot assume that the person will recognize your voice, and many people become anxious when a caller does not give his or her name.
5. *Use your best vocalization and articulation skills.* Speak clearly, enunciate carefully, and use changes in pitch, loudness, and rate to reinforce the meaning of your words. It is more difficult to distinguish between some sounds on the phone than it is in person.
6. *Keep calls to a reasonable length.* Monopolizing the phone is not considerate to other members of your household. Lengthy phone calls may also be inconvenient for the person you are talking to.

complete the activities on their own as independent practice. Allow class time for students to act out their responses and to discuss the results.

Assessment

Because the information in this segment is very practical and relates to everyday speaking skills, you might consider how well students use the guidelines in functional situations in addition to evaluating the four activities. You can be especially observant of students' abilities to give and receive information and to make announcements.

Receiving a Social Call. Just as there are procedures to follow when you are making a social call, so are there procedures to follow when receiving a social call.

1. *Answer appropriately.* The best way to answer the telephone is simply to say, "Hello," and wait for the caller to speak. If you hear nothing, hang up. If the caller is not someone you recognize, you will need to be cautious about disclosing personal information. You might ask, "Who is speaking, please?" or "What number are you calling?"
2. *Respond to the situation.* If the caller has dialed a wrong number, respond courteously as you inform the caller of the mistake. If the call is for another person in your household, you might ask, "May I say who's calling?" and then ask the caller to wait while you tell the other person that he or she has a phone call. If the person whom the caller wishes to speak to is not available, offer to take a message. When there is a message, record it clearly and post it where it can be seen.
3. *Do not provide strangers with your name or number.* If a caller is not someone you know, seems confused, or demands your name or number, ask, "What number are you dialing?" If the caller has misdialed, say, "I'm sorry. You've reached the wrong number." If the person in fact dialed your number correctly, suggest a call to directory assistance for the correct number he or she actually wants.
4. *Be honest but courteous.* If you are short of time or are expecting another call, tell your caller. To avoid being rude, you might provide a brief explanation for the reason you need to get off the phone. You might say, "Elena, I just sat down to eat dinner. Can I call you back in about an hour?" or "Sam, I've enjoyed talking to you, but I need to go now. My brother wants to use the phone to get some information about a homework assignment."

Integrating the Language Arts

Grammar Link

Review with students the predicate nominative and how it applies to telephone manners. Explain that the forms "This is he" and "This is she" are the appropriate forms to use in answering the telephone when the caller asks for the person who answers the call by name. If students find the predicate-nominative form awkward or unnatural sounding, suggest alternative forms that are grammatically correct. For example, students could say "This is *(name)* speaking" or "I'm *(name)*."

Reteaching

You can reteach all of the objectives for this segment by using audiocassettes and videotapes of people giving directions, making and receiving phone calls, and making announcements. You can ask volunteers to make the tapes or you can record them from television shows. Game shows, news segments, and dramatized stories may effectively show these communication interchanges.

Play the tapes one at a time and then ask students to list the good and bad features of each one. Encourage students to use their textbooks for ideas. Then discuss the lists and point out additional good and bad features that students have missed.

Ongoing Assessment

Activity 2

Evaluation can be based on the suggestions on pp. 162–163 for making and receiving social calls.

Making Connections

Technology

Ask students to report on the telephone technology that is available now or that will be available in the near future for answering calls, taking messages, forwarding calls, and so on. Part of the research for the reports can be based on interviews with people who have used these services to find out the pros and cons associated with the services.

Activity 2 Practicing Social Calls

Act out the following situations with a partner, showing how you would handle each call. Then ask for and respond to feedback from your classmates.

1. You are baby-sitting for your neighbors, the Garcias, who have gone out for the evening. The phone rings, and the caller asks to speak to Mr. Garcia.
2. There is a new student at school whom you would like to get to know better. You telephone this person and extend an invitation to go bowling with you.
3. Someone whom you would like to get to know just telephoned you for the first time, but you have to get off the phone right away because your mother is expecting an important call.
4. You are visiting a friend's house, and everyone is in the back yard. As you walk back into the house, the phone rings.

Making a Business Call. A **business call** is a call made to a company or organization to request information or help, to make a complaint, or to take care of some other business matter.

In most cases, the same procedures apply to making business calls as apply to making social calls, except that business calls often require you to be more formal. When calling a business, be prepared to identify yourself and to state your purpose promptly.

EXAMPLE: Hello, my name is Ted Begosian. I'm president of the Student Council at North High School. May I speak with Mr. Moniz? He asked to be informed when we had a calendar of school events available.

In addition, businesses often transfer or route calls. If your call is

- answered by an operator or a secretary, identify the person or department you need to reach
- answered by voice mail (a computerized answering system), leave your name, phone number, and purpose for calling
- put on hold, wait patiently (for a reasonable time)
- transferred to another person, state your name and your purpose again
- cut off accidentally, call back
- answered by a computerized routing system, listen carefully to the options and select the one that will direct your call to the correct person or department

Respond appropriately when the phone is answered. Choose what to say based on whom you have reached and whether the person ought to hear your purpose in full detail.

See p. 167 for **EXTENSION, ENRICHMENT,** and **CLOSURE.**

1. *Be sure you are talking to the right person.* It does you no good to explain your business to the person who answers the phone if he or she is not the proper person. To make sure that you are connected with someone who can help you, you might say something like, "Hello, this is Ellen Cheng. I'm having a problem with a hair dryer I bought from your company recently. Whom should I speak with about this matter?"
2. *Be specific about what you want.* State your request clearly and directly. For example, if you were calling a business-supply store to ask about a specific product, you might say, "Hello, my name is Ellen Cheng. I'm calling to see whether you carry $9\frac{1}{2}$- by 6-inch spiral notebooks with college-ruled paper."
3. *Make sure that the person understands your request.* If the person repeats your request incorrectly or in some other way shows a lack of understanding, stop the person and repeat your request. If you have a complaint, explain what you expect to happen to resolve the difficulty.
4. *Be patient.* No matter how many times you have been transferred, cut off, or put on hold, always be polite as you explain your business clearly and firmly.

Receiving a Business Call. You may receive business calls on the job or at home. If you have a job that includes answering the telephone, your employer will give you specific instructions for taking calls. Usually, you will answer the phone by giving the company's name rather than your own.

When you are at home, most of the business calls you receive are **telemarketing** calls, telephone calls from individuals or businesses that want to sell you services or products. Many of these calls

An Alternative Approach

Some state legislatures and the U.S. Congress have considered laws regulating unsolicited calls from telemarketing agencies. Ask students who are interested to research the status of these laws and to report on their research to the class.

TEACHER'S RESOURCE BINDER

Skills for Success 2
Answering a Business Telephone

MEETING INDIVIDUAL NEEDS

Students with Special Needs

Many students with disabilities lack the wide range of experiences that other students have. Often, these missed experiences prevent students from recognizing key information. Activities that require students to summarize or paraphrase information are useful because they provide the students with opportunities to practice identifying key information and paraphrasing it.

For this section, have the students practice leaving concise messages for whomever they choose. This may be done aloud as an answering machine message or in writing. Then have partners provide constructive feedback.

COOPERATIVE LEARNING

Ask students to work in groups of four to write several sets of instructions that could be recorded on answering machines. The messages should be simple and clear, but they can incorporate humor, references to current events, holiday messages, or other features that help make them interesting. Let the groups share their work. They could even compile an anthology of instructions for future reference.

are made by professional telemarketing agencies. Such agencies hire people to make calls for the purpose of selling products or getting contributions. If you know you are not interested in buying the product or pledging a contribution, say politely but firmly, "I'm not interested," and hang up. Some calls are generated by computers. For these you need only to hang up if you are not interested.

Using Answering Machines. When you call many businesses, as well as some individuals, you may find yourself communicating not with a human but with an answering device. There are several different devices that answer telephone calls.

One common device is an **answering machine,** an independent mechanism hooked up to a telephone line that responds to calls with a tape-recorded or digitally reproduced message.

Voice mail is an electronic system that provides the caller with a number of options from which to select, usually by using numbers on a touch-tone telephone pad. A voice-mail system often allows callers the option of recording a message. Voice mail also allows callers to route calls to a specific extension in a business office or request particular information, such as the weather forecast or the caller's bank balance.

Most answering devices follow these procedures.

1. The machine answers the phone.
2. The caller listens to prerecorded instructions. (For voice mail, you may be asked to use your touch-tone keys to route your call.)
3. A tone, a beep, or a series of beeps signals the caller to begin a message.
4. A second tone or beep indicates that the recording time has been used up and that the machine has stopped recording.

EXTENSION

Have students imagine that they are in a foreign country in which they are unfamiliar with the language. Ask them to work out pantomime routines they might use to ask directions to a hospital, a restaurant, or a zoo. Have volunteers present their routines to the class without indicating the places they are trying to locate and let the rest of the class try to guess the place each presenter wants to go. You might add to the activity by inviting students to discuss experiences they have had trying to understand or give directions when they have traveled in foreign countries or met foreign travelers.

When you record a message, listen very carefully to the taped instructions. In most cases, you will be asked to state who you are, as well as the date and time you called. Since you will have a limited amount of time to state your message, make sure it is brief and to the point. If you want someone to return your call, be sure to leave your phone number.

When communicating by answering machine or voice mail, there is always a possibility that a message will be lost. If you leave a message and the person does not return your call within two days or so, you may want to try again.

ACTIVITY 3 Practicing Business Calls

Working with a partner, act out one of the following situations. After demonstrating an appropriate response to the situation, ask for and respond to feedback from your classmates on how effectively you have communicated your message.

1. Your parents are buying a new kitchen appliance, and they want you to help them. You call a department store to find out whether it has a specific model of the appliance in stock, what its price is, what its features are, and what colors are available.
2. You headed a drive at your school to collect food and clothing for the homeless. You are calling a local agency to find out where and when you should drop off the donated items.
3. You recently bought a shirt. It shrank and faded the first time you washed it. You call the department store to complain and are directed to leave a recorded message.
4. You get a call from a telemarketer offering you a good deal on a five-year subscription to a magazine that your family does not usually buy.

Relaying Messages. When you answer a phone call intended for someone else, it is important to relay an accurate message to the other person. In some cases, passing on the message may be a simple courtesy; in other cases, the message may be of critical importance.

ONGOING ASSESSMENT

Activity 3

Students can act out these situations in the form of simple dialogues. The dialogues should follow the suggestions on pp. 164–166 for making and receiving business calls.

Enrichment

Invite a sales representative of the local telephone company to address the class on the kinds of special telephone services and equipment that are available now and on the new services that will probably be available in the future. If specialized equipment is available, ask the sales representative to demonstrate to the class ways to use the equipment. As a follow-up, lead the class in a discussion of how the new technology may affect telephone skills in the future.

Common Error

Problem. Some messages are never received in some households because no system for delivering messages has been established.

Solution. Ask students to share how messages are delivered in their households. Compile a list of these ideas (and of additional ones generated through brainstorming) for future reference.

When taking a message, try to make a written note rather than trust your memory, and keep the following points in mind.

1. Take the caller's name and phone number. Even when a return phone call is not requested, the person receiving the message may need to return the call.
2. Offer to take a message. Once the caller has given you the message, it is a good idea to repeat it and make sure that you have recorded it accurately.
3. Make sure that you give the message to the person or post it in a place where it can be clearly seen.

If you take messages from an answering machine, check the directions on the machine before playing back the messages. Some answering machines tape new messages over ones that have been replayed, so it is important to have a pencil and paper ready to note the messages and phone numbers as you hear them.

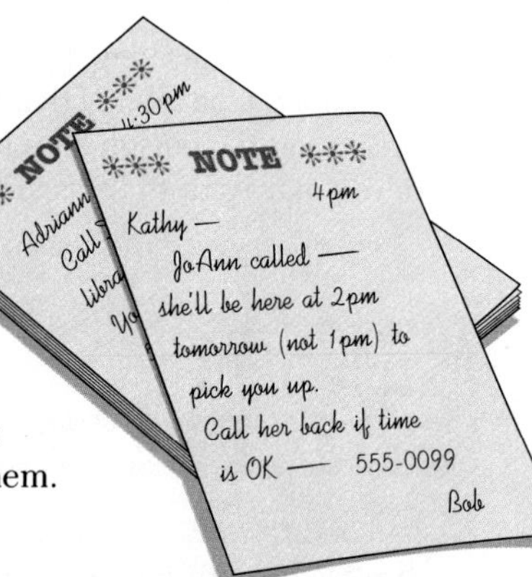

Making Announcements

You may need to make announcements in class, at a school assembly, or over the public-address system. When you are asked to make an announcement, follow these guidelines.

1. *Include all important information.* To make sure you have all the information you need, you might use the reporter's 5W-*How?* questions: *Who? What? When? Where? Why? How?*
2. *Write out your announcement.* By writing and revising your wording, you can be sure not to forget any major points, and you can make your message interesting. Get your audience's attention by beginning in an interesting or unexpected way.
3. *Rehearse.* Practice emphasizing the key words in your announcement. Speak slowly and clearly. Have someone listen to you as you practice and give you feedback to help you improve your delivery. If you will be using a microphone or public-address system, determine how close to the microphone your mouth should be to get the best sound level.
4. *Deliver your announcement effectively.* Wait until the audience is quiet to begin. Speak loudly enough that everyone can hear you clearly.

CLOSURE

To review the material in this segment, ask the class to construct charts that list pitfalls and provide tips on how to give directions, make telephone calls, and make announcements. You can write the charts on the chalkboard and let volunteers contribute ideas.

ACTIVITY 4 Giving Messages and Announcements

Imagine yourself in each of the situations that follow. For each situation, prepare an appropriate response.

1. When you come home one afternoon, you hear the following message on your family's answering machine: "Hello. This is the principal, Mr. Ames, calling from Kaiser Elementary School. It's 2:30 P.M. Shirlene said she wasn't feeling well, so we took her temperature. It was 102 degrees. We have her lying down now in the school nurse's office, but she's definitely a sick little girl. Could somebody come and get her as soon as possible? The phone number here is 555–5100." You realize that the caller made an error, because you do not know anyone named Shirlene.
2. You want to start a new club at school. Your school principal has given you permission to go to each classroom to announce the introductory meeting for the club. In your announcement, give information that students might need in order to motivate them to attend the first meeting. Your announcement should create interest in the club since the school will not sponsor the club unless it has at least ten members. Be sure to state the time and location.

ONGOING ASSESSMENT

Activity 4

Students can draft and revise paragraphs describing how they would respond to these situations. Evaluate whether students' responses solve the problems in both situations.

GUIDELINES for Practical Communication

- When I give directions, do I select the simplest route and explain chronological steps in visual terms?
- Do I ask for directions courteously, listen carefully when they are given, and repeat them to make sure that I have understood them?
- When I make a social telephone call, am I considerate of the person receiving the call, and do I identify myself?
- When I make a business telephone call, do I identify myself and state my purpose clearly?
- When I make or receive a business telephone call, am I efficient and courteous?
- When I leave a message on an answering device, is my message clear, specific, and concise?
- Do I relay messages accurately and completely?
- Do I make announcements that are interesting and that are loud enough to be heard by everyone in my audience?

Segment 2 *pp. 170–179*

- **Speaking for Social Purposes**
- **Resolving Disagreements Using Constructive Feedback**

Performance Objectives

- To develop introductions for a variety of social and business situations
- To develop and apply evaluation criteria to personal conversational skills
- To analyze and to draw conclusions about a conversation
- To act out situations and to apply problem-solving methods to settle disputes

MEETING INDIVIDUAL NEEDS

Cultural Diversity

The etiquette of making introductions differs from culture to culture. Ask students who are familiar with different cultures to explain to the class how people make and respond to introductions in other cultures.

In some cultures, it is considered impolite to use personal names, even in introductions. Ask students who are interested in cultural traditions to research the rules for using personal names in various societies and to report their findings to the class.

Teacher's Resource Binder

Skills for Success 3
Making Introductions

Speaking for Social Purposes

Making Introductions

When you meet people you do not know, or when you are with people who do not know each other, you will need to make introductions. The ability to make an **introduction**—to present one person to another or to a group—identifies you as a person who is self-confident and competent.

Introducing Yourself to Others. You will sometimes be faced with situations in which you have to introduce yourself. For example, you might be attending a new school and have to introduce yourself to some other students at a table in the cafeteria, or you might be at a party and not see anyone you know. In such situations, you can introduce yourself by

- greeting the other person
- giving your name
- saying something about yourself and asking a question

EXAMPLE: Hi, I'm José Morales. Mrs. Bellini, our club sponsor, asked me to meet you here and go with you to our school. How was your flight?

When introducing yourself in a business situation, you should greet the other person, give your name, and then state your purpose.

EXAMPLE: Hello. My name is Amy Yamoto. I'm a student at West Township High School, and I would like to ask you how I may apply for a summer job here.

MOTIVATION

To get students thinking about the material on conversation in this segment, read them the following anecdote about Franklin D. Roosevelt. The anecdote relates an incident that occurred during his presidency.

Roosevelt hated small talk at social gatherings at the White House because he was convinced nobody paid attention to what was said. To prove his point, he occasionally greeted people by saying that he had murdered his grandmother that morning. Most people would smile and mumble some polite but meaningless reply. One time, though, an attentive listener replied that the grandmother had it coming to her.

Ask students if they've ever found themselves in conversations in which people didn't seem to be listening. How did they handle the situations? Ask them if they think comments such as

Introducing Others. Even though the opportunity or the occasion to introduce people to each other comes up frequently, you might feel rather uncomfortable about how you should go about it. The purpose of introductions is to exchange information, primarily people's names. In years past, people followed elaborate rules regarding introductions, but today, people are usually not as demanding about observing every dictate of formal etiquette in social situations.

In general, any introduction that is conducted in a smooth, comfortable manner and that allows the people involved to exchange names and greet one another politely is considered a successful introduction. Knowing a few simple guidelines about the order of names and the wording of an introduction will help you to manage introductions without awkwardness or embarrassment.

The first issue in making an introduction concerns the **order of names**—the order in which people are presented to each other. The person named first is the person to whom the other person is being introduced.

EXAMPLE: In the following introduction, Tarik is being introduced to Amy: "Amy, I'd like you to meet Tarik Armani. Tarik, this is my neighbor, Amy Beaulieu."

According to tradition, you should first state the name of the person

- who is of higher achievement or earned status ("Dr. Mora, this is my little sister, Ruth.") [Dr. Mora is the school principal and therefore has higher status.]
- who is older ("Mrs. Rosenberg, I'd like to introduce you to Tom Karas, my classmate.") [Mrs. Rosenberg is a retired art teacher.]

If the rules for status and age conflict or do not apply, simply start your introduction by naming the person who is more familiar to you. For example, "Mom, I'd like you to meet my friend, Margaret Browne." As another example, you might say, "Leroy, I want to introduce my next-door neighbor LaKeesha."

MEETING **INDIVIDUAL** NEEDS

An Alternative Approach

Some students may be interested in the more formal rules of social etiquette for making introductions. You can have interested students research the matter in etiquette books and then have the students report their research to the class. Suggest that students consult several different sources to compare how various etiquette authorities deal with the matter of introductions.

Roosevelt's would be noticed in conversations with their friends. You can point out that good conversational skills such as listening and responding will be considered in this segment.

Teaching the Lesson

This segment consists of three distinct topics, but you can probably handle the material in two class periods. Teaching the information on conversation will probably take the equivalent of a full period, while the material on introductions and constructive feedback can probably be taught together in one period.

Cultural Diversity

The etiquette of greeting with a handshake differs from culture to culture. For example, the French clasp hands lightly and shake once, and the Germans shake hands with people they see every day. Ask students who are familiar with different cultures to explain to the class how and when people shake hands in the different cultures. Foreign-language teachers and foreign-exchange students may also be able to provide information on this subject.

The second issue in making an introduction is what wording to use. Although there are many acceptable variations, formal situations usually call for formal language, as well as the use of last names and titles.

Formal Wording:
Dr. Klein, I would like to present my friend, Tuan Chin.
Felicia Hernandez, I'd like to introduce Chip Johansen.

Informal Wording:
Paula, have you met Mike?
Bill, this is Sam.
Janelle, Shula.

Responding to an Introduction. The best way to respond to an introduction is to politely acknowledge your pleasure at meeting the other person. The simplest response is "Glad to meet you." However, if the person introducing the two of you has added some details about the other person to the introduction, you can express interest by asking a question that allows you to get a conversation started.

Example: Brian introduces his brother Matt to Angelina: "Angelina, I'd like you to meet my brother Matt. He plays in the school band." Angelina might then say, "Glad to meet you, Matt. What instrument do you play?"

Appropriate behavior during introductions is largely a matter of good manners and good sense. For example, if someone you are introduced to offers to shake your hand, you should do so. However, if shaking hands is inconvenient, it makes sense to ignore the custom and to respond politely in some other way. For example, you might simply smile and nod rather than shake hands in some circumstances. The main idea is to be polite.

Example: You are at a party. You have food in one hand and a beverage in the other. Because both your hands are encumbered, it makes sense to nod and smile in greeting when you are introduced rather than to try to shake hands. However, if the person you are being introduced to really seems to want to shake hands, then you should put everything down in a gracious manner that does not in any way suggest that you find this maneuver inconvenient. Then you should shake hands politely and cheerfully.

Good sense also dictates when you should stand up for an introduction. In general, you should stand up to indicate respect when you are introduced. However, if standing is awkward, as it might be in a bus or in a theater, it makes better sense to ignore this convention.

◆ Real-Life Speaking Situations

PERFORMANCE OBJECTIVES

- To plan and write telephone responses that include directions to a location and outlined techniques to keep a prospective buyer interested
- To act out a situation involving selling a car by telephone
- To prepare and present a dialogue using constructive feedback to resolve a disagreement

REAL LIFE Speaking Situations

1 At one time or another, you will likely own an automobile. If you do come to own one, the day will eventually come when you want to get rid of it. Instead of trading your car in, you may decide to sell it yourself.

You have placed advertisements to sell your car, and you are expecting phone calls from people interested in buying it. When they call, what information will you give them over the phone? If a caller wants to see your car, what directions will you give? When someone arrives, what will you say about your car? How will you describe it? How will you handle discussing its price? How friendly a manner do you feel is appropriate for you to take toward the caller?

Plan your telephone responses, and write directions that interested parties can follow to find the location where they can see your car. Outline the techniques you would use to keep a conversation going with a prospective buyer. Also outline techniques you might use to resolve any disagreements over the price. Be prepared to present the information on your outline as if you were speaking to the buyer. Be ready also to read your directions aloud.

2 Because we are all unique individuals, each of us sees the world differently from anyone else. Most of the time, people find individual differences interesting and even intriguing. In fact, these differences make for life's excitement. Occasionally, however, differing viewpoints can lead to disagreements in any aspect of our lives. Learning to settle disagreements through discussion is vital to both business relationships and personal ones.

You are a college student with a summer job, working part-time in a clothing store. You and another clerk have had a disagreement concerning the sharing of responsibilities in the department—stocking shelves, organizing merchandise, answering the phone, waiting on customers, and taking care of minor paperwork.

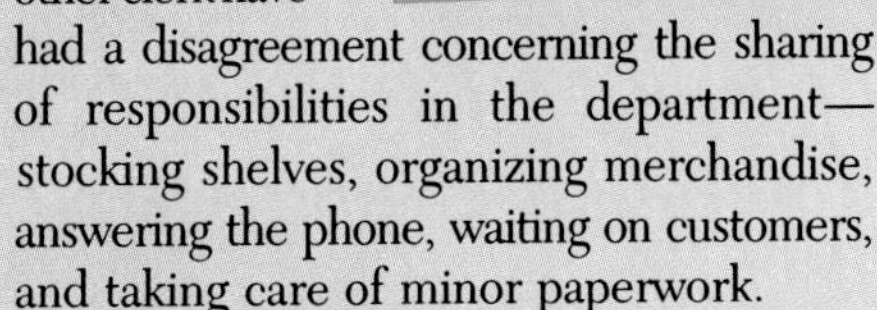

What would you try to do to reach some sort of agreement? Identify your point of view and the point of view of the other clerk. Then think of the strategies you could use to solve the problem. Prepare a short dialogue in which you use constructive feedback to resolve your disagreements, and present your dialogue for your classmates.

ASSESSMENT GUIDELINES

1. Students will need to work in pairs on this activity. The telephone responses should answer the potential buyers' questions clearly, directly, and completely. The directions to the location of the car and the buyers' responses should follow the suggestions for giving and receiving directions on pp. 160–161, and the techniques for keeping a conversation going should include open questions and paraphrasing.
2. The dialogues should sound natural, and they should incorporate the ideas given in the steps on p. 178 for using constructive feedback.

Chapter 8
Interviewing
pp. 186–211

Chapter Overview

This chapter discusses job interviews, school interviews, and informative interviews. The first segment covers preparing for an interview and includes reading the advertisement carefully, preparing a résumé, scheduling an appointment, determining the purpose of the interview, researching for the interview, knowing what to say and what to ask, and rehearsing the interview.

Teacher's Resource Binder

The following materials are identified at their point of use in this chapter:

- Skills for Success
  1 *Preparing to Be Interviewed*
  2 *Being Interviewed*
  3 *Identifying People to Interview*
  4 *Identifying and Preparing Interview Questions*
- Chapter 8 Vocabulary
- Chapter 8 Test/Answer Key

AV Audiovisual Resource Binder

The following materials are identified at their point of use in this chapter:

- Transparency 14
  Job Interviews: Questions and Answers
- Transparency 15
  Selecting Sources to Interview
- Audiotape 1, Lesson 6
  The Interview

The first segment also includes information about being interviewed and helps students to analyze what interviewers are looking for and what kinds of questions they ask. In the second segment students learn to interview others by identifying good sources, by scheduling appointments, by preparing and organizing questions, and by practicing specific interviewing skills. The chapter also explains how to follow up an interview.

Introducing the Chapter

During high school, students will begin taking part in interviews for jobs and schools and in interviews to obtain information. Tell students that this chapter will provide them with specific skills for being interviewed and for interviewing.

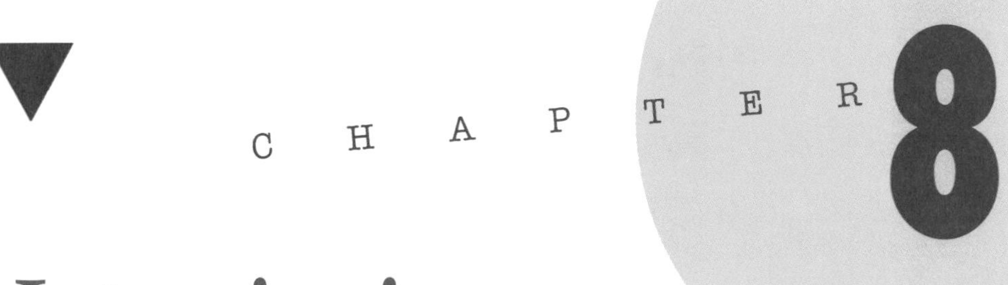

Interviewing

OBJECTIVES

After studying this chapter, you should be able to

1. Prepare to be interviewed for a job or for school admission.
2. Recognize the qualities interviewers look for in an applicant.
3. Anticipate the kinds of questions interviewers will ask.
4. Conduct an informative interview to gather information about a topic.
5. Follow up an interview effectively.

What Is an Interview?

An **interview** is a formal meeting, usually face to face, in which people obtain information by asking questions. The **interviewer** is the person who conducts the interview by asking questions. The **interviewee** is the person who responds to the interviewer's questions. However, an interview is not a one-way form of communication. The interviewee can also ask questions. Three common types of interviews are

- the **job interview,** in which a personnel director or other person responsible for hiring employees reviews an applicant's qualifications for a job
- the **school interview,** in which an admissions officer interviews an applicant for schooling after high school graduation, such as business, technical, and trade schools; community colleges; or colleges and universities
- the **informative interview,** in which the interviewer gathers information about a topic from a knowledgeable, experienced person

In this chapter, you will learn how to be interviewed for a job or for school admission and how to conduct an informative interview.

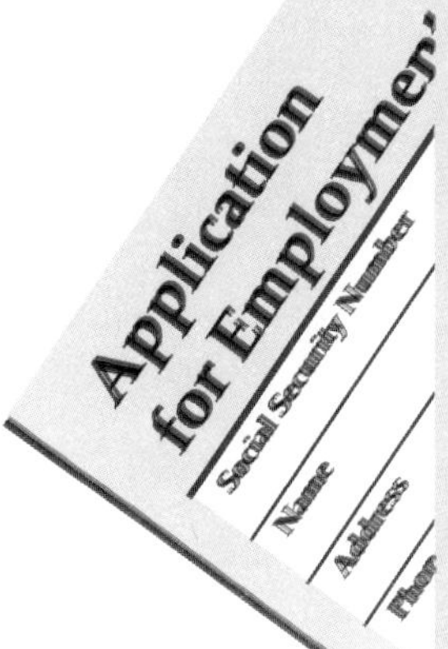

Bibliography of Additional Materials

Professional Readings

- Allen, Jeffrey. ***How to Turn an Interview into a Job.*** New York: Simon & Schuster.
- Stewert, Charles. ***Teaching Interviewing for Career Preparation.*** Annandale, VA: Speech Communication Association.

Audiovisuals

- ***Effective Answers to Interview Questions***—Quiet Advantage, Anaheim, CA (videocassette, 35 min.)
- ***Interviews***—Films for the Humanities and Sciences, Princeton, NJ (two filmstrips with audio, 15 min. each)
- ***The Journalistic Interview***—Nebraska ETV Council for Higher Education, Lincoln, NE (videocassette, 30 min.)
- ***A Professional Talks About Interviewing***—Indiana University Audio-Visual Center, Bloomington, IN (videocassette, 25 min.)
- ***Sell Yourself: Successful Job Interviewing***—The Learning Seed, Lake Zurich, IL (videocassette, 23 min.)

Segment 1 *pp. 188–199*

- **Preparing to Be Interviewed**
- **Being Interviewed**

PERFORMANCE OBJECTIVES

- To identify and make notes about factors affecting a future career or further education
- To report an interview experience
- To write a résumé
- To prepare for, rehearse, and analyze an interview
- To define qualities needed for a specific job

TEACHING NOTE

You may want to post job advertisements from local newspapers on a communication bulletin board for students to use as they study this segment. For example, they could analyze the ads to determine the types of jobs being advertised and the qualifications the applicants must have. In addition, they could use the ads as a basis for finding out more about the advertisers and for composing sample interview questions and answers.

TEACHER'S RESOURCE BINDER

Skills for Success 1
Preparing to Be Interviewed

Preparing to Be Interviewed

Since you can expect to face a number of important interviews, you will want to be well prepared for them. The following suggestions can help you get ready for an interview for a job or for school admission.

Reading the Advertisement Carefully

Often you'll learn about jobs or educational opportunities through advertisements. When reading these advertisements, make sure you understand two things: (1) the type of job or courses being advertised and (2) the qualifications that an applicant must have for the job or courses. Here are two sample advertisements:

RECEPTIONIST
Summer Replacement
Generic Products is looking for a person with a good phone voice to handle our six incoming phone lines. Person must be a good typist. We will train on CRT. Application forms will be provided on Wed. and Fri. at 2693 Spring Ave. Write for interview.

The two qualifications for this job as a receptionist are a good telephone voice and good typing skills. If you met these qualifications, you could fill out an application and write a business letter requesting an interview.

SUMMER BUSINESS PROGRAM
Southern Ohio College is offering the following courses:
Summer Session I: Intro to Business 101, Accounting 101, Finance 111
Summer Session II: Intro to Business 102, Accounting 102, Finance 112
For more information on admissions and registration, call 555-1234.

By reading this ad, you could tell whether Southern Ohio College was offering a course you wanted. By calling the number provided, you could also learn how to apply for admission as well as how to register.

- To plan and conduct a job interview
- To evaluate an interview

Motivation

Tell students to imagine that they have applied for the ideal jobs and have just received calls requesting that they appear for interviews tomorrow. How do the students feel about the upcoming interviews? How would they prepare? Ask volunteers to share the steps they would follow to get ready.

Preparing a Résumé

A **résumé** is a brief account of an applicant's educational background and employment experience. Some employers want to receive a cover letter and a résumé before they will ask you to interview. Even if you have sent a résumé ahead, bring a copy to the interview. The résumé will provide a quick overview of data about you and will remind the interviewer of your qualifications after the interview is over.

A résumé is seldom more than one page long. It should include the following information:

- your name, address, and telephone number
- your education, including honors, awards, or special courses
- your previous work experience

Résumé

Name: Angela Thompson
Address: 1632 Morgan Drive
Cincinnati, Ohio 45211
Telephone: (513) 555-5971

Work Experience:
Clerk, Danson's Department Store, Cincinnati (part-time), 1991–1992.
Newspaper carrier, Cincinnati Post, 1988–1990.

Education:
Junior, Central High School

School Experience and Activities:
Played the lead in spring production of My Fair Lady, 1992.
Reporter, Central High News, 1990.

Interests:
Theater, drill team, basketball, creative writing.

References:
Mrs. Judith Miller, Director, School Plays, Central High School, Cincinnati, Ohio 45219.
Mr. Paul Shuman, Manager, Danson's Department Store, 4962 Glenway, Cincinnati, Ohio 45238.
Ms. Donna Groves, Homeroom Teacher, Central High School, Cincinnati, Ohio 45219.

Additional Activity

You may want to invite your principal to spend fifteen to twenty minutes in your classroom playing the role of interviewer as you play the role of a recent college graduate applying for a teaching position. Let the principal know the purpose of the activity and that you will be asking questions about the position as an actual candidate would. To add authenticity to the performance, perhaps a student could play the role of receptionist. He or she could greet you as you enter, allow you to introduce yourself and tell your purpose, and then introduce you to the principal.

TEACHING THE LESSON

You may want to introduce the section on interview preparation by having students scan the boldfaced heads on pp. 188–194. The heads represent the steps in preparing to be interviewed. As guided practice for **Activity 1**, you may want to describe an interviewing experience that you have had. Then assign **Activity 1** for independent practice.

Because **Activity 2** on p. 194 could prove especially helpful to students, you may want to spend time preparing them for it. You could provide all students with the same advertisement and help them to write résumés geared to that advertisement. Discuss appropriate qualifications and questions for the interviewer. Then assign **Activity 2** for independent practice. Students should be able to locate personally appealing advertisements and to adapt their résumés accordingly.

Students with Special Needs

Before students complete the **Communication Journal** assignment, you may want to help students with learning disabilities to recognize their personal strengths. Discuss job aspirations with each student and provide a variety of job descriptions related to each student's interests. Then help students to identify the specific qualities and skills they possess that would facilitate success at these jobs.

Activity 1

Students' reports of interview experiences should specify the purpose of the interview, identify the interviewer and his or her position, and describe the outcome of the interview.

In your communication journal, make notes about your qualifications, interests, and goals for a job, a career, or further education. As new ideas occur to you, add them to your notes. What do your notes show you about the kind of job or schooling you would enjoy?

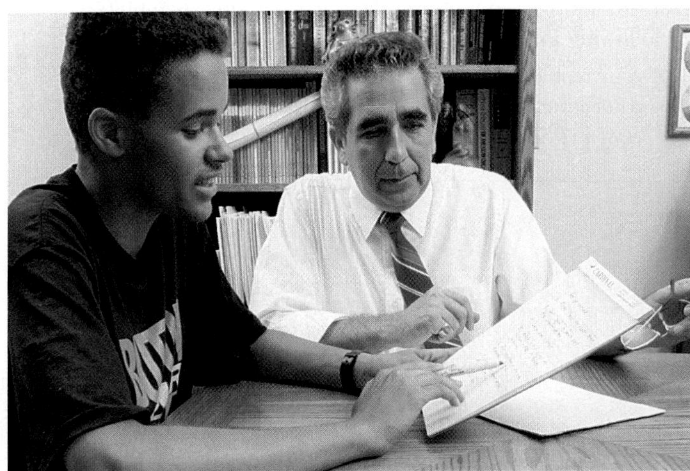

When preparing a résumé, you may want to get advice from a school counselor, job counselor, or other adult.

Scheduling an Appointment

Usually the business's personnel director or the school's admissions officer will schedule your interview for a specific time. However, if you are asking for an interview, you should set up a time with the interviewer or with his or her assistant. Volunteering to just "show up any time" suggests a lack of understanding of business etiquette. To appear professional, always make an appointment.

Reporting an Interview Experience

Have you ever been interviewed for a job or for admission to a school? If so, tell your class about your experience and specify the purpose of the interview. Identify the interviewer, and describe the outcome of the interview. If you have not been interviewed, talk with someone who has and report that person's experience.

You will probably want to set aside class time for students to work together on **Activity 3** on p. 194. Circulate throughout the classroom to offer assistance as needed.

After students have read the information in **Being Interviewed,** starting on p. 195, encourage them to share any personal experiences with interviewing that might benefit their classmates.

You may want to work with the class to write an advertisement, identify applicants' desirable qualities, and prepare appropriate interview questions before you assign **Activity 4** on p. 196 and **Activity 5** on p. 199 as independent practice.

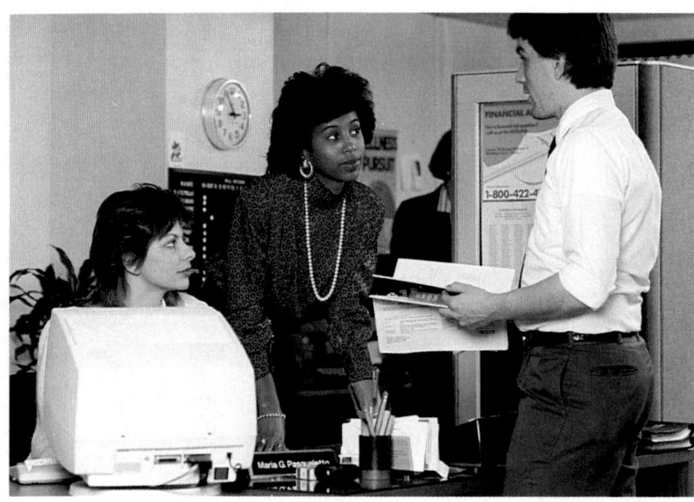

Determining the Purpose of the Interview

Whether you are being interviewed for a job or for school admission, the interviewer may have several purposes.

Primary, or main, purposes:

- to make sure that you are qualified for the job or school
- to decide if you are the kind of person the company hires or the school admits

Secondary, or additional, purposes:

- to do a preliminary screening interview to determine whether you may proceed in the interview process
- to gather additional information about you

Try to learn the purpose of the interview beforehand so that you can prepare for it.

Finding Out Information for the Interview

The more you know about the company, the school, or the interviewer, the better you can anticipate and answer questions as well as pose your own. Interviewers will see your knowledge as a sign of interest, initiative, and responsibility; consequently, they will be more likely to feel that talking with you is worth their time. Good sources of useful information include brochures, catalogs, and newspaper and magazine articles. Information may also be available in your school library or career counseling office.

Cooperative Learning

You may want to give students some experience in finding information for an interview. Allow students to work in groups of three, and give each group a list of five local businesses. Tell students to imagine that they have upcoming interviews with employers from the businesses on their lists; therefore, they need to gather some information about the businesses.

Students will probably need several days to complete their research. You may want to have each group report their methods and findings to the class.

Assessment

You can assess students' understanding of writing résumés by checking **Activity 2.** By observing the interviews and considering classmates' suggestions in **Activity 5,** you can assess students' understanding of the roles of the interviewer and the interviewee.

Reteaching

Through observation of the interview rehearsals, you may discover that some students appear overly anxious and nervous when being interviewed. You may want to refer these students to the section in **Chapter 13: "Presenting Your Speech"** on pp. 321–323 that deals with stage fright. Although the section refers to overcoming stage fright when giving a speech, many of the

Writing to Learn

You may want to put special emphasis on the importance of writing specific qualifications for any jobs students apply for. They can label the list "Why I Am Qualified to Be ____ ." They may want to organize their lists into categories such as similar work experience, personal qualities, and ambitions and goals. Suggest that as students gain more work and interview experience, they may want to update their lists and revise their résumés for the specific positions they seek.

Knowing What You Want to Say

What do you want the interviewer to remember about you? Make sure that you are prepared to provide sufficient information about your qualifications, goals, and interests. General information is information you would use for any interview. Specific information is information that applies only to the particular job or school. You will need both kinds.

- **Qualifications:**
  What makes you a good candidate for this job or school? Generally, you might state that you have good communication skills. But specifically you could note that you type sixty words per minute.
- **Goals:**
  What do you hope to achieve with this job or at this school? Your general goal might be to find a challenging, rewarding career. Your specific goal might be to become a programmer for a computer software company, to design interactive computer games, or to earn a degree in computer science.
- **Interests:**
  How do you spend your spare time? You might say that you generally enjoy several hobbies, but you could specifically mention belonging to your school computer club. Be sure to put special emphasis on those interests that relate to the job or school.

same techniques apply to being interviewed. You could set up individual practice sessions in which you or trusted partners interview students who need help. Encourage positive feedback from the interviewers.

See p. 197 for **EXTENSION, ENRICHMENT,** and **CLOSURE.**

Knowing What You Want to Ask

A job or school interview is not a one-way form of communication. Although its main focus is on finding out about you, you may also want to ask questions. In order to make good decisions about the job or school, you should feel knowledgeable about the situation. More information may help you decide whether to take the job if it is offered or to attend the school if you are accepted.

Strictly Classified reprinted by permission: Tribune Media Services.

One technique you can use to be sure you obtain the information you need is to prepare a list of questions ahead of time. If your questions are not answered during the interview, request a few moments to ask questions. The following questions are some of the ones you may want to ask.

Job

What will be my specific duties?
Who will be my supervisor?
If I have questions, whom should I ask?
What kinds of clothes are required? If uniforms are required, who pays for them?
Is there a union?
Will I be expected [*or* will I have the opportunity] to work overtime?
Is there any on-the-job training?

School

How long is the course of study?
How many credits am I expected to handle [*or* am I allowed to take] each term?
What is the balance between required courses and electives?
Are there any work-study programs?
Besides books, tuition, and fees, what other expenses can I expect?
How can I apply for financial aid and for scholarships?
Are there any job placement services?

MAKING CONNECTIONS

Community Involvement

You could invite the personnel director from the school district or from a local company to describe to the class the traits employers look for in job candidates. Ask the speaker to include remarks on the communication skills that pertain to interviewing. Encourage students to ask questions.

Ongoing Assessment

Activity 2

Responses should be appropriate to the ads students have chosen. Students should be honest and should not exaggerate their qualifications. Their questions should be relevant and should cover important details regarding the selected jobs.

Making Connections

Community Involvement

Invite someone from an employment agency or an executive search firm to talk to the class about how they help clients rehearse for interviews. Encourage the guest to engage student volunteers in actual interview situations.

Ongoing Assessment

Activity 3

You may want to have students write brief reviews of their interview experiences. Ask them to include their own assessments as well as the comments of their interviewers.

ACTIVITY 2 Writing a Résumé and Preparing for an Interview

In the classified section of your newspaper, find an advertisement for a job that appeals to you and for which you feel you are qualified. Using the format shown in the example on page 189, write a résumé that you could use if you were applying for this job. Then list both your qualifications and any questions you would ask.

Rehearsing the Interview

Even though you cannot anticipate every question you may be asked in an interview, rehearsing answers to possible questions and devising follow-up questions will still be helpful. You may want to plan two or three practice sessions before you go. Rehearsing the interview will help you appear to have **poise,** the quality of looking confident and prepared to handle any problem.

ACTIVITY 3 Rehearsing the Interview

Ask a classmate, a parent, or a trusted adult to play the role of interviewer and to ask you questions about the résumé you have developed in Activity 2, above. Try to answer the questions in the same manner that you would answer them in an actual interview. Then review your answers with your partner. Were your answers clear and concise? Which answers do you feel you handled best? Does your interviewer agree that these were your best responses?

Being Interviewed

After you prepare for being interviewed, you are ready to consider the qualities interviewers look for in applicants and the kinds of questions they may ask.

What Do Interviewers Look For?

The interviewer wants to know about your knowledge, your interests, and your attitudes. In addition, he or she will be looking for qualities that indicate you are a candidate to consider seriously.

What Interviewers Look For	
Promptness	• Arrive on time. • Give yourself more time than you need to get there. • If you know you'll be late, call ahead to tell the interviewer. • If you know you will not be there at all, call ahead to reschedule the interview.
Appearance	• Dress appropriately. • Groom yourself well. • Do not chew gum.
Poise	• Maintain an assured, confident manner throughout the interview. • Be prepared. The more prepared you are, the more poised you are likely to be. • To deal with nervousness, focus on the questions one at a time, and on your answers to them.
Flexibility	• Give answers that reflect your ability to adapt to new situations. • Give at least one specific example to support your answers.
Honesty	• Be honest. • Avoid the temptation to exaggerate. • If you don't know the answer to a question, say so.
Initiative	• Give answers that show you are willing to take on new tasks and enterprises.
Communication Skills	• Develop good written and oral communication skills. • Give answers that reflect your ability to take directions from supervisors; to communicate with fellow employees, teachers, and other students; and to express your thoughts effectively in writing.

Making Connections

Technology

After students have rehearsed, you may want to videotape their interviews. Play the tapes back and have students identify one area per interview that needs improvement. Explain to students that focusing on improving just one aspect is more beneficial than trying to identify everything they would like to improve.

Building a Portfolio

If students keep videotapes in their portfolios, encourage students to include videotaped interviews. As the year progresses and students become more comfortable speaking in front of groups, you will probably want to videotape interviews again. Encourage students to compare their performances.

Using the Chart

You may want to tell students that the **What Interviewers Look For** chart is an important reference tool when preparing for any interview. You could have students copy the chart in their communication journals so that they can refer to it in future years.

Ongoing Assessment

Activity 4

Students should address each of the characteristics listed in the chart on p. 195 and should explain why each characteristic is or is not important for the jobs they are advertising.

Cooperative Learning

You may want to give students some practice in considering questions that interviewers ask. Have students work in groups of four or five, and give each group a classified ad for a job that calls for a teenager in your area. Have the group brainstorm examples of all four types of questions interviewers might ask. A student recorder should write down the questions. You may want to have each group present its ad and questions to the class.

Audiovisual Resource Binder

Transparency 14
Job Interviews: Questions and Answers

ACTIVITY 4

Playing the Role of a Job Interviewer

Imagine that you are hiring someone for a job. First, write the advertisement detailing the job responsibilities and requirements. (You can get ideas by reviewing the ads in your local newspaper.) Then, discuss with your class the qualities mentioned on page 195 that you would consider the most important in a person applying for this job. Also explain your reasons for choosing these qualities. Finally, discuss with your classmates the similarities and differences in your ideas.

What Do Interviewers Ask?

Interviewers obtain information by asking questions. No two interviewers will ask exactly the same questions, but you can anticipate four types of questions that they usually will ask:

- questions that request information
- questions that probe deeper
- questions that check understanding
- questions that require you to take a stand

Questions That Request Information. Questions that request information consider your current status, background, interests, and goals for the future.

1. **Current status:** Questions about your current status seek to discover where you stand at the moment in school or at work.

   EXAMPLES: What grade are you in now?
   What kind of program are you taking in school?
   What are your duties on your current job?

2. **Background:** Questions about your background seek to learn about your work and school experience, places you have lived, and things you have done.

   EXAMPLES: What experiences have you had that prepare you for this job?
   What courses have you taken that prepare you for this program?
   What are you particularly good at?

3. **Interests:** Questions about your interests seek to gain insight into the kind of person you are.

   EXAMPLES: What do you do in your spare time?
   What are your hobbies?
   If you could travel anywhere in the world, what places would you like to visit?

EXTENSION

Ask students to imagine the following interview situations:

1. A high school student has an interview with the manager of a public-access radio station for a job as a disc jockey.
2. A new aerospace manufacturing plant is moving into the area. A high school student has an interview with the personnel director.
3. A high school student wants to work in the city youth camp program for the summer and has an interview with the park director.

Have students discuss effective preparation and appropriate conduct for each of these interview situations.

ADDITIONAL ACTIVITY

You may want to invite three or four college freshmen who are home on a holiday to speak to your class about their perspectives on interviewing for college admissions. Encourage the college students to be specific about questions they were asked. Let the guidance counselors know of your plans, and recruit their support. Be sure to follow up every guest presentation with class discussion combined with focused journal writing. These two activities give students a chance to participate in giving feedback.

4. **Goals:** Questions about your goals seek to discover your hopes and plans for the future.

    EXAMPLES: If you are hired, how long would you expect to work here?
    In five years, what position would you like to hold?
    After you graduate from high school, what do you see yourself doing?

Questions That Probe Deeper. Interviewers ask questions that probe deeper to find out more about your answers to other questions. These questions are meant to challenge statements you have made and to find reasons for your actions.

EXAMPLES: You say you quit your newspaper delivery job after three weeks. Why?
You say math is your favorite subject. What in particular do you like about math?
Why do you think that you would be able to handle dictation if you have not had a course in shorthand?

Questions That Check Understanding. Interviewers ask questions to check their understanding of what you have said.

EXAMPLES: Though you took typing, you are not sure that you understand letter-format rules?
Did you say that your grades in English accurately reflect your communication skills?
What I hear you saying is that you would not be able to work on weekends. Is that correct?

ENRICHMENT

You may want to have students write cover letters (letters of application) to accompany the résumés that they wrote for **Activity 2** on p. 194. Explain that a letter of application is a sales letter that tells what the applicant can do and that refers to the enclosed résumé. The letter serves additional purposes: It names the specific person who should read the letter, states the exact job, states the applicant's reasons for applying, conveys the applicant's interest in the company, and requests an interview. (If the name of the person who should read the letter is not listed in the advertisement, suggest ways for students to find it: by telephoning the company to ask for the name of its personnel manager or human-resources director, by checking a business directory in the public library, or by contacting an acquaintance in the company.)

COMMON ERROR

Problem. Because of overpreparation or because of failure to listen carefully, some people do not answer exactly the questions asked in interviews.

Solution. You may want to set up sessions in which students can practice specific interview situations. First, have students write out questions they anticipate being asked in the interviews and answers they would give to the questions. Then have each student give his or her list of questions to a partner who will play the part of the interviewer. However, the partner should deviate from the written questions so that the interviewee's prepared answers will not be completely correct. Such practice should help students to listen carefully to the questions presented.

Questions That Require You to Take a Stand. Interviewers ask questions that require you to take a stand to see how you respond under pressure.

EXAMPLES: Why do you want to work for this company?
Why do you want to attend this school?
What kind of pay do you expect?

[Note: The Equal Employment Opportunity Commission, the EEOC, has written guidelines for the kinds of questions that may or may not be asked. In general, questions about marital status, family, race, physical characteristics, age, and other personal information are not allowed unless they directly bear on an applicant's ability to do the job.]

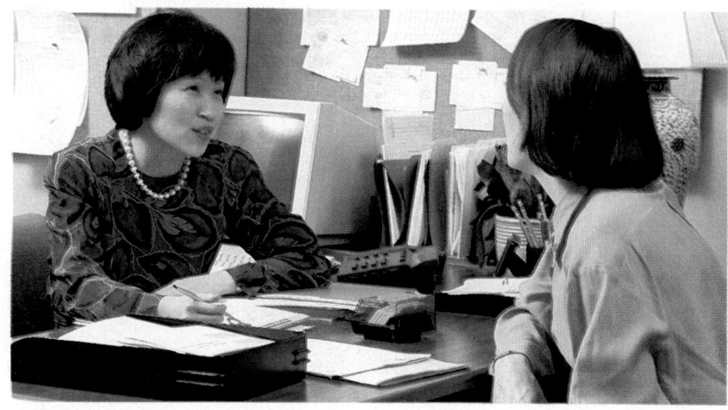

HOW TO *Answer an Interviewer's Questions*

1. **Answer the question the interviewer actually asked.** Listen carefully to be sure you understand the question. Then answer the question the interviewer actually asked, not the one you wish the interviewer had asked. Feel free to use questions that check understanding to clear up any misperceptions.
2. **Answer questions as fully and as honestly as you can.** Don't be afraid to take a few moments to frame, or shape, your responses. Avoid answering simply "yes" or "no" or giving only one- or two-word responses, but keep to the point. Don't go into long-winded explanations. Also, keep in mind the EEOC guidelines mentioned above. You don't have to answer personal questions unless they concern your qualifications for the job.
3. **Frame your answers to present yourself in the best possible light.** Emphasize the reasons that make you a good candidate for the job or the school.

TEACHER'S RESOURCE BINDER

Skills for Success 2
Being Interviewed

AV ➤ *Audiovisual Resource Binder*

Audiotape 1, Lesson 6
The Interview

Tell students to limit their letters to one page each and to follow the conventions for a business letter. You will probably want to have sample letters of application for students to study.

Closure

Ask the class to identify the steps involved in preparing for a job or a college interview. Then ask several students to name the most helpful things they learned about being interviewed.

Activity 5

Planning and Conducting a Job Interview

Look again at the job advertisement you wrote in Activity 4 on page 196. Write at least five questions you would ask an applicant for that job. Then, working with a partner, use your questions to conduct an interview, with one of you as the interviewer and the other as the interviewee. Present the interview to the class. Finally, ask your classmates to assess the strengths and weaknesses of the interview and to suggest how the questions and the responses could be improved.

"I'd just like to say, sir, that I always make a bad first impression."

Guidelines for Being Interviewed

- Do I have a résumé to give the interviewer?
- Have I identified my qualifications, goals, and interests?
- Have I allowed enough time to get to the interview?
- Have I dressed appropriately for the interview?
- Am I prepared to ask and answer questions clearly, honestly, and carefully?
- Do I have questions to ask the interviewer?
- Am I relaxed, enthusiastic, and confident?
- Do I speak clearly?

Timesaver

You may want to have students use a rating scale such as the one below to evaluate the strengths and weaknesses of the interviews in **Activity 5.**

Rating Scale	
Interviewer:	
Asked appropriate questions	1 2 3 4 5
Covered various types of questions	1 2 3 4 5
Exhibited poise	1 2 3 4 5
Spoke clearly	1 2 3 4 5
Comments:	
Interviewee:	
Answered questions precisely	1 2 3 4 5
Asked appropriate questions	1 2 3 4 5
Exhibited poise	1 2 3 4 5
Spoke clearly	1 2 3 4 5
Comments:	

Ongoing Assessment

Activity 5

You will probably want to consider the classmates' comments about the interviews as well as students' performances. A rating scale such as the one suggested above could help with your assessment.

Segment 2 *pp. 200–205*
- **Interviewing Others**
- **Following Up an Interview**

Performance Objectives
- To brainstorm a list of speech topics
- To identify and limit a speech topic
- To select appropriate interviewees
- To write and organize interview questions
- To conduct and evaluate an informative interview
- To write a follow-up letter to an interviewer

MEETING INDIVIDUAL NEEDS

Linguistically Diverse Students

The text suggests that interviewing an expert is a good way to gather information. This strategy is particularly useful for nonnative speakers of English because the interviewing process offers practice in all four basic skills: speaking, listening, writing, and reading (their own notes and questions). Strongly suggest that students use the interviewing process as often as possible when researching information for their speeches. Encourage them to take written notes rather than to record the interviews on tapes.

Teacher's Resource Binder

Skills for Success 3
Identifying People to Interview

Audiovisual Resource Binder

Transparency 15
Selecting Sources to Interview

Interviewing Others

You can conduct an informative interview with a knowledgeable person to gather information about a topic for an informative speech (see Chapter 14) or a persuasive speech (see Chapter 15). For example, for a speech about placing a local bird on the endangered species list, you could interview a biologist. Identifying the person you want to interview and planning what questions you want to ask will help you prepare for an interview.

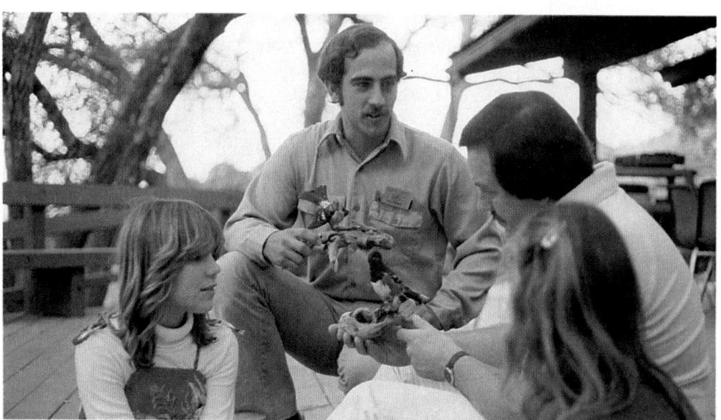

Brainstorm a list of possible topics for a speech and jot them down in your communication journal. Then, for each topic, try to think of a person whom you could interview to gather information. Write the names or job titles beside the topic.

Identifying Likely Sources

For any topic, you can probably find several people who can provide good information. Start by listing three or four likely sources. You want someone who can be a **reliable source**—someone who can be depended upon to give accurate information about the subject. A **primary source** is someone who provides information from direct experience. A **secondary source** is someone who provides information that originated with other people.

MOTIVATION

Discuss various interview situations on television. Examples are late-night celebrity talk shows and interviews in news programs. Include questions such as these in your discussion: What are the purposes of the various types of interviews? How do interviews to entertain differ from interviews to get information? Who are some interviewers who are effective in getting information? What types of questioning strategies do these interviewers use? Point out that in this segment students will learn to conduct effective informative interviews.

HOW TO *Select Sources to Interview*

1. **Is the person knowledgeable about the information you want?** For example, a buyer for a local department store would be a knowledgeable source for a report about the latest fashions.
2. **Is the person a primary source or a secondary source?** Can this source give you information from direct experiences, or does the source obtain information from other people? For example, if a chef tells you how he prepares his famous soufflé, he is a primary source; however, if he tells you how another chef says she prepares the soufflé, he is a secondary source.
3. **Is the person a reliable source?** Can you trust your source to give you dependable, accurate information? For example, a dietician would give accurate information about safe ways to lose weight. You should carefully consider three aspects of reliability:
   - Age: An older person is likely to have had more experience than someone younger and is therefore often perceived as being a more reliable source. However, a younger person may have more recent information that may be more reliable than an older person's experience.
   - Memory: As a rule, the longer ago an event took place, the less reliable a person's remembrance of details about the event will be.
   - Bias: Even the most reliable source will usually have a point of view that may affect the accuracy of information.

Making an Appointment

Call or write the person you want to interview. Explain why you would like an interview with him or her and what you hope to gain from the interview. Try to arrange an in-person interview. If the person lives far away or if the person's schedule does not permit a face-to-face visit, you may have to conduct the interview by telephone. In either case, set up a specific time and place for the interview. Tell the person how to contact you in case he or she needs to reschedule.

Preparing a List of Questions

Gather background information about your topic and about the person you are interviewing. Then use this knowledge to prepare intelligent questions. The types of questions you will ask will depend on the information you want.

TEACHING NOTE

The textbook emphasizes identifying the best person to use as a reliable source of information for an interview. As an alternative, you might suggest that if a student knows of a particularly interesting person or someone with a fascinating job, the student might first choose the person for the interview and then develop an appropriate topic. The remaining procedures, such as preparing questions, would not change.

TEACHER'S RESOURCE BINDER

Skills for Success 4
Identifying and Preparing Interview Questions

TEACHING THE LESSON

Invite students to read the first part of the segment to learn the stages of preparing for an informative interview. As you lead students through the section on selecting a source to interview, you might model the selection process by using names of familiar people from your school or your community who could be approached about specific topics.

As you lead students through the section on preparing and organizing questions, you might wish to model the process by using the topic and interviewee already selected. Pay particular attention to the distinction between neutral questions and leading questions.

If you have followed the steps above, you have already modeled most of the skills practiced in **Activity 6,** so you may want to assign it as

CRITICAL THINKING

Analysis

You may want to bring to class question-and-answer interviews from magazines and have students identify the types of interview questions that were used: open, closed, neutral, leading, and follow-up. Have students analyze answers to identify particularly effective questions.

ONGOING ASSESSMENT

Activity 6

Students' sources and questions should be appropriate for eliciting information about the chosen topics.

Types of Interview Questions

Type of Question	Description	Example
Open Questions	encourage a person to talk at length, to share feelings and impressions	"How did you first become interested in medicine?"
Closed Questions	can be answered with "yes" or "no" or a few words; used to obtain specific information quickly	"Where did you do your internship?"
Neutral Questions	promote objectivity by giving the interviewee no hint of what particular answer you want	"How do you respond when a patient refuses to follow orders?"
Leading Questions	suggest the answer you expect or desire	"Doesn't it upset you when a patient refuses to follow orders?"
Follow-up Questions	probe for additional information about a previous question	"What was it about being in medicine that interested you?"

Organizing Your List of Questions

You can arrange your questions so that your interview will have a beginning, a middle, and an end.

- Beginning: Try to relieve any tension the interviewee may have by asking easy-to-answer questions.
- Middle: Include questions that aim for specific information and that may take more time for the interviewee to answer.
- End: Conclude by thanking the interviewee for taking time to answer your questions. Give him or her a chance to make additional comments. A good final question is "Is there anything else you think I should know about this topic?"

Gathering Information from Others

You are going to give a speech on the popularity of a sport, a television show, or a place to eat. Choose and limit your topic, and then list three people who would be good sources of information about it. Which person would you choose to interview? Why? Next, write six questions to ask this person, and organize them into the most effective order.

homework. Students will use the results of this as a basis for **Activity 7**, an in-class activity.

Emphasize the importance of following up an interview. You may want to model the content for several follow-up letters before assigning **Activity 8** on p. 205.

Assessment

You could use **Activities 6** and **7** to assess students' abilities to formulate interview questions and to conduct interviews. You could assess students' understanding of writing follow-up letters by checking **Activity 8.**

Conducting an Interview

1. **Come prepared to record the interview.** To prevent distortion of facts, keep a careful record of the interview. If you plan to take notes, leave enough space between the questions you prepared so that you can write down brief answers. If you plan to tape-record the interview, first ask the interviewee's permission. Also be sure that your tape recorder is working well.
2. **Be courteous.** Show patience, encouragement, and respect as the interviewee answers your questions.
3. **Listen carefully.** At various points in the interview, paraphrase out loud any answers that seem unclear to you. **Paraphrasing** means stating in your own words the idea or feeling you get from another person's words.
4. **Monitor your nonverbal communication.** Make sure that your nonverbal reactions—your facial expressions and your gestures—reflect the tone you want to convey. Keep good eye contact, nod to show understanding, and smile occasionally to maintain the friendliness of the interview.

ACTIVITY 7

Conducting an Informative Interview

Working with a partner, conduct the informative interview you developed in Activity 6 on page 202. Present your interview in front of the class. After you finish, discuss with your classmates how effective your questions were and how you might have conducted the interview better.

Cooperative Learning

You may want to arrange in-class interview opportunities for students. First, divide the class into groups of five. You could query students about people in the community that they would like to interview, or you could assign an individual to each group. Contact the individuals (or have the students do so) and schedule interview times. Each group should locate information about its assigned individual, prepare interview questions, and choose one group member to act as the interviewer.

After the interview, each group should prepare an evaluation of its performance. In addition, you will probably want the groups to send thank-you notes to their interviewees.

Ongoing Assessment

Activity 7

Following the class discussions, you may want to have students do self-evaluations of their interview performances.

RETEACHING

You may want to videotape several effective informative interviews from television. Play the interviews for students and stop to evaluate each one. Point out any techniques students could adapt to their own interview situations.

ENRICHMENT

Ask each student to choose a historical character whose identity the student will assume in an interview situation. Then pair students to plan their interviews. Each pair will participate in two interviews, as each student will play the roles of interviewer and interviewee. Each pair should decide on a particular incident or period in each historical character's life on which to focus the

INTEGRATING THE LANGUAGE ARTS

Library Link

Have students look in the school library or in the public library to find books on applying for work. Ask students to find examples of follow-up letters and to read their examples to the class. Point out similarities and differences, and assess the level of formality in each letter.

Following Up an Interview

After an interview, you should write a short letter to the person who interviewed you or whom you interviewed. This is a courtesy letter to thank the interviewer or the interviewee for taking the time to talk with you.

In a letter to an interviewer, indicate that you look forward to hearing from the company or school as soon as possible. If you interviewed someone, offer to send the interviewee a copy of your article or report as well.

1632 Morgan Dr.
Cincinnati, OH 45211
June 4, 1995

Mr. Richard Parker
Director, Marketing Division
Generic Products
2847 Spring Ave.
Cincinnati, OH 45227

Dear Mr. Parker:

Thank you for taking the time to talk with me about the opening for a clerical position in the Marketing Divison of Generic Products. I look forward to hearing from you about my application.

Sincerely yours,

Angela Thompson

Angela Thompson

interview. To prepare for the interviews, each student will need to research not only the character they will portray but also the character they will interview.

Encourage students to rehearse their interviews and to include props and costumes before presenting the interviews to the rest of the class.

CLOSURE

Ask volunteers to identify helpful tips concerning interviewing others. List the most popular ones on the chalkboard.

ACTIVITY 8

Writing a Follow-up Letter

For Activity 2 on page 194, you selected a job advertisement in the newspaper. Suppose that you have already gone on an interview for the advertised job. Write a follow-up letter to the interviewer. What impression of yourself would you want the interviewer to get from your letter? How would you write your letter in order to give this impression?

ONGOING ASSESSMENT

Activity 8

Before students write their letters, you may want to have them write brief notes about the kinds of impressions they want to make on the interviewers. Then you can evaluate their letters in terms of students' effectiveness at conveying the intended impressions.

GUIDELINES

for Interviewing Others

- Do I have a knowledgeable and reliable person to interview for information about my topic?
- Do I have an appointment scheduled at a time that is convenient for the interviewee?
- Do I have an organized list of questions?
- Do I have permission to tape-record the interviewee's responses?
- Do I appear courteous and attentive and listen carefully to the interviewee's answers?
- Do I send appropriate nonverbal messages to the person I am interviewing?

◆ Profiles in Communication

Performance Objectives

- To prepare for an informal interview
- To write a dialogue involving a disagreement

Teaching the Feature

Before students read the information about Amy Baragar, you may want to ask them if they have ever been in the position of calming another person in a stressful situation. If so, what techniques did they use? Then have students read the profile to determine the techniques that an employment supervisor for a large corporation uses. After students have read the profile, you may want to ask them to evaluate Ms. Baragar's methods: Would your students do anything differently than Ms. Baragar does?

Activity Note

Assessment should focus on the effectiveness of each student's participation in the dialogue. Is the student honest, pleasant, and tactful? Is the student likely to make a good impression?

PROFILES IN COMMUNICATION

Amy A. Baragar

Most interviewers try to help job seekers and college applicants feel at ease. Amy Baragar, employment supervisor for a large corporation, says, "Being interviewed is stressful for the applicant, so I usually begin by chatting about a casual topic." After the applicant feels comfortable, Ms. Baragar explains how the interview will proceed: First, she'll ask about the person's education, work history, and goals. Next, she'll describe the position to be filled. Last, she'll explain any tests that the applicant might be asked to take. The entire interview may take from twenty minutes for a clerical position to an hour for an executive position.

What's the best way to create a good impression? "Before your interview, do some serious preparing," advises Ms. Baragar. "Of course, you'll list the main points you want to get across. But also practice making these points out loud, so that your words will flow smoothly and you'll project confidence."

Ms. Baragar, too, prepares thoroughly for each interview, because it's just as important for the employer to hire well as it is for the applicant to get the job. She considers the specific requirements of the position to be filled and develops questions designed to bring out those qualities in the applicant. What is the most important requirement for her own job? "I have to be a very good listener!"

ACTIVITY

Many social situations have similarities to a formal interview. Suppose your best friend has asked you to spend a week at his grandparents' farm. First, you are invited to meet the grandparents over dinner at a nice restaurant. Naturally, you want to make a good impression. How would you prepare for the meeting? Then consider how you would present yourself in a conversation in which your friend's grandfather makes a statement you disagree with. Write a dialogue of the discussion.

CHAPTER 8

S☆U☆M☆M☆A☆R☆Y

INTERVIEWING is a form of communication in which people obtain information by asking questions or by answering questions. A person who is conducting an interview is the interviewer; the person being interviewed is the interviewee.

- **Prepare to be interviewed** for a job or for school admission by determining the requirements for the job or the school, preparing a résumé, and scheduling an appointment with the interviewer. You should also determine the purpose of the interview and find information about the company, the school, or the interviewer. Think about what you want to say and what you want to ask the interviewer. Then rehearse the questions and answers so that you will be less nervous during the actual interview.
- **Understand qualities** interviewers look for: promptness, appearance, poise, flexibility, honesty, initiative, and communication skills. Also anticipate the kinds of questions the interviewer will probably ask.
- **Prepare to conduct an interview** by determining a knowledgeable and reliable source to interview, making an appointment, and preparing and organizing a list of varied types of questions. Record the interviewee's responses in written notes or in a tape-recording. Be courteous and listen carefully. Also be sure to use nonverbal language that maintains an appropriate tone for the interview.
- **Follow up an interview** with a thank-you letter.

Vocabulary

Look back through this chapter and find the meaning of each of the following terms. Write each term and its meaning in your communication journal.

closed question, *p. 202*
follow-up question, *p. 202*
informative interview, *p. 187*
interview, *p. 187*
interviewee, *p. 187*
interviewer, *p. 187*
job interview, *p. 187*
leading question, *p. 202*
neutral question, *p. 202*
open question, *p. 202*
paraphrasing, *p. 203*
poise, *p. 194*
primary source, *p. 200*
reliable source, *p. 200*
résumé, *p. 189*
school interview, *p. 187*
secondary source, *p. 200*

TEACHER'S RESOURCE BINDER

- Chapter 8 Vocabulary

Review Questions

Answers

1. Questioners from an audience usually are chosen randomly and ask only one question each. Interviewers ask a series of planned questions.
2. Read the ad carefully, schedule an appointment, determine the purpose of the interview, gather information for the interview, plan what you want to say and ask, and prepare a résumé.
3. your name, address, telephone number, work experience, education, personal interests, and references
4. General information could be used for any interview; specific information applies only to a particular job or school.
5. It will help you appear to have poise.
6. promptness, appearance, poise, flexibility, honesty, initiative, and communication skills

Discussion Questions

Guidelines for Assessment

Student responses may vary.

1. Your attire for the interview reflects your personal taste. Particularly because clothing is the employer's product, you need to look stylish.
2. A job interview should center on objective questions regarding the qualifications for the position and not on the applicant's personal life.
3. Horace Mann would advise any prospective interviewee to be prompt.
4. Students might interpret the quotation to mean that insight can be gained into a person's character by evaluating the questions he or she asks because formulating effective questions can often be more difficult than answering the questions. In an interview, both parties draw conclusions about the other person's characteristics, such as honesty, knowledge, and enthusiasm, based on the questions that the person asks.
5. Being hired based on false information is apt to lead to trouble later. One way interviewees can establish their honesty is by admitting openly that they lack certain skills (if asked about the skills) or by admitting that they lack the answers to particular questions.

CHAPTER **8**

Review Questions

1. How is an interview different from a question-and-answer session in which an audience asks questions of a speaker?
2. What are at least three things you should do to prepare for an interview?
3. A résumé is a brief account of your experience. In general, what information should you include in your résumé?
4. What is the difference between the general information and the specific information you provide about your qualifications, goals, and interests?
5. Why is it important to rehearse for an interview?
6. What are at least five qualities interviewers look for in an applicant?
7. What are the four types of questions you may be asked during an interview?
8. What three questions should an interviewer ask before choosing a person for an informative interview?
9. What is the difference between an *open* question and a *closed* question? What is the difference between a *neutral* question and a *leading* question?
10. How should you follow up an interview?

Discussion Questions

1. You are interviewing for a job selling clothing at a department store. Discuss the importance of good appearance in interviewing for that job.
2. The Equal Employment Opportunity Commission (EEOC) does not allow employers to ask prospective employees questions about marriage, religious preference, ethnic background, and other personal matters. Discuss why you think such questions are disallowed.
3. The famous U.S. educator and politician Horace Mann once wrote, "Unfaithfulness in the keeping of an appointment is an act of clear dishonesty. You may as well borrow a person's money as his time." Do you agree or disagree with Mann? Why? What advice do you think Mann would give to a person preparing for an interview?
4. The French philosopher Voltaire suggested, "Judge a man by his questions rather than by his answers." What do you think this quotation means? Discuss what the interviewee can learn from the questions the interviewer asks. Then discuss what the interviewer can learn from the questions the interviewee asks.
5. Interviewers look for honesty in applicants. Discuss with your classmates why this trait is so important and what an applicant can do to establish his or her honesty.

7. questions that request information, probe deeper into a topic, check understanding, and require the interviewee to take a stand
8. Is the person knowledgeable? a primary source or a secondary source? a reliable source?
9. An open question encourages a person to talk at length; a closed question can be answered with a yes or a no or with a few words. A neutral question gives the interviewee no hint of what particular answer the interviewer wants; a leading question suggests the answer the interviewer expects or desires.
10. with a brief and direct letter of thanks

ACTIVITIES

1. **Analyzing Interviewing Skills.** Watch an interview on a television talk show or news program, and tell your class about it. What kinds of questions did the interviewer ask? How effective were these questions in getting the interviewee to talk? How could the questions have been more effective?

2. **Understanding and Answering a Job Advertisement.** Read the following job advertisement. What type of job is being advertised? What qualifications does an applicant need? List the steps that you would follow in applying for this job. Then, compare your list with a partner's to see if you have included all the necessary steps.

SUMMER HELPER
Fast-paced and growing florist and gift delivery business looking for a sharp, self-motivated, cheerful customer service clerk. Must have: professional appearance, pleasant phone voice, ability to handle light typing and filing. Must be dependable and reliable. Good pay, some benefits. Send résumé to:
Blooms and More
9258 NW Parkway
Cincinnati, OH 45233

3. **Preparing for and Practicing for a School Interview.**
   A. Choose a school in which you are interested—a business, technical, or trade school; a community college; or a college or university. Write questions that an interviewer from that school might ask you. Then write your answers to these questions. Compare your questions and answers with those of your classmates.
   B. Write a letter to the school of your choice asking for an interview.
   C. Working with a partner, conduct a school interview. Have one person act as the interviewer and the other as the interviewee. Then, invite and respond to feedback from your classmates.

4. **Preparing for a Celebrity Interview.**
   A. Imagine that you are a journalist. Your next assignment is to interview one of the celebrities shown below or another celebrity of your own choosing. What would your readers be most interested in knowing about the person you interview? Think of at least four general topics that you might have your interviewee address.

   B. Using the list of general topics that you made for Part A, think of ten specific questions to ask your interviewee. Try to make most of your questions open ones to encourage the person to talk at length. [For examples of the different types of interview questions, see the chart on page 202.]

ACTIVITIES

Guidelines for Assessment

1. Make sure that students consider questions that request information, that probe deeper, that check understanding, and that require the interviewee to take a stand.
2. The ad is for a customer service clerk. The applicant should be sharp, self-motivated, cheerful, dependable, and reliable; should have a professional appearance and a pleasant phone voice; and should be able to handle light typing and filing. Steps include preparing a résumé, sending a résumé with a cover letter requesting an interview, finding out information about the company, planning what you want to say and ask in the interview, and rehearsing the interview.
3. A. Students' questions should cover all relevant aspects of attending the school.
   B. Students' letters should each follow business-letter format, name the specific person who should read the letter, state the intended course of study, state an interest in the school, and request an interview.
   C. Both the interviewer and the interviewee should be well prepared and poised, ask appropriate questions, and give appropriate answers.
4. See next page.

SUMMATIVE EVALUATION

Your **Teacher's Resource Binder** contains a reproducible **Chapter 8 Test** that may be used to assess students' mastery of the concepts presented in this chapter.

PORTFOLIO ASSESSMENT

For future reference and evaluation you may want to have students keep in their portfolios any skill sheets or evaluation forms that you have used with this chapter along with any other recorded or written materials that students have created.

4. A. You may need to give some guidance regarding appropriateness of topics. You could discuss the issue of what the public is entitled to know about public figures and what it is not.

B. Make sure that most of the questions are open-ended and that they are all organized in a logical manner.

C. Students should follow the business letter format shown on p. 204. In their letters, students could offer to send copies of their articles to the interviewees.

5. A. You may want to specify a particular number of questions that each student must list.

B. You may want to have each pair write an evaluation of its performance.

6. Encourage students to review the section on **Controlling Stage Fright** on pp. 321–323 and to draw from personal experience in making up their lists.

7. Each student's questions should be appropriate for the topic and should elicit a complete picture from the interviewee.

8. Encourage each student to choose two diverse types of jobs for this activity.

C. Imagine that your interview has taken place. Follow it up with a thank-you letter. Write a letter to your interviewee, thanking him or her for talking with you. [Use the letter on page 204 as a model of a business letter.] Notice that you will need to make up the interviewee's address.

5. Preparing for and Practicing for a Job Interview.

A. Imagine you are going to interview for a summer job. List the questions you would expect an interviewer to ask you. Then list your answers to these questions. Compare your questions and answers to those of your classmates.

B. Working with a partner, conduct an interview for a summer job. Have one person act as the interviewer and the other as the interviewee. After the interview, listen to and respond to feedback from your classmates.

6. Identifying Techniques for Reducing Nervousness. Discuss with your classmates techniques you can use to help reduce your nervousness before an interview. Compile a class list of these techniques, and copy the list in your communication journal. Try to refer to it before you participate in an interview.

7. Preparing for an Informative Interview. Think of a sport, a profession, a craft, or a hobby that would make an interesting topic for a speech. [You may wish to refer to pages 216–220 in Chapter 9 for more about generating topic ideas.] Next, identify three people in your community who would be knowledgeable subjects for an informative interview on this topic. Finally, develop at least five questions you might ask each person to gather information about your topic.

8. Analyzing Nonverbal Communication in an Interview. In a job interview, an experienced personnel director or other business person who does a great deal of hiring will often form opinions about a job applicant even before the applicant says a word. Such opinions are based on the interviewer's first impression of the applicant. Obviously, creating a good first impression is important to getting an interview off to a positive start.

Think of two different jobs that you would like to apply for. Imagine that you have an interview for each job. How would you try to create a good first impression at each interview? What would you wear to each one? How would you act? Notice the ways in which you adapt your appearance or behavior to each setting. For example, you would probably not wear the same clothes to apply for a pizza delivery driver job that you would wear to an interview for a position as a sales clerk in a department store.

◆ Real-Life Speaking Situations

PERFORMANCE OBJECTIVES

- To write a résumé
- To prepare for a job interview
- To identify important personal qualities to be shared with an interviewer
- To write and present an interview dialogue
- To conduct a question-and-answer session

REAL LIFE Speaking Situations

1 Whether you are a teenager or an adult, when you hunt for a job, you want to make every effort to find one that is right for you. Making a positive impression during an interview can determine your success in getting the job you want.

Imagine that you see an ad in the newspaper for a job that you think would suit you perfectly. Stop for a minute and identify such a job. Assume that you meet the job qualifications, and write a résumé, just as you would if you were actually replying to the ad. Make sure that your résumé is complete and shows that you meet the requirements for the job. (Also be sure to refer to the information on preparing a résume on page 189.) If you were invited to interview for this job, how would you make a favorable impression on the interviewer? What would you wear? What would you present as your strongest qualifications for the job? your goals for the job?

At an interview for this job, the interviewer might ask why you want the job and why you think you should be hired for it. Prepare brief answers to these questions. Be ready to discuss your answers with your classmates.

2 People who interview job applicants need to have a strong command of verbal and nonverbal skills. Along with these skills, interviewers also need to have personal qualities that enable them to communicate effectively with applicants. What are some of these qualities?

Make a list of the five most important personal qualities that an interviewer needs to deal effectively with applicants. Then use this list and illustrate how these qualities might be used in the interview situation that follows.

You are an interviewer asking questions of an applicant for a summer job. So far, the applicant has given only very short answers, and you want the person to become more at ease and more talkative because you feel that he or she would be a good candidate for the job.

Write a short dialogue that you can present in three or four minutes to show how you would draw out this applicant. Give your dialogue in class, and then conduct a short question-and-answer session in which you discuss the personal qualities that you feel are necessary for an interviewer to have.

ASSESSMENT GUIDELINES

1. Résumés should show students' qualifications clearly. You may want to organize the class into groups of four or five so that students can discuss why they want the jobs and why they think they should be hired.
2. The class could develop a master list of personal qualities an interviewer should have. You may want to allow the students to rate the effectiveness of the dialogues.

Unit 3 • Public Speaking

Public Speaking

Chapter 9
Getting Ready
pp. 214–239

Chapter Overview

This chapter presents the planning stages of the process students will follow to create effective speeches. The steps explained in this chapter are choosing your topic, knowing your purpose, writing a thesis statement, knowing your audience, knowing your occasion, and supporting your thesis statement.

Teacher's Resource Binder

The following materials are identified at their point of use in this chapter:

- Skills for Success
  1 *Limiting the Topic*
  2 *Writing a Specific Purpose Statement*
  3 *Analyzing Audience*
  4 *Adjusting to Suit Your Occasion*
- Chapter 9 Vocabulary
- Chapter 9 Test/Answer Key

AV ➤ Audiovisual Resource Binder

The following materials are identified at their point of use in this chapter:

- Transparency 16
  Exploring Subject Areas for Speech Topics
- Transparency 17
  Developing Thesis Statements
- Transparency 18
  Finding Support for a Thesis
- Audiotape 1, Lesson 7
  Brainstorming

The chapter begins by discussing subject areas that students may be interested in or have knowledge about. It provides strategies to develop topics and to narrow those topics for a specific purpose. The chapter shows students how to write thesis statements that express the key points and how to support thesis statements with corroborating details. Analysis of the audience and occasion helps students tailor the appeals for their speeches.

INTRODUCING THE CHAPTER

When given an assignment to prepare and deliver a speech, many students are at a loss as to how to begin. Tell students that this chapter provides an orderly process for developing and organizing their thoughts. Remind students that they will apply many of the same skills they use in planning a paper when they get ready for a speech.

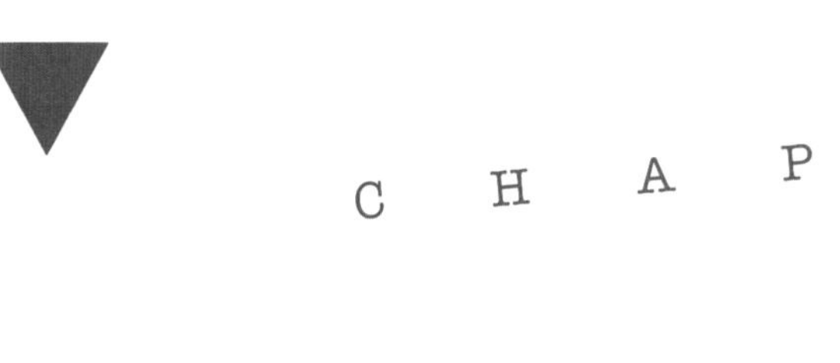

C H A P T E R 9

Getting Ready

OBJECTIVES

After studying this chapter, you should be able to

1. Select a suitable topic for a speech.
2. Identify qualities that make a good topic for a speech.
3. Tell the difference between a general purpose and a specific purpose.
4. Write a thesis statement.
5. Draw conclusions about the knowledge, interests, and attitudes of your audience.
6. Determine how your occasion will affect your speech.
7. Identify the kinds of information you can use to support your thesis statement.

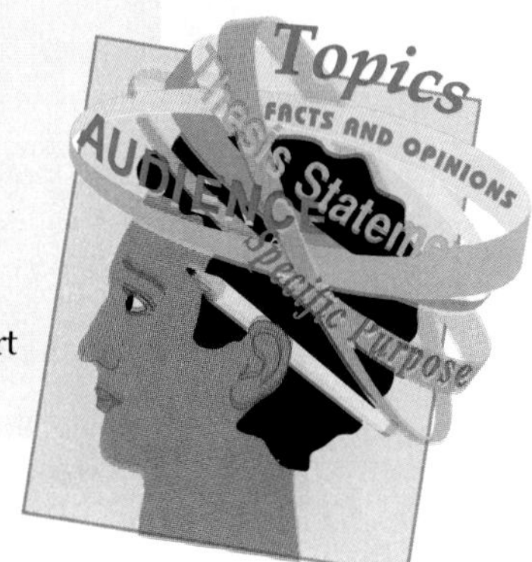

How to Prepare for a Speech

Your teacher has just given you an assignment: You are to make a five-minute speech to your class a week from today. You probably have many questions. Where should you begin to plan your speech? What topic should you speak about? What do you need to know about your audience, and what will interest them? What kinds of information can you use in your speech?

The key to making a successful speech is to prepare, prepare, prepare. Speakers sometimes think they are so familiar with their topics that they can simply get up and speak about them. But planning a successful speech means thinking about several separate but interrelated parts: choosing your topic; writing your thesis statement; knowing your purpose, audience, and occasion; and supporting your thesis statement. In this chapter, you will learn several useful techniques that will help you with each of these steps.

Bibliography of Additional Materials

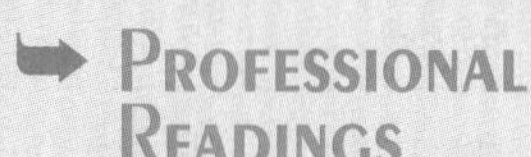

PROFESSIONAL READINGS

- Johannesen, Richard L. ***Contemporary American Speeches.*** Dubuque, IA: Kendall/Hunt Publishing Company.
- ***Vital Speeches of the Day.*** This bimonthly publication reprints the text of important current speeches. These transcripts can be used as models for identifying and discussing speech topics, purposes, thesis statements, audiences and occasions, and reasons supporting thesis statements.

AUDIOVISUALS

- ***JJ Gets Ready***—Journal Films, Evanston, IL (videocassette, 10 min.)
- ***Planning Your Speech***—Coronet/MTI Film & Video, Deerfield, IL (videocassette, 13 min.)
- ***Preparing to Speak***—Films for the Humanities and Sciences, Princeton, NJ (videocassette, 17 min.)
- ***Public Speaking***—Michigan State University, East Lansing, MI (videocassette, 16 min.)

Segment 1 *pp. 216–224*

- **Choosing Your Topic**
- **Knowing Your Purpose**
- **Writing a Thesis Statement**

PERFORMANCE OBJECTIVES

- To generate a list of topics of personal interest
- To select subject areas and to brainstorm for ideas
- To choose and limit a subject
- To limit topics for effective coverage
- To write a specific speech purpose
- To distinguish between specific purpose sentences and thesis statements
- To write thesis statements to accompany specific purposes

MEETING INDIVIDUAL NEEDS

Learning Styles

Visual Learners. Many students, especially visual learners, generate ideas successfully by clustering and branching. In addition to generating ideas, students see the connections between topics, subtopics, and details, as well as how ideas can lead to dead ends. Students might use a different-colored pen each time they divide a topic for clustering or branching. Using different colors will enable students to classify and locate topics more easily.

TIMESAVER

A collection of recent popular magazines and newspapers is a handy resource for generating and limiting topics and writing thesis statements.

AV Audiovisual Resource Binder
Audiotape 1, Lesson 7
Brainstorming

Choosing Your Topic

Generating Topic Ideas

You can begin to find a topic for your speech by thinking about **subject areas,** or general categories, that are interesting and familiar to you. Some common subject areas are jobs and careers, hobbies and activities, past events, current issues, places, processes, and people. However, a general subject area, such as *movies,* is too broad to be covered effectively in one speech. A **topic** suitable for a speech is a specific category within a subject area. A number of techniques can help you get ideas for your topic:

- flipping through magazines and newspapers
- scanning entries of your diary or writing journal
- skimming through an encyclopedia
- interviewing others
- **brainstorming,** or quickly listing possibilities without stopping to evaluate each one

EXAMPLE: For his first speech, Joel Foster selected the subject area *hobbies and activities* and brainstormed the following ideas about the subject *football* to find a topic for his speech.

Football

players	offense	defense	passing
tackling	plays	calling plays	stadiums
rules	injuries	equipment	stretching
zones	positions	cheerleaders	coaching
practice	strategy	numbers	the ball
placekicking	punting	pass patterns	blocking

Motivation

Ask students, "If you could have a free subscription to any magazine, which magazine would you choose and why?" Write some of the responses on the chalkboard. Students will probably say that the magazines they chose cover subjects of particular personal interest. Point out that the variety of magazines selected illustrates the variety of interests in the classroom. Encourage students to concentrate on what interests them when they are searching for appealing speech topics.

As you participate in your daily activities—going to classes, talking to friends, watching television, reading—note subject areas or specific topics that interest you. This list of topics can furnish useful ideas for speech topics.

Limiting Your Topic

Limit your topic enough so that you can cover it effectively in one speech. Focus on specific aspects, examples, parts, uses, or other features of the topic.

EXAMPLE: After brainstorming, Joel selected three topics: *calling plays, pass patterns,* and *placekicking.* Since Joel liked *placekicking* best, he chose this topic for his speech. But this topic is too broad to be covered effectively in one speech because there are so many different features of placekicking—its use in football strategy, famous plays involving placekicking, and the two different styles of placekicking. For his speech, Joel further limited his topic to *soccer-style placekicking.*

The chart on the following pages shows how you can use questions to narrow a general subject to a suitably limited topic.

Meeting Individual Needs

An Alternative Approach

To help students discover topics and to express ideas, you might want to suggest topics or to display magazines, newspapers, or books to give students ideas about various subjects. Give students individual assistance by asking probing questions such as "What do you most enjoy?" and "What are some of your favorite subjects?" Then encourage students' thinking by asking "What comes to your mind when you think of this subject?" and "How do you feel about this?" Questions such as these will give students practice in expressing and expanding ideas.

Critical Thinking

Synthesis

You might involve your class in a brainstorming session to generate topics. Ask students to name current issues that are discussed in the news. As students name topics, show how current problems relate to each other. For example, failure to recycle aluminum cans not only wastes money but also leads to shortened lives for city landfills.

Teacher's Resource Binder

Skills for Success 1
Limiting the Topic

TEACHING THE LESSON

Because the information in this segment is essential to preparing a speech, you may want to model the steps as they are presented in the textbook. Involve students in the modeling process by having them agree on a subject that interests them. Then brainstorm with the class to generate topic ideas about the subject. Work together to limit the topic so it can be covered effectively in one speech.

The chart below demonstrates how general subject areas can be explored and limited to speech topics. Continue guiding students in determining a general purpose and a specific purpose for giving a speech about the selected topic. Finally, work with students to write a thesis statement for the limited topic.

INTEGRATING THE LANGUAGE ARTS

Library Link

You might have students look in the subject category of the *Readers' Guide to Periodical Literature* to analyze some of the categories used and to find ideas for speech topics.

USING THE CHART

You may want to have students create charts to explore subject areas after you have brainstormed with the class to come up with a few general subject areas. You could have students work in groups of four or five to develop sample limited topics.

***AV* ▶ Audiovisual Resource Binder**

Transparency 16
Exploring Subject Areas for Speech Topics

Exploring Subject Areas to Find Speech Topics

General Subject Areas	Questions to Ask Yourself About This Subject Area	Sample Subjects	Sample Limited Topics
Jobs and Careers	1. Have you ever had a part-time job during the summer or on weekends? If so, what knowledge or experience have you gained that might interest others?	pet-sitting	Five Pointers Every Pet-Sitter Should Know
	2. Are you interested in a specific career? What do you know about it that might interest others?	chemistry lawn care	Why I Want to Become a Research Chemist What I Learned About Lawn and Garden Care in My Summer Job
Hobbies and Activities	1. What hobby or activity do you enjoy? (Possibilities include coin collecting, raising cats, playing an instrument, or painting.)	baseball cards	How to Collect and Display Baseball Cards
	2. Have you ever participated in an activity or hobby that others might like to know more about?	community theater scuba diving	Participating in Community Theater How I Learned to Scuba Dive
Past Events	1. Is there a specific historical event that interests you and that you think would interest others?	the Battle of Gettysburg	How the Battle of Gettysburg Affected the Civil War
	2. What event in your life or someone else's life is significant to you and could be meaningful to others?	my new baby sister	New Baby in the House

(continued on next page)

Assessment

By evaluating **Activities 1, 2,** and **4,** you can assess each student's ability to choose a subject, narrow a topic, state a specific purpose, and write a thesis statement. Check **Activity 3** to ensure that students can differentiate between purpose sentences and thesis statements.

Reteaching

You might copy onto a transparency the beginning of a speech from a publication such as *Vital Speeches,* or read the introduction of the speech aloud. Guide students in identifying the speaker's topic, general purpose, specific purpose, and thesis. Discuss and evaluate how clear the speaker's purpose is.

General Subject Areas	Questions to Ask Yourself About This Subject Area	Sample Subjects	Sample Limited Topics
Current Issues	1. Is there a recent event in world or national news that you think is important?	peace in the Middle East	Why Resolving the Arab-Israeli Conflict Is Important
	2. What significant events are taking place in your city, county, or state?	our county's programs	Our County's New Youth Activities Program
Places	1. What specific place appeals to you for a particular reason?	a fishing location	The Best Place on Lake Texoma to Fish for Bass
	2. What place have you heard about or studied that has importance or significance for others?	the Panama Canal	The Panama Canal's Importance in World Trade
Processes	1. What do you know how to do or to make that you could describe to someone else?	models	How to Build a Model Airplane
	2. Are you familiar enough with the way something works that you could explain it to others?	TV sets	How a Television Set's Color Gun Works
People	1. Is there a person whose courage, skill, honesty, thoughtfulness, or other quality impresses you?	my grandfather	Why I Admire My Grandfather
	2. What famous person do you find notable or admirable? Why?	Hatshepsut	Hatshepsut, the Woman Who Became Pharaoh

Building a Portfolio

Students might include their brainstorming activities in their speech portfolios so that they will have their collections of ideas for future planning and assessment.

See p. 223 for **EXTENSION, ENRICHMENT,** and **CLOSURE.**

ONGOING ASSESSMENT

Activity 1

Lists should show that each student has explored a variety of subject areas before choosing one topic per area. Lists might be done linearly or in clusters.

MEETING INDIVIDUAL NEEDS

Students with Special Needs

Students with learning disabilities may have difficulty with narrowing a topic. Thus, it is important to provide positive reinforcement, guidance, and explanations of vocabulary. It is especially important that the student choose a topic of interest.

Allow the student to look through newspapers and magazines to help with brainstorming. Once the student has several ideas, help him or her choose a topic. Then discuss this topic in detail with the student and make a list of key words and phrases. This will provide the student with the necessary vocabulary as well as a structure to use for further development of ideas. Not only will this help the student with a poor vocabulary, but it will also help the student who has a poor short-term memory.

ACTIVITY 1

Choosing a Subject and Limiting It to a Speech Topic

Select two subject areas and brainstorm ideas about each subject area. When you run out of ideas, put your lists aside. Later, return to your lists to see if you can add more items. After completing your two lists, choose the three items from each list that interest you most. Next, from each group of three items, find the one that you would most like to develop into a speech topic for this subject area. Finally, limit each topic so that it can be covered effectively in one speech.

Knowing Your Purpose

Your **purpose** is what you intend to achieve in your speech. You will have both a general purpose and a specific purpose.

General Purpose

Your **general purpose** is the overall intent of your speech. Speeches may be given for several different general purposes, but primarily speeches are intended to inform, to persuade, to entertain, or to suit a special occasion.

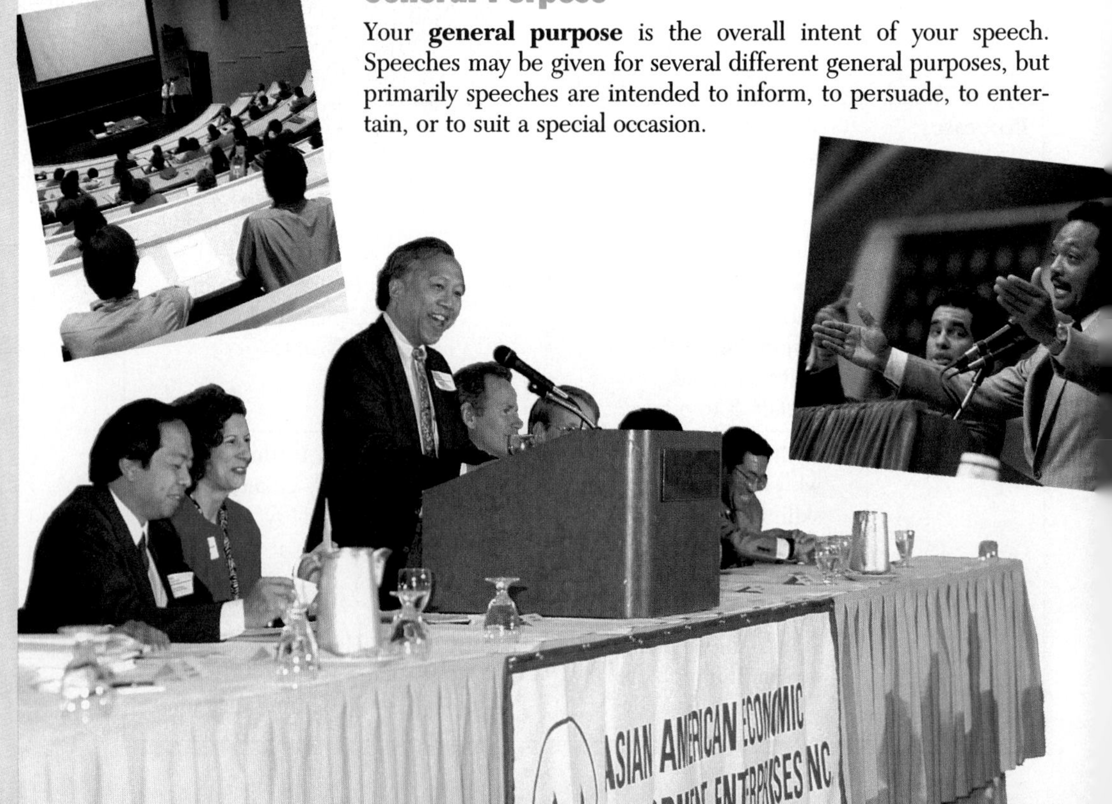

General Purposes for Speeches		
Purpose	**Description**	**Examples**
Speech to Inform	presents new information to an audience or gives new insights into information that an audience already has	• teachers giving class lectures • announcers broadcasting news • supervisors explaining work • procedures [See pages 355–381 for more information about speeches to inform.]
Speech to Persuade	tries to change an attitude or a belief, or to move an audience to action	• politicians urging voters to support them • lawyers addressing a jury • salespeople convincing consumers to buy products [See pages 383–415 for more information about speeches to persuade.]
Speech to Suit a Special Occasion	entertains or amuses an audience or recognizes a specific reason for the audience being present and promotes group bonding or social cohesion	• club officers giving a "roast" to a member at a banquet • valedictorians addressing their graduating classmates and parents • officials commemorating the unveiling of a memorial statue [See pages 417–445 for more information about speeches to entertain or to suit a special occasion.]

Specific Purpose

The **specific purpose** of a speech is its goal, stated in a complete sentence. If the general purpose of your speech is to inform, then your specific purpose will be a statement of the particular information you will present to the audience.

EXAMPLE: Joel's general purpose in his speech about placekicking is to inform. His specific purpose could be stated in a complete sentence: "I want to explain the steps in soccer-style placekicking."

INTEGRATING THE LANGUAGE ARTS

Literature Link

To help students see the relationship between writing and speaking purposes, have students bring examples of nonfiction essays from their literature textbooks to class. Have each student try to find at least one example of each general speaking purpose: to inform, to persuade, and to suit special occasions (to express ideas or to use language creatively). Then have students work in small groups to compare and contrast the three different kinds of essays. They could examine such elements as tone and word choice.

TEACHER'S RESOURCE BINDER

Skills for Success 2
Writing a Specific Purpose Statement

Enrichment

Students might create collages of all the ideas they have generated as speech topics. The collages could be displayed in the room.

Closure

Ask each student to share a topic for a speech. Have the class suggest a purpose and a thesis sentence for each topic.

Critical Thinking

Analysis

Choose a limited topic and have each student write a specific purpose statement for this topic for each type of speech—informative, persuasive, and special occasion. Then the student should write a thesis statement for each specific purpose. Students should share their responses and analyze how the thesis statements changed with the change in purpose.

An Alternative Approach

Have more-experienced students perform persuasive, informative, or special-occasion speeches for other class members to analyze and evaluate for topic, purpose, and thesis statement. As an alternative to live speeches, use videotapes of students from last year's classes.

Ongoing Assessment

Activity 4

Each thesis statement should be stated in a complete sentence and should express the key idea to be presented about a topic.

EXAMPLE: Knowing the steps involved in soccer-style placekicking, Joel Foster can complete his thesis statement at this stage of preparation.

Subject Area: football

Topic: placekicking

Limited Topic: soccer-style placekicking

General Purpose: to inform

Specific Purpose: I want to explain the four steps in soccer-style placekicking.

Thesis Statement: The four steps in soccer-style placekicking are to spot the ball, to mark off the steps, to approach the ball, and to kick the ball.

Writing Thesis Statements

Write a thesis statement for each of the specific purposes you stated in Activity 2 on page 223.

CATHY **by Cathy Guisewite**

Even when you are allowed little preparation time, identifying your purpose, writing a clear thesis statement, and thinking about your audience and the occasion will help you speak more effectively than not planning at all.

Segment 2 *pp. 225–227*

• Knowing Your Audience
• Knowing Your Occasion

PERFORMANCE OBJECTIVES

- To analyze an audience and to draw conclusions about its knowledge, interests, and attitudes about a topic
- To determine how the occasion will affect a speech

Knowing Your Audience

The people who will hear your speech are your **audience.** Knowing about your audience will help you determine the information you need to include in your speech. You will need to know some defining characteristics of your audience, or **demographic data,** which may include average age, educational background, and cultural heritage. You will also need to determine your audience's knowledge, feelings, and beliefs about the topic.

Questions About Your Audience

1. Who will be in the audience? Teenage students, elderly retirees, or a mixed group?
2. Are most members of the audience from an urban, a suburban, or a rural environment?
3. How much will the audience know about the topic—a great deal, a moderate amount, or very little?
4. Will the listeners be familiar with specific terms, concepts, or references you will use?
5. Will the audience need any background or technical information in order to understand your speech?
6. Will the audience be very interested, somewhat interested, or uninterested in this topic?
7. Will the audience's attitude toward this topic be positive, neutral, or negative?

MEETING **INDIVIDUAL** NEEDS

Linguistically Diverse Students

Speakers of Spanish and other Romance languages have an advantage in analyzing audience because of a familiar, formal designation built into their pronoun systems. One set of second-person pronouns is used with audiences of family members, friends, and children. Another set is used in formal contexts with older persons, authority figures, and so on. Several cultures emphasize defining the audience this way to assure appropriate and effective communication. Point to this example to encourage students who may not recognize the skill they bring to this task.

TEACHER'S RESOURCE BINDER

Skills for Success 3
Analyzing Audience

Motivation

Have groups of four or five students describe a complicated machine such as a CD player, a laptop computer, or a telephone for a variety of audiences such as a six-year-old cousin, an alien scientist, a dictionary maker, or a time traveler from the old west. Each group should describe the item for its chosen audience. Then the class can evaluate how effective each group's explanation is.

Teaching the Lesson

Have students read **Knowing Your Audience** and **Knowing Your Occasion.** Then students can refer to their topics from **Activity 1** for discussion of **Activity 5** and **Activity 6.** Students might work in groups of four to discuss the implications of their analyses of audience and occasion for their topics.

Meeting Individual Needs

An Alternative Approach

Some students may need further explanation about what demographic information is and how speakers use it. Students might use an almanac or a yearbook to develop demographic reports on their state or region.

They might include information from questions like these: What is the average age? How many people are in each age range? What is the age range of parents? grandparents? What is the gender breakdown? Which occupations are the most prominent? What is the average educational level? What are the major religious groups? What is the political makeup? the ethnic or cultural makeup? the socioeconomic makeup? A few students can share their information with the class.

Ongoing Assessment

Activity 5

Responses should reflect a consideration of the questions on demographic data, audience attitudes, and opinions.

For instance, if Joel Foster knows that his audience has no knowledge of soccer-style placekicking, he will need to provide important background information. If Joel plans to speak to the Northside Parents Club, he should select details and information that appeal to the parents' interests. For example, he might explain how soccer-style placekickers learn to focus on the task despite tremendous distractions and pressure. If Joel plans to speak on the same topic to freshman football players, he might actually explain learning how to placekick.

In most speaking situations, you will have to suit your speech to your audience—not find an audience that suits your speech.

Activity 5 — Analyzing an Audience

Considering your classmates as your audience, apply the questions in the chart on page 225 to one of the topics that you chose in Activity 1 on page 220. Explain what effect the answers to these questions will have on the material you will use to present your topic. Also be prepared to discuss your answers with your classmates to see how accurate your analysis is.

Knowing Your Occasion

Every speech that you prepare will be given for some occasion. The **occasion** of a speech includes the time, place, and all of the other conditions that define the setting in which you will deliver the speech. Knowing the occasion will help you make choices as you develop your speech.

To assess, have students write about how their analyses of audience and occasion affected their topics. Then have students turn in the papers so you can briefly check them.

To reteach, find a sample speech in this textbook, a speech anthology, or *Vital Speeches,* and help students evaluate the speaker's topic selection in relation to audience and occasion.

CLOSURE

Ask students to list in their communication journals the audiences and occasions that may prove challenging for them as speakers. Have students explain why these audiences and occasions pose problems. Let a few volunteers share their lists with the class. Have the class discuss what specific steps they would need to follow to prepare a speech for those audiences and occasions.

HOW TO *Think About the Occasion*

1. **When will your speech be given?** Consider both the date and the time of day. The date of your speech may be the reason for the speech. For example, you might give a speech about Martin Luther King, Jr., on his birthdate or one about the role of women in the work force on a date close to Labor Day. The time of day also affects your speech. At an early morning speech, some members of your audience might be sleepy. Therefore, you might include some audience participation and avoid dimming the lights for a long slide presentation.
2. **Where will your speech be given?** The size of the room, the seating arrangement, and the presence of a speaker's stand can affect your presentation. For example, in a large room, any visual materials should be much larger than those you would use in a small room.
3. **What are the restrictions for your speech?** Any limitations placed on your speech will affect your preparation. For example, a time limit will determine the amount of material you can present. Whether or not you may use notes affects the way you will deliver your speech.

ACTIVITY 6 Determining the Effect of Occasion on a Speech

Apply to your own speech each of the questions in the chart above concerning occasion. Then discuss how this information will affect the kind of material you will use in your speech.

ADDITIONAL ACTIVITY

To further explore the effect of audience and occasion on speeches, students might interview three or four teachers to find the following information: times of day most productive for classes; times least productive for classes; days of the week best for teaching; days worst for teaching; the relationship of students in a class to the teacher's presentation; the impact of time restrictions; and any other elements of audience and occasion analysis.

Students can write their findings in their communication journals and report to the class. Then the class can draw some conclusions about what they discovered and include the conclusions in their journals for future reference in speech preparation.

ONGOING ASSESSMENT

Activity 6

Responses should demonstrate that students have explored each question in **How to Think About the Occasion.**

TEACHER'S RESOURCE BINDER

Skills for Success 4
Adjusting to Suit Your Occasion

Segment 3 *pp. 228–233*

• Supporting Your Thesis Statement

Performance Objective

- To identify different kinds of supporting information that are useful in preparing speeches

Motivation

Ask students how it feels when people make promises they do not keep. List students' reactions on the chalkboard. Then explain that a thesis in a speech is much like a pledge that must be carried out, for if it is not, the audience will feel the emotions listed on the chalkboard. This should prepare students to study the many ways a speaker can fulfill the promise of his or her thesis.

Meeting Individual Needs

An Alternative Approach

You may need to work closely with students who cannot easily distinguish between fact and opinion. Have them find some newspaper editorials or articles in which they can locate and identify both the opinion statements and the factual statements. Using colored markers to underline and identify the different methods of support should help students recognize how variety enhances a writer's or a speaker's main idea.

Making Connections

Community Involvement

Invite to class a lawyer, legal assistant, or paralegal who can speak about the kinds of supporting material lawyers use and how they go about collecting such data.

Audiovisual Resource Binder

Transparency 18
Finding Support for a Thesis

Supporting Your Thesis Statement

You need to find information to support your main idea as expressed in your thesis statement. The types of details commonly used to support a thesis include facts, opinions, examples, illustrations, anecdotes, statistics, comparisons, definitions, descriptions, and quotations.

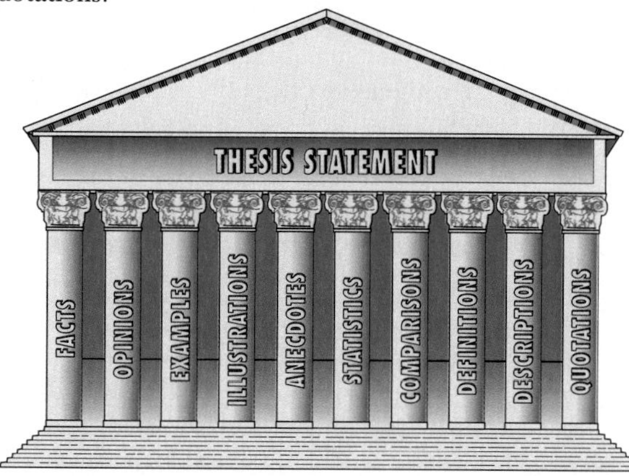

Facts and Opinions

Statements of **fact** contain information that can be proved, or verified, by testing, by observing, or by consulting reference materials.

EXAMPLES:

1. **Fact:** Tin weighs more than aluminum.
   To verify: Look up their weights on a periodic chart of elements, or weigh equal amounts of these substances.
2. **Fact:** Some rodents can fly and glide.
   To verify: Observe bats and flying squirrels, or read about them in a reference source.
3. **Fact:** Dodecahedrons are twelve-sided.
   To verify: Consult a dictionary for a definition, or get a dodecahedron and count the sides.

TEACHING THE LESSON

Have students discuss the difference between facts and opinions, and then have them examine the examples of opinions and expert opinions. They might practice writing their own opinions to share with the class. You might have student volunteers read orally the other kinds of supporting information for a thesis (pp. 230–233). Allow time to discuss the examples and to consider any other examples.

Give some time to the section on comparisons, especially figurative comparisons. Have students complete **Activity 7** on p. 233 by bringing newspapers to class or by using resources in the classroom to look for examples of the different kinds of supporting information.

Statements of **opinion** express personal beliefs or attitudes. Such statements contain personal judgments, which include information that cannot be proved.

EXAMPLE:

1. **Opinion:** Roses are more beautiful than tulips.
   Why? Beauty is a matter of personal preference.
2. **Opinion:** Spaghetti tastes better than ravioli.
   Why? Taste is a matter of personal preference.
3. **Opinion:** The Braves will win tomorrow's game.
   Why? Predictions are always opinions.

In some situations, you may seek an expert opinion. An **expert opinion** is a statement of belief about a subject from a person who is recognized as an authority on that subject. For example, a rocket scientist could offer an expert opinion on space travel. Experts can also supply facts. For instance, a high school coach can report on how many college recruiters have visited players on the team. To get an expert's opinion, you could read books or articles written by the expert, request information in a letter, or interview the expert in person or by telephone.

EXAMPLES:

1. **Expert opinion:** Book publisher—how the nonfiction market will grow
2. **Expert opinion:** Coach—how college recruiters will judge the team
3. **Expert opinion:** Dietitian—how low-fat cooking improves health

CRITICAL THINKING

Analysis

Statements of fact and statements of opinion often use different language. Have students explore these differences by providing the class with example statements of fact and opinion. Students should analyze how the word usage varies in facts and opinions. For example, facts use concrete and specific words, whereas opinions tend to use relative, general, or even vague descriptive words.

Assessment

Have each student present a couple of examples of facts and opinions to the class and have the students explain how they identified each example. As an alternative, bring to class a list of ten or more facts and opinions from a publication such as the local or school newspaper. Present the items one at a time to check students' ability to distinguish fact from opinion.

Present examples, illustrations, anecdotes, statistics, comparisons, definitions, descriptions, and quotations in the same way. Have students identify the methods used.

Examples and Illustrations

An **example** is a single instance that supports or develops a statement. An **illustration** is a detailed example.

EXAMPLE: Joel Foster might want to support the idea that soccer-style placekickers are often smaller than other players on a football team. Through reading, Joel might discover this example: Placekicker Jim Breech, at 5′7″ and 165 pounds, was the smallest player on the Cincinnati Bengals in 1992. Joel could expand the Jim Breech example into the following illustration.

Many people who are relatively small are aware that they have little chance of becoming college or professional football players—unless they can placekick. Today, placekickers are the smallest players on the team. For example, consider Jim Breech of the Cincinnati Bengals. Standing only 5′7″ tall and weighing only 165 pounds, he was by far the smallest player on the team's 1992 roster.

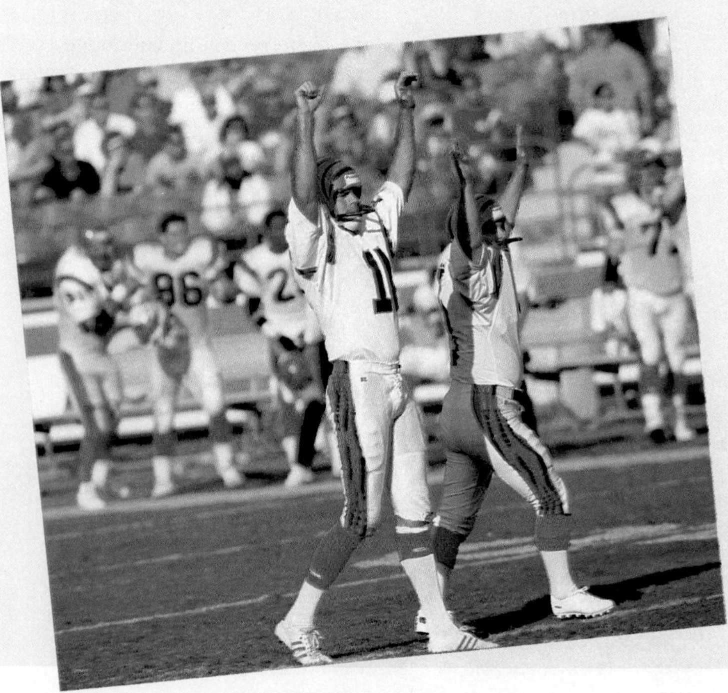

Reteaching

Choose a speech from the appendix of this textbook. Then help students identify the different types of information that the speaker uses.

Anecdotes

Anecdotes are brief, often amusing, stories. The purpose of an anecdote is to give information in a form that an audience will remember. Because anecdotes are often entertaining, they can help make your speech more interesting and enjoyable as well as informative.

EXAMPLE: Joel might recall a humorous incident that had happened to him the first time he kicked off in a game. He might use that story as part of his speech introduction.

Bill Cosby has entertained millions of people with his anecdotes, which usually contain a kernel of wisdom.

Most people assume that placekicking is simple. I did, in my first game. When the kickoff whistle blew, I ran up to the ball. Just as I launched into a kick hard enough to boot the ball all the way to the end zone, the ball fell off the kicking tee. I kicked at nothing and fell flat on my back. Luckily, the referee had already blown his whistle, so I got a chance to try again. But I never thought of a place kick as simple again.

Statistics

Statistics are numerical facts: "Only six out of every ten registered voters voted in the last school election" or "unemployment recently dropped 2 percent." Citing a few statistics may make your speech more informative, but giving too many statistics can be boring or distracting. Use statistics carefully to add interest or to emphasize a point.

EXAMPLE: In his speech on placekicking, Joel could use statistics to show that a large percentage of college placekickers prefer the soccer style: "In the last year, more than 85 percent—that's more than eight out of every ten placekickers on major college teams—kicked soccer style."

EXTENSION

Ask students working in groups of four or five to come to a consensus for a topic and then to write a purpose statement and a thesis sentence. Then have them spend no more than a day researching in the library to find supporting material. Students should find at least one example of each type of supporting data. Have each group report to the class about what they accomplished.

INTEGRATING THE LANGUAGE ARTS

Figurative Comparisons

To help students realize how many figurative comparisons are commonly used, brainstorm for comparisons in class. Discuss how speakers use comparisons to make information clear and interesting to an audience. You may want to review some examples of figures of speech such as similes and metaphors.

Literal Comparisons

Students might benefit from practice developing literal comparisons. Give the class a fact such as a car having skidded fifty yards on wet pavement and tell each student to write a literal comparison that would help the listener visualize how far the car skidded. One logical comparison is to compare the skid to half the length of a football field.

Comparisons

A **comparison** is a statement that shows the similarities between people, places, things, events, or ideas. Comparisons help listeners relate new ideas to familiar concepts.

A **figurative comparison** imaginatively shows similarities between things that are essentially not alike. For example, you may say someone is "as slow as molasses in January" to point out that the person moves slowly.

A **literal comparison** shows the real similarities between things that are essentially alike. For example, if you say, "Tom runs slower than Jorge," you are making a literal comparison.

Occasionally, a comparison is phrased as a **contrast,** highlighting the differences between two things. For instance, you might say, "Unlike last year's ecology club, which consisted primarily of seniors, this year's club has mostly sophomores and juniors as members."

Definitions

A **definition** explains what a word or a concept means. You should define carefully any words or concepts your audience may not understand.

EXAMPLE: Joel Foster might define *soccer style* this way: "*Soccer style* means approaching the ball at an angle and kicking the ball with the instep as the leg crosses the body."

Descriptions

A **description** is a word picture of a person, place, thing, or event. Accurate descriptions help people in your audience form mental pictures that correspond to the actual thing described.

EXAMPLE: Joel might describe the proper posture for placekicking: "Before kicking, kickers stand with their arms swinging freely at their sides, weight on the left foot, which is placed slightly ahead of the right, shoulders square to the ground, and eyes fixed on the point where the ball is placed."

Enrichment

Students might create posters of the different types of supporting material for display in the classroom and for future reference in preparing speeches.

Closure

Tell students to close their textbooks and ask the class to list all the types of details to support a thesis. Then have students double-check their lists against the textbook.

Quotations

A **quotation** expresses someone's exact words. Usually, you express your ideas in your own words. However, in some cases you will use a quotation to express the opinion of an authority or to include a particularly well stated idea. When you use quotations, you must give credit to the source from which the words were taken. (See pages 256–257.) To avoid boring your audience, limit the number and the length of quotations you use.

> **EXAMPLE:** To sum up the importance of sportsmanship in football, Joel might use the following quotation by Grantland Rice in *Alumnus Football:* "When the One Great Scorer comes to write against your name—/He marks—not that you won or lost—but how you played the game."

7 Recognizing Different Kinds of Supporting Information

Read the editorial page of your newspaper. Find examples, illustrations, anecdotes, statistics, comparisons, definitions, descriptions, and quotations that writers use to support main points or to clarify ideas. Share your findings with classmates.

Ongoing Assessment

Activity 7

Samples and explanations should demonstrate that the students have applied the explanations for the various types of supporting material.

GUIDELINES for Getting Started

- Have I chosen a topic that interests me?
- Have I thought about my own knowledge of this topic?
- Do I know my general purpose?
- Have I clearly identified my specific purpose?
- Do I have a well-worded thesis statement?
- Have I considered my audience—their backgrounds and interests and their knowledge of and attitudes toward my topic?
- Have I considered the occasion of the speech?
- Do I know what types of information I will need to support my main point?

◆ Profiles in Communication

Performance Objectives

- To analyze an audience for a sales presentation
- To create and deliver a sales presentation
- To evaluate the effectiveness of classmates' sales presentations

Teaching the Feature

Have students read the profile of auctioneer Dave Manor. Then ask students to list the qualities a good sales presentation should include based on their analysis of Mr. Manor's comments. Students might note Mr. Manor's preparation, his friendly approach to gain audience trust, and his attempt to put himself "in the other person's place." Before assigning the activity, you might show a videotape of an auction or another sales presentation.

Activity Note

Each presentation should include a clear purpose and thesis with adequate support to make the sales pitch convincing. Students should include personal anecdotes to make their audience feel more at ease.

You might want students to write about the processes they followed as they prepared their presentations. Students should include how they analyzed the prospective audience.

PROFILES IN COMMUNICATION

Auctioneer Dave Manor believes in preparation. "In the auction business, you have to know your product," he says, "because in an auction, you introduce an item, set the price, and sell it in minutes."

Even though Dave Manor sometimes goes to great lengths to learn about a product he is going to sell, he refrains from talking too specifically about items during a sale because he feels he cannot be a specialist in everything. "You need to know enough about a product to answer customers' questions," he comments, "but, of course, you can't be an expert in everything."

Since the auctioneer is an arbitrator between the buyer and the seller, Mr. Manor believes it is important to gain the trust of the audience quickly. He says, "First I tell a personal story to make the people feel comfortable, like we're old friends. I also try to put myself in the other person's place and have compassion. Most people react differently in situations they're unaccustomed to. I try to take that into account."

Mr. Manor, of course, uses the auctioneer's traditional rapid-fire delivery, which includes about one-half filler words, plus repeated numbers. He says that the rapid chant keeps the action going and the excitement high.

Besides chanting, Mr. Manor's training included nonverbal communication—always standing not too far above the audience, establishing eye contact, and dressing to suit the audience.

You, like Dave Manor, are going to sell a product—perhaps a car, a personal computer, or a stereo component. What type of questions might your audience ask? What could you do to prepare for their questions? What personal story might appeal to your audience? What features might motivate a customer to buy your product?

Give your "sales" presentation to your class, and ask your classmates to participate as if they were buyers. Then ask them for feedback about your effectiveness.

S☆U☆M☆M☆A☆R☆Y

GETTING READY for a speech involves a systematic approach to selecting a suitably limited topic, developing a thesis statement, and finding information to support your thesis. Whether you are giving a speech to inform, to persuade, or to entertain, you can prepare by doing the following activities.

- **Identify subject areas** that are interesting and familiar to you.
- **Determine your topic** and limit it to a manageable size.
- **Identify your general purpose** (to inform, to persuade, or to entertain) and your specific purpose (your particular goal stated in a declarative sentence).
- **Write a thesis statement** that expresses the most important idea you wish to present to your audience.
- **Consider the makeup of your audience:** their demographic features and their knowledge, feelings, and attitudes about your topic.
- **Determine the significance of the occasion** for your speech, and make sure that you know any restrictions that may apply.
- **Support your thesis statement** with appropriate information: facts and opinions, examples and illustrations, anecdotes, statistics, comparisons, definitions, descriptions, or quotations.

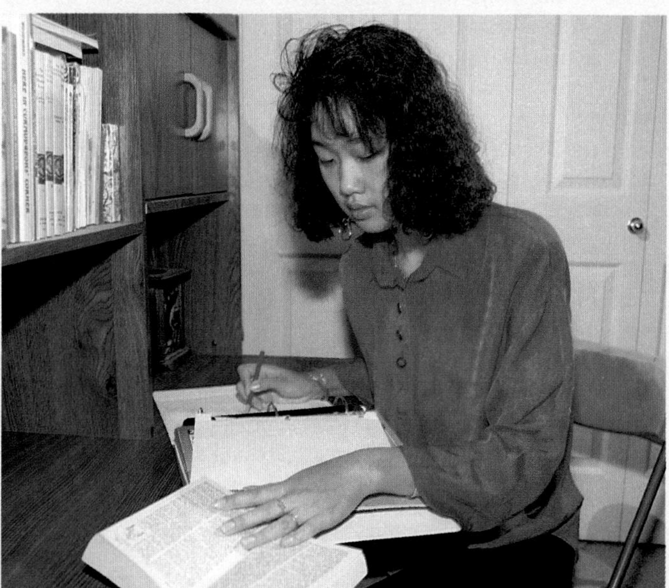

CHAPTER 9

Vocabulary

Look back through this chapter to find the meaning of each of the following terms. Write each term and its meaning in your communication journal.

anecdote, *p. 231*
audience, *p. 225*
brainstorming, *p. 216*
comparison, *p. 232*
contrast, *p. 232*
definition, *p. 232*
demographic data, *p. 225*
description, *p. 232*
example, *p. 230*
expert opinion, *p. 229*
fact, *p. 228*
figurative comparison, *p. 232*
general purpose, *p. 220*
illustration, *p. 230*
literal comparison, *p. 232*
occasion, *p. 226*
opinion, *p. 229*
purpose, *p. 220*
quotation, *p. 233*
specific purpose, *p. 221*
statistics, *p. 231*
subject area, *p. 216*
thesis statement, *p. 223*
topic, *p. 216*

TEACHER'S RESOURCE BINDER

- Chapter 9 Vocabulary

Review Questions

Answers

1. so information can be effectively covered in one speech
2. hobbies and activities, past events, current issues, places, processes, and people
3. to inform, to persuade, and to suit a special occasion
4. The general purpose of a speech is the speaker's overall intent to inform, to persuade, or to suit a special occasion. The specific purpose states in a declarative sentence the particular goal and topic the speaker will address in the speech.
5. A specific purpose states what the speech is about; a thesis statement identifies the main idea and the key points developed in the speech.

Discussion Questions

Guidelines for Assessment

Student responses may vary.

1. A speech topic is specific and has a focus; a new idea is often not specific or focused. Brainstorming sessions can be useful alone, but real productivity occurs when several people brainstorm together.
2. Students might add subject-area headings such as animals or pets, modes of transportation, machinery, or similar subjects.
3. a. This audience needs specific information. Demonstration and audience participation is appropriate.
   b. This audience needs to hear a reason to listen; the speaker might compare traditional kicking and soccer-style kicking.
   c. The speaker can build on the listener's willingness to learn by demonstrating techniques and by involving the audience as participants.
   d. The speaker could use questions to determine what the listeners already know and then build on that knowledge to increase their receptiveness to the speech.
4. Emerson expresses his dislike for using the words and thoughts of others instead of generating original words and thoughts. However, carefully selected quotations in a speech introduction can keep listeners interested and attentive. In the body, quotations can lend credibility to the speaker's information. In the conclusion, a quotation can give a feeling of finality and provide a memorable summary of the speech's focus.

CHAPTER **9**

Review Questions

1. After you choose a topic, why should you limit it?
2. List five sources of ideas for speech topics.
3. What are three general purposes for giving a speech?
4. What is the difference between the general purpose and the specific purpose of a speech?
5. How does a specific purpose differ from a thesis statement?
6. Identify the kinds of information that you need to know about your audience.
7. What are three questions you should ask yourself about the occasion of a speech?
8. How does a statement of opinion differ from a statement of fact?
9. How does an illustration differ from an example?
10. How does a literal comparison differ from a figurative comparison?

Discussion Questions

1. Discuss why brainstorming is likely to produce better topics for your speeches than just sitting down and trying to come up with a topic. What were the results of your past brainstorming sessions? In what specific ways could you have made these sessions more productive?
2. Discuss with your classmates why it is important to find a topic that interests you and that you know something about. Then discuss the seven subject areas listed in the chart on pages 219–220. What subject areas would you add to this list? Why?
3. You are giving a speech on soccer-style placekicking. Discuss how the following audiences would affect either your specific purpose or your approach.
   a. Boys ages 9–14—very interested in soccer-style placekicking but with very little knowledge of the subject
   b. Senior citizens—not very interested in soccer-style placekicking but with some knowledge of football
   c. Exchange students from China—very interested in learning about football but with little direct knowledge of the game
   d. Male and female high school students—somewhat interested in learning about soccer-style placekicking and with some knowledge of football
4. Ralph Waldo Emerson advised, "Stay at home in your mind. Don't recite other people's opinions. I hate quotations. Tell me what you know." Do you agree with Emerson's statement? Discuss when and where quotations can be used effectively in a speech.

6. demographic data; audiences' knowledge, feelings, and beliefs
7. When will the speech be given? Where will the speech be given? What are the restrictions for the speech?
8. A statement of opinion expresses personal beliefs or attitudes; it cannot be proved to be true or false.
9. They differ in length; an illustration is an example developed in detail.
10. A literal comparison shows similarity between essentially alike objects, people, or places; a figurative comparison imaginatively shows similarities between things that are essentially not alike.

ACTIVITIES

1. **Identifying Facts and Opinions.** Identify the following statements as fact or opinion. If an opinion is an expert opinion, explain why it qualifies as one.
   a. Ronald Reagan first took office as president on January 20, 1981.
   b. The mechanic informed my father that our truck needs a new fuel pump.
   c. Cheerleading is an enjoyable high school activity.
   d. Over 60 percent of the students who take a speech course in our school go on to college.
   e. In this school, athletes must maintain a B average to play on teams.
   f. As soon as photoelectric cells become more efficient, auto manufacturers will build more electric-powered cars.
   g. The decision to close the park was a bad one.
   h. According to the almanac, we had a record rainfall last year.
   i. That comic strip is very funny.
   j. My uncle, who repairs electronic office equipment, thinks voice-operated typewriters will be on the market before the middle of the next decade.
2. **Identifying Comparisons.** Identify each of the following comparisons as either figurative or literal. Explain your reason(s) for classifying each comparison as you did.
   a. The cheerleading squad worked as smoothly as a well-oiled machine.
   b. Ed Kitt, Central High's center, was about the same size as Miller High's center.
   c. A basketball is slightly larger than a soccer ball.
   d. Derrick Williams was a tiger on defense during the entire game.
   e. The crowd at game time was larger than any other crowd that had attended a Central High game in more than a year.
3. **Limiting a Topic and Developing It into a Thesis Statement.**
   A. Choose a subject of your own, select a subject suggested by the photographs below, or select one of the following subjects: basketball, cars, mountains, dogs, or college.

ACTIVITIES

Guidelines for Assessment

1. a. fact
   b. expert opinion; the mechanic is an expert in his field
   c. opinion
   d. fact
   e. fact
   f. opinion
   g. opinion
   h. fact
   i. opinion
   j. opinion
2. a. figurative; comparison of two unlike things
   b. literal; comparison of two similar things
   c. literal; comparison of two similar things
   d. figurative; comparison of two unlike things
   e. literal; comparison of two similar events
3. Responses should illustrate students' understanding of the narrowing process:
   A. A general subject is selected.

SUMMATIVE EVALUATION

Your **Teacher's Resource Binder** contains a reproducible **Chapter 9 Test** that may be used to assess students' mastery of the concepts presented in this chapter.

PORTFOLIO ASSESSMENT

For future reference and evaluation you may want to have students keep in their portfolios any skill sheets or evaluation forms that you have used with this chapter along with any other recorded or written materials that students have created.

B. A list of twenty-five to thirty topics is then limited to one specific topic.

C. For the limited topic, each student should write a purpose statement and a clear thesis statement and should compile a list of at least five kinds of information to support the thesis statement.

4. Students should demonstrate that they understand the process of choosing a topic and determining a specific purpose for that topic. They should each have a clear thesis. The facts should be provable, and the opinions should be credible.

5. Students might photocopy their articles so that they can underline the statistics. On the backs of the copies, they can write their responses as to whether the articles needed statistics.

CHAPTER 9

B. Working with classmates who have chosen the same subject, brainstorm to come up with a list of twenty-five to thirty topics. Then choose one topic from the list and limit it. Compare your limited topic with your classmates' limited topics.

C. For the limited topic you selected in Part A of this activity, write a purpose statement. Then turn your purpose statement into a thesis statement. Finally, compile a list of at least five different kinds of information to support your thesis statement. Share your list with your classmates.

4. Planning a Speech on a Personal Topic.

A. Take a personal inventory and choose a speech topic from the information you gather on your inventory. Completing the following statements may help you discover a suitable topic.

1. On a Saturday afternoon, I most like to . . .
2. You can always count on me to tell you my opinion about . . .
3. My friends think I'm talented when it comes to . . .
4. If I could be anything I want, I would be . . .
5. I will read almost any book about . . .
6. One day, I hope to be able to . . .
7. I spend most of my spare time . . .
8. My favorite (or least favorite) school subject is . . .
9. When I go to the movies, I most like to see . . .
10. If I could tell you only one thing about me, it would be that I . . .

B. Imagine that your general purpose for your speech is to inform your listeners about the topic you have chosen. Brainstorm and identify a specific purpose for your speech.

C. Using the specific purpose you stated in Part B of this Activity, write your thesis statement and list five kinds of information you would use in your speech to support this thesis statement.

5. Analyzing the Use of Statistics in an Article. Read an article about a local sports team's most recent game. Underline all the statistics used in the article. Could any of the points in the article have been made without statistics? If so, identify which ones.

◆ Real-Life Speaking Situations

PERFORMANCE OBJECTIVES

- To tell a story suitable for a specific purpose, audience, and occasion
- To choose an appropriate subject for a classroom setting
- To analyze an audience's interests
- To adapt a subject to suit a specific audience
- To give a short informative speech

REAL LIFE Speaking Situations

1 In the course of conversation, people often tell amusing personal anecdotes and secondhand stories about the escapades of others. At a party and in other group situations, someone skilled in storytelling often becomes the center of attention, using a range of verbal abilities to entertain appreciative listeners.

You are seated in class with a group of friends, and you want to entertain them by telling an amusing story to make a point. To generate ideas for a good story to tell, ask yourself the following questions.

- Which friends are you with?
- What story do you think will appeal to them the most? (Pick a story that will be suitable for telling in class.)
- What point do you plan to illustrate with this particular story?
- What parts of this story will amuse these specific friends?

Practice telling your story, and be prepared to present it in class. Also be ready to take part in a discussion on how you and your classmates planned your stories to suit your purpose (to entertain), your audience (classmates who are your friends), and the occasion (a class activity).

2 A teacher is usually aware of two things: one, who is in the "audience" in the classroom, and two, what style of speech is needed to communicate with that audience. Having attended school for a number of years, perhaps you have thought about how you would teach a class.

You have been asked to teach a one-hour class on a subject that interests you and that you are knowledgeable about. What subject would you choose?

You can choose a hobby, a vocational skill, a process, or any other subject of interest that you feel you could teach to others. Who will be your audience? Children at a summer camp? High school students? Adults taking a community education course? Write a short outline of what you would say to your class. Then, based on your outline, prepare a three- to five-minute speech summarizing

- what you would teach (your topic)
- what you would say (what you would teach your students)
- what approach you would take to teach your students (how you would tailor your speech to your students)

After giving your speech, ask your classmates for feedback on your plan for teaching your class.

ASSESSMENT GUIDELINES

1. Students might introduce their stories by telling what audience they are addressing and how they planned their stories to suit a purpose.

The stories should reflect the appropriate subject matter for audience and occasion, and the point of the story should be clear whether it is stated or implied.

2. Each outline should include the specific purpose statement and a clear thesis statement. Students should also include the key points of instruction and appropriate support and details.

In the speech, each student should explain the subject area and support elements and tell what process would be used to teach that particular topic to the chosen audience. Allow time for sharing and evaluation.

Chapter 10
Gathering Information
pp. 240–263

Chapter Overview

This chapter shows students where to look for information as they plan their speeches. The discussion of personal experience and observation emphasizes that the first source from which to begin gathering information is oneself. Other informative sources—interviews, surveys, and letters of request—are also discussed.

Teacher's Resource Binder

The following materials are identified at their point of use in this chapter:

- Skills for Success
  1 *Gathering Information*
  2 *Planning a Survey*
  3 *Using the Library for Print Sources*
  4 *Using the Library for Nonprint Sources*
- Chapter 10 Vocabulary
- Chapter 10 Test/Answer Key

AV Audiovisual Resource Binder

The following materials are identified at their point of use in this chapter:

- Transparency 19
  Using Your Knowledge and Experience
- Transparency 20
  Conducting a Survey

The second segment of the chapter introduces students to the various reference materials and technologies available in the library or media center. The chapter ends with a discussion of how to record information on note cards and how to credit sources.

Introducing the Chapter

After they select speech topics, students often need a systematic information-gathering routine for investigating the topics. Tell students that this chapter gives an overview of research techniques and provides new ideas about making discoveries. Students will also learn to consider personal experiences and other people's knowledge when they assemble information.

CHAPTER 10

Gathering Information

OBJECTIVES

After studying this chapter, you should be able to

1. Find information for speeches by using your own experience and observations.
2. Obtain information from others by interviewing, by surveying, or by writing a request letter.
3. Use the library or media center to locate information.
4. Select and use appropriate reference books.
5. Locate newspaper and magazine articles in the library.
6. Use the technologies available in your library (on-line catalog, InfoTrac and other electronic databases, or the interlibrary loan service) to obtain information.
7. Prepare note cards for speeches and identify your sources appropriately.

Where to Look for Information

We live in the "age of information." Facts, statistics, details, theories, practical advice, studies, and reports are readily available in a variety of media. With a little effort, anyone researching a speech can find enough information to give an interesting and informative presentation. How do you begin to look for the specific information that you need for your speech? Where do you go to find this information? You have three major sources:

- yourself
- other people
- reference materials

In this chapter you will learn how to use these sources and how to record the information you find so that you can incorporate it into your speech.

Bibliography of Additional Materials

Professional Readings

- Applewhite, Ashton, et al. ***And I Quote: The Definitive Collection of Quotes, Sayings, and Jokes for the Contemporary Speechmaker.*** New York: St. Martin's Press.
- Gates, Jean Key. ***Guide to the Use of Libraries and Information Sources.*** New York: McGraw-Hill Publishing Company.
- Mills, Glen E. ***Putting a Message Together.*** New York: Macmillan Publishing Company.
- Sheehy, Eugene P., ed. ***Guide to Reference Books.*** Chicago: American Library Association.

Audiovisuals

- ***Confident Public Speaking: Volume 2***—Quiet Advantage, Anaheim, CA (videocassette, 93 min.)
- ***Know Your Library***—Coronet/MTI Film & Video, Deerfield, IL (videocassette, 13 min.)
- ***Research***—Films for the Humanities and Sciences, Princeton, NJ (two filmstrips with audio, avg. 10 min. each)

Reteaching

Distributing and discussing several good examples of surveys and request letters might help students who are having difficulty using these sources. You will probably want to discuss the style and content of the request letters and the wording of the survey questions.

Extension

Public opinion of government policy can be measured by electronically polling voters. First, have students find information about electronic polling. Then, invite students to discuss this method of gathering information from voters. Do they see any drawbacks? What are the benefits? How could the information be used?

Making Connections

Mathematics

If your students work together to conduct a survey, encourage students with special math skills to set up the mathematical parameters for the survey, to determine the random sampling method, and to tabulate the results.

Ongoing Assessment

Activity 2

Students' survey questions should be clear and concise. Explanations of how students organized their questions and how they chose their survey participants should reflect an understanding of the material in this segment. Classmates' evaluations of the surveys could also help with your assessment.

Timesaver

You may want to compose a checklist that includes the steps for gathering information with a survey. Have students use the checklists when they evaluate their classmates' survey methods in **Activity 2.**

Activity 2: Gathering Information with a Survey

Conduct a survey in your school on the popularity of a certain sport, a particular television show, or a well-known place to eat. First, choose one of these topics. Next, write six survey questions that you will ask about your topic. Organize these questions in the most effective order. Use these questions to survey the student body in your school. Tell your class how many people you surveyed and how you conducted the poll. Report your findings. Ask for and respond to your classmates' evaluations of your survey.

The Request Letter

If your speech topic is unusual or specialized in some way, you may not have access to people who have information about this topic. An interview or a survey might not be an appropriate method of collecting information from others. However, if you can locate the names of organizations that have knowledge about your topic, you might write a **request letter,** one that asks for information about your topic. Examples of request letters include

- a letter to a political cartoonist, inquiring how he or she began his or her drawing career
- a postcard to a government agency, requesting a free information pamphlet
- a letter to a tourism bureau, seeking information on a state
- a note to a computer company, asking questions about its new computer models

Enrichment

Invite to class a math teacher or a math student with knowledge of statistics to explain more about sampling techniques for conducting surveys. You might ask the guest to cover the ideas of validity and reliability or to suggest common sampling techniques for polls. If your students are interested, have the speaker explain the mathematical formulas involved.

Closure

Ask students to recall the information-gathering methods presented in this segment. Invite discussion of the methods that students favor. Ask them to explain why they think these particular information-gathering methods would be most useful. Then have students discuss the drawbacks of the ones they feel would be least beneficial.

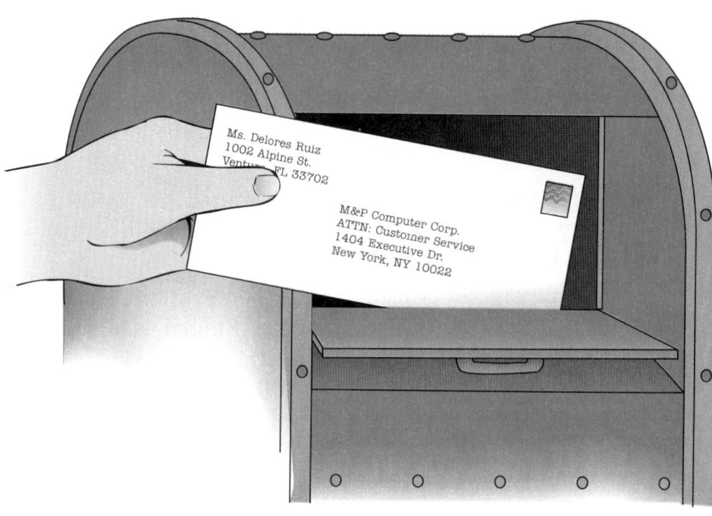

HOW TO Write a Request Letter

1. **Allow enough time for the recipient to answer.** You should allow time for the person or organization from whom you are requesting information to receive your letter, to read and respond to your request, and to send you the information you want.
2. **Be clear about what information you need.** Make sure that your request is reasonable and that the recipient will understand exactly what information you need.
3. **Help to make the response easier to send.** You might include a self-addressed, stamped envelope so that it will be easier for the person or organization to mail your reply.

ACTIVITY 3 Gathering Information by Letter

With your classmates, brainstorm a list of organizations and individuals that you think might provide helpful information for speech topics. Then select a specific topic, such as the topic you selected for Activity 1 (page 244) or another topic of your own choosing. Identify a particular source from the brainstormed list and compose a request letter, asking for information about this topic.

Integrating the Language Arts

Library Link

You will probably want to offer students assistance in obtaining addresses of government organizations and bureaus that provide information. The U.S. Government Printing Office in Washington, D.C., has many pamphlets and books available. Check with the school librarian for help in getting current addresses. In addition, *The New York Public Library Desk Reference* has many useful addresses for private, state, and national organizations.

Ongoing Assessment

Activity 3

The requests that students make in their letters should be reasonable, clear, and concise. If you plan to evaluate form and neatness, you will probably want to review the process of writing business letters before students write their letters.

Segment 2 *pp. 248–257*

- **Using the Library or Media Center**
- **Recording Your Information**
- **Identifying Your Sources**

PERFORMANCE OBJECTIVES

- To use the card catalog or on-line catalog to locate books on a topic
- To use a magazine index to look up articles on a topic
- To locate information in an encyclopedia or specialized reference
- To prepare note cards
- To write appropriate citations for sources

MEETING INDIVIDUAL NEEDS

Learning Styles

Visual Learners. To help familiarize students with library research, you (or artistic volunteers) could prepare several posters. You may want to include in these posters information on the Dewey decimal system or the Library of Congress system, a floor plan of the library showing where the subject areas are located, sample card-catalog entries, and charts of media available.

Alternative Approach

If you find that some students need extra help in developing research skills, you could pair them with peer tutors. Ask each pair to choose a speech topic of mutual interest. Then send pairs to the school library (or to the public library, if necessary). Ask students to make lists of the steps they follow in finding relevant information about their topics. Have students keep copies of this step-by-step process as a guide for future assignments.

Using the Library or Media Center

In many instances, particularly in planning informative and persuasive speeches, you will need to research and read about your topic. By researching, you will be able to

- verify facts that you have already discovered
- find new information that gives your speech depth
- provide background for your topic

Today's library is often called a **media center** because it holds such a wide variety of information resources. Printed material is no longer the only medium for reference sources. In your library you may find reference material in the form of

- books
- magazines, newspapers, and pamphlets
- electronic databases accessed by computer
- videotapes or audiotapes
- photographs, filmstrips, and slides

The Librarian

Often, the most valuable resource in the library is the librarian. Think of the librarian as an information specialist—someone who can direct you to the most useful tools for your particular research. Make a list of questions that you need to answer about your topic, and show these questions to your librarian. The librarian will be able to suggest the best sources for the information you need.

Motivation

Ask students who collect stamps, comic books, or coins about their methods of organizing their collections. Then question computer users about organizing their disks or arranging their computer files. Next, ask avid readers how they organize their own shelves of books. Explain that the library is arranged systematically so that materials can be located quickly.

Teaching the Lesson

As students work through this segment, you may want to plan an orientation of a school or a community library by arranging for a field trip or a visit with a librarian. Explain that just as libraries have become media centers with the additional technologies available, librarians have become specialists in a wide variety of media. Librarians are often the sources that can 

The Card Catalog or On-Line Catalog

The **card catalog** lists all the books contained in a particular library. In the card catalog, cards providing information about books are filed alphabetically in three different ways:

- by subject
- by author
- by title

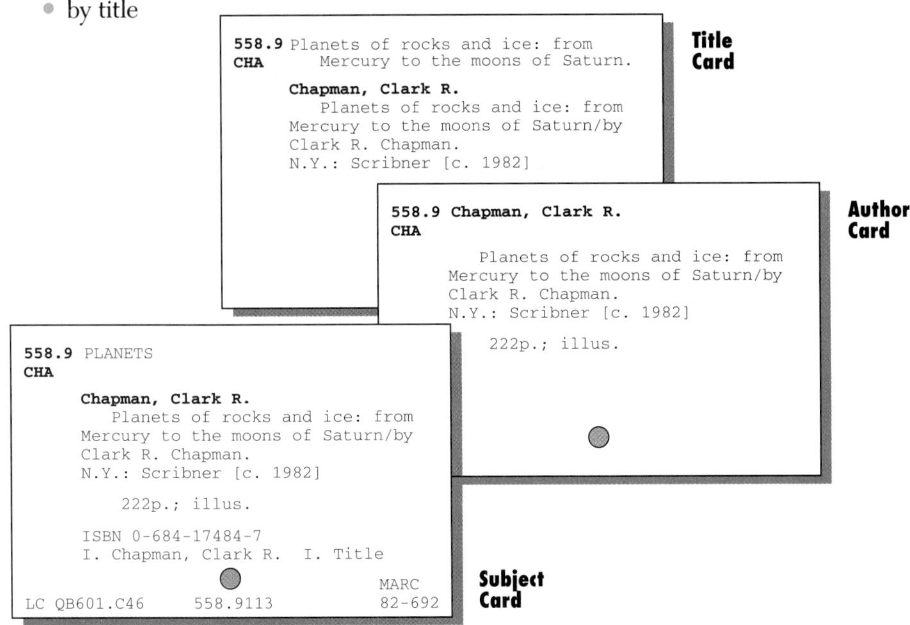

Some libraries have a **microform catalog** (a microfilm or a microfiche machine) that contains the library's entire listing of books. By turning the dial on a viewer, you can locate the same book information that you would find on card-catalog cards.

Some libraries have an **on-line catalog,** or a computerized card catalog. To use the on-line catalog, you type in the author, title, or subject to find information about the library's resources. The on-line catalog often tells you if the book is checked out or if it is available in

Common Error

Problem. Students sometimes go to the library without good research plans.

Solution. Explain that experienced researchers avoid wasting time by knowing the kinds of information they want to find when they begin researching. Suggest that in addition to having clearly limited topics, students should have lists of questions or points they want to find out about. Such lists will give the librarian a better idea how to help students who ask for assistance. In addition, the lists should shorten students' research time.

Teacher's Resource Binder

Skills for Success 3
Using the Library for Print Sources

help determine what other media-center materials will be most helpful.

Before you discuss the usual materials available in a library, you might want to discuss with students the varieties of libraries that are found in your community. Then adapt the presentation of the library catalog system to the method used by the libraries most students will visit. You will also want to discuss the call-number system that your students will use.

You might gather reference books from your collection or from the library to discuss with students. If you have space available, leave the books out for students to peruse. You might want to rely on the librarian to demonstrate the use of a magazine or newspaper index and to show any electronic database search methods or interlibrary loan services available. Make students aware of any special sources that are available in their school or community libraries.

Making Connections

Technology

If your library has an on-line catalog, demonstrate its use and give students time to use it to locate information. You might suggest that students keep note cards with the instructions or the commands necessary for locating books with the on-line catalog.

Linguistically Diverse Students

Some of your students might be accustomed to using library classification systems other than the Dewey decimal system and the Library of Congress classification system, both of which were developed in and are primarily used in the United States. For example, some students may have been exposed to the Universal Decimal Classification system, which is popular in Europe. You may want to spend extra time with linguistically diverse students when introducing the two American systems to make sure the students understand both systems.

another library branch. You can ask your librarian to show you how the cataloging system works.

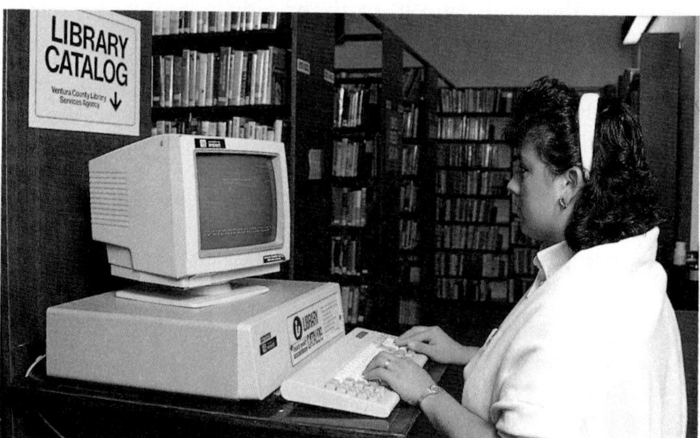

The key to finding a book is the **call number,** a number-and-letter code assigned to a book according to the classification system used to organize books in the library. All nonfiction books are organized by number, following either the Dewey decimal system or the Library of Congress classification system. Books of fiction are arranged according to the last names of the authors.

Reference Works

Reference works are publications containing useful facts and information. Used for ready reference in the library, many reference books cannot be checked out. The chart on page 251 shows a few reference works that are useful sources for general information.

If you have preferences for recording information, explain how you would like students to make note cards. Read aloud the examples of source citations on p. 257 so students will become familiar with the language used. You might also want to compare citations for a speech with citations in newspapers and news magazines.

Before you assign **Activity 4** on p. 255 and **Activity 5** on p. 257, model how to find information in the library on a particular topic by locating books, magazine articles, and encyclopedia references on your topic. Create a collection of note cards from your research and suggest some ways to cite the sources in a speech; post the cards in the classroom as references. You could do the research ahead of time and prepare the materials for demonstration in either the classroom or the library. Then assign **Activities 4** and **5** as independent practice.

Reference Works

Type	Description	Examples
Encyclopedias	• multiple volumes • articles arranged alphabetically by subject • good sources for general information	*Encyclopaedia Britannica* *Encyclopedia Americana* *The World Book Encyclopedia*
Specialized Encyclopedias	• helpful in researching specialized fields • contain in-depth information and little-known facts about specific topics	*Reader's Encyclopedia of American Facts and Dates* *The Encyclopedia of World Costume* *The Sports Encyclopedia*
Biographical Sources	• information about the lives and accomplishments of outstanding people	*Current Biography* *The International Who's Who* *Webster's New Biographical Dictionary*
Atlases	• maps and geographical information	*Atlas of World Cultures* *National Geographic Atlas of the World*
Almanacs	• facts, statistics, dates, and general information	*The Information Please Almanac, Atlas and Yearbook* *The World Almanac & Book of Facts*
Dictionaries	• contain information about how words are spelled, pronounced, or used	*Random House College Dictionary* *Webster's New World Dictionary*
Books of Quotations	• famous sayings of well-known people • often categorize sayings by subject matter or theme	Bartlett's *Familiar Quotations* *The Oxford Dictionary of Quotations*
Books of Synonyms	• list more interesting or more exact words to express ideas • may group entries into categories by subject	*Roget's International Thesaurus* *Webster's New Dictionary of Synonyms*

MEETING INDIVIDUAL NEEDS

Students with Special Needs

Students with learning disabilities might have trouble remembering how to use a large variety of reference works. You may want to select a few that will be most beneficial to students and to steer students toward these books for research. The more familiar students are with a few sources, the more likely they are to utilize the sources extensively and to feel comfortable doing so.

USING THE CHART

Have students brainstorm to list the advantages and disadvantages of using the types of reference works listed in the chart. (Some of the advantages are included in the chart.) Have several students compile the results to create a handout for the class.

Assessment

By checking **Activities 4** and **5,** you can assess each student's understanding of the skills covered in this second segment. You might want to work with students to create evaluation checklists for the quality of their source references and library skills. Then have students use the checklists to rate themselves as fair, good, or excellent in each category.

Reteaching

Students might have difficulty deciding which sources to credit. To help students see the difference between general information and information that needs a citation, divide the class into several groups. Assign each group a different subject for which information is widely available.

Ask each group member to consult reference sources and to write down one fact about the

Making Connections

Mass Media

Remind students that in addition to using newspapers for research, reading newspapers daily is a good practice for gathering ideas and materials for speeches. Politicians, comedians, ministers, consultants, educators, and journalists must constantly scan newspapers to keep their presentations fresh. You might encourage students to bring to class interesting items or current events for discussion. You might also provide a place for students to share and compare newspapers.

Writing to Learn

As students read newspapers and magazines, encourage the students to record or save interesting information in their communication journals. Remind them to make notes about how the information could be used and to make comments about how the events affect them personally.

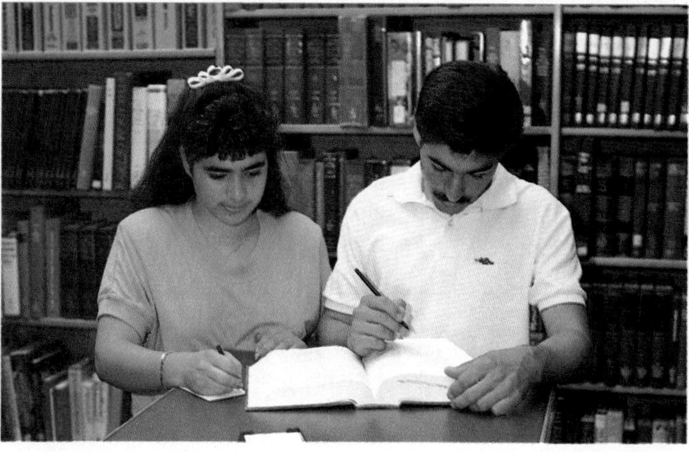

Newspaper and Magazine Articles

For current topics, the best sources of information are likely to be newspapers and magazines.

1. Newspapers. Your local library probably has an index of articles appearing in the nearest major daily newspaper and an index of articles appearing in the *New York Times.* Even if your library does not carry back issues of the *New York Times,* you will find that when the *Times* index refers to an article on a particular subject, your local paper may have an article on that subject appearing that same day.

assigned subject that needs to be cited and one fact that does not need a citation. Group members should discuss the information to make decisions about whether or not to write citations. You will probably want to circulate throughout the classroom to offer guidance as needed.

See p. 255 for **EXTENSION, ENRICHMENT,** and **CLOSURE.**

2. Magazines. Your library probably carries both current and back issues of popular magazines. The *Readers' Guide to Periodical Literature* gives complete reference information for articles in over one hundred popular magazines and journals. The *Readers' Guide* is published yearly with indexes for articles from magazines and journals published the previous year. For each year in progress, the *Readers' Guide* prepares monthly and quarterly indexes.

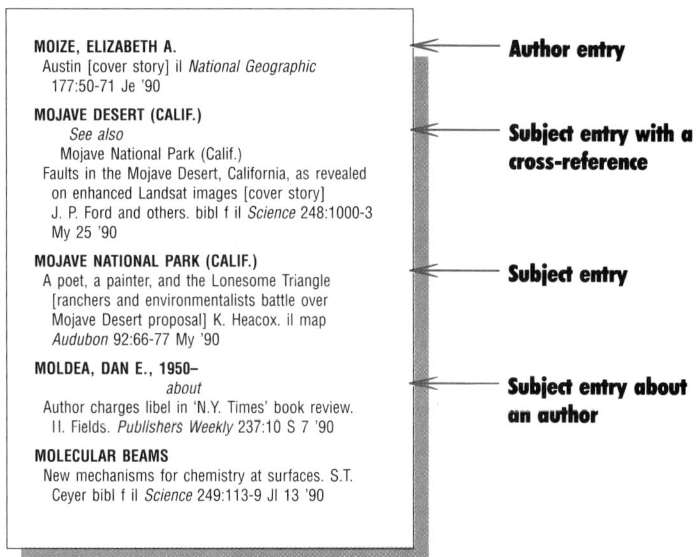
MOIZE, ELIZABETH A.
Austin [cover story] il *National Geographic* 177:50-71 Je '90

MOJAVE DESERT (CALIF.)
See also
Mojave National Park (Calif.)
Faults in the Mojave Desert, California, as revealed on enhanced Landsat images [cover story] J. P. Ford and others. bibl f il *Science* 248:1000-3 My 25 '90

MOJAVE NATIONAL PARK (CALIF.)
A poet, a painter, and the Lonesome Triangle [ranchers and environmentalists battle over Mojave Desert proposal] K. Heacox. il map *Audubon* 92:66-77 My '90

MOLDEA, DAN E., 1950–
about
Author charges libel in 'N.Y. Times' book review. I. Fields. *Publishers Weekly* 237:10 S 7 '90

MOLECULAR BEAMS
New mechanisms for chemistry at surfaces. S.T. Ceyer bibl f il *Science* 249:113-9 Jl 13 '90

Author entry

Subject entry with a cross-reference

Subject entry

Subject entry about an author

Each *Readers' Guide* entry gives the article title, author (if the magazine lists one), illustration information, magazine title, volume, page, month, and year. Just as some card catalogs have now been moved to microform and computer, periodical indexes have also been modernized. *The Magazine Index* on microfilm lists articles for hundreds of magazines. Each month, the editors of *The Magazine Index* feature a number of "hot topics" that are arranged in a loose-leaf binder and that are usually kept near the microfilm machine.

A popular magazine and newspaper article index on compact disk is InfoTrac. It is updated monthly and provides an index of general interest magazines from 1985 to the present. To access InfoTrac, use the computer to locate your subject, find the references available, and determine which are the best sources. Often, headings and an **abstract** (a brief statement of the key ideas) are available on the computer. The machine can then print out a listing of just the periodicals that you think will be useful for your speech.

CRITICAL THINKING

Evaluation

If you have access to a computerized magazine index such as InfoTrac, designate students to compare the computerized version with the *Readers' Guide to Periodical Literature* and to present their comparisons to the class. In small groups, students can select and narrow topics, look up the topics in both sources, and analyze which system is most helpful. Have students include the benefits and the drawbacks of both systems.

An Alternative Approach

Both the *Readers' Guide* and computerized magazine indexes use peculiar abbreviations and present material in ways that may baffle some students. The reduced type and close printing might also cause reading difficulty. You may want to read a few entries with students and explain the format and abbreviations.

Making Connections

Community Resources

Encourage students to use the resources of your local library and, if possible, to explore nearby college or university libraries. Students can usually take advantage of the research facilities available and can often obtain library cards.

Common Error

Problem. Students sometimes spend too much time looking up periodical sources and then discover that the sources they want are not available.

Solution. Before students begin their research, have them explore the magazine sources available in the library they are using. In your school library, show students where current issues are located on the shelves and provide information about how long the periodicals are kept. Show students how to locate and use the microforms and the microform machines. Remind students how materials should be left to best meet your library's needs.

Teacher's Resource Binder

Skills for Success 4
Using the Library for Nonprint Sources

3. Databases. Some libraries also have access to **electronic databases,** which are extensive collections of information on computer. On-line search services can give you access to more than five hundred databases. There is sometimes a fee charged for the search service, so ask your librarian about it.

4. Interlibrary Loan Services. Libraries, both large and small, may provide **interlibrary loan services.** By means of computers, libraries across the country can access each other's on-line catalogs. Your librarian can check the listings and can then tell you if a branch library or a library in another city has a book you want. Then, through the interlibrary loan service, your library can request the book for you. Libraries that use this service can increase the number of books available to their borrowers by obtaining materials from more than six thousand other libraries. Sometimes you must pay a fee to use this service.

Specialty Sources

1. Microforms. To save storage space, many libraries miniaturize numerous newspapers and magazines on film. **Microforms** are various types of photographic film bearing the reduced-scale record of printed or graphic material. The two most common types of microforms are **microfilm** (a roll or reel of film) and **microfiche** (a sheet of film).

Microfilm usually comes on a spool holding what looks like a filmstrip. Microfiche is usually on reduced-size pages. Both kinds of microform are used on special microform readers, which magnify the pages to about half the size of an actual newspaper or magazine page. In many cases, you can make copies of the pages you need. If you do not know how to use one of the readers, ask your librarian for help.

Extension

To give students practice in thinking about ways to use the library, divide the class into groups. Give each group the following research questions about speech topics:

1. What percentage of high school students drop out before graduation? (for a graduation speech)
2. Which computer programs are preferred by accountants? Why? (for a sales presentation)
3. Which breeds of horses make better sprinters? (for an informative speech on horse racing)
4. How does recycling benefit your community? (for a persuasive speech on a local issue)

Have each group list the library resources that might help students to answer the questions. Groups could compete to see who can come up with the most sources of information.

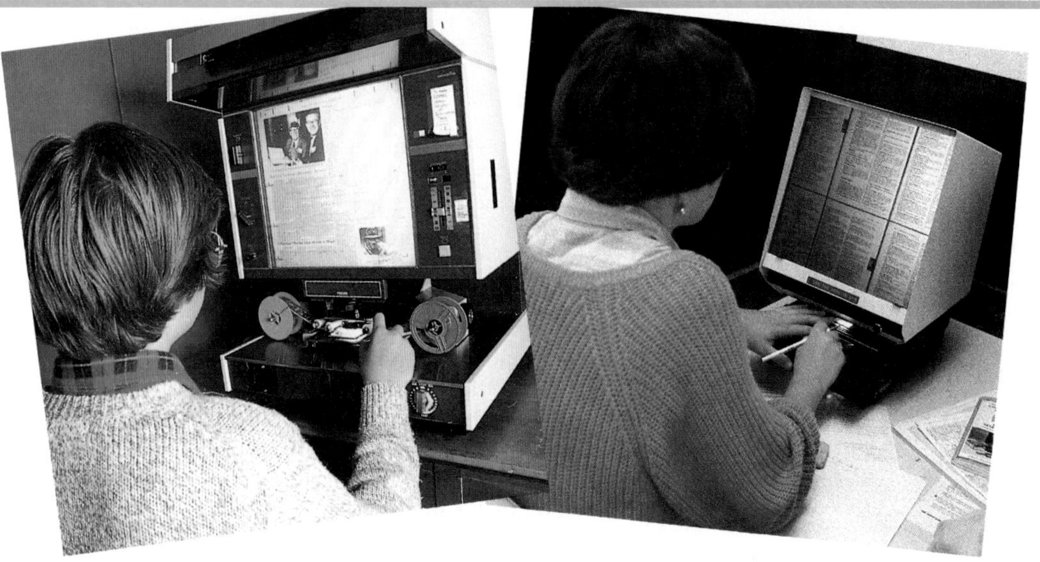

Additional Activity

Although many libraries no longer use vertical files, you can start a class vertical file with information received from students' request letters, newspaper or magazine clippings, survey results from various class projects, and interview notes students have collected. Have a committee decide what to include in the file and how to organize it.

2. Audiovisual Materials. Your library may offer recordings, books on audiotape, videocassettes, films, or other audiovisual materials that contain information on your subject. Because each library is different, you will need to check with a librarian to see what is available.

3. Vertical File. The **vertical file** is a collection of pamphlets, photographs, and clippings. These materials are not cataloged and are kept in vertical filing cabinets. Many libraries have abandoned the vertical files, but smaller and specialized libraries still maintain the collections. For example, a history library might have a vertical file containing old photographs, newspaper clippings, and other odd-sized material about historical places in the community. Ask your librarian whether your library has a vertical file and how to use it.

Activity 4

Finding Information in a Library

Identify a speech topic. Use the card catalog or on-line catalog to find several books on your topic. For each book, write the call number, title, author, and date of publication. Next, use the *Readers' Guide, The Magazine Index,* or a computerized magazine index to find articles about your topic. List several articles that you think will contain information you can use. Finally, consult several encyclopedias. If any of these have articles on your topic, list the articles under the name of that encyclopedia.

Ongoing Assessment

Activity 4

You may want to check over their information to see if students are on the right track in researching their topics. If the information sources seem too broad, too dated, or too far from the topics students have selected, you may want to make suggestions for further research.

Enrichment

Because new reference books are often added to the library's collection, students might take turns presenting a weekly or monthly library-reference seminar to show how to use new materials. As students use the library for research, ask them to select references that they feel are particularly useful for finding facts and to give brief reports to the class. Have students explain how to use the references and what kinds of information they include. You might keep in a notebook or in a computer database records of the information presented.

Critical Thinking

Application

You may want to have students practice paraphrasing. Copy part of a short article or a notice from a newspaper or a magazine and have students paraphrase it. Then discuss what information students should include so that their paraphrasing accurately reflects what the article says.

Additional Activity

Students might not be aware of how useful quotations can be to speakers. They also might not know that many quotation books include subject or word indexes. These indexes make searching for a relevant quotation simple. Work with students to select a few topics. Look up in books of quotations the topics, main ideas, or related ideas to find relevant quotations. Remind students to vary the ways the sources are cited. (Refer them to the examples on the next page.)

Recording Your Information

As you find information that you can use in your speech, you will need to record it. One way to do this is to make **note cards** on which you copy the information (or a summary of it) and its source. Use 4- x 6-inch cards, and record each idea separately.

On each card, note the name of the source, the author (if one is given), and the page number. If you have several cards from one source, you might code the cards by number so that you do not have to write the same source information on every card.

Note cards give you flexibility in sorting and arranging information. Remember, though, that you will probably not use all the information you have recorded on your note cards. Before you write your speech, you will select from your note cards only the specific information that is most useful.

Famous people who were cheerleaders

Former President Dwight D. Eisenhower, Jimmy Stewart, Cheryl Ladd, and former Miss America Phyllis George were all cheerleaders.

Randy Neil, Official Cheerleader's Handbook, p. 16

Identifying Your Sources

How many sources should you use for a speech? If you are relying on research to give your speech authority, you should probably not have fewer than three. Using only one or two sources may not give you a broad enough range of viewpoints.

The information you use from various sources needs to be credited. Be careful to avoid **plagiarism,** the presentation of another person's words or ideas as if they were your own. You do not need to credit general information—facts that are widely known or that can be found in any number of sources. However, you do need to credit exact quotations, opinions, and information gained from the research or insight of others.

CLOSURE

Ask students to identify the most-helpful ideas about library research covered in this segment. List the most frequently mentioned ones on the chalkboard. Ask students why it is necessary to record research information [so the source can be adequately cited in the speech and so there is no possibility of plagiarism]. Then discuss the necessity for accuracy in recording information and in citing sources.

A statement giving credit to the source of quoted material is called a **citation.** In your speech you can give appropriate credit to a source by using a short citation.

EXAMPLES:

- According to an article about interest rates in last week's *Newsweek,* . . .
- In a speech before the Habitat for Humanity organization, former President Carter said . . .
- Martina Browne, in her interesting book on parrots, presents the idea that . . .
- Jim Hawkins, in his book entitled *Cheerleading Is for Me,* suggests that . . .

ACTIVITY 5

Preparing Note Cards and Source Citations

Consult the sources you listed for Activity 4 (page 255). Gather information from these sources as if you were going to use it in a speech. Prepare separate note cards for three items of information from these sources. Then, on each note card, write an appropriate citation for each source.

GUIDELINES for Gathering Information

- Have I called upon my prior knowledge or personal experiences for information?
- Have I gained information from my observations?
- Have I interviewed others to gain information?
- Have I conducted surveys as a way of gathering information?
- Have I written to any sources that have information about my subject?
- Have I used the library effectively?
- Have I recorded information on note cards?
- Do I know how to cite information from reference sources or from individuals appropriately in my speech?

MAKING CONNECTIONS

Technology

Although recording information on note cards is generally recommended, students with messy handwriting might try taking notes on computers. They can set up hanging indents, use boldface type to highlight information, and bullet important points. This method also allows students to reorder information and to delete unwanted material quickly.

ONGOING ASSESSMENT

Activity 5

Each note card should contain the name of the author (if one is given), the page number, and an appropriate citation.

Segment 1 pp. 266–274

- **Organizing the Body of Your Speech**
- **Planning the Introduction**
- **Planning the Conclusion**

PERFORMANCE OBJECTIVES

- To write a specific purpose for a speech
- To organize the main points of a speech in chronological, topical, or spatial order
- To analyze the appropriateness of an organizational pattern for a speech
- To prepare and present a speech introduction and a speech conclusion

COMMON ERROR

Problem. Students might believe that they should always prepare their speeches in sequence: first, the introduction; then, the body; then, the conclusion.

Solution. Explain that the first priority is to shape a speech's message, its main ideas. These ideas are presented in the body of the speech. Afterwards, the student can attach an appropriate introduction and conclusion.

INTEGRATING THE LANGUAGE ARTS

Listening Link

You may want to tell students that effective listeners generally focus on the main ideas when listening to speeches. Have students listen to a lecture, a news report, or the school's daily announcements (if they are broadcast over the public-address system). Ask students to jot down the main points in these speeches. Then have students choose partners to compare responses.

Organizing the Body of Your Speech

The **body** of a speech is the portion in which the main points are developed. To organize the body of a speech, you will need to

1. determine the main points you want to stress
2. organize the main points in a consistent pattern the audience can follow
3. outline all the material you plan to use in the speech

Because the body of a speech contains the most important ideas that will be presented, many experienced speakers prepare it first. Then, after they know the development of the main ideas, they usually find the introduction and conclusion easier to prepare.

Introduction
- Gains the attention and the goodwill of the audience
- Develops interest in the topic

Body
- Presents the main points in an organized pattern
- Gives supporting information for the main points

Conclusion
- Emphasizes key idea or ideas of the speech
- Leaves the audience with greater interest in the topic

Determining the Main Points

The **main points** of a speech are the major ideas under which the supporting information is organized. If you have composed a well-written specific purpose (or a clear thesis statement), then determining the main points of your speech should be fairly easy. [See Chapter 9 for more about identifying a specific purpose and developing a clear thesis statement.] The specific purpose or the thesis statement leads to the wording of the main points.

EXAMPLES:

1. If your specific purpose is to explain the three ways that dogs have earned their title as our "best friends," each of the main points of your speech would be one of the three ways that dogs have earned this title.
2. If your specific purpose is to explain the development of the modern bicycle, your main points would be the steps in the historical progress of the bicycle's evolution.

- To analyze the effectiveness of speech introductions and conclusions
- To write an anecdote about a personal experience

Motivation

You may want to write the following statement on the chalkboard: "Every message, no matter how brief, requires a beginning, a middle, and an end." Ask students to think about how this statement applies to the following messages: a telephone message, a friendly letter, and a TV ad for breakfast food. Encourage volunteers to give examples of such messages and to identify 

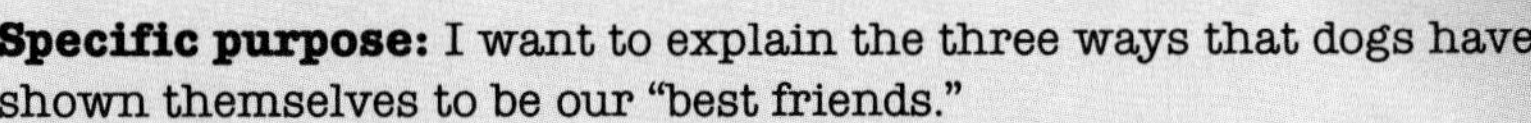

Specific purpose: I want to explain the three ways that dogs have shown themselves to be our "best friends."

Thesis statement: Dogs have earned their place as our "best friends" by working with people, by protecting people and their property, and by showing love and devotion to people.

Main points:
I. Dogs work with people.
II. Dogs protect people and their property.
III. Dogs show love and devotion to people.

Types of Organizational Patterns

The main points of your speech may be organized in any of a number of logical patterns. The three most common methods of arrangement are chronological order, spatial order, and topical order.

Chronological order: the order in which events happen in time (often used for giving directions, showing how things are made, or explaining the history of something in terms of a sequence of events)

Specific purpose: I want to explain the five stages in the evolution of the bicycle.

I. The first stage is the origin.
II. The second stage is the development of a steering device.
III. The third stage is the attachment of pedals to the front wheel.
IV. The fourth stage is the addition of chain drive.
V. The fifth stage is the development of modern safety features.

Cooperative Learning

You could have students work in small groups to practice organizing events in chronological order. Ask each group to choose a fable, a myth, or a well-known story and to set up a chronology of the story's events. In writing the chronologies, students should succinctly list the main events and avoid specific details. On completion, you may want to ask the groups to share their lists and to discuss any difficulties they might have encountered.

AV Audiovisual Resource Binder
Transparency 21
Organizational Patterns

the beginning, the middle, and the end of each one. Tell students that in this segment they will learn how to organize the introduction (beginning), the body (middle), and the conclusion (end) of a speech and how to develop each part effectively.

Teaching the Lesson

Invite students to read the first part of the lesson to learn about organizing the body of a speech. Show the relationship of the specific purpose to the main points of a speech by examining and discussing the examples provided.

To help students choose appropriate organizational patterns, discuss the types and their uses.

Critical Thinking

Analysis

Ask the class to brainstorm for several speech topics of interest to them. (Ideas that were generated in **Chapter 9: "Getting Ready"** and **Chapter 10: "Gathering Information"** can be used here.) Write the topics on the chalkboard. Then have students list at least three main points for each topic.

Spatial order: the organization of things according to their position in space (often used in describing places)

Specific purpose: I want to describe the three levels of the Community Center.

I. The basement contains various recreational facilities.
II. The main floor contains restaurants and administrative offices.
III. The second floor contains an auditorium, smaller meeting rooms, and a banquet room.

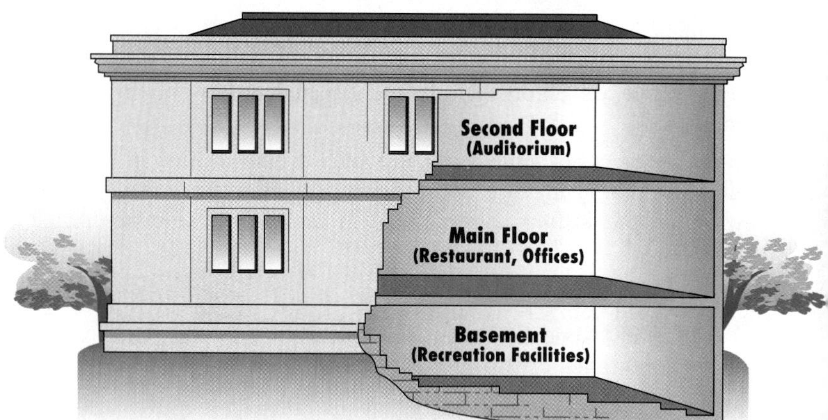

Topical order: a pattern of organization in which a topic is broken down into parts that are then arranged in an order determined by the speaker (used to examine parts of a whole such as a series of reasons or a list of major features)

Specific purpose: I want to discuss three measures of the strength of the United States as a world power.

I. One measure of U.S. strength is its natural resources.
II. A second measure of U.S. strength is its military.
III. A third measure of U.S. strength is its technology.

Provide guided practice by asking the following questions: What pattern might be appropriate to organize a speech on a scientist's life? [chronological] on the qualities of a good leader? [topical] on the beauty of a tropical island? [spatial] Then help students to select one of the three organizational patterns for the following speech topics: how to help the environment [topical], a ride down the Amazon River [spatial], my first day of high school [chronological]. Then use **Activity 1** on p. 270 as independent practice.

As you proceed through the second part of the lesson, you may want to have students work in small groups to discuss the different kinds of introductions and conclusions presented in the charts on pp. 272–274. Have the groups answer the following questions: Which introduction and conclusion would be the simplest to prepare? the most difficult to prepare? the most commonly used?

Other Organizational Patterns

Sometimes a particular speech may call for another kind of organizational pattern. Other organizational patterns that you may use include

- climactic order
- cause and effect
- comparison and contrast

[For more information about these organizational patterns, see Chapter 14.]

The following patterns of organization, discussed in Chapter 15, are effective in developing persuasive speeches:

- deductive approach
- inductive approach
- statement of reasons
- problem/solution
- comparative advantage
- criteria satisfaction
- negative method
- Monroe's motivated sequence

Developing the Main Points

Once you have determined the main points of your speech and have made an informal plan of organization, you can arrange your supporting information under appropriate headings. Remember that the main points provide a basic structure that you fill out with supporting information. As you sort and arrange your supporting material to group related ideas, take care to keep **unity** in mind.

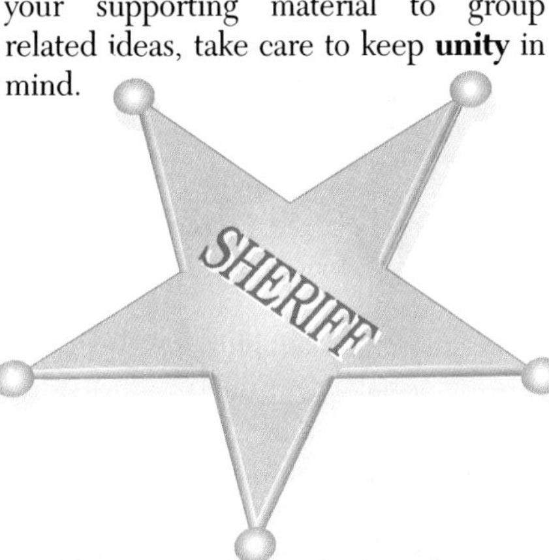

"And so you just threw everything together? ... Mathews, a posse is something you have to *organize*."

INTEGRATING THE LANGUAGE ARTS

Literature Link

You may want to have students look for famous speeches in literature and identify the organizational patterns used. Encourage students to look for different types of patterns such as the additional ones listed on this page.

Learning Styles

Visual Learners. To make the concepts of main points and supporting details more concrete, you may want to draw the following diagram on the chalkboard:

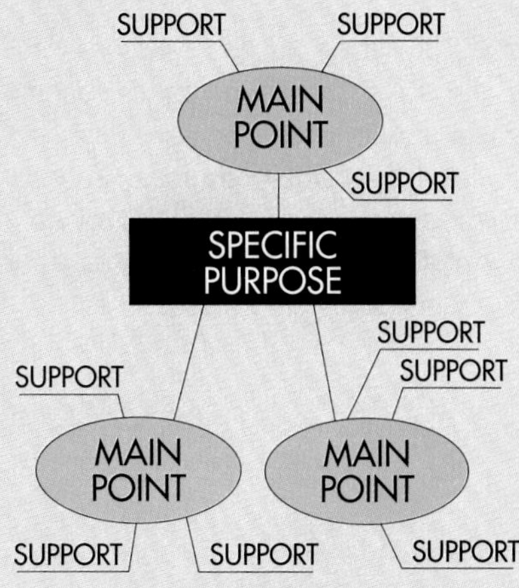

Then assign **Activity 2** on p. 273 and **Activity 3** on p. 274 as independent practice. Allow class time for your student audience to evaluate the introductions and conclusions.

Assessment

Using **Activities 1–3,** assess students' abilities to organize the main points of a speech and to present an effective introduction and conclusion.

Unity means "oneness." A speech is unified when all its parts fit together to make a whole and all of the information contained in the speech relates to the specific purpose. You will find that one of the best ways to plan a unified speech is to prepare an informal outline. Any information that does not fit under one of the main headings in the outline does not belong in the speech.

Ongoing Assessment

Activity 1

As you listen to the reasons students give for choosing a specific organizational order, evaluate the suitability of their choices. In your evaluations, you will probably want to consider the comments of students during the discussions.

Activity 1: Organizing the Main Points of a Speech

Write a specific purpose for a speech that you might give to your class. Under the specific purpose, organize the main points for the speech in chronological, spatial, or topical order. What makes the organizational pattern you have chosen the most appropriate one for your speech? Discuss your answers with your classmates.

Planning the Introduction

The beginning section of your speech is the **introduction.** An introduction can be as short as a few sentences and should usually be no longer than 10 percent of the speech.

An introduction serves three very important purposes. It should

1. get the attention of the audience
2. gain the goodwill of the audience
3. develop the audience's interest in the topic of the speech

Reteaching

To help students understand the three ways to organize main points, you may want to write the following speech titles and organizational patterns on the chalkboard: (1) How to Set Up a Bird Feeding Station: chronological order; (2) Our Town—Where to Eat, Shop, and Play: spatial order; (3) What Is School Spirit?: topical order.

Then proceed as follows: **Topic 1**—Elicit a discussion of possible content for the speech. Why would chronological order be a good organizational pattern? [Assembly of the station would follow specific steps.] **Topic 2**—Discuss attractions in your town. What visual aid would help others find them? [A large map might help.] Why is spatial order a good choice for this speech? [People need to know how to proceed from one part of town to the other.] **Topic 3**—

Attention means sustained interest. You need to find a way to focus the audience's attention on the subject matter of your speech. Then, when you get into the body of the speech, your audience will continue to listen.

Goodwill is the audience's respect or positive feeling for the speaker as a person. What you say in your opening remarks and the way in which you say it—your tone, your inflection, and other nonverbal signals—are important. If your audience likes or trusts you, they will likely be willing to listen to what you have to say and to think about your message.

Interest refers to the involvement or concern your audience shows about your topic. As you plan your introduction, include facts, examples, and other information that will hold your audience's attention.

How you get attention, build goodwill, and develop interest in your topic takes ingenuity. As you can tell by listening to speakers on the radio and on television, there are dozens of ways to begin a speech. The following chart lists and illustrates the most effective types of speech introductions. Each one of these can get your audience interested in the topic of your speech.

Critical Thinking

Synthesis

Ask students to give examples of weak introductions they have read or heard. To get the discussion moving, ask students to develop a "don't" list. Begin with the following points:

1. Don't open with an apology—if you are not prepared, the audience will know it.
2. Don't open with a canned joke—the joke may offend someone or fall flat. It also may have nothing to do with your speech.

Discuss the variety of opinions inherent in this topic. What kind of order would be appropriate? [A variety of opinions can best be arranged in topical order.]

Evaluate responses and elaborate on areas students do not seem to understand.

An Alternative Approach

Some students may need additional practice in determining the best techniques to use to introduce their topics. You may want to give students several broad topics and work with the class to suggest ways in which the topics could be introduced with any of the techniques for introductions on this page.

For example, if you list the general topic "baseball," students might suggest the following introductions:

1. Question: Why is baseball considered America's national pastime? Why are baseball players called the boys of summer?
2. Startling statement: In the first rules of baseball, the batter was considered out if a fielder caught the ball either on the fly or on the first bounce. Much has changed in the rules of baseball. . . .

TEACHER'S RESOURCE BINDER

Skills for Success 1
Using Techniques for Introductions

Audiovisual Resource Binder

Transparency 22
Techniques for Introductions

Techniques for Introductions

1. Startling statement: Begin your speech with a brief statement that surprises your audience and thus catches their attention.

EXAMPLE: There are an estimated fifty million dogs in the United States. That's approximately one dog for every two families in the country. In my speech today, I want to look at the ways dogs have become humans' "best friends."

2. Question: Ask a question. Your audience will listen carefully so that they can hear the answer.

EXAMPLE: Why is it that roughly one out of every two families in the United States has a pet dog? What is it about dogs that makes them far and away the leading pet and humans' "best friends"?

3. Story: Tell a brief story, or anecdote. An audience, young or old, is "hooked" by a story. However, finding stories that are relevant and short enough to fit a speech takes effort.

EXAMPLE: The house was filled with smoke. The father led his wife and children into the yard—everyone was gasping for breath. As smoke cleared from his eyes, he looked around only to discover that Julie, his five-year-old daughter, was missing. Just as the father was about to rush back into the house, he saw Kelly, the family's German shepherd, pull Julie through the doorway.

Is this just a story? No, it's the kind of actual occurrence that happens several times every year and represents just one of the ways that dogs have shown themselves to be true friends. Today I want to talk with you about the ways in which dogs have earned their place as humans' "best friends."

4. Quotation: Open with a quotation that fits your topic. You might quote a recognized expert on your topic or you might use a quotation because it expresses an idea in a creative way. [See more about finding quotations on page 251.]

EXAMPLE: These lines from a speech given to the U.S. Senate by George Graham Vest describe the way many people feel about their dogs.

> The one absolutely unselfish friend that man can have in this selfish world, the one that never deserts him, the one that never proves ungrateful or treacherous, is his dog. . . .When all other friends desert, he remains.

In my speech today, I want to look at the ways in which dogs have become humans' "best friends."

5. Personal reference: Give a personal reference in the introduction. This relates the speech topic directly to the audience's experience.

EXAMPLE: I'm sure many of you have pets—perhaps you have a cat or a parakeet. Some of you may go in for more exotic pets like monkeys, snakes, or rare tropical fish. But unless I miss my guess, more of you own dogs than own any other kind of family pet. Today I want . . .

(continued on next page)

EXTENSION

Have students gather short articles about subjects they are interested in (unusual pets, sports, music). Then have students remove (and save) the conclusions from the articles. Have students work in groups to write new conclusions by using one or more of the techniques on p. 274. Have students discuss the effectiveness of the conclusions they wrote and compare theirs with the originals.

ENRICHMENT

Introduce students to sources for effective introductions by bringing to class specific reference books such as a book of quotations, the *Guinness Book of World Records,* and an almanac. Point out that speechwriters usually keep such books on hand to provide themselves with startling facts, impressive statistics, or authoritative quotations that fit the mood of a

Techniques for Introductions

6. Audiovisual materials: Use audiovisual materials to support your words of introduction and to add variety and interest to your speech.

EXAMPLE: Look at this picture of Border collies herding sheep in Montana. Here's another picture that shows a Doberman pinscher on guard at a warehouse complex. And finally, here's a picture of a German shepherd playing with his human owners. As these pictures show, there are at least three ways dogs have become humans' "best friends."

ACTIVITY 2 Planning Speech Introductions

Prepare an introduction that you can use for the speech that you planned for Activity 1 on page 270. Present it to your class. When everyone has given his or her introduction, have the class evaluate the introductions. Which ones are especially effective in capturing attention, gaining goodwill, and developing interest in the topic of the speech?

Planning the Conclusion

The **conclusion** is the final portion of a speech. Although a conclusion is seldom longer than a few sentences, it is very important. The goals of an effective conclusion are

1. to emphasize the key idea or ideas of the speech
2. to intensify the emotions, or feelings, of the audience

Bring your speech to a conclusion as soon as you have covered the main points. Don't make the mistake of concluding your speech and then adding to it. The following methods are three of the most effective ways of concluding a speech.

ONGOING ASSESSMENT

Activity 2

You may want to help students devise a rating scale for evaluating capturing attention, gaining goodwill, and developing interest. Then students' rating scales could be included in your evaluation of the introductions.

BUILDING A PORTFOLIO

You may want to suggest that students include their introductions and conclusions from **Activities 2** and **3** in their portfolios. Urge students also to include any helpful ideas gleaned from classmates' evaluations.

TEACHER'S RESOURCE BINDER

Skills for Success 2
Using Techniques for Conclusions

guided practice for **Activity 6** on p. 281, you may want to show students how the note cards on p. 280 were derived from the formal outline on pp. 277–278. Then assign **Activity 6** as independent practice.

Assessment

Use **Activities 4–6** to assess the following skills: using transitions, creating an outline, and rehearsing a speech.

Additional Activity

You may want to have students analyze contemporary writing to understand how it is organized. Provide the class with magazine articles and have students highlight the specific purpose of each article. Then have students find and highlight related ideas. Have students use different colors for each main point. Challenge students to make an outline of the article by using the highlighted main points.

	C. Dogs can find people who commit crimes. **1.** Dogs have a remarkable sense of smell that enables them to track people. **2.** Dogs remember a scent for a long time. **D.** Dogs can rescue people in danger. **1.** Stories of dogs' heroic sacrifices are well documented. **2.** The opening story about Kelly was a good example of such a feat. **E.** Dogs can guide people with physical disabilities. **1.** Dogs are used to guide people who are visually impaired. **2.** Dogs are used to guide people who are hearing impaired.
Transition in parentheses	(Finally, there is one more way, perhaps the most important way, that dogs are our "best friends.")
Main point	**III.** Dogs give people unquestioning love and devotion. **A.** Dogs will greet their owners joyfully. **B.** Dogs will sit on their masters' laps or at their masters' feet for an entire evening. **C.** Dogs will play with members of the family for hours. **D.** Dogs may provide the best key to mental health. **1.** People with dogs as pets are basically better adjusted. **2.** People with emotional disturbances who are given dogs for pets improve in mental health.
Conclusion separated from body	**CONCLUSION** **I.** So we can see that dogs work with people, dogs protect people and property, and dogs show love and devotion to people. **II.** Final quotation.

Ongoing Assessment

Activity 5

As criteria for your evaluation, you may want to use the five points in **Preparing a Formal Outline** on p. 276.

Creating a Speech Outline

Review your responses to Activity 1 through Activity 4 to create a complete outline for your speech. Use the preceding outline as a model. Refer to the suggestions for preparing an outline on page 276 and include transitions at the appropriate points.

Reteaching

Students who do not understand transitions or how to use them may be helped by a discussion of common uses:

1. Use synonyms to recall words or phrases used earlier. (Dogs give unquestioning love. These *canine friends* . . .)
2. List or enumerate points. (First, . . .; second, . . .; third, . . .)
3. Repeat a key word or phrase. ("But as I said before, we must go forward.")

Translating Your Outline into a Speech

Your complete outline usually contains enough information to make up one third to one half of your speech. To prepare for the delivery of your speech, you need to flesh out this skeleton in a number of practice sessions, or **rehearsals.**

Setting the Stage for Speech Rehearsal

Complete your outline at least two days before you plan to deliver your speech so that you will have time to rehearse.

Only you can determine how many rehearsals you will need. Some speakers do well with just two or three rehearsals. Others need more. For a classroom speech, you will probably need at least two rehearsals over a two-day period.

HOW TO *Rehearse for a Speech*

1. **Create a situation as much like the actual speech situation as possible.** For instance, rehearse standing up or rehearse with a speaker's stand (or something like one) if your speech will be delivered in this manner.
2. **Present your speech just as you hope to deliver it.** Check your watch to note how long you take to give the speech. As you rehearse, pretend that objects around the room are members of the audience and practice maintaining eye contact. [See pages 36–37.]
3. **Evaluate your performance.** Which parts seemed to go especially well? Which parts need more development? What could you say that you did not say during your first rehearsal?
4. **Plan for improvement with additional rehearsals.** A second rehearsal is likely to be both longer and better than your first. Compare your rehearsals. Where did you improve? Were there any parts that did not go as well as the first time? Put the speech aside for several hours—or even until the next day. If you have identified problem areas, ideas for improvement may occur to you during the time between rehearsals.

An Alternative Approach

Some students may need additional work in preparing outlines and translating them into speeches. As a reteaching strategy, you may want to write an outline and a short speech with students. As they help you make decisions or discuss your work, you will be able to tell whether they understand the steps in the process. This activity also enables you to model each step of the speech-writing process.

Technology

If you have access to tape recorders, you may want to have students tape-record their rehearsals. They can listen to their readings as they follow their outlines. Encourage students to analyze the taped rehearsals and to work on weak points.

Extension

Rehearsals of a speech are usually more effective if one or two classmates can attend the rehearsal and make suggestions. Ask students to create a checklist to fill out at a speech rehearsal. The checklist should include the topics studied in this chapter (introduction, main points, transitions, and so on).

Enrichment

Pass out copies of the Gettysburg Address. Have students discuss the work with partners or in small groups to uncover the outline of the speech. A suggested outline follows:

Introduction: Eighty-seven years ago, a new nation was born.

I. We as a nation are being tested by a great war.

Writing to Learn

Tell students to ask parents, friends, and other teachers to listen as the students rehearse their speeches. Have students record in their communication journals the responses they get and the effort they make to correct their errors.

The Role of Notes in Rehearsal

Whether or not you are allowed to use notes during your presentation, you will probably feel safer using notes during practice. A formal outline is too long to use as speaker notes. The handiest way to manage speaking notes is with note cards containing a series of single words or phrases in outline form. The examples shown below are acceptable note cards for the outline on pages 277–278.

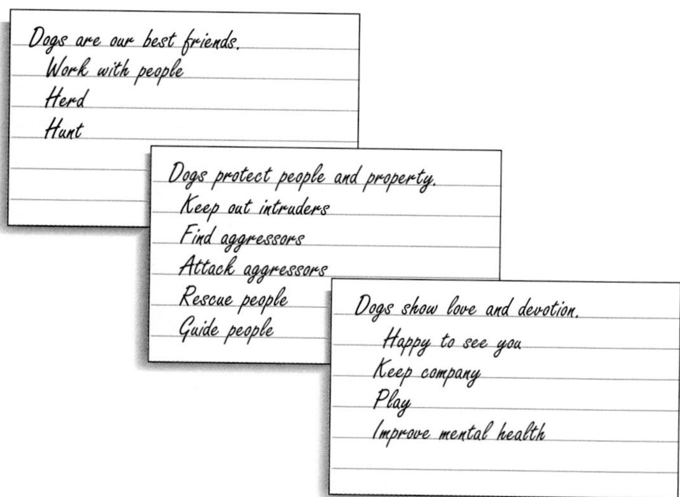

Avoid Memorizing

Many speakers fall into a trap of memorizing without even knowing it. If you try to say key ideas exactly the same way each time you rehearse, you will begin to memorize the entire speech even if you are not trying to do so. To avoid this trap, develop a method of practice that will help you to master your speech without memorizing it. Each time you rehearse, try to say various parts of your speech in different ways. Remember that your goal is to know your speech, not to memorize it.

What is the difference between knowing a speech and memorizing it? Look at the examples below. In the first practice, the speaker rehearsed the speech exactly as it was written.

Example:

Let's take a look at the common pencil. My pencil consists of a wooden shaft with six sides that has a cylinder of graphite running the length of its center. An eraser is attached to one end of the shaft with a brass band. The other end of the shaft is sharpened to a point.

II. We are here to dedicate a battlefield for those who died in the war.
III. We cannot. They have dedicated it with their blood.
IV. We can only make sure they have not died in vain.

Conclusion: Let us pledge that freedom and democracy will live forever.

Closure

You may want to ask each student to share with the class the most helpful thing learned in this lesson. List their responses under the headings "Transitions," "Outlines," and "Rehearsals."

In the second practice, the words have been changed, but the meaning is the same.

EXAMPLE:

Have you ever looked closely at a pencil? Most pencils are very similar. Mine consists of a six-sided wooden shaft encasing a piece of graphite that's about $\frac{1}{16}$ of an inch in diameter. At one end of the shaft is a slightly worn eraser that is attached to the shaft with a brass band. At the other end, the shaft is sharpened to a point.

As the preceding example shows, rehearsing a speech can help you to sound natural and relaxed. By contrast, memorization can make you sound wooden. The familiarity that comes from careful practice can also help you to adapt to your audience's mood and to recover smoothly when you forget a word or a point.

ACTIVITY 6 Creating and Using Note Cards to Rehearse a Speech

Make note cards from your formal outline. Using these note cards, rehearse your speech at least three times. To avoid memorization, work on improving your wording in each rehearsal.

Ongoing Assessment

Activity 6

To assess understanding of creating note cards, you will need to see students' formal outlines to compare the information.

GUIDELINES

for Preparing Your Speech

- Is my specific purpose clear?
- Does my introduction get attention and lead into the speech?
- Are my main points clearly stated?
- Do my points follow a consistent pattern?
- Is each of my points developed with supporting material?
- Does my conclusion summarize and leave the audience with heightened interest in the topic?
- Have I used an effective technique to develop my introduction and my conclusion?
- Have I practiced the speech enough to be familiar with the main ideas and supporting information?

◆ Profiles in Communication

Performance Objectives

- To select the desired effect, the main points, and the organizational method for a pep talk
- To prepare an outline, an introduction, and a conclusion for a coach's pep talk
- To rehearse and present an inspiring talk
- To evaluate a pep talk for its effectiveness

Teaching the Feature

You may want to have a student read aloud the profile of Natalie Gunter. Ask students if they have known any coaches like Ms. Gunter who feel that preparation and organization are a big part of the sports program.

Encourage students to recall experiences they have had in athletics that involved spirited pep talks before, during, or after challenging games. What methods, moods, or inspiring phrases do they recall? What effect did the pep talk have on the team? Did the speech make a difference in how the team played?

Activity Note

This activity is a good opportunity for students to prepare short speeches to show mastery of the organizational skills presented in this chapter. Each student should start with a determined effect, plan and organize the main points, outline the message, write an effective introduction and conclusion, rehearse the speech, present it to classmates, and respond to comments from the student audience.

PROFILES IN COMMUNICATION

Natalie Gunter

According to Natalie Gunter, head track coach at a large high school, clear communication is essential. Her thirty years of coaching girls' basketball and track and five years of coaching cross country have given her much valuable practice in polishing her communication skills.

Coach Gunter believes in organization. She says, "The success of my program centers around preparation. I carefully outline each practice, but experience has taught me the value of spontaneity."

Although her communication to individual players is often impromptu, Coach Gunter sometimes uses an outline when she is addressing the team as a whole. Ms. Gunter says that her outline is her assurance that she will remember to cover every important point in the order that the points need to be raised.

On game days Coach Gunter extemporaneously delivers pep talks to her team. "Much emotion is involved," she reports, "because playing well means as much to me as it does to the team." She adds that nonverbal communication is particularly important during a game because she can send important messages to her players with just a nod or a gesture.

ACTIVITY

Imagine that you coach a little league team. For the day of the championship game, you must prepare a pep talk. First, decide how you want your speech to affect your team. Do you want to inspire emotional frenzy or do you want to calm and reassure your team? Next, determine your main points and organize them in a consistent pattern. Prepare a brief outline of what you want to say. How will you get the team's attention and gain goodwill with your introduction? What is the goal of your conclusion?

Practice your speech before presenting it to your classmates. Ask for feedback on the effectiveness of your presentation.

SUMMARY

PREPARING A SPEECH includes planning its parts: the introduction, the body, and the conclusion.

- **Organize the body** of the speech by determining the main points. Often, the main points of the speech are stated in the specific purpose. The main points should be arranged in a logical pattern, such as chronological, spatial, or topical order.
- **Plan the introduction** of the speech so that it gets the attention of your audience, makes them interested in your topic, and gains their goodwill. Kinds of speech introductions include startling statements, questions, stories, quotations, personal references, and audiovisual materials.
- **Plan the conclusion** so that it emphasizes the key idea or ideas of a speech and leaves the audience with heightened interest in the topic. Kinds of conclusions include the summary, the recommendation, and the stirring ending.
- **Use transitional devices** to connect parts of a speech and to help emphasize the points you are making.
- **Outline your speech** to test the logical structure of the speech, to provide an organization that your audience can follow, to help you in your practice, and to provide a base for speaker notes.
- **Rehearse your speech** in a number of practice sessions. Rehearse in the same way that you plan to give the speech. In every rehearsal, time your speech, deliver the speech in its entirety, and analyze your progress. Avoid memorizing your speech.

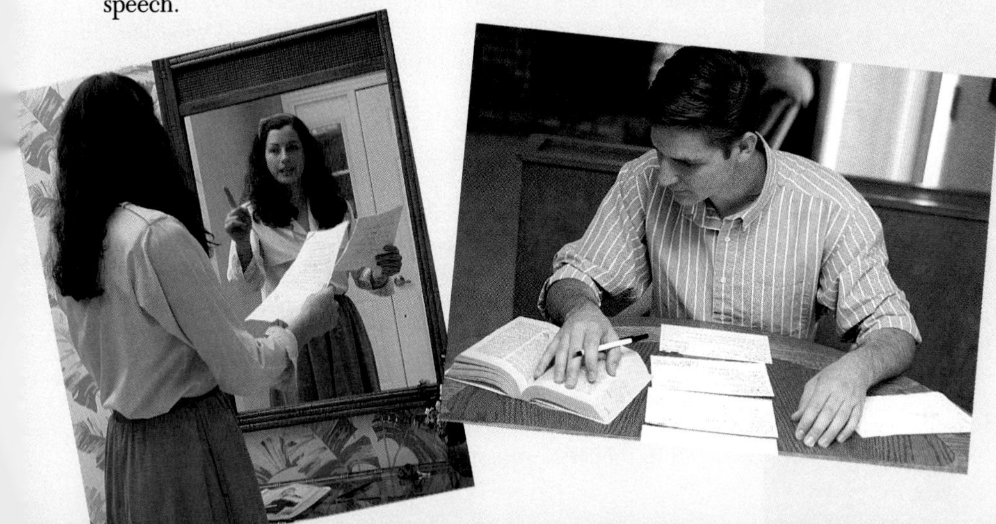

CHAPTER 11

Vocabulary

Look back through this chapter to find the meaning of each of the following terms. Write each term and its meaning in your communication journal.

attention, *p. 271*
body, *p. 266*
chronological order, *p. 267*
conclusion, *p. 273*
formal outline, *p. 275*
goodwill, *p. 271*
interest, *p. 271*
introduction, *p. 270*
main points, *p. 266*
personal reference, *p. 272*
recommendation, *p. 274*
rehearsal, *p. 279*
spatial order, *p. 268*
startling statement, *p. 272*
stirring ending, *p. 274*
summary, *p. 274*
topical order, *p. 268*
transitional devices, *p. 275*
unity, *p. 269*

TEACHER'S RESOURCE BINDER

- Chapter 11 Vocabulary

REVIEW QUESTIONS

Answers

1. introduction: serves as an attention-getting device; body: contains the main ideas and supporting information; conclusion: serves as a review of key ideas and leaves the audience on a high point of interest
2. chronological order, spatial order, and topical order
3. develop interest in the topic, get the audience's attention, and gain goodwill
4. a startling statement, a question, a story, a quotation, a personal reference, and audiovisual material
5. summary, recommendation, and a stirring ending
6. connect parts of a speech and help emphasize points in a speech
7. to test the organizational structure of the message; to help in organizing information so that the audience can readily follow the speech; to

DISCUSSION QUESTIONS

Guidelines for Assessment

Student responses may vary.

1. Preparing the body of the speech first allows the speaker to use key ideas in the speech as a bridge for developing the introduction and conclusion. Responses will vary concerning the most difficult section to prepare.
2. Students will probably say that a short speech requires a brief introduction such as a question or a quotation. In a longer speech, the speaker can spend more time introducing the main topic with a story, a personal reference, or audiovisual material.
3. Although interpretations will vary, students will probably relate the quotation to speakers by saying that the treatment is the pattern of organization chosen for the piece. The effect is the purpose of the speech: to inform, to entertain, or to persuade. The main idea of the quotation is that speakers should begin their preparation of speeches by analyzing purpose and audience.
4. Students might say that an idea is well conceived when it is clear and fully understood by the writer or speaker. Only then can a writer or speaker present the idea effectively. A good outline is the proof that an idea is well conceived.
5. Emerson's notion that practice is a significant part of the job is proved by the skilled speaker who rehearses conscientiously.

CHAPTER 11

Review Questions

1. What are the three parts of a speech, and what function does each serve?
2. Identify three common patterns you can use to organize your speeches.
3. What are at least two goals you should try to achieve in a speech introduction?
4. What are at least three effective methods that you can use to begin a speech?
5. What are three of the kinds of conclusions that you can use to end your speech?
6. What are the two main purposes for using transitional devices in a speech?
7. What are three reasons you should make an outline of your speech?
8. State two of the five guidelines you should follow for making a formal outline.
9. How much rehearsal should a speaker have before delivering a speech?
10. How is knowing a speech different from memorizing it?

Discussion Questions

1. Discuss with your classmates why the body of the speech should be prepared before the introduction and the conclusion. Then discuss which of these sections of a speech is likely to be most difficult to prepare. Give the reasons for your choice.
2. Discuss which kind of speech introduction you would choose for a short speech. What kind would you choose for a longer speech? Give reasons for your choices.
3. In *Fundamentals of Good Writing*, Robert Penn Warren writes, ". . . one begins a piece of writing by asking himself what kind of treatment is natural to the subject and what kind of effect he wants to work on the reader." Although his comment is directed toward writers, it could easily be applied to speakers. First, discuss the meaning of the quotation. Then, discuss how it applies to people preparing speeches.
4. The French poet and critic Nicholas Boileau-Despréaux once wrote, "Whate'er is well conceived is clearly said." First, discuss the meaning of the quotation. Then, discuss whether or not you agree with it. Finally, discuss how it relates to the need to outline your speech.
5. Ralph Waldo Emerson, the American essayist and poet, once wrote, "Practice is nine-tenths [of the job]." First, discuss whether you agree with this quotation or not. Then, discuss how it relates to the need to rehearse your speech.

help in rehearsing a speech and providing a base for good speaker notes

8. Write all points in complete sentences. Use Roman numerals to indicate main points. Write main points in parallel language. Express only one idea in each main point and each subtopic. Try to have no more than five main points.
9. The amount of rehearsal time a speaker needs varies; however, a beginning speaker should rehearse the speech at least twice over a two-day period.
10. Memorizing is trying to say a speech exactly as it is written. Knowing a speech means mastering your information so that you can adapt what you say to your audience's mood.

ACTIVITIES

1. Preparing a Speech

A. Choose a topic you know very well and for which your main source of information would be your own experience. Use a topic suggested by these photographs, or select a topic of your own, such as getting along with a kid sister, valuing a particular film, or planning a perfect weekend. Write your specific purpose and your thesis statement for a speech on this topic. Write a startling statement you might use to begin this speech.

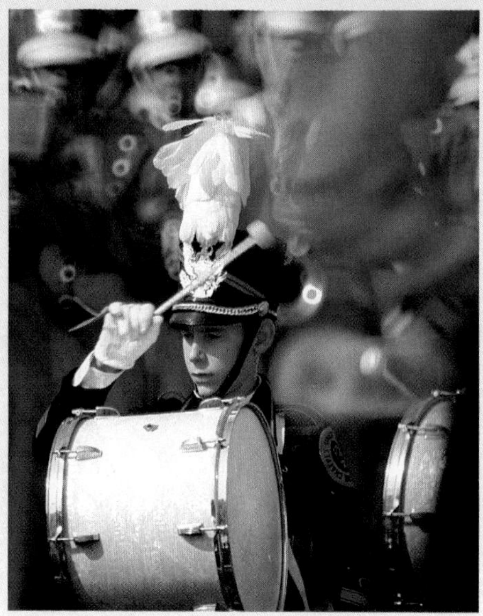

B. Think again about the topic you have selected for Part A. Write a question that you might use as part of the introduction for your speech.

C. Jot down the information that you would include in this speech. Arrange this information according to one of the following orders: chronological order, spatial order, or topical order.

D. Write a summary that you could use to conclude your speech.

E. Write a stirring ending that you could use as part of the conclusion of your speech.

F. Find five quotations you could use to end your speech.

ACTIVITIES

Guidelines for Assessment

1. Students should demonstrate a working knowledge of the different types of introductions and conclusions and the different patterns for organizing the main points of a speech. You may want to have students work in groups if they seem to have trouble creating topic ideas.

SUMMATIVE EVALUATION

Your **Teacher's Resource Binder** contains a reproducible **Chapter 11 Test** that may be used to assess students' mastery of the concepts presented in this chapter.

PORTFOLIO ASSESSMENT

For future reference and evaluation you may want to have students keep in their portfolios any skill sheets or evaluation forms that you have used with this chapter along with any other recorded or written materials that students have created.

2. a. spatial order
b. topical order
c. chronological order
d. topical order *or* chronological order
e. spatial order
f. chronological order *or* topical order
g. chronological order
h. spatial order

3. a. question
b. startling statement
c. personal reference
d. quotation
e. question

4. a. summary
b. recommendation
c. stirring ending
d. recommendation
e. summary

CHAPTER **11**

2. Identifying Different Organizational Patterns for Speeches. Identify the following speech patterns as *chronological order, spatial order,* or *topical order.*

a. Blue is on top.
Pink is in the middle.
Green is on the bottom.

b. One feature of playing baseball is hitting.
A second is running.
A third is throwing.

c. First, dig a furrow in the ground.
Then, plant the seeds.
Finally, water the seeds.

d. The Greeks established the basis of law.
The Romans codified laws.
Modern societies have reworked laws.

e. As you enter, you see a hallway on the left.
To the right is the family room.
Directly ahead is the kitchen.

f. One step in sewing a garment is selecting an appropriate pattern or design.
Another step is laying out and cutting the fabric.
A third step is assembling and sewing the garment.

g. In spring, the farmer plows the field and plants the seeds.
In summer, the farmer weeds, tends, and irrigates the crops.
In early autumn, the farmer gathers the harvest.

h. Closest to the batter in a baseball diamond is the home plate.
In the center of the baseball diamond is the pitcher's mound.
At the far end of the diamond is second base.

3. Identifying Kinds of Speech Introductions. Identify the following speech introductions as *startling statement, question, quotation,* or *personal reference.*

a. What do you do when you get home from school each afternoon?

b. Twenty-two great civilizations have risen and disappeared during the course of history.

c. I think I feel much the same way you do about having to make that long climb up to the fourth floor for art classes. We're all huffing and puffing long before we get there.

d. Harriet Tubman reacted to her escape from slavery in this way: "When I found I had crossed that line, I looked at my hands to see if I was the same person. There was such a glory over everything."

e. The term "global warming" has been widely used by scientists and the general public alike. What does this term really mean?

4. Identifying Different Types of Speech Conclusions. Identify each of the following speech conclusions as *summary, recommendation,* or *stirring ending.*

a. As you have seen, the three main skills in baseball are hitting, running, and throwing.

b. Therefore, take the bus to school.

c. He looked at us and said, "It's not the color of the balloon that matters; it's what it's made of."

d. If you are going to take up a sport, try racquetball.

e. Registering to vote, learning about the candidates and the issues, and actually voting—these are three ways in which U.S. citizens can actively participate in their government.

◆ Real-Life Speaking Situations

PERFORMANCE OBJECTIVES

- To create an outline and to use it in a brief oral report to a selected group
- To use an outline to organize a short presentation such as a sales pitch
- To conduct a question-and-answer session to address prospective buyers' questions

REAL LIFE Speaking Situations

1 How many oral reports do you remember giving in school? You have probably delivered reports on countries, famous people, historical events, and books, to name a few. On many jobs and in many social situations, informational reports are an important part of group communication. Take a moment to consider the occupation and the social activities you might want to pursue after you complete your high school education. What kinds of reports would you need to give in those pursuits?

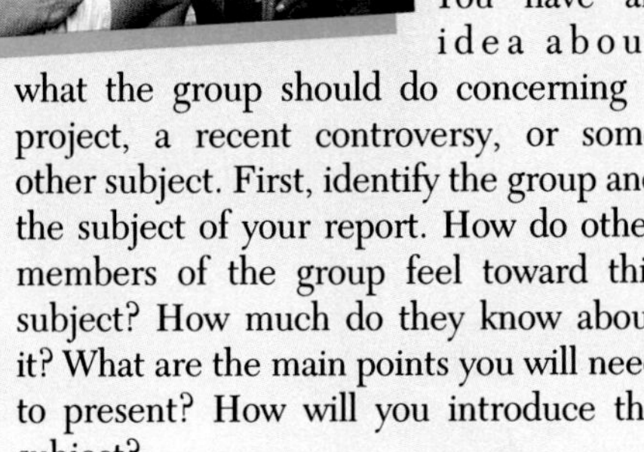

Think of a service club, a political committee, or a community group that you might belong to after graduating from school. You have an idea about what the group should do concerning a project, a recent controversy, or some other subject. First, identify the group and the subject of your report. How do other members of the group feel toward this subject? How much do they know about it? What are the main points you will need to present? How will you introduce the subject?

Write an outline for a three- to four-minute oral report on your subject. Be prepared to deliver your report in class.

2 When people buy, sell, or rent a place to live, they are likely to hire the services of a real estate agent. In helping their clients, these agents give reports on property, present deals to buyers and sellers, conduct meetings and discussions, and engage in many other activities that require effective verbal communication skills.

You are a real estate agent. You have been hired to sell a house or an apartment like the one in which you are now living (or would like to live in). How would you present the house or apartment to prospective buyers? How would you discuss the issue of price? What desirable qualities would you discuss? How would you point out weaknesses and flaws in the property? (Note: Real estate agents are bound by ethical standards to be honest and forthright in presenting a property.)

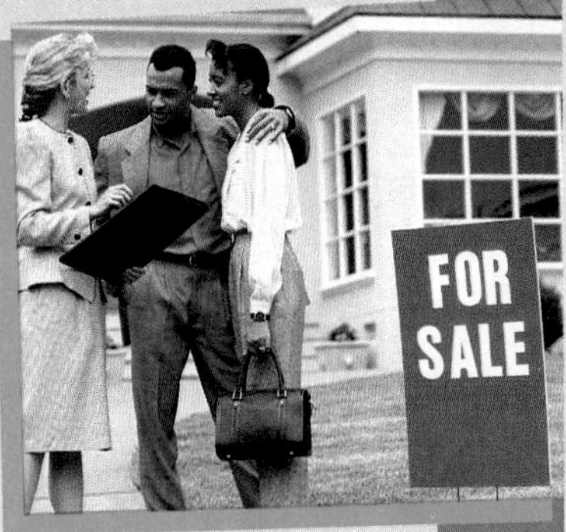

Make an outline of what you would say. Be prepared to use your outline to deliver a short presentation in class as if you were showing the property to a prospective buyer. When you have finished, conduct a question-and-answer session in which your classmates ask questions from a prospective buyer's point of view.

ASSESSMENT GUIDELINES

1. If the reports are delivered to the class, students may want to introduce their speeches by identifying the intended audience and the subject of the reports. Look for outlines that address the main points and for reports that follow the outlines.
2. Tell students to think of the questions that will be asked at the question-and-answer session. These questions can be useful in preparing an outline because they represent what the prospective buyer really wants to know. Students might choose effective presentations and tell which property they would be interested in buying as a result of the sales pitches.

Chapter 12
Using Effective Language
pp. 288–315

Chapter Overview

The chapter begins by discussing the differences between spoken and written language. It then presents guidelines for choosing words to communicate with an audience and includes discussions of simple, precise, specific, and concrete words.

The next segment deals with using language expressively. It includes information on sensory words and figurative language and strategies for

Teacher's Resource Binder

The following materials are identified at their point of use in this chapter:

- Skills for Success
  1 *Choosing the Right Words*
  2 *Choosing Specific Words*
  3 *Using Language Expressively*
  4 *Using Figurative Language*
  5 *Adjusting Your Vocabulary*
  6 *Avoiding Common Language Problems*
- Chapter 12 Vocabulary
- Chapter 12 Test/Answer Key

AV ➤ Audiovisual Resource Binder

The following materials are identified at their point of use in this chapter:

- Transparency 23
  Choosing the Right Words
- Transparency 24
  Using Language Expressively
- Transparency 25
  Achieving Emphasis

Detail from METAMORPHOSE III © 1967/'68 M.C. Escher / Cordon Art–Baarn–Holland developing emphasis and adjusting tone. The third segment explores issues related to the selected audience for a speech. These include ways of adjusting vocabulary for a particular audience, involving the audience, and avoiding common language problems such as jargon, clichés, euphemisms, slang, and unintended meanings.

INTRODUCING THE CHAPTER

Students may have difficulty framing the best language to present their ideas. Tell them that exploring this chapter will help them balance the formal requirements of speaking with their individual needs as speakers. Explain that the chapter will discuss aspects of word use that are similar in spoken and written language, but will emphasize spoken language.

CHAPTER 12

Using Effective Language

OBJECTIVES

After studying this chapter, you should be able to

1. Explain the differences between good speaking and good writing.
2. Choose the words that most clearly express your thoughts.
3. Explain the difference between specific and general words.
4. Explain how the use of sensory words and figurative language makes language more vivid.
5. Define and give examples of exaggeration, understatement, and irony.
6. List and use different ways to emphasize ideas.
7. Adjust language and tone to suit an audience.

What Is Effective Language?

Effective language is language that is appropriate for your audience and purpose. The different kinds of language that you use for various audiences and purposes are called **levels of usage.** In English, the levels of usage range from very formal to very informal. For most speakers and occasions, language usage falls somewhere in between the two extremes.

The most widely used variety of English is called **standard American English.** Standard American English allows people from many different regions and cultures to communicate clearly with one another. It is the variety of English that you read and hear most often in books and magazines and on radio and television. It is also the kind of English that people are expected to use in most school and business situations.

As you rehearse a speech, you will need to focus on the language you plan to use when you deliver your presentation.

Bibliography of Additional Materials

PROFESSIONAL READINGS

- Cook, Jeffrey S. ***The Elements of Speechwriting and Public Speaking: An Indispensible Guide to Anyone Who Speaks in Public.*** New York: Macmillan Publishing Company.
- Jeffreys, Michael. ***America's Greatest Speakers Reveal Their Secrets.*** Los Angeles: Powerful Magic Publishing Company. *Representative American Speeches Series.* New York: H. W. Wilson.

AUDIOVISUALS

- ***Effective Communication Skills, Program 17: Choosing the Ideas and Words***—Wisconsin Foundation for Vocational, Technical, and Adult Education, Middleton, WI (videocassette, 28 min.)
- ***The Speeches of Martin Luther King, Jr.***—MPI Home Video, Oak Forest, IL (videocassette, 60 min.)
- ***Your Speaking Image, Program 5: Words That Work***—Agency for Instructional Technology, Bloomington, IN (videocassette, 30 min.)

Segment 2 pp. 296–303

- **Using Language Expressively**

Performance Objectives

- To identify the senses to which sensory words appeal
- To change similes to metaphors
- To identify kinds of figurative language
- To identify the methods for achieving emphasis in statements
- To adjust the tone of a speech for different audiences

Meeting Individual Needs

An Alternative Approach

To provide more practice in finding sensory words, have students read sports articles from a local newspaper or a magazine. Suggest that they underline the words that appeal to the senses. After students have completed two or three paragraphs, discuss the words they have underlined to determine why the words are sensory.

Ongoing Assessment

Activity 3

Each student should produce a list of words that appeal to the senses and then the student should indicate to which senses the words appeal.

Teacher's Resource Binder

Skills for Success 3
Using Language Expressively
Skills for Success 4
Using Figurative Language

Audiovisual Resource Binder

Transparency 24
Using Language Expressively

Using Language Expressively

Sometimes ideas are clear, but they lack force—they are not lively or memorable. **Vividness** is the quality of being full of life—of being vigorous or exciting. Good speakers know how to use vivid language that

- captures the imagination
- appeals to the senses
- creates mental pictures

Sensory Words

One way to make your speech more vivid is to use sensory words. **Sensory words** appeal to one or more of the five senses. To find sensory words, look in a dictionary or a book of synonyms for words that have roughly the same meaning as the word you intend to use but that create a more vivid picture.

Original Description	More Vivid Description
Lena *walked* out of the room.	Lena *stomped* out of the room.
The snake *moved* through the grass.	The snake *slithered* through the grass.
The *noise* was *loud*.	The *explosion* was *deafening*.
Hungrily, Chris *ate* his slice of *fruit*.	Hungrily, Chris *crunched* his slice of *apple*.

Activity 3: Analyzing Sensory Words

Find a paragraph in a book, magazine, or newspaper that you think is particularly vivid because of its use of sensory words. Identify the senses that these words appeal to. Share your findings with your class.

Figurative Language

Another way to express an idea vividly is to use figurative language. **Figurative language** consists of figures of speech—words and phrases that are not literally true, but that create a fresh, lively understanding of an idea.

MOTIVATION

Write the words *simile, metaphor, exaggeration, understatement,* and *irony* on the chalkboard, and ask volunteers to give examples of each. Point out that in this segment students will learn how to use these familiar figures of speech as well as other language techniques to make their speeches more vivid.

TEACHING THE LESSON

This segment introduces two goals for students to strive toward in their speeches—vividness and emphasis—and several techniques they can use to achieve both of these goals. You may want to treat each of the goals separately on successive days to help students see how the techniques are related to each goal.

Some of the types of figurative language that you can use to create vivid images in your speeches include

- similes
- metaphors
- exaggerations
- understatements
- irony

Simile. A **simile** is a comparison of two essentially unlike things. In a simile, the comparison is introduced by *like, as,* or a similar word (*seem* or *appear,* for example).

EXAMPLES:
- Vicky's criticism was *as sharp as a knife edge.*
- His smile was *as warm as a down comforter.*
- She's got a mind *like a computer.*
- The snow appeared *as flour sifted over the mountains.*

Eagle's Flight by Bev Doolittle © 1982 The Greenwich Workshop, Inc., 30 Lindeman Dr., Trumbull, CT 06611

This painting is a visual representation of a simile from Shakespeare's poem "Venus and Adonis"—"through his mane and tail the high wind sings, / Fanning the hairs, who wave like feathered wings."

Metaphor. A **metaphor** is also a comparison between essentially unlike things. Unlike a simile, a metaphor does not contain the word *like* or *as.* For example, "The lion's eyes glowed like candles in the dark" is a simile; "The lion's eyes were candles in the dark" is a metaphor. Here are some other examples of metaphors.

EXAMPLES:
- *The snow was a blanket* over the field.
- *Manuel is a tiger* when he competes.
- *Our offensive line is a wall* of determined players.
- *The sky is a bowl* of pea soup.

INTEGRATING THE LANGUAGE ARTS

Literature Link

Give students copies of poems that contain figurative language, and ask students to identify the figures of speech. One poem that is especially good for this activity is "Metaphors" by Sylvia Plath. English teachers can probably suggest others, and the library probably has poetry books with sections on figurative language to use as resources. Ask students to comment on why poets use figures of speech.

CRITICAL THINKING

Synthesis

Find similes that are not immediately obvious (or have students find or write them). Let students supply an explanatory sentence telling why the analogy is appropriate. Here is an example: "That artist works like an icemaker." "After long periods of seeming inactivity, she regularly produces quantities of paintings."

ADDITIONAL ACTIVITY

Nicknames are often disguised metaphors. For example, Charles Schulz's Pigpen in *Peanuts* is so named because he is always dirty. Have students develop a list of metaphorical nicknames for sports stars or celebrities.

You can have students read the material on sensory words and figurative language, pp. 296–299, for homework and then spend class time the next day discussing the examples in the text and eliciting additional examples from students. You might assign the activities for the next night's homework and go over them the following day in class. The material on emphasis and tone could be presented in the same way.

To provide guided practice for **Activity 3** on p. 296, work with the class to analyze a paragraph for sensory appeals. You can give guided practice for the other activities by using the first item in each activity for class discussion. Completing the rest of the activities on their own will give students sufficient independent practice.

Ongoing Assessment

Activity 4

Answers will vary. Here are some possibilities:

1. He is a bear sleeping soundly in the dead of winter.
2. The icy hill in front of school was glass. People kept slipping and sliding.
3. In the bright green spotlight, Donna was a frog standing on a lily pad.
4. The baby's cry was a siren in the night.
5. Her deep thoughts were mountain canyons.

Meeting Individual Needs

An Alternative Approach

Students who are adept at using exaggeration might benefit from researching American folklore characters like Paul Bunyan, Johnny Appleseed, Annie Oakley, and Davy Crockett. Have students report on the characters' adventures and discuss how exaggeration is used in stories to make characters and their adventures appealing.

Activity 4

Changing Similes to Metaphors

Each of the following sentences contains a simile. Revise each sentence by changing the simile into a metaphor. The first one has been done for you.

Simile: Howie moved like a cat to get to the ground ball.
Metaphor: Howie was a cat as he pounced on the ground ball.

1. He sleeps as soundly as a bear in the dead of winter.
2. The icy hill in front of school was like glass. People kept slipping and sliding.
3. The bright green spotlight made Donna look like a frog standing on a lily pad.
4. The baby's cry was like a siren in the night.
5. Her thoughts ran as deep as mountain canyons.

Exaggeration. **Exaggeration,** or **hyperbole,** emphasizes or enlarges a description of actions, emotions, or other qualities, such as size or speed. Hyperbole is appropriate only if your listeners know that you are stretching the truth for effect. In its simplest form, hyperbole involves selecting words that magnify to create an effect, usually ironic or humorous.

EXAMPLES:

1. Rather than saying that you are "hungry," you could say that you are "on the verge of starvation."
2. Instead of saying that someone was "embarrassed," you might say that he was "certain that he'd sink into the earth and disappear."
3. Rather than saying that you are "mad" at someone, you could say that you "will never speak to her again in a million years."

Exaggeration plays a major part in many folk tales, such as the tall tales about the giant Paul Bunyan and his blue ox, Babe.

ASSESSMENT

You can use the activities in this segment to assess students' ability to use language effectively. You can also assess competence related to the objectives by noting whether your students incorporate vividness and emphasis in their speeches throughout the school term.

RETEACHING

To reteach methods for achieving vividness, videotape students giving speeches. As you play these for the class, stop after each sentence to ask how the speaker achieved vividness or how the speaker could have changed the speech to make it more vivid. Let students use their textbooks to look up the various methods the speaker employed or could have employed. You

Understatement. **Understatement** is the opposite of exaggeration. By describing an idea, an event, or a thing in terms that intentionally diminish or lessen its importance, you can create an ironic or humorous effect.

Actual Situation	Understatement
The batter has struck out five times in one baseball game.	The batter has not done too well today.
Yori is running for class president, trying out for the debate team, and auditioning for the school play.	Yori tries to stay busy.
Lily ate five sandwiches and drank a quart of milk.	Lily had a hearty snack.

Irony. **Irony** is the use of words to imply something different from, perhaps even the opposite of, what is actually meant.

EXAMPLE: A person may be speaking ironically when he or she says, "I noticed yesterday that Michael just accidently happened to be in the hall by the lockers when Mary Harper walked by on her way to class."

When irony becomes cutting or bitter it is called **sarcasm.**

EXAMPLE: After a boring play, someone leaving the theater may sarcastically say, "That was really an exciting performance. In the middle of the second act, the lady behind me accidentally hit me with her program and woke me up."

Identifying Kinds of Figurative Language

Identify each of the following uses of figurative language as *simile, metaphor, exaggeration, understatement,* or *irony.*

1. The peace was like the eye of a hurricane.
2. Tilly is so strong that she could knock Jupiter out of its orbit.
3. We had a little breeze yesterday—I think it was called a tornado.
4. When he's boxing, his arms are pistons.
5. Don took one of his little naps after dinner last night. I woke him up to go to work this morning.

COOPERATIVE LEARNING

Have pairs of students each write ten sentences containing exaggeration. Then have pairs exchange sentences to rewrite by using understatement.

COMMON ERROR

Problem. Some students think of all verbal irony as sarcasm.

Solution. Point out to students that sarcasm is always ironic, but not all irony is sarcastic. Sarcasm is the kind of irony that can hurt another person or ridicule a person, idea, or thing.

ONGOING ASSESSMENT

Activity 5

1. simile
2. exaggeration
3. understatement
4. metaphor
5. irony

can reteach methods of achieving emphasis by having students analyze any repetition and announcement used in the speeches. Then have students make other suggestions for the use of these techniques for emphasis.

Integrating the Language Arts

Mechanics Link

When they write speeches, remind students of the punctuation used to show emphasis. Exclamatory sentences end with exclamation marks. Emphasis on individual words can also be shown by using italics or underlining.

Critical Thinking

Analysis

Have students read newspaper editorials to find examples of repetition, restatement, parallelism, and announcement used to create emphasis. Also, have students note places in the editorials where emphasis would be appropriate but is not used.

AV➤ *Audiovisual Resource Binder*

Transparency 25
Achieving Emphasis

Emphasis

Emphasis is the force or special attention given to a particular word or point. You can use emphasis to signal to your audience exactly what you want them to remember.

Since emphasis is such a powerful device, you should use it sparingly. If you overuse it, your audience can no longer tell what you intend to stress. Too much emphasis then becomes no emphasis at all.

In Chapter 2, you learned how you can use your gestures and the sound of your voice to create emphasis. You can also create emphasis through repetition and announcement.

Repetition. **Repetition** is saying something more than once. It is the easiest and most common means of showing emphasis.

By using repetition, you tell an audience, "Pay attention—this is really important."

EXAMPLE: If you were giving a speech on deforestation in the Amazon, you might say the following: "Scientists estimate that as many as fifty million acres of tropical rain forest are destroyed annually. Imagine that—fifty million acres!"

You can use repetition without repeating a statement word for word. Two other forms of repetition are *restatement* and *parallelism.*

Restatement is the repetition of an idea using different words.

EXAMPLE: You might say, "During the last 200 years, more than 125 species of birds and mammals have become extinct. That's not 125 individuals, but 125 different kinds of animals gone forever." With this restatement, the idea is repeated, but the language is different.

"'What I Did This Summer.' This summer, I went to camp. I hated it. I hated every minute of it. I hated my counsellor. I hated the food. I hated the woods. I hated the nature walks and the nature talks. I hated the outings. I hated the campfires. I hated the overnights. I hated . . ."

Extension

Ask students to bring to class paragraphs or essays they have written for other classes and to revise their writing by using the methods of achieving vividness and emphasis they have learned in this segment.

Parallelism is the repetition of words, phrases, or sentences to emphasize an idea or a series of ideas.

EXAMPLE: Dr. Martin Luther King, Jr., used parallelism in many of his speeches to add power to his statements. Note the use of parallelism in the following excerpt from "I Have a Dream" (reprinted in full in the Appendix of Speeches).

> *There are those who are asking the devotees of civil rights, "When will you be satisfied?" We can never be satisfied as long as the Negro is the victim of the unspeakable horrors of police brutality. We can never be satisfied as long as our bodies, heavy with the fatigue of travel, cannot gain lodging in the motels of the highways and the hotels of the cities. We cannot be satisfied as long as the Negro's basic mobility is from a smaller ghetto to a larger one. We can never be satisfied as long as a Negro in Mississippi cannot vote and a Negro in New York believes he has nothing for which to vote.*

Announcement. Another way of emphasizing a point is to precede what you intend to say with an **announcement** that clearly states your evaluation of that point. For instance, you might use any of the following statements as an announcement.

- Now I come to what I consider my most important point.
- This second idea is the key to understanding the material.
- Pay close attention to the steps of this process. They are a little tricky to follow.
- The formula that I am about to give you is the one that you will use the most in this entire unit.

Identifying Methods for Achieving Emphasis

Read each of the following items. For each item, tell whether it achieves emphasis through *repetition*, *restatement*, or *announcement*.

1. Three new cases of this deadly disease are reported each week—that's 156 new cases a year!
2. Everyone was amazed by Koslov's margin of two million votes—that's two million votes.
3. Lucas hit .287 last year, just about .300!
4. The United States Coast Guard traces its history back to 1790—that means it is almost as old as this country.
5. Pay attention to this next step. It is crucial to the success of your project.

Integrating the Language Arts

Listening Link

Ask students to listen carefully to teachers in other classes and to report on instances when the teachers use repetition, restatement, and announcement to achieve emphasis.

Ongoing Assessment

Activity 6

1. restatement
2. repetition
3. restatement
4. restatement
5. announcement

Enrichment

Invite to class a person well-known locally for his or her public-speaking ability, and ask the guest to discuss how he or she adds vividness and emphasis to speeches. Likely candidates include ministers, public officials, and members of the Toastmasters Club.

Another idea for an enrichment activity is for students to compile lists of figures of speech they hear people using in conversation. A master list can be compiled and duplicated for each student to have for future reference.

Making Connections

Mass Media

In movies and TV shows, the tone is often communicated with the help of music. Ask students to describe the music in recent movies and TV shows and to evaluate how music contributes to the tone. Or you could play videotapes of the opening credits of movies without letting students see the TV screen. Ask them to identify the kind of movie (for example, comedy, drama, or action-adventure) the music suggests.

Tone

By using **tone,** speakers express their attitudes toward their subjects and their audiences. You can communicate to your audience how you feel about your topic by the tone of your speech. Your tone should also let your audience know how you want them to feel about your topic. You can express tone in two ways:

1. through the sound of your voice
2. through your choice of language

Vocal Tone. Choosing the appropriate tone of voice is essential in delivering the message you intend.

> **EXAMPLE:** If your speech topic is about the dangers of air pollution, you will have a greater appeal to your audience if your tone is concerned and sincere rather than nagging.

Choice of Language. The language you use in your speech will help you to express how you feel about your topic and about your audience. Your language can be *formal, informal,* or somewhere in between. By using informal language, you will express an informal tone. Whichever language you choose needs to be appropriate for the occasion and for your audience.

> **EXAMPLE:** You are speaking before a group of parents and teachers on a formal occasion, such as a ceremony honoring the parent who has volunteered the most time in behalf of the school. For this audience and on this occasion, it would probably not be appropriate to use slang or colloquial expressions, even in an attempt at humor. Instead, choose your words and expressions carefully and use formal language.

Closure

Write the headings *vividness* and *emphasis* on the chalkboard. Call out one of the methods for achieving these qualities, and ask a student to write the name of the method under the appropriate heading. Then ask the student to give a definition or an example of the method. If the student gives a definition, let him or her call on another student for an example, and vice versa.

Uses of Formal and Informal Language

Occasion	Audience	Tone	Language Use
Awards Ceremony	school officials and fellow classmates	dignified, polished	*Formal:* Use your best vocabulary, grammar, and syntax. Avoid slang and colloquial expressions.
Meeting to Schedule Events	student committee	serious, but not stuffy	*Formal to informal:* Use good vocabulary, grammar, and syntax. You may use some slang, colloquial expressions, and personal references (*I, you, we, they*).
Dinner at Home	family members	chatty, personal	*Informal:* You may use slang, colloquial expressions, and personal references.

KUDZU by Doug Marlette. By permission of Doug Marlette and Creators Syndicate.

ACTIVITY 7

Adjusting Tone for Different Audiences

Prepare a short statement describing how you feel about a school dress code. Prepare this statement as part of the remarks you might make for the following occasions and audiences:

- a class report for your teacher
- a student committee meeting with your peers
- lunch with your friends

Then tell your class how the tone of each statement differs.

Using the Chart

You might discuss the information in the **Uses of Formal and Informal Language** chart with students and help them to draw some conclusions about how the speaking situation affects the formality of language. For example, in general, the larger the group becomes, the more formal the language used becomes. Or the more familiar a speaker is with the audience, the less formal the language must be.

Ongoing Assessment

Activity 7

The class report should be relatively formal, the statement for the committee should be less formal than the class report but more formal than the lunch conversation, and the lunch conversation should be completely informal. The degree of formality should be obvious both from the tone of voice used to present the statements and from the vocabulary used in the statements.

Segment 3 pp. 304–309

- **Adjusting Your Vocabulary to Suit Your Audience**
- **Avoiding Common Language Problems**

Performance Objectives

- To identify a speaker's use of words or phrases suitable to an audience
- To rewrite sentences for an audience of classmates
- To identify common language problems in speeches

Integrating the Language Arts

Usage Link

When students use personal pronouns, remind them to avoid the use of noninclusive, or sexist, pronouns. In addition, you may want to point out that some usage experts now favor the use of plural pronouns (*they, their, them*) with words that are technically singular but that clearly imply plurality (for example, *everyone, everybody, anyone, anybody*). These experts argue that using plural pronouns is less distracting to listeners and readers than continually saying "his or her" and similar constructions.

Teacher's Resource Binder

Skills for Success 5
Adjusting Your Vocabulary

Adjusting Your Vocabulary to Suit Your Audience

Like all groups of people, audiences differ from one to another. You need to be able to adapt your vocabulary to suit your audience. [See Chapter 9 for more information on how to gather important data about your audience.]

Use words that are appropriate for your audience. Obviously, the words you use in a speech to kindergarten students will differ from the words you use in a speech to city council members. Choosing a word that is accurate, specific, and vivid will not matter if your audience does not understand that word.

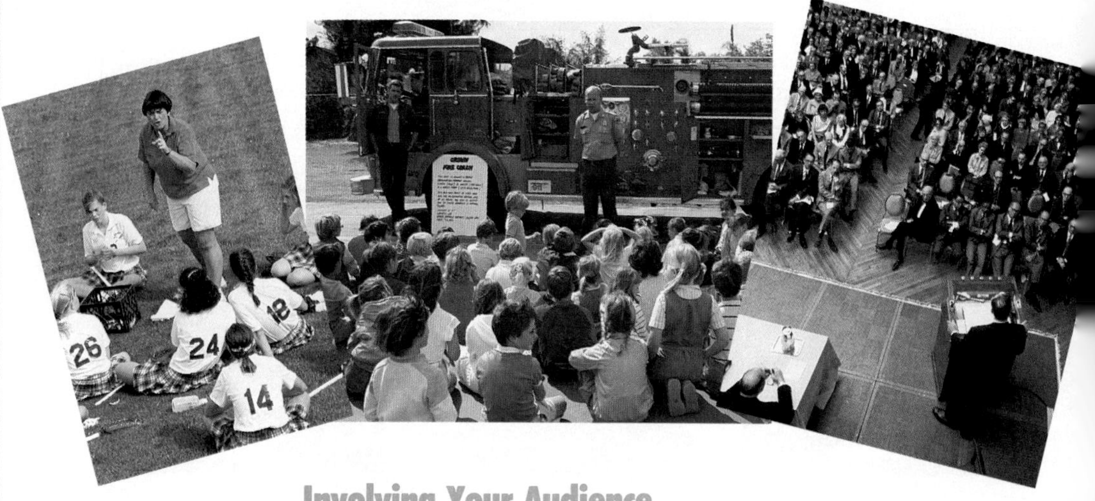

Involving Your Audience

Audiences remember more about your speech and respond more favorably to your message when you actively involve them.

You can accomplish this by

- selecting material that relates to your audience's experience
- using personal pronouns to address your audience
- asking rhetorical questions to involve your listeners

Relate to Your Audience's Experience. Whenever you have a choice, use material that is closely related to your audience's experience.

EXAMPLE: If you can use only one of two examples—driving a car or flying an airplane—in a speech to your classmates, you will probably want to discuss driving a car, an example that will be more likely to relate to your audience's experience.

Motivation

Write *pig, hog,* and *swine* on the chalkboard and ask students to decide which word would be the greatest insult. Then write *thin, slender, skinny,* and *lean* on the chalkboard and ask students to identify the words that are most flattering and least flattering.

Ask students why they made these choices. If no one volunteers the idea of connotation, tell students that even though the definitions are almost identical, all of the words have strong connotations, or implied meanings, that go beyond the literal meanings. Point out that connotation is one aspect of language students will study as they adjust their vocabularies to their audiences.

Use Personal Pronouns. You give each speech to a specific audience—not to some general or unknown group, but to people who are sitting in front of you. You always want your audience to feel that you are talking with them. One way to do this is to use the personal pronouns *you* and *we* freely.

The pronoun *you* makes an audience feel that you are talking directly to them. The pronoun *we* makes an audience feel that they are joining with you for some shared purpose.

EXAMPLE: Instead of saying, "*One* would think that . . .," say, "*You* would think that. . . ." Instead of saying, "*People* often find that . . .," say, "*We* often find that. . . ."

Ask Rhetorical Questions. A **rhetorical question** is one that is not meant to be answered but that is asked only for effect. Phrasing some key points in the form of rhetorical questions helps to involve your audience by getting them to think actively.

Suppose you are practicing a speech on the history of the bicycle. Instead of beginning, "The bicycle originated in the year . . .," you might try the following phrasing: "Do you know when the first bicycle was built? Can you come up with a specific date? If you think it was during the 1800s, you're absolutely right!"

Original Phrasing	More Audience-Centered Phrasing
Across the country, parents are telling their children to turn off the TV set. However, television can actually help children learn.	Across the country, parents are telling their children to turn off the TV set. But did you know that television can actually help children learn?
Although some people think that cars are unreliable, 40 to 45 percent of cars are still on the road after ten years of operation.	Do you think that cars are unreliable? Did you know that 40 to 45 percent of cars are still on the road after ten years of operation?
Some people might say, "Don't worry. We've had hurricanes before." But hurricanes are costly. In 1992 Hurricane Andrew cost Floridians more than $10 billion.	Some people might say, "Don't worry. We've had hurricanes before." But hurricanes are costly. Did you know that in 1992 Hurricane Andrew cost Floridians more than $10 billion?

Integrating the Language Arts

Literature Link

Many poems use rhetorical questions to make a deeper impression on readers. One such poem is W. B. Yeats's "No Second Troy," which is composed exclusively of rhetorical questions. If a copy of the poem is available, lead the class in discussing whether the rhetorical questions in the poem are effective or distracting.

Summative Evaluation

Your **Teacher's Resource Binder** contains a reproducible **Chapter 12 Test** that may be used to assess students' mastery of the concepts presented in this chapter.

Portfolio Assessment

For future reference and evaluation you may want to have students keep in their portfolios any skill sheets or evaluation forms that you have used with this chapter along with any other recorded or written materials that students have created.

B. Synonyms may vary. *happy:* blissful, delighted, glad, joyful, elated; *said:* spoke, uttered, exclaimed, announced, replied; *ran:* rushed, sprinted, bounded, sped, dashed; *hit:* punch, rap, jab, strike, whack; *friend:* acquaintance, chum, companion, confidant, crony

4. Students should examine the speaker's vocabulary and the techniques used for gaining audience involvement, especially the speaker's use of personal pronouns and rhetorical questions.

5. Students should listen to and analyze at least two news stories to get a fuller picture of the newscaster's use of language. Since many news stories are written by someone other than the newscaster, students should probably listen to and analyze a live report rather than a staged report by a news anchor.

Students' analyses should include the key concepts of the chapter: word choice; tone; and use of figurative language, emphasis, personal pronouns, rhetorical questions, slang, jargon, clichés, and euphemisms.

6. Answers will vary. Students should concentrate on being apt and original in their comparisons.

7. While analyzing the speeches, students can concentrate on all three techniques for achieving emphasis: repetition, restatement, and announcement. Students' analyses should consider whether the ideas emphasized deserve emphasis and whether the speaker chose the best techniques for particular ideas.

4. Ruben felt *angry* because he had thought that Sal was his friend.
5. When we saw Clara *walk* to the podium, we could tell that she thought that her speech would be the *best* one.

B. Using either a dictionary or a book of synonyms, list five words that you think would be good, vivid choices to replace the following words:

happy
said
ran
hit
friend

4. Analyzing the Language in a Political Speech. Many politicians are effective speakers. They have to be effective to win elections. Listen to a political speech. Analyze the speaker's use of language. How does the speaker use language effectively? Can you find any weaknesses in the speaker's use of language? If so, identify those weaknesses. Share your findings with your classmates.

5. Analyzing a Newscaster's Use of Language. News stories on television can be considered short informative speeches. Listen to your favorite newscaster deliver the top story on the nightly news. In what ways does the newscaster use language effectively? In what ways does he or she use language ineffectively? What advice would you give this person for improving his or her use of language? Share your advice with your classmates.

6. Completing Similes. Complete each of the following similes by creating an original comparison. Avoid writing clichés, such as "as sound as a dollar" for the first item.

a. The economy of a nation needs to be as sound as . . .
b. She was a great woman, as courageous as a . . .
c. A tall man, he looked like a . . .
d. Reading a book is like . . .
e. After the war, the peace between the two nations was as fragile as . . .
f. After helping clean up the house all day, I was as tired as . . .
g. That old car he bought looks like . . .
h. When the sun comes out after several days of rain, I feel as . . . as . . .
i. The waves washing up on the loose sand sounded like . . .
j. The light, cool breeze felt like . . .

7. Analyzing Methods for Achieving Emphasis. Analyze the methods used to achieve emphasis in two of the student speeches included in the Appendix of Speeches on pages 658–683. Begin by copying the specific words that the speakers use. Then identify whether these words achieve emphasis through repetition or through announcement. Next, briefly state the idea or ideas that are being emphasized in each case. Finally, evaluate the effectiveness of each speaker's use of emphasis, and compare how emphasis was used in each of the two speeches.

Record all of this information in your communication journal and be prepared to share your findings in class discussion.

◆ Real-Life Speaking Situations

PERFORMANCE OBJECTIVES

- To write a dialogue using characteristic speech patterns of three people
- To present and respond to dialogues
- To identify and define five jargon terms
- To report how jargon terms help people in an occupation communicate effectively

REAL LIFE Speaking Situations

1 After graduation, you will probably lose track of many of your high school friends. However, in the course of your business and personal activities, you may run into some of these friends over the years. One common experience that brings old friends together is a high school reunion.

Imagine that you have just arrived at the twenty-year reunion of your graduating class. As you look around, you notice many people who seem familiar, but they have changed in appearance. Despite these changes you still recognize the familiar voices and speech patterns of friends you haven't seen for a long while.

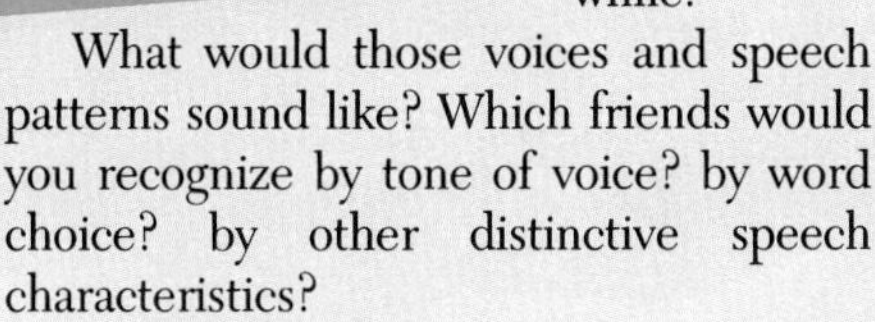

What would those voices and speech patterns sound like? Which friends would you recognize by tone of voice? by word choice? by other distinctive speech characteristics?

Using the speech characteristics of two of your friends, write a two-page dialogue depicting the three of you meeting at your class reunion. Be prepared to present this dialogue in class and to respond to your classmates' feedback on how well you have captured your two friends' speech patterns.

2 Nearly all occupations have their own jargon. Because jargon terms often have other, more common, meanings, people not familiar with the jargon meaning of a term may be puzzled or misled by the jargon usage of that term. For example, you may be surprised to hear housepainters complain about *holidays*. You may wonder: Do painters enjoy their work so much that they don't like to take vacations? No, painters look forward to their time off, just as most people do. A *holiday* is painters' jargon for a spot that has been left uncovered on a painted surface.

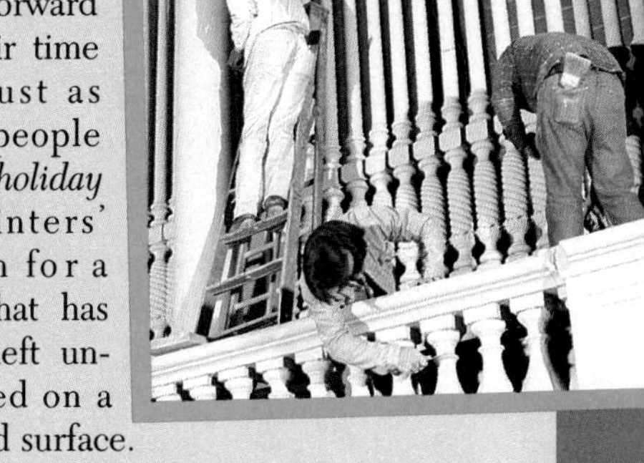

Think of jargon terms you know for various occupations, such as food preparation, mechanics, teaching, sports, computer programming, and retail sales. Identify five jargon terms used in a particular occupation. Find the definitions for these terms and determine what relationship, if any, the jargon meaning has to a more common meaning of each term.

Be prepared to report to your class on the terms you chose and on how these terms help people within the occupation communicate more efficiently.

ASSESSMENT GUIDELINES

1. If students have trouble identifying speech characteristics of their friends, suggest they consider such features as dialect, use of slang, sentence structure and length, and vocabulary. The dialogues should sound natural and should convey a distinct sense of characterization. There should be no narration.
2. The jargon terms will vary. Students who are not familiar with jargon from any particular field may want to talk with someone they know who practices an occupation that uses jargon terms. In addition to the occupations mentioned in the assignment, students may want to speak with members of specialized crafts. Possibilities are printers, plumbers, and electricians. *Newsweek* magazine periodically publishes the latest jargon of various groups in the work force. This may also be a useful source of jargon for students to investigate.

Chapter 13
Presenting Your Speech
pp. 316–351

Chapter Overview

This chapter defines and discusses four different methods of delivering a speech: impromptu, manuscript, memorized, and extemporaneous. Techniques for coping with stage fright are presented. Methods to improve nonverbal behavior and vocal skills are provided, and the use of speaker's equipment and audiovisual materials is explained. The chapter shows how timing,

Teacher's Resource Binder

The following materials are identified at their point of use in this chapter:

- Skills for Success
  1. *Controlling Stage Fright*
  2. *Decoding Nonverbal Messages*
  3. *Using Voice Effectively*
  4. *Using Audiovisual Materials*
- Chapter 13 Vocabulary
- Chapter 13 Test/Answer Key

AV Audiovisual Resource Binder

The following materials are identified at their point of use in this chapter:

- Transparency 26
  Evaluating Vocal Skills
- Transparency 27
  Using Equipment and Materials
- Audiotape 1, Lesson 3
  Problems in Articulation
- Audiotape 1, Lesson 8
  Vocalized Pauses

audience feedback, and distractions affect the delivery of a speech. Finally, a set of guidelines for evaluating speech delivery is provided.

Introducing the Chapter

Even the most superb message is diminished, if not destroyed, by poor delivery. Because of inexperience in public speaking, students often suffer from stage fright and are overwhelmed by giving a presentation in class. You might want to reassure students by telling them that feeling anxious about giving a speech is normal. Even an experienced speaker is often nervous before giving a speech. Tell students that the information in this chapter will help them overcome their fears by giving them a chance to practice the skills that are needed for the successful delivery of a speech.

CHAPTER 13

Presenting Your Speech

OBJECTIVES

After studying this chapter, you should be able to

1. Describe the four methods of delivering a speech and explain the advantages and disadvantages of each.
2. Use effective methods to control stage fright.
3. Explain the effect of your appearance, eye contact, facial expressions, and other nonverbal behavior on your audience.
4. List and explain ways you can improve your vocal skills.
5. Improve your verbal message by concentrating on diction and grammar.
6. Use equipment and materials efficiently.
7. Practice delivering a speech to experience aspects of delivery that include timing, audience feedback, distractions, and unexpected occurrences.
8. Evaluate your delivery of a speech, analyzing both the strengths and the weaknesses.

How to Present Your Speech

It is your turn to make your first speech in class. You rise from your seat and walk to the front of the room. Setting your notes on the speaker's stand, you pause to look at the audience before you begin. How do you feel? Are you ready?

To present a successful speech, you will need to be well rehearsed and to sound interested in and enthusiastic about your subject. If you are enthusiastic about your subject, you will be less likely to be unnerved by the prospect of giving a speech. In addition, thorough rehearsal will help you to develop the best nonverbal behavior and vocal skills for your particular speech and audience. Careful preparation will even help you to handle unexpected mishaps and distractions that may occur during your speech.

Bibliography of Additional Materials

Professional Readings

- Axtell, Roger E. ***Do's and Taboos of Public Speaking: How to Get Those Butterflies Flying in Formation.*** New York: John Wiley and Sons.
- Cooper, Pamela, ed. ***Activities for Teaching Speaking and Listening: Grades 7–12.*** Annandale, VA: Speech Communication Association.
- Wohlmuth, Ed. ***Overnight Guide to Public Speaking.*** Philadelphia: Running Press.

Audiovisuals

- ***Aids to Speaking***—Coronet/MTI Film & Video, Deerfield, IL (videocassette, 15 min.)
- ***Communication: The Nonverbal Agenda***—CRM Films, Carlsbad, CA (videocassette, 20 min.)
- ***Effective Aids to Speaking***—Resources for Education and Management, Decatur, GA (videocassette, 14 min.)
- ***Say It Better: Fearless Public Speaking***—The Learning Seed, Lake Zurich, IL (videocassette, 22 min.)
- ***Stage Fright***—Coronet/MTI Film & Video, Deerfield, IL (videocassette, 13 min.)

Segment 1 pp. 318–324

- **Comparing Methods of Delivery**
- **Controlling Stage Fright**

Performance Objectives

- To identify the four methods of delivering a speech
- To compare and contrast the effectiveness of the methods of delivery
- To identify effective steps to manage stage fright
- To practice and evaluate the use of relaxation techniques

Making Connections

Community Involvement

You may want to invite a local public speaker (for example, a lawyer, actor, TV anchor, or politician) to share his or her experiences in delivering speeches. Prior to the guest's appearance, have students meet in groups to brainstorm for possible questions to ask the visitor. Some of the questions should address the effectiveness of the four methods of delivery discussed in this segment.

Additional Activity

You might conduct impromptu speaking as an ongoing class activity. Provide the topics yourself, or ask each student to write a topic on a slip of paper for submission. Have each student select a topic by drawing one at random from the collection. Discourage students from submitting inappropriate topics by requiring that they sign the topics they submit.

Comparing Methods of Delivery

A speech can be delivered in one of four ways: impromptu, manuscript, memorized, or extemporaneous.

Although most experienced speakers prefer extemporaneous speaking, each of the four methods of delivery is appropriate for certain circumstances.

Impromptu

An **impromptu speech** is given on the spur of the moment with no preparation.

EXAMPLE: Sometimes, when a celebrity is stopped by reporters and asked to comment on a particular subject, the celebrity's remarks are delivered impromptu. In these instances, the celebrity cannot take the time to prepare a response but simply speaks the words as they come to his or her mind.

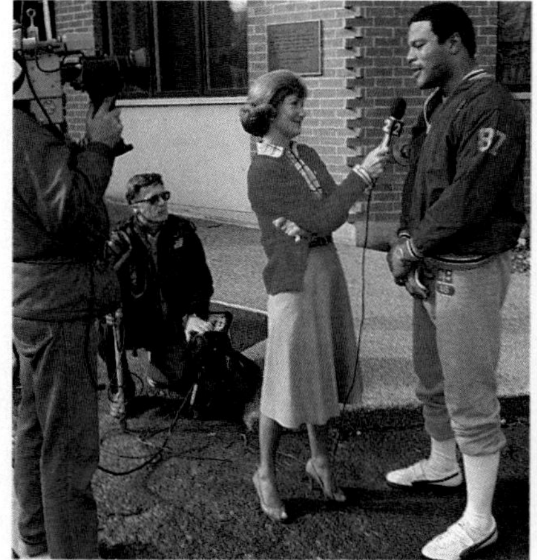

Manuscript

A **manuscript speech** is written out completely and read to the audience.

EXAMPLE: Most political speeches are manuscript speeches. By using manuscripts, the speakers avoid the risk of making errors. Reading from their manuscripts provides them assurance that they will not leave out any important points.

Motivation

Introduce the lesson by asking students to think about different ways to deliver a speech. Write the following list on the chalkboard:

1. Read the speech.
2. Write the speech out and memorize it.
3. Make up the speech as you go.
4. Prepare the speech, but talk from a few notes.

Discuss with students which methods might be used by the following speakers:

1. the president of the PTA
2. a lawyer pleading a case
3. a coach giving a pep talk
4. a member of Congress
5. a talk-show host
6. a speaker at a graduation

Tell students that in this segment they will learn more about ways to deliver a speech.

Memorized

A **memorized speech** is written out completely and recited word for word. A memorized speech is actually a manuscript speech committed to memory.

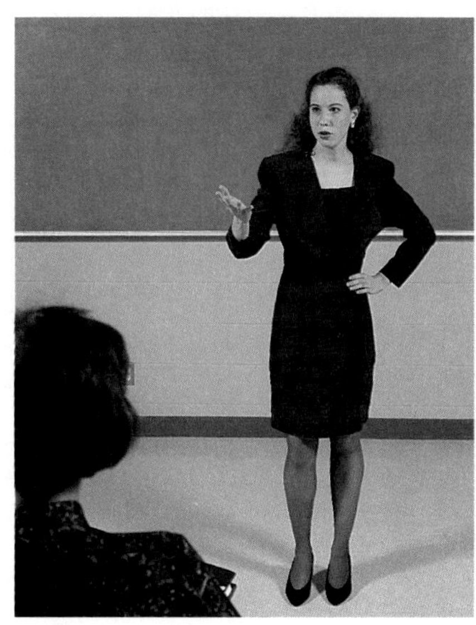

EXAMPLE: Contestants in certain competitive speech events often prefer to memorize their speeches because their choice of words plays a large part in how their performances will be evaluated. When writing and revising their written speeches, they take care to choose their words very carefully. By memorizing their speeches, contestants can ensure that their ideas are expressed in the manner they want.

Extemporaneous

An **extemporaneous speech** is fully outlined and practiced but not memorized. Because the exact wording is left until the speech is given to an audience, the speaker's words sound spontaneous and natural.

EXAMPLE: Most professional speakers prefer to speak extemporaneously. They use only a few note cards or perhaps a brief outline. These speakers are thoroughly familiar with their subjects, and they have rehearsed their material. Therefore, they are free to listen and to pay close attention to their audiences' reactions.

Integrating the Language Arts

Vocabulary Link

Most students will understand the difference between a memorized and a manuscript speech; however, some may not be able to distinguish between an impromptu and an extemporaneous speech. You may wish to have volunteers check an unabridged dictionary for definitions of the terms. [*Impromptu* refers to suddenness or haste in doing or making something without any previous preparation, possibly creating an impression that one is caught off guard. *Extemporaneous* suggests previous planning but delivery with the use of few or no notes.]

Making Connections

Mass Media

Students are probably familiar with newscasters, actors in commercials, and politicians who speak directly into the camera without notes. Students may admire the prodigious memories these TV personalities seem to possess because students may not realize that the speaker may be reading from a teleprompter, an off-camera machine that unrolls a script line by line. Encourage students to discuss other devices, such as cue cards, that allow TV people to speak fluently without relying on notes.

TEACHING THE LESSON

You may wish to begin the lesson by inviting students to give impromptu speeches as suggested in the **Additional Activity** on p. 318. Encourage students to discuss the benefits and risks of an impromptu speech. [While a speaker may have a chance to speak naturally and sincerely, he or she may forget something important or confuse the delivery.]

Discuss the three remaining methods of delivery and the benefits and problems associated with each. You could use the **Methods of Delivering Speeches** chart below to compare and contrast the four methods. Then introduce **Activity 1** by presenting an excerpt from a prepared speech and asking students which method they think the original speaker used to deliver the speech. Then ask students to complete **Activity 1** as homework. After they have had time to listen

USING THE CHART

You may want to tell students that the **Methods of Delivering Speeches** chart is a handy reference when they need to decide which type of delivery is most suitable for a specific audience or situation.

Methods of Delivering Speeches

Type of Delivery	Description	Advantages	Drawbacks
Impromptu	given on the spur of the moment, with no preparation	• allows speaker to respond quickly • sounds natural, spontaneous	• can seem disorganized • may not include all of the important points on the topic • limits a speaker's time to think before responding • may lead to blunders
Manuscript	written out completely and read to the audience from a prepared script	• can be revised until wording is exact • can be researched so that every key point is supported by details and examples • can be rehearsed and timed exactly	• often sounds stiff, unnatural • may be boring for audience • requires time to plan, write, and revise
Memorized	written out completely (like a manuscript speech) and then thoroughly memorized	• can be revised until wording is exact • can be researched so that every point is supported by details and examples • can be rehearsed and timed exactly	• must be memorized well enough to sound smooth and natural • requires time to memorize • may increase nervousness and cause speaker to forget
Extemporaneous	fully prepared (outlined and researched) but not memorized; speaker may use brief outline or note cards	• sounds spontaneous and natural • can be organized in a logical manner • can be researched so that main points are supported • allows for greater flexibility of response to audience feedback	• requires time to prepare outline or notes • requires time to rehearse

to the five speeches, allow some class time for students to discuss findings.

You might guide students through the section on stage fright by having a volunteer read the guidelines on pp. 321–323 for understanding and preventing stage fright. Demonstrate the muscle-relaxation techniques for students. You may wish to have students meet in cooperative groups to complete **Activity 2** on p. 324.

ASSESSMENT

Using the **Methods of Delivering Speeches** chart on p. 320, assess students' understanding by asking the following questions: Which kind of speech can sound unnatural or uninteresting? [manuscript] Which kind of speech needs to be rehearsed? [extemporaneous] Which kind of speech might seem disorganized? [impromptu] 

ACTIVITY 1

Analyzing Methods of Delivery

Keep a record of the next five speeches you hear. Identify the method that you think was used to deliver each speech: impromptu, manuscript, memorized, or extemporaneous. Which of the speeches are the most effective? What relationships do you notice between effectiveness and method of delivery? Discuss your findings with your classmates.

Controlling Stage Fright

Are you nervous when you give a speech? If you ask people how they feel about speaking in public, most will admit having feelings of anxiousness. **Stage fright** is the nervousness that speakers feel before and during the presentation of their speeches.

What You Should Know About Stage Fright

1. **Stage fright is normal.** Beginners as well as experienced speakers feel stage fright before and during a speech. Experienced speakers know that some nervousness is actually beneficial, since people who are a little nervous are more likely to be alert and ready to do their best.
2. **Your audience is not likely to notice your nervousness.** Often, beginning speakers report that they confided in friends that they had felt nervous while speaking, only to hear their friends say, "You didn't seem nervous at all."
3. **Experience and practice will help.** Take advantage of every opportunity you have to speak. With each speech, you will make fewer and fewer mistakes, and your confidence will grow.

For Better or For Worse® **by Lynn Johnston**

ONGOING ASSESSMENT

Activity 1

Students should be able to support the evaluations they make of the five speeches they hear. Ask them to give reasons for their decisions about the effectiveness of the various methods of delivery.

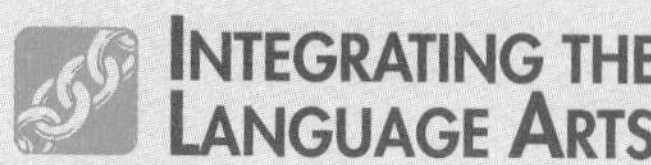

INTEGRATING THE LANGUAGE ARTS

Library Link

Point out that stage-fright management is another form of anxiety management. Students may wish to look in the *Readers' Guide* for articles on anxiety management and coping strategies. Students may also benefit from perusing texts on stage fright. These books are available in the library's fine-arts section.

PRESENTING YOUR SPEECH 321

Which kind of speech might increase nervousness? [memorized]

To assess students' mastery of the section on stage fright, ask students to share their communication journals with you if they feel comfortable in doing so.

Reteaching

To reteach how preparation can help remedy stage fright, write the heading *Remedies for Stage Fright* on a transparency. Under it list these items and discuss them: your preparation, the way you look, your relaxation, your self-talk, your self-confidence, your opening lines, your concentration, your comfort in saying lines, and your focus on the message.

MEETING **INDIVIDUAL** NEEDS

Learning Styles

Kinetic Learners. It may be helpful to have students go through **Six Steps for Relaxing Tense Muscles** together. After students have practiced, have volunteers who are adept with relaxation techniques demonstrate the steps for the class or lead the class in relaxation exercises.

Making Connections

Mass Media

If students have not witnessed stage fright in a real-life setting, obtain a copy of the movie *Broadcast News.* Show the clip (about midway through the film) in which the character played by Albert Brooks gets to anchor the news. Instead of performing well, he falls victim to catastrophic stage fright. Invite students to comment on the scene.

Teacher's Resource Binder

Skills for Success 1
Controlling Stage Fright

Before Your Speech

1. **Prepare for your speech carefully and completely.** Be sure to set aside enough time to allow yourself to become completely familiar with your material. Leave yourself one or two days just for rehearsal. During that time, even the breaks between rehearsals will help you. Your mind will be working on your speech even when you are not consciously rehearsing.
2. **Look your best.** Dress in the way that gives you the greatest confidence. As a rule, the better you look, the better you will feel. Being appropriately dressed and well groomed when you give your speech will help boost your assurance and lessen your nervousness.
3. **Relax tense muscles.** You are likely to feel most tense shortly before you speak. Therefore, the time immediately before your speech should be spent applying relaxation techniques. Use the techniques shown below.

Six Steps for Relaxing Tense Muscles

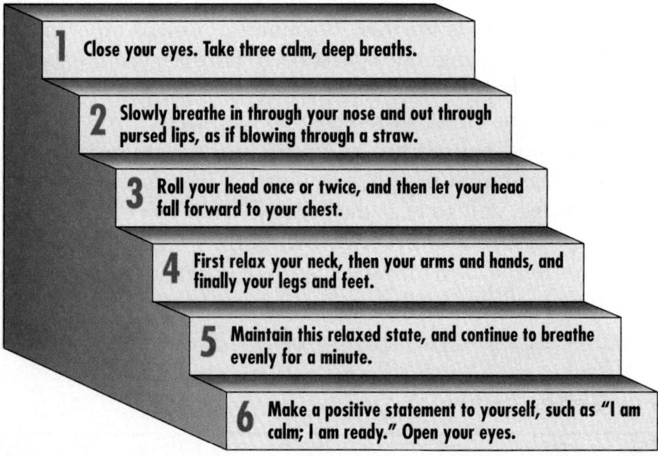

4. **Give yourself a pep talk.** Immediately before your speech, remind yourself that you are well prepared and that the audience is going to profit from what you have to say.
5. **Be self-assured.** Walk to the speaker's stand with confidence. Let your movements and posture tell your audience that you are prepared to present your speech. Pause a few seconds before you start speaking. Take a deep, steady breath. Then begin your speech.

ENRICHMENT

So that the students in the audience will feel compelled to give impromptu comments, suggest that the class set up a mock talk show. Appoint a planning committee to select the guests; choose a host; and identify an issue of the day such as curfews, homework, clothes, cars, politics, or music. Guests should represent extreme views—for example, three students who refuse to do homework.

CLOSURE

To close the lesson, ask the class to identify the four methods of delivering a speech. Then ask several students to name the most helpful things they have learned about managing stage fright.

During Your Speech

Regardless of how well prepared you are, when you begin to speak, you may still be nervous. Consider the following list of some of the most common sensations. Remember that each of these is a perfectly normal response that is shared by many people. In most cases, you can learn to control your response to these sensations so that they do not affect your delivery.

1. **Queasy feeling, butterflies, sweaty palms, general weakness.** These symptoms may feel strong when you begin speaking, but they lessen quickly once you get into your speech. Remember that these sensations have no direct effect on your delivery. Ignore them and concentrate on expressing your message to your audience.
2. **Dry mouth.** Licking your lips and swallowing often will not diminish the dryness, but they will detract from your appearance. Instead, start your speech slowly and concentrate on what you are saying. As you continue, the dryness in your mouth will subside.
3. **Stumbling over words at the start.** Word fumbles often result from trying to recall the exact words you wrote to express an idea. Practice saying your opening lines several different ways so that you will feel comfortable with a variety of openings as you deliver your speech.
4. **Perspiration, squeaky voice, slight trembling.** Ignore these reactions and focus on your message; your body will return to normal.
5. **Strong desire to quit.** Finish your speech no matter how painful the experience seems at the moment. You will build your confidence by proving to yourself that you can reach your goal and finish your speech.

Keep a record of the kinds of nervousness you experience before and during your speeches. Apply the suggestions given in this chapter for handling stage fright. Note which of these suggestions helps you most in managing your nervousness. List other advice or techniques that you have been taught or that you have discovered yourself. Make note of the suggestions that you feel to be most helpful.

COOPERATIVE LEARNING

You may want to have students share some personal experiences of stage fright. By conducting the discussion in small groups, you could help students who might be embarrassed talking about their experiences in front of the whole class. To add organization to the activity, have each group answer the following questions:

1. Would you rather speak to a group of strangers or a group of your friends? Why?
2. Which type of speech is most comfortable for you? Why?
3. What strategy do you find most successful for controlling stage fright?

You could have each group report to the class about the coping strategies that they found to be most helpful.

WRITING TO LEARN

Have students write about stage-fright experiences they have witnessed on film or in real life. Ask them to describe what happened and to analyze what went wrong. Have students identify specific techniques that might have been effective in reducing and controlling stage fright.

Segment 2 *pp. 324–332*

- **Improving Nonverbal Behavior**
- **Improving Vocal Skills**
- **Improving Verbal Messages**

Performance Objectives

- To evaluate nonverbal behavior
- To evaluate the effect of vocalized pauses
- To analyze and evaluate an effective public speaker's diction and use of standard American English

Ongoing Assessment

Activity 2

Monitor the class discussion to make sure students discuss all the relaxation techniques. If students omit any of the techniques from the discussion, ask them to discuss the problems they experienced in trying to follow the plan.

Common Error

Problem. Some students believe a new outfit is the ideal thing to wear when giving an important speech. New clothing may be uncomfortable or perhaps even stiff and unflattering.

Solution. Explain to students that experienced speakers try to wear something attractive but well broken in. The outfit should be something that always looks good, is not too trendy, and has a comfortable fit and feel. The speaker can then focus all of his or her energies on giving an effective speech.

Teacher's Resource Binder

Skills for Success 2
Decoding Nonverbal Messages

Activity 2 Managing Nervousness

At home, practice the relaxation techniques that are recommended for use before your speech. In class, discuss these techniques with your classmates. Tell why you find these techniques helpful. Also ask your classmates for suggestions about managing any specific problems that you may have found when applying these techniques.

Improving Nonverbal Behavior

Certain nonverbal behaviors can affect your impact on your audience and your ability to achieve your purpose in your speech. Experienced speakers know that their nonverbal behavior has as much—sometimes even more—effect on achieving their goals as the words they speak. For example, if you give your speech with a "deadpan" face or with a scowl, if you shuffle about nervously, or if you look at the floor or at the ceiling, your audience is not going to trust you. Make sure that your nonverbal presentation sends the appropriate message.

Appearance

Your **appearance** is how you look to your audience. Two key features of your appearance are your clothing and your grooming.

Good appearance is not going to guarantee a good speech, but poor appearance can lessen your chances of achieving your goal. Proper appearance depends on the situation of the speech, but you should always be clean and well groomed, and your clothes should look neat and tidy.

Common Attire for Specific Speaking Situations

Situation	Men	Women
Informal	depending on the occasion, jeans or slacks and perhaps a tie or jacket	possibly a skirt or pants and blouse; or a dress
Formal	perhaps slacks and a jacket; or suit, dress shirt, and tie	perhaps a suit (coordinated skirt or dress pants and jacket) and blouse; or a dress and jacket

Motivation

On the chalkboard, list the names of TV personalities your students enjoy. Discuss the TV stars' nonverbal behavior: smile, posture, walk, and eye contact. Which stars are effective in using nonverbal behavior? Discuss each star's voice. Which one is the easiest to listen to? Why? Point out that students will learn more about these techniques that help create star quality.

Teaching the Lesson

Invite students to read the first part of the segment to learn the role that nonverbal factors such as clothing, facial expression, gestures, posture, and eye contact play in public speaking. Follow up with questions such as these: How can you avoid the "conflicting expression" pitfall? What exercises will help you make eye contact? How does good posture enhance your speaking ability?

Eye Contact

Eye contact is direct visual contact with the eyes of members of your audience. Your goal in making eye contact with your audience is to give every person listening to you the impression that you are speaking to him or her personally.

Good speakers look randomly at individuals and at groups of individuals distributed widely in the audience. For instance, for a few seconds you might talk to people on the left side of the front row. For the next few seconds you might talk to people at the right rear of the room. By moving randomly from group to group, you can develop a bond with the entire audience. The key is to look at someone or some group at all times.

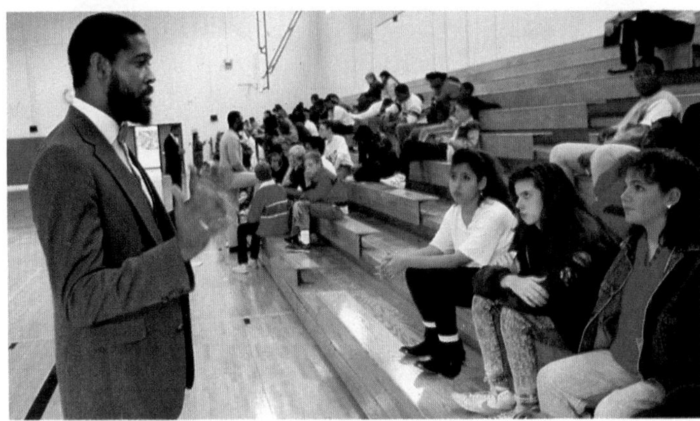

Facial Expressions

Your facial expression gives your audience clues about the content of your speech. The key to using appropriate facial expressions is to concentrate on what you are saying, not on the fact that you are giving a speech. If you do this, you will be able to avoid two common expression problems: the deadpan and the conflicting expression.

Deadpan. A **deadpan** is an expressionless facial appearance that never changes, regardless of what is being said.

Conflicting Expression. A **conflicting expression** is a facial appearance that does not match a speaker's words or actual feelings. For example, some people develop the habit of smiling when they feel angry or scared. Therefore, if they are a little nervous at the start of a speech, they may start smiling regardless of what they are saying. The conflict between a speaker's verbal expression and facial expression can confuse or annoy an audience.

Additional Activity

Ask a volunteer to recite a short speech for the class while looking randomly about the audience as suggested in **Eye Contact.** Then tell the speaker to look at the foreheads or at a line above the heads of the listeners instead of making direct eye contact. Before you ask the class to evaluate the effectiveness of this variation, let several volunteers try this strategy.

Making Connections

Mass Media

Ask students to evaluate the facial expressions of people in the news—newscasters, politicians, or local celebrities who may be interviewed. Suggest that for the next several days students look particularly for examples of people with smiling faces reporting sad or catastrophic news. Discuss how conflicting expressions make the audience feel.

As you lead students through the part of the segment on vocal skills, you might model good articulation and pronunciation. Have students form small groups to discuss the **Correcting Vocalization Problems** chart (p. 330). Encourage students to evaluate each other's pitch and volume to achieve the recommended optimum level.

Before you assign **Activity 3** on this page and **Activity 4** on p. 330, model how you would read a paragraph and ask students to evaluate your nonverbal behavior. In preparation for **Activity 5** on p. 332, have students note your vocalized pauses and evaluate your other vocal skills from the same reading. Then assign **Activity 5** for independent practice.

Additional Activity

You might want to have students work in teams to coach each other during practice for their speech presentations. Together, the pairs can agree on hand motions or facial expressions to serve as codes. Suggest, for example, that the two agree on signals that say "slow down," "speak louder," "smile," "watch your posture," "prolong eye contact," or "use more gestures."

Ongoing Assessment

Activity 3

You might want to provide students with an evaluation guide or checklist so that they can quickly evaluate all aspects of their partners' nonverbal behavior. Leave a short space for additional comments or have students plan oral critiques that include personal comments.

Effective Gestures

Beginning speakers often worry about what to do with their hands. When you are standing in front of an audience, you should use the same natural gestures that you use in ordinary conversation.

Since nervousness can affect your gestures, begin your speech with your hands in a neutral position at your sides or resting comfortably on the speaker's stand. Then, as you start to talk, your hands will be free to move normally.

Good Posture

Good posture creates an impression of confidence and authority. At the start of your speech, stand up straight with both feet firmly on the ground. As you speak, you will naturally shift position, but you should never slump, slouch, or look sloppy.

Activity 3 — Evaluating Nonverbal Behavior

Select a partner with whom to exchange feedback about your effective use of nonverbal behavior. Taking turns, let each partner practice approaching the podium, pausing, and then reading the first two paragraphs on the previous page as if they were a brief speech. Have your partner, acting as an audience member, evaluate your nonverbal behavior. Ask for suggestions for improvement.

ASSESSMENT

By checking **Activities 3, 4,** and **5,** you can assess each student's achievement in the skills covered in this segment. You may wish to have students evaluate themselves. Create an evaluation checklist and have students rate themselves as good, fair, or excellent in each category.

RETEACHING

Students who are having difficulty mastering the concepts in this segment may benefit from a more personal approach. Using a familiar poem as your subject, deliver three ineffective readings. Each time, exaggerate some undesirable nonverbal behavior (poor posture or eye contact) or verbal skill (poor articulation, pronunciation, or enunciation). After students point out the

Improving Vocal Skills

The sound of your voice plays a major role in your success as a speaker. If you deliver your speech with enthusiasm, your audience will probably share your positive feelings. However, if you are hesitant and seem uncertain, your audience will share your doubt and discomfort.

Enthusiasm

Show enthusiasm through your voice. **Enthusiasm** is the strong positive feeling speakers show for their topics. Almost all studies show that enthusiasm is the most important factor in determining how much confidence an audience has in a speaker. Listeners who believe that a speaker is truly enthusiastic will become enthusiastic themselves about the speech and about the speaker.

The key to enthusiasm is a positive attitude. You will be enthusiastic about giving your speech if you believe

- your topic is a good one
- you have found excellent supporting material
- your audience will be interested in the material

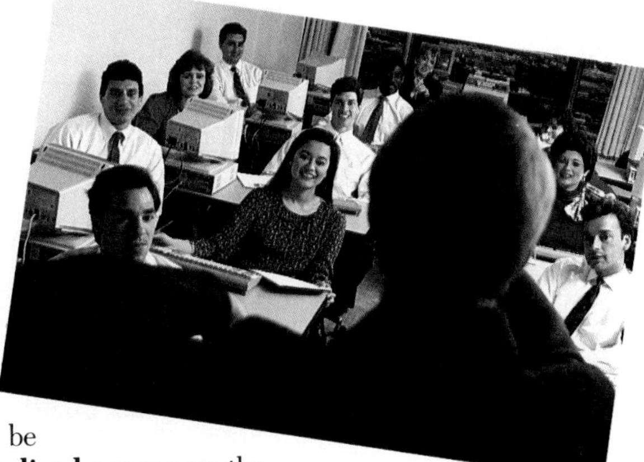

Vocalized Pauses

Your effectiveness as a speaker can be weakened by vocalized pauses. **Vocalized pauses** are the meaningless speech sounds that speakers use to fill time. The most common vocalized pauses are *uh, well uh, um,* and *you know.*

Everyone uses these fillers at one time or another in conversation. Most of us do not even hear our vocalized pauses. Because these sounds are not directly related to the meaning of what we are saying, our minds do not usually pay any attention to them. You are likely to insert one or more vocalized pauses when you are

- unprepared for your speech
- searching for the right word
- flustered or embarrassed
- in too much of a hurry

WRITING TO LEARN

Tell students to ask their parents, friends, and other teachers to help identify vocalized pauses in their speech. Have students record in their communication journals the feedback they get and the efforts they make to eliminate those pauses.

AV ➤ *Audiovisual Resource Binder*

Audiotape 1, Lesson 8
Vocalized Pauses

problems, encourage a volunteer to read the poem more effectively. Discuss the changes made in verbal and nonverbal behavior in the student's delivery.

See p. 330 for **EXTENSION, ENRICHMENT,** and **CLOSURE.**

TEACHING NOTE

Pepper your delivery with intentionally ineffective delivery habits, including vocalized pauses, poor articulation, and poor pronunciation. Avoid exaggerating the problems so that students will not be readily aware that you are playing a role. After a few minutes, call their attention to what you have been doing and encourage students to discuss delivery problems.

Decrease Your Use of Vocalized Pauses

1. **Find out whether you overuse vocalized pauses.** Focus on overuse, not on the informal slips that nearly everyone makes now and then. You are overusing vocalized pauses if your audience becomes aware of them. You might ask people (including your teacher), "When I talk, are you aware of my use of *uh's*, *well uh's*, *um's*, or *you know's*?"
2. **Train your ear to hear your vocalized pauses.** Set up a practice session with a partner who will raise one hand whenever he or she hears you use a vocalized pause. By having someone call your attention to your use of vocalized pauses, you will begin to tune your ear to them.
3. **Train yourself to speak with fewer vocalized pauses.** Once you can hear yourself using vocalized pauses, you can limit their use through practice sessions. As you become more successful at limiting them during rehearsals, you will be able to limit them in your regular speaking.

For Better or For Worse® **by Lynn Johnston**

Articulation, Pronunciation, and Enunciation

In public speaking, you must be careful of your articulation and pronunciation. As you learned in Chapter 3, **articulation** is the shaping of distinct speech sounds into recognizable words. **Pronunciation** is the grouping and accenting of the sounds. [If you have problems with articulation and pronunciation, review the exercises in Chapter 3.]

When you deliver your speech, do your best to enunciate clearly. **Enunciation** refers to the distinctness of the sounds you make.

AV ➤ Audiovisual Resource Binder

Audiotape 1, Lesson 3
Problems in Articulation

Good enunciation is clear and precise. Many people suffer from sloppy enunciation. For example, they say

- *probly* for *probably*
- *gimme* for *give me*
- *commere* for *come here*
- *liberry* for *library*
- *gunna* for *going to*

Although sloppy enunciation causes few problems in casual conversation, it is not acceptable when delivering a formal speech.

HOW TO Improve Articulation, Pronunciation, and Enunciation

- If you have any doubt about the pronunciation of a word, look it up in a dictionary.
- If you have the common faults of slurring sounds and leaving off word endings, practice will help to improve your enunciation. Take ten to fifteen minutes a day to read passages aloud, trying to overaccentuate each of the sounds that give you difficulty.
- If you have a persistent problem of distorting, omitting, substituting, or adding sounds, you may want to work closely with a speech therapist.

MEETING INDIVIDUAL NEEDS

Linguistically Diverse Students

Pronunciation may be a key area in which ESL students need extra help. Because they are more familiar with their native-language pronunciations, students with different language backgrounds may experience difficulty pronouncing English words even if the students make an effort to consult a dictionary. Keeping this in mind, try to provide tutorial sessions for those students who need individual help. Your assistance and encouragement can help in the improvement of their pronunciation skills.

Extension

Copy onto a transparency the following negative statements:

The speaker is poorly educated.
The speaker is not well informed.
The speaker does not like us.
The speaker is bored or upset.

Ask students to determine what nonverbal behavior or vocal problem might lead an audience to one of these conclusions. [For example, a speaker with a deadpan expression might appear bored.]

Using the Chart

If recordings of students' speeches are readily available, you might have students use **Correcting Vocalization Problems** to analyze their own speech problems. You could have students write their observations in their communication journals for future reference.

Ongoing Assessment

Activity 4

Have students determine which speakers come closest to eliminating vocalized pauses. Encourage the class to use a checklist when evaluating each student in the group. Have students check for the criteria listed in the activity.

Audiovisual Resource Binder

Transparency 26
Evaluating Vocal Skills

Correcting Vocalization Problems

Vocal Category	Description	Common Problems	Problem Correction
Pitch	highness or lowness of vocal sounds	• monotone—a melody pattern that consists of only one tone	Speak at your optimum pitch, the pitch at which you feel the least strain and have the best resonance.
Volume	loudness or intensity of speech tones; determined by the force exerted to produce it	• speaking too softly • speaking too loudly	1. Practice controlling your speaking volume. 2. Observe your audience closely. (Are people in the back row straining to hear you? Do people in the front row cringe as if you were shouting at them?) 3. Adapt your volume to suit the audience and the speaking environment.
Rate	the speed at which a speaker speaks	• speaking too quickly • speaking so slowly that the audience is bored	1. Practice speaking at a steady rate. 2. Observe your audience. closely. (Does your audience seem to be struggling to keep up with you? Do your listeners seem to be impatient for you to speed up?)

Activity 4 Evaluating Vocal Skills

Working in small groups of four or five members, have each person stand and talk to the group for two minutes about his or her favorite class. Every time the person says *uh, well uh, you know,* or some other vocalized pause, the other members of the group should each raise a hand. Can anyone get through the entire two minutes without using one vocalized pause? Have the members of the group evaluate and give specific feedback about each speaker's enthusiasm, articulation, pronunciation, enunciation, pitch, volume, and rate.

Enrichment

Students might create a bulletin board featuring pictures of speakers from TV or film who exemplify the speech qualities presented in this segment. For example, one corner could be labeled "Great Appearance," another could be labeled "Fine Articulation," and a third "Excellent Posture." Students should write out the reasons for their choices under each picture.

Closure

Ask students to identify the most helpful ideas covered in the unit. List the most popular ones on the chalkboard.

Improving Verbal Messages

A verbal message consists not only of the meaning of its words but also of the arrangement of the words in sentences. [You will find more information about verbal messages in Chapter 2.]

Diction

Diction refers to both the words a speaker selects and the specific ways in which the speaker uses these words. No matter what audience you are speaking to, your choice of words can make the difference between a vague, uninteresting message and a clear, effective message.

If you take care when selecting your words, you are more likely to express the precise meaning you intend. Your words should

- be precise, specific, concrete, and simple enough for your listeners to understand your message
- be vivid so that your listeners are able to use your words to create clear mental images of what you are saying
- place emphasis on the most important points of your message
- be fresh, avoiding clichés and overuse of euphemisms or slang

BLOOM COUNTY **by Berke Breathed**

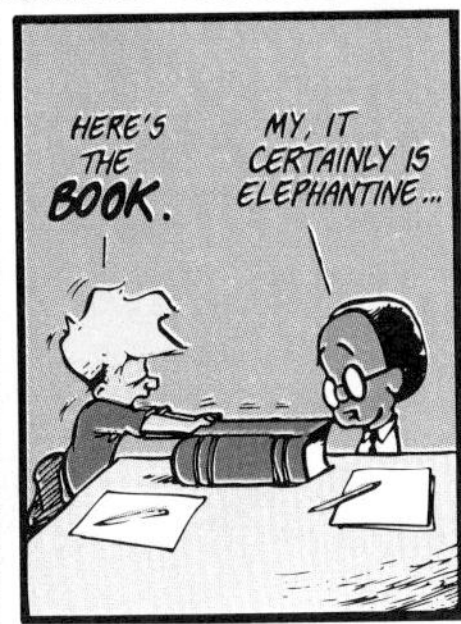

Grammar

Grammar refers to the rules and conventions for speaking and writing English. When you deliver a formal speech, use standard American English. [See Chapter 12 for additional information about using standard American English.]

Meeting Individual Needs

Students with Special Needs

Students with learning disabilities may find peer evaluation as suggested in **Activity 4** very intimidating. Also, if students have problems with expressing themselves verbally, those problems may interfere with the performance factors being evaluated.

To help build confidence, have students practice this activity with a tape recorder and then have them do self-evaluations. Encourage students to focus on enthusiasm, rate, and vocalized pauses. Then have students make another recording to check for improvement. You may want to give suggestions for improvement as well as provide positive reinforcement.

Teacher's Resource Binder

Skills for Success 3
Using Voice Effectively

Segment 3 *pp. 332–345*

- **Using Speaker's Equipment and Materials**
- **Controlling Other Factors That Affect Delivery**
- **Evaluating Your Delivery**

Performance Objectives

- To practice using a lectern and a microphone
- To practice how to stand and move during a speech
- To evaluate the effectiveness of audiovisual materials used by a professional speaker
- To practice speaking with partners to learn control techniques for delivery

Ongoing Assessment

Activity 5

Students' findings should reflect understanding of good diction as well as familiarity with standard American English. Encourage students to compile a list of effective public speakers and to annotate the list with comments about speakers' use of diction and grammar.

An Alternative Approach

Challenge students who feel at ease at the lectern to try walking a few feet from it and returning to it without losing their poise. Suggest that they walk to address one side of the audience, return to the lectern, and then walk to the other side to make another point.

Explain that this technique brings them closer to the audience and is also a physical way to effect a relaxed transition from one point to the next.

Using Standard American English

Guideline	Example
Use the nominative case for pronouns used as subjects.	*He* and *I* saw an accident.
Use the objective case for a pronoun used as the object of a preposition.	The problem is between Jim and *me*.
Make sure that a verb agrees with its subject in number.	*One* of the books *is* missing.
Use adjectives to modify nouns and pronouns; use adverbs to modify verbs, adjectives, and adverbs.	Her speech was *very good*. He was doing *really well*.

Evaluating a Speaker's Diction and Grammar

Watch an effective public speaker give a speech. Concentrate on the speaker's diction and grammar. Does the speaker use standard American English? How did the speaker's diction and grammar affect the message of the speech? Share your findings with your classmates.

Using Speaker's Equipment and Materials

Speaker's Stand

A **speaker's stand,** or **lectern,** is a piece of furniture designed to hold a speaker's notes or manuscript. The lectern may be an elaborate structure made out of wood or a portable boxlike object that sits on a table, or it may resemble a metal music stand. The top is often slightly tilted so that the speaker can easily see his or her notes, which are kept out of sight of the audience.

- To deliver an extemporaneous speech
- To evaluate delivery of an extemporaneous speech

MOTIVATION

Write *1907* on the chalkboard. Point out that prior to this year, no speaker could effectively talk to more than a hundred people at a time. Speakers often had to shout and use exaggerated gestures to convey their messages. In 1907, Dr. Lee De Forest changed public speaking forever with the invention of the microphone. Today, a speaker using a microphone can talk to thousands.

HOW TO *Use a Lectern Properly*

1. Practice with a lectern until it becomes an aid, not a crutch. Avoid leaning on or clutching the lectern.
2. If you are allowed notes, you may want to rest them on the stand. You may, instead, prefer to hold your note cards in one hand. This method will give you the freedom to move away from the lectern as you give your speech.
3. Look at your notes when you need to, but do not read from them continuously.
4. As you speak, feel free to stand behind the lectern, beside it, or in front of it.

Microphone

When speaking to a large audience or in a large auditorium, you will probably want to use a **microphone,** which is simply an electronic device for broadcasting sound. In class you may be asked to use a microphone for one of your speeches just for practice.

Microphones are of three basic types.

1. **The Standing Microphone.** A **standing microphone** is a microphone attached to a stand or lectern. Because this type of microphone picks up sounds only from a narrow range, you will need to speak directly into the microphone for it to work. Do not lean over or put your face too close to the microphone, though. Ordinarily, you will want to maintain a distance of eight to twelve inches from the microphone. To be sure that you are speaking from the correct distance and angle, you should practice with a microphone before giving your speech.

   While you are speaking, a standing microphone can sometimes become a distraction, since it may tend to limit your movement. In order to learn how to speak comfortably, you will probably need a few practice sessions to become comfortable with using a standing microphone.

But using a microphone has its own set of problems. Initiate a discussion of "mike mishaps" and urge students to recall when a microphone gave constant feedback, was not loud enough, died out, or created problems for the speaker. Point out that such events even occur on nationwide TV where, presumably, top technicians are on call. Conclude by telling students they will learn more about microphones and audiovisuals in this segment.

Teaching the Lesson

Make sure students understand that while a lectern can be a valuable aid, a professional speaker can make a speech without one. Discuss what a speaker can do with his or her hands when no lectern is available, and demonstrate some solutions.

The section on microphones presents an opportunity for students who sing in bands or

Teaching Note

Both hand-held and clip-on microphones are available as special wireless models. They transmit radio signals to nearby receivers that hook into the public-address system. A wireless microphone provides unrestricted mobility within its transmitting range.

You might explain to students that wireless microphones are powered by batteries, so it is a good idea to ensure that the batteries are fresh before beginning a presentation. Most wireless microphones have two switches. One switch turns on the power for the microphone; the other switch activates the transmitter in the microphone. Both switches have to be on before the microphone will work.

2. **The Hand-held Microphone.** A **hand-held microphone** gives you greater freedom of movement. However, it can be difficult to juggle both the microphone and your speech notes. Some hand-held microphones have long cords that may get caught around objects in the room or may cause you to trip.

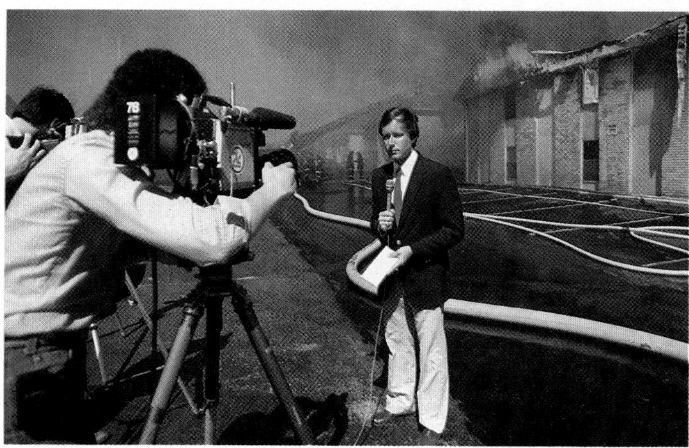

3. **The Lavaliere or Clip-on Microphone.** A **lavaliere microphone** is much easier to use than a standing or hand-held microphone because it hangs around your neck. A **clip-on microphone** is attached to your clothing in such a way that it remains at the same distance from your mouth and at the same angle. Once you have either type of microphone properly adjusted, you will have considerable freedom of movement.

who have specialized knowledge about sound systems to explain to the rest of the class how those systems work. For guided practice for **Activity 6,** you might provide students with opportunities to examine the various kinds of microphones that might be available in the school gym, auditorium, or band room. Demonstrate how to use the microphones that are available and have volunteers practice using the microphones. Show students how plosives and sibilants can cause pops and hisses and how volume can be adjusted to reduce audio feedback.

Allow students to practice independently using the lectern and microphone and have them practice plosives and sibilants. Let them experiment with their volume as well.

Students who are skilled in the visual arts can explain the kinds of materials and lettering styles that are used to produce effective visual materials. To prepare students for analyzing audiovisual

Ongoing Assessment

Activity 6

Allow students enough time to practice individually at the lectern. Remind them that a lectern can give them both mobility and freedom from managing notes. If a variety of microphones are available, have students experiment with the different types to see which are best suited for various occasions, audiences, and speakers.

Practicing with a Microphone

Situation	What to Watch
Pronouncing plosives (*p*, *b*, *d*, *t*, *k*, and *g*)	The *p* and *b* sounds, especially, can pop and be distorted by a microphone.
Pronouncing sibilants (*c*, *ch*, *s*, *th*, and *z*)	The *c* and *s* sounds, especially, can hiss into the microphone.
Raising pitch or volume	The microphone may distort sounds or "boom" if your pitch or volume is excessive.

Activity 6: Using a Lectern and Microphones

Practice all or a portion of your speech in a classroom that has a lectern. Determine how you will stand at the beginning of your speech. Practice moving away from the lectern and then moving back to it.

If your school has a standing microphone, a hand-held microphone, a clip-on microphone, or all three, practice a part of your speech using one or all of these. For a standing microphone, determine how close to it you should be to achieve the best vocal sound. Find out how much you can move without losing the necessary projection. For a hand-held microphone, determine how close to your mouth it must be to give you the best projection. Walk around with it. Does movement affect your ability to project? For a clip-on microphone, find out how your movements affect the microphone's ability to pick up your voice.

Audiovisual Materials

Audiovisual materials are resources that a speaker uses to clarify or add to the verbal presentation of a speech. Examples include

- an audio recording (cassette or CD)
- a prerecorded videotape or videodisc
- a film (usually 8mm or 16mm)
- 35mm slides or a 35mm filmstrip
- transparencies
- posters or charts

materials in a TV broadcast or speech in **Activity 7,** you might tape a televised news segment that includes a map, a chart, or some similar visual. Discuss what each visual display adds to the overall presentation. Or you could show effective audiovisual materials students have used in the past. Then assign **Activity 7** for independent practice.

You might want to guide students through the rest of the segment by setting up an idea web on the chalkboard. You could start off the idea web with the following key terms: *timing, feedback, distractions,* and *unexpected events.* As students read, encourage them to add to the web suggestions gleaned from their reading. (For example, link the word *rehearse* to *timing.*) You will probably want to review the **Guidelines for Delivering a Speech** on p. 345 before students make presentations in class.

Cooperative Learning

To show how different audiovisual materials can improve the presentation of a speech, you might have the class develop a list of informative speech topics. Then divide the class into groups of four or five and have each group name at least three audiovisuals for each topic.

Encourage students to suggest materials that the speaker could prepare as well as equipment he or she could use.

Teacher's Resource Binder

Skills for Success 4
Using Audiovisual Materials

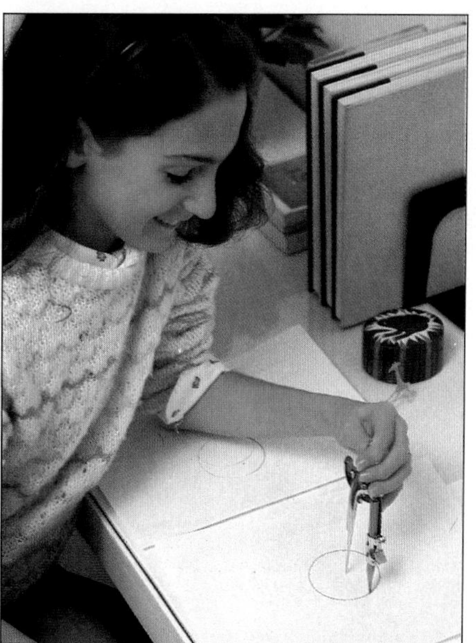

Audio resources are materials that an audience can hear, such as CDs, records, or cassette tapes. **Visual resources** (sometimes called visual aids) are materials that an audience can see, such as slides, pictures, transparencies, videotapes, or films. In some instances, a person could be considered an audiovisual resource, such as in situations when he or she gives a demonstration or when he or she dresses up in costume to portray a particular role.

You may be able to create many of your own visual resources by drawing, pasting, tracing, or by using other common artistic techniques. If you keep the following guidelines in mind, you do not have to be an artist to create effective drawings.

HOW TO *Make a Visual Aid*

- Make the visual aid large enough so that everyone in your audience is able to see it clearly.
- Make the lettering large enough for your audience to see the information clearly, even at a distance.
- Use contrasting colors on your audiovisual materials to make details easy to recognize.

Do not reveal a visual aid during your speech unless you actually want your audience to be looking at it. If you display all of your visual resource materials at the beginning of your speech, or if you pass these materials around while you are giving the speech, your audience is more likely to look at the visuals than to listen attentively to you.

Carefully consider the number of visual materials you will use. You should have enough visuals to illustrate necessary information in your speech clearly and vividly—but no more.

Assessment

Use **Activity 9** on p. 345 to assess students' presentation skills. **Guidelines for Delivering a Speech** on p. 345 provides a means of developing a complete assessment profile for each student. In addition, you may wish to conduct impromptu speaking days as an ongoing class activity. Keep records on the date, subject, and effectiveness of each speech.

Reteaching

For class discussion, list on a transparency the following unnerving experiences that could occur during a speech:

1. You drop your materials.
2. A loud noise occurs outside.
3. You discover you have left some of your materials at home.
4. You forget to make a point.

Questions About Using Audiovisual Materials
Will you save time by using an audiovisual aid? If using an audiovisual aid will save you time in presenting your information, you should probably use it.
Will an audiovisual aid help you to clarify a point? Some ideas are easily explained verbally, but others need audiovisual resources to clarify them.
Will an audiovisual aid help the audience to remember a point? Not every point in your speech is equally important. Decide which points in your speech will be most clearly and economically emphasized by audiovisual materials.

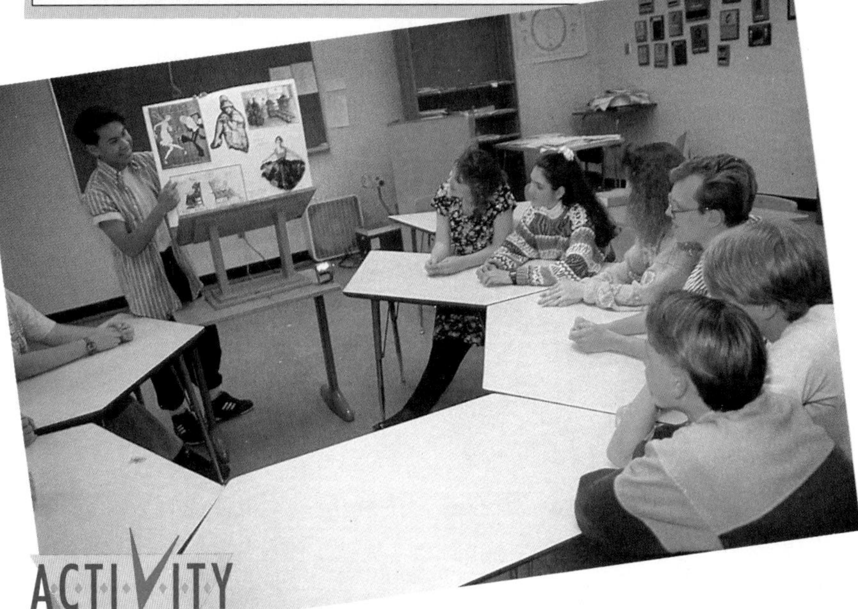

ACTIVITY 7

Analyzing a Speaker's Use of Audiovisual Materials

Watch a television broadcast or a speech in which the speaker uses audiovisual materials. Determine whether these materials are appropriate for the speech. Are they well prepared? Are they used effectively? Would the speech have been as effective without these materials? How does the speaker use these materials—to create interest, to explain, to give examples, or to achieve some other purpose(s)? Share your findings with your classmates.

Critical Thinking

Analysis

Challenge students to list the pros and cons of each of the following audiovisuals: a chalkboard, a chart, an overhead projector, 35mm slides, a videotape, and computer-generated graphics.

Encourage students to consider the size of an audience, the size of a room, the nature of the speech material, and possible technical difficulties.

Ongoing Assessment

Activity 7

Students should demonstrate an awareness of the effectiveness of audiovisual materials. Encourage students to be analytical about understanding how speakers may use audiovisuals to their advantage and in determining the best uses for different materials.

AV Audiovisual Resource Binder

Transparency 27
Using Equipment and Materials

See p. 344 for **EXTENSION, ENRICHMENT,** and **CLOSURE.**

TEACHING NOTE

In pointing out the varieties of charts students might design, you might mention the importance that clarity and readability play in emphasizing a point or helping an audience to remember. For example, the **Informational Chart** shown here might not be readable on a poster from the back of a room. But if a speaker presented it on an overhead projector and used a pointer to focus on facts, the same chart would be a clear and effective tool.

AUDIOVISUAL MATERIALS

CHARTS

Line–Staff Chart

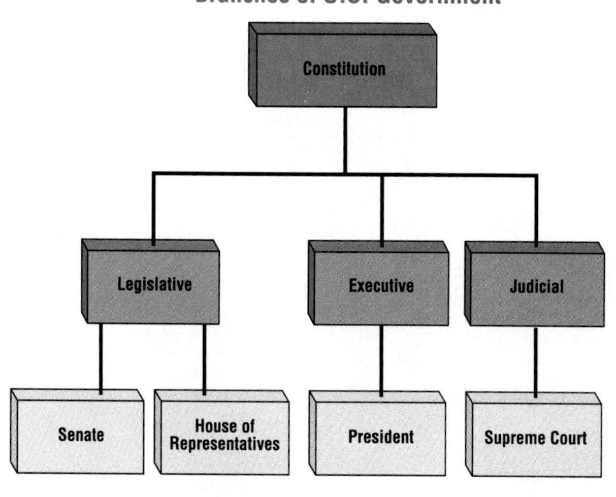

Flow Chart

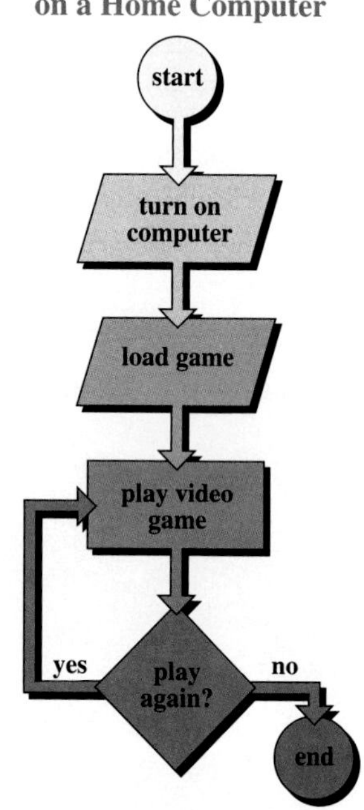

Informational Chart

Average Weight of Americans by Height and Age

MEN						
Height	Age					
	20-24	25-29	30-39	40-49	50-59	60-69
5'2"	130	132	138	140	141	140
5'3"	136	140	143	144	145	144
5'4"	139	143	147	149	150	149
5'5"	143	147	151	154	155	153
5'6"	148	152	156	158	159	158
5'7"	153	156	160	163	164	163
5'8"	157	161	165	167	168	167
5'9"	163	166	170	172	173	172
5'10"	167	171	174	176	177	176
5'11"	171	175	179	181	182	181
6'0"	176	181	184	186	187	186
6'1"	182	186	190	192	193	191
6'2"	187	191	195	197	198	196
6'3"	193	197	201	203	204	200
6'4"	198	202	206	208	209	207

WOMEN						
Height	Age					
	20-24	25-29	30-39	40-49	50-59	60-69
4'10"	105	110	113	118	121	123
4'11"	110	112	115	121	125	127
5'0"	112	114	118	123	127	130
5'1"	116	119	121	127	131	133
5'2"	120	121	124	129	133	136
5'3"	124	125	128	133	137	140
5'4"	127	128	131	136	141	143
5'5"	130	132	134	139	144	147
5'6"	133	134	137	143	147	150
5'7"	137	138	141	147	152	155
5'8"	141	142	145	150	156	158
5'9"	146	148	150	155	159	161
5'10"	149	150	153	158	162	163
5'11"	155	156	159	162	166	167
6'0"	157	159	164	168	171	172

GRAPHS

Pie Graph

Kinds of Jobs Performed by Workers Aged 16 to 17

Male Workers 16–17

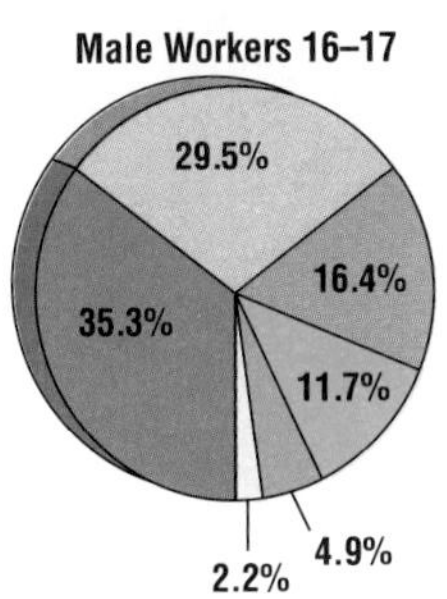

Female Workers 16–17

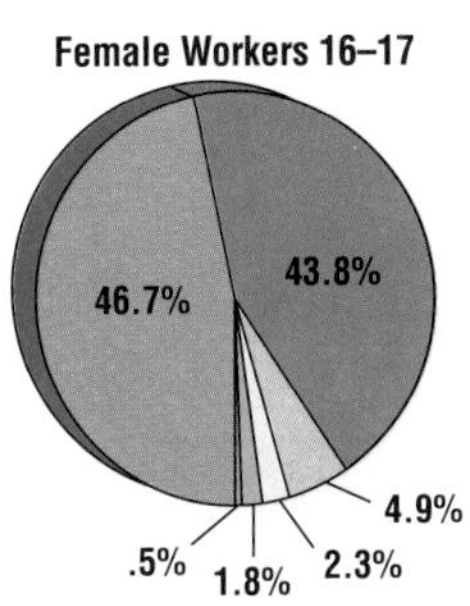

All Workers 16–17

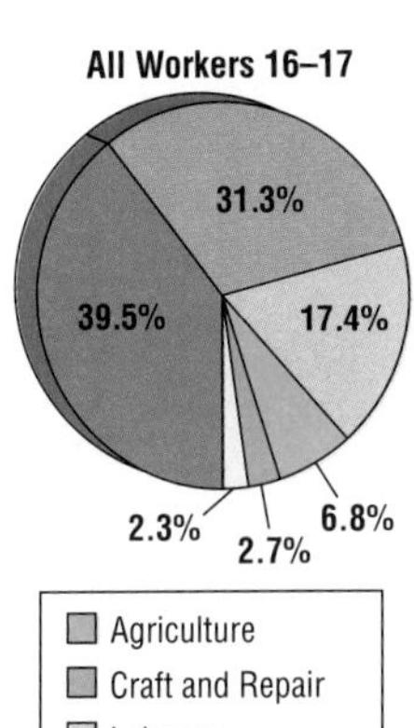

Line Graph

Living Arrangements for Children

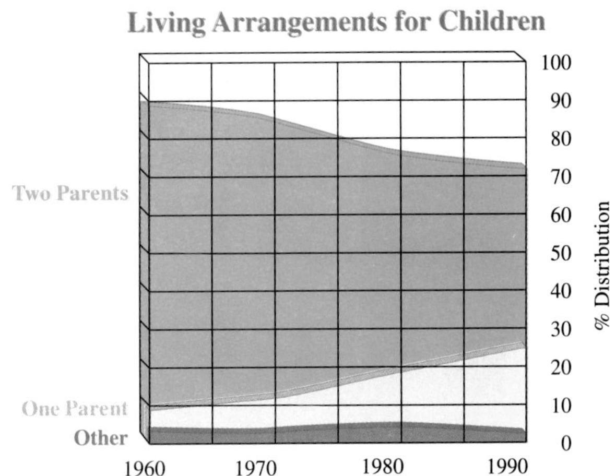

Bar Graph

Percentage of 5–17 Year Olds Compared with Other Ages

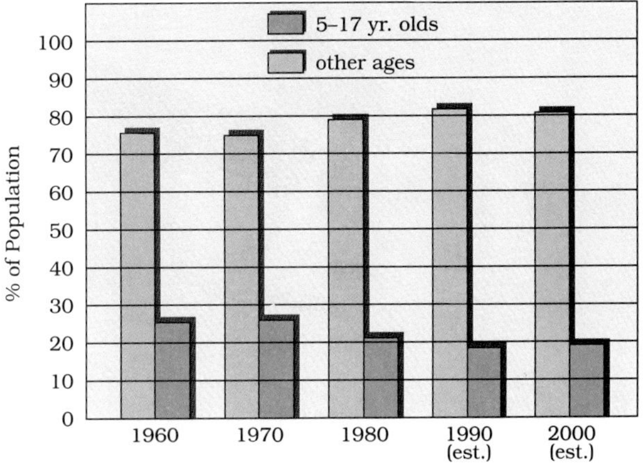

TEACHING NOTE

Color may help make differences on visuals more visible to audiences, and graphs may be more visually stimulating to viewers than charts. Point out how important it is for lettering to be large enough to be seen and legible to all the audience. You might want to illustrate some lettering methods students might use to show the students how useful standardized lettering can be in helping the audience read and remember.

DIAGRAMS

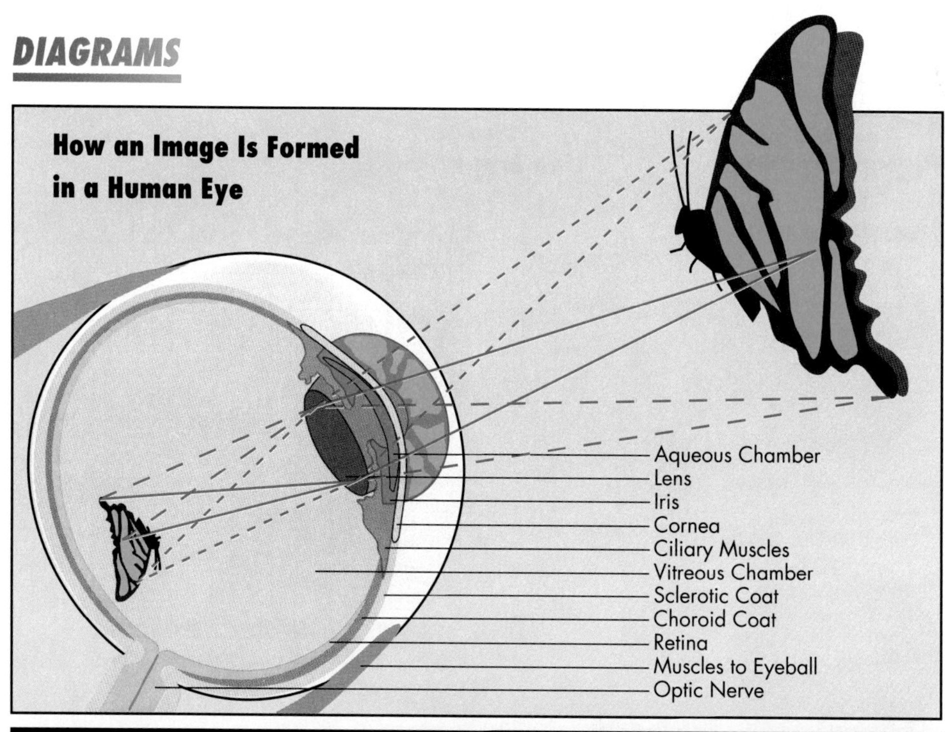
How an Image Is Formed in a Human Eye
Aqueous Chamber
Lens
Iris
Cornea
Ciliary Muscles
Vitreous Chamber
Sclerotic Coat
Choroid Coat
Retina
Muscles to Eyeball
Optic Nerve

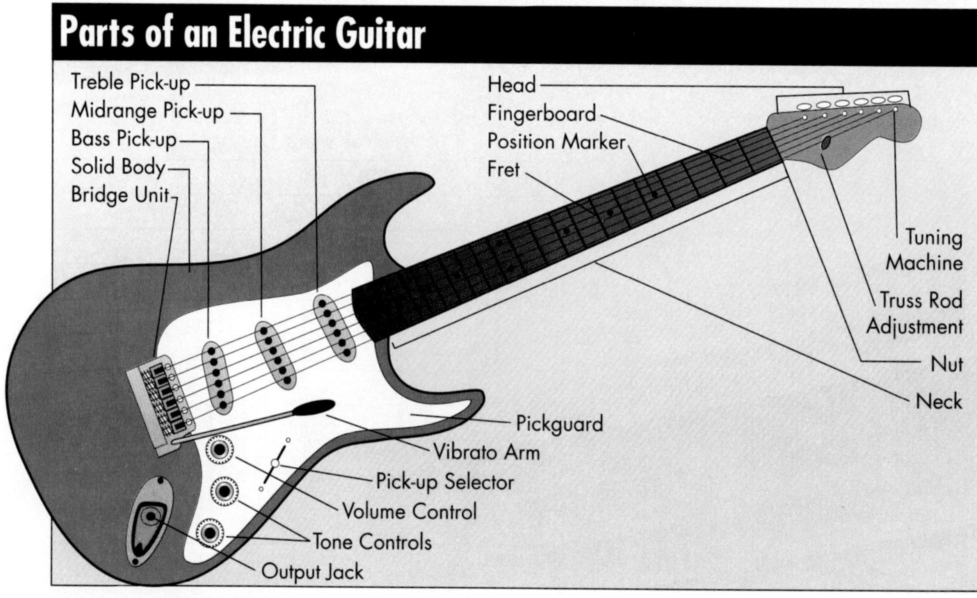
Parts of an Electric Guitar
Treble Pick-up
Midrange Pick-up
Bass Pick-up
Solid Body
Bridge Unit
Head
Fingerboard
Position Marker
Fret
Tuning Machine
Truss Rod Adjustment
Nut
Neck
Pickguard
Vibrato Arm
Pick-up Selector
Volume Control
Tone Controls
Output Jack

Controlling Other Factors That Affect Delivery

Stage fright and nonverbal, vocal, and verbal messages are not the only factors that may affect the delivery of your speech. You will also need to consider several other factors, such as your timing, your response to audience feedback, your need to handle distractions, and your response to any unexpected events that may affect the delivery of your speech.

Timing

Timing is the controlled pacing of a speech. You time your delivery in two ways: by pacing your delivery so that it fits within a specific time limit and by pacing your delivery of particular words or phrases to give them special attention.

During your rehearsals, you will get an approximate sense of the length of your speech. Experience will help you to judge whether the actual delivery of your speech is likely to take more or less time than your rehearsals take.

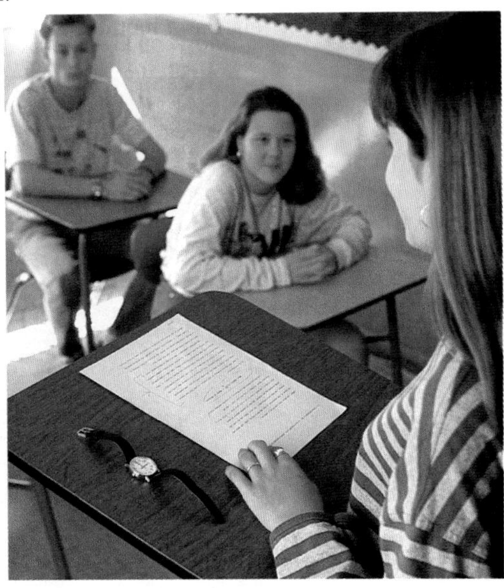

During your speech, your teacher or a classmate may use "countdown" cards so that you can keep track of the time remaining. For example, if the time limit for your speech is five minutes, your timekeeper may hold up a card numbered *4* after the first minute, *3* after two minutes, and so on—to tell you how much time you have left. If you have no timekeeper, you can set a watch on the lectern so that you can glance at it occasionally.

Timing also means pacing your delivery of specific material in your speech to achieve maximum effect. Consider Henny Youngman's old one-line joke, "Take my wife—please." As many times as he tells this joke, it still gets a laugh because of his timing, the way he pauses before he says "please." As you gain experience as a speaker, you will learn how to time the delivery of key sentences in your speech so that you will get the maximum effect out of them.

INTEGRATING THE LANGUAGE ARTS

Literature Link

Find a recording of a literary piece read by an actor. Have students listen for pauses. Ask how the pauses affect both the reading and the meaning of the passage. Then ask students how pauses make them feel. Would they change any of the pauses? Have students imitate the recording in groups to develop a sense of timing. Explain that timing can change the meaning or emphasis of a speech.

Extension

Select a current issue of interest to the class such as a sports controversy or a dispute over a music award. Ask students to give impromptu speeches for or against the issue while a class recorder takes notes on the chalkboard. With the class, evaluate the rationale of each impromptu speech and select the best presentation.

Common Error

Problem. Many students panic when they lose or drop part of their speech material.

Solution. Mention to students that good speakers always have a backup system. Tell students to write important points on index cards and to place them in a pocket. Then if a student should drop or lose any part of the speech, he or she can simply retrieve the index cards from the pocket, glance at them, and continue.

Ongoing Assessment

Activity 8

Students should demonstrate an understanding of pacing their delivery so that it fits within a time limit and pacing the delivery of particular words or phrases for special emphasis. Encourage a class discussion on effective ways to deal with distractions.

Although you cannot anticipate all the frustrating things that might happen, you should consider what you would do in the case of the following unexpected events.

Dropping Material. Whether you drop two or three note cards or a stack of papers, try to go on with your speech as if nothing had happened. If you must retrieve the material, do so as gracefully as possible and continue as if nothing had happened.

Speaking Without Key Material. After starting your speech, you may realize that you do not have with you an important bit of material you need for your speech.

- If the material is readily available—such as at your desk—and is a necessary part of your speech, then excuse yourself to the audience, get the material, return to the lectern, and go on as if nothing has happened.
- If the material is unavailable, either skip any reference to it or think of a way to present the same information in some other manner. If the missing material is a visual aid, for instance, you might give a detailed description of what it would have shown.

Forgetting a Key Point. Anyone is likely to unintentionally leave out some part of a speech. Unless what you have omitted is vital to your audience's understanding, go on without it. However, if the omitted material is vital to the meaning of the speech, then you need to make a comment such as "I forgot to mention a very important point. Let me go over it with you, tell you where it fits, and then go on."

Practicing Delivery

With two or three partners, take turns coping with factors that can affect your delivery of a speech. To practice timing, select a quotation from Bartlett's *Familiar Quotations* and present it to your partners as if you were delivering a short speech. Be sure to pause and add emphasis to convey the meaning of the words as expressively as possible.

Have your partners give you feedback on your performance. For example, they may ask you to repeat a word or to speak more slowly. Respond appropriately to your listeners' feedback.

Take turns practicing how to deal with distractions, such as a pretended interruption for an announcement over the loudspeaker. Discuss with classmates the strategies that you feel were most effective.

Enrichment

You might wish to arrange for students to learn how to make slides by using desktop publishing equipment. If no one in the school has such equipment, contact a local design studio and ask if they will help with a demonstration. Make sure students prepare a few charts or graphs for the professional designers to use. Ask if students may experiment with the equipment.

Closure

Ask each student to recall at least one helpful idea learned in this segment. It might be an idea about equipment—microphone techniques or the use of visual materials. Or it might be something about handling hecklers or unexpected distractions. Ask members of the class to contribute ideas. List the ideas on the chalkboard.

Evaluating Your Delivery

After you finish giving your speech, you should evaluate your delivery. What do you think were your greatest strengths? What do you think were your weaknesses? Use the Guidelines for Delivering a Speech, below, as a basis for making your evaluation. You may want to have one or two of your classmates help you in making your analysis. Your teacher may give you oral or written comments that you can use, too.

Activity 9: Evaluating Delivery of an Extemporaneous Speech

Using the extemporaneous method, deliver a formal speech to your class. Use the Guidelines for Delivering a Speech listed below to evaluate your delivery. Then have the members of your audience identify two aspects of your delivery that you might improve and two aspects of your delivery that they feel are your greatest strengths.

Guidelines *for Delivering a Speech*

- Do I approach the front of the room with confidence?
- Is my appearance appropriate?
- Do I show enthusiasm?
- Is my speaking free of excessive vocalized pauses?
- Do I look at the audience as I talk?
- Are my facial expressions appropriate, and my gestures and movements smooth and natural?
- Are my articulation and pronunciation correct?
- Do I stay within the time limit?
- Do I use the speaker's stand well?
- Do I handle unexpected distractions with ease?
- Do I use audiovisual materials effectively?

Meeting Individual Needs

Students with Special Needs

Presenting a speech to the class may be stressful for students with emotional problems or learning disabilities. You can help students gain confidence by having them participate in small group discussions or in other cooperative activities. If another student is working on a related topic, you might want to have the two students work together.

If a student is a visual learner, you may want to have him or her construct the visual materials for another student's speech and present a brief talk explaining the materials.

Ongoing Assessment

Activity 9

Make sure students consider every point in **Guidelines for Delivering a Speech** that is relevant to their speeches, both when they speak and when they evaluate their peers' speeches.

◆ Profiles in Communication

Performance Objectives

- To plan a speech to accompany a school tour
- To list essential information, helpful hints, and interesting facts to outline in a speech
- To list visual materials that a new student could use for a school tour
- To plan appropriate verbal and nonverbal behavior to use in presenting a speech

Teaching the Feature

This activity is designed so that the skills presented in this chapter can be pulled together in the preparation of a speech. Ask students to plan all aspects of the presentations including designing handouts or obtaining other appropriate audiovisual materials. If time is limited, however, you may want to allow students to share what they have prepared without actually having students deliver formal speeches.

Activity Note

Evaluation should center on students' outlines, visuals, and delivery. In addition, you might want to consider students' responses to the presentations.

PROFILES IN COMMUNICATION

Oshea Spencer

Working as a tour guide at a state capitol, Oshea Spencer says she always aims to be both informative and creative when she delivers her presentations.

To accomplish these goals, Ms. Spencer practices a variety of communication skills. "The most important skill," she reports, "is adapting my speech to my audience." She encourages audience participation and strives to "give every question the same attention."

Adapting her speeches to suit her audience is a challenge, Ms. Spencer says. Her listeners often vary widely in age, background, and interests. Frequently, her audiences contain citizens of other countries. As she begins each tour, Ms. Spencer must evaluate her audience quickly and then focus her speech on the types of information that she thinks may be of particular interest to her listeners.

Because her audience must be able to understand what she is saying, Ms. Spencer always pays close attention to her enunciation and her grammar.

Ms. Spencer finds that she relies on many nonverbal skills to help deliver her message. "Eye contact is important, especially with younger audiences," she says. With her winning smile, Ms. Spencer makes visitors feel welcome and encourages them to enjoy their tour.

ACTIVITY

What if you were chosen to give a new student a five-minute but thorough tour of your school? How would you use your communication skills to welcome, inform, and reassure your nervous guest? Begin by listing the various things a student at your school must know, such as certain rules and important locations. Then add helpful hints and interesting facts to the essentials.

Think about what items you would offer the new student (for example, a map) and list those items. Make an outline of your tour, keeping your time limit in mind. Ask your classmates how they think that the new student would respond to your presentation.

S☆U☆M☆M☆A☆R☆Y

PRESENTING YOUR SPEECH requires effective delivery. There are four methods of delivering a speech: impromptu, manuscript, memorized, and extemporaneous.

- **Control stage fright** by reminding yourself that nearly all speakers are nervous, that audiences are seldom aware of a speaker's nervousness, and that with greater speaking experience, you will learn to control nervousness. Plan and practice your speech carefully. While speaking, you may feel normal symptoms of nervousness. You should ignore them and concentrate on your message.
- **Improve nonverbal behavior** by making sure you present a good appearance, by keeping eye contact with the audience, by maintaining appropriate facial expressions, by using appropriate gestures, and by maintaining good posture.
- **Improve vocal skills** by showing enthusiasm for your topic; by working to eliminate vocalized pauses; and by improving your articulation, pronunciation, and enunciation. Use an appropriate volume, rate, and pitch.
- **Improve verbal messages** by paying attention to your diction and grammar.

- **Use speaker's materials** efficiently. Practice with a speaker's stand, or lectern, and with the various types of microphones. Prepare audiovisual materials, if appropriate.
- **Control other factors that affect delivery** of your speech through practice. Develop a sense of timing, adjust your delivery to respond to audience feedback, and learn to anticipate distractions and unexpected events.
- **Evaluate your delivery** after giving a speech, concentrating on specific areas in which you might make improvements.

CHAPTER 13

Vocabulary

Look back through this chapter to find the meaning of each of the following terms. Write each term and its meaning in your communication journal.

appearance, *p. 324*
articulation, *p. 328*
audiovisual materials, *p. 335*
conflicting expression, *p. 325*
deadpan, *p. 325*
diction, *p. 331*
enthusiasm, *p. 327*
enunciation, *p. 328*
extemporaneous speech, *p. 319*
eye contact, *p. 325*
grammar, *p. 331*
hand-held microphone, *p. 334*
heckler, *p. 343*
impromptu speech, *p. 318*
lavaliere or clip-on microphone, *p. 334*
lectern, *p. 332*
manuscript speech, *p. 318*
memorized speech, *p. 319*
microphone, *p. 333*
pronunciation, *p. 328*
speaker's stand, *p. 332*
stage fright, *p. 321*
standing microphone, *p. 333*
timing, *p. 341*
visual resources, *p. 336*
vocalized pauses, *p. 327*

TEACHER'S RESOURCE BINDER

- Chapter 13 Vocabulary

REVIEW QUESTIONS

Answers

1. manuscript, memorized, and extemporaneous
2. extemporaneous delivery
3. Prepare carefully and completely, look your best, relax your muscles, give yourself a pep talk, and be self-assured.
4. general weakness; a queasy feeling, butterflies, sweaty palms; dry mouth; stumbling over words; perspiration, trembling, a squeaky voice; a strong desire to quit
5. Proper attire and good grooming will help boost confidence and lessen nervousness.
6. "Conflicting expression" is a facial appearance that does not agree with a speaker's words or feelings.
7. Vocalized pauses are the meaningless speech sounds that speakers use to fill time. Vocalized pauses cause the audience to become aware of the pauses instead of the message, and the

DISCUSSION QUESTIONS

Guidelines for Assessment

Student responses may vary.

1. Students may share comments they have read or heard made by parents, other adults, or professional performers. Most novices will believe that no one else gets as nervous as they do. Some students will have had dance or piano recitals that they can discuss.
2. Students may mention speaking too quietly, vocalized pauses, no enthusiasm, or poor audiovisuals. Require students to be specific in what they find annoying.
3. Students may mention good preparation, interesting topics, pleasing appearance, and enthusiasm. Have them be specific as to why they are impressed.
4. (a) Acknowledge what happened and retrieve the material without becoming flustered. Then continue as if nothing happened.
   (b) Acknowledge the noise and repeat yourself, if necessary. If the noise is momentary, pause until it ends and then continue. If you anticipate that the noise will last more than a few seconds, announce that you will pause until it is over.
   (c) If the delivery is to be extemporaneous, you may remember enough to go ahead. If the delivery is to be from a manuscript, you cannot present the speech as planned. A memorized speech is unaffected if your notes are at home. If you misplaced an audiovisual, you can describe it or omit reference to it.

Review Questions

1. One way of delivering a speech is the impromptu method. What are three other ways of delivering a speech?
2. Which of the ways of delivering a speech allows for the most adaptation to the audience?
3. What are five techniques that you can use to reduce nervousness before giving a speech?
4. What are five kinds of nervous sensations that speakers may experience when giving their first few public speeches?
5. Your appearance has a crucial effect on the success of your speech. Why is appearance such an important aspect of nonverbal behavior?
6. Facial expression is another important nonverbal behavior. What is meant by "conflicting expression"?
7. What are vocalized pauses? What is the effect of too many vocalized pauses in a speech?
8. Beginning speakers often have trouble knowing what to do with their notes when they are speaking. What two ways can you handle your notes during your speech?
9. Microphones help you to be heard clearly; however, they can also cause problems. How can a standing microphone cause a distraction?
10. What are three examples of audiovisual materials?

Discussion Questions

1. Do you believe that most people are nervous about speaking in public? Why do people feel the way they do about public speaking? Working in a small group, share your opinions. On what evidence do you base those opinions?
2. Identify and discuss the kinds of behavior that you find most annoying in public speakers. Why are these kinds of behavior especially annoying?
3. Identify and discuss the kinds of behavior that impress you most in a speaker. Why do they impress you? How might you adopt the behaviors you find particularly impressive?
4. Discuss what you should do if the following situations were to occur while you were giving a speech: (a) you drop material; (b) a loud noise occurs outside; (c) you discover that you have left material at home; (d) you forget to make a certain point.
5. Ralph Waldo Emerson wrote, "There are men whose language is strong and defying enough, yet their eyes and their actions ask leave of other men to live." Working in a small group, discuss the meaning of the quotation. Then discuss how it relates to your own delivery of a speech.

speaker's effectiveness is destroyed.

8. Use a lectern or use your hands to hold your notes.
9. A standing microphone can limit your movement if you are accustomed to moving around freely when delivering a speech.
10. transparencies, recordings, and charts

ACTIVITIES

1. **Identifying Ways of Coping with Nervousness.** Talk with people who give speeches as part of their jobs. Are they nervous before they speak? If so, under what circumstances? How do they cope with that nervousness? Compile a class list of ways to cope with nervousness. Copy this list in your communication journal.
2. **Analyzing Others' Delivery.** While others are giving speeches in class, make notes on their delivery. After everyone has given a speech, review your notes. Identify specific behavior that helped each speaker be more effective and specific behavior that caused the speaker to be less effective. Share your findings with your classmates.
3. **Analyzing Your Own Delivery.**
   - **A.** After you have given your first class speech, use the Guidelines for Delivering a Speech (page 345) to analyze your delivery. Identify your strengths and weaknesses. Once you have arrived at some conclusions about your delivery, ask at least three of your classmates to comment on your conclusions.
   - **B.** If your school has videotape equipment, videotape all or a part of one of your final practice sessions or your actual delivery to the class. Use the Guidelines for Delivering a Speech (page 345) to analyze your delivery. Discuss your conclusions with classmates who saw your delivery.
4. **Analyzing a Professional Speaker's Delivery.**
   - **A.** Watch a professional speaker deliver a speech. Make a list of any vocal or verbal behavior that interferes with or adds to the speaker's effectiveness. Share your findings with your classmates.
   - **B.** Look at each of these photographs. Make a list of the nonverbal behaviors that you think might add to or detract from the impact each of these speakers would have on his or her audience. Share your findings with your classmates.

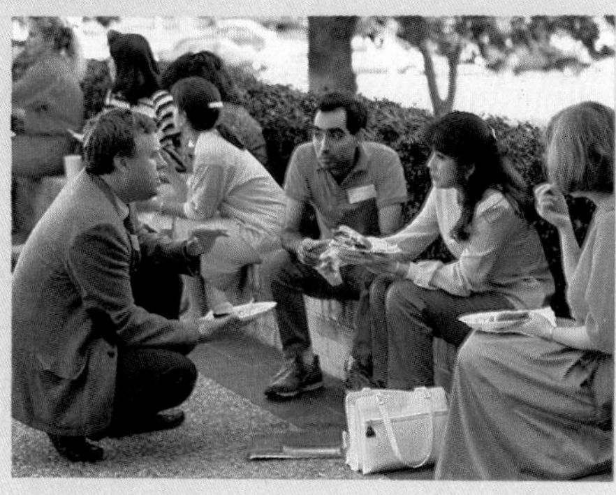

(d) If the forgotten point is a key one, stop and acknowledge the lapse, explain the point and how it fits in the total message, and go on speaking. If the point is not vital, do not bring it up.

5. To get a discussion started, tell the class that Emerson is noting that although some speakers prepare strong speeches, their nonverbal messages destroy the impact of their messages. Ask students how this quotation relates to what they have learned.

ACTIVITIES

Guidelines for Assessment

1. Encourage each student to interview one person and to identify one method for dealing with nervousness. Interview sources can be coaches, store managers, hairdressers, clergypersons, parents, or relatives.
2. Tell the class to listen to and observe the speakers with open minds and to avoid being overly critical. Encourage students to concentrate on the positive aspects of speeches.
3. A. Direct the class to review the guidelines on p. 345. Encourage students to identify at least two specific areas of strength and at least two areas that need more work.

   B. Students should use the guidelines on p. 345 as criteria for evaluating speeches. Using videotape allows students to evaluate their performances and not rely on the critiques of others.

Summative Evaluation

Your **Teacher's Resource Binder** contains a reproducible **Chapter 13 Test** that may be used to assess students' mastery of the concepts presented in this chapter.

Portfolio Assessment

For future reference and evaluation you may want to have students keep in their portfolios any skill sheets or evaluation forms that you have used with this chapter along with any other recorded or written materials that students have created.

4. A. The **Correcting Vocalization Problems** chart on p. 330 should help students identify vocal behaviors.

B. Answers will vary, but students may identify some of the following nonverbal behaviors: Each of the speakers maintains eye contact with the audience, has a pleasant and encouraging expression, and uses body language that invites audience feedback.

5. Students should be able to identify ten possible speech topics and specific materials to use as audiovisual support for the topics.

6. Remind students that this activity is intended to help student speakers become comfortable with the unexpected events that may occur during a speech. A spirit of fun is essential on the part of the speaker as well as for the audience. The audience should not become so rowdy or unruly that the speaker is unable to speak.

7. Interpretations for the gestures shown may vary, but most students will agree with the meanings cited. For their own gestures, students should use a variety of expressions and movements, but the gestures should also be clearly understandable to others.

5. Using Audiovisuals. Working in a small group, develop a list of informative speech topics or use a list that you've already made. Select ten topics, and list at least five audiovisuals to use with each topic. Try to come up with a variety of materials that a speaker could prepare, such as photographs, illustrations, and charts or graphs of statistical information. In addition, list manufactured materials that a speaker might use, such as tape recordings, compact discs, videocassettes, slides, and filmstrips. You may wish to talk to the media specialist at your school about the availability of such materials.

6. Preparing for the Unexpected. An unexpected event, whether it is a fire drill or a simple memory lapse, can fluster a beginning speaker. To recover gracefully from such an event, you need to be prepared. But how can you prepare yourself for the unexpected? One way is to act out "What-if?" situations.

With a small group of classmates as your audience, deliver a speech that you've prepared or given before. It is the job of your group to try to fluster you. They might rearrange or remove your notes, make noises, appear to be asleep, or even heckle you. As each person in the group delivers his or her speech, try coming up with new and different ways to distract the speaker. Remember, the more situations you can imagine and act out, the better prepared you'll be when the unexpected happens.

7. Inventing Effective Gestures. Long ago, students of elocution (public speaking) were required to learn and to use a number of standard gestures when they gave speeches or recited pieces of literature in public. These gestures were often quite formal and theatrical: They had to be. Before the invention of the microphone and loudspeaker, an orator could not be certain that everyone in a large auditorium was always able to hear the speech. By watching the speaker's gestures and facial expressions, people in the audience could fill in any parts of the speech they hadn't heard.

Here are two illustrations from an elocution textbook published in 1874. What do you think these gestures mean?

The gesture shown on the left expresses anger and determination. The gesture shown on the right shows the first of a series of seven items that the speaker will mention, with gesture to match, in order of each item's importance.

Working on your own, invent five gestures for speakers today to use. Remember, gestures can reveal a speaker's attitude to a subject, his or her physical position in relation to the subject, and even the relationships among various examples or ideas. Demonstrate each of your gestures to a partner to find out if the meaning is as clear to another person as it is to you.

◆ Real-Life Speaking Situations

PERFORMANCE OBJECTIVES

- To practice controlling nervousness while delivering a short speech
- To write a dialogue for an imaginary situation that employs both verbal and nonverbal interaction skills

REAL LIFE Speaking Situations

1 Outside of school, when was the last time you had to speak before a group of people? How many times have you been in such speaking situations? How did you feel as you stood before the group you were to address? If you are like most people, you probably felt rather nervous. What did you do to keep your nervousness under control?

You have been asked to speak before a group that you belong to—perhaps a scout troop, a sports team, a hobby club, or a group of family members. What could you do to control your nervousness?

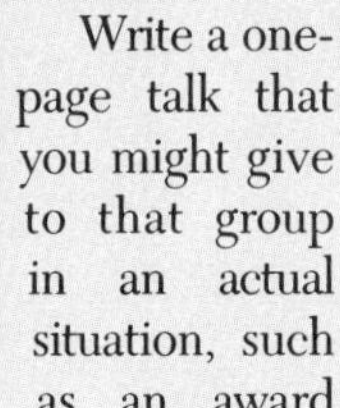

Write a one-page talk that you might give to that group in an actual situation, such as an award ceremony, a victory party, a meeting, or a special occasion. First, deliver your talk to your classmates as if you did not have your nervousness very well under control. Then deliver your talk again, this time showing that you have your nervousness very well under control.

Discuss with your classmates the differences between your two talks. Explain to the class and discuss with your classmates the effectiveness of the methods that you used during your talk to control your nervousness.

2 Travelers often need to call upon hotel staff members for directions and for information. All staff members are expected to give helpful, courteous replies to guests' inquiries. In addition to helping guests, giving such replies is one of the surest ways that a staff member has of earning a generous tip.

Imagine that you are working in a hotel and an impatient guest stops you in the hall to ask for help. You are in a hurry yourself because you must be in a staff meeting in the manager's office in less than five minutes.

How will you respond to the guest so that your reply is courteous and helpful, yet also brief? Describe the situation. What is the guest's inquiry? Is the guest a child or an adult? Is the person alone or with his or her family? Write a one- or two-page dialogue of your exchange with the guest. Be prepared to present your dialogue to the class (don't forget to include appropriate nonverbal behavior).

Ask your classmates for feedback on how well you handled the situation. You might ask how much of a tip each of them would have given you if he or she had been the guest.

ASSESSMENT GUIDELINES

1. Students might introduce their speeches by telling the class what audiences the speeches are intended for. Have the class consider this when commenting on the two speeches.
2. You may want to have students work in pairs to act out the dialogues they have created. Have the partners present their dialogues in class.

Unit 4 • Speaking for a Purpose

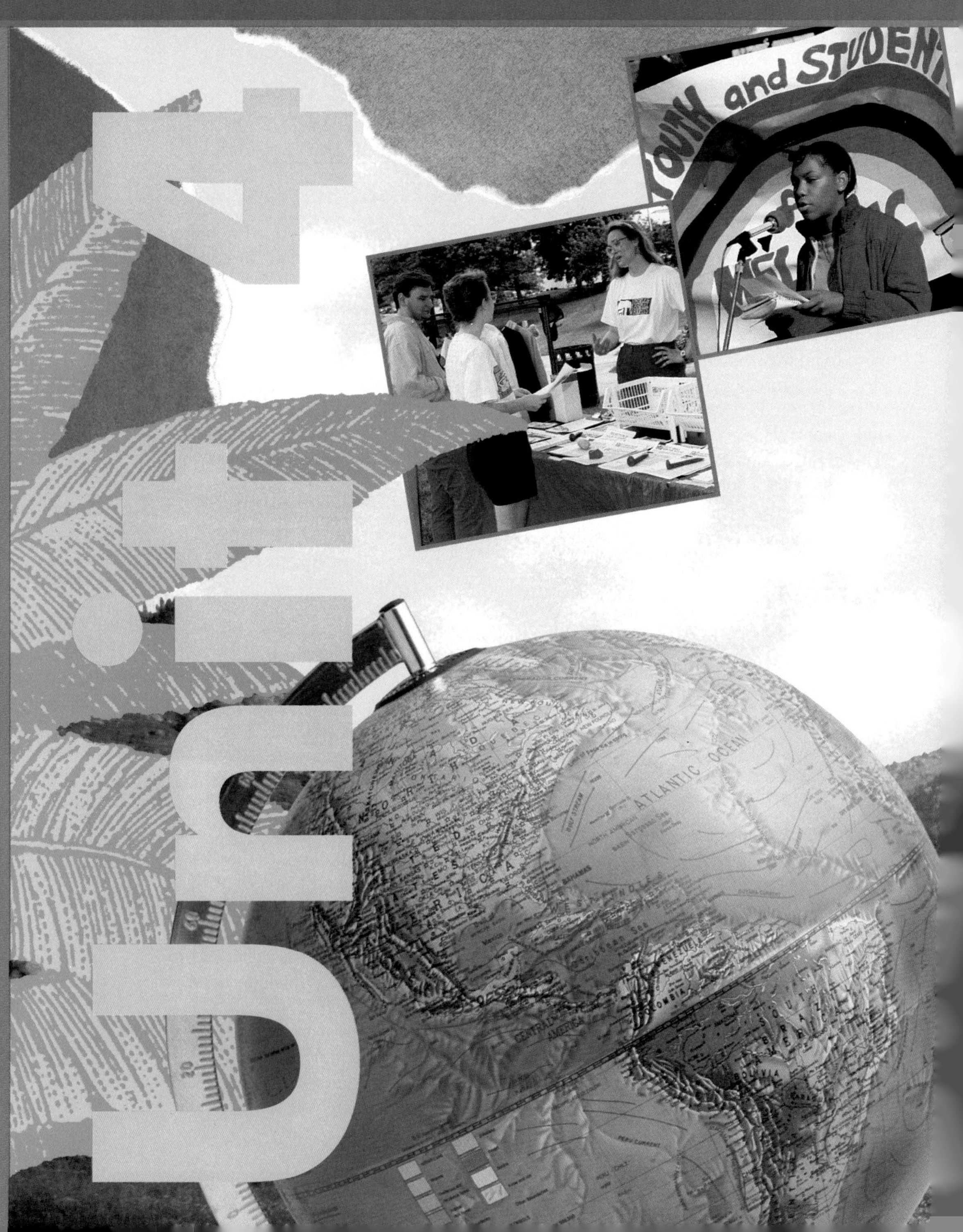

Speaking for a Purpose

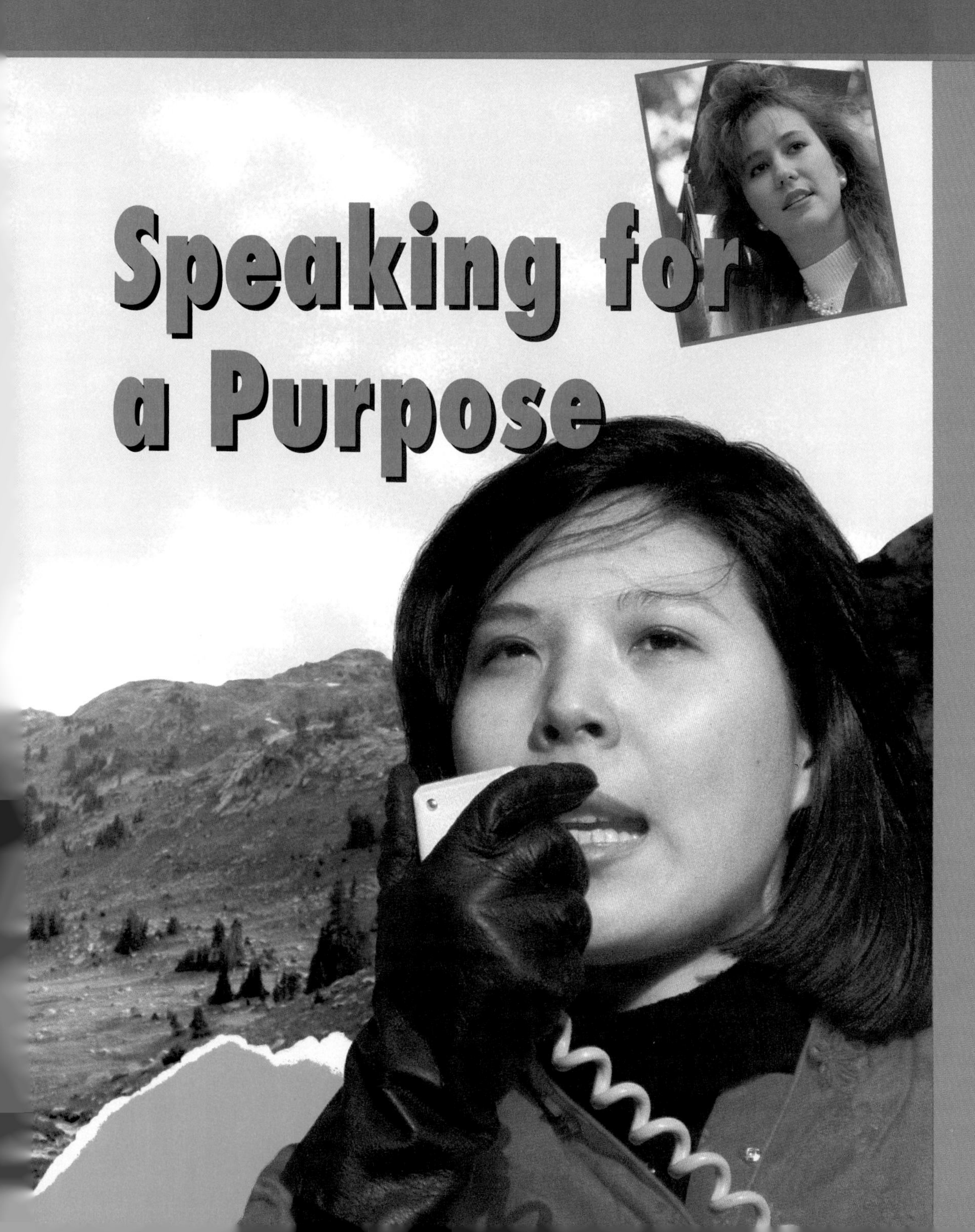

Chapter 14
Speaking to Inform
pp. 354–381

Chapter Overview

The first segment of this chapter covers the process of planning and presenting an informative speech. The second segment presents methods for adapting speeches to specific audiences and discusses ways to help listeners retain information. Students learn tips for delivering speeches and for conducting question-and-answer sessions. Finally, the chapter presents guidelines for evaluation.

Teacher's Resource Binder

The following materials are identified at their point of use in this chapter:

- Skills for Success
  1 *Planning an Informative Speech*
  2 *Organizing an Informative Speech*
  3 *Adapting the Message to Your Audience*
  4 *Helping Your Audience to Remember Information*
  5 *Conducting a Question-and-Answer Session*
  6 *Responding to Feedback*
- Chapter 14 Vocabulary
- Chapter 14 Test/Answer Key

AV Audiovisual Resource Binder

The following materials are identified at their point of use in this chapter:

- Transparency 28 *Developing an Informative Topic*
- Transparency 29 *Evaluation Checklist for Informative Speeches*
- Audiotape 2 contains recordings of informative speeches. The complete text of each speech is printed in the Appendix of Speeches in this textbook.

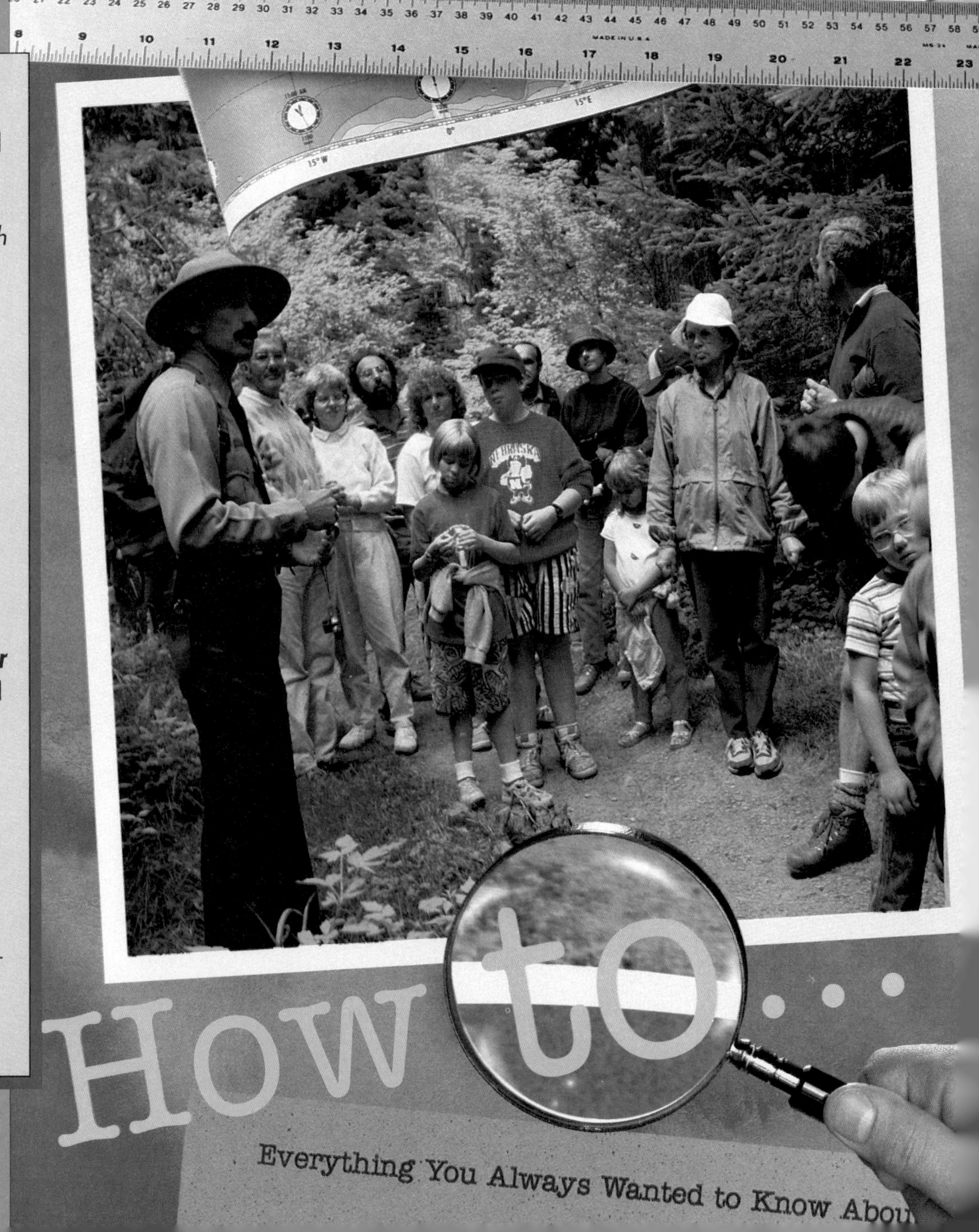

Introducing the Chapter

Presenting information is one of the chief purposes of public speaking, and this chapter discusses two types of informative speeches: the expository speech and the process speech. In addition to information on planning and delivering a speech, the chapter includes material on evaluating informative speeches that students hear and that they present themselves. Mastering the content of this chapter should prepare students to succeed in clearly presenting information to a variety of audiences.

CHAPTER

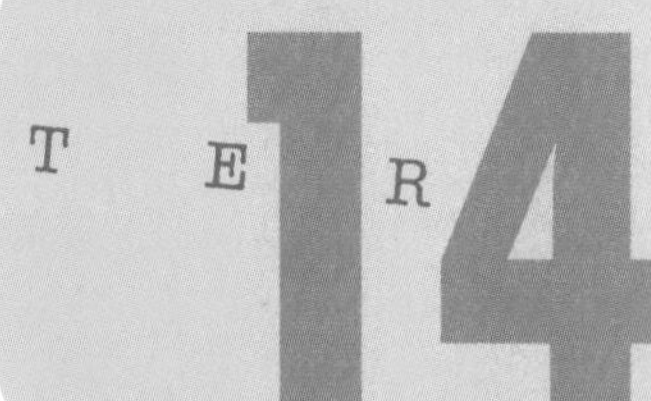

Speaking to Inform

OBJECTIVES

After studying this chapter, you should be able to

1. Identify the defining features of an informative speech.
2. Identify the aims of an informative speech.
3. Identify two types of informative speeches.
4. Develop an informative speech, using an appropriate topic.
5. Adapt information to help an audience understand and retain information.
6. Conduct a question-and-answer session.
7. Evaluate an informative speech.

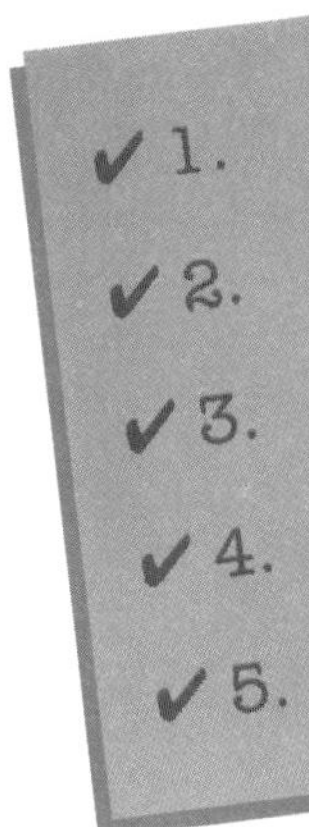

What Is an Informative Speech?

An **informative speech** provides information to an audience. The aims of an informative speech are to help your audience to understand and to remember the information you are presenting.

The two most common types of informative speeches are

- the **expository speech,** which gives information about a specific subject
- the **process speech,** or how-to speech, which explains how to do something, how to make something, or how something works

Some common informative speaking situations include a college recruiter telling graduating seniors about scholarships, a paramedic explaining how to perform CPR, a firefighter telling about household safety tips, and a student reporting on advertising in presidential elections.

In this chapter, you will learn how to develop both types of informative speeches. In addition, you will find suggestions about ways to present information that will increase your audience's understanding.

Bibliography of Additional Materials

Professional Readings

- Hunsaker, Richard A. ***Understanding and Developing the Skills of Oral Communication.*** Englewood, CO: Morton Publishing Co.
- Vasile, Albert J., and Harold K. Mintz. ***Speak with Confidence: A Practical Guide.*** New York: HarperCollins.

Audiovisuals

- ***Informative Speaking***—Films for the Humanities and Sciences, Princeton, NJ (two filmstrips with audio, 15 min. each)
- ***Reporting and Briefing***—Coronet/MTI Film & Video, Deerfield, IL (videocassette, 16 min.)
- ***The Speeches of Dwight D. Eisenhower***—MPI Home Video, Oak Forest, IL (videocassette, 60 min.)
- ***The Speeches of Franklin D. Roosevelt***—MPI Home Video, Oak Forest, IL (videocassette, 60 min.)
- ***When You Have to Get Up and Talk***—Bureau of Business Practice, Waterford, CN (videocassette, 21 min.)

Segment 1 *pp. 356–364*

- **Planning an Informative Speech**
- **Preparing to Speak**

Performance Objectives

- To select and limit a topic and to state a specific purpose for an informative speech
- To list possible sources of information for an informative speech
- To describe a speaking situation and to analyze its appeal

Cooperative Learning

You may want to let your students work in groups of four for five minutes to practice generating speech topics. Each group must come up with eight topics, two from each member. You can then write some of these topics on the chalkboard and evaluate them with the class to determine whether they are good topics for informative speeches.

Integrating the Language Arts

Listening Link

Remind students that they can gather information from nonprint sources such as interviews, television and radio broadcasts, and classroom lectures. To help students develop their skills in gathering information from nonprint sources, read aloud a short magazine or newspaper article. Have students write down the most important facts as you read. Then ask volunteers to share the information they gained from listening.

Teacher's Resource Binder

Skills for Success 1
Planning an Informative Speech

Planning an Informative Speech

Choosing a Topic

For any type of informative speech, you should select a topic that you are interested in and that you already know something about. The following charts list appropriate topics for the two types of informative speeches.

Possible Topics for Expository Speeches
• Education of women in colonial America
• The influence of African masks on modern sculpture
• Changes in the ozone layer above Antarctica
• Cliff dwellings of the Anasazi
• Three types of extrasensory perception
• Cartoon images in American pop art

Possible Topics for Process Speeches	
How to Do Something	• How to use a compass • How to select in-line skates • How to repair a bicycle hand brake
How to Make Something	• How to prepare healthy snacks • How to build a bookcase • How to make origami flowers
How Something Works	• How an automatic teller machine works • How a microwave works • How a helicopter flies

In some cases, you will not be able to choose a topic of your own. You may be assigned a broad subject area from which you will be expected to select a specific topic, or you may be assigned a topic that needs to be limited further.

Always look carefully at a topic you have been assigned to see if it has been limited to a manageable size. If the topic is too broad, consider particular features or a specific perspective from which the topic can be examined. [For more information about limiting a topic, see pages 217–219.]

- To prepare an introduction and a conclusion for an informative speech
- To organize information according to topic and purpose

Motivation

Ask students to think back to what they have learned in English classes about writing and to name the first stage of the writing process [prewriting]. Then ask them to describe the steps they follow during prewriting. [Answers may vary, but they should generally include selecting and limiting a topic, gathering information about the topic, and organizing the information.] You

Knowing Your Purpose

Your general purpose in an expository or a process speech is to inform your audience. Your specific purpose relates to your topic and to the specific information you want to convey. [For more information on stating a specific purpose and writing a thesis statement, see pages 221–224 of Chapter 9.]

EXAMPLES:

1. For an expository speech, you might state your specific purpose as "I want to explain the three major steps in the evolution of the computer."
2. For a process speech, you could state your specific purpose as "I want to explain how to perform a soccer-style place kick."

Gathering Information

The more convincingly you can show your listeners that you know about your topic, the more likely they are to pay attention and to remember what you say.

You might begin gathering information by thinking of what you already know about your topic. To locate more information, use library resources, interview a knowledgeable person, survey a group of people, or write a request letter to obtain information. [For more help on sources of information, see pages 242–255 of Chapter 10.]

Developing a Topic for an Informative Speech

Make a list of five subjects that interest you. Then select one and limit it to a suitable topic (see pages 217–219). Is the topic more appropriate for an expository speech or a process speech? State a specific purpose for your speech, and list at least two sources of information you would use to gather material for your speech.

Meeting Individual Needs

Linguistically Diverse Students

Interviewing is a particularly useful strategy for linguistically diverse students because it offers them invaluable practice in all four basic skill areas: speaking, listening, writing, and reading (their own notes). Strongly encourage students to use the interviewing process; require that they take written notes rather than record interviews on tape.

Ongoing Assessment

Activity 1

Students should limit each subject to a topic that could be covered effectively in one speech. Each specific purpose should contain only one idea and should be as precise as possible.

AV ➤ *Audiovisual Resource Binder*

Transparency 28
Developing an Informative Topic
Audiotape 2, Informative Speeches

can write these steps on the chalkboard and then have students flip through the pages of segment 1. Point out that the information in the segment outlines steps that are almost identical to the prewriting stage of the writing process and that students should have little difficulty understanding it.

TEACHING THE LESSON

If your students are well grounded in the writing process, they should have little difficulty handling the segment. If students need additional help, the segment refers students to information in previous chapters. If your students do not understand the writing process well or if you have not taught the referenced chapters, you may find it necessary to proceed through this segment slowly to make sure

WRITING TO LEARN

Suggest that students jot down the questions they ask themselves and the key points that come to mind as they develop their introductions. For example, a student might think, "I listen more carefully when the speaker tells an introductory joke, so I'll try to think of something funny to say in my introduction." Or a student might pose questions such as "How familiar will my classmates be with origami? Will I need to give some background information?"

Explain that the purpose of the assignment is for each student to become more aware of his or her creative process. Assure students that the assignment will not be graded as formal writing.

Preparing to Speak

Preparing Your Introduction

Introductions for informative speeches can vary in length depending on the topic, the audience's interest level, and the audience's knowledge about the subject. Keep in mind that an introduction for an informative speech should

- attract the audience's attention
- focus attention on the subject
- gain the audience's goodwill

You can use any of the common methods for beginning a speech—a startling statement, a question, a quotation, a story, or a personal reference—in an informative speech. [See pages 271–273 of Chapter 11 for a discussion of these methods.] You might try different introductions and then choose the one that you think would most appeal to your audience.

EXAMPLE: Latice chose a topic for a process speech—how to fold napkins. She thought of two approaches to interest others: the first based on people's curiosity and the second based on people's desire to please others.

➤ Have you ever seen and admired the special ways napkins are folded for elegant dinners shown on television programs? Have you wanted to know how to make beautifully folded napkins? Actually, napkin folding is not as difficult as it may seem. In the next few minutes, I will show you two of the most attractive ways of folding napkins.

➤ Think of a time when your family prepared a meal for a special occasion. Did you ever wonder what you could have done to give that meal a memorable touch? One way is to use a technique seen at elegant dinners on television programs: Fold the napkins in a unique, formal manner.

students understand the concepts that deal with planning and organizing a speech.

As guided practice for **Activity 1** on p. 357, you may want to select a topic that interests you and model for students the process of limiting it to a suitable topic. Then state a specific purpose and discuss various sources of information you would use to gather material about your topic. Students should then be ready to complete **Activity 1** as independent practice.

As guided practice for **Activity 2** on p. 364, you could have students help you to prepare an introduction and a conclusion for a speech about the topic you chose in **Activity 1.** In addition, discuss the type of organization that would best fit your topic and purpose. As students complete **Activity 2** for independent practice, you may want to circulate throughout the room to offer assistance as necessary.

Reprinted with permission of the authors from *Stockworth: An American CEO*, by Sterling and Selesnick.

Jot down a brief description of a speaking situation in which you were interested in listening to information about a topic. Why did you want to learn more about this specific topic? In what ways did the introductions contribute to your interest?

Organizing the Body of an Informative Speech

You can select from a variety of ways to organize the body of your informative speech. [For a general discussion of these methods, see Chapter 11.] The following list gives specific suggestions about applying these methods to organize an informative speech.

1. Chronological Order. **Chronological order** arranges details or events according to the order in which they occurred in time. Chronological order is often useful for expository speeches that present a history of something, as in the following outline.

Specific Purpose: I want to explain the three major steps in the evolution of the computer.

I. The first electronic computers used vacuum tubes and were so large that each took up an entire room.
II. The second electronic computers used transistors and were considerably smaller than the earlier computers.
III. The third generation of computers uses microchips and has been further reduced in size.

Critical Thinking

Synthesis

After students have completed the **Communication Journal** assignment, ask them to share with the class their reasons for being interested in a topic. Make a list of these reasons on the chalkboard. Ask students to study the list to determine common threads that seem to run through the reasons. Ask students to arrive at a generalized statement about interest. An example is "People are interested in listening to informative speeches if the people think the information will improve their lives in some way."

Teaching Note

Before you begin a discussion of the six organizational methods described in the textbook, you may find it helpful to review the information on pp. 221–222 in **Chapter 9: "Getting Ready"** about writing statements of specific purpose. Usually, a good specific purpose will dictate which organizational pattern is most appropriate for a given topic.

Teacher's Resource Binder

Skills for Success 2
Organizing an Informative Speech

Assessment

Depending on your students' ability levels, you may want to hold individual conferences to assess **Activities 1** and **2.** By doing so, you can evaluate students' understanding of planning and organizing informative speeches as well as students' expertise in writing introductions and conclusions.

Reteaching

To approach the concepts in this segment a different way, you could give students copies of an informative speech to use when answering the discussion questions that follow. Help students analyze the speech to arrive at answers.

1. What is the topic and the specific purpose of the speech?

Making Connections

Taking Tests

Emphasize that students should keep in mind these methods of organizing ideas when deciding how to answer essay questions on tests. Tell students that choosing the best method of ordering ideas can help to make answers clearer and more effective.

You could have students work in pairs to analyze several essay questions in a textbook and to decide which way of ordering ideas would be most effective.

Chronological order is also used in process speeches that explain procedures or events step by step.

To make remembering easier for your audience, group the steps in chronological order under broad headings. Your audience members can remember four main points, each with four subdivisions, much better than they can remember sixteen main points.

EXAMPLE: The first outline in the chart on page 361 shows a series of twelve steps. The second outline shows how these steps can be grouped under major headings.

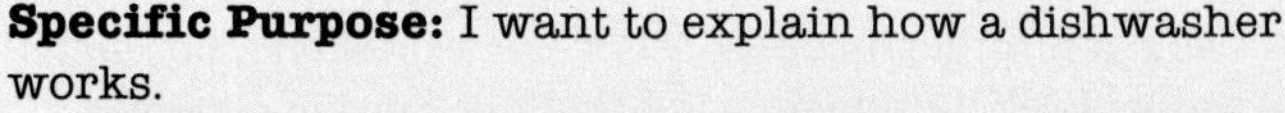

Specific Purpose: I want to explain how a dishwasher works.

I. In the first step, the drain is closed and soapy water fills the lower portion of the washer.

II. In the second step, an electric coil heats the soapy water.

III. In the third step, the heated, soapy water is siphoned through rotating blades and sprayed onto the dishes.

IV. In the fourth step, the soapy water is drained, and clean water is heated and then used to rinse the dishes.

2. What sources might the writer have used to gather information?
3. What methods are used in the introduction?
4. How is the body of the speech organized?
5. What methods are used in the conclusion?

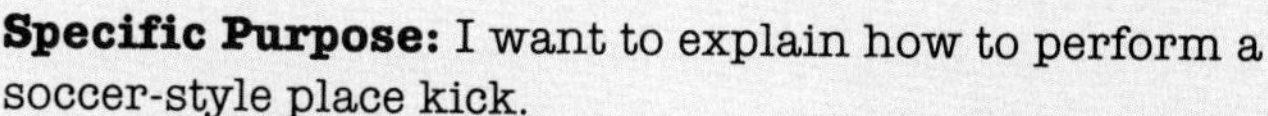

Specific Purpose: I want to explain how to perform a soccer-style place kick.

WEAK: 12 steps

I. Spot the ball on the tee.
II. Face the goal posts.
III. Take three steps back.
IV. Take two steps left.
V. Stand facing right goal post.
VI. Take three steps toward the ball.
VII. Contact ground on left heel.
VIII. Swing right leg through.
IX. Keep toe pointed.
X. Lock knee.
XI. Strike ball at a spot one third up from ground.
XII. Kick with instep.

BETTER: 4 steps with subdivisions

I. Spot the ball on the tee.
II. Mark off steps.
  A. Face the goal posts.
  B. Take three steps back and two to the left.
  C. Stand facing right goal post.
III. Step toward the ball.
  A. Take three steps, beginning with left foot.
  B. On third step, contact ground with left heel.
IV. Kick the ball.
  A. Swing right leg through.
  B. Keep toe pointed.
  C. Lock knee.
  D. Strike ball at a spot one third up from ground.
  E. Kick with instep.

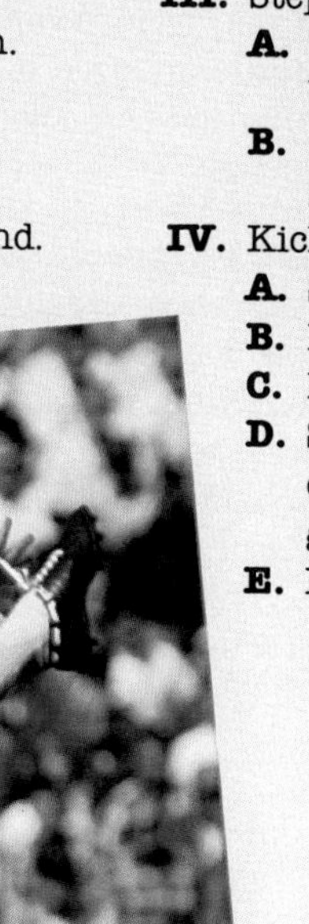

EXTENSION

You can encourage students to use the higher-order thinking skill of evaluation by having them view a videotape of a speech to determine whether the topic, organization, introduction, and conclusion are effective. A good source of speeches for this activity is the C-Span cable TV network, which routinely presents speeches by government officials and others.

Before students view the tape, you will probably want them to collaborate to develop an evaluation scale.

Learning Styles

Kinetic Learners. To help students determine the most effective way to organize their informative speeches, suggest that they write each detail on a separate index card. Then students can lay the index cards out on their desks and rearrange the cards until they find the most effective order.

2. Topical Order. In **topical order,** a topic is broken down into its parts and then arranged in an order determined by the speaker and stated in the specific purpose. This is the most common method for organizing expository speeches.

Specific Purpose: I want to explain the three major types of extrasensory perception.

I. One type is telepathy.
II. A second type is clairvoyance.
III. A third type is precognition.

Topical order is also used for a process speech that addresses more than one main point. In this method of organization, the main points are arranged in topical order, and then their subdivisions are arranged chronologically.

Specific Purpose: I want to explain two simple but attractive ways of folding napkins.

I. One way is the fan fold.
  A. The first step is . . .
  B. The second step is . . .
  C. The third step is . . .
II. A second way is the turtle fold.
  A. The first step is . . .
  B. The second step is . . .
  C. The third step is . . .

3. Spatial Order. In **spatial order,** details are arranged according to their position in space. This arrangement is often used for descriptions.

Specific Purpose: I want to explain what a typical word-processing unit looks like.

I. Immediately in front of the operator is a standard computer keyboard.
II. Directly above the computer keyboard is a monitor screen.
III. Below or to the right of the computer keyboard is a disk drive.

Enrichment

You can hold a "guess the character" contest by having your students write and deliver one-paragraph introductions to speeches in the styles they think might be used by famous people or characters from literature. Have each student use one or two simple props or costume elements, and let the members of the class try to guess who the character is based on the content of the introduction and the way it is delivered.

Animal Crackers by Roger Bollen. Reprinted by permission: Tribune Media Services.

4. Climactic Order. **Climactic order** arranges items according to their order of importance, usually starting with the least important item of information and ending with the item of information that is the most important.

Specific Purpose: I want to explain three requirements for being a good football coach.

I. A good coach must have an ability to recognize raw talent in new players.

II. More important, a good coach must understand the mechanics of the sport.

III. Most important, a good coach must be able to motivate players to do their best.

5. Cause-and-Effect Order. In **cause-and-effect order,** information is arranged to show causes or conditions and the effects or results of those causes or conditions.

Specific Purpose: I want to explain the relationship between high interest rates for consumers and the onset of a recession in the general economy.

I. High interest rates for consumers make consumers more reluctant to borrow and drive down consumer demand for financing to make purchases.

II. A reduction in consumer purchases calls for a decrease in production of manufactured goods, which then causes more unemployment.

III. The result is a recession, or a downward trend in the overall economy.

Critical Thinking

Analysis

Although the text suggests that climactic order usually proceeds from the least important to the most important item, special circumstances related to the audience may require the use of most important to least important item as an organizational scheme. Ask your students to analyze their audience. Are there special factors (age, attention span, conditions in the place where the speech will be delivered) that make the most-to-least pattern more desirable?

Teaching Note

Cause-and-effect order often moves chronologically from one event to the next. Point out to students that the emphasis in cause-and-effect order is on showing how one event causes the next, rather than on simply describing events in the order in which they occurred. You can also point out to students the danger of the "false cause" fallacy, which assumes that any event that happens after another event occurs is caused by the previous event. In fact, the cause of the second event may be something completely unrelated to the event that preceded it.

CLOSURE

Ask students to respond to the following questions:

1. What's the difference between an expository speech and a process speech? [An expository speech presents factual information; a process speech tells "how to."]
2. What are some ways to gather information for a speech? [Think about, read about, and talk to others about the topic.]
3. What should a good introduction accomplish? [It should motivate the audience to learn more about the topic.]
4. What's the most important factor in selecting an organizational pattern? [the speaker's specific purpose]
5. What should a good conclusion accomplish? [It should summarize the main points of the speech.]

TEACHING NOTE

You may want to remind students that comparison-and-contrast order can be organized in two different ways. The following chart might help to clarify the two strategies:

Block Method
Item 1: Sojourner Truth
  Point 1: Background
  Point 2: Personality
  Point 3: Achievements
Item 2: Harriet Tubman
  Point 1: Background
  Point 2: Personality
  Point 3: Achievements

Point-by-Point Method
Point 1: Background
  Item 1: Sojourner Truth
  Item 2: Harriet Tubman
Point 2: Personality
  Item 1: Sojourner Truth
  Item 2: Harriet Tubman
Point 3: Achievements
  Item 1: Sojourner Truth
  Item 2: Harriet Tubman

ONGOING ASSESSMENT

Activity 2

Students' introductions should attract the audience's attention, focus attention on the subject, and gain the audience's goodwill. The types of organization students choose should be appropriate for their topics and specific purposes. Their conclusions should summarize the main points of their speeches.

6. Comparison-and-Contrast Order. In **comparison-and-contrast order,** items of information are arranged to show the similarities and differences between the items.

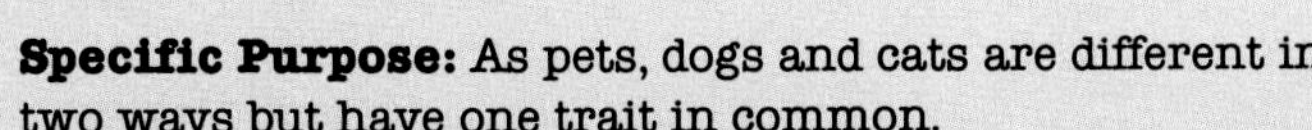

Specific Purpose: As pets, dogs and cats are different in two ways but have one trait in common.

I. Dogs tend to show more devotion to owners than most cats do.
II. Cats generally show more independence and self-sufficiency than most dogs do.
III. Both dogs and cats can be affectionate pets.

Preparing Your Conclusion

The conclusion of an informative speech usually includes a summary of the main points. [See Chapter 11 for more on conclusions.]

EXAMPLE: The expository speech on extrasensory perception, outlined on page 362, might end with this statement: "So we can see that extrasensory perception includes telepathy, clairvoyance, and precognition."

Since a process speech aims to have the audience master the key steps of the process, an effective conclusion often includes a summary of those steps.

EXAMPLE: The speech about how high interest rates contribute to starting a recession might conclude with the statement, "When high interest rates reduce consumer spending, the decrease in sales causes cutbacks in production, resulting in layoffs and the beginning of a recession."

Many speakers end with a quotation, an anecdote, or a final thought that makes the conclusion more memorable.

Preparing Your Informative Speech

Using the topic and the specific purpose you developed in Activity 1 (page 357), prepare an introduction for your speech. Next, decide which type of organization will best fit your topic and purpose. Be prepared to explain your decision. For a process speech, list the main points of the information or the main steps in the process. If your list has more than five steps, group the steps into categories. Finally, prepare a conclusion for your speech.

Segment 2 *pp. 365–369*

- **Adapting Your Speech to Suit Your Audience**

Performance Objectives

- To prepare and administer a survey to determine audience awareness about a topic
- To write a paragraph explaining adjustments made to a speech on the basis of an audience survey
- To prepare and explain a memory device for a speech

Adapting Your Speech to Suit Your Audience

To help your listeners understand and recall the information you present, you will often need to adapt your speech to suit their experience, needs, and interests.

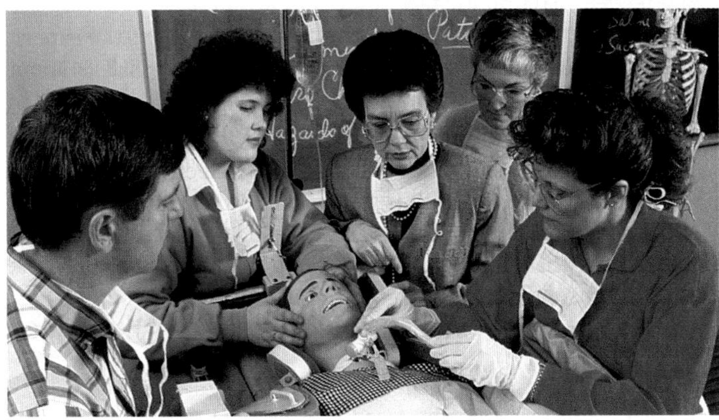

Experience

Since your listeners may lose interest if they cannot figure out what your information has to do with them, you will need to relate your speech to your audience's experience. Some topics are easy to relate to an audience's needs and interests—for instance, telling high school seniors how to improve their SAT scores.

When your audience is not knowledgeable about your topic, you should relate it to a topic that they may know more about. For example, an expository speech about building the Egyptian pyramids might be more interesting to an audience if you compare ancient and modern building methods.

Familiarity

Your audience is unlikely to be familiar with all of the information you plan to include in your speech. You might poll some of the members of your audience before giving your speech to find out the extent of their knowledge.

EXAMPLE: Rico, who raises show dogs, had planned to give a speech on the different types of dogs. He had assumed everyone in class knew that dogs were classified into six groups:

Teaching Note

Students often have little sense of who their audience will be for a speech, so audience analysis is difficult. Suggest to students that they consider their audience to be the other students in speech class. Then students can gather data about audience background on particular topics by asking classmates what they know about the topics.

Teacher's Resource Binder

Skills for Success 3
Adapting the Message to Your Audience

Assessment

Activities 3 and **4** can be used to assess students' performance. Another method of assessment is to observe how well the audiences understand and remember the information when students deliver speeches. You can base your evaluations on these questions: Does the information seem appropriate for the audience? Does the student use memory devices?

Reteaching

Students might have difficulty adapting their information to their audiences' needs. Provide students with copies of an informative speech written by you or by a former student. With the class, determine the targeted audience for the speech. Then decide on a different audience and discuss how to change the speech to accommodate that audience.

Cooperative Learning

A third type of mnemonic device that students might find helpful in remembering information is a sentence in which the first letter of each word stands for something the student wants to remember. A classic example is from music theory: *"Every good boy deserves fun." E, G, B, D,* and *F* represent the bars on the lines of the treble clef musical notation.

Have students work in small groups to create similar devices for one or more of their informative speech topics. Then have groups share their sentences with the class.

Teaching Note

During demonstrations such as the demonstration of napkin folding that was used as an example in segment 1, members of the audience can practice the skill as the speaker demonstrates it. Encourage students to consider audience practice if their topics lend themselves to using it.

Teacher's Resource Binder

Skills for Success 4
Helping Your Audience to Remember Information

Helping Listeners Retain Information

You can use a number of methods and devices to help your audience understand and remember the information you are presenting.

1. Mnemonic Devices. A **mnemonic device** helps the memory by providing easy-to-remember associations.

Mnemonic Devices

Type	Examples
Rhyme—a short poem or rhymed phrase	In fourteen hundred and ninety-two, Columbus sailed the ocean blue. *(to remember date of Columbus's voyage)*
Acronym—a word made out of the first letters of the words in a phrase or the items in a list	H.O.M.E.S. *(to remember the names of the five Great Lakes:* ***H****uron,* ***O****ntario,* ***M****ichigan,* ***E****rie, and* ***S****uperior)*

2. Audiovisual Materials. **Audiovisual materials** are resources that a speaker uses to

- save time in explanation
- clarify a point
- help an audience remember important material

Sometimes you can find audiovisual materials—such as charts, diagrams, photographs, cassette tapes, graphs, or maps—already prepared. For example, you may obtain audiovisual materials through your local, state, or national government agencies. You can also make suitable visuals yourself. [See Chapter 13, page 336, for more about making visual materials.]

3. Demonstrations. In a **demonstration,** a speaker performs the steps of a process to help listeners understand it and learn how to perform it themselves. A speaker might also ask a well-qualified person to demonstrate. For a speech on giving artificial respiration, for example, you could ask a paramedic to demonstrate while you explain the process.

Using a demonstration is appropriate when

- the process to be demonstrated is relatively simple and has a manageable number of steps
- the demonstrator is able to complete the demonstration smoothly
- the audience can see everything that is being done

ENRICHMENT

TV meteorologists use visuals to present daily weather reports. Invite a local TV meteorologist to talk to the class about how the visuals are developed and how he or she helps the audience understand the symbols used in the visuals. If a meteorologist is not available, videotape a local weather program and ask your students to evaluate how the meteorologist uses visuals.

CLOSURE

Ask a volunteer to suggest an appropriate topic for an informative speech. Ask a second volunteer to evaluate the topic in terms of the experience, familiarity, and technical knowledge of the class as an audience. Then ask a third volunteer to come up with an idea for a memory device that could be used in delivering a speech on the topic.

In a **partial demonstration,** either some of the parts of the demonstration are already completed or the size of items is exaggerated so the audience can see them clearly.

EXAMPLES:

1. To show how to patch a hole in plasterboard, you could avoid delay by bringing two containers with premeasured amounts of water and dry plaster and demonstrating how to mix them. While giving more details about the mixture, you could show a third container with the proper mixture ready to use. Then you could go on to your next step.
2. To show how to sew a button on a coat, you might use items of an exaggerated size: a cardboard button about the diameter of a dinner plate, and a sharpened pencil with string tied to the end to represent the needle and thread. Then everyone in your audience could see the process.

ACTIVITY 4 — Preparing a Memory Device

Using the topic you began to prepare in Activity 2 on page 364, create a device to help your audience understand and remember information about your topic. Be prepared to explain how this memory device would help you present information more effectively than you could with words alone.

MEETING INDIVIDUAL NEEDS

Learning Styles

Kinetic and Tactile Learners. Demonstrations seem particularly well suited for students whose primary learning channels are kinetic and tactile. Encourage these students to plan demonstration speeches and to practice their demonstrations several times before they deliver their speeches.

ONGOING ASSESSMENT

Activity 4

One of the essential qualities of a memory device is ease of use. The devices your students create should be easy to remember if they are mnemonic devices and convenient to manipulate if they are audiovisuals or props.

TIMESAVER

You may want to develop a simple rating scale for **Activity 4** that students can use to evaluate each other's memory devices. Then you can collect the ratings for assessment purposes.

Segment 3 *pp. 370–375*

- **Delivering Your Speech**
- **Conducting a Question-and-Answer Session**
- **Responding to Feedback**
- **Evaluating Informative Speeches**

PERFORMANCE OBJECTIVES

- To record a rehearsal of an informative speech and to evaluate the recording
- To rehearse giving answers to questions following an informative speech
- To write a description and an evaluation of audience behavior during a speech
- To deliver an oral and a written critique of an informative speech

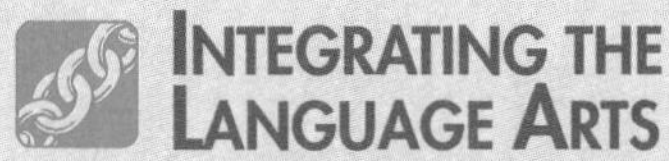

INTEGRATING THE LANGUAGE ARTS

Vocabulary Link

The term *ethos* refers to the distinguishing character, attitudes, beliefs, and nature of a speaker. Point out to students that these qualities all work together to enhance a speaker's credibility.

Ask students to discuss what makes them believe or disbelieve what others say in informal communications. What traits make people believable?

TEACHING NOTE

Like other good habits, steady eye contact between speaker and listener can be learned. Encourage students to maintain eye contact with you and with one another during class discussion and routine class proceedings. Also, check yourself to see that both as a speaker and as a listener, you model steady eye contact with your students.

Delivering Your Speech

Any speech will be more effective if it is delivered well. [In preparing to deliver your informative speech, keep in mind the guidelines discussed in Chapter 13.]

1. Credibility. A speaker's **credibility** is the amount of trust and belief the speaker inspires in an audience. You want to establish yourself as a speaker whom the audience can trust to give accurate information. One way to do this is to tell the audience a little about your background or experience to let your audience know what makes you qualified to talk about your topic. Be thoroughly prepared, but if you do not know something or if experts are still debating a point, freely admit this.

2. Enthusiasm. Be enthusiastic about your topic. Your audience will probably find it difficult to become excited about the topic you are speaking about if you do not seem to find it important or interesting. The more enthusiasm you show, the more likely you are to get and to hold the audience's attention.

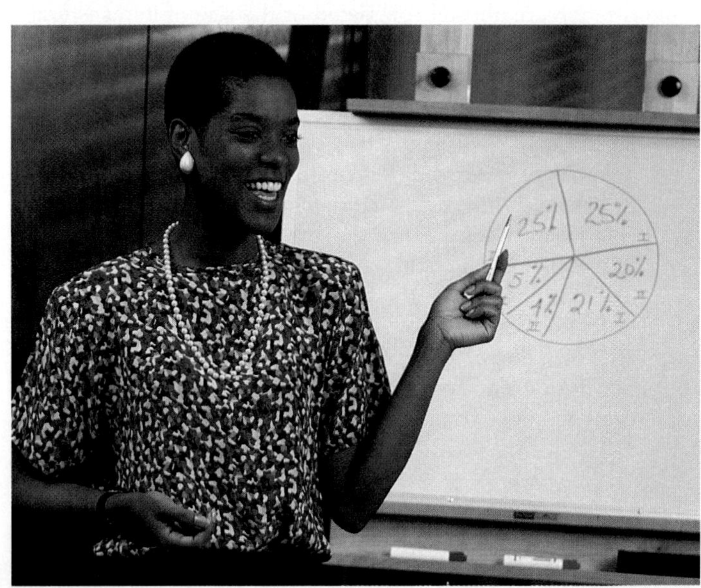

3. Eye Contact. Establish eye contact with your listeners. If you look at the members of your audience, they will look at you. If you fail to establish eye contact, the members of the audience will let their eyes—and their attention—wander. [See Chapter 13 for more information about eye contact.]

Motivation

Ask students to share situations in which they had questions but did not get chances to question the speakers. Then ask them to share situations in which their questions were not answered to their satisfaction. Tell students that conducting an effective question-and-answer session takes practice and that there are guidelines they can follow to do a good job of handling questions. Point out that answering questions is part of a speaker's responsibility and that students will learn how to do it correctly in this segment.

4. Vocal Variety and Emphasis. Vary your tone, rate, volume, and pitch to emphasize key points and to make your speech more interesting. [See Chapter 3 for more about using your voice effectively.]

5. Clear Articulation and Enunciation. Be careful not to slur your words. When you speak clearly, your audience will find listening to your message easy and enjoyable.

6. Good Pronunciation. Your pronunciation can either help or hurt your credibility. If you mispronounce key words in your speech, your listeners will begin to question whether you have a thorough knowledge of your subject.

Evaluating Your Delivery

Record a rehearsal of your informative speech (or have someone listen carefully to your rehearsal). Rate yourself (or have your partner rate you) on your enthusiasm, your vocal emphasis and variety, your articulation and enunciation, and your pronunciation. Identify two specific improvements that you plan to make in delivering your speech.

Conducting a Question-and-Answer Session

Question-and-answer sessions often follow informative speeches. These sessions allow the audience to clarify ideas and to get more information. Plan to set aside one third to one half of your time for questions and answers—for example, for a thirty-minute speech, reserve ten to fifteen minutes for questions.

People are sometimes reluctant to ask questions, so you will need to let the audience know in advance that you are truly interested in answering their questions. For example, you might say, "As I'm going along, make note of any places where I haven't been clear or where you would like more detail—and I'll answer your questions at the end."

Another way to encourage your audience to answer questions is to conclude by saying something like this: "What I've said may have started you thinking about ideas that I didn't cover or that you'd like to have explained further. I'll be happy to answer your questions."

Additional Activity

Most students are inexperienced at speaking through amplification systems. You may want to allow your class to practice using public-address systems so the students can become familiar with how their voices sound when amplified.

Ongoing Assessment

Activity 5

A uniform rating scale devised by the students (as suggested in **Teaching the Lesson** on p. 372) should facilitate your assessment of students' delivery and students' ability to evaluate delivery. You can have students write down the improvements they plan to make and keep this information in their portfolios for future reference.

Building a Portfolio

You may want to have students keep the completed rating scales and projected improvements from **Activity 5.** At a later date, students could again use the rating scale to evaluate their delivery and then could compare the two scales to assess their progress.

Teacher's Resource Binder

Skills for Success 5
Conducting a Question-and-Answer Session

Teaching the Lesson

This segment refers to information from several other chapters as it applies to informative speeches. If you have not covered **Chapters 3, 4,** and **13,** you may want to provide brief explanations of these chapters before students begin work on this segment. Before you assign **Activity 5** on p. 371, you may want to have the class work together to devise a rating scale to be used for the activity. Discuss the use of the scale and then assign **Activity 5** as independent practice.

You could model a question-and-answer session for the class by reading a passage from a speech or another source and by letting students ask questions. As you answer the questions, point out how you are implementing the four **"How to"** points. Then assign **Activity 6** as independent practice. Model the evaluation process by reading aloud an informative speech and by

Teaching Note

Encourage students who are conducting question-and-answer sessions to repeat in a highly condensed form the questions they are asked. This practice enables the speaker to check his or her understanding of the questions and to focus the audience's attention on the questions. In large rooms, some members of the audience may not be able to hear the original question, and by repeating a concise version of it, the speaker draws the whole audience into the exchange.

Ongoing Assessment

Activity 6

The questions that students ask should be relevant, and the answers should be brief and easy to understand. All questions and answers should be delivered politely.

Teacher's Resource Binder

Skills for Success 6
Responding to Feedback

HOW TO Conduct Question-and-Answer Sessions

1. **See to it that people ask questions rather than give speeches.** If someone starts talking but no question comes forth within the first few sentences, interrupt politely to make sure that the person has a question.
2. **Call on people from all parts of the audience.** Avoid calling only on those in the middle of the audience or those seated in the first few rows. Give everyone a chance to ask a first question before calling on those with second questions.
3. **Try to answer all questions briefly.** Remember that you have a time limit. Reply succinctly to give as many people as possible a chance to ask their questions.
4. **If you cannot answer a question, feel free to say so.** It is much better to say, "I'm sorry, I really don't have an answer for that" than to stall or try to answer questions you are not prepared to answer. You can always offer to locate the information and provide it later.

Rehearsing Answers to Potential Questions from Your Audience

After you rehearse your speech, rehearse answers to potential questions. Either ask yourself questions or have a friend listen to your speech and then ask you questions. Locate any additional information the questions raise that your speech did not answer.

Responding to Feedback

In an informative speech, you are trying to reach as many people as possible with your information, so you should watch for signs of inattention or lack of understanding: yawning, papers rustling, feet shuffling, and coughing. If you see your listeners adopting these behaviors, begin at once to think of ways to recapture their attention, such as varying your voice, increasing your movements, and making gestures.

As you gain speaking experience, you will become more aware of audience behavior. The mark of a truly effective speaker is the ability to adapt to these signs and regain the audience's interest quickly and smoothly.

having students evaluate it with the checklist on p. 375. Then discuss how to use the checklist to create oral and written critiques. If students present their informative speeches at this time, the audience can prepare oral and written critiques as independent practice. If not, you can assign **Activity 7**.

Assessment

You can use the activities in the segment to assess students' performance on the objectives. In addition, if students present informative speeches at this time, you can assess their deliveries, their question-and-answer sessions, and their responses to feedback.

When you speak, how aware are you of what your audience is doing? When your next speech is over, write down some of the behavior that you observed during your speech. What behavior, if any, affected your delivery? What did you do to keep or regain the audience's attention?

Evaluating Informative Speeches

After your classmates have presented their speeches, you will probably be called upon to give an oral or a written critique of each speaker's effectiveness. [For a more detailed discussion of oral and written critiques, see Chapter 4.]

Remember that the purpose of an informative speech is to help an audience understand and remember the information presented. Therefore, a critique of an informative speech should focus on the effectiveness of what the speaker said and did to help the audience understand and remember information.

Giving a Critique of an Informative Speech

Working with a partner, find an informative speech in an issue of *Vital Speeches of the Day*. Have your partner deliver this speech to you as if he or she were presenting it to an entire audience. Then, using the Evaluation Checklist on page 375, give an oral critique. Finally, provide a written critique.

Meeting Individual Needs

Learning Styles

Visual Learners. You may want to have your students create charts for the **Communication Journal** exercise. The first column can contain each behavior the students observed. The second column can contain a check if the behavior in the first column affected the delivery. The third column can contain a brief description of what they did to regain or keep the audience's attention.

Ongoing Assessment

Activity 7

In their oral critiques, students should be specific, concentrate on only one or two negative criticisms, mention what the speaker could do to improve, and give positive feedback. The written critiques should take a more detailed look at the areas of organization, content, language, and delivery.

Reteaching

To reteach the sections on the question-and-answer session and audience feedback, videotape a volunteer presenting a speech and a question-and-answer session to the class. Analyze the videotape with students by stopping the tape where necessary to comment on problems and their solutions.

Extension

Show a videotape of a news conference or a political forum. After each question, stop the tape and ask students to consider whether the answer will require the speaker to give or repeat information (knowledge), to apply ideas to new situations (application), to break down an idea into its parts (analysis), to put together parts of ideas to create a new idea (synthesis), or to

Students with Special Needs

Delivering a speech might be a frightening experience for some of your students. Therefore, encourage students by providing many opportunities for success.

One modification is to allow students to give their speeches before small groups. Another suggestion is to have students focus on three or four speech techniques at a time. As students gain confidence and increase knowledge about what makes speeches effective, you can increase the number of techniques on which they will be evaluated.

GUIDELINES

FOR INFORMATIVE SPEECHES

for an Expository Speech

- Have I selected and limited an appropriate topic?
- Have I clearly stated a specific purpose?
- Have I gathered information from a variety of sources?
- Does the topic relate to my audience's experience?
- Does the introduction spark my audience's interest in learning more about my topic?
- Is the material well organized?
- Is the information new, or does it offer new insights?
- Can I use audiovisual materials to help my audience understand and remember information?

for a Process Speech

- Have I selected a process that interests me and that I know how to perform?
- Have I clearly stated a specific purpose?
- Have I organized the steps in the process clearly?
- Will my presentation help the audience visualize the process?
- Have I adapted the speech to my audience?
- Can I deliver the speech confidently?
- Can I respond appropriately to audience feedback?

judge the value of an idea (evaluation). After the class agrees on what the question requires, play the answer to determine whether the speaker did what the class predicted.

CLOSURE

Ask volunteers to explain the meaning of the following terms as they are used in the segment: *credibility, eye contact, vocal variety and emphasis, clear articulation and enunciation, good pronunciation, audience feedback,* and *signs of inattention.*

EVALUATION  CHECKLIST

for Informative Speeches

Organization:

Was the purpose of the speech clear?
Did the introduction gain attention? Did it clarify the purpose?
Was each of the main ideas or major steps easily identifiable?
Did the main ideas follow a consistent pattern?
Did the speaker use good transitions?
Did the conclusion summarize the key ideas? Did it close the speech on a high note?

Content:

Did the speaker seem to understand the topic?
Did the speaker consider the audience's interest, knowledge, and attitude?
Was enough information given to make the key ideas or points of the speech understandable?
Were audiovisual materials used effectively?
Were materials provided to help the audience remember the key ideas?

Language:

Was the language precise?
Were the words specific and concrete?
Did the speaker use words that the audience could understand?
Did the speaker emphasize key ideas?
Was the tone appropriate for the audience and the occasion?

Delivery:

Did the speaker seem confident?
Was the speaker's appearance appropriate?
Did the speaker show enthusiasm?
Did the speaker look at the audience during the speech?
Were facial expressions, gestures, and movements natural?
Were the speaker's articulation, enunciation, and pronunciation correct?

Additional Comments:

Evaluation:

Audiovisual Resource Binder

Transparency 29
Evaluation Checklist for Informative Speeches

◆ Profiles in Communication

Performance Objective

- To prepare and deliver a training speech by considering audience, topic, and method of presentation

Teaching the Feature

Have students read the profile of Officer Herman Ward. Then ask a volunteer to list the steps that Officer Ward must go through to adapt his presentations to his various audiences.

Activity Note

Discuss the activity with students so they understand the steps involved. You will probably want to set a time limit for the presentations. Even if you do not require students to write their training speeches out in full, you could have them write down their answers to all of the questions listed in the assignment before they deliver their speeches. Suggest that students refer to the **Guidelines for a Process Speech** on p. 374 before they deliver their speeches to their classmates.

Topics should be appropriate for students' audiences. Presentations should fit the time frame and be clear and enthusiastic. You may want to use the **Evaluation Checklist for Informative Speeches** on p. 375 to assess presentations. In addition, you will probably want to consider the audience's feedback in your assessments.

PROFILES IN COMMUNICATION

Herman Ward

After he completed his training at the Texas Highway Patrol Academy, Officer Herman Ward's public speaking responsibilities began almost immediately. He had been on the job less than three months when he was asked to speak to the Lions Club about the Highway Patrol's training program.

Since that time, giving public information speeches has been an integral part of Officer Ward's professional duties. He is frequently asked to talk to a variety of audiences: public-service groups, business and social organizations, church groups, and students.

Some audiences request that Officer Ward speak on a specific topic, such as radar operations or accident investigation; others leave the topic selection up to him. Once he has a definite topic, he reviews the information he wants to present. Then he writes an outline, decides "when to show and when to tell," and practices fitting the presentation into the time frame he has been given.

ACTIVITY

Imagine that you have been called upon to give a training session. First, identify your audience. Are your listeners interested in education, business, military service, sports, or some other field? Second, identify your audience's level of experience. Are they beginners or experts? Third, identify the information or process you will teach. Choose a topic you know well—perhaps a process such as changing a tire, giving first aid, or preparing a meal. List the main points or the steps of the process. Fourth, decide on the best way to present your ideas clearly and completely. Consider presenting a visual aid or two. Finally, give your training session in class. Ask for feedback from your classmates on the effectiveness of your presentation.

S·U·M·M·A·R·Y

AN INFORMATIVE SPEECH helps an audience understand and remember the material presented. The two types of informative speeches are expository speeches and process speeches. An expository speech gives information on a specific topic. A process, or how-to, speech tells how to do something, how to make something, or how something works. Use the following pointers to develop an informative speech:

- **Choose a topic** that you are interested in and that you already know something about. Limit your topic to a manageable size.
- **Gather information** from a variety of sources: your own experience and observations, interviews or surveys, and written sources.
- **Organize your speech** into three parts: an introduction, a body, and a conclusion. Organize the body of your speech in one of the following orders: chronological, spatial, topical, climactic, cause-and-effect, or comparison-and-contrast.
- **Adapt your speech** to your audience's experience, interests, and knowledge.
- **Deliver your speech** expressively. Use audiovisual materials if they save time, clarify an idea, or emphasize a point. Throughout the speech, evaluate and respond to audience feedback. After the speech, leave time for a question-and-answer session. Answer questions carefully and fully.
- **Evaluate an informative speech** with an oral or written critique by focusing on what the speaker did to help the audience understand and remember the information presented.

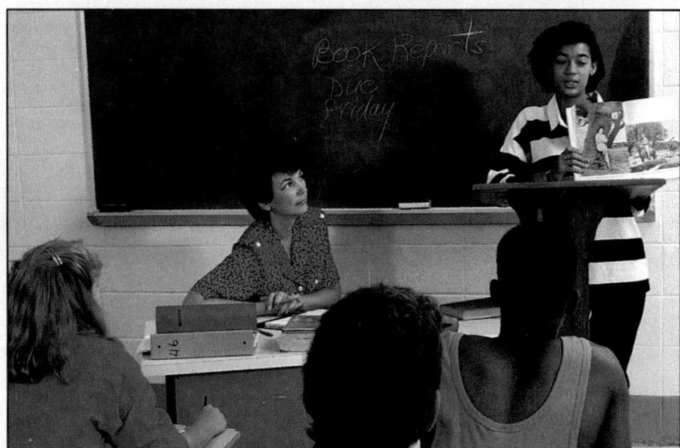

Vocabulary

Look back through this chapter to find the meaning of each of the following terms. Write each term and its meaning in your communication journal.

audiovisual materials, *p. 368*
cause-and-effect order, *p. 363*
chronological order, *p. 359*
climactic order, *p. 363*
comparison-and-contrast order, *p. 364*
credibility, *p. 370*
demonstration, *p. 368*
expository speech, *p. 355*
informative speech, *p. 355*
mnemonic device, *p. 368*
partial demonstration, *p. 369*
process speech, *p. 355*
spatial order, *p. 362*
topical order, *p. 362*

TEACHER'S RESOURCE BINDER

- Chapter 14 Vocabulary

Review Questions

Answers

1. for the audience to understand and to remember information
2. how to do something, how to make something, and how something works
3. attract the audience's attention, focus attention on the subject, and gain the audience's goodwill
4. in expository speeches that explain the history of something and in process speeches that explain procedures or events step by step
5. group the steps under broader headings
6. summarizes the main points of the speech
7. consider your audience's experience, needs, and interests
8. to save time in explanation, to clarify a point, and to help an audience remember important material

Discussion Questions

Guidelines for Assessment

Student responses may vary.

1. Students might suggest using a startling statement, a question, a quotation, a story, a personal reference, or audiovisual materials.
2. Students' responses should reflect that demonstrations help listeners to understand processes and to learn how to perform the processes themselves.
3. A summary ties main ideas together, helps listeners recall information, signals the end of a speech, and offers a sense of completion.
4. The quotation suggests that knowledge empowers individuals and makes them strong; the strength gained from knowledge is more forceful than physical strength. When developing informative speeches, speakers should choose topics that they know something about but should consult sources to fill gaps in knowledge.
5. Most students will probably say that people learn better by seeing something in addition to hearing about it. This suggests that demonstrations should be included in speeches whenever possible.

CHAPTER **14**

Review Questions

1. What are the major goals that an effective informative speech should accomplish?
2. Identify the three kinds of processes that can be explained in process speeches.
3. What should an effective introduction to an informative speech accomplish?
4. In what cases would chronological order be an especially good organizational pattern to use in developing the body of an informative speech?
5. What should you do when you find you have as many as fifteen steps in a process speech?
6. What does an effective conclusion of an informative speech accomplish?
7. What are three ways that you can adapt your speech to your audience?
8. When should audiovisual materials be used in an informative speech?
9. What is the difference between a demonstration and a partial demonstration?
10. "Call on people from all parts of the audience" is one guideline for handling the question-and-answer session following an informative speech. What are three other guidelines?

Discussion Questions

1. You are giving a speech on a subject that interests you a great deal, but you think that this subject might not have a very strong appeal to your audience. Discuss with your classmates how you might prepare an introduction that would arouse your audience's interest in this subject.
2. Think of the courses that you take in school. In which of these courses would you like to see more demonstrations? How would additional demonstrations make it easier for you to learn? Discuss your answers with your classmates.
3. Discuss the reasons for including a summary as part of the conclusion of an informative speech.
4. Samuel Johnson once wrote, "Man is not weak, knowledge is more than equivalent to force. The master of mechanics laughs at strength." First, discuss the meaning of this quotation. Then, discuss how various types of knowledge can be used in developing an informative speech.
5. Long ago, the Greek philosopher Heraclitus claimed, "Eyes are more accurate witnesses than ears." Discuss how this quotation relates to the need to include a demonstration in your process speech.

9. In a demonstration the speaker performs the steps in a process; in a partial demonstration either some of the parts of the demonstration are completed prior to the presentation or the size of the items is exaggerated so the audience can see them clearly.

10. See to it that people ask questions, not give speeches; try to answer all questions briefly; and if you cannot answer a question, feel free to say so.

ACTIVITIES

1. **Testing Your Memory.** Read the following paragraph in order to remember it.

   Go straight until you come to a fork in the road. Then turn left and keep going until you see the third four-way stop. Now turn right and go until you come to an overpass. Turn right again at the street immediately before the overpass. Continue for three stop signs and you will see a church with a steeple. You want the white building directly across from the church.

   Now cover the paragraph and write the directions as you remember them. After you finish, check your version of the directions against the paragraph.

2. **Using Spatial Order to Organize Details for a Speech.**

   A. Select an object, a location, or a landscape (such as one shown in the pictures on this page) as the topic for an informative speech. You may also select a topic of your own. Identify the component parts of the topic you have selected, and arrange the details of your description in a specific spatial order.

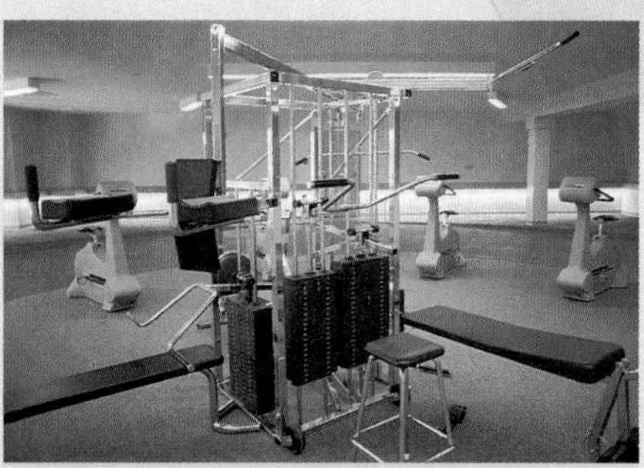

   B. Present your informative speech to your classmates. After you complete your speech, ask your listeners to draw a sketch and label the parts of the object or location you are describing. Was your description clear enough to help your audience to visualize the object or location clearly?

3. **Giving an Informative Speech.** Choose a common object in your classroom, such as an eraser, a wastebasket, or a window; or choose an idea or emotion such as courage, equality, or anger. Write a short definition of the object or idea you chose. Present your definition as a short informative speech. Ask your listeners to use the Evaluation Checklist for Informative Speeches (page 375) to evaluate your delivery. Conduct a question-and-answer session following your speech, and respond to your listeners' feedback.

ACTIVITIES

Guidelines for Assessment

1. You may want to make this a timed activity. Give students three minutes to study the paragraph, and award a point to everyone who gets all steps correct. The steps include
   a. Go straight to a fork in the road.
   b. Turn left and go to the third four-way stop.
   c. Turn right and go to the overpass.
   d. Turn right at the street before the overpass.
   e. Go through three stop signs to the church.
   f. Find the white building across from the church.
2. A. Students' descriptions should be organized in an obvious spatial order.
   B. You may want to have students write evaluations of their presentations after they have studied the drawings of their classmates.
3. You may want to have students compile the data from the **Evaluation Checklist** and the question-and-answer sessions to arrive at written conclusions about the effectiveness of their speeches.

SUMMATIVE EVALUATION

Your **Teacher's Resource Binder** contains a reproducible **Chapter 14 Test** that may be used to assess students' mastery of the concepts presented in this chapter.

PORTFOLIO ASSESSMENT

For future reference and evaluation you may want to have students keep in their portfolios any skill sheets or evaluation forms that you have used with this chapter along with any other recorded or written materials that students have created.

4. You may want to see written evidence of research. You can have students write one-paragraph self-evaluations based on the evaluation checklists they receive. If it is convenient, consider asking colleagues who teach the subjects the speeches deal with to allow students to present the speeches in their classes.

5. Students can write brief self-evaluations based on the responses indicated on the evaluation checklists. In each self-evaluation, ask the student to identify one aspect of the speech that was well done and one aspect that could use improvement.

6. Using the evaluation checklists, students can evaluate their performances in one- or two-paragraph assessments. You may want to review the notes students compile for this activity.

7. You may want to have students compile the **Evaluation Checklist** data into self-evaluation reports. You can evaluate the written material for clarity, unity, coherence, and mechanical accuracy.

8. You may want to require students to indicate in writing the kind of demonstration each job would require and to name the equipment the demonstration would require.

9. The oral critiques should be specific, concentrate on only one or two negative criticisms, mention what the speaker could do to improve, and give positive feedback.

4. **Giving an Informative Speech.** Choose a topic you are studying in another class, such as the discovery of radioactive elements by the Curies or a landmark Supreme Court ruling. Research this topic by consulting three different sources. Using your notes from your research, prepare a brief extemporaneous report on your topic. Include citations for at least two of your sources. Present your report in class. Ask your listeners to critique your speech by using the Evaluation Checklist for Informative Speeches (page 375).

5. **Giving a Process Speech on How to Do Something.** Write a list of five processes that you know how to do well. Which process can you explain completely in less than five minutes? Jot down the steps of the process, and using only this brief list, deliver a short extemporaneous speech explaining the process. If necessary, use audiovisual materials in your speech. Ask your classmates to use the Evaluation Checklist for Informative Speeches (page 375) to evaluate your presentation.

6. **Giving a Process Speech on How to Make Something.** Think back to a project you have completed in which you made something, such as a special meal, a computer program, a video, or a piece of art. Review the steps in the process and write them down in order. Also list all the materials you needed. Organize your lists into an outline that you can use to present a speech giving complete directions for following the process. Deliver your speech to your classmates. Try to use notes as little as possible, but be careful not to leave out any steps or materials. Ask your listeners to use the Evaluation Checklist for Informative Speeches (page 375) to give you a critique of your presentation.

7. **Giving a Process Speech on How Something Works.** Think of the many simple tools and devices you commonly use (for example, a pencil sharpener, a can opener, an eraser, or a bicycle pump). Read two or three short explanations of how one of these common tools or devices works. Using the best information from your sources, write a two- or three-page explanation of your own. Present your explanation in a speech to your class. Use audiovisual materials to demonstrate the item that you are explaining. Conduct a question-and-answer session following your speech, and respond to your audience's feedback. Ask your listeners to use the Evaluation Checklist for Informative Speeches (page 375) to critique your presentation.

8. **Identifying the Uses of Demonstrations.** Prepare a list of twenty jobs that would require a demonstration of something. For example, a vacuum-cleaner salesperson would likely be required to demonstrate how a vacuum cleaner works or a person selling a time-saving food processor might be required to demonstrate how easily or simply the processor works. Share your list of jobs with your classmates. After eliminating duplications, select a combined list of twenty jobs that the class feels are most likely to require demonstrations.

9. **Giving an Oral Critique of an Informative Speech.** Using the Evaluation Checklist for Informative Speeches (page 375), prepare a careful critique of an informative speech delivered by one of your classmates. Present your critique orally in class. Ask your classmates to evaluate your critique, and respond to the feedback they give you.

◆ Real-Life Speaking Situations

PERFORMANCE OBJECTIVES

- To write and present a critique as advice for a friend
- To prepare and deliver a training speech by considering audience, topic, and method of presentation

REAL LIFE Speaking Situations

1 Whenever you get something new, don't you often ask your friends for their own opinions of it? Although everyone welcomes favorable critiques, you probably want more than simple flattery from your friends. Instead, you look to them for honest evaluations and helpful criticism. One of the best ways to ensure that you get thoughtful critiques is to be able to give such critiques yourself.

Your best friend has asked you for advice about something he or she has received as a gift, has purchased, or has made. Your reaction is generally favorable, but you see some flaws. What will you say to your friend?

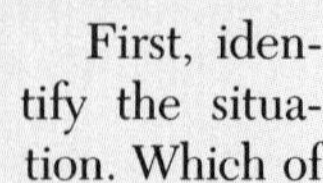

First, identify the situation. Which of your friends has asked your opinion? What have you been asked to critique—a bike, a hairstyle, a musical recording, an idea, a decision? What specifically is good about it? What is flawed? How will you express your overall favorable impression and your reservations as well?

Write a one- or two-page critique giving your opinion. Be prepared to present your critique in class. Ask your classmates for feedback on the helpfulness and tactfulness of your comments.

2 Engineers often need to present complex information in a readily understandable form. To explain the features of a machine, a road plan, or any other engineering product, an engineer must be able to translate technical data so that it can be understood by nonspecialists. While you are not an engineer, you probably have specialized technical knowledge about some machine or procedure.

You have been asked to teach a classmate, a co-worker, or someone else how to operate a particular piece of machinery. How will you go about doing so? First, identify the person you will teach. Then, identify a specific machine that you think you could teach someone to operate.

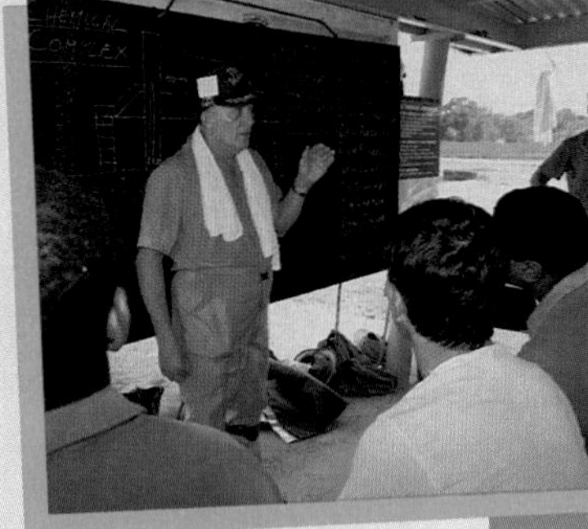

Make a list of the steps that have to be followed to operate this piece of equipment, along with any other details that you think would be helpful to a learner. Adapt your instructions to suit the experience, familiarity, and technical knowledge of your listener. Be prepared to present your lesson in class and to respond to feedback on how well you have explained the process of operating the equipment.

ASSESSMENT GUIDELINES

1. Both the written and oral presentations should include comments about both the strengths and weaknesses of the situations under consideration. When students present their critiques to the class, have the other students use the **Evaluation Checklist** on p. 375 to offer suggestions to the student presenting the critique.
2. When students present their training speeches to the class, ask the other students to use the **Evaluation Checklist** on p. 375 to provide them with feedback. The students who make the presentations can then compile a self-evaluation summary based on the checklists.

Chapter 15

Speaking to Persuade

pp. 382–415

CHAPTER OVERVIEW

This chapter defines and discusses the three types of questions that persuasive speeches address—fact, belief, and policy. Four persuasive techniques are included: applying logical reasoning, developing emotional appeals, establishing credibility, and meeting ethical standards. The chapter leads students through the steps in presenting persuasive speeches and also deals with concerns

TEACHER'S RESOURCE BINDER

The following materials are identified at their point of use in this chapter:

- Skills for Success
  1. *Preparing a Persuasive Speech*
  2. *Using Persuasive Techniques*
  3. *Determining Audience Attitudes*
  4. *Using a Deductive or an Inductive Approach*
- Chapter 15 Vocabulary
- Chapter 15 Test/Answer Key

AV ➤ Audiovisual Resource Binder

The following materials are identified at their point of use in this chapter:

- Transparency 30
  Evaluating Reasons and Evidence
- Transparency 31
  Evaluation Checklist for Persuasive Speeches

Audiotape 2 contains recordings of persuasive speeches. The complete text of each speech is printed in the Appendix of Speeches in this textbook.

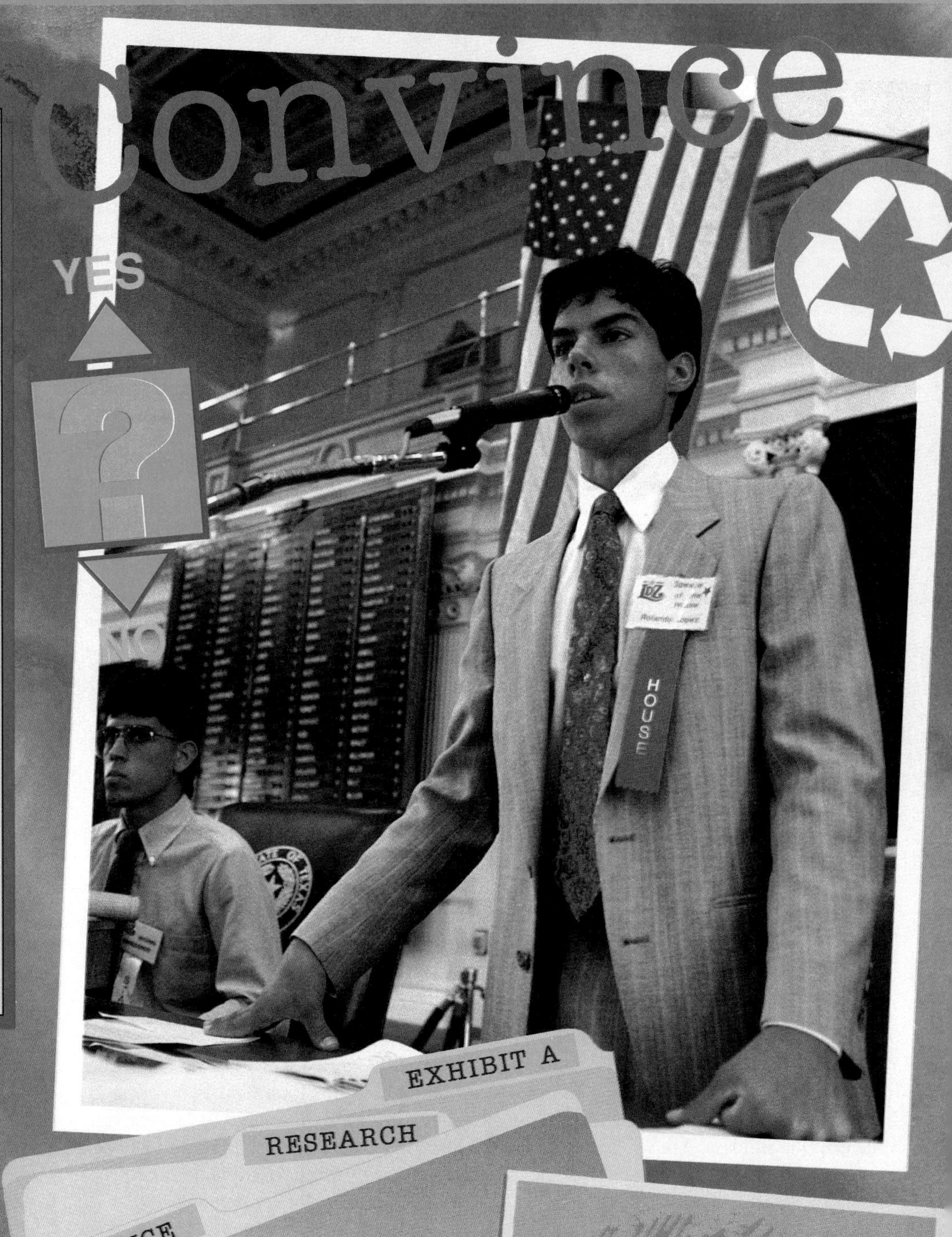

such as how to persuade an audience that is favorable, neutral, apathetic, or hostile. Finally, the chapter provides a set of guidelines for evaluating persuasive speeches.

Introducing the Chapter

Some researchers say that most information a person processes has a somewhat persuasive nature. The degree of influence of such messages varies widely. To deal with this steady onslaught of persuasive messages, students need to know about the strategies, both ethical and unethical, that people use to be convincing. Students also need to know how to evaluate persuasive information intelligently. Explain to students that by mastering the art of persuasion, they will accomplish two purposes: presenting their views effectively and responding appropriately to others.

CHAPTER 15

Speaking to Persuade

OBJECTIVES

After studying this chapter, you should be able to

1. Define *persuasive speaking.*
2. Select a persuasive speech topic and develop it into a persuasive speech.
3. Use logical reasoning, consisting of reasons and evidence, to support and develop points in your speech.
4. Develop appropriate emotional appeals to support and develop points in your speech.
5. Establish your credibility while meeting ethical standards for public speaking.
6. Evaluate a persuasive speech.

DON'T TRASH'EM.
CASH'EM.
RETURNING BEER AND SODA EMPTIES MAKES GOOD CENTS.

What Is a Persuasive Speech?

Any time you try to convince someone to think, believe, or act as you want them to, you are speaking to persuade. A **persuasive speech** is one that

- establishes a fact
- changes a belief
- moves an audience to act on a policy

How successful you are in presenting a persuasive speech depends on what you say and how you say it—your content and delivery.

In this chapter you will learn how to select and limit a suitable topic and to develop it into a persuasive speech. You will also learn how to apply logical reasoning by developing reasons and supporting them with evidence, how to develop emotional appeals to support your ideas, and how to establish your credibility with your listeners. You will learn how to adapt your speech to your audience and how to deliver it convincingly.

Bibliography of Additional Materials

Professional Readings

- Bradley, Bert E. ***Fundamentals of Speech Communications: The Credibility of Ideas.*** Dubuque, IA: William C. Brown Publishers.
- Brembeck, Winston L., and William S. Howell. ***Persuasion: A Means of Social Influence.*** Englewood Cliffs, NJ: Prentice-Hall.

Audiovisuals

- ***The Language of Leadership: The Winston Churchill Method***—Films for the Humanities and Sciences, Princeton, NJ (videocassette, 60 min.)
- ***Persuasive Speaking***—Films for the Humanities and Sciences, Princeton, NJ (two filmstrips with audio, 15 min. each)
- ***The Speeches of John F. Kennedy***—MPI Home Video, Oak Forest, IL (videocassette, 60 min.)
- ***You're On: Persuading Your Audience***—Center for Video Education, North White Plains, NY (videocassette, 78 min.)

Segment 1 pp. 384–396

- Preparing a Persuasive Speech
- Using Persuasive Techniques

Performance Objectives

- To identify persuasive statements as statements of fact, belief, or policy
- To develop a topic for a persuasive speech
- To write a thesis statement for a persuasive speech
- To generate reasons and evidence to support a thesis statement

Making Connections

Mass Media

Magazine and newspaper ads are excellent sources of persuasion to analyze. Have students bring examples that they find appealing to class. Encourage students to record television and radio ads, political speeches, and editorials.

Teaching Note

As your class studies persuasive speaking, point out examples from your class interactions. For example, if students ask for extra time to prepare an assignment, point out that they are speaking to persuade; then analyze the techniques they use.

Teacher's Resource Binder

Skills for Success 1
Preparing a Persuasive Speech

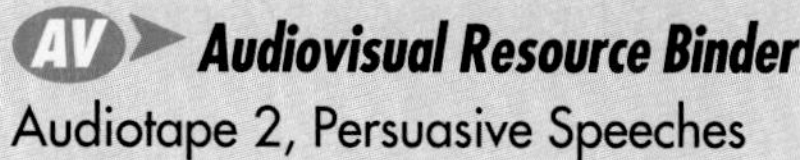

Audiovisual Resource Binder

Audiotape 2, Persuasive Speeches

Preparing a Persuasive Speech

In planning a persuasive speech, you consider the same elements you do for any type of speech: topic, purpose, and audience. You already know what the general purpose of your speech is: to persuade. Knowing your choices within that general purpose will help you make decisions about the other elements of your speech, such as the organizational pattern you use.

Understanding the Types of Persuasion

Persuasion stems from the idea that people can hold different views on a topic and that it is open to question as to which viewpoint is the better one. Your goal as a speaker is to support your viewpoint so that the audience will adopt it. In this way, persuasive speeches deal with three types of questions that can be answered in more than one way:

- questions of fact
- questions of belief
- questions of policy

A **question of fact** concerns statements that can be seen as either true or false. You offer proof to support a statement of fact, but the audience determines whether you have convincingly proved that the statement of fact is true.

Examples:

1. Recycling can (cannot) save local communities money.
2. Coffee drinkers have (do not have) a higher risk of heart disease.
3. The space program does (does not) contribute to our national security.

A **question of belief** focuses on what is right or wrong, good or bad, best or worst, moral or immoral. While you cannot prove that a belief is true or false, you can supply convincing information to justify a belief.

Examples:

1. Small schools are (are not) better for most students than large schools are.
2. Elvis Presley was (was not) the greatest rock-and-roll performer ever.
3. It is (is not) wrong to avoid jury duty.

A **question of policy** focuses on a particular action. You try to convince the audience to act on some policy or to agree that some policy should be changed.

- To use evaluation guidelines to evaluate reasons and evidence
- To analyze emotional appeals and logical reasoning used in advertisements
- To develop emotional appeals and methods of credibility for a persuasive speech

MOTIVATION

Display for the class a magazine advertisement that uses persuasion effectively to promote an item of interest. Read the copy and ask students to discuss their reactions to the ad. Ask students whether it would motivate them to take action—to purchase the item. Tell students that in this lesson they will learn some of the characteristics of persuasion that are used in effective advertising

EXAMPLES:

1. The senior class should (should not) vote for Ann Welch.
2. High school athletes should (should not) be required to maintain a B average to compete interscholastically.
3. Funding for space exploration should (should not) be increased.

ACTIVITY 1 Identifying Persuasive Statements

Identify each of the following statements as a question of fact, a question of belief, or a question of policy.

1. Seattle does not deserve its reputation for having an extremely rainy climate.
2. The United States should abolish the electoral college.
3. South High has a better basketball team than North High.
4. You should watch the documentary about jobs for teenagers.
5. Illiteracy continues to be an important national problem.

Choosing and Limiting a Topic

With the techniques you learned in Chapter 9 (pages 215–239), you can find many topics for persuasive speeches. A good persuasive topic is one that

- you feel strongly about
- other people may have different views on

EXAMPLE: For her persuasive speech, Gloria Marcus chose the subject area *current events* and brainstormed about upcoming events at her school. From her list of ideas, she chose *the election of class officers* and limited it to the topic *Ann Welch's candidacy for senior class president.* Gloria felt strongly that Ann should be elected, and she knew that other students supported other candidates.

CRITICAL THINKING

Analysis

Ask students to focus on strong beliefs that they hold—not necessarily on a controversial issue. Ask students how they came to have the opinions—experience, parents' influence, or friends' opinions. Have they ever had to argue for their opinions? If so, how did they defend their beliefs? What would it take for them to change their minds? Have students write their ideas in their communication journals.

ONGOING ASSESSMENT

Activity 1

Students might complete this activity independently, but take the time to discuss students' reasoning. **(1)** fact **(2)** policy **(3)** belief **(4)** policy **(5)** fact

CRITICAL THINKING

Application

Students may need practice using persuasive methods. Ask the class to brainstorm for issues that they discuss and argue with friends, family, and teachers. Then ask students to rephrase the issues so that each is phrased as a statement of fact, value, or policy.

You may want to have brief conferences with students as they work on **Activity 2** on p. 386 to make certain that their topics are appropriate. Students can then write their thesis statements in **Activity 3** on p. 387 independently.

You might want to base your presentation of **Using Persuasive Techniques** from p. 387 on the graphic model below. You could copy the model on the chalkboard as you discuss reasons and evidence. Use the examples to show how they fit the model and strengthen an argument. You might want to have volunteers read through **How to Evaluate Reasons.** Students could complete **Activity 4** on p. 391 as homework and then use **How to Evaluate Reasons** on p. 389 and **How to Evaluate Evidence** on p. 391 to evaluate and revise their work.

Introduce **Developing Emotional Appeals** on p. 392 by discussing the examples that show how appeals can be improved. In addition to

Making Connections

Philosophy

An extension of the study of persuasive speaking is examining religious sermons or philosophical arguments students may have heard for the persuasive techniques used.

Example: You want to persuade your classmates to see the drama club's production of *Grease.* You might use statements such as these as your reasons:

- *Grease* is one of the most popular musicals of all time.
- The music is excellent.
- The acting and dancing are outstanding.

Evidence is material that establishes the soundness of each reason. For instance, to establish that *Grease* is one of the most popular musicals of all time, you could cite the fact that the *World Almanac* lists *Grease* as one of the longest-running Broadway shows ever.

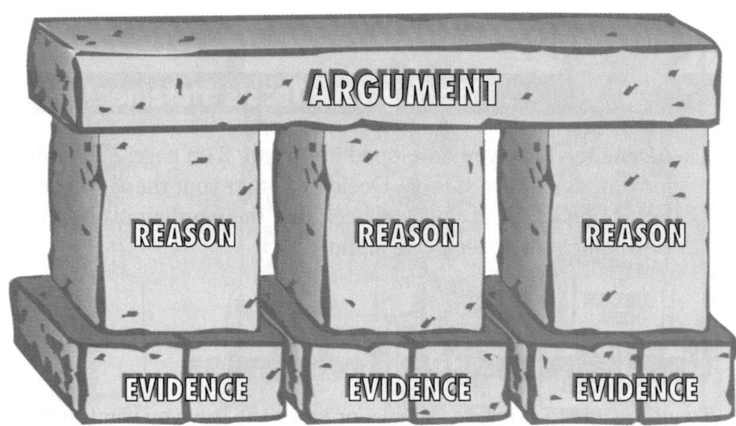

Finding and Evaluating Reasons. To find reasons to support your thesis, you can use three sources:

- yourself
- other people
- reference materials

[For help with finding and using different sources of information for a speech, see pages 242–255 of Chapter 10.] For some topics, you can begin drawing on your own knowledge and experience. For other topics, you will also need to talk to other people and to conduct research using a variety of reference materials.

Example: From Gloria's own experience, she knew that Ann Welch had held a variety of elective and appointive positions. As one of her reasons, she listed Ann's leadership experience.

Next, Gloria talked to other people—students, teachers, and school officials—about Ann's candidacy. Many of these people discussing the examples in the text, you may want to encourage students to discuss familiar ways of making emotional appeals. You might have students work with partners to complete **Activity 5** on p. 396.

ASSESSMENT

By checking **Activities 2** and **3**, you can assess students' abilities to narrow topics and to write theses. Students' abilities to generate and evaluate reasons and evidence to support a thesis will be evident from evaluation of **Activity 4**. By checking **Activity 5**, you can assess students' abilities to develop emotional appeals and to build credibility for speeches.

mentioned Ann's efforts on behalf of her fellow students. (Such comments are called **testimonials,** statements attesting to the worth of someone or something.) These comments led Gloria to her second reason: Ann's willingness to work hard.

Finally, Gloria found several articles and editorials by and about Ann in current and back issues of the school paper. From them she learned about Ann's hopes for the senior class. As her third reason Gloria listed Ann's interesting ideas for the coming school year.

HOW TO Evaluate Reasons

1. **Is each reason relevant to your thesis?** Each of your reasons should directly support your thesis. Set aside any that don't answer the question "Why?" in relation to your thesis. For example, Gloria might have listed as one of her reasons Ann's ambition to become the first woman to be elected president of the United States. That ambition does not directly support Gloria's thesis that Ann should be elected president of the senior class.
2. **Is each reason distinct?** Each reason should be separate from each of your other reasons and from your thesis. For example, the statement "Ann Welch has held several elective and appointive positions" merely restates Gloria's first reason, Ann's leadership experience, and should be set aside.
3. **Does each reason provide strong support for the thesis?** For example, if Gloria discovered that Ann's leadership experience was actually very limited, she would need to look for reasons that provided stronger support for her thesis.
4. **Will the audience consider the reason important?** For example, Gloria had to decide whether her fellow seniors would consider leadership experience, hard work, and fresh ideas important factors in selecting a class president.
5. **Do you have just enough reasons?** An effective persuasive speech usually presents two or three reasons. If you present fewer, your audience may feel that you have not answered the question "Why?" to their satisfaction. If you present more than five or six, they may be overwhelmed and lose the thread of your argument.

BUILDING A PORTFOLIO

Students might include in their speech portfolios a chart taken from **How to Evaluate Reasons.** Students could include this in an outline form to use with persuasive speeches. They will only need to list the main questions. As they compile reasons to include in their speeches, they can refer to the chart.

Audiovisual Resource Binder

Transparency 30
Evaluating Reasons and Evidence

Another approach to assessing students' understanding of the sections on emotional appeals, establishing credibility, and using logical reasoning is to ask students to share their communication journal entries in which they analyze advertisements.

Reteaching

Prepare a videotape that includes televised advertisements and speeches that demonstrate the effective use of persuasive techniques. As you show the video, point out examples of strong reasons and evidence. You might ask students to point out effective use of vivid language, citation of specifics, and establishment of credibility.

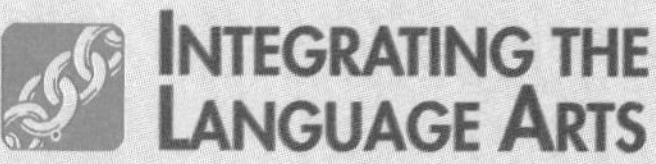

Integrating the Language Arts

Library Link

Point out to students that some of their topics may be especially appropriate for using library resources to discover evidence. You may want to suggest specific resources or allow students to do the research independently.

Students with Special Needs

Students with learning disabilities often have difficulty distinguishing between fact and opinion. It is important to provide them with many examples. For practice, ask the class or a small group of students to brainstorm and list facts and opinions about a popular movie. Make two lists on the chalkboard—one of facts and one of opinions. Then give students who need additional work a list of sentences and have the students label the facts and opinions. Students should explain their answers.

Supporting Reasons with Evidence. In your speech you will support each of your reasons with evidence. For a persuasive speech, two of the types of details you learned about in Chapter 9 (pages 228–229) are particularly effective evidence: facts and expert opinions. You should offer at least two pieces of evidence for each of your reasons. If you offer any fewer than two pieces of evidence, the audience may not take your reasons seriously.

BORN LOSER reprinted by permission of NEA, Inc.

A **fact** is an item of information or a statement that can be verified, or checked, by testing, by observing, or by consulting reference materials.

EXAMPLE: As evidence of Ann's leadership experience, Gloria cited two facts: that Ann was vice-president of her sophomore class and that Ann is editor of the school paper. Both of these statements can be verified.

An **expert opinion** is a statement of belief about a subject by a knowledgeable person recognized as an authority on that subject. Such statements cannot be proved, because they express value judgments. Expert opinion is not always perceived by an audience to be as strong as factual evidence. In some cases, however, expert opinions are as effective as facts.

EXAMPLE: One of Gloria's reasons is that Ann is a hard worker. Gloria could support that reason with factual evidence: what posts Ann has held and what she has accomplished. Still, the term *hard worker* involves a value judgment about what constitutes hard work. That is, different people can hold different views about what characterizes hard work.

To further support her point, Gloria could interview the school paper's faculty adviser. That teacher's testimonial that Ann is a hard worker would be considered an expert opinion because of the teacher's years of experience working with other student editors.

See p. 394 for **Extension, Enrichment,** and **Closure.**

HOW TO *Evaluate Evidence*

1. **Is the evidence relevant to the reason it supports?** The facts or expert testimony you present should relate to the particular reason you are trying to support. For example, saying that Ann Welch is an honor roll student would not help Gloria support her first reason, Ann's leadership experience. However, Gloria could state that Ann helped establish a volunteer tutoring service.
2. **Is the evidence verifiable and reliable?** You should be able to check the accuracy of any facts you cite to support a reason. An expert opinion should come from someone knowledgeable about the topic—someone recognized as an authority on the subject. For example, Ann's piano teacher would not be a reliable source for information about Ann's willingness to work hard on school projects.
3. **Is there enough evidence?** Your purpose is to persuade your audience. You want your listeners to adopt your point of view or to take a specific action. To get them to do so, you must provide sufficient proof—usually two pieces of evidence for each reason.

ACTIVITY 4 — Building and Evaluating Your Argument

List at least two reasons to support the thesis statement you wrote for Activity 3 on page 387. Using the questions on page 389, evaluate your reasons to determine whether they build the argument you want to make. Then gather at least two pieces of evidence to support each reason, and evaluate your evidence with the questions above. Remember to use the sources of information you learned about on pages 242–255 of Chapter 10.

Building a Portfolio

The questions in **How to Evaluate Evidence** could be added to the outlines of students' persuasive speeches.

Ongoing Assessment

Activity 4

You may want to have students go over their reasons and evidence with you to discuss their evaluation strategies. Suggest revisions as needed.

INTEGRATING THE LANGUAGE ARTS

Vocabulary Link

Most students need practice in identifying and using vivid language. Have them find examples in advertisements and in magazine and newspaper articles. You may want to brainstorm with students to create an ongoing list of vivid words and phrases. Students can record their favorites in their communication journals and then compile a class list. The goal is for students to incorporate vivid words effectively in their speeches.

TEACHER'S RESOURCE BINDER

Skills for Success 2
Using Persuasive Techniques

Developing Emotional Appeals

An **emotional appeal** is a statement that arouses strong feelings—pleasure or anger, joy or sadness, pride or shame—in an audience. This type of statement may be effective for a persuasive speech that focuses on urging action. In such a speech, you don't simply want your listeners to agree with you; you want them to translate that agreement into action. And many people will not do so until their emotions become involved. For example, some of Gloria's classmates might believe that Ann would make a good senior class president, but they will not take the time to vote. Gloria needs to spur them to action.

You can develop emotional appeals for any persuasive speech in three ways:

- by citing specifics
- by using vivid language
- by including personal references

Citing Specifics. When you cite specifics, you mention or refer to details or examples that clearly illustrate a point you want to make. By citing specifics, you may remove any uncertainty your audience may have about your meaning.

GENERAL STATEMENT: Ann Welch is a hard worker.

SPECIFIC EXAMPLE: When Ann thought that students weren't being rewarded for their efforts to clean up the schoolyard, she arranged to take the principal on a tour of the school grounds and pointed out exactly what the students had done.

The words *hard worker* alone are not likely to arouse strong feelings. Most people are accustomed to hearing these words without giving them much thought. But by specifying *how* Ann works hard on behalf of her fellow students, Gloria appeals to her classmates' pride, thus getting them emotionally involved.

Using Vivid Language. When you use descriptive language effectively, you enable your listeners to picture situations that you are referring to. [For more information on using vivid language, see pages 296–303 of Chapter 12.]

BLAND STATEMENT: Ann Welch knows how to stay cool in an emergency.

VIVID DEVELOPMENT: Last April 25 during lunch, Ann was outside enjoying the fresh air along with hundreds of other students. Suddenly, the wind picked up, coal-black clouds began building, and lightning crackled the sky. Recognizing the threat of a tornado and the danger of panic, Ann quickly got a few friends together and worked out a plan to lead the students calmly to the school basement. As a result of her swift action, not a single person was injured in the move to safety.

Including Personal References. When you refer to the audience directly or when you relate the topic you are discussing to the audience's direct experience, you are using personal references. By using personal references, you make your listeners feel that they have a personal stake in the topic and you increase their interest.

TOO IMPERSONAL: Ann Welch plans to make graduation ceremonies better.

PERSONAL REFERENCE TO AUDIENCE: You've worked hard for your diploma, and you deserve to have your achievement recognized in front of the school community and your family and friends. Ann Welch will propose a graduation policy that calls for every one of you to receive your diploma in person. School officials will individually name graduates and award their diplomas. This policy will guarantee you the individual recognition you deserve.

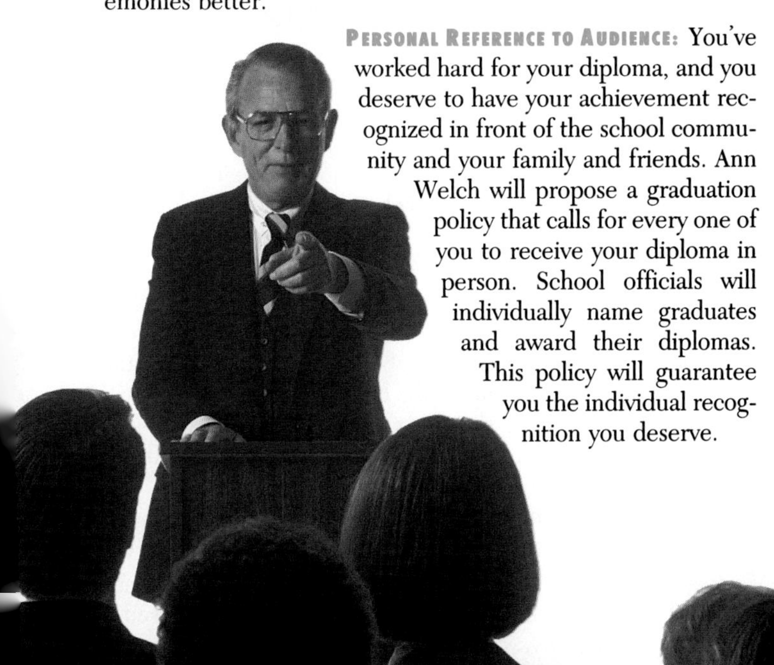

CRITICAL THINKING

Analysis

Distribute copies of a persuasive speech that relies primarily on logical arguments and that uses few emotional appeals. Read the speech to the class. Then ask students to locate places in the speech where emotional appeals could be added to make the speech more persuasive. Have students specify the kind of emotional appeal that would be most effective.

EXTENSION

Ask students to listen to the following speech occasions and discuss effective persuasive techniques to use for a given audience. The audience is given in parentheses.

1. A student wants to take a weekend trip with a school organization such as a band. (parents)
2. A movie critic on television wants people to avoid seeing a certain movie. (viewers)
3. You believe you shouldn't be fined for making a U-turn the first day the new sign announces such turns are illegal. (a traffic-court judge)

Have students determine which techniques would be most effective in each situation.

COOPERATIVE LEARNING

Have students work in groups of three or four to discuss how to establish credibility for their various topics. Each person should read his or her selected thesis statement to the group. Then the group can discuss the speaker's competence and sincerity about the topic.

Establishing Your Credibility

Credibility is the quality of being believable. Think about the people you trust. You probably consider them trustworthy because you see them as competent, sincere, and dynamic. Your success as a speaker hinges on convincing your audience that you possess those three characteristics.

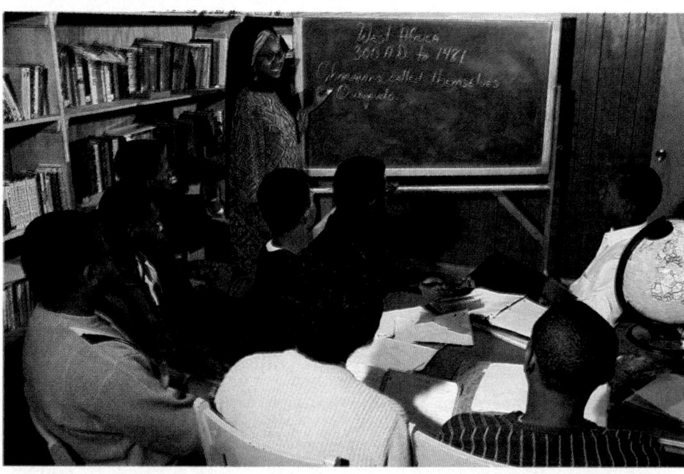

Competence. **Competence** is the state of being well qualified. It comes from knowledge and preparation. To establish your competence, you have to *know* your topic thoroughly and *show* that you are knowledgeable. The more you know about a topic and the better prepared you are, the more likely it is that your audience will believe you.

EXAMPLES:

1. You want to convince your classmates to buy a certain brand of running shoes. To establish your competence, you could show how much you know about the construction of these shoes and the anatomy of the human foot. Showing how this particular type of shoe protects the runner's foot would more likely persuade the audience than just saying that the shoe looks good or is popular.
2. Gloria established her competence by showing that she knew Ann's experience, achievements, and ideas in detail.

Sincerity. **Sincerity** is the quality of being genuine. It is primarily conveyed by your tone of voice, and it usually can't be faked. To establish your sincerity, you have to genuinely care about both your topic and your audience.

Enrichment

Suggest that the class set up a mock trial to practice using effective persuasive techniques. Have a committee establish a crime such as rudeness in the classroom, inappropriate behavior in the cafeteria, or tardiness. Have students take turns playing the roles of judge, defendant, attorney, and prosecuting attorney. Have students evaluate the persuasive techniques used by the various characters. If some students are effective in a variety of roles, have the class identify their strengths in persuasion.

Example: If Gloria truly cares about the senior class and really thinks that Ann is the best candidate, her speech will probably sound sincere. If not, her delivery will lack the sincerity necessary to establish her credibility.

Dynamism. **Dynamism** is the quality of being energetic and enthusiastic. It is expressed by your tone of voice as well as by your nonverbal behavior—your appearance, eye contact, facial expressions, gestures, and posture. Enthusiasm is contagious. The more dynamic you are, the more receptive to your ideas your audience is likely to be.

As you watch television and listen to the radio, make notes in your journal about the emotional appeals advertisers use to convince you to buy their products. Also try to note when advertisers use logical reasoning and how they try to establish their credibility with you as a consumer.

Meeting Ethical Standards

Ethical standards are society's guidelines for right, just, and moral behavior. Violating ethical standards can destroy a speaker's credibility. It is unethical for public speakers

- to lie or deceive
- to distort
- to engage in name-calling
- to attack a person or an idea without giving evidence
- to deny the opposition the right to reply

Critical Thinking

Evaluation

Before you discuss how ethics affect communication, you might want to offer the following scenario as a basis for discussing ethical choices:

Tino, a teenage boy, covers up for his friend Ann, who has stolen money from the school office. Although Tino knows that stealing and covering up for it are both wrong, he also knows that his friend's father does not understand why she needs spending money and will not understand her stealing. Tino knows why Ann stole the money, and she has promised him she will never steal again.

Discuss questions such as the following ones: Does it matter that the father doesn't understand the need for spending money? Does it matter what the money is for? Should Tino speak in private to a teacher or a counselor about the theft? Should Tino offer to go with Ann to a teacher or a counselor if she refuses to go alone? Should the problem be dropped since Ann promised not to steal again?

Closure

To close the lesson, ask the class to identify the three types of questions that can be addressed in persuasive speeches. Have students describe the process of choosing and limiting a topic for a persuasive speech. Then have them summarize the techniques to use in persuasive speeches—applying logical reasoning, developing emotional appeals, and establishing credibility.

Cooperative Learning

To increase students' awareness of how facts and figures can be manipulated, have students work in groups of four or five to explore the difference between persuasion and manipulation. Give each group statistical information about a current issue of interest such as the relationship between teenage alcohol use and car insurance rates. The task is for students to interpret the same material in both a persuasive way and a manipulative way. Have two speakers from each group present their interpretations to the class.

Ongoing Assessment

Activity 5

You may want to have students go over the emotional appeals they intend to use in their speeches. Then have them explain how they intend to establish their credibility. Make suggestions for improvement as appropriate.

Your goal is to persuade the people in your audience, not to manipulate them. Persuasion uses logical reasoning and emotional appeals to convince your listeners to agree with you of their own free will. You want them to adopt your viewpoint or to take specific action, but you are not coercing, or forcing, them to do so. By contrast, **manipulation** is the shrewd or devious management of facts for your own purpose. It is based on the unethical distortion of information: withholding key information, presenting half-truths, or purposely misrepresenting ideas and details.

Calvin and Hobbes, copyright 1989 Watterson. Distributed by Universal Press Syndicate. Reprinted with permission. All rights reserved.

If you try to manipulate your audience or follow any other unethical practices, you will probably fail to achieve your goal. Once your listeners discover that you have deceived them, you lose your credibility and become totally ineffective. As you develop any persuasive speech, be aware of the close relationship between manipulation and the use of propaganda techniques. Take care to base your argument on sound logical reasoning and valid emotional appeals. [For information on spotting propaganda techniques, see pages 92–95 of Chapter 4.]

Activity 5: Developing Emotional Appeals and Credibility for a Persuasive Speech

Identify at least one emotional appeal that you can use to develop your thesis statement. Why do you think this method will be effective? What do your classmates think about its effectiveness?

Next indicate the best method you can use to establish your credibility on your topic. What information can you give to show your competence? What can you do to establish your sincerity?

Segment 2 *pp. 397–409*

- **Adapting Your Persuasive Speech to Your Audience**
- **Organizing Your Speech**
- **Delivering Your Speech Convincingly**
- **Evaluating a Persuasive Speech**

Performance Objectives

- To use a questionnaire to identify audience attitudes
- To select a method of organization for a persuasive speech and to outline the main points

Adapting Your Persuasive Speech to Your Audience

Before you decide how to organize your material, you ought to consider two things: one, the possible makeup of your audience, and two, how best to adapt your speech to that particular audience. With the persuasive speech more than with any other, adapting your speech so that it both reaches and moves your audience is crucial to your success.

Although the individual members of any audience may have many different attitudes about a topic, an audience as a whole can be classified as

- mostly favorable
- mostly neutral
- mostly apathetic
- mostly hostile

To determine your audience's attitude toward your topic, you can use the questions in Chapter 9 (page 225). You may also want to conduct a poll.

EXAMPLE: A few days before delivering her speech, Gloria gave each person in class the questionnaire on the next page. Gloria's goal was to determine how her audience felt about the candidates for senior class president. Knowing her audience's attitudes, Gloria could make adjustments in her reasons and evidence to build a more convincing argument.

Making Connections

Community Involvement

Invite to class a panel of professional "persuaders" such as a college recruiter, a sales representative, and a local politician. Ask the panel to talk to the class about how they use information differently to suit the needs of the various audiences they meet.

Help students prepare interview questions to ask the guests. Appoint a student moderator to conduct a question-and-answer session in which students can ask their questions.

Teacher's Resource Binder

Skills for Success 3
Determining Audience Attitudes

- To gather and prepare visual materials
- To rehearse and present a persuasive speech
- To note one's daily encounters with persuasive speaking
- To evaluate and critique orally a persuasive speech

Motivation

You may want to begin this lesson with a dramatic portrayal of the four types of audiences: favorable, neutral, apathetic, and hostile. Draw a stick figure on the chalkboard with a large speech balloon. In the balloon write a controversial message that has immediate relevance to your class. An example is "Our school must have a strict dress code. The administration will let you

Using the Questionnaire

You may want to modify the questionnaire to include names of students in the class or in your school who are candidates or possible candidates for student government positions. Each student can use the letters to rate the candidates. Then you might tally the results and ask students to describe how they would use the information in speaking to the class in favor of each of the four candidates.

Making Connections

Mass Media

You may want to have students search popular magazines for examples of other types of questionnaires. Have the students create a list of examples and have them show where the questionnaires can be found. Perhaps students can use the questionnaires with speeches they are currently planning or as a source of ideas for future topics.

QUESTIONNAIRE FOR STUDENT ELECTIONS

1. If elections for senior class president were held today, who would you vote for?

____

2. For each candidate, indicate the letter of the phrase that best summarizes your feelings about that person:

Bill Garver ______
Jack Phillips ______
Laura Simpson ______
Ann Welch ______

A. I am strongly in favor of his/her candidacy.
B. I am somewhat in favor of his/her candidacy.
C. I have no strong feelings one way or the other about his/her candidacy.
D. I don't know much about him/her, or I am not interested in the election.
E. I am somewhat opposed to his/her candidacy.
F. I am strongly opposed to his/her candidacy.

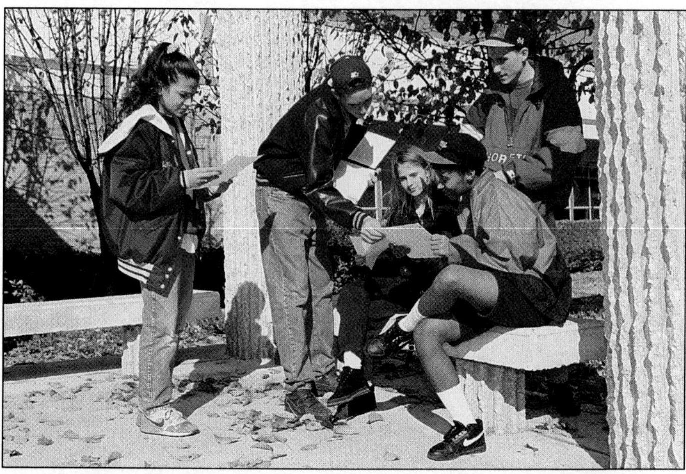

When you cannot circulate such a questionnaire, base your prediction of your audience's attitude on what you do know about their interests and values.

know what the policy is this afternoon. Monday we expect students and teachers to dress according to regulations." Have four volunteers each slowly read the message as you react, nonverbally and verbally, with the four types of audience attitudes.

TEACHING THE LESSON

Invite students to read the first section of the segment to learn about the types of audience attitudes they may encounter when they make persuasive speeches. Follow up with discussion questions such as these: How might the size of an audience affect the way a speaker handles a group? What responses (effective and ineffective) to a student audience have you observed teachers

MAKING CONNECTIONS

Community Involvement

Selecting juries gives attorneys opportunities to work with audiences they help choose. Invite an attorney to class to talk about tailoring an audience to a message and adapting a message to an audience. Another guest who has served on a jury could add an interesting perspective to the discussion.

Adapting to a Favorable Audience

A **favorable audience** is one in which the majority of the listeners agree, from slightly to completely, with your thesis. Listeners with this type of favorable attitude need to have their existing feelings strengthened to such a degree that they will act on their feelings.

EXAMPLE: Gloria found that most of the class already seemed to favor Ann Welch. Yet, no one can ever be sure what voters will do. Thus, Gloria's goal was to sustain and build on her listeners' favorable attitude so they would, indeed, vote for Ann.

Adapting to a Neutral Audience

A **neutral audience** is one in which the majority of the listeners have not reached a decision about your thesis. Neutral audiences will generally give all sides an equal hearing. They need information to persuade them to take a stand.

EXAMPLE: If Gloria faced a neutral audience, she could supply her listeners with such a wealth of information that they would decide that their best course was to vote for Ann.

Adapting to an Apathetic Audience

An **apathetic audience** is one in which a majority of the listeners have no interest in your thesis. Other than a hostile audience, an apathetic audience is the most difficult to persuade. Such listeners need to be shown how your thesis affects them personally.

EXAMPLE: If Gloria faced an apathetic audience, she could show her listeners how voting—and, specifically, voting for Ann—would give them a say in how the senior class is run.

use? How might you modify a questionnaire to collect oral responses?

Activity 6 requires students to use questionnaires to tabulate class opinions. If it's difficult because of time or logistics for students to give written questionnaires to each other, have them write questionnaires for their topics and then allow time for students to read their questionnaires aloud. Have the class respond by a show of hands, which the speakers can then tabulate.

When you discuss **Organizing Your Speech,** use the boxed examples to discuss the six deductive and inductive approaches. To further explain the inductive and deductive methods of organizing persuasion, you may want to model examples of each approach by selecting topics and guiding students through the process. This will serve as guided practice for **Activity 7** on p. 405, which students can complete independently.

Cooperative Learning

Have students work in groups of three or four to act out ways to give persuasive speeches to hostile audiences. Suggest a few situations that might involve hostile audiences. For example, a consumer wishes to return a faulty product, but the store manager rudely refuses to give a refund. Have groups act out their situations for the class and have the class discuss how the messages are effectively adapted for the audience. This activity can provide useful practice with extemporaneous delivery as well as with persuasive methods of speaking.

Ongoing Assessment

Activity 6

The effectiveness of the questionnaires will be apparent from students' discussions. You may want to help students use the information they gain to modify their planned reasons and evidence.

Adapting to a Hostile Audience

A **hostile audience** is one in which the majority of the listeners oppose your thesis. With some topics, especially highly controversial ones, you may notice that many people in a hostile audience may specifically object to your proposal, while others may favor a different one. Such listeners need to be shown that they are being fair in listening to you, that what you have to say matters to them, and that you are worth listening to. One speech probably will not sway them completely, but it may open their minds to your thesis.

> **EXAMPLE:** If Gloria faced a hostile audience, she could compliment her listeners on their fairness in listening to her and acknowledge the validity of their point of view. Establishing her credibility would be particularly important, as would using logical reasoning.

This approach also works well when you address a radio or television audience. It is unlikely that you will drive away any listeners who already favor your proposal, and your approach may convince some neutral listeners and stir some apathetic ones.

Using a Questionnaire to Identify Audience Attitudes

Make up a questionnaire on your topic. Your questionnaire can be similar to the one on page 398. Hand out your questionnaire to every person in your audience. Then collect the questionnaires, and tabulate the responses with a chart like the following one. Use the results to determine the final wording of your thesis statement and to review the appropriateness of your reasons and evidence.

____ Strongly in favor	____ Apathetic or uninformed
____ Slightly in favor	____ Slightly against
____ Neutral	____ Strongly against

After you tabulate your results and consider how they might affect your argument, discuss your findings with your classmates. What did they learn by using a questionnaire?

Organizing Your Speech

For the most part, the way you organize your speech will be guided by your impression of your audience's attitude and by the nature of your material. Persuasive speeches are organized according to two approaches: deductive and inductive.

To discuss **Delivering Your Speech Convincingly** on p. 405, you may want to use charts, graphs, or pictures to model how to use visuals effectively in a speech. Demonstrate basic skills such as propping up visuals securely, making sure everyone can see the material, and holding visual materials steadily in your hands.

You may want to suggest that students complete **Activity 8** on p. 406 (rehearsing their speeches) in private several times. Then it might be helpful for students to present their speeches to family members or friends (or even before mirrors) to further revise and refine their material and their presentations. Suggest that they become very comfortable using any visual materials they intend to use.

You will probably want to review the **Evaluation Checklist for Persuasive Speeches** on p. 409 before students present their speeches to the class.

Deductive Approach

THESIS

Supporting Reason

Supporting Reason

Supporting Reason

Inductive Approach

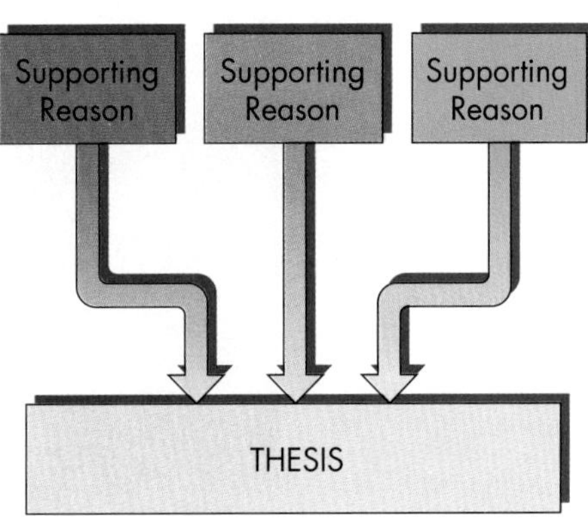

With the deductive approach, the thesis is stated first and then reasons are presented that support the thesis. With the inductive approach, a number of reasons are stated which then build to the statement of the thesis.

Using a Deductive Approach

In a **deductive approach,** you begin with your thesis and then present reasons to support it. When you organize your material deductively, you try to move your audience from the general to the specific. Three types of deductive approaches are

- the statement-of-reasons method
- the problem-solution method
- the comparative advantage method

While all of these methods are deductive, each of them has its own special format for presenting information, making it particularly useful in certain circumstances.

Statement-of-Reasons Method. The **statement-of-reasons method** is the classic deductive approach in which the thesis is stated directly and followed by supporting reasons. This method works well with a favorable audience, since your listeners are not likely to be turned off by a direct approach.

Thesis: You should vote for Ann Welch for senior class president.

I. Ann Welch has proven leadership experience.
II. Ann Welch is a hard worker who will work for you.
III. Ann Welch has fresh ideas that will benefit you.

Critical Thinking

Application

If your students have made a list of current controversial issues in the **Critical Thinking Application** on p. 385, refer to the propositions they wrote. Ask students to decide on the biggest stumbling block to persuading an audience on each of the propositions. Then ask them to decide on the best way to organize the information (comparative advantage, statement of reasons, and so on) to make it convincing to a specific audience—teenage males, homeowners, working mothers, or other audiences of students' own choosing. Lead the class in a discussion of the methods that are chosen.

Teacher's Resource Binder

Skills for Success 4
Using a Deductive or an Inductive Approach

Before assigning the **Communication Journal** activity on p. 407, write on the chalkboard a few examples of persuasive speaking. Episodes from classroom teaching might be effective examples to use.

To prepare students for **Activity 9** on p. 408, you might select a brief speech and model how you would critique it. Use the questions in the **Evaluation Checklist for Persuasive Speeches** to guide your critique.

ASSESSMENT

You might want to evaluate **Activities 6** and **7** informally and to use **Activities 8** and **9** for formal evaluation. Use students' critiques in **Activity 9** to assess students' mastery of the material in this segment. In their evaluations, students should focus on the checklist questions on organization, content, and language.

CRITICAL THINKING

Analysis

Plan a class period of impromptu speeches on topics that offer more than one point of view. After the speeches, have students analyze the styles of organization that were used and how well the information suited the audience.

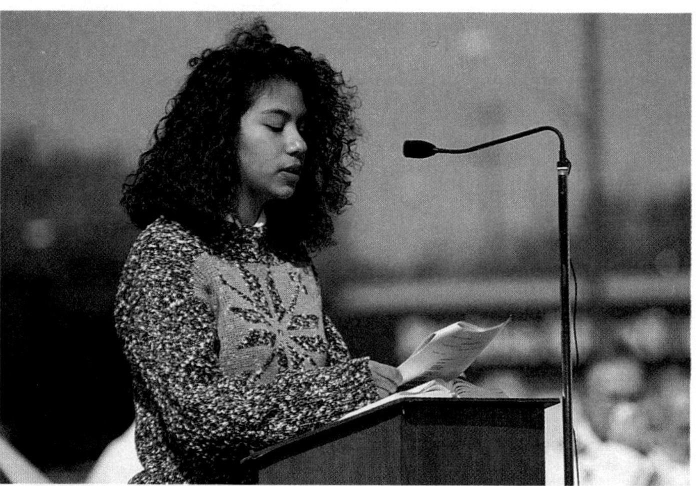

Problem-Solution Method. With the **problem-solution method,** you first present a problem and then offer at least one possible solution for that problem. You continue with this pattern for each problem you have identified.

This method works well with both favorable and neutral audiences. It can also succeed with apathetic audiences if you personalize both the problem and the solution convincingly.

Thesis: You should vote for Ann Welch for senior class president.

I. Our senior class members face several problems. [Problem]

- **A.** Students don't feel they have any input.
- **B.** Teachers don't respect student opinion.

II. Ann Welch can solve each of these problems. [Solution]

- **A.** Ann Welch can generate student interest.
- **B.** Ann Welch is respected by the faculty.

Comparative Advantage Method. The **comparative advantage method** presents each reason as a benefit to the audience. Sometimes the advantage of each reason is stated directly, using words like *more* or *better;* other times it is simply implied, or suggested. This method works well with neutral audiences. By directly presenting the benefits, you might sway a neutral audience to adopt your viewpoint.

RETEACHING

To help students practice tailoring their material to favorable, neutral, apathetic, and hostile audiences, have the class act out the following scenario: A group of students wants to set up a lounge area for seniors to use when they are not in class.

Students are to take turns playing the roles of principal, teachers, sophomores, juniors, seniors, and custodial staff. Students should adapt their comments to specific audiences. After students present their dialogues, have them discuss how they modified their approaches to convince the various audiences.

MAKING CONNECTIONS

Mass Media

You may want to have students view videotaped recordings of political speeches and to analyze the methods of organization the tapes use.

Thesis: You should vote for Ann Welch for senior class president.

- **I.** Ann Welch has more experience than any other candidate.
- **II.** Ann Welch has shown the ability to work harder than any other candidate.
- **III.** Ann Welch's fresh ideas will benefit you more than any other candidate's ideas will.

Using an Inductive Approach

In an **inductive approach,** you begin with your reasons and lead up to your thesis. When you organize your material inductively, you try to move your audience from the specific to the general. The inductive approach is the opposite of the deductive approach you have just read about. Three types of inductive approaches are

- the criteria-satisfaction method
- the negative method
- the Monroe motivated sequence

Criteria-Satisfaction Method. The **criteria-satisfaction method** has the purpose of getting the audience to agree to the soundness of certain criteria, or standards. Then you show how your proposal satisfies those criteria. This method is especially useful with hostile audience members who need to be shown that what you have to say matters to them and that you are worth listening to.

- **I.** Most of us are likely to agree on the criteria for class president.
  - **A.** A class president should have proven leadership experience.
  - **B.** A class president should have a record as a hard worker.
  - **C.** A class president should have fresh ideas.
- **II.** Ann Welch meets all three of these criteria.
  - **A.** Ann Welch has considerable leadership experience.
  - **B.** Ann Welch has proven to be a hard worker.
  - **C.** Ann Welch has fresh ideas that will benefit you.
- **III.** **Thesis:** You should vote for Ann Welch for senior class president.

See p. 408 for **EXTENSION, ENRICHMENT,** and **CLOSURE.**

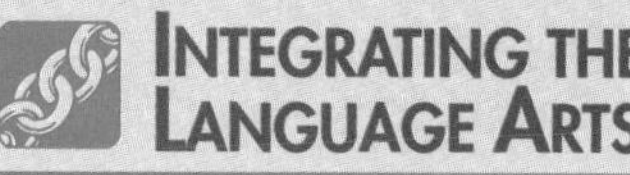

INTEGRATING THE LANGUAGE ARTS

Literature Link

You might wish to have students study plays, short stories, speeches, nonfiction essays, and novels they have read to find examples of persuasion. For example, you might use Patrick Henry's "Speech to the Virginia Convention" or passages from *Black Elk Speaks* by John G. Neihardt. Have students study the passages to analyze the use of the concepts they have learned in this chapter—types of persuasion, logical reasons and emotional appeals, and organizational methods.

You have to satisfy criteria in all areas of life. This photograph shows an example of a vehicle that did not meet the clearance criteria for this bridge.

Negative Method. With the **negative method,** you show that no option other than the one you propose is acceptable. This method can work well with a hostile audience if you give your listeners enough solid evidence to convince them to agree with every one of your reasons.

I. Bill Garver has no real leadership experience.
II. Laura Simpson has no real leadership experience.
III. Jack Phillips has a little experience but has not shown an inclination to be willing to pitch in with the work.
IV. Ann Welch has leadership experience, has proven herself to be a hard worker, and has fresh ideas.
V. **Thesis:** You should vote for Ann Welch for senior class president.

Monroe Motivated Sequence. The **Monroe motivated sequence,** developed by Professor Alan H. Monroe, is based on the premise that in order to convince an audience to act, a speaker must

1. draw *attention* to the problem
2. show a *need* for some action
3. outline a plan that will *satisfy* that need
4. help the audience *visualize* the benefits of that plan of action
5. suggest a specific *action* that puts the plan into practice

I. We all saw how last year's senior class floundered for lack of leadership. [Attention]
II. Yet, the senior class is the class with the greatest expectations in high school. [Need]
III. A strong leader can restore class spirit and help our class accomplish its goals. [Satisfaction]
IV. Led by a president with a clear vision of this class's potential, proven leadership experiences, and a commitment to hard work, this class can go down in history. [Visualization]
V. **Thesis:** You should vote for Ann Welch, a hard-working, proven leader with a vision. [Action]

Organizing Your Persuasive Speech

Select one of the six methods of organization, either deductive or inductive, and outline the main points of your speech. Be prepared to explain why you chose this method.

Delivering Your Speech Convincingly

Delivery is important in any speech, but it is especially critical in a persuasive speech. Anything less than your most dynamic delivery will diminish your chances of persuading your audience.

Using Visual Materials

Since an audience can grasp information better by seeing and hearing it than by hearing it alone, look for opportunities to use visual materials in your persuasive speech.

Charts, graphs, films, slides, and photographs can help listeners visualize a need, motivating them to action. For example, to persuade an audience to support relief efforts for hurricane victims, a speaker could dramatize the need by showing photographs of people left homeless by the storm.

However, if you include visuals, beware of their overuse. No doubt you have had the experience of sitting in a darkened room as a speaker showed slides. The first few slides may have aroused your

BUILDING A PORTFOLIO

Have students keep the preparative work for their persuasive speeches in their portfolios. As students complete the activities in the chapter, have them label their work to indicate any plans they are making, including the type of organization they will use.

Activity 7

You may wish to check the outlines in advance to help students if they have not chosen the most effective organizational methods for their speeches.

COOPERATIVE LEARNING

Have students work in groups of four or five to practice using their visual materials before they actually present their speeches. Students should take turns practicing and receiving suggestions about ways to improve.

MEETING INDIVIDUAL NEEDS

Learning Styles

Kinetic Learners. Have students brainstorm for ways of boosting the energy level of a speech's delivery if an audience begins to seem bored. You may want to model techniques such as moving from one part of the room or stage to another, pausing for dramatic effect, using more eye contact, or employing gestures.

interest, and the next few may have held it. Beyond that, however, you were probably more ready to go to sleep than to pay attention to the speaker.

Responding to Feedback

While you speak, your audience will be giving you subtle (and at times, not-so-subtle) feedback that will help you determine how you are doing. Be sure to respond to that feedback. For example, if your audience shows signs of boredom, boost the energy level of your delivery. Also be alert for shifts in attitude. For example, if a neutral audience begins to show signs of doubt, spend more time detailing your evidence.

Don't treat your speech as though it were engraved in stone. Feel free to add to a point, shorten a point, speed up, slow down, or even insert some humor if the feedback from your audience suggests the need for it.

ONGOING ASSESSMENT

Activity 8

Students will rehearse their speeches out of class. Their degree of success in rehearsing their speeches will become apparent as you evaluate their later presentations.

Rehearsing Your Persuasive Speech

Using the outline you developed for Activity 7 on page 405, rehearse your persuasive speech thoroughly. Mark the ideas that you feel should be given special vocal emphasis, and work to achieve that emphasis. Then decide what kinds of visual materials, if any, you will use, and gather or prepare those materials. Be prepared to give your persuasive speech in class.

Evaluating a Persuasive Speech

Both oral and written critiques are as essential for persuasive speeches as they are for informative speeches. However, while an informative speech critique focuses on the speaker's efforts to help the audience understand and remember the information, a critique of a persuasive speech focuses on the speaker's efforts to motivate the audience to believe a thesis or to act upon it. Such a critique, whether oral or written, evaluates the speaker's organization, content, language, and delivery.

You can use the Evaluation Checklist on page 409 as the basis for an oral or written critique of a persuasive speech. [For more about oral or written critiques, see pages 96–99 of Chapter 4.]

In your communication journal, make notes about the instances of persuasive speaking that you encounter daily. For example, did you try to convince a parent to let you go to the football game or to the dance on Saturday? What reasons and evidence did you present? What emotional appeals did you use? How did you try to establish your credibility, so you would be allowed to go? Perhaps you have seen a political advertisement on television lately. What was the ad trying to convince you to do or to believe? What reasons and emotional appeals did it use? What did the ad do to make you want to believe it?

CRITICAL THINKING

Analysis

Have students analyze how they have responded as an audience for a persuasive speech or for another speech occasion. For example, have them recall their first day in class with a new teacher. As an audience, were they favorable, neutral, apathetic, or hostile? How did the teacher respond to students' reactions? If there have recently been any speakers at school assemblies, have students recall the types of audience reactions and attitudes and have them note any adaptations the speakers made.

EXTENSION

Select a current issue of interest to the class. Possibilities are smoking or a dispute over parking. Ask students to give impromptu speeches for or against the issue. Students should analyze the speeches to determine the types of organization (deductive or inductive) that are used. Then they can select the best presentations.

ONGOING ASSESSMENT

Activity 9

Students should demonstrate an awareness of persuasive techniques. Their critiques should reflect understanding of the points in the **Evaluation Checklist for Persuasive Speeches.**

ACTIVITY 9

Giving an Oral Critique of a Persuasive Speech

In an issue of *Vital Speeches of the Day,* find a persuasive speech that you think is especially effective. Prepare and give an oral critique of this speech. Be sure your critique explains why you think the speech is particularly effective. What reasons and evidence does the speaker give? What emotional appeals does the speaker use? How does the speaker establish his or her credibility and adapt to the audience?

The best way to develop a persuasive argument is to be persuaded yourself, like the people shown in this photograph.

GUIDELINES

for Persuasive Speeches

- Is my specific purpose clearly stated in my thesis?
- Have I provided good reasons to support my thesis?
- Have I provided evidence to support each reason?
- Have I provided enough reasons and evidence to build a convincing argument?
- Have I analyzed my audience?
- Have I adapted my material to meet audience attitudes?
- Have I used emotional appeals appropriately?
- Have I organized my speech in a way that is likely to motivate the audience?
- Have I established my credibility on my topic?
- Can I use verbal and nonverbal skills to present my speech convincingly?

Enrichment

You might wish to help students in preparing visual materials for their persuasive speeches. If the media center has related filmstrips or slides, you could teach students to use projectors. Perhaps you can get materials from an art teacher for students to make creative visuals to illustrate points in their speeches.

Closure

Ask each student to recall at least one helpful idea learned in this segment. It might be an idea about adapting speeches to different types of audiences. Or it might be information about the various kinds of inductive and deductive organizational patterns for speeches.

EVALUATION  CHECKLIST

for Persuasive Speeches

Organization:

Did the introduction gain the audience's attention?
Did the thesis statement clearly indicate the specific purpose of the speech?
Was each of the reasons clearly identifiable and logically organized?
Did the conclusion summarize the key points? Did it close the speech on a high point?

Content:

Did the speaker seem knowledgeable about the topic?
Did the speaker consider the audience's interest, knowledge, and attitudes?
Was enough specific information given to make the key points of the speech understandable?
Did visual materials help the audience remember the key ideas?
Were reasons presented to support the thesis?
Did the evidence strongly support the reasons presented?
Did the speaker use any emotional appeals to motivate the audience?
Did the speaker build or maintain credibility?
Did the speaker present the speech ethically?

Language:

Was the language precise?
Were the words specific and concrete?
Did the speaker use words that the audience could understand?
Did the speaker emphasize key ideas?
Was the tone appropriate for the audience and the occasion?

Delivery:

Did the speaker seem confident and enthusiastic?
Did the speaker look at the audience during the speech?
Were the speaker's facial expressions, gestures, and movements natural?
Were the speaker's articulation, enunciation, and pronunciation correct?

Additional comments:

Evaluation:

Audiovisual Resource Binder

Transparency 31
Evaluation Checklist for Persuasive Speeches

◆ Profiles in Communication

Performance Objectives

- To select an extracurricular activity to evaluate
- To devise a set of criteria for an evaluation
- To apply the criteria to the evaluation process
- To prepare a persuasive speech that evaluates an extracurricular activity

Teaching the Feature

This activity is designed so that the skills presented in this chapter can be pulled together in the preparation of another persuasive speech. If time is limited, however, you may want to allow students to share what they have prepared without actually having them deliver formal speeches. Ask students to prepare all aspects of their presentations, including using visuals, in the same way County Extension Agent Hebert advises his judges to do.

Activity Note

Students' evaluations should include both the evaluation criteria students develop for their particular topics and assessment of the persuasiveness of their evaluations.

PROFILES IN COMMUNICATION

Jay Hebert is County Extension Agent for a state university's Institute of Food and Agricultural Sciences. His favorite part of the job is teaching 4-H Club members to become winning horse judges.

Mr. Hebert has his teenage judges begin by establishing priorities, or standards for judging, that their listeners will accept or agree to. "Don't make your talk complicated," he advises. "Know what's most important to your audience, and use language they'll understand." Using the criteria-satisfaction method, the teenage judges then establish how their horses satisfy each point.

To hone their presentation skills, the student judges practice in groups. "I ask them to sell me and the group on each point about a horse," Mr. Hebert explains, "to help them build self-confidence and sharpen their speaking skills."

Mr. Hebert has his teenage judges first write out their evaluations and read them aloud. As they progress, they use fewer notes until they can present their evaluations extemporaneously.

Jay Hebert wouldn't trade his job for any other. "When those young people can stand in front of a judge at a competition and express themselves with confidence, that's what it's all about."

ACTIVITY

What if you were chosen to be a judge for some kind of extracurricular activity at your school? What standards or criteria would convince your listeners that your evaluation is the one they should accept? First, select an extracurricular activity. Perhaps you could effectively evaluate poems and stories submitted to your school newspaper or literary magazine, drawings and paintings for the annual student art exhibit, or gymnastic routines. Then, devise a set of criteria you would use for evaluation, and apply these standards to whatever you are judging. Finally, prepare a short persuasive speech in which you present your evaluation of the activity.

S·U·M·M·A·R·Y

A SPEECH TO PERSUADE establishes a fact, strengthens or changes a person's beliefs, or moves a person to action.

- **Choose a topic** that you feel strongly about and that other people may have different views on.
- **Write a thesis statement** that addresses a question of fact, of belief, or of policy.
- **Use persuasive techniques** to convince your audience. You might (1) use logical reasoning by providing sound reasons and valid evidence, including facts (verifiable statements) and expert opinions (statements by knowledgeable people); or (2) appeal to your listeners' emotions by citing specifics, using vivid language, and including personal references.
- **Establish your credibility** by emphasizing your competence, knowledge of the topic, sincerity and goodwill toward the audience, and enthusiasm about the subject.
- **Meet ethical standards** when you speak. Lying, distorting, and name-calling have no place in persuasive speaking.
- **Adapt your speech** to your audience's attitude toward your topic—favorable, neutral or undecided, apathetic, or hostile.
- **Organize your speech** to present your reasons and evidence in either a deductive or an inductive pattern.
- **Deliver your speech** as convincingly as possible. Use visual materials, and respond to audience feedback.
- **Evaluate a persuasive speech** by focusing on how the speaker motivated the audience to believe the thesis or to act upon it.

CHAPTER **15**

Vocabulary

Look back through this chapter to find the meaning of each of the following terms. Write each term and its meaning in your communication journal.

apathetic audience, *p. 399*
comparative advantage method, *p. 402*
competence, *p. 394*
credibility, *p. 394*
criteria-satisfaction method, *p. 403*
deductive approach, *p. 401*
dynamism, *p. 395*
emotional appeal, *p. 392*
ethical standards, *p. 395*
evidence, *p. 388*
expert opinion, *p. 390*
fact, *p. 390*
favorable audience, *p. 399*
hostile audience, *p. 400*
inductive approach, *p. 403*
logical reasoning, *p. 387*
manipulation, *p. 396*
Monroe motivated sequence, *p. 404*
negative method, *p. 404*
neutral audience, *p. 399*
persuasive speech, *p. 383*
problem-solution method, *p. 402*
question of belief, *p. 384*
question of fact, *p. 384*
question of policy, *p. 384*
reason, *p. 387*
sincerity, *p. 394*
statement-of-reasons method, *p. 401*
testimonials, *p. 389*

TEACHER'S RESOURCE BINDER

- Chapter 15 Vocabulary

Review Questions

Answers

1. A persuasive speech presents information to change a belief or an opinion or to motivate the audience to action.
2. change a belief or prompt action on a specific policy
3. facts and expert opinions
4. using emotional appeals and establishing credibility
5. using vivid language and including personal references
6. competence, sincerity, and dynamism
7. Persuasion involves convincing people to agree of their own free will. Manipulation involves shrewd or devious distortion of information to deceive people into agreeing.
8. statement-of-reasons method, problem-solution method, and comparative advantage method

Discussion Questions

Guidelines for Assessment

Student responses may vary.

1. The speaker needs to know demographic information about the audience and the ideas and beliefs that listeners hold about the topic so that the speaker can determine which supporting information listeners will find most convincing. The speaker also needs to determine the most effective way to approach a specific audience to establish credibility. A speaker needs to adapt a persuasive speech to complement the audience's general attitude toward the topic.
2. You can let students have free rein in making their choices, or you can establish guidelines. For example, require that the people in two of the audiences be essentially the same in their personal traits but not in their views toward the topic. Or assign the students to work with an audience that is hostile to the speaker but not to the topic.
3. Some students will believe unequivocally that there is no adequate justification for unethical means. Others may see the question as a matter of degree: How much are ethical standards violated? Others might see the end itself as the deciding factor in the question. For example, boosting the spirits of an ill person by saying he or she looks better, even though the person's appearance has not improved, may be seen as justifiable. Encourage students to identify specific instances when an audience has been manipulated.

CHAPTER **15**

Review Questions

1. Both an informative and a persuasive speech provide information. What makes a persuasive speech different from an informative speech?
2. One kind of persuasive speech establishes a fact. What do the two other kinds of persuasive speeches do?
3. You should support your thesis with reasons. What two types of evidence should you use to support your reasons?
4. Using logical reasoning is one technique of persuasion. What are two other techniques of persuasion?
5. One way of appealing to emotions is to use specific words and details. What are two other ways of appealing to emotions?
6. To give your speech effectively, you must establish credibility. What are the three elements of speaker credibility?
7. What is the difference between persuading and manipulating an audience?
8. When you use deductive organization, you state your thesis first and then give your reasons. What are three types of deductive organization?
9. When you use inductive organization, you state your reasons first and lead up to your thesis statement. What are three types of inductive organization?
10. A critique of an informative speech focuses on the speaker's ability to help the audience understand and remember the material. On what does a critique of a persuasive speech focus?

Discussion Questions

1. Audience analysis is extremely important for effective persuasive speaking. Discuss why a speaker needs to approach each audience differently.
2. You are giving a speech to three different audiences. First identify these audiences. Then discuss what you would do differently to adapt your speech to each of them.
3. All of us have encountered unethical speakers at one time or another. First discuss the question, "Does the end ever justify the means in public speaking?" Then discuss the methods used by unethical speakers to manipulate their audiences.
4. Blaise Pascal, a French mathematician, wrote, "People are generally better persuaded by the reasons which they have themselves discovered than by those which have come into the minds of others." Discuss how this quotation relates to the persuasive speech.
5. In the eighteenth century, an English writer who used the pseudonym of Junius (and whose identity is still uncertain) wrote, "By persuading others, we convince ourselves." Discuss how this quotation relates to you as a persuasive speaker.

9. criteria-satisfaction method, negative method, and Monroe motivated sequence
10. the speaker's efforts to motivate the audience to believe the proposition or to act on it

ACTIVITIES

1. **Identifying Types of Persuasion.** Identify each of the following statements as a question of fact, a question of belief, or a question of policy.
   a. The Lindale Eagles will win the regional football championship.
   b. Students should receive job training while they are in high school.
   c. The defendant did commit the crime of which he is accused.
   d. We must act globally to combat the "greenhouse effect."
   e. Katherine Hepburn single-handedly changed Hollywood's rather narrow image of a leading lady.

2. **Examining Techniques of Persuasion.**
   A. Find five different advertisements. Label each one according to its primary audience appeal. Is its appeal based on logical reasoning? emotional appeals? the credibility of the source? Explain your answers.

   B. Select a persuasive speech from an issue of *Vital Speeches of the Day.* Identify portions of the speech that contain logical reasoning, make emotional appeals, and establish credibility. Be prepared to read these portions to the class and to discuss the techniques of persuasion they use.

3. **Identifying Logical and Emotional Appeals.** Identify each of the following statements as representing a logical appeal or an emotional appeal.
   a. According to one study, illiteracy costs the U.S. government and taxpayers approximately $120 billion a year.
   b. Sixty percent of prison inmates are unable to read.
   c. You and I have to spend our hard-earned dollars on taxes to pay for prisons.
   d. Literacy programs benefit everyone in the community by lowering crime rates and increasing local workers' abilities to handle higher-skilled employment.
   e. You can make a difference in your community by volunteering to become a reading tutor and helping someone who is illiterate learn to read or someone whose reading is deficient improve his or her skills.

4. **Giving a Persuasive Speech That Establishes or Changes a Belief.** First, look at the photograph below (or another picture of your own choosing), and think of an issue that the scene in the photograph raises. Then, think of an improvement that would address the issue, and write it as a thesis that addresses a question of belief. For instance, you might state, "Community involvement is the best way to combat our litter problem." Outline a logical argument for making the improvement, and present it in an extemporaneous speech to your class. Finally, ask your classmates to use the Evaluation Checklist for Persuasive Speeches on page 409 to give an oral critique of your speech.

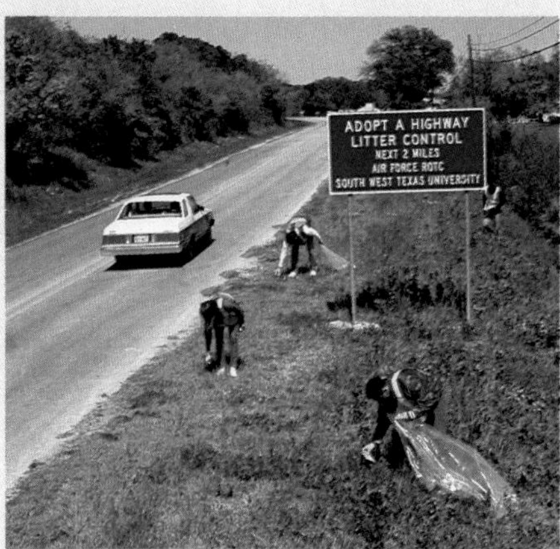

4. Pascal's statement can relate to the persuasive speech in this way: Specific, verifiable facts and vivid examples frequently lead one to discover reasons for taking a position or for reaching a conclusion. By presenting these facts and examples to support the reasons for taking a certain position, a speaker can help listeners discover these same reasons for reaching the same conclusion.
5. Junius realized that when preparing a persuasive message, a speaker gathers evidence, evaluates reasons, develops emotional appeals, and makes ethical decisions before the message is presented. The process of preparing the speech helps the speaker collect and assimilate the knowledge and become a proponent.

ACTIVITIES

Guidelines for Assessment

1. a. question of belief
   b. question of policy
   c. question of fact
   d. question of policy
   e. question of belief
2. A. You may want to have students work in groups to discuss their advertisements and their analyses of the appeals used.
   B. Sincerity and dynamism are difficult credibility methods to judge from the written text of a speech; students may need to focus on evidence of competence to show credibility. Have students identify the types of reasons and evidence

SUMMATIVE EVALUATION

Your **Teacher's Resource Binder** contains a reproducible **Chapter 15 Test** that may be used to assess students' mastery of the concepts presented in this chapter.

PORTFOLIO ASSESSMENT

For future reference and evaluation you may want to have students keep in their portfolios any skill sheets or evaluation forms that you have used with this chapter along with any other recorded or written materials that students have created.

included. Students should correctly identify specific portions of the speeches they select.

3. a. logical appeal
b. logical appeal
c. emotional appeal
d. logical appeal
e. emotional appeal

4. Students' theses should state a belief and the outlines should show a logical application of reasoning.

5. a. deductive; problem-solution method
b. inductive; criteria-satisfaction method
c. inductive; negative method

6. Analyses should reflect the organizational patterns of the speeches students choose. Discussions should identify specific strengths and weaknesses and should use these to justify judgments of the arguments' effectiveness.

7. Tell students to listen to the speeches with open minds. They should not be overly negative in their oral critiques.

8. Have students listen to their classmates' speeches with open minds. For the evaluation discussion, you may want to have students raise their hands to show how many agree with the policy change suggested before the presentation and how many change their minds after the speech.

CHAPTER **15**

5. Identifying Inductive and Deductive Approaches. Identify each of the following arguments as inductive or deductive in approach. Then label each argument according to its method of organization.

a. **Thesis:** My family should buy a new car.
 I. Our old car is giving us problems.
  A. It gets poor gas mileage.
  B. It breaks down regularly.
 II. A new car would solve these problems.
  A. It would get better gas mileage.
  B. It would be less likely to break down.

b. I. Our family agrees on the criteria for a family car.
  A. A family car should get good gas mileage.
  B. A family car should be reliable.
  C. A family car should have room for the whole family.
 II. This minivan meets all these criteria.
  A. This minivan gets good gas mileage.
  B. It is reliable.
  C. It has room for the whole family.
 III. **Thesis:** My family should buy this new minivan.

c. I. That sports car doesn't have room for the whole family.
 II. That station wagon has room for the whole family, but it doesn't get good gas mileage.
 III. That sedan has room for the whole family, but it has very little cargo space.
 IV. This minivan has room for the whole family, gets good gas mileage, and has plenty of cargo space.
 V. **Thesis:** Our family should buy this minivan.

6. Analyzing a Persuasive Speech. Briefly outline the main points of a persuasive speech from *Vital Speeches of the Day.* Which of the six organizational patterns (deductive or inductive) did the speaker use? How effective was the speaker's argument? What were its strengths and weaknesses? Be prepared to discuss the main points you outlined and your analysis of the speech.

7. Giving a Persuasive Speech That Establishes a Fact. Think of a statement that concerns you and that can be proven true or false—for example, homework does (or does not) help students learn a subject thoroughly. First, state your thesis to address a question of fact. Organize your information and identify whether you use a deductive or an inductive approach. Deliver your speech to your class. Ask your classmates to use the Evaluation Checklist for Persuasive Speeches (page 409) to give you an oral critique of your speech.

8. Giving a Persuasive Speech That Changes a Policy. Think of a policy you would like to see changed at your school. Clearly identify the policy and the change you would like to see made. Then state this change in a thesis that addresses a question of policy. Organize your supporting facts and other information in a brief outline that will fit easily on a 3- x 5-inch or 4- x 6-inch card. Using only the outline on your card, deliver your speech to your class. Then conduct a question-and-answer session about the policy change you presented as well as the strengths and weaknesses of your speech.

◆ Real-Life Speaking Situations

PERFORMANCE OBJECTIVES

- To outline and analyze a past discussion
- To revise dialogue to include a more effective presentation of a position
- To present a dialogue and to explain the changes effected
- To respond to classmates' presentations
- To write and present a sales talk for a selected product that is tailored to a particular buyer

REAL LIFE Speaking Situations

1 Think of the various discussions you have had during the past week. You can probably recall several in which persuasive speaking played a part. Can you think of circumstances when others were trying to convince you of something? Were there any occasions when you were trying to persuade others? After some of these discussions, did you think of what you should have said to present your position more effectively?

Here is your chance to relive a persuasive discussion and bring all of the good ideas you had later into play. Begin by outlining the original discussion. Who was involved? Who said what? What was the outcome of the discussion? Study your outline, and decide exactly when and how you should have presented the ideas you had later.

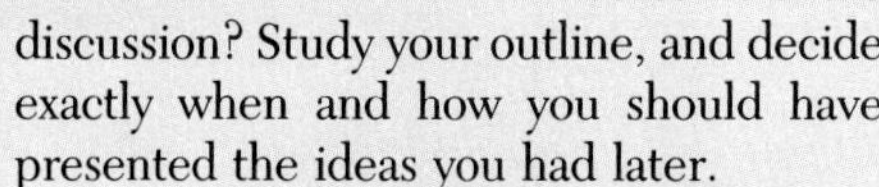

Write a brief dialogue of the discussion, inserting your later ideas where they would have had the greatest effect. Also be prepared to explain the differences between your dialogue and the actual discussion that took place. Present your dialogue in class, and ask for feedback on how effectively you presented your opinions in the two situations.

2 People who work in sales need strong persuasive skills to overcome all kinds of customer resistance. In some situations, potential buyers may object to the price of the product, they may not believe that they need the product or service, or they may prefer a competing brand. Successful salespeople have the skills to analyze the customer's resistance and find a way to overcome it.

You have just taken a job selling a product or service you believe in. Write a brief (three- to four-minute) sales talk to present to your first customer or buyer tomorrow. Begin by identifying your product or service. Choose one that you use and that you regard as the best of its kind. Next, identify your customer—a shopper in a mall? a mechanic in a service station? a buyer for retail stores? Try to anticipate your customer's resistance. List the three strongest objections you think your customer might have. Make sure you address these objections in your sales talk.

Present your sales talk in class, using visual materials, if possible. Ask your classmates to give you feedback about the persuasiveness of your sales talk.

ASSESSMENT GUIDELINES

1. Students might want to work in pairs to revise dialogues so that both sides of the interchange can be strengthened. One person can present one side of the argument while the other presents opposing reasons. Classmates can analyze how persuasive speaking can improve with preparation.
2. Sales presentations should be specific as to the product or service sold (topic) and audience selected (attitude). Students might introduce their sales talks with this information. Ensure that students address the three objectives in their sales talks and that they use visual material, if appropriate. The student audience might respond as prospective customers would with decisions to buy or not to buy the product or service.

Chapter 16
Speaking for a Special Occasion
pp. 416–445

Chapter Overview

This chapter discusses special-occasion speeches. The first segment presents general information about planning, preparing, delivering, and evaluating speeches. The second segment gives specifics about various kinds of special-occasion speeches.

Teacher's Resource Binder

The following materials are identified at their point of use in this chapter:

- Skills for Success
  1 *Analyzing the Occasion*
  2 *Analyzing the Audience*
  3 *Preparing a Speech of Introduction*
  4 *Preparing a Speech of Acceptance*
- Chapter 16 Vocabulary
- Chapter 16 Test/Answer Key

AV Audiovisual Resource Binder

The following materials are identified at their point of use in this chapter:

- Transparency 32
  Evaluation Checklist for Special-Occasion Speeches
- Audiotape 2 contains recordings of special-occasion speeches. The complete text of each speech is printed in the Appendix of Speeches in this textbook.

INTRODUCING THE CHAPTER

Write the words *special occasion* on the chalkboard. Ask students to name events in their lives that were special and that were marked by parties, celebrations, or public gatherings of some sort. You may want to write some of the occasions on the chalkboard. Tell students that these important events are often accompanied by speeches that promote bonding and social cohesion. This chapter will explain how to give such special-occasion speeches.

CHAPTER 16

Speaking for a Special Occasion

OBJECTIVES

After studying this chapter, you should be able to

1. Choose and limit a topic, identify purpose, think about an appropriate tone, gather information, and prepare to deliver a special-occasion speech.
2. Adapt a special-occasion speech to an audience.
3. Evaluate a special-occasion speech.
4. Plan and deliver the following types of special-occasion speeches: a graduation speech, a speech of introduction, a speech of presentation, a speech of acceptance, a commemorative speech, and an "after-dinner" speech.
5. Recognize the rules for extemporaneous and impromptu speeches in a competition.

What Is a Special-Occasion Speech?

In an informative or persuasive speech (see Chapters 14 and 15), you have a definite purpose—to inform or to persuade. Accordingly, your purpose as a speaker is the most important factor in determining what you say and how you say it. However, not every speech is controlled by purpose. In a **special-occasion speech** the occasion itself sets the tone of the speech and determines its content. These occasions are often rituals that mark important events in our lives and promote group bonding or social cohesion.

Special-occasion speeches are given in a wide variety of real-life speaking situations: Speaking at a graduation ceremony, introducing a speaker to your club, and presenting your coach with a gift at a sports banquet are all examples of special-occasion speeches. In this chapter you will learn how to develop various kinds of speeches for special occasions.

Bibliography of Additional Materials

PROFESSIONAL READINGS

- Booher, Dianna. ***The Executive's Portfolio of Model Speeches for All Occasions.*** Englewood Cliffs, NJ: Prentice-Hall.
- Filson, Brent. ***Executive Speeches: Fifty-One CEOs Tell You How to Do Yours.*** Williamstown, MA: Williamstown Publishing.
- Prentice, Diana, and James Payne. ***More Than Talking.*** Topeka, KS: Clark Publishing.

AUDIOVISUALS

- ***Confident Public Speaking: Volume 1***—Quiet Advantage, Anaheim, CA (videocassette, 87 min.)
- ***Impromptu Speaking***—Films for the Humanities and Sciences, Princeton, NJ (two filmstrips with audio, 15 min. each)
- ***Speak Up with Confidence***—National Educational Media, Chatsworth, CA (videocassette, 30 min.)

Segment 1 *pp. 418–426*

- **Planning a Speech for a Special Occasion**
- **Preparing Your Speech**
- **Delivering Your Speech**
- **Evaluating Special-Occasion Speeches**

CRITICAL THINKING

Analysis

Ask the class to brainstorm several speech topics, such as high school memories or future challenges, that would be appropriate at a graduation. Write the topics on the chalkboard and have students decide if the topics are too broad or too limited for a graduation speech. If a topic is too broad, encourage students to suggest ways to limit it.

Learning Styles

Visual Learners. Help students learn how to limit topics by using idea webs. Have students make idea webs about graduation speeches by starting with general topics in the center and moving outward toward specific ideas and experiences such as playing baseball or acting in school plays. Explain to students that the outer parts of their idea webs should contain ideas for limited topics.

Planning a Speech for a Special Occasion

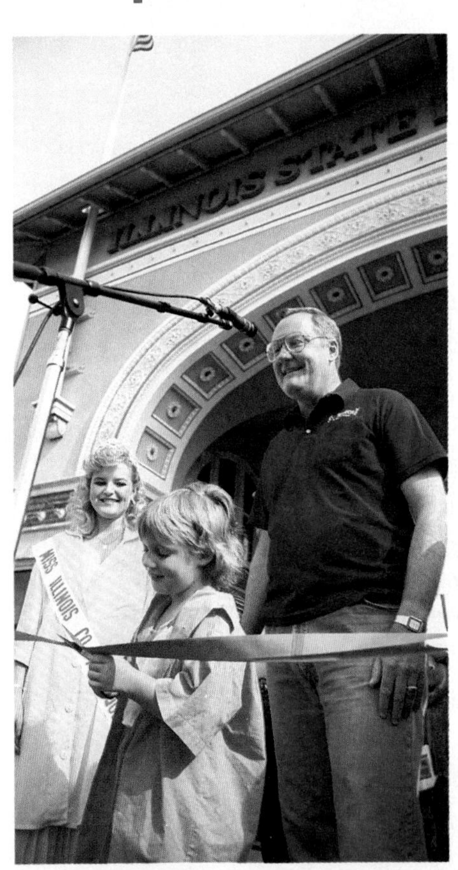

Most special-occasion speeches are not impromptu. You usually know that you will be asked to speak and have time to plan what you are going to say. You can use the suggestions on pages 418–426 to develop any kind of special-occasion speech. [For specific suggestions regarding several common types of special-occasion speeches, see pages 427–437.]

Choosing and Limiting a Topic

Choosing a topic is often not a problem for special-occasion speeches because the occasion itself frequently determines the topic. For example, in a graduation speech, you will probably talk about your school experience or about what graduation means to you. Try to focus on something specific. Limit your topic to a small, coherent piece of the larger topic.

Special-Occasion Topics

Occasion	Large Topic	Limited Topic
Graduation speech	Your experience at Shaw High School	A few specific experiences and why you'll always remember them
Introducing a speaker	The speaker's whole life and career	Four reasons why you should listen carefully to this speaker
Presenting an award	The recipient's whole life and career	The recipient's actions and qualities that led to this honor

Performance Objectives

- To analyze the purpose and tone of a special-occasion speech
- To prepare a special-occasion speech
- To develop attention-getting introductions for speeches
- To self-analyze speech rehearsals
- To evaluate a special-occasion speech

Motivation

Tell students to imagine that they have been asked to speak at going-away parties for best friends. How would they go about planning their speeches? What factors would they consider in deciding what to say? Explain that in this segment students will learn how to plan, prepare, deliver, and evaluate special-occasion speeches.

Identifying Your Purpose

Knowing your purpose will help you to decide on the tone and content of your speech. Two questions can help you to identify whether your purpose is to inform, to persuade, or to entertain your audience.

- **What does the occasion require?** Most occasions have a built-in purpose. For example, suppose that for an upcoming assembly you have been asked to introduce the main speaker, an astronaut who had graduated from your high school. Your purpose is to inform: to give the audience information about the astronaut's accomplishments and career.
- **What does the audience expect?** Rude and sarcastic jokes in a graduation speech would be out of place—even shocking. However, the audience would probably expect some humor as a graduation speaker prepared the way for his or her more serious or reflective remarks. In the same way, some humor about the guest of honor would be expected in some "after-dinner" speeches in which the audience expects to be entertained.

Thinking About Tone

Because occasions vary, some speeches for special occasions are informal and humorous, while others are both formal and serious. The tone of a speech should fit the occasion. **Tone** is the feeling a speaker reveals or conveys about his or her topic. The tone you adopt is determined by the content of your speech, the language you use, and the amount of humor you include.

Teaching Note

You may want to tell students that the information in **Identifying Your Purpose** and **Thinking About Tone** refers to general concepts about special-occasion speeches. In segment 2 of this chapter (pp. 427–439), students can expect to find specific material on occasion, audience, content, and tone for the following special-occasion speeches: graduation, introduction, presentation, acceptance, commemorative, "after-dinner," competitive extemporaneous, and competitive impromptu.

Teacher's Resource Binder

Skills for Success 1
Analyzing the Occasion
Skills for Success 2
Analyzing the Audience

TEACHING THE LESSON

Because the first segment outlines the procedure for speaking for a special occasion, you may want to maintain a working outline on the chalkboard. List the following main topics: Choosing and Limiting a Topic, Identifying Your Purpose, Thinking About Tone, Gathering Information, Adapting Your Speech to Your Audience, Delivering Your Speech, and Evaluating Your Speech. As you proceed through the segment, have students suggest topics and subtopics for the outline.

You may want to use the first item of **Activity 1** to give students guided practice in analyzing special-occasion speeches. Then assign the remainder of the activity for independent practice.

To guide students through the procedure of preparing a special-occasion speech, you could use the speech occasion mentioned in the first

Tone	How Tone Is Achieved
Formal tone (often used for a graduation speech, a speech of introduction, or similar types of speeches)	• complete sentences • an appropriate amount of humor • no slang or idioms • serious ideas • often impersonal but can include personal reflections • serious attention to structure of speech
Informal tone (often used for an "after-dinner" speech, a story, or similar types of speeches)	• slang, idioms, contractions • humorous anecdotes • other kinds of humor • a few sentence fragments • personal—tell about yourself • structure less important

Gathering Information

For most special-occasion speeches, you carry around all the information you need right in your head—in your memories and thoughts. In Chapter 9 (see pages 216–219) you learned some techniques for getting that information on paper. Here are some additional ways to gather information for your speech.

- **Idea starters:** For the introduction, the body, and the conclusion of your speech, you may be able to use facts, quotations, anecdotes, humorous incidents, definitions, personal experiences, personal opinions (beliefs, hopes, wishes), current events (newspaper stories, magazine articles, TV or radio news), and audiovisuals (posters, photos, charts, music).
- **Talking to people:** Because no two people experience an event in exactly the same way, others may be able to fill in specific details you do not recall about an event. For example, as preparation for your speech at a sports banquet, you might ask several teammates, "What were you thinking when Melissa threw that final pitch in the last inning of the championship game?" For most speeches, teachers and other trusted adults can also advise you on the kinds of information your speech should contain as well as give you other tips on how to make your speech successful.

MAKING CONNECTIONS

Technology

Ask students to discuss national computer networks that allow subscribers to communicate by means of electronic bulletin boards. While much of the information that is exchanged is content-heavy, humor is highly prized. Extremely funny jokes and anecdotes are often responded to with the anagram *ROFL* (rolling on the floor laughing). Many professional speakers are aware of the material that comes from these bulletin boards and explore it for ideas for speeches.

item of **Activity 1.** Work with students to complete the **Planning a Special-Occasion Speech** chart on p. 425 and to develop two different attention-getting introductions. Then assign **Activity 2** on p. 424 for independent practice.

As guided practice for **Activity 3** on p. 426, you may want to have the class watch a videotaped special-occasion speech. (You could videotape a student or a colleague presenting one of the special-occasion speeches in the **Appendix of Speeches.**) Then work with students to complete the **Evaluation Checklist for Special-Occasion Speeches** on p. 439. In addition, address the questions listed in **Activity 3.** Then assign **Activity 3** as independent practice. (You may want to have an additional special-occasion speech on videotape for students to evaluate independently.)

Activity 1: Analyzing Special-Occasion Speeches

For each speech outlined below, tell what you think the purpose is and what the tone of the speech should be. Then jot down two ideas or details you might include in each speech.

1. You are the president of the drama club. For the upcoming last club meeting of the school year, you have been asked to present an award to the club's faculty adviser.
2. You have been asked to present the main speaker at your state's annual student government association meeting. Teachers and students from the entire state are in the audience. The main speaker is your state's first woman governor.
3. You have been chosen to give a two-minute speech on scholarship at the induction ceremony of the National Honor Society. Other speakers will talk about membership qualifications and service projects for the year. In the audience are current National Honor Society members, students who are about to be inducted, and their parents and friends.
4. You have won the essay contest on free enterprise sponsored by business owners in your community. The award will be presented to you after lunch at the business club's next monthly meeting.
5. You are the captain of your high school's swimming team. You have been asked to speak at the dedication ceremony for your community's recently built natatorium. Because the new facility was funded by state and local sources, prominent state and local politicians, as well as teachers, students, and community members, will be present.

Ongoing Assessment

Activity 1

Students should be able to explain their choices for the purpose and tone of each speech. Base evaluations of students' ideas and supporting details on their relevance to the speech topics.

Assessment

You could use **Activities 1–3** to assess students' abilities to analyze, to prepare, and to evaluate special-occasion speeches.

Reteaching

Some students might have difficulty writing effective introductions. First, you could refer students to the information on pp. 270–273 in **Chapter 11: "Preparing Your Speech."** The **Techniques for Introductions** chart on p. 272 should prove especially helpful. Then provide students with copies of speeches written for special occasions. (You could use speeches written by former students

Common Error

Problem. Students may not appreciate that speeches for special occasions need formal structure such as introductions, conclusions, main points, or general outlines.

Solution. Point out to students that any speech that is effective has structure, no matter how short or informal it may be. You may want to analyze with students a special-occasion speech that has an obvious introduction, clear main points in the body, and an obvious conclusion.

Preparing Your Speech

Once you have clearly identified your purpose and your audience and have made some notes about what you might include in your speech, you are ready to transform your rough notes and general ideas into a speech.

HOW TO *Prepare a Special-Occasion Speech*

1. **Focus on what is important.** No matter how much your topic interests them, everyone in your audience has a limited attention span. If you ramble, they will start to daydream or fall asleep. As you prepare your speech, avoid wordiness. Get to the point.
2. **Keep it simple.** Everyday conversation is generally easy to listen to and to understand, but speeches often contain complex ideas. Listeners cannot go back to something that has confused them in a speech. Keep your language simple and make your ideas easy to follow. Explain complicated ideas carefully.
3. **Support what you say with specifics.** Back up your statements with examples, anecdotes, facts, or statistics. When you state a fact or opinion, your audience needs to hear reasons or evidence to understand why you believe the statement to be true.
4. **Pay attention to structure.** Experienced speakers advise: "Tell them what you're going to tell them; then tell them; then tell them what you told them." Start with an intriguing introduction, and end with a definite conclusion. [See pages 270–274 of Chapter 11 for information on writing introductions and conclusions.]

   One device that lends structure to a speech is **repetition,** the repeating of a sentence or a phrase that runs like a refrain throughout the speech—for example, the "I have a dream" refrain in the famous speech by Dr. Martin Luther King, Jr. (page 680). Speech writers aim for a slogan or sentence that the audience will remember. A graduation speaker, for example, might repeat "We are the future" at appropriate places in the speech.

Adapting Your Speech to Your Audience

When you give a special-occasion speech, your audience is likely to consist of your peers—fellow students who share common interests and experiences. They may be members of your club, your graduating class, or your tennis team. Since you know them fairly well, you can draw on your own observations and experience to adapt your speech to fit your classmates' interests, needs, and expectations.

or refer students to specific speeches in the **Appendix of Speeches.**) Help students to determine which introductory techniques were used and how effectively they were used. You may want to allow students to work in small groups to evaluate and, if necessary, to rewrite the introductions of their speeches. Circulate throughout the groups to offer assistance as needed.

See p. 425 for **EXTENSION, ENRICHMENT,** and **CLOSURE.**

Attention Span. A captive audience sitting through a long program, such as a graduation ceremony, will not pay attention for very long to a dull speech. Recapture lost attention by using your voice with power and cadence. You might also consider cutting some material and proceeding to the end.

Attention span is usually not a problem if your audience is there by choice. If you are talking to the computer club about a contest for developing new software, for instance, the members will listen carefully because they are interested in what you are saying. If you are presenting an award to this year's outstanding school soccer player, the members of the soccer team will probably pay close attention to your comments.

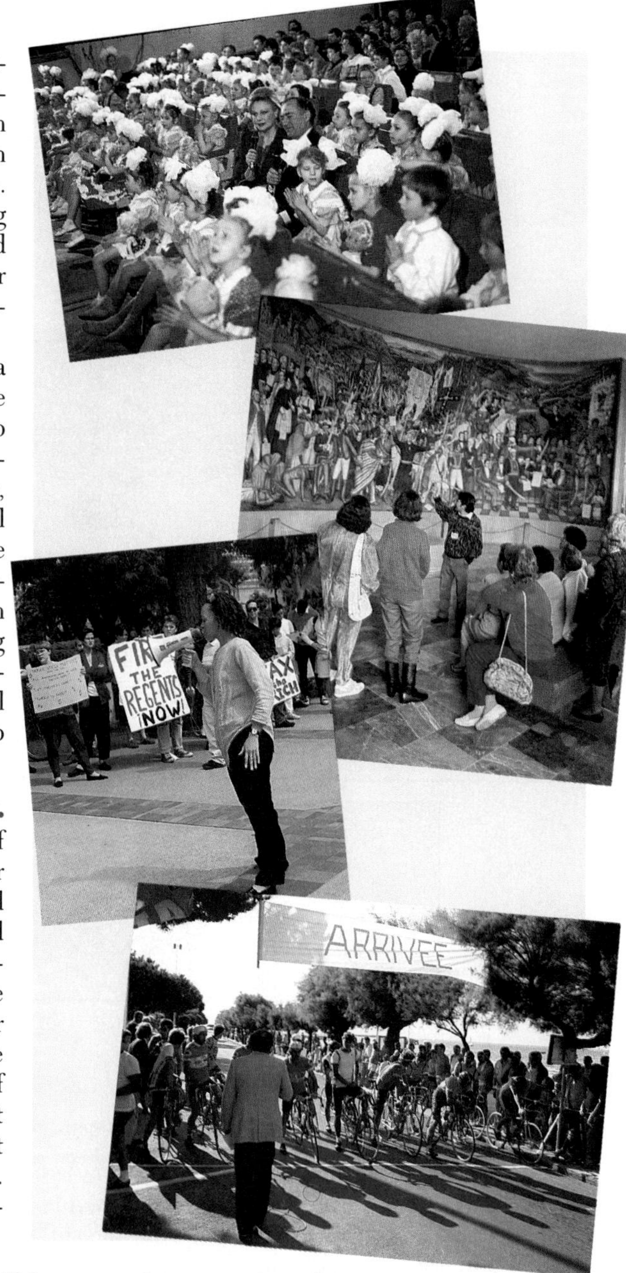

Knowledge, Needs, and Interests. Every listener should feel as if you are talking directly to him or her. For this reason, you should include specific suggestions and examples, provide needed background information, and define technical terms. For example, for a speech introducing a state representative to a group of high school seniors, you might identify the specific district that the elected official represents. You might also mention committees on which he or she serves.

Expectations. Your audience will have certain expectations that you should aim to meet. For instance, an audience would not expect to hear a graduation speech made up primarily of jokes.

COOPERATIVE LEARNING

Ask each student to list five special occasions at which speeches might be given. Then divide the class into groups of three. Have each group choose from each of the lists one special occasion for which they should determine a speaking purpose; identify the probable knowledge, needs, interests, and expectations of the audience; identify the appropriate tone; and suggest content. Ask each group to share its findings with the rest of the class.

Encourage students to make notes about this activity in their communication journals as material for future speeches.

Here are three ways to determine what your audience will expect from your speech:

1. Refer to the suggestions on pages 427–437 for developing the type of special-occasion speech you plan to make.
2. Listen to other people's speeches for similar occasions, and pay attention to the audience's reactions.
3. Ask for advice from teachers and advisers, especially those who have listened for many years to the kind of speech you are going to make.

PEANUTS reprinted by permission of UFS, Inc.

ACTIVITY 2 Preparing a Special-Occasion Speech

Look back at the five speech occasions listed in Activity 1 on page 421. Choose one situation and fill out a chart like the one at the top of the following page. You may also want to work with a classmate to develop two different attention-getting introductions for the speech you have chosen. [Review pages 270–273 in Chapter 11 for more help with writing introductions.]

(continued on next page)

Ongoing Assessment

Activity 2

The charts that students prepare should present topics that are appropriate for the audiences and occasions. Each introduction should get the attention of the audience, gain the goodwill of the audience, and develop the audience's interest in the topic. You may want to encourage students to save their charts to use as broad outlines for speeches they will give later in the chapter.

EXTENSION

Introduce students to two world-famous special-occasion speeches: Nehru's eulogy for Mahatma Gandhi called "A Glory Has Departed" and William Faulkner's acceptance speech given when he received the Nobel Prize. Encourage students to study these classic speeches for their overall effectiveness.

ENRICHMENT

Ask each student to choose a historical event at which to present a special-occasion speech. Encourage creativity. For example, a student may choose a parent's graduation ceremony. Students will need to assume identities as the speakers, either as actual characters present at the events or as imaginary characters. Encourage students to learn as much as possible about

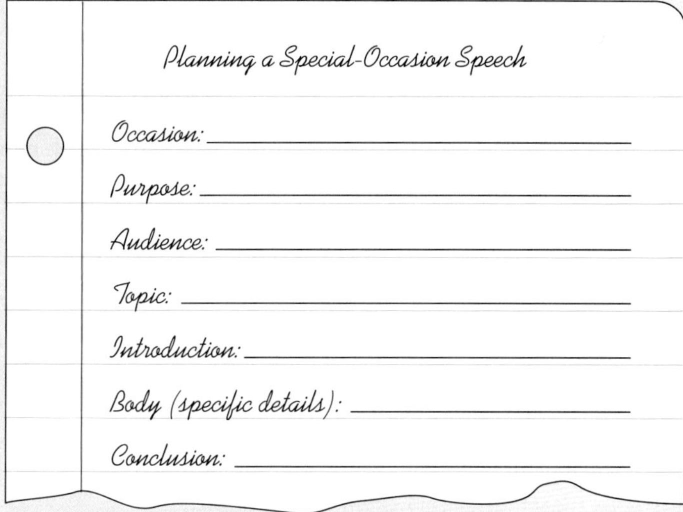

Delivering Your Speech

All the principles of effective delivery that you studied in Chapter 13 (pages 317–345) apply to several different types of speeches, including special-occasion speeches. Rehearsing is one way to increase the chances that you will present your speech with the most effective delivery possible. The more you rehearse, the more comfortable you will be when you deliver your speech. By knowing your speech well, you will be able to maintain eye contact with your audience while only occasionally glancing down at your manuscript or notes. Keep the following suggestions in mind as you rehearse your speech.

- **Rehearse by yourself.** Say your speech aloud in front of a full-length mirror. Figure out where to pause, where your voice should rise for emphasis, and where it should fall. You may even want to mark your manuscript with a colored pencil to show word groupings, pauses, and inflections for emphasis. [See pages 63–64 for more information on inflection.]

  Remember that many special-occasion speeches are for pleasant occasions. In such cases, a deadly serious, wooden tone of voice is inappropriate. Always try to give your speech a dash of liveliness. Keep your volume up as you vary your tone and phrasing.

Linguistically Diverse Students

To help students with pronunciation and intonation, give students audiocassettes and have the students record their speeches. Have each student submit a written copy of his or her speech to you. Afterwards, you too should use clear, standard language to record students' speeches on audiocassettes. Ask students to compare the two versions by listening carefully and to make written notes on any discrepancies in expression. They should then record final versions and make appropriate suggestions for practice in areas that remain troublesome.

the events they have chosen. If speeches were given at the events, encourage students to study the speeches. Then have students present their speeches for the rest of the class. Students may want to don period costumes or to use appropriate props.

CLOSURE

Ask students to identify the three things to take into account when adapting a special-occasion speech to a specific audience [the audience's attention span; the audience's knowledge, needs, and interests; and the audience's expectations]

COMMON ERROR

Problem. Some students might think that they will not experience stage fright or that they will not need to rehearse if they are presenting special-occasion speeches to their peers.

Solution. Tell your students that rehearsal is important in performing anything well. Have them review the section on stage fright on pp. 321–323 in **Chapter 13: "Presenting Your Speech"** to ensure that they know how to cope with the potential problem.

ONGOING ASSESSMENT

Activity 3

Students' answers should reflect an understanding of the material covered in this segment. If some answers seem weak, ask students to give reasons for their evaluations.

- **Rehearse before an audience.** Find people who are similar to the members of your expected audience, and ask them for some suggestions on what might improve your speech. You might get together with five or six classmates, listen to each other's speeches, and comment on them. [See the Evaluation Checklist on page 439.] If the drama or speech department in your school has a video camera you can borrow, ask someone to film you as you practice delivering your speech. Then watch the video carefully and critically.

Thinking about your rehearsals for a speech will help you deliver your speech better. In your communication journal, make notes about your rehearsals by yourself in front of a mirror and those before an audience. What do you think you do well when you give your speech? What do you need to improve?

Evaluating Special-Occasion Speeches

In real life, there are no grades at the end of a special-occasion speech. Your audience may applaud politely or enthusiastically or not at all. In speech class, however, you may often be asked to critique your classmates' speeches. Whether oral or written, your critique should evaluate the speaker's organization, content, language, and delivery. [See pages 96–98 for more information on oral and written critiques.]

You can use the Evaluation Checklist on page 439 to evaluate a special-occasion speech. Because special-occasion speeches vary a good deal, not all of the questions apply to every type of speech.

Evaluating a Special-Occasion Speech

Using the Evaluation Checklist on page 439, evaluate a special-occasion speech you have heard on television or on the radio, at school or a community event, or at a family gathering. What did you notice about what the speaker said? about the tone of the speech? about the audience at that occasion? about the speaker's delivery of the speech? Was the speech memorable or outstanding in any way? Why?

Segment 2 pp. 427–439

- **Understanding Types of Special-Occasion Speeches**

PERFORMANCE OBJECTIVES

- To plan, write, and critique a graduation speech
- To write and present a speech of introduction
- To prepare speeches of presentation and acceptance
- To prepare a commemorative speech
- To plan an "after-dinner" speech

Understanding Types of Special-Occasion Speeches

In this section you will focus on specific types of special-occasion speeches. If someday you accept an Oscar for an Academy Award or nominate a candidate for president of the United States, you can apply the principles you learn in this section to plan your speech.

Preparing a Graduation Speech

Occasion. A **graduation speech** is a formal address made at a commencement ceremony in honor of the occasion. Actually, a graduation ceremony may include several speeches, such as those given by students, administrators, and a featured or main speaker. After the speeches, the graduates receive their diplomas.

Audience. The audience at a graduation ceremony is usually made up of graduating students, their families, friends, and teachers. The graduates are often excited, and their parents and families are proud and happy. Thus, although typically cheerful and positive in attitude toward the speaker, the listeners may likely be restless. Remember that your listeners are eagerly waiting for the presentation of diplomas. They will be grateful for a short speech: ten to twenty minutes long. Your senior-class adviser will tell you how long your speech should be.

Content and Tone. Certain ideas and approaches are expected in a graduation speech. Use the following suggestions to develop your speech.

- Tell brief anecdotes, not long stories.
- Include some humor, but avoid silliness and disrespect.
- Evaluate the school experience without slapstick or anger.
- Include expected topics: congratulating graduates, acknowledging teachers, looking back, looking ahead.
- Offer optimistic and inspirational advice.
- Use formal and dignified language.

MAKING CONNECTIONS

Community Involvement

You may want to invite local persons from your school who spoke at their graduation ceremonies to share their experiences with the class. Prior to the guests' visit, have students prepare a list of questions pertaining to preparing and delivering a graduation speech. Encourage your guests to share anecdotes that might help students prepare graduation speeches.

AV Audiovisual Resource Binder

Audiotape 2, Graduation Speech

- To prepare and give an impromptu speech
- To discuss evaluative techniques for impromptu speeches at a competition

Motivation

Ask students to imagine that they are on a high school swim team that has won national recognition; their coach not only has been inspirational and supportive but also has been a friend to all. However, she plans to leave the school at the end of the year. Ask students how they would choose to honor her. Would they give her a plaque in private without saying a word, or

Ongoing Assessment

Activity 4

You may want to have students write down their critiques of their partners' speeches. You can collect the critiques for assessment purposes.

Integrating the Language Arts

Vocabulary Link

You may want to have students research the etymology of the word *introduce. Introduce* is a hybrid of two Latin words: *intro,* meaning "on the inside," and *ducere,* meaning "to lead." Ask students how these Latin roots explain the job of introducing a speaker. [An introduction should lead to the inside facts about the speaker.]

Teacher's Resource Binder

Skills for Success 3
Preparing a Speech of Introduction

AV *Audiovisual Resource Binder*

Audiotape 2, Speech of Introduction

Activity 4

Preparing a Graduation Speech

You are a featured speaker at your class's graduation from high school. Plan and write a five-minute speech. Find a partner and listen to each other's graduation speeches. Then use the Evaluation Checklist on page 439 to critique each other's speeches, providing three or four specific, positive suggestions for improvement.

Preparing a Speech of Introduction

Occasion. A **speech of introduction** is a formal speech for the purpose of gaining the audience's attention and setting the stage for the speaker or program that follows. For example, a speech of introduction may precede a dramatic reading or oral interpretation to provide background for the audience that will help them understand the dramatization they are about to hear. In many cases, a speech of introduction is used to introduce the main speaker that an audience has come to hear.

Purposes. Your first purpose is to inform the audience about the speaker and the topic: to tell them just enough to pique their curiosity and to convince them that the speaker is worth listening to. A second purpose is to make the speaker feel welcome.

Audience. Most audiences have a wide range of attention spans. You need to capture your listeners' attention immediately and to keep your introduction brief. Most introductions should run no longer than two minutes; some may be as short as half a minute. Remember that the audience still has to listen to the speaker's speech.

would they arrange a special event to honor her? Students will probably say that the coach deserves public recognition. If so, the person who presents the plaque will deliver a speech of presentation. Tell students that this type of speech, along with other special-occasion speeches, is discussed in this segment.

TEACHING THE LESSON

Lead students through the reading material provided for each type of speech. As you do, ask students to note that each section deals with the occasion, audience, content, and tone for that particular type of speech. Have students summarize key ideas about each of the four components. You may want to chart the information in columns on the chalkboard.

Content and Tone. Your audience will expect answers to three basic questions: *Who is the speaker? What will the speaker talk about? Why should I listen?* Use the following suggestions to develop your speech.

- Make your speech brief.
- Pronounce the speaker's name and official title correctly.
- Use the title the speaker wants you to use—for example, Dr. Janice Goodstein.
- Include accurate facts about the speaker's qualifications and experience, but avoid too many details and too much personal information.
- Adopt a formal, respectful tone.
- End your speech of introduction with a formal welcome: "I'd like you to welcome Dr. Janice Goodstein to our psychology club meeting."

ACTIVITY 5 Introducing a Speaker

Choose a classmate and write a one- or two-minute speech of introduction that you would give if that classmate were the main speaker at a school assembly. Think of a topic your classmate will speak about, and tell why he or she is an expert on that topic. Use factual information about your classmate. Practice your speech and then deliver it before the class.

Preparing a Speech of Presentation

Occasion. People often receive awards, honors, or gifts for special achievements or for special occasions. For example, your principal might present a plaque to the school's outstanding student volunteer, or an actor might receive an Oscar for a movie role. At these times, a speaker gives a **speech of presentation** to honor the person who is being recognized and to present the actual award or gift.

Audience. Whether friends, family members, or colleagues, the audience members for a speech of presentation are usually people who either know or care about the person receiving the award. They are interested in hearing about the person's accomplishments that led to the honor. They are also eager to see the person receive the award or gift, so a brief speech of presentation—no more than five minutes long—is appropriate.

ONGOING ASSESSMENT

Activity 5

As students deliver their speeches, you may want to have the rest of the class critique the speeches by using the **Evaluation Checklist** on p. 439. Then you can consider in your assessment both your observations and students' evaluations.

MEETING INDIVIDUAL NEEDS

Students with Special Needs

Students who find speaking in front of the class stressful may respond by misbehaving. To help them participate with appropriate behavior, design a contract for students. The focus of the contract should be a mutually agreed-on assignment that the students will complete. The contract should include a list of the steps necessary to complete the assignment. It should also include an outline of positive and negative consequences that will occur according to the level of completion.

AV ➤ *Audiovisual Resource Binder*

Audiotape 2, Speech of Presentation

Activities 4–7 ask students to prepare and give various kinds of special-occasion speeches. As guided practice, you could use **Activity 4** on p. 428 to work through the steps of planning and delivering a graduation speech. Then assign **Activity 5** on p. 429, **Activity 6** on p. 431, and **Activity 7** on p. 433 as independent practice. Remind students to consider the different audience, content, and tone for each kind of speech. (Because of time constraints, you might choose to have students complete just one of the activities.)

Because students might need extra exposure to incorporating anecdotes in speeches, you may want to model the process of planning an "after-dinner" speech before assigning **Activity 8** on p. 434 as independent practice.

As guided practice for **Activity 9** on p. 437, you could take the first turn at choosing a topic

CRITICAL THINKING

Synthesis

Ask each student to develop a "don't" list for a speech of presentation and for a speech of acceptance. You could share the following tips for a speech of presentation:

1. Don't overpraise—avoid phrases such as "the best in the world!"
2. Don't emphasize the value of the award—it is not important to the purpose of the award.
3. Don't mention those who nearly won—it can do more harm than good and could bring about hard feelings.

Ask students to share their lists with the rest of the class.

TEACHER'S RESOURCE BINDER

Skills for Success 4
Preparing a Speech of Acceptance

AV ➤ *Audiovisual Resource Binder*

Audiotape 2, Speech of Acceptance

Content and Tone. Unless it is important to surprise the award's recipient, the speaker usually names the person early in the speech. Use the following suggestions to develop your speech.

- Explain why the award or gift is given, who gives the award, and how the person's qualities or achievements led to this honor.
- Tell a brief anecdote to illustrate the recipient's actions or personal qualities.
- Read aloud the inscription on a plaque or trophy to satisfy the audience's curiosity.
- Adopt a respectful tone, but also consider using a warm and personal tone, depending on the award itself and on how well you and the audience know the recipient.

Preparing a Speech of Acceptance

Occasion. A **speech of acceptance** is one given by a person who has received an honor, an award, or a gift. In the speech, the recipient usually expresses his or her appreciation.

Audience. Like the audience for a speech of presentation, the audience for a speech of acceptance is usually made up of the recipient's friends, family members, and colleagues. The audience members are certainly interested in the speaker's thank-you remarks, but they would most enjoy a brief speech of acceptance—two to three minutes long at most.

and giving an impromptu speech. Before students give speeches in their groups, you may want to scan the suggested topics for appropriateness.

ASSESSMENT

You could use any or all of **Activities 4–7** to evaluate students' abilities to plan and deliver special-occasion speeches. You may want to give a completion grade for **Activity 8;** students are being asked to generate ideas and to develop techniques and would probably benefit most from supportive comments. Because students give their speeches in groups in **Activity 9,**

Content and Tone. A speech of acceptance acknowledges the people who have given the award or gift, as well as the people who helped the speaker to achieve it. You might use one or some of the following suggestions in your acceptance speech.

- Convey a simple, direct thank you.
- Include a brief anecdote to entertain your listeners and perhaps strengthen your connection with them.
- Mention what you think the honor might mean to you in the future.
- Accept with a sense of pride and honor, not false modesty and embarrassment.
- Adopt a warm, personal tone.

ACTIVITY 6

Preparing Speeches of Presentation and Acceptance

Working with a partner, identify a speech occasion for receiving an honor or award. Prepare a speech of presentation, giving the award to your partner. Next, have your partner prepare a speech of presentation to give you the award. Each of you should then become a recipient, and prepare a speech of acceptance for the award. Refer to the Guidelines for Special-Occasion Speeches on page 438 as you prepare your speeches.

ONGOING ASSESSMENT

Activity 6

As students deliver their speeches, assess the appropriateness of occasion, audience, content, and tone. In addition, you may want to have pairs write brief evaluations of their performances.

you may want to ask each group to write a short summative evaluation of the group members' performances.

RETEACHING

Students who do not understand how to select anecdotes or stories for speeches may be helped by reviewing a videotape on great moments from the Academy Awards. As you review the tape, ask students to watch and listen for anecdotes—stories about personal experiences or funny things that happened to the stars. Ask students to note how the anecdote works for the

ADDITIONAL ACTIVITY

Have students choose famous people about whom they would like to write testimonials. Before they research their characters, explain to students that the testimonial speaker focuses on evoking emotions rather than on relating facts. Students may want to relate scenes from their characters' lives, but remind students that they are not giving informative speeches.

Depending on the amount of time you want to spend, you could have students present their testimonials in small groups or for the whole class.

AV➤ *Audiovisual Resource Binder*

Audiotape 2, Commemorative Speech

Preparing a Commemorative Speech

Occasion. A **commemorative speech** is given to mark an important event or to honor a person. For example, your mayor may give a commemorative speech to dedicate a monument at a local Civil War battlefield. A commemorative speech that honors a living person is called a **testimonial speech;** one that honors a person who has died recently is called a **eulogy.**

Audience. The audience at a commemorative speech usually has some vital interest in the event or in the person being honored. You may attend the mayor's dedication speech, for example, because one of your ancestors played an important role in the battle that is being remembered. While the audience wants to hear what the speaker has to say, the speaker should still strive to be brief. There may be other speakers who are also presenting their comments about the event or the person.

Content and Tone. Commemorative speeches can be given at occasions that range from being joyful to being very sad. Use the following suggestions to develop a commemorative speech for a particular occasion.

- Discuss the significance of the event or the person being honored.
- Include brief anecdotes to illustrate your points. Even in the case of a eulogy, which is often given at a funeral service, you may include a light anecdote to illustrate the person's best qualities.
- Include details and ideas that honor the person or the event.
- Adopt a respectful tone. Depending on the specific occasion and your connection to the person or event, you may also want to convey a warm, personal tone. Try to avoid slang and informal language, however.

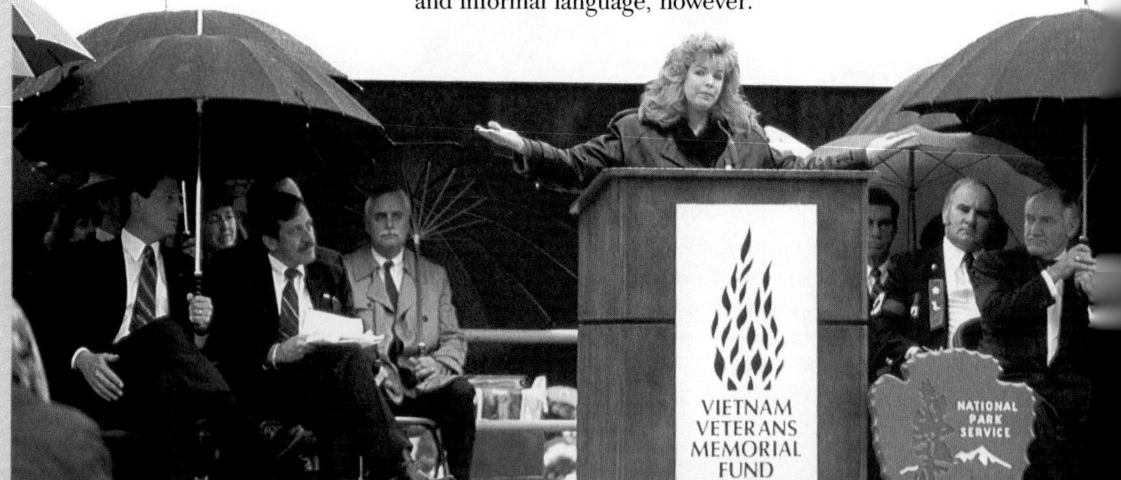

presenter. Does it set a relaxed tone? Does it tie two or more ideas together? Does it make the audience more comfortable? Ask volunteers to try retelling some of these anecdotes to the class.

See p. 438 for **EXTENSION, ENRICHMENT,** and **CLOSURE.**

ACTIVITY 7

Preparing a Commemorative Speech

Your school has just built a new facility that will improve the quality of education you and your classmates receive (for example, a new media center or a computer lab). Decide what kind of facility you would like to talk about, and prepare a commemorative speech to mark and celebrate its opening.

Preparing an "After-Dinner" Speech

Occasion. An **"after-dinner" speech** is the featured entertainment at a meeting or at a special occasion, such as an awards banquet. Usually, the audience eats first; then there may be a brief business meeting, followed by one or more speakers.

Audience. Members of the audience may know each other and share a common experience (owning a business) or interest (drama). If they have just eaten a meal, they have been sitting still for a long time. They may listen patiently for a while but may become restless before very long. Your purpose is to entertain them briefly—no more than five minutes if there are several speakers, and no more than ten minutes if you are the only speaker.

ONGOING ASSESSMENT

Activity 7

You may want to have students evaluate themselves on this activity. Then have a short conference with each student to review his or her evaluation.

Ongoing Assessment

Activity 8

Make sure that every student understands that the purpose of an "after-dinner" speech is to entertain. A topic can be serious and still be treated with some humor. Have students hand in their topics and anecdotes. Assess the topics and anecdotes according to the material in this segment.

Cooperative Learning

As mentioned in the textbook, extemporaneous speaking teams amass folders of information about various topics. You may want to have students work in groups of three to choose topics for which to gather information. For each topic, require students to provide a specific number of articles from a variety of sources. Then have each group compile its information in a folder. Store the folders in a central location. Such a class library could prove invaluable throughout the year for students who are searching for topics and information for speeches.

Content and Tone. Choose a topic that will appeal to your audience's interests and concerns. For example, for an audience of amateur photographers, you might talk about the topic "Great Pictures That Got Away." For an audience of parents, you might choose a serious topic, such as "How to Talk to Your Teenager," and treat it lightly. Use the following suggestions to develop your "after-dinner" speech.

- Include an introduction that captures your audience's interest and communicates that your speech is intended to be amusing.
- In the body of your speech, use a series of brief stories and examples related to your topic.
- Convey a light and amusing tone by using informal language.

Planning an "After-Dinner" Speech

You have been invited to be the only speaker at the next meeting of a school club. (For this speech you can choose a club that you currently belong to or one you are interested in joining.) Brainstorm possible topics that would appeal to your audience—perhaps a serious topic that you would like to treat humorously. Then choose one topic and think of at least three brief anecdotes and examples to include in your "after-dinner" speech.

Preparing an Extemporaneous Speech for Competition

Occasion. The National Forensic League sponsors high school speech and debate competitions all over the country. [See Chapter 18 for more about debate.] An **extemporaneous speech** for a competition is one that requires speakers to give seven-minute speeches after only thirty minutes of preparation time. Speakers compete in two divisions with topics that have a persuasive purpose and that deal with either international or domestic (United States) issues, such as nuclear war or national health insurance.

An extemporaneous speaking team amasses current evidence about the topics—newspaper and magazine articles, statistics, quotations, and excerpts from books. Each piece of evidence has a **citation** that tells its source and date, and files are updated throughout the year. Team members study each folder carefully to become familiar with the evidence.

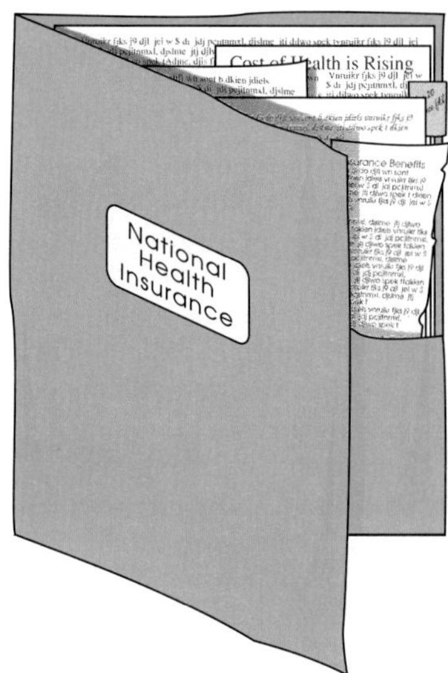

The heart of an extemporaneous speaking competition is the preparation room or area, where speakers wait until it is their turn to speak. Thirty minutes before their turn to speak, the speakers reach into an official envelope and draw out three topics. They must immediately choose one of the three. Speakers consult the team's files on the topic, make notes, and quickly rehearse the speech. Speakers are not allowed to look at any written material when they deliver their speeches.

Audience. A judge or panel of judges listens to each speech and awards points based on the speaker's content and delivery. After several preliminary rounds (with different topics for each round), the highest-ranking speakers compete in quarterfinal, semifinal, and final rounds.

Content and Tone. Use the following suggestions to develop an extemporaneous speech.

- Take a stand and line up supporting evidence. State an opinion clearly, and back it up with statistics, facts, and examples.
- Stick to the topic. **Topicality,** or relating everything directly to the topic you have chosen, is a requirement in extemporaneous speeches. You will lose points if you wander from your topic as stated in the question.
- Pay attention to tone and structure. Create a definite beginning, middle, and end. Make sure that you state the topic in your introduction.
- Sound confident. You want your audience to believe that you are in control and that you know what you are talking about. Send these messages nonverbally by keeping your voice steady, showing enthusiasm, and having a relaxed body posture.
- Express your ideas clearly. Remember that you don't need to choose "difficult" words to show that you know what you are talking about. Use simple, direct language and complete sentences.

Additional Activity

You may want to set up a mock extemporaneous speech contest. Create enough topics so that each student can draw one from an envelope. Take the class to the school's library and allow students twenty minutes to prepare their speeches. Then groups of three students can take turns delivering two-minute speeches without notes. The remaining group members should rate both content and delivery with a score of 1 (excellent), 2 (good), or 3 (fair). Encourage students to consider the short preparation time and the difficulty of the topic when they make their evaluations.

Completing the activity in one class period is important; otherwise, students will have extra time to prepare for their speeches. If one class period seems impossible, you may want to consider this alternative: Each day, let four or five students choose topics, go to the library, and present their speeches to the class for evaluation.

Critical Thinking

Analysis

Ask students to compare and contrast the concept of an extemporaneous speech with the concept of an impromptu speech. How are the speeches alike? How are they different? Which is more difficult to deliver? What do audiences expect of both kinds of speeches?

Giving an Impromptu Speech in a Competition

Occasion. An **impromptu speech** for a speech contest requires speakers to give a five-minute speech after five minutes or less of preparation. With so little preparation time, impromptu speakers rely almost entirely on their ability to "think on their feet." They must formulate their ideas quickly. Their goal is simple: to be articulate, or to express their ideas clearly. Impromptu speakers must also maintain their poise to convey the impression that they can calmly and coherently speak on any topic.

Impromptu speakers do not prepare evidence folders: They would not have time to look at them, and impromptu topics are not often about current events for which speakers would require evidence. Topics in impromptu speech competitions vary widely and are usually a single word or phrase. Some contests require speakers to respond to a quotation, question, or statement.

From the three topics drawn from an envelope, an impromptu speaker chooses the one he or she knows most about. In most impromptu speech tournaments, speakers have up to five minutes to prepare, but sometimes they must begin speaking right after they choose a topic.

Audience. Judges award each speaker points for content and delivery. Just as in extemporaneous speech contests, the highest-ranking speakers move into the final rounds.

Content and Tone. Use the following suggestions as you prepare for an impromptu speech in a competition.

- Follow a simple structure: an attention-getting introduction, then the main ideas with supporting details, and finally an effective conclusion.
- Use clear, coherent language.
- Try to project confidence.
- Adopt a tone that is appropriate to the topic, from personal topics (responsibility, friends) to formal ones (world hunger, voter apathy).

"The picture's pretty bleak, gentlemen. ... The world's climates are changing, the mammals are taking over, and we all have a brain about the size of a walnut."

ACTIVITY 9 Giving an Impromptu Speech

Work with five or six students. Put at least twenty slips of paper with impromptu speech topics into an envelope. Topics can be single words, phrases, quotations, questions, or statements. Have each person pick three topics and choose one for a two-minute impromptu speech. Allow for five minutes of preparation time. Take turns until each person has given an impromptu speech. Then, discuss how you would evaluate each speech if you were a judge at a competition.

COMMON ERROR

Problem. Students might feel the need to apologize because they are not better prepared to deliver impromptu speeches.

Solution. Explain to students that starting off with an apology makes a speech seem weak and unprofessional. Instead, students should begin speeches with attention-getting introductions that clearly state the topics.

ONGOING ASSESSMENT

Activity 9

You may want to help students develop a checklist (a simplified version of the one on p. 439) to use when evaluating the impromptu speeches. (Consider using the items in the bulleted list at the top of this page.) Then you can base your assessment both on your observations and on students' evaluations.

BUILDING A PORTFOLIO

Videotaped speeches can be a valuable assessment tool for both you and your students. If possible, videotape students' special-occasion speeches and have students keep the videotapes in their portfolios.

EXTENSION

The following activity requires students to consider all of the types of special-occasion speeches covered in this segment. Bring in a newspaper section that lists or describes local community events. First, have students analyze the events to determine the kinds of speeches that might be given at each event. Then ask each student to choose one of the occasions and to develop an appropriate speech. Students can present their speeches in small groups or for the entire class.

GUIDELINES for Special-Occasion Speeches

- Have I chosen a limited topic appropriate for the occasion?
- Have I identified my purpose?
- Have I gathered information to support what I say?
- Have I written an attention-getting opener and a strong conclusion?
- Have I adapted the speech to my audience's needs, knowledge, interests, and expectations?
- Is my speech too long or too short?
- Is my tone appropriate for the occasion?
- Have I practiced the speech enough so that I can deliver it confidently and maintain eye contact with the audience?
- Can I use humor to make my speech more entertaining?

ENRICHMENT

You may want to have students find out if anyone in the school has ever participated in a National Forensic League extemporaneous speech competition. Encourage students to invite the speaker to your class to talk about his or her speaking experience. Who won the competition? Where was it held? What are some helpful hints for others interested in competing?

CLOSURE

Have students discuss the different kinds of speeches they have studied.

EVALUATION  **CHECKLIST**

for Special-Occasion Speeches

Organization:

Did the introduction catch the audience's attention?
Were the speaker's ideas easy to follow?
Did the speaker use good transitions between major points?
Was there an effective conclusion?

Content:

Was the speech an appropriate length for the particular occasion?
Did the speaker provide any necessary background information the audience might need?
Was the content appropriate for the occasion?
Did the speaker consider the audience's interests, needs, and expectations?
Was the tone appropriate for the occasion?

Language:

Did the speaker choose words that created a tone appropriate for the particular occasion?
Did the speaker use words that the audience could understand?
Did the speaker define any technical terms?

Delivery:

Did the speaker seem confident?
Was the speaker's attitude appropriate for the occasion?
Did the speaker look at the audience during the speech?
Was the speaker easy to hear and understand?
Did the speaker pronounce words and names correctly?

Additional Comments:

Evaluation:

Audiovisual Resource Binder

Transparency 32
Evaluation Checklist for Special-Occasion Speeches

◆ Profiles in Communication

Performance Objectives

- To prepare and present a "bon voyage" speech
- To evaluate classmates' "bon voyage" speeches

Teaching the Feature

Before students read the profile on Paul C. Hudson, you may want to ask students who are familiar with Toastmasters to share their information about the organization. After students have read the profile, have them discuss the pros and cons of belonging to such an organization. You might ask if any students would consider joining a local chapter sometime in the future.

Activity Note

You may want to have students review the guidelines on p. 438 and the **Evaluation Checklist** on p. 439 before they prepare their speeches. If you have students evaluate their classmates' speeches with the checklist on p. 439, you can use both your observations and students' evaluations to assess each speech.

PROFILES IN COMMUNICATION

Paul C Hudson

As president of Capital City Toastmasters, Paul C. Hudson presides over a special occasion each time he opens one of his club's weekly meetings. "Toastmasters International has about eight thousand clubs all over the world," he explains. At each meeting, Mr. Hudson introduces the day's Toastmaster, who has the responsibility of introducing several members who give short, timed speeches. Afterwards, each speaker is evaluated orally by another member, who offers constructive criticism about the speech and the delivery.

Toastmasters International, founded in 1924, has developed a series of speech manuals that members can use to sharpen their expertise in speaking. When developing his or her speech, a Toastmaster will use the manual's guidelines to write a speech of a specific type and length.

Toastmasters are often asked to speak on special occasions in the community. For example, they may be requested to write and deliver speeches to motivate people to contribute to community charities. Whatever the occasion, a Toastmaster will gladly and confidently rise to it.

ACTIVITY

A friend in your class has been chosen to be a foreign exchange student. You have been asked to prepare a speech for your friend's going-away party. You want to congratulate your friend, wish him or her well, and express your feelings about the event. Some of your reactions may be difficult to talk about. For example, you will probably wish that your friend were not leaving the country. How will you be honest without detracting from the celebration? Using wording and tone appropriate to the occasion, prepare your "bon voyage" speech. Then present it to the class. Ask your classmates how they think your friend and the other guests at the going-away party would react to your speech.

S•U•M•M•A•R•Y

SPEAKING FOR A SPECIAL OCCASION involves a situation in which the occasion itself sets the tone of the speech and determines its content.

- **Plan a special-occasion speech** by limiting your topic and identifying your purpose and tone according to the occasion. Some special-occasion speeches require a formal tone, while others require an informal tone. Gather information by using idea starters and by talking to other people.
- **Prepare your special-occasion speech** by focusing on your key ideas, supporting your ideas with specifics, eliminating wordiness, and keeping your language and ideas easy to understand.
- **Adapt your speech** to the audience's expectations, attention span, knowledge, needs, and interests.
- **Rehearse your speech** by yourself and before an audience so that you can deliver it without reading it. Mark your speech for pauses, emphasis, and word groupings. Deliver your speech in a relaxed manner, maintaining eye contact and varying your voice. Be sure to pronounce words correctly and to enunciate clearly.
- **Evaluate a special-occasion speech** using the Evaluation Checklist on page 439.
- **Understand that different types of speeches are appropriate** in various special occasions. Be familiar with the kinds of special-occasion speeches presented in this chapter.

CHAPTER **16**

Vocabulary

Look back through this chapter to find the meaning of each of the following terms. Write each term and its meaning in your communication journal.

"after-dinner" speech, *p. 433*
citation, *p. 434*
commemorative speech, *p. 432*
eulogy, *p. 432*
extemporaneous speech, *p. 434*
graduation speech, *p. 427*
impromptu speech, *p. 436*
repetition, *p. 422*
special-occasion speech, *p. 417*
speech of acceptance, *p. 430*
speech of introduction, *p. 428*
speech of presentation, *p. 429*
testimonial speech, *p. 432*
tone, *p. 419*
topicality, *p. 435*

TEACHER'S RESOURCE BINDER

- Chapter 16 Vocabulary

REVIEW QUESTIONS

Answers

1. to inform: introduction; to persuade: competitive extemporaneous; to entertain: "after-dinner"
2. a graduation speech and a speech of introduction; by using serious ideas in complete sentences, by avoiding slang and excessive humor, and by paying attention to structure
3. an "after-dinner" speech and a story; by using slang, humor, idioms, contractions, and incomplete sentences; by being personal; and by paying less attention to structure
4. Because no two people experience an event in exactly the same way, others may provide many specific details.
5. A well-structured speech helps focus the audience's attention and makes the speaker's points easy to follow.

DISCUSSION QUESTIONS

Guidelines for Assessment

Student responses may vary.

1. Students should be able to support their choices with valid reasons.
2. The type of audience and the formality or informality of an occasion help a speaker to decide on the tone and the type of speech to be given.
3. Anecdotes are particularly appropriate in speeches of acceptance, commemorative speeches, and "after-dinner" speeches. Tasteful humor is generally appropriate in a special-occasion speech. Humor may not be appropriate for occasions that derive their strength from formality and seriousness. Generally, the occasion and the audience dictate the appropriateness of humor.
4. Students might interpret the quotation to mean that too much praise lessens its value. A person giving a speech of presentation should not praise the recipient to the extent that the praise has little meaning. A person giving a speech of acceptance should be sincere, but not effusive, in his or her acknowledgments.
5. Your school counselors or principal could be a good source for students who are unfamiliar with the graduation traditions of your school.

CHAPTER **16**

Review Questions

1. Identify two specific purposes a special-occasion speech might have. Give an example of each.
2. Name two types of special-occasion speeches for which a formal tone is appropriate. How would you achieve a formal tone?
3. Name a type of special-occasion speech for which an informal tone is suitable. How would you achieve an informal tone?
4. Why would talking to other people sometimes be helpful in gathering information and details for a special-occasion speech?
5. Why is structure important in a special-occasion speech?
6. What are three considerations you should take into account when adapting your special-occasion speech to your audience?
7. What topics are appropriate in a graduation speech? in a speech of introduction?
8. How are a speech of presentation and a speech of acceptance related?
9. What is the main purpose of a commemorative speech? of an "after-dinner" speech?
10. What is the difference between extemporaneous and impromptu speeches for competition?

Discussion Questions

1. Of all the special-occasion speeches mentioned in this chapter, which one do you think you would be most comfortable giving? Which one would make you feel most uncomfortable? Discuss your responses with your classmates. See if you can find reasons why certain types of speeches make you feel more comfortable.
2. Discuss how the occasion itself determines the type of speech you give in a particular situation. Also discuss how the occasion affects the tone you adopt in your speech.
3. Discuss the role of anecdotes and humor in special-occasion speeches, and tell when both are or are not appropriate.
4. Samuel Johnson, the English essayist and poet, wrote "Praise, like gold and diamonds, owes its value only to its scarcity." First, discuss the meaning of this quotation. Next, discuss how this quotation applies to a speech of presentation. Then, discuss the ways in which this quotation relates to someone who is making a speech of acceptance.
5. Discuss with your classmates the meaning of the ceremony held by your school to commemorate the graduation of the senior class. Who participates in this ceremony? How many speakers usually give speeches, including speeches of introduction? How many speeches could be considered main or featured speeches? What expectations does the audience have of the speeches made on this occasion?

6. the audience's expectations; the audience's attention span; and the audience's knowledge, needs, and interests
7. graduation: congratulating graduates, acknowledging teachers, looking back, looking ahead; introduction: accurate facts about the speaker's qualifications and experience without too much detail or personal information
8. A person honored with a speech of presentation usually gives a speech of acceptance.
9. to mark an important event or to honor a person; to provide entertainment
10. Extemporaneous speakers prepare for thirty minutes and speak for seven. Impromptu speakers prepare for five minutes and speak for five.

ACTIVITIES

1. **Preparing a Graduation Speech.** Prepare a three-minute graduation speech to be given before the graduates of an extracurricular program, such as a museum art class, a gymnastics team, or a community music program. Be sure to include topics that will interest the graduates and their friends and families. Deliver your speech to your classmates. Then ask them to use the Evaluation Checklist on page 439 to determine the strengths and weaknesses of your speech.
2. **Preparing a Speech of Presentation.**
   A. Using a literature or humanities textbook or current magazines and newspapers, select an author, an artist, or a musician you would like to honor. Decide what type of award you would like to bestow on this person. The award may be real or imaginary, serious or humorous. For example, you might choose to award your favorite columnist a Pulitzer Prize. Or, you might "honor" the rock musician whose guitar riffs are the most repetitive, by presenting him or her with a Golden Snore Award.
   B. Prepare a three-minute speech of presentation for the award. In your speech, be sure to explain the significance of the award and to state the reasons why the recipient deserves the honor. Deliver your speech to a group of classmates. Ask them to use the Evaluation Checklist on page 439 to evaluate your speech.
3. **Giving a Commemorative Speech.**
   A. Using a social studies or history textbook, select a historic event that interests you and that you would like to commemorate. If you are not very familiar with the event, do some research to learn more about the event's participants, its causes and outcomes, and its lasting significance.
   B. Prepare a three-minute commemorative speech in which you dedicate a monument erected to honor and remember this historic event. Be sure to take into account your audience's knowledge (or lack of knowledge) of the event. Also, point out what, specifically, makes this event worthy of commemoration. Deliver your speech to a small group of classmates, and ask them to use the Evaluation Checklist on page 439 to evaluate your speech.
4. **Preparing an "After-Dinner" Speech.** Prepare a five-minute "after-dinner" speech for a banquet. For example, you might prepare a speech for your swim team's awards banquet or for your youth group's annual retreat. Deliver your speech to a small group of classmates. After you speak, ask your classmates to evaluate your speech with the Evaluation Checklist on page 439.
5. **Observing and Critiquing Special-Occasion Speeches.** Watch an awards presentation on television. For example, you might choose a ceremony for one of the awards

ACTIVITIES

Guidelines for Assessment

1. Have students announce who their intended audiences are before they deliver their speeches. After students complete each evaluation, you may want to open a discussion about the speech's strengths and weaknesses. Listen to the discussion to determine if students' assessments are on target.
2. A. You may want to check the appropriateness of the awards before students prepare their speeches. Remind students to review the bulleted list of suggestions on p. 430.
   B. If you cannot observe the delivery of every speech, you can base your assessments on the completed checklists.
3. Evaluate the speeches based on the speakers' research and on the criteria in this chapter for giving a commemorative speech.
   A. You may want to look over students' choices of events before students prepare their speeches. Remind students to review the bulleted list of suggestions on p. 432.
   B. If you cannot observe the delivery of every speech, you can base your assessments on the completed checklists.
4. The presentations and the evaluations should give you a good gauge for measuring students' understanding of the "after-dinner" speech.
5. See next page.

Summative Evaluation

Your **Teacher's Resource Binder** contains a reproducible **Chapter 16 Test** that may be used to assess students' mastery of the concepts presented in this chapter.

Portfolio Assessment

For future reference and evaluation you may want to have students keep in their portfolios any skill sheets or evaluation forms that you have used with this chapter along with any other recorded or written materials that students have created.

5. Students' critiques should reflect an understanding of the criteria for presentation speeches and acceptance speeches. Suggest that students refer to the bulleted lists on pp. 430 and 431.

6. Students' standards or criteria should demonstrate a working knowledge of the material in this chapter. Encourage students to consider their past speaking experiences when they develop the standards for others.

7. As each group offers suggestions to its speakers, ask a member of the group to record the suggestions. You can use these notes in your assessments.

8. Assessment should be based on how well students support their opinions. You will also want to consider topicality and the logic of the speeches' structures.

like the ones shown in these photographs or for another prestigious award of your own choosing. Prepare a short written critique of one presentation speech and one acceptance speech you observe during the program. What could each speaker have done differently? Refer to the Evaluation Checklist on page 439 to develop your critiques.

6. **Developing Standards for Impromptu and Extemporaneous Speech Contests.** In impromptu and extemporaneous speaking competitions, judges evaluate each speaker's performance, considering the short preparation time and the tense situation. For each type of speech, develop at least three standards, or criteria, you would use if you were a judge evaluating speakers. Be prepared to explain why speakers should meet each standard in the competition.

7. **Giving an Impromptu Speech.** Using a five-minute preparation time, prepare a two-minute impromptu speech. In your speech, you should try to explain the meaning of any one of the following quotations. Deliver your speech to a small group of your classmates. After you speak, discuss with your classmates specific suggestions for making improvements in your impromptu speaking style.

   a. "This above all: to thine own self be true, / And it must follow, as the night the day, / Thou canst not then be false to any man."
   —William Shakespeare, from *Hamlet*

   b. "Iron rusts from disuse; stagnant water loses its purity and in cold weather becomes frozen; even so does inaction sap the vigor of the mind."
   —Leonardo da Vinci, from *The Notebooks [1508–1518]*

   c. "I started with this idea in my head, 'There's two things I've got a right to . . . death or liberty.'"
   —Sarah Bradford, from *Scenes in the Life of Harriet Tubman*

   d. "'Hope' is the thing with feathers— / That perches in the soul— / And sings the tune without the words— / And never stops—at all—"
   —Emily Dickinson, from *No. 254*

   e. "Conversation . . . is the art of never appearing a bore, of knowing how to say everything interestingly, to entertain with no matter what, to be charming with nothing at all."
   —Guy de Maupassant, from *Sur l'Eau (On the Water)*

8. **Planning an Extemporaneous Speech for a Competition.** Using a thirty-minute preparation time, plan a seven-minute extemporaneous speech that outlines your opinion and reasons that support it. Use the following question for your topic: "Should this state pass a law limiting the times and number of hours teenagers can work during the school year?" In your plan, also indicate how you would gather information to support your reasons.

◆ Real-Life Speaking Situations

PERFORMANCE OBJECTIVES

- To prepare and deliver a three-minute speech of presentation
- To prepare and deliver a two-minute speech of introduction
- To evaluate speeches of introduction

REAL LIFE Speaking Situations

1 Academy Awards, Nobel Prizes, Medals of Honor—all these awards and honors have one thing in common. They all recognize an individual's outstanding achievement in some particular area. Such awards are bestowed at special ceremonies during which presentation speeches are given. Customarily, a presentation speech is brief and formal. It explains the importance of the honor or award, and it states why the recipient deserves it.

You are the student representative on your community's board of education. The board members have asked you to present the community's "Teacher of the Year" award to this year's recipient, Mr. Yarnell, the band director. The award is a plaque that bears this inscription: "With gratitude for your willing leadership and encouragement of all student musicians." The recipient will also receive season tickets to your community symphony. You will present the award at the board's last meeting of the school year. The meeting will also be televised. Prepare and deliver a three-minute speech of presentation for Mr. Yarnell's "Teacher of the Year" award.

2 Parents and teachers sometimes complain that young people today just don't care about social and political issues. In your opinion, how valid is this complaint? How important is it that young people take an interest in politics? What are some ways to make politics more interesting and meaningful to all citizens, including high school students?

Imagine that you are the representative to your school council from your homeroom. To increase awareness of local issues, the student council is sponsoring a series of speeches by representatives in your community. You have been asked to introduce a community representative who will speak to your school at an assembly. Prepare a two-minute speech of introduction for a community representative (select a real person, if possible). In your speech, briefly give the representative's background, and identify the topic about which he or she will speak. You may need to do some research to find specific information about the person or to clearly identify the topic. Then deliver your speech to your class. Afterwards, ask your classmates to evaluate your performance.

ASSESSMENT GUIDELINES

1. After students present their speeches, have each student hand in a rough outline and any notes he or she used either during the speech or for preparation. Assess each student's preparation and how he or she followed the material.
2. You may wish to have students evaluate their own performances. Using the **Evaluation Checklist** on p. 439, students could rate themselves as fair, good, or excellent in each category.

Unit 5 • Democratic Processes

Democratic Processes

Chapter 17
Group Discussion
pp. 448–477

CHAPTER OVERVIEW

Group discussion is a goal-oriented communication in which a small number of people interact face to face to share information, to solve a problem, or to arrive at a decision.

The first segment of this chapter presents steps for planning a group discussion: determining purpose and format; choosing a topic; defining a

TEACHER'S RESOURCE BINDER

The following materials are identified at their point of use in this chapter:

- Skills for Success
  1 *Planning a Group Discussion*
  2 *Developing Types of Discussion Questions*
  3 *Analyzing Leadership Qualities*
  4 *Preparing to Participate*
  5 *Managing Group Conflict*
  6 *Evaluating Group Discussion*
- Chapter 17 Vocabulary
- Chapter 17 Test/Answer Key

AV *Audiovisual Resource Binder*

The following materials are identified at their point of use in this chapter:

- Transparency 33
  Analyzing Discussion Questions
- Transparency 34
  Developing Discussion Outlines
- Transparency 35
  Evaluating a Group Discussion

discussion question that is well-worded, limited, and objective; and preparing an outline.

In the second segment, students will learn to perform the roles of leader, recorder, and participant in a group discussion.

Finally, in the third segment, strategies for managing group conflict, reaching group decisions, and evaluating group discussions are presented.

Introducing the Chapter

Group-discussion skills are important for students in their school work, their personal lives, and their occupational pursuits. Students are likely to be involved in group discussions both in and out of school. Tell students that in this chapter they will learn personal skills to draw on when participating in group discussions.

C H A P T E R 17

Group Discussion

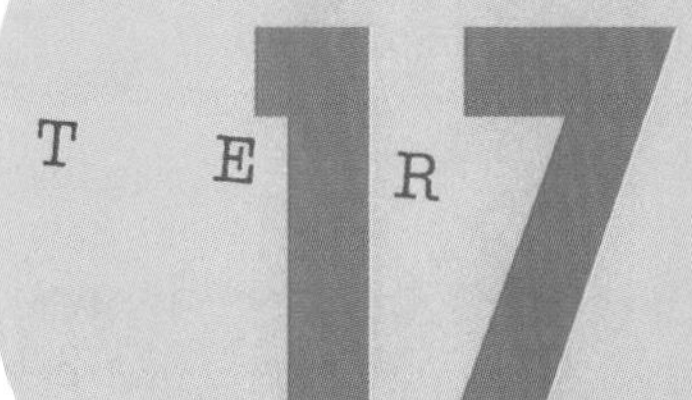

OBJECTIVES

After studying this chapter, you should be able to

1. Define *group discussion.*
2. Plan a discussion by determining a purpose and format, choosing a topic, wording a discussion question, and preparing an outline.
3. Carry out the roles of leader, secretary, and participant in group discussions.
4. Resolve conflict in discussions.
5. Reach group decisions by decree, by voting, or by consensus.
6. Evaluate a discussion.

What Is Group Discussion?

More than likely you have participated in group discussion in many of your cooperative learning projects. **Group discussion** is a goal-oriented form of communication. It is the face-to-face communication of a small number of people who meet for a specific purpose, such as to arrive at a decision, to brainstorm ideas, to share information, or to solve a problem.

In planning a group discussion, it is important to consider the *who, where,* and *when* of the meeting. Five to seven people are enough to stir up a lively discussion but not so many that members will feel uncomfortable. Also, an odd number of members prevents tied votes, or deadlocks. Members should work in a comfortable, well-lighted environment and should sit either in a circle (for a private discussion) or in a semicircle (for a public discussion with an audience). To be effective, members should be well rested and should limit their sessions to short time periods, usually no more than an hour in length.

Bibliography of Additional Materials

Professional Readings

- Beebe, Steven A., and John T. Masterson. ***Communicating in Small Groups: Principles and Practices.*** Glenview, IL: Scott Foresman.
- Brilhart, John K., and Gloria J. Galanes. ***Effective Group Discussion.*** Dubuque, IA: Wm. C. Brown Publishers.
- Johnson, David, and Frank Johnson, eds. ***Joining Together: Group Theory and Group Skills.*** Englewood Cliffs, NJ: Prentice-Hall.
- Johnson, David, et al. ***Circles of Learning: Cooperation in the Classroom.*** Alexandria, VA: Association for Supervision and Curriculum Development.

Audiovisuals

- ***Groupthink***—CRM Films, Carlsbad, CA (videocassette, 22 min.)
- ***Team Building***—CRM Films, Carlsbad, CA (videocassette, 18 min.)
- ***You Know What I Mean?***—CRM Films, Carlsbad, CA (videocassette, 21 min.)

Segment 1 *pp. 450–458*

• Planning a Group Discussion

Performance Objectives

- To brainstorm topics for a group discussion
- To decide on a discussion format to use for each selected topic
- To choose a purpose, format, and discussion topic for a group discussion
- To prepare a discussion question and an outline for a group discussion

Teaching Note

Students may think that a group discussion is only a vehicle for solving problems and that a final decision must always be reached.

Point out that group discussions also allow people to share information, brainstorm, stimulate thought, or strengthen bonds. The desired outcome is not necessarily a final decision or solution; an exchange of ideas and impetus for future ideas are legitimate outcomes.

Planning a Group Discussion

Planning and participating in an effective group discussion means thinking about and dealing with several interrelated parts of the discussion:

- determining a purpose and a format
- choosing a topic
- wording a discussion question
- identifying the types of discussion questions
- preparing an outline

Determining a Purpose and a Format

Members of a discussion group do not meet simply for the sake of discussion. The group has a goal or a purpose, and the discussion is intended to accomplish that goal or purpose. The following chart lists several of the many purposes that group discussions can serve.

Purposes for Discussion	
• to arrive at a solution to a problem	• to negotiate agreements
• to brainstorm ideas	• to resolve conflicts
• to learn cooperatively	• to share information
• to make a decision	• to stimulate thought or action
• to make plans	• to strengthen bonds among people

Teacher's Resource Binder

Skills for Success 1
Planning a Group Discussion

Motivation

Write the following statement on the chalkboard: "Whether we realize it or not, we rarely make decisions alone; usually, we obtain information from others before making a final decision." Ask students to discuss the statement in terms of how they choose clothing to buy, a movie to see, a class to take, a book to read, or a way to handle a social problem. Lead them to see that they have informal group discussions on the way to school, at parties, and in the lunchroom.

To be successful, your discussion group needs more than a purpose, or reason, for meeting. You must also choose an appropriate **discussion format.** Group discussion formats may be either public or private.

Public Discussion Formats. When group discussions are held in front of an audience, you can use one of the following public discussion formats: panel, symposium, or forum.

- A **panel format** is used when a group of experts discusses a topic to provide information and opinions that another group can use to reach a decision or to find a solution.

  EXAMPLE: A town council invites a panel of experts, such as engineers, waste disposal experts, and environmentalists, to discuss the plans for building a new incinerator plant.

- A **symposium format** is used when several people present short, prepared speeches on the same topic and then discuss among themselves the ideas presented in the speeches.

  EXAMPLE: A university invites a symposium of people, such as a campus police officer, a college student, and a professor, to discuss ways to improve campus security.

- A **forum format** is used when a panel or a symposium is opened up to questions or comments from the audience.

  EXAMPLE: A company invites a symposium of productivity and time-management experts to discuss ways of improving worker efficiency. After the experts have presented their prepared speeches, the moderator invites questions from the audience.

TEACHING THE LESSON

You may wish to begin the lesson by reading aloud the five items listed at the beginning of the segment under **Planning a Group Discussion** on p. 450. Point out that these items will be covered in this chapter.

Have students discuss the purposes listed on p. 450. Make sure students understand that the purpose usually precedes the discussion. In other words, a problem needs to be solved, a conflict must be resolved, or a decision needs to be made. These situations lead people to come together for a group discussion.

In discussing private and public formats, point out that content usually determines the choice. If the town, city, or community wants to know about the issue, a public discussion will be held. In school, club, or family matters, a private format is usually appropriate.

MAKING CONNECTIONS

Mass Media

You may want to have students watch TV talk shows to analyze the various types of group discussions. Explain to students that a forum always includes either a panel or a symposium.

Private Discussion Formats. When group discussions are held in closed session, you can use one of the following private discussion formats: free-form, moderated free-form, standing committee, ad hoc committee, round-table, or progressive.

- A **free-form format** is used when group members discuss a topic at will in no particular order.
- A **moderated free-form format** is used when a moderator, or leader, introduces the topic to be discussed and recognizes individuals to speak.
- A **standing committee format** is used when a small group of people is asked to study problems that fall within their scope of duties or functions and then to make recommendations to the organization of which they are a part.

  EXAMPLE: An organization asks its budget committee to discuss a problem related to dues. The members of the committee discuss the problem in a private meeting and then present their proposed solution to the organization's leaders or perhaps to the entire organization.
- An **ad hoc committee format** is used when a group is formed to study a single issue or to accomplish a single task. Unlike a standing committee, which handles various issues or tasks over a long period of time, an ad hoc committee is formed to do a particular job and then is disbanded when its job is completed.

  EXAMPLE: A college board of trustees forms an ad hoc committee to search for a new college president.
- A **round-table format** is used when each member of a group discussion gives a brief report on some aspect of a topic and then the group as a whole discusses the separate reports.

  EXAMPLE: A museum of African American culture holds a round-table discussion on "African Americans in the Arts." After reports by each member on the different arts—for example, music, dance, painting, sculpture, and theater—the group as a whole discusses the breadth and depth of the African American contribution to the arts in the United States.
- A **progressive format** is used when a large group of people is divided into smaller groups, each of which discusses a different aspect of the topic. This format is particularly helpful when everyone in the group is not prepared to discuss the entire question.

Encourage students to brainstorm questions of fact, value, or policy that affect them personally. Possibilities are questions about class procedures, dating, curfews, and exams.

To prepare students for **Activity 1** on p. 454, pick a topic and guide the class through the process of choosing a discussion format for the topic. Then assign **Activity 1** as independent practice.

As you present **Wording a Discussion Question** on p. 454, **Identifying Types of Discussion Questions** on p. 455, and **Preparing an Outline** on p. 456, discuss the examples in the textbook. Next, using the topic you used to prepare students for **Activity 1,** guide the class through the steps of creating a discussion question, identifying its type, and preparing an outline. Students should then be ready to complete **Activity 2** on p. 458 as independent practice.

"Oddly enough, language has proved no problem."

Choosing a Topic

Without a topic, there is nothing to discuss. A discussion can be held on almost any topic. Often the topic is chosen for the group.

EXAMPLES:

1. A principal asks a group of teachers to find possible solutions to the problem of an overcrowded student parking lot.
2. A nonprofit organization asks a group of architects to devise a workable plan for adding a new wing to the public library.

Sometimes a group is asked to select its own topic. If you are in a group that is given this opportunity, here are a few guidelines that you should keep in mind to help you choose an appropriate topic.

HOW TO *Choose a Discussion Topic*

1. **Choose an interesting topic.** The topic should be interesting to all or most members of the discussion group and to the audience if the discussion is to be public.
2. **Choose a topic about which group members are informed.** The members of the discussion group should know enough about the topic to be able to make a valuable contribution to the discussion.
3. **Choose a significant topic.** Members should feel that time spent discussing the topic is time well spent.
4. **Choose a properly limited topic.** The topic should be narrow enough to be dealt with effectively in the time available.

Assessment

To assess students' understanding of how to choose topics and formats, have a representative from each group share the group's topics and formats with the class. You may want to have groups exchange the outlines and discussion questions developed in **Activity 2** on p. 458. Students will benefit from comparing their work to that of other students.

Reteaching

If students are having difficulty understanding what is meant by questions of fact, value, and policy, ask them to bring to class clippings about a current issue in the news. Ask your class, "What do we know about this issue?" List whatever facts are available. Then ask, "How do different groups feel about it?" List the pertinent values and the criteria on which they are based.

Ongoing Assessment

Activity 1

Have each group present a list of the ten topics and the format to be used for each topic. Challenge students to come up with a wide range of topics. Give credit based on the originality of the topics and on the appropriateness of the formats.

Writing to Learn

Have students explain the following statement in their communication journals: A discussion topic must be both interesting and significant. What is an example of a topic that is interesting but not significant? Significant but not interesting? Encourage students to list topics they consider to be both interesting and significant.

AV ▶ Audiovisual Resource Binder

Transparency 33
Analyzing Discussion Questions

Activity 1

Choosing Topics and Formats

Form a discussion group of five to seven classmates. Brainstorm to come up with a list of ten group discussion topics. For example, you might list censorship of movies as one topic. Then decide within your group which discussion format you would use to discuss each topic.

Wording a Discussion Question

Once you have chosen the topic for your group discussion, you will need to phrase, or word, the topic as a question. A well-phrased discussion question should meet the following requirements.

1. The question's wording should be clear and concise. If the wording is vague, the group will not know what it is trying to achieve or how to proceed.

VAGUE: Should the curriculum be looked into?
CONCISE: Should each course in the high school's curriculum be reevaluated to make sure that it meets the goals set by the state board of education?

2. The question's wording should promote objective discussion. If the wording is subjective, it could sway the group to reach the answer or solution implied by the question.

SUBJECTIVE: Should our ridiculously low standards for high school athletic eligibility be raised?
OBJECTIVE: Should our high school's minimum standards for athletic eligibility be revised?

3. The question's wording should allow for more than a yes or no answer. If the wording requires only a yes or no answer, the group may not fully discuss all of the issues of the topic.

REQUIRES YES OR NO: Should a student who cheats on a test receive an F?
REQUIRES A DISCUSSION: What should the policy be for dealing with students who cheat on tests?

In your communication journal, keep a list of questions that could be used for a group discussion. Add ideas to this list as they occur to you.

Finally ask, "What should we do?" List possible policies that could be adopted.

Identifying Types of Discussion Questions

There are three major types of discussion questions: questions of fact, questions of value, and questions of policy. Understanding the category that a discussion question belongs to helps the group to determine an effective organization, or plan, for dealing with the topic.

- A **question of fact** asks for evidence that can be gathered from observation, experimentation, or authoritative sources to determine what is true.

  EXAMPLES:
  1. How much has the space program cost Americans, and what return have they received for their investment?
  2. What effect did the arrival of the Europeans have on the native peoples of the Americas in the late fifteenth and early sixteenth centuries?

- A **question of value** asks for an evaluation of one or more persons, places, things, or ideas and often contains words such as *effective, good, worthy, better,* or their opposites. To answer a question of value, a group must make a judgment.

  EXAMPLES:
  1. Has the space program brought about better living conditions for ordinary Americans?
  2. What valuable aspects of indigenous culture disappeared as a result of contacts between Europeans and the native peoples of the Americas?

- A **question of policy** asks what action, if any, should be taken and often includes the word *should.* By far the greatest number of questions examined by discussion groups in everyday situations are questions of policy.

  EXAMPLES:
  1. Should funding for the space program be increased, decreased, or maintained at current levels?
  2. What efforts should be made to restore parts of the indigenous cultures that were destroyed by the coming of Europeans to the Americas?

COOPERATIVE LEARNING

Divide the class into small groups. Ask each group to decide on a discussion topic. (Possible topics are extracurricular functions, after-school jobs, and peer pressure.) Have groups exchange topics. Then have each group develop the topic into a discussion question. Have groups exchange topics again. This time, have each group use the criteria on p. 454 to evaluate the discussion question that they have received.

BUILDING A PORTFOLIO

Have students look through newspapers and magazines for current accounts of important questions under discussion. Have the students cut out the articles and label them "fact," "value," or "policy" questions. Encourage students to save the clippings in their portfolios for further ideas for group discussions.

TEACHER'S RESOURCE BINDER

Skills for Success 2
Developing Types of Discussion Questions

EXTENSION

Have students watch a public discussion on television. Have them identify the topics, formats, and discussion questions; then have the students classify the discussion questions.

MEETING **INDIVIDUAL** NEEDS

An Alternative Approach

Some students may have trouble understanding how a discussion outline works. Explain to them that an outline works like a map.

If you were to drive from California to Florida, a map would show you the fastest and easiest way to get there. If you were on a leisurely vacation, though, you might not want to adhere to a strict schedule. When an interesting side trip suggested itself, you could get off your planned route and return to it later.

Point out that using a discussion outline is much like using a map: The outline allows the group to get off the track for a while to explore new ideas but still leads the group toward a goal.

Audiovisual Resource Binder

Transparency 34

Developing Discussion Outlines

Preparing an Outline

The next step in planning a discussion is to prepare an outline. A **discussion outline** usually consists of questions about the topic that the group members should address. Group members should decide on the specific wording and order of these questions or issues for the outline they will follow. Very few groups follow an outline point by point throughout a discussion. However, following the main points of the outline will help group members avoid straying from the topic and from their purpose. There are three ways to prepare an outline, depending on whether the discussion question is one of fact, of value, or of policy.

Outline for Questions of Fact. The main points in this type of outline should ask group members

1. to define key words
2. to find information that supports the definitions
3. to determine what circumstances might affect the answer

Discussion Question: Does our high school adequately prepare students for their lives after graduation?

I. What do we mean by *adequately?*

II. How can we measure students' employment or academic experiences after graduation?

III. What effect might current economic conditions have on students' lives after graduation?

Enrichment

Ask your students these questions: How do doctors figure out the best way to treat a disease? How do lawyers develop plans to defend clients?

Have students recall TV stories or movies that show lawyers conferring to develop plans or that show doctors meeting with a medical team to solve a problem.

Promote a brief discussion of reasons why professionals rely so heavily on group discussion. [One person doesn't know all the variables or possibilities. Much research is available, but no one person has a command of it all. Problem solving is hard work; group members support each other, give each other energy, and keep each other focused.]

Outline for Questions of Value. The main points in this type of outline should ask group members

1. to determine the criteria, or standards of value, for making the judgment
2. to determine the information relevant to the discussion question
3. to match the information with the criteria
4. to determine what circumstances might affect the decision

Discussion Question: Is our high school the best high school in the area?

I. What are the criteria for determining the "best" high school?
II. What facts need to be considered in comparing our high school to other high schools in the area?
III. Do the facts show that our high school meets more of the criteria than other high schools in the area meet?
IV. Are there any other circumstances that affect the evaluation?

Outline for Questions of Policy. The main points in this type of outline are based on John Dewey's five steps of reflective thinking. These steps are particularly useful if the group purpose is to solve a problem. Group members should

1. define the problem
2. analyze the problem
3. suggest possible solutions
4. select the best solution
5. suggest ways of carrying out the solution

Discussion Question: What should be done to lower student absenteeism in our high school?

I. How many students are absent each day?
II. What are the effects of absenteeism?
III. What are some possible solutions to the absenteeism problem?
IV. Which solution will reduce the problem and limit its effects?
V. How will the solution be carried out?

Teaching Note

John Dewey (1859–1952) was an American educator and philosopher who had a strong influence on education in the first half of the century. He believed that learning must address the interests of children. He discouraged memorization of facts and encouraged problem solving and reflective thinking. While these ideas seem fairly commonplace today, they were revolutionary in Dewey's time.

CLOSURE

Have students list criteria to use in choosing a discussion topic. Then have students list the types of discussion formats and the types of discussion questions.

ONGOING ASSESSMENT

Activity 2

Have groups exchange their discussion questions and outlines. Ask the groups to evaluate each other's work. Are the discussion questions well thought out? Are the question types (fact, value, or policy) properly categorized? Are the outlines well developed? Have each group support its responses.

Because no two discussion questions are the same, no two outlines will follow exactly the same format. Each of the outlines that have been provided on the preceding pages applies only to the specific discussion question that it illustrates. However, as you can tell from these examples, every outline should help the discussion group to

- define key terms
- present relevant information
- address all relevant facets of the question
- allow for opposing views
- conclude with a tangible outcome

ACTIVITY 2 Planning a Discussion

Form a discussion group with four or six of your classmates. With the other members of your group, decide on a purpose, format, and discussion topic. If your group has difficulty deciding on a topic, you may want to review the information on how to choose a discussion topic on page 453. Then write a discussion question on your topic and tell whether the question is a question of fact, a question of value, or a question of policy. Finally, work as a group to develop a tentative outline for a discussion of your topic.

Segment 2 *pp. 459–465*

• Performing Different Roles in a Discussion

Performance Objectives

- To identify and analyze a particular style of leadership
- To hold a problem-solving group discussion

Performing Different Roles in a Discussion

Each member of a discussion group has some role, or task, to perform. In most discussion groups, there are three distinct roles: the leader, the secretary or recorder, and the participants.

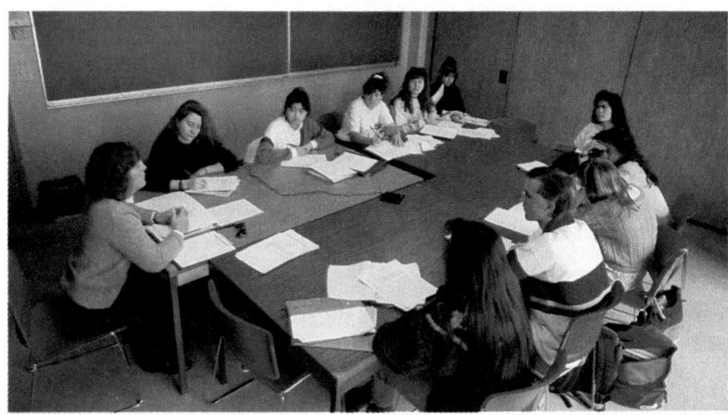

Leading a Discussion

Leadership is the ability to guide a group toward its goal. When a person is appointed leader, he or she may adopt one of the following styles of leadership.

Styles of Leadership

Style	Description	Advantages	Disadvantages
Laissez-faire (or **nondirective**) **leadership**	responsibilities are shared by all members of the group	works well if several members assume the leadership role	may not provide sufficient guidance
Authoritarian (or **directive**) **leadership**	responsibilities are given to one leader	works well if time is short and all members want or need total direction	can be oppressive, create resentments, and hinder communication
Democratic (or **supportive**) **leadership**	leader suggests procedures, asks other members for ideas	works well if members are willing to contribute	may take too long; can be ineffective if members do not contribute

Additional Activity

Divide the class into two or three groups. Assign each group a task such as determining the average height of the members of the class. After they achieve their goals, encourage members of the groups to discuss specific difficulties, solutions, and instances of interaction that took place. Discuss whether a leader emerged. If so, how? Was a leader appointed? How? Was the group leaderless? If so, by decision or by lack of need? Finally, discuss with the class how working in a group either helped or hindered completion of the task.

Teaching Note

Laissez faire is a French phrase that translates literally as "let do." It is an economic theory that states that the government should not interfere with decisions made in an open market. Ask students how the sense of this economic theory applies to leading a group discussion.

Teacher's Resource Binder

Skills for Success 3
Analyzing Leadership Qualities

MOTIVATION

Write the word *leader* on the chalkboard. Underneath it write some common synonyms: *chief, head, boss, superior, guide, ruler, master,* and *motivator.* Ask students which of these synonyms might describe a discussion leader. Promote a lively discussion. [Most students will agree that *head, guide,* and *motivator* partially describe a discussion leader.] Point out that the role of a discussion leader is one of the topics for study in this unit.

CRITICAL THINKING

Analysis

Discuss with students their views on leadership. What constitutes leadership? Do they believe that leadership is a talent that one is born with or that it is an ability that can be developed? What qualities are most important in a leader? Have a student write the main points of the discussion on the chalkboard.

Cultural Diversity

Students tend to function well when the curriculum is made relevant to their experiences. Therefore, as often as possible, create a link between information being presented and the students' native cultures. For example, when discussing styles of leadership, encourage students to comment on the predominant styles of leadership in their native countries. What have been the outcomes politically, socially, and economically of various types of leadership? Ask for specific examples.

A leader's responsibilities include selecting a time and place to meet, distributing an outline in advance of the meeting, and making sure that the meeting place is set up properly. When conducting a group discussion, a leader is responsible for

- introducing the discussion
- keeping the discussion moving
- moderating the discussion
- keeping the discussion on track
- concluding the discussion

Introducing the Discussion. Usually, the leader introduces the discussion question and reviews the tentative outline. After a brief discussion of the outline, the group may decide to change it or to follow it closely. Then the group leader presents any essential background information that the group needs and moderates a brief discussion of key terms related to the discussion question.

Keeping the Discussion Moving. An effective leader keeps the discussion moving by having a prepared list of questions that are related to the group's outline and that encourage others to contribute their own ideas, facts, and opinions.

An effective leader also summarizes when the group reaches a decision or agreement. For example, the leader may say, "Then we are all agreed that the class gift will be a world atlas for the library." By summarizing, the leader helps the group keep track of its progress.

"And now at this point in the meeting I'd like to shift the blame away from me and onto someone else."

TEACHING THE LESSON

You may wish to use the chart on p. 459 to illuminate the very different kinds of leadership styles that can be effective. If students feel that the democratic style is the only acceptable one, help them think of examples of special situations that justify another kind of leadership.

Present **Leading a Discussion** on pp. 459–461 by having a volunteer read the text aloud. To prepare students for **Activity 3** on p. 462, show a videotape of a meeting of some group. Lead the class in analyzing the leader's style by using the questions in **Activity 3,** and then assign **Activity 3** as independent practice.

Continue the discussion of roles by presenting the material on pp. 462–465 on the roles of secretary and participant. As you discuss the preparation required of participants, ask students to consider real-world discussions such as those 

Moderating the Discussion. Another important responsibility of the group leader is making sure that everyone has an equal chance to participate. The leader should recognize speakers, solicit reactions from members who have not contributed, and moderate interchanges between members.

Moderating interchanges between members sometimes means calming tensions that arise. In any good discussion, some group members are likely to pursue their points aggressively. An effective leader breaks in before individuals become angry.

EXAMPLES:

1. When one person interrupts another person, the leader might say, "Kim, I don't think you are letting José make his point. Would you go over that again, José?"
2. When two members are building up to an argument, the leader might say, "You two are on opposite sides of this issue, but let's discuss possible points of agreement."

Keeping the Discussion on Track. Whenever a group discussion veers off course, the leader should steer the conversation back to the question and issues at hand. In this way the leader helps to ensure that the group will accomplish its purpose.

Concluding the Discussion. Accomplishing the purpose of the discussion often requires taking a final vote or summarizing what has been said. It is the group leader's responsibility to conduct the vote and to summarize the major points made during the entire discussion. Sometimes a leader may ask the group's secretary to summarize the discussion. After the vote and summary, the leader gives members a chance to comment on the summary and modify it.

INTEGRATING THE LANGUAGE ARTS

Literature Link

Obtain a copy of Reginald Rose's play "Twelve Angry Men" or a videotape of the movie based on the play. Have students analyze the role played by each juror. How did a leader emerge? Was his leadership effective?

held in the United Nations and in Congress. Point out that the welfare of many people may depend on the effectiveness of an individual participant.

For guided practice, model for the class the process of defining a problem as a clearly stated question. Then assign **Activity 4** on p. 465 as independent practice.

ASSESSMENT

Use students' performances on **Activities 3** and **4** to assess students' understanding of the material in this segment. Have a representative from each group share the group's problem and solutions with the class.

ONGOING ASSESSMENT

Activity 3

Students should be able to explain how they arrived at their conclusions by citing material from this segment. Evaluate the analyses to see if students understand the styles of leadership.

Analyzing Leadership

Listen to a group discussion in a class, at work, or in a club meeting. What kind of leadership style does the leader use: laissez-faire, authoritarian, or democratic? How can you tell? What are some examples that illustrate that kind of style? How effective is the leader? How do you account for the leader's effectiveness or ineffectiveness? If you had been the leader, what would you have done differently? Share your findings with your classmates.

Serving as a Secretary, or Recorder

Sometimes members of a discussion group agree on six or eight points during a meeting, but a week later no one remembers precisely what those decisions were. A good written record can eliminate confusion and prevent disagreement.

A **secretary,** or **recorder,** for the group should record

- major points of agreement or decisions made
- definitions of key terms
- issues that the group wishes to return to at a later time
- major points of disagreement
- issues that seem important during the discussion

At the end of the discussion, the secretary will either record the summary given by the group leader or present a summary at the leader's request.

RETEACHING

Some students may have difficulty listening critically to others in the group. Such students may benefit from watching a videotape in which a group discussion is key to solving a problem. Begin by having students view the entire discussion while they take notes on what the speakers say. Then repeat the video in segments. Stop to discuss the reasons given for certain statements, any facts that are contradicted by other facts, and statements that beg for proof.

Participating in a Discussion

Participating in a discussion is more than just being present. Communicating effectively in a group discussion involves

- preparing to participate
- taking an active part
- listening carefully
- listening critically
- respecting all group members
- using an appropriate speaking voice

Preparing to Participate. Before group members take part in a discussion, they should prepare for the discussion by

- studying the outline
- thinking about the discussion question
- doing research on the discussion question, if necessary

Research can include considering one's own experiences, asking others for information and opinions about the discussion question, and studying relevant materials in a library or media center. [See Chapter 10 for more information on research.]

Before the group discussion, evaluate your understanding of the discussion outline, the discussion question, and any background research. Then take some time to strengthen any area in which you are weak. You are reasonably well prepared for a discussion if you have completed the tasks in the following chart.

HOW TO Prepare for a Group Discussion

1. **Define the topic to be discussed or the problem to be solved.** Know exactly what it is that the group must make decisions about.
2. **Analyze the problem.** Break the discussion question down into its parts.
3. **Evaluate the facts you have gathered.** Separate fact from opinion. Eliminate facts that are not relevant to the ideas being considered.
4. **Sort your notes.** Select the most important facts and arrange them in a logical order.
5. **Identify incomplete information.** Make plans to complete your research.
6. **Consider several different solutions.** Think of a number of different ways to resolve the problem.
7. **Keep an open mind.** Don't decide the issue until you have heard all the facts.

INTEGRATING THE LANGUAGE ARTS

Library Link

Remind students to start with their experiences and thoughts when preparing for a group discussion. Have students write down their ideas and opinions about a discussion topic and then have them go to the library for more information. In the library, they can look through encyclopedias, almanacs, atlases, biographical sources, dictionaries, newspapers, and magazines to check their information and to obtain new information pertinent to the discussion topic.

TEACHER'S RESOURCE BINDER

Skills for Success 4
Preparing to Participate

EXTENSION

Have students discuss the leader's obligation to make sure every group member has an equal chance to participate. Let them recall examples of teachers, coaches, club leaders, etc., who had excellent skills in this area. What did those leaders do and say? Why were these actions effective? How did the groups feel about the leaders?

MEETING INDIVIDUAL NEEDS

An Alternative Approach

Some students may already be comfortable with their responsibilities in group discussions. You could have these students observe a group discussion to perform a more sophisticated analysis of the roles members play in the group. One person may assume many roles and some roles may defy categorization. Provide the following list to see if students can recognize these roles as they are played:

1. information/opinion seeker
2. information/opinion giver
3. summarizer
4. procedural technician
5. reality tester
6. boundary tester
7. mediator

TEACHING NOTE

Students may let personal feelings about other group members affect the discussions. To avoid this pitfall, remind students to stay focused on the issues and to put personal feelings, positive or negative, aside during the discussions.

Taking an Active Part. During the discussion, participate fully. Share information that you have gathered about the discussion topic, ask questions often to clarify what other group members are saying, and respond directly to the statements made by other group members.

Listening Carefully. Participants in discussions often concentrate so hard on what they want to say that they do not listen closely to other group members. Yet, some of the best participants are those who concentrate on understanding what is being said. This allows them to ask penetrating questions, to give appropriate examples, and to recognize areas of agreement or disagreement.

Listening Critically. Listening critically involves weighing and evaluating comments made by other group members. You can do this by asking yourself the following questions.

- What was the source of the information presented, and was it reliable?
- What were the reasons, or bases, for that conclusion or opinion?
- Are any facts or ideas contradictory?
- Does the conclusion or opinion follow logically from the evidence presented?

As you listen to other group members, take notes on what they say. Doing so will help you to avoid misinterpreting other speakers' statements and to refer specifically to what other speakers have said when you are speaking.

Enrichment

Find out if any parents of your students are involved in policy-making groups at work or in the community. Invite one of these parents to share his or her experiences with the class. Make sure your guest knows the topics students have covered in this chapter. Encourage the guest to offer personal experiences that make these speech principles come alive for students.

Closure

Ask students to name three styles of leadership [laissez faire, authoritarian, and democratic]. Then ask students to name some responsibilities of discussion group members [preparing, taking an active part, listening carefully and critically, respecting all group members, and using an appropriate speaking voice]

Respecting All Group Members. When you are in disagreement with someone else in a group, you may have difficulty restraining negative emotions. However, doing so is essential to the effectiveness of the group.

- Don't stifle group creativity by making negative evaluations of others' ideas.
- Let others finish talking before you comment.
- Even if you feel frustrated, avoid becoming abusive or short-tempered.
- Never make personal remarks. Instead, focus your comments on facts and issues.
- Show in your attitude that you respect others' opinions, values, beliefs, and ideas.

Using an Appropriate Speaking Voice. In all discussions, public or private, it is important that you

- speak loudly enough to be heard
- enunciate clearly
- adopt a tone that is appropriate for the audience and the occasion of the discussion

Solving Problems Through Group Discussion

In your discussion group, brainstorm a list of problems that exist in your school or community. Then select one of the problems and follow these steps to arrive at a possible solution.

1. Define the problem as a clearly stated question that contains one main idea. For example: *How can we stop automobile thefts from occurring in the school parking lots?*
2. Analyze the problem by examining its details. For example: *Under what specific circumstances have automobile thefts occurred? Have there been witnesses? Have students kept their cars locked?*
3. Determine possible solutions. Brainstorm as many solutions as possible—no matter how bizarre and far-fetched some may seem—to encourage creativity among all participants.
4. Select the best solution or combination of solutions. Consider how much the solution will cost, how easily it can be implemented, and whether it will create other problems.
5. Present a brief summary to your class of the problem your group has discussed and the solution or solutions suggested.

Meeting Individual Needs

Students with Special Needs

Students with behavioral or learning problems may feel uncomfortable in group discussions. To help put students at ease, select the members of the groups carefully; make sure there are students in the group with whom the special-needs students feel comfortable. Also, provide any necessary background information to the students so that they are able to discuss the topics. You may want to set a three-minute time limit for each person to ensure that everyone has an equal opportunity to speak. Another effective measure is for you to participate in the discussion to model appropriate behavior.

Ongoing Assessment

Activity 4

You may want to have each group do a self-evaluation. Ask students to give their groups a 1 (fair), 2 (good), or 3 (excellent) on each of the five steps in the activity.

Segment 3 pp. 466–471

- Managing Group Conflict
- Reaching a Group Decision
- Evaluating Group Discussion

Performance Objectives

- To analyze conflict in a group discussion
- To analyze a group's decision-making process
- To evaluate a group discussion

Common Error

Problem. Some group members may think that recognizing and resolving conflict during a discussion is solely the responsibility of the leader.

Solution. Remind students that recognizing conflict within the group is the responsibility of all group members, not just the leader. By recognizing the conflict and acting to resolve it quickly, the entire group can move on to meeting its goal.

Managing Group Conflict

Conflict is a form of disagreement. In any group discussion, conflict may arise between members of the group. Some conflict is desirable because it leads group members to put forward their best efforts and arguments. However, too much conflict can make constructive discussion impossible. To prevent conflict from becoming disruptive, group members need to

- recognize when conflict is developing
- diagnose the nature of the conflict
- help the group to defuse or resolve the conflict

Recognizing Conflict

Conflict often begins innocently as a genuine disagreement over some point.

EXAMPLE: In a meeting of the editorial board of a school newspaper, two editors might disagree about which of two stories deserves the leading place on the first page. If their agreement remains a healthy exchange about the pros and cons of the two choices, there is no problem. However, if the disagreement goes beyond an objective weighing of the two positions, someone, usually the group leader, will recognize that a disruptive conflict is developing.

One sure sign of disruptive conflict is the unwillingness of one group member to hear another out. Other signs include the use of derogatory remarks rather than logical argument and the inability or unwillingness of one group member to recognize the worth or reasonableness of another member's statement or idea.

Motivation

Write the words *debate* and *discussion* on the chalkboard. Tell students that in a debate, two sides clearly oppose each other. In a group discussion, the idea is to discuss differences until the group can agree on a single solution or policy.

However, groups can become divided as they discuss topics. Tell students that managing conflict is the subject of this segment.

Teaching the Lesson

Have students read the material on group conflict. Be sure they understand that conflict is to be expected in a lively group discussion. It is a sign that group members have brought many points of view to the discussion.

After students complete the **Communication Journal** activity (p. 468), review their journal entries. If any students seem unclear about conflict issues, 

Diagnosing and Resolving Conflict

Once conflict is recognized, it should be diagnosed so that it can be resolved. Usually this means redirecting the attention of the people who are in conflict toward the issue at hand.

Managing Group Conflict

Problem	Cause	Possible Solution
Group members arguing about what to discuss next	Conflict concerning outline for discussion	Refer to outline for discussion.
Group members arguing about a point that has been discussed	Conflict over differences in recollection	Read record of discussion, and review facts and reasoning.
Group members arguing about whether something is true	Conflict concerning factual information	Analyze and evaluate information; if necessary, find additional supporting information.
Group members arguing over the meaning or significance of facts or other points of discussion	Conflict over interpretation	Analyze facts or points of discussion and their relationships to each other and to the topic of discussion.
Group members arguing over what is "more important" or "better"	Conflict concerning value of information	Identify and establish criteria for determining value of information.
Group members arguing about solution to question	Conflict over goals, methods of discussion, or results of discussion	Review and evaluate goals, methods used to reach solutions, and solutions.
Group members interrupting	Group members being disrespectful	Remind group of purpose of discussion and call on all members to show tolerance and respect.
Group members trying to defeat one another rather than focusing on ideas or issues	Group members competing rather than cooperating	Focus attention on the ideas or issues being disputed; remind group members that they should attack the problem or question, not one another.

Cooperative Learning

Divide the class into small groups. Have each group brainstorm polite ways of phrasing statements or questions to help resolve group conflicts. You could help students get started by giving them an example such as the following one: When a group member interrupts, you can say, "It's great that you're enthusiastic, but I think Maria needs a chance to finish explaining her point." The class may wish to make a list of the most effective statements or questions developed by their groups.

Teacher's Resource Binder

Skills for Success 5
Managing Group Conflict

you may want to guide them through analyzing the television programs by using the **Managing Group Conflict** chart on p. 467.

Model **Activity 5** with a group discussion from your life to show students how to analyze conflict. Then assign **Activity 5** as independent practice.

As you lead into the material on decision making, point out that an effective leader shows respect to all group members. Such a group leader is most likely to be effective when it is time to set aside differences and reach a consensus.

Have a volunteer read aloud **Reaching a Group Decision.** To prepare students for **Activity 6** on p. 470, again model the process with an example from your life. Then assign **Activity 6** as independent practice.

To teach the material on evaluating a group discussion, you could discuss the material with the class and diagram the class discussion as it

Watch a television discussion program. Make notes in your journal about any conflicts that arose during the discussion. Determine what caused the conflict in each case and then note what could have been done to resolve it. Also note whether the members of the discussion group and the moderator of the group dealt with the conflict effectively.

Ongoing Assessment

Activity 5

Students should be able to support their answers based on the material in this segment. Evaluate answers to see if students understand how to diagnose and resolve group conflict. Reteach the material if necessary.

Integrating the Language Arts

Vocabulary Link

Tell students that another way a decision can be reached is by compromise. A compromise occurs when each member of a group gives up a certain part of the solution he or she wants. In exchange, each member gets a part of the solution that he or she favors. Have students discuss examples of compromises they have made in their lives.

ACTIVITY 5 Analyzing Conflict in Group Discussions

Recall a group discussion in which you participated and in which conflicts developed among group members. What were the factors that contributed to the conflicts? How effective were the group leader and the other members of the group in dealing with the conflicts? Were the conflicts resolved? If so, how? If not, what do you think could have been done? Share your experiences and your views with your classmates.

Reaching a Group Decision

Very often, the major goal of a group is to reach a decision. Groups usually arrive at decisions in one of three ways: by decree, by voting, or by consensus.

Decision by Decree

A decision by **decree** occurs when the group leader dictates the group's decision. Often when a group is being run in a directive, authoritarian way, the leader will listen to group comments and then state a decision. Decision by decree is quick and easy, but it tends to be counterproductive because it lowers group morale. If the members of a group have no voice in the decision making, then they are unlikely to work hard to carry out the decision.

Decision by Voting

There are times when a group just cannot seem to agree on key points, and yet the group must arrive at a decision. In such circumstances, the group should take a **vote.** Before the group votes, its occurs. This process will also provide guided practice. Assign **Activity 7** on p. 471 as independent practice.

Assessment

Evaluate students' understanding of the material in this segment by assessing the responses to **Activities 5–7.** You may want to have students share their responses in small groups rather than with the whole class.

leader should state clearly the options being voted on. The option that receives a **majority** (more than half) of the votes wins. Unfortunately, voting inevitably results in winners and losers. Since losers can sometimes become disgruntled, voting is not always the ideal way to come to a decision.

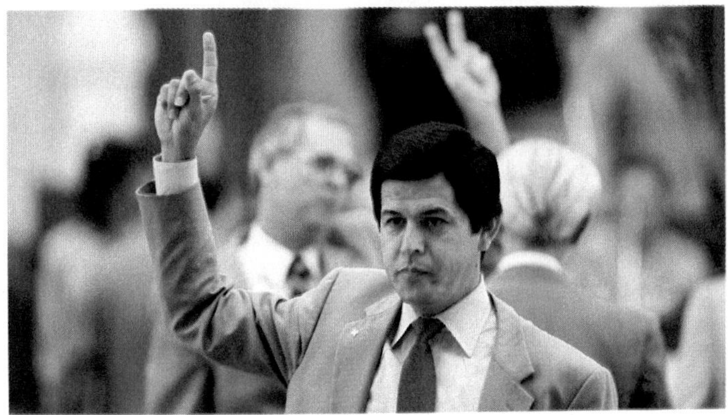

Decision by Consensus

By far the best way of arriving at a decision is by consensus. A **consensus** is arrived at when the group's decision is worded in such a way that the entire group can agree on it. If the members of the group cannot agree on a point, but the group desires that a consensus be reached, then the group should reword the point or continue discussion until consensus is reached.

Groups must be careful, however, to avoid achieving a **false consensus,** one that does not reflect the actual views of the group members. This can occur when a question or option is made so vague that it causes conflict in interpretation. [See chart on page 467.]

"Then, gentlemen, it is the consensus of this meeting that we say nothing, do nothing, and hope it all blows over before our next meeting."

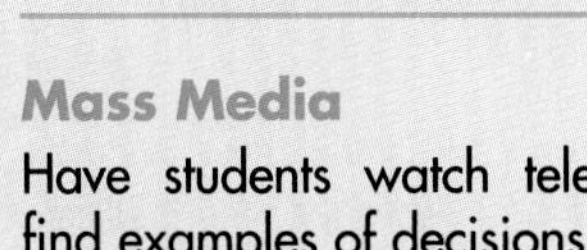

Making Connections

Mass Media

Have students watch television to find examples of decisions made by decree, by voting, or by consensus. Suggest that students consider the various types of group discussion seen in newscasts, movies, trials, or congressional sessions.

Teaching Note

A false consensus occurs when group members keep serious disagreements to themselves but vote with the majority just to maintain unanimity. A false consensus usually does the group more harm than good.

Reteaching

One way to reteach the material in this segment is to have a group of students hold a discussion and tape-record it. They could play back the tape and work together to analyze conflict and decision making and to evaluate the discussion.

Extension

Have students discuss whether they think that any of the strategies for resolving conflicts and reaching decisions in groups would be useful in one-to-one relationships. Have students explain their answers.

Ongoing Assessment

Activity 6

Have students evaluate their group's decision from **Activity 4.** If there was no conflict, ask them to explain why. Listen to the class discussion and make notes for your files.

Teacher's Resource Binder

Skills for Success 6
Evaluating Group Discussion

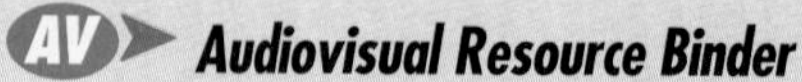

Audiovisual Resource Binder

Transparency 35
Evaluating a Group Discussion

Activity 6 — Analyzing Group Decision Making

Think about the last group that you worked in. Were the group's decisions made by decree, by vote, or by consensus? What effect did the method of arriving at decisions have on the group's morale? Discuss your views with your classmates.

Evaluating Group Discussion

How much you improve your discussion skills will depend on how you take advantage of criticism. Group discussions are evaluated by observers. Each observer takes careful notes of what happens. Since you are likely to work as both an observer and a participant, you should know how group discussions are evaluated.

Individual Participation. One way to evaluate a group discussion is to concentrate on what each person in the group is doing. Each speaker can be rated on a scale of 1 to 5 on the characteristics that have been discussed. The evaluation shows the observer's reactions to each group member's performance.

Sample Evaluation Form for Group Discussion

Name	Contributed Information	Asked Questions	Followed Plan	Paid Attention	Showed Courtesy

The Discussion Process. A second way to evaluate a group discussion is to focus on the discussion process. To do this, you should have some record of who is talking and to whom he or she is speaking. Then after the discussion, you can make your judgment about the balance of participation.

An effective method for keeping this record is to diagram the discussion process. On a sheet of paper, draw separate boxes to represent each of the individuals involved in the discussion. Then label each box with a participant's initials. Place the leader's initials at the top. Draw an arrow from each box to each one of the other boxes. (The resulting diagram will look something like a multi-pointed star with the boxes at the points.)

Each time one of the participants speaks to another individual, place a mark on the line that connects the boxes containing these individuals' initials. (Place this mark closest to the box of the

ENRICHMENT

Challenge students to study the dynamics of TV situation comedies and family shows in which the humor depends on group discussions gone awry. Have the students watch a favorite show several times while taking notes on the way discussions develop and then dissolve into conflict. Then have students explain to their classmates the dynamics of these discussions.

CLOSURE

Ask students what they have learned about group discussions and how they can apply what they have learned to their everyday lives.

individual who made the remark. However, if a speaker makes a comment intended for the entire group, place a mark inside the box containing that speaker's initials.) Using this method, you can evaluate whether the discussion involved the entire group.

Quality of the Discussion. A third way to evaluate a discussion is to focus on the quality of the discussion. To do so, you should answer the following questions.

- Was the group goal clearly stated as a question of fact, of value, or of policy?
- Did the group have a discussion outline?
- Were conclusions that were drawn based on information presented in the discussion?
- Was the decision defensible?

ACTIVITY 7 Evaluating Group Discussion

Listen to a group discussion, either a live discussion or a radio or television program. Choose a method of evaluation and evaluate the discussion. Share your evaluation with your classmates.

GUIDELINES for Participating in Group Discussion

- Am I prepared?
- Do I share information objectively?
- Do I ask questions?
- Do I try to help the group stay on track?
- Do I evaluate information that is presented?
- Am I respectful of others' views?
- Do I cooperate?
- Do I speak loudly and clearly enough for everyone to understand?
- Do I understand and carry out the responsibilities of leadership?
- Am I able to identify and help manage conflict?

MEETING INDIVIDUAL NEEDS

An Alternative Approach

Invite management people such as a mayor, a hospital administrator, and a school superintendent to present a symposium to the class on how they use private group discussions in their work. Have students chart the group interaction while they listen. Afterward, discuss not only the topic of the symposium but the group interaction as well.

ONGOING ASSESSMENT

Activity 7

You could have students work in groups and have different groups use different methods for evaluating discussion so that all three types of evaluation are used. Ask students to keep notes on their evaluations and to share their notes with you.

◆ Profiles in Communication

Performance Objectives

- To prepare an outline and a list of questions for a group discussion
- To participate in a democratically led group discussion
- To evaluate a group discussion

Teaching the Feature

Have students read the profile of architect Gary Hoyt. Ask students what other professions they think would use group discussions as a regular part of conducting business. Point out that most kinds of work involve some group discussions, either formal or informal.

Activity Note

Allow students to refer to the textbook and the work they did in **Activity 2** to remind themselves how to prepare for participation in a group discussion. You could give students time to go to the library to complete their research. Circulate through the room as groups hold their discussions. Assess students' mastery by monitoring participation and by checking their notes.

PROFILES IN COMMUNICATION

A self-employed architect, Gary Hoyt must often participate in group discussions with clients, engineers, bankers, and government officials. "One of the keys to holding a successful meeting," says Mr. Hoyt, "is putting together a good group of people with a variety of perspectives to approach the matter at hand." He comments that the whole can be greater than the sum of its parts. "Often, when several people talk together, sounder decisions are reached and exciting new ideas are generated."

The first thing to do in any meeting, advises Mr. Hoyt, is to introduce the participants and make them feel comfortable. It's important to be organized, he finds. "Have a specific goal in mind for your meeting. Then, as the discussion gets underway, don't let it bog down. Keep the pace brisk and the mood relaxed." Afterwards, he says, "Always follow up; let the participants know that things went well." He offers a final suggestion: Keep good records of the proceedings.

Group discussions can't solve every problem. However, group discussions are an important part of most business negotiations, and Gary Hoyt has found them vital in achieving success.

ACTIVITY

Prepare to participate in a group discussion of the question, "Should all students be required to attend high school until age eighteen?" Begin by making a discussion outline, and then research the topic, using the methods suggested in this chapter. Add the facts, ideas, and information you gather to the discussion outline. Finally, make a list of questions to ask other group members.

With three or four classmates, discuss the question. Appoint or elect a discussion leader. Classmates acting as observers should evaluate the discussion, using an evaluation form such as the one shown on page 470 or the Guidelines on page 471 as a basis for their critiques.

S U M M A R Y

GROUP DISCUSSION is the face-to-face communication of a small number of people who meet for a specific purpose. You can plan and participate in a group discussion by thinking about and dealing with the interrelated parts of the discussion.

- **Plan a group discussion** by determining a purpose and a format, choosing a topic, wording the discussion question appropriately, indentifying the type of discussion question, and preparing an outline for the discussion.
- **Perform the different roles in a discussion** by selecting a specific role to play. The discussion leader should introduce the discussion, keep it moving, moderate the discussion, keep it on track, and conclude the discussion. The secretary should record major points of agreement and decisions made by the group, definitions of key terms, issues to be discussed at a later time, major points of disagreement, and important issues raised during the discussion. Participants in a discussion should prepare by studying the discussion outline, thinking about the discussion question, and doing research on the discussion question, if necessary.
- **Manage group conflict** by recognizing that a conflict is developing, by diagnosing the nature of the conflict, and by helping the group to defuse or resolve the conflict.
- **Reach a group decision** by decree, by voting, or by consensus. Consensus is preferred but cannot always be achieved.
- **Evaluate a discussion** by analyzing the contributions of all of the participants.

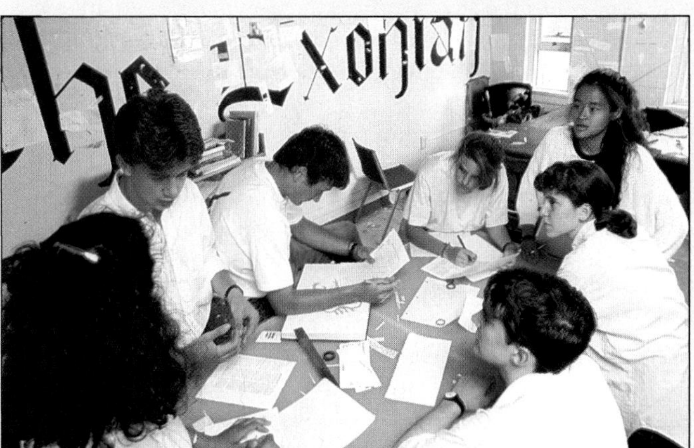

CHAPTER 17

Vocabulary

Look back through this chapter to find the meaning of each of the following terms, and write it in your communication journal.

ad hoc committee format, *p. 452*
authoritarian (or **directive) leadership, *p. 459***
conflict, *p. 466*
consensus, *p. 469*
decree, *p. 468*
democratic (or **supportive) leadership, *p. 459***
discussion format, *p. 451*
discussion outline, *p. 456*
false consensus, *p. 469*
forum format, *p. 451*
free-form format, *p. 452*
group discussion, *p. 449*
laissez-faire (or **nondirective) leadership, *p. 459***
leadership, *p. 459*
majority, *p. 469*
moderated free-form format, *p. 452*
panel format, *p. 451*
progressive format, *p. 452*
question of fact, *p. 455*
question of policy, *p. 455*
question of value, *p. 455*
round-table format, *p. 452*
secretary (or **recorder), *p. 462***
standing committee format, *p. 452*
symposium format, *p. 451*
vote, *p. 468*

TEACHER'S RESOURCE BINDER

- Chapter 17 Vocabulary

REVIEW QUESTIONS

Answers

1. goal-oriented, face-to-face communication of a small number of people who meet for a specific purpose
2. to arrive at a decision, to brainstorm ideas, to share information, to solve a problem
3. panel: group of experts discusses a topic to provide information and opinions for another group; symposium: members present brief, prepared speeches and then discuss the ideas
4. The moderated free-form format has a leader, and the free-form format has no particular order. An ad hoc committee is formed to study a single issue only. A standing committee exists over a long period of time.
5. questions of value and questions of policy
6. authoritarian and democratic; laissez faire: sharing responsibilities with all group members;

DISCUSSION QUESTIONS

Guidelines for Assessment

Student responses may vary.

1. Democracies require an informed public. Discussion groups provide a forum and support. Members can help take responsibility for a discussion's course.
2. Answers will come out of students' experiences. Encourage shy students to respond to this question.
3. To recognize conflict early, pay attention to nonverbal messages, verbal interruptions, or members talking all at once or talking out of turn. A leader can tactfully remind members to follow the rules of order and to be courteous toward each other. The leader should emphasize the points of agreement between disputing members and should make sure that all members get to express their opinions.
4. Laissez-faire leadership is effective in small groups of close friends. Authoritarian leadership is effective when the leader has special information or skills. Democratic leadership is effective in most other situations.
5. The quotation implies that a horse planned in committee would be poorly designed. Decision by committee can be muddled and inefficient. Each situation has to be decided individually.

CHAPTER **17**

Review Questions

1. What is a group discussion?
2. What are some purposes that a discussion can serve? (Name at least four.)
3. A panel is a group of people who discuss a topic of mutual interest to them and to their audience. What is the difference between a panel and a symposium?
4. What is the difference between a free-form discussion format and a moderated free-form format? between a standing committee format and an ad hoc committee format?
5. One type of discussion question is a question of fact. What are two other types?
6. One style of leadership is laissez-faire. Name two other styles of leadership. What are the responsibilities of a group leader using each of these styles?
7. What is the job of the secretary, or recorder?
8. One major responsibility of a participant is to share information. What are three other responsibilities of a participant in a group discussion?
9. Disagreements between group members can turn into disruptive conflicts. What can a group leader do to manage conflict in a discussion?
10. A group decision can be reached by decree, by voting, or by consensus. Why is consensus the most effective method?

Discussion Questions

1. Discuss with your classmates why discussion groups are a necessary part of a democratic society. In what ways do discussion groups help participants voice their opinions? How do group members keep the power of leaders in check?
2. Some people feel too shy to express their opinions in group discussions. Discuss ways in which a person can overcome shyness. Then discuss ways in which an effective leader can help and encourage a shy group member.
3. Conflict is likely to arise in group discussions. Discuss ways to recognize a conflict before it becomes a serious disagreement. Then discuss ways in which a good leader can manage the conflict.
4. Compare and contrast the effectiveness of groups led by laissez-faire, authoritarian, and democratic leaders. List some specific examples of situations in which each type of leadership would be appropriate.
5. *Vogue* magazine once defined *camel* as "a horse planned by a committee." First, discuss the meaning of this comment. Then discuss how the comment illuminates certain weaknesses of the group decision-making process. Finally, discuss whether the strengths of the group decision-making process outweigh its weaknesses.

authoritarian: taking all leadership responsibilities; democratic: suggesting procedures, supporting members' ideas

7. record major points of agreement or disagreement, decisions made, definitions of key terms, issues to return to at later time, issues that seem important during discussion
8. prepare for discussion, take active part, listen carefully and critically, respect all group members, and use appropriate speaking voice
9. Employ any of possible solutions listed in the **Managing Group Conflict** chart on p. 467.
10. because all members are in agreement and therefore are more likely to remain committed to the decision

ACTIVITIES

1. **Choosing Topics and Questions for Group Discussion.**
   A. Think about your school. List five issues facing your school that would be suitable for group discussion. For example, you might list pass/fail grading, the need for new gym equipment, changes in graduation requirements, or the dress code.
   B. Turn each of the topics you listed in Part A of this Activity into a discussion question. Then identify each question as a question of fact, of value, or of policy.
2. **Analyzing Your Role in a Group.** On a sheet of notebook paper, copy the pattern of circles shown below. Write your name and a personal description in the center circle. Then, in the outer circles, write the names of the different groups to which you belong, such as your family and your speech class. On your paper, describe your role in each group. What effect do other group members have on the way you see yourself in the group? Do you act sometimes as a leader and sometimes as a participant? What is your main leadership style?

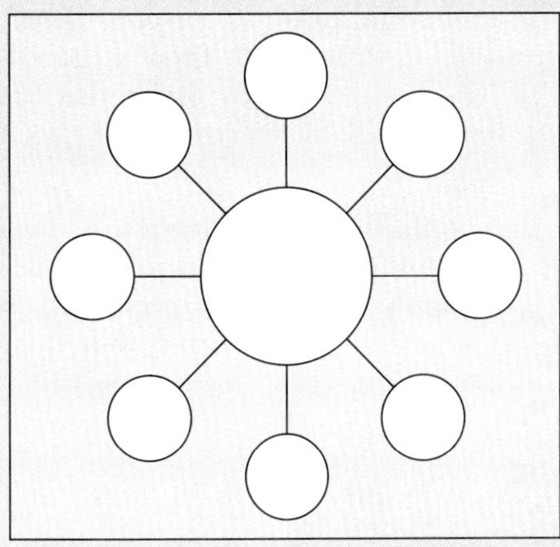

3. **Analyzing a Public Meeting.** Attend a public forum, a city council meeting, a school board meeting, or any other type of public meeting such as the one shown below. Report afterward on such items as the number of people in attendance, the number of participants, the way the meeting was conducted, the topics discussed, and the action taken.

4. **Preparing an Outline for Group Discussion.** First read each of the following questions. Decide whether each is a question of fact, a question of value, or a question of policy. Then prepare an outline for a group discussion on each of the questions. You may want to refer to the example outlines on pages 456–457.
   a. What are the advantages and the disadvantages of a liberal arts education?
   b. What role should the federal government play in supporting the arts in this country?
   c. In what ways are young children influenced by television?
   d. What should the foreign language requirement be for high school students?
   e. What was the funniest movie produced last year?

ACTIVITIES

Guidelines for Assessment

1. To assess students' understanding of discussion questions, have each student read his or her discussion question and then ask a volunteer to identify the question as one of fact, value, or policy.
2. Have students share their self-analyses in small groups.
3. You may want to suggest to students that they use the **Sample Evaluation Form for Group Discussion** on p. 470 when making their reports. You can use this checklist when assessing the reports.
4. Students should first identify the type of discussion question before they make their outlines.
   a. value
   b. policy
   c. fact
   d. policy
   e. value
   Make sure that the outlines cover all the points given in the models on pp. 456–457.

SUMMATIVE EVALUATION

Your **Teacher's Resource Binder** contains a reproducible **Chapter 17 Test** that may be used to assess students' mastery of the concepts presented in this chapter.

PORTFOLIO ASSESSMENT

For future reference and evaluation you may want to have students keep in their portfolios any skill sheets or evaluation forms that you have used with this chapter along with any other recorded or written materials that students have created.

5. Have each group appoint a recorder to take notes. Circulate through the room to monitor students' participation.

6. Have students share their research and conclusions in small groups.

5. Understanding the Effect of Seating Arrangements. A group's seating arrangement can affect both the interaction among group members and the kind of leadership that is appropriate for the group.

A. Working with a group of your classmates, answer the following questions. Then compare your answers to those of others in the class.

1. In your experience, how does where a person sits affect the way he or she acts in a group?
2. Which of the seating arrangements shown below is best suited to a private group discussion? to a public group discussion?
3. The seating arrangements shown below are just a few of the many arrangements that are possible. Think of some other arrangements and the situations in which they might be used, such as a panel discussion with two opposing factions or a pep talk before a football game. Draw a simple diagram of each arrangement you think of.

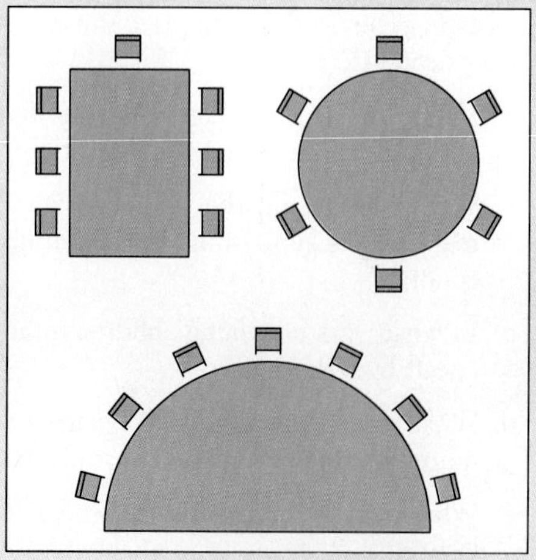

B. With your group, answer the following questions. You may want to rearrange your own chairs in order to experiment with some different seating arrangements.

1. In each of the seating arrangements shown in the diagram on this page, where would the discussion leader most likely sit?
2. Which of the seating arrangements shown would best suit an authoritarian leader? a laissez-faire leader? a democratic leader? Give reasons for your answers.
3. How important is it for the leader to be in a position where he or she can see and be seen by all of the group members?
4. One of the discussion leader's responsibilities is to arrange the meeting space. If you were leading a discussion group, which of the seating arrangements shown here would you choose to encourage active participation from all group members? Explain your choice.

6. Analyzing Public Group Discussion.

A. Study your daily newspaper. Look for reports of meetings of Congress, of the state legislature, of the city council, and of local clubs. Then prepare a list of eight or ten topics that are being resolved through public group discussion.

B. Classify the level of interest of each topic as local, state, national, or international. Then identify specific groups that would be concerned with these topics.

◆ Real-Life Speaking Situations

PERFORMANCE OBJECTIVES

- To write and present an informative speech on how to lead a family meeting
- To write a dialogue of a problem-solving employee group discussion
- To present a dialogue in class and to respond to feedback

REAL LIFE

Speaking Situations

1 Many families hold meetings to discuss vacation plans, household chores, family projects, and other issues that families face. If your family has such conferences, you may likely have wished that you were the discussion leader.

Picture yourself as head of your own family, with your own husband or wife and your own children. Your family needs to make a decision, and you have called a conference to discuss it.

First, identify the members of your family. Next, identify the issue that your family needs to discuss. Write an informative speech (two or three minutes long), about how you would lead the discussion. [See Chapter 14 for more information on informative speeches.]

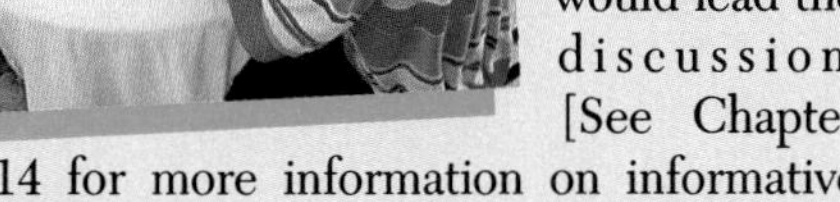

In your speech, be sure to discuss your leadership style, the method your family would use to arrive at a decision, the part that each family member would play in the discussion, and the decision that would be reached through the discussion. Present your speech in class. Invite feedback from your classmates on the accuracy of your role-playing and the effectiveness and appropriateness of your leadership style.

2 To succeed, the owner of a small business must be skilled not only at providing a particular product or service but also at running the business itself. One way that owners of small businesses meet the demands they face is by calling their employees together to discuss how the business can best meet the wants and needs of customers.

Imagine that you run a small business. You have had a good year, but lately business has slowed down. To help you decide how to deal with this decline, you gather your employees for a group meeting. What issues do you plan to discuss with your employees? How will you prepare for and conduct the meeting?

Begin by identifying the business you are running. Next, specify who your employees are and what each of them could contribute to the discussion. Write a three- or four-page dialogue of your group discussion that ends with a conclusion about what caused your business to decline and a decision on what to do to reverse the decline. Present your dialogue in class, and respond to feedback on the effectiveness of your discussion.

ASSESSMENT GUIDELINES

1. Evaluate the informative speeches on how well the student describes the following points: issue to be decided, leadership style, method used to arrive at a decision, part played by each family member, and final decision.
2. Point out to students that in this scenario there may be some group conflict because business is slow. Students should be able to apply what they have learned in this chapter to their dialogues. Evaluate both the dialogues and the responses given by the class. Keep records for your files.

Chapter 18

Debate

pp. 478–517

CHAPTER OVERVIEW

This chapter presents the complex process of formal debate. Students will need to use their best listening, reasoning, and speaking skills. The chapter explains the types of debate such as traditional debate, cross-examination debate, and Lincoln-Douglas debate. The chapter also explains features of debate such as the proposition, issues, affirmative and negative cases, refutation, and

TEACHER'S RESOURCE BINDER

The following materials are identified at their point of use in this chapter:

- Skills for Success
  1 *Wording Debate Propositions*
  2 *Preparing Yourself for Debate*
  3 *Refuting an Argument*
  4 *Developing a Rebuttal*
- Chapter 18 Vocabulary
- Chapter 18 Test/Answer Key

A Debate supplement provides additional instructional material and activities for this chapter.

AV Audiovisual Resource Binder

The following materials are identified at their point of use in this chapter:

- Transparency 36
  Evaluating Proposition Statements
- Transparency 37
  Evaluating Evidence in Debate
- Transparency 38
  Debate Flow-Sheet Chart

rebuttal. Students will also learn the types of evidence, strategies for gathering evidence and using proofs, the patterns for developing cases, techniques for questioning, and methods for creating debate briefs and flow sheets. Finally, students are exposed to the judging criteria and procedure for debates.

Introducing the Chapter

Because many issues in this country are resolved through debate, students will benefit from studying the formal processes for arguing one's position and defending it effectively. Explain to students that this chapter will give them experience in honing their persuasive tactics and their analytical and reasoning capabilities.

C H A P T E R

Debate

OBJECTIVES

After studying this chapter, you should be able to

1. Identify the specialized features of debate.
2. Identify three kinds of propositions.
3. Identify three debate formats.
4. Prepare to debate by discovering issues and organizing proof.
5. Recognize the responsibilities of the affirmative and negative sides in constructive speeches.
6. Define *refutation* and *rebuttal.*
7. Recognize criteria, or standards, for judging a debate.

What Is Debate?

Debate is formalized public speaking in which participants prepare and present speeches on opposite sides of an issue to determine which side has the stronger arguments. Even if you do not participate in competitive debate, knowing its principles of clear thinking will help you in many speaking situations.

Debate as a means of decision making goes back to the ancient Greeks. Today, debate is an essential element of the democratic process in the United States: In legislative assemblies, courtrooms, and other public forums, debates have led to decisions on personal freedom, civil rights, and war and peace. In the past thirty years, presidential debates have also played a prominent role in elections.

In this chapter you will learn about the features and principles of debate as they are used in three different debate formats:

- formal or traditional debate
- cross-examination debate
- Lincoln-Douglas debate

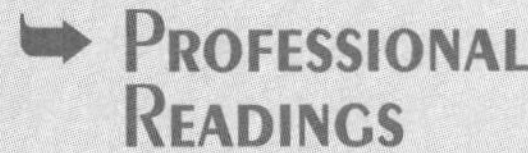

Bibliography of Additional Materials

Professional Readings

- Brown, Wayne, and Howard Prost. ***Directing Successful Speech Tournaments.*** Grandview, MO: Dale Publishing Company.
- Klopf, Donald W. ***Coaching and Directing Forensics.*** Lincolnwood, IL: National Textbook Company.
- Smith, Craig R., and David M. Hunsaker. ***The Bases of Argument: Ideas in Conflict.*** New York: Macmillan Publishing Company.

Audiovisuals

- ***Debate: An Introduction***—Dale Publishing Company, Grandview, MO (videocassette, 19 min.)
- ***Debate in Video***—Dale Publishing Company, Grandview, MO (two videocassettes, about 60 min. each)

  Videocassettes of final rounds of the National Forensic League's annual national tournaments are available from Dale Publishing Company, Grandview, MO.

Segment 1 *pp. 480–493*

- **Understanding the Features of Debate**
- **Understanding Debate Formats**
- **Preparing Yourself for Debate**

Performance Objectives

- To identify the affirmative and negative positions in debate
- To make journal entries about the use of debate features by speakers on television and radio
- To identify the three types of propositions
- To develop reasons and evidence for a policy debate

Teaching Note

Your students may enjoy engaging in an informal two-minute debate each day during this unit. You can draw propositions from current community or school affairs—even a bulletin board that presents school announcements may suggest suitable topics. Call on two volunteers to present opposing views on a topic. This strategy offers nonthreatening guided practice for skills such as extemporaneous delivery, concise expression, speedy organization, and quick rebuttal.

Understanding the Features of Debate

As a specialized form of public speaking, debate has several unique features. These features include speakers on two sides of a controversial issue who present speeches that build arguments for and against a proposition.

Controversy

Debate begins with a controversy expressed in a proposition. A **proposition** is a statement that asserts a fact, makes a value judgment, or recommends a policy. A proposition must deal with a controversial question—one that has valid evidence for two sides of an issue that divides public opinion. [For more information on propositions, see pages 482–484 of this chapter.]

Speakers on Two Sides

The two sides in a debate are called the *affirmative* and the *negative.* The affirmative side supports the debate proposition. The negative side opposes it. For instance, if the proposition to be debated were "*Resolved,* That the minimum age for obtaining a driver's license should be raised to eighteen," the affirmative side in the debate would support the change, and the negative side would oppose it.

The speakers on opposing sides take turns presenting their arguments. In formal debate and cross-examination debate, each side has two speakers. The two speakers work as a team with each person having different responsibilities at different times. In Lincoln-Douglas debate, each side has only one speaker. In the cross-examination and Lincoln-Douglas debate formats, speakers also question, or cross-examine, the opposing speaker. In all debate formats, the affirmative side always begins and ends the debate.

Motivation

Invite students to write in their communication journals about times in their lives when they have been in arguments to defend positions or to argue against other positions. They might respond to the following questions:

1. What was your position?
2. How did you support that position?
3. What were the arguments against you?
4. How successful were you?
5. If you were unsuccessful, why?

Have a few students share their experiences, and then tell students that in this segment they will learn about formal arguing, or debate.

Activity 1

Identifying Affirmative and Negative Positions in Debate

Imagine that you will participate in a debate on the proposition "*Resolved,* That public schools should adopt a year-round schedule." (1) What will be the affirmative side? (2) What will be the negative side? (3) Which side will go first?

Ongoing Assessment

Activity 1

The affirmative side will argue for adopting a year-round schedule, the negative will argue against, and the affirmative side will go first.

Status Quo

The existing state of affairs is called the **status quo.** Debate assumes that the status quo is satisfactory until proven otherwise.

> **Example:** The minimum age for obtaining a driver's license in most states is sixteen. Sixteen is neither the only age that could be considered nor necessarily the best age. However, sixteen is the status quo. It will continue to be the law until enough evidence is presented to change it.

Because the affirmative side seeks a change from the status quo, speakers on that side have the **burden of proof,** the obligation to present arguments for changing the status quo. Until this burden of proof is met, the negative side has nothing to do. Therefore, the affirmative goes first and presents a strong enough argument in favor of the change to force the negative to reply.

Constructive and Rebuttal Speeches

Any debate format is based on two kinds of speeches: a **constructive speech,** which builds an argument, and a **rebuttal speech,** which rebuilds it.

Calvin and Hobbes by Bill Watterson

Integrating the Language Arts

Vocabulary Link

Students may not understand the joke in the *Calvin and Hobbes* cartoon if they don't know the meaning of *forensic.* Check to see if anyone in the class can define the word. If not, have students look it up in a dictionary. [According to *Webster's New World Dictionary,* Third College Edition, *forensic* means "...suitable for a law court, public debate, or formal argumentation."]

TEACHING THE LESSON

Begin the lesson by discussing how debate differs from everyday disagreements and arguments. Then guide students through the material on p. 480, which will prepare them to complete **Activity 1** on p. 481 as independent practice. You may want to have a few student volunteers read aloud the information on pp. 481–484 because it covers many challenging terms. Stop periodically to clarify any difficult concepts and terms. Guide students through identifying the first proposition in **Activity 2** on p. 484 and demonstrate your reasoning processes. Then assign the rest of **Activity 2** as independent practice.

Introduce the formats for various debates on pp. 484–487, and ask students to note the major differences between the formats. You probably will want to point out that traditional debate is seldom used, especially in most educational competitions,

During the constructive speeches, the affirmative and negative speakers establish reasons for the superiority of their side. During the rebuttal speeches, each speaker does two things: rebuilds arguments that have been questioned or attacked and refutes, or attacks, an argument raised by the other side. Refutation leads to verbal clashes that make debate exciting.

Besides being used in high school contests, debate is basic to public discussion. In your communication journal, take notes about how speakers on television and radio use the features of debate. For example, listen to news analysis programs and talk shows. What issues do the speakers discuss? How controversial are the issues? How clear is each speaker's position on the issue? What kinds of propositions do they argue? Do the speakers build arguments to establish the superiority of their positions? Do they refute arguments raised by the other side? How effective are the speakers?

The Proposition

Debate focuses on a controversial topic stated in a proposition, or resolution. Every year, national debate organizations select the propositions that high school debaters will use in their contests. There are three types of propositions:

- propositions of fact
- propositions of value
- propositions of policy

Propositions of Fact. **Propositions of fact** make statements about what has happened, is happening, or will happen. This type of proposition is most common in courts of law, where people search out reasons and evidence to prove or disprove the proposition—to determine what is true or false.

EXAMPLES:
- Anita Jones is not legally bound by the terms of the contract.
- Chris Smith is guilty of damaging clothes at the Plaza Department Store.
- Tom Green is the legal owner of the 1987 automobile in question.

TEACHER'S RESOURCE BINDER

Skills for Success 1
Wording Debate Propositions

and ask students to decide why. [Traditional debate does not allow for cross-examination and is therefore less lively.] Then you can discuss the steps to prepare for a debate on pp. 488–493.

To prepare students for **Activity 3** on p. 493, guide them through some of the work for each of the three steps. Work with the class to list subissues under the stock issue of *ill,* to list one affirmative and one negative reason, and to prepare four evidence cards. Then assign the rest of the activity as independent practice. You could have students work with partners. You may need to provide some library time for students to complete the activity.

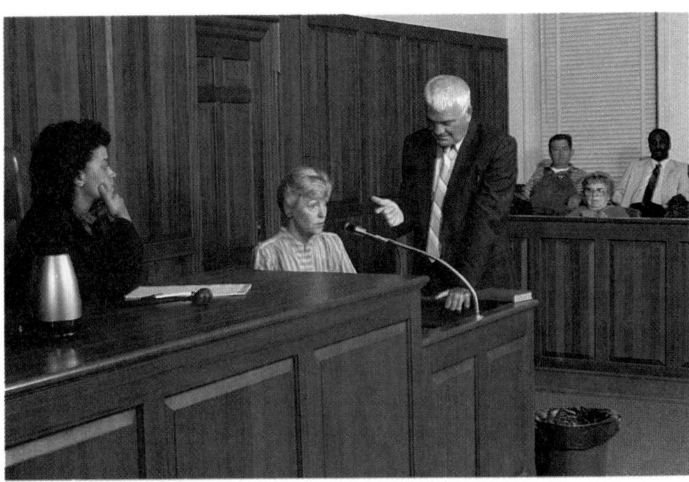

COOPERATIVE LEARNING

Divide the class into groups of four or five. Tell each group to decide on an issue and to write three propositions, one of each kind on that issue. Then each group will share their issues and propositions. Allow time for discussion about the issue and the features of good propositions. The class might choose the best ones and discuss why they made those choices.

Propositions of Value. **Propositions of value** express judgments about the relative merit of a person, place, or thing—the value object. Propositions of value always include evaluative words such as *effective, good, worthy, better,* or their opposites. Although debaters can set up criteria for determining what is "best," "effective," or "easier" and can measure the objects against those criteria, they cannot verify the findings. Therefore, the result is a matter of judgment, not a matter of fact.

EXAMPLES:

- *Resolved,* That Parker High has the best football team in the state.
- *Resolved,* That personal freedom is more important than law.
- *Resolved,* That computer language is easier to master than a foreign language.

Propositions of Policy. **Propositions of policy** focus on specific plans of action. The word *should* in propositions of policy makes this type of proposition the easiest to recognize and the easiest to phrase.

EXAMPLES:

- *Resolved,* That solar-energy research should be significantly increased.
- *Resolved,* That the United States should adopt a national health insurance program for all citizens.
- *Resolved,* That more vigorous academic standards for language arts and mathematics should be established in United States secondary schools.

Assessment

Responses to **Activities 1** and **2** should enable you to assess students' understanding of the two sides of a debate and of the kinds of propositions. Evaluate students' work in **Activity 3** on p. 493 to assess mastery of developing reasons and gathering evidence. You might ask students to present their subissues and reasons to the class and then to turn in their evidence cards.

Reteaching

Find portions of news articles that each present two sides of an issue. Allow students to work in groups of three or four on one article. They should identify the proposition, list the reasons for and against, and make note of the evidence used by both sides. Ask the groups to read their articles to the other groups and to share their findings. Then provide time for the class to discuss

HOW TO *Evaluate a Proposition*

1. **Does the proposition give the burden of proof to the affirmative?** The proposition should be worded to change an idea, an institution, or a current policy or to express a value judgment. For example, the proposition of policy "*Resolved,* That the federal income tax should be abolished" is stated correctly because abolishing the tax would be a change from current policy. If the proposition were worded, "*Resolved,* That the federal income tax should be continued," it would be incorrect because this statement would place the burden of proof on the negative side.
2. **Does the proposition contain only one topic?** The proposition "*Resolved,* That the Murray High School football and basketball programs should be abolished" is incorrect because it contains two topics. Either topic (the football program or the basketball program) is debatable, but both cannot be debated at the same time.
3. **Are the words used in the proposition clear?** For instance, the proposition "*Resolved,* That qualifications for welfare recipients should be reevaluated" is not clearly stated. The words *should be reevaluated* do not suggest a specific plan of action. The word *reevaluated* needs to be replaced with a word or phrase that specifies the reevaluation, such as *broadened* or *made more restrictive.*

Ongoing Assessment

Activity 2

Students should identify the propositions as follows:

1. policy
2. value
3. value
4. policy
5. value (Students may identify number 5 as a proposition of fact and cite evidence such as a win-loss record, but what constitutes *better* is a question of value.)

Audiovisual Resource Binder

Transparency 36
Evaluating Proposition Statements

Activity 2: Identifying the Types of Propositions

Identify each proposition below as a proposition of fact, of value, or of policy.

1. All high school students should be required to take a foreign language.
2. The advantages of wearing seat belts outweigh any risks.
3. Ann Welch is an effective president of the senior class.
4. All young people should be required to participate in a year of public service.
5. Park Hills has a better football team than North Hills has.

Understanding Debate Formats

High school students usually participate in three different debate formats:

- formal or traditional debate
- cross-examination debate
- Lincoln-Douglas debate

whether each group was accurate and thorough in its examination.

To reteach identifying the types of propositions, you might have students create propositions of fact, value, and policy.

See p. 492 for **EXTENSION, ENRICHMENT,** and **CLOSURE.**

These debate formats differ in three important ways:

1. number of speakers
2. time schedules for the speakers
3. types of propositions used

While the time schedules vary, the affirmative and negative sides in each format speak for the same total amount of time.

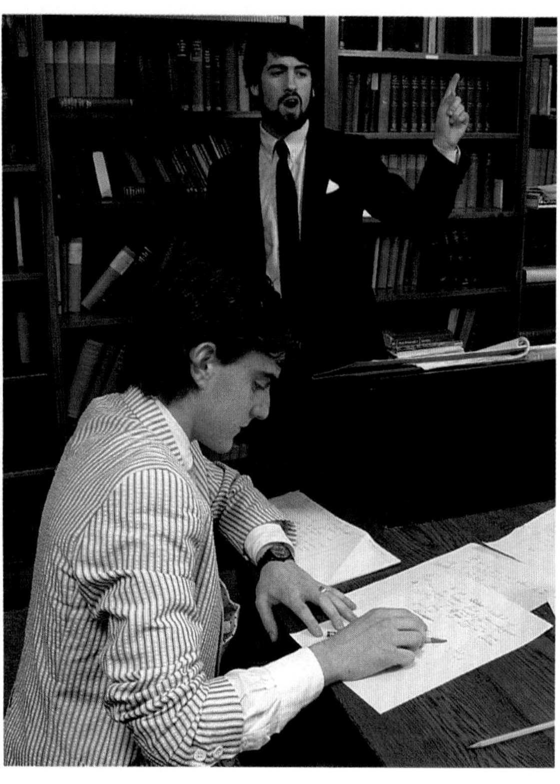

Traditional Debate

Traditional, or **formal, debate** involves two affirmative speakers and two negative speakers who argue a proposition of policy. Each speaker speaks twice within set time limits—once in a constructive speech and once in a rebuttal speech. The two affirmative speakers act as one team, and the two negative speakers act as the other. The two teams typically follow this schedule.

Traditional Debate

Constructive Speeches		Rebuttal Speeches	
1st Affirmative	10 minutes	**1st Negative**	5 minutes
1st Negative	10 minutes	**1st Affirmative**	5 minutes
2nd Affirmative	10 minutes	**2nd Negative**	5 minutes
2nd Negative	10 minutes	**2nd Affirmative**	5 minutes

Cross-Examination Debate

Cross-examination debate takes place between two affirmative speakers and two negative speakers who argue a proposition of policy. It differs from traditional debate by including brief cross-examination periods in which the participants question their opponents. This give-and-take between speakers provides for a lively

MEETING INDIVIDUAL NEEDS

An Alternative Approach

If you have students who feel confident that they can put together a debate after practice, offer them as much opportunity as possible to prepare, observe, and judge debates. Challenge these students to prepare arguments for both sides of a proposition and to prepare a case on the side of a proposition with which they do not personally agree.

Critical Thinking

Analysis

Divide the class into groups of three or four and have students analyze the characteristics of the three debate formats. Each group should discuss these elements and then determine the advantages and disadvantages of each format. Groups can also list the types of organizations that would use the different formats and explain why. Then each group should share its conclusions.

exchange of ideas. The cross-examination period specifically allows a speaker to clarify issues and to highlight the opposing side's weaknesses for the judge. Although time limits may vary, the following schedule is frequently used.

Cross-Examination Debate	
1st Affirmative	8-minute constructive speech
2nd Negative	3-minute questioning of 1st Affirmative
1st Negative	8-minute constructive speech
1st Affirmative	3-minute questioning of 1st Negative
2nd Affirmative	8-minute constructive speech
1st Negative	3-minute questioning of 2nd Affirmative
2nd Negative	8-minute constructive speech
2nd Affirmative	3-minute questioning of 2nd Negative
1st Negative	5-minute rebuttal speech and summary
1st Affirmative	5-minute rebuttal speech and summary
2nd Negative	5-minute rebuttal speech and summary
2nd Affirmative	5-minute rebuttal speech and summary

Lincoln-Douglas Debate

Lincoln-Douglas debate involves one affirmative speaker and one negative speaker who argue a proposition of value. The name of this format comes from a series of debates between Abraham Lincoln and Stephen A. Douglas in the 1858 Illinois senatorial race.

The Lincoln-Douglas format is well suited to classroom practice, because it focuses on the skills of individual debaters and takes less time than formal debate. At the same time, it includes all the same elements of argument, reasoning, refutation, and rebuttal as the other two debate formats. It also includes cross-examination periods. In a typical Lincoln-Douglas debate, each speaker has thirteen minutes for constructive and rebuttal speeches, as well as a three-minute cross-examination period.

Lincoln-Douglas Debate	
Affirmative	6-minute constructive speech
Negative	3-minute questioning of the Affirmative
Negative	7-minute constructive speech and refutation
Affirmative	3-minute questioning of the Negative
Affirmative	4-minute rebuttal speech
Negative	6-minute rebuttal speech and summary
Affirmative	3-minute rebuttal speech and summary

Lincoln-Douglas debate deals with values, not policy. The word *should* never appears in a proposition of value because the affirmative side is not called upon to prove the need for a policy change. The affirmative side simply argues the truth or merit of its proposition, and the negative side argues the falsity of that proposition. Neither side considers solutions or new policies to enact. While the arguments in formal debate rely on factual evidence, the arguments in Lincoln-Douglas debate emphasize evidence consisting of the logical analysis of philosophical issues. This format promotes exploration and increased understanding of our values and beliefs.

Lincoln-Douglas debate argues four basic types of values: moral, utilitarian, social, and aesthetic. Any combination of these values may be used to either defend or deny a proposition of value.

EXAMPLES:

- In the proposition "*Resolved,* That war is a moral way to settle disputes between nations," the debaters may argue the morality of war, the utility of war, or the social necessity of war.
- In the proposition "*Resolved,* That protection of the environment is more desirable than economic development," the debaters may argue the morality of endangering the environment, the usefulness of the environment as opposed to the usefulness of development, society's need to grow economically, and the aesthetic values of preserving nature.

Making Connections

Mass Media

To show how television has influenced the presentation of presidential debates, you could show some videotaped portions of debates such as those of Kennedy-Nixon, Carter-Reagan, or Clinton-Bush-Perot. Afterwards, students can discuss the ways debate has been affected by the media, especially by television news shows. You might ask students to consider the following questions: How has debate changed because of television? What roles do personal style and delivery have in the debate process?

MAKING CONNECTIONS

Legal Proceedings

Invite a local attorney to speak to the class on the role of debate in the legal profession. Ask this person to explain in detail how trials are conducted and what kinds of arguments are admissible. The attorney might also explain what rules of evidence are and how evidence might differ according to the type of case. Your guest might also address how a court case can be lost even though the evidence presented is sound.

TEACHER'S RESOURCE BINDER

Skills for Success 2
Preparing Yourself for Debate

Preparing Yourself for Debate

Your preparation for the debate—regardless of the debate format you are using—will include identifying or discovering the key issues that are central to your proposition. You will also have to find reasons and evidence that relate to the debate proposition. [See pages 248–255 of Chapter 10 for more help on gathering information.]

Recognizing Key Issues

In order to debate effectively, debaters need to identify the key issues that are central to the proposition. **Key issues** are the points of disagreement in the debate—questions that a speaker must answer satisfactorily in order to justify the adoption or rejection of a proposition. The affirmative must answer *yes* to the questions; the negative must answer *no*. Whether yes or no, each answer must be supported with reasons and evidence.

Using Stock Issues

Since the time of the ancient Greeks, debaters have looked for help in discovering key issues. One method that continues to be helpful, regardless of which of the three types of propositions the speakers are debating, is the use of stock issues. **Stock issues** are a formula of set questions that are adapted to the particular debate topic. Different sets of stock issues apply to propositions of policy and to propositions of value.

Stock Issues for Propositions of Policy. In formal debate and cross-examination debate, debaters use four basic stock issues to discover the key questions in a proposition of policy. These stock issues are:

1. **Ill:** Is there a problem with the current situation?
2. **Blame:** Is the current policy responsible for the problem?
3. **Cure:** Will the proposition solve the problem?
4. **Cost:** What are the costs of the proposition?

Both the affirmative and the negative speakers can use these stock issues to analyze the proposition and construct their cases.

EXAMPLE: *Resolved,* That Social Security benefits for the elderly should be lowered significantly.

I. Is the level of Social Security benefits for the elderly causing a problem? [This question meets the stock issue of ill: *Are there significant harms or needs within the present situation to warrant a change in policy as specified in the proposition?*] Subissues suggest potential problems with the status quo:

A. Is the economy being adversely affected?

B. Are the benefits received by the elderly unfair?

II. Is the current policy on Social Security benefits responsible for the ills? [This question meets the stock issue of blame: *Is the present system inherently responsible?*]

III. Are there facts to support the statement that lowering benefits will solve the problems? [This question meets the stock issue of cure: *Will the proposal remove the ills?*]

A. Will lowering benefits help the economy?

B. Will lowering benefits make for more equitable treatment of the elderly?

IV. What are the consequences of lowering benefits? [This question meets the stock issue of cost: *What are the consequences of changing the system?*]

A. Will lowering benefits work? [This subissue questions the practicality of the solution.]

1. Is it feasible to lower benefits?

2. Will lowering benefits upset the system?

B. Are there facts to prove that the advantages of lowering benefits outweigh the disadvantages? [This subissue questions the desirability of decreasing benefits.]

1. Will the proposal alienate the elderly?

2. Will the economy be stimulated?

Additional Activity

You might wish to create a debate proposition and to write it on the chalkboard. Then put students into groups of three or four and assign each group the position of either affirmative or negative. Let the groups brainstorm how they would defend their sides. Then tell them to determine what type of evidence would best suit their reasons and also to decide where they could find such evidence. Each group can share with the other groups by writing their information on the chalkboard. Allow time for discussion.

Stock Issues for Propositions of Value. In Lincoln-Douglas debate, speakers can use the following stock issues to explore a proposition that affirms a value judgment or evaluation.

1. What are the criteria, or standards of judgment, for making the evaluation?
2. Does this particular case meet the criteria?

EXAMPLE: *Resolved,* That SAT tests are effective predictors of college success.

- **I.** What are the criteria for determining whether a test is an "effective predictor of college success"? [This question asks *By what criteria is the value object to be judged?*] The subissues offer possible criteria:
  - **A.** Is the correlation of high test scores with high college grades an important criterion?
  - **B.** Is the correlation of low test scores with low college grades an important criterion?
- **II.** Does the available information show that SAT tests meet the key criteria? [This question asks *Do indicators show that the value object conforms to the criteria?*]
  - **A.** Is there information to show that people with high scores do well in college?
  - **B.** Is there information to show that people with low scores do poorly in college?

The Proof

In a debate, **proof** is the reasons and evidence given to answer the questions in the stock issues. You should gather more reasons and evidence than you will be able to use in the debate's time period.

For Better or For Worse® **by Lynn Johnston**

Reasons. **Reasons** are statements that justify the proposition. As you conduct your research, be sure to take note of reasons that support both the affirmative and the negative positions, regardless of which side of the debate you are on. Knowing the reasons for the opposition's point of view will make you aware of the evidence that may be used against your argument. This will help you to strengthen your own case. Also, you may be asked to argue either side of a proposition.

EXAMPLE: *Resolved,* That law enforcement agencies should be given greater freedom in investigating and prosecuting crime.

Stock Issue: Is there a problem?

A. To what extent are law enforcement agencies hampered by restrictions placed on how they investigate and prosecute crime?

B. What potential harms may result from the current restrictions?

C. What are the limits of an individual's rights?

D. What criteria are used to determine when current restrictions are too strict?

E. Can the problem be solved under the status quo?

Affirmative Reasons:

1. Recent Supreme Court decisions have unduly restricted law enforcement agencies in investigating and prosecuting crime.
2. Judicial restrictions have caused much of the increase in crime.
3. Criminal suspects are able to take advantage of various technicalities in the current system of laws to escape jury trial.

Negative Reasons:

1. Law enforcement agencies are not unduly restricted in their investigation and prosecution of crime.
2. Judicial restrictions contribute very little to increasing the crime rate.
3. Suspects and defendants who profit from limits imposed on law enforcement agencies are taking advantage of rights guaranteed by the Constitution.

Stock Issue: Would greater freedom for law enforcement agencies solve the problem?

A. Would the plan for granting greater freedom to law enforcement agencies be practical?

B. Would greater freedom be the best way of solving the problem?

EXTENSION

Write a list of debate propositions. Word some correctly, and in others purposely make errors such as stating more than one issue in a single proposition or failing to place the burden of proof with the affirmative. Give the list to your students and ask them to identify each proposition as correct or incorrect. For those propositions that are wrong, tell students to identify the problem and to write corrections in their communication journals. Have them share their work in class.

Affirmative Reasons:

1. Greater freedom for law enforcement agencies would allow more evidence to be gathered and put before juries.
2. Greater freedom for law enforcement agencies would lead to more convictions, which in turn would reverse the alarmingly high crime rate.
3. Greater freedom for law enforcement agencies would not create new problems.

Negative Reasons:

1. Those who commit crimes can be convicted within the existing framework if law enforcement agencies respect the law in collecting evidence.
2. Greater freedom would have little effect on crime.
3. Greater freedom would give law enforcement agencies too much power, which some officials would be tempted to abuse.

Evidence. To debate, you also need **evidence,** the facts and opinions given to support each reason. You need to gather examples, statistics, and quotations that support your reasons. Write your pieces of evidence on note cards following the guidelines discussed on page 256 in Chapter 10.

EXAMPLE: You might create the following note card about giving greater freedom to law enforcement agencies. Then you could evaluate this particular piece of evidence using the questions in the how-to chart on page 493. [For more information on reasons and evidence, see pages 387–391 of Chapter 15.]

Undue Restrictions

According to William Long, Superior Court Judge, King County, Washington, the question of unlawful searches and seizures "has become so highly technical that an officer who goes into a hotel room with a search warrant for one piece of evidence and finds something else can't use that other evidence. It's suppressed, so the criminal can go free."

"How Much Crime Can America Take?"
U.S. News and World Report,
April 20, 1964, p. 66

AV ➤ Audiovisual Resource Binder
Transparency 37
Evaluating Evidence in Debate

Enrichment

Encourage students to attend debates held in court, at city commission meetings, at school board meetings, or in some other public forum. Ask the students to note similarities to and differences from the techniques of debate described in this chapter. Students should report to the class their observations on the debates they attended.

Closure

To close the lesson, ask students to identify the two sides of a debate, the types of propositions, and the questions to ask when using stock issues. Allow students to consult their textbooks.

HOW TO *Evaluate Evidence*

1. **Is the evidence recent enough to be relevant to today's problems?** Out-of-date evidence is likely to be irrelevant to a current debate. For instance, the quotation in *U.S. News and World Report* is dated 1964. Criminal law has changed a great deal since then.
2. **Is the evidence well documented?** Where did the evidence come from? Who said it? The quotation from *U.S. News and World Report* is well documented.
3. **Is the source reliable?** Can you believe the source? In this example, *U.S. News and World Report* is a widely quoted, credible national news magazine. The source of the quotation, a superior court judge from Washington, is a reliable source on legal matters.
4. **Is the evidence objective?** Is the evidence inclined to be partial to either side of an issue? For the quotation in the example, you would need to determine whether William Long had an objective viewpoint.

ACTIVITY 3 Developing Reasons and Evidence

Using the steps given below, develop reasons and evidence for a policy debate on the following proposition: "*Resolved,* That the United States government should increase preservation of wilderness areas."

1. List potential questions (subissues) under the four stock issues (ill, blame, cure, and cost) that are relevant to the proposition.
2. List three affirmative and three negative reasons under your proposition. (These reasons are likely to relate to at least one of the stock issues—see pages 491–492 for examples.)
3. Prepare fifteen evidence cards to be turned in to your teacher. Record your information as suggested in the sample note card on page 492.

Meeting Individual Needs

Students with Special Needs

Students with learning disabilities may experience difficulty with **Activity 3** because they often have problems categorizing information.

Place students in small mixed-ability groups to work the activity.

Ongoing Assessment

Activity 3

Students should be able to develop several questions for each issue in question 1. You could allow library time before students list sound affirmative and negative reasons for question 2. Evidence cards should support the affirmative and negative reasons.

Segment 2 *pp. 494–511*

- Developing the Constructive Speech
- Considering Refutation and Rebuttal
- Creating a Flow Sheet
- Preparing the Debate Brief
- Judging Debates

ADDITIONAL ACTIVITY

Encourage students to attend a debate tournament. This activity will give students the opportunity to experience all the elements of debate in one setting. Have students report to the class on their observations.

Developing the Constructive Speech

Your next step in preparing for a debate is to develop a constructive speech, which builds an argument for an affirmative or a negative case. A **case** consists of the reasons and evidence on which you base your position.

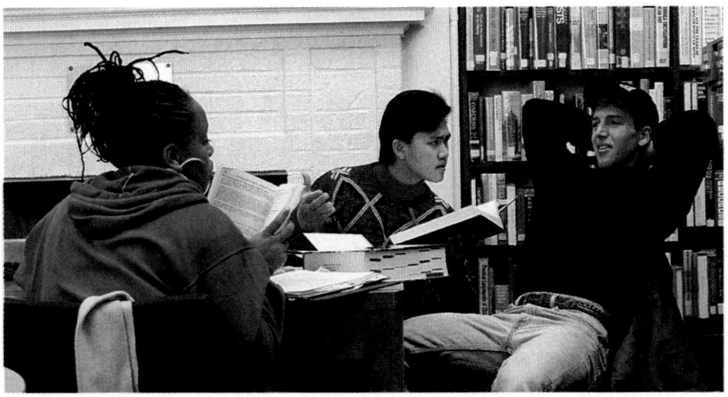

The Affirmative Case

The **affirmative case** presents reasons and evidence that support a proposition. In formal or cross-examination debate, the affirmative case indicates a problem with the present system and shows why the plan of action in the proposition offers the best solution. In Lincoln-Douglas debate, the affirmative case defends the criteria for making the value judgment stated in the proposition.

Because the affirmative always has the burden of proof, the affirmative argument needs to present a ***prima facie* case,** one that contains enough reasons and evidence to win a debate if the other side presented no argument. (*Prima facie* means "at first sight.") A *prima facie* case convinces a debate judge that the affirmative argument is valid. If the affirmative side cannot build a *prima facie* case, there is no need for negative argument and, consequently, no reason for debate.

After you have gathered reasons and evidence, you should select the most powerful ones for presenting your case in a limited time—probably two to four reasons. In Lincoln-Douglas debate, you will organize the affirmative case in a straightforward way: Define any terms, outline the issues to be debated, and justify why those are the key issues. For traditional or cross-examination debate, you should also consider a pattern of organization: the problem-solution pattern or the comparative advantages pattern.

Performance Objectives

- To select reasons for different patterns of argument
- To identify types of arguments and to question their reasoning
- To list in a journal ideas for debate topics and to state the ideas as propositions
- To write a debate brief
- To judge a debate

Motivation

Ask students to name television commercials that use evidence to support their claims. List these commercials on the chalkboard. Then discuss the effectiveness of the evidence and the commercials. Tell students that in this segment they will learn more about how to use good reasoning and evidence in arguing for or against a proposition or position.

Problem-Solution Pattern. The **problem-solution pattern** (also called the "need-plan pattern") organizes information to present both a problem and a solution to that problem. This pattern has at least three parts that attempt to prove

- that a significant problem exists
- that adopting the proposal will help to solve the problem
- that adopting the proposal is the best way to solve the problem

EXAMPLE: *Resolved,* That law enforcement agencies should be given greater freedom in investigating and prosecuting crime.

I. Restrictive Supreme Court rulings on government law enforcement agencies have resulted in an increase in the crime rate.

II. Our plan for greater freedom for these agencies would work to solve this problem.

III. Our plan for greater freedom would be the best way to solve this problem.

Comparative Advantages Pattern. The **comparative advantages pattern** organizes information to demonstrate that the proposal would have significant advantages over the status quo. This pattern differs from the problem-solution pattern in two important ways:

- The plan is always presented and discussed in detail at the beginning of the proposal.
- The plan focuses on the two to four advantages of the proposition over the status quo.

EXAMPLE: *Resolved,* That law enforcement agencies should be given greater freedom in investigating and prosecuting crime.

I. [A detailed explanation of the specific points of the proposal is given here.]

II. The proposal would be comparatively advantageous to the status quo for the following reasons:

A. Greater freedom for law enforcement agencies would contribute to protection of all citizens by lowering the crime rate.

B. Greater freedom for these agencies would create more effective deterrence to crime, thereby helping to prevent young people from pursuing criminal activities.

In the comparative advantages pattern, you still must consider whether a problem exists. However, instead of identifying a serious problem that cannot be solved by the status quo and then giving a

Teaching the Lesson

You will probably want to guide students slowly through the information in this segment as there are many challenging terms. Be sure students understand how to build an affirmative case before they tackle a negative case and refutation and rebuttal. You may want students to work in small groups for **Activity 4** on p. 498. As you circulate among the groups to monitor the activity, have a few groups do the problem-solution pattern while the other groups do the comparative advantages pattern. Then have each group share and discuss their cases. Then the whole class can play the negative side and compile reasons against the affirmative cases.

When presenting **Considering Refutation and Rebuttal** on pp. 498–504, you may want to list on the chalkboard the four types of reasoning, their characteristics, and the questions that can

Cooperative Learning

Have students find some speeches on contemporary problems. Then, working in groups of three, students can prepare outlines of affirmative or negative cases as presented in the speeches. To find the texts of speeches, students can consult *Vital Speeches, Representative American Speeches,* the *New York Times,* or *U.S. News and World Report.* Groups can share their speeches and outlines with the class.

solution, you suggest a new proposal whose benefits would be so significant that the plan should be adopted whether a problem exists or not.

EXAMPLE: If you are able to show your friend that another route to school is shorter, has fewer traffic lights, and will get him to school faster than the route he now takes, your friend may try the route because it is comparatively advantageous. The question is not whether something is wrong with the old route, but whether the new route is *significantly* better. Your friend will not adopt the new route to save only fifteen seconds on a thirty-minute drive.

The Negative Case

The negative side's main goals are to develop the negative constructive case and to attack the affirmative's argument. The **negative case** gives reasons and evidence that

- act as straight refutation of the affirmative case
- defend the status quo
- for policy propositions, present a counterplan

The organization of negative speeches depends on which of these three courses the speech will take.

Straight Refutation. **Straight refutation** means that the entire negative case will be a denial of each affirmative argument stated—whatever reasons the affirmative team presents.

EXAMPLE:

Affirmative Case:

I. Restrictive Supreme Court rulings on law enforcement agencies have resulted in a continued increase in the crime rate.

II. Our plan for greater freedom for these agencies would work to solve this problem.

III. Our plan for greater freedom would be the best way to solve this problem.

Negative Case Using Straight Refutation:

I. Supreme Court rulings have not been the cause of the increase in the crime rate.

II. Giving greater freedom to law enforcement agencies would not work to solve this problem.

III. Giving greater freedom to law enforcement agencies would actually create more problems.

be used to refute each type. Guide students through the first question in **Activity 5** on p. 503 and then assign the rest of the activity as independent practice.

As you present the material on pp. 505–508, model the process of preparing a debate brief to prepare students for **Activity 6** on p. 509. You might choose the proposition and let the whole class help you construct the brief on the chalkboard or overhead projector. Students might benefit from working in pairs for **Activity 6.** To prepare students for **Activity 7** on p. 511, show a videotaped debate and guide the class through using a ballot to judge the debate. Then assign **Activity 7** as independent practice. You could have students take turns debating and judging until each student has had a chance to do both.

Defense of the Status Quo. To defend the status quo, the negative team explains the status quo and shows either how it is already meeting the problem or how it could meet the problem.

EXAMPLE:

Negative Case Defending the Status Quo:

I. Under the present system, police have the tools to cope with the increase in the crime rate.

II. The present system works better than would giving greater freedom to law enforcement agencies.

III. The present system has more benefits and fewer disadvantages than would giving greater freedom to law enforcement agencies.

The defense of the status quo has a major advantage. The negative team stands for something rather than simply being against the affirmative. This forces the affirmative to go on the defensive. Instead of just supporting its own case, the affirmative side must also attack the constructive arguments of the negative side. The major disadvantage of defending the status quo is that it requires the negative side to construct two arguments: one for the status quo and one against the proposition for change.

Counterplan. A **counterplan** is a different solution. Ordinarily, only the solution suggested in the policy proposition is debated. However, if the negative side agrees that a problem exists, it can present a solution that differs substantially from the affirmative's proposition. The debate then becomes a clash between the relative merits of the two solutions.

EXAMPLE:

Negative Case Counterplan:

I. The negative agrees that the crime rate has risen.

II. The best solution to this problem would be to involve more citizens in crime prevention programs.

III. Increased citizen participation in crime prevention would work better to lower the crime rate than would giving law enforcement agencies greater freedom.

IV. More citizen participation in crime prevention would have more benefits and fewer disadvantages than would giving law enforcement agencies more freedom.

The advantage of the counterplan is that it may catch the affirmative side off guard. In effect, when the negative side proposes a counterplan, the first affirmative speech has been wasted. If the negative side believes that the status quo has weaknesses, it is better off presenting a minor repair than defending the status quo.

Assessment

By monitoring and observing responses to **Activity 4,** you can assess students' understanding of building cases. You can check **Activities 5** and **6** to evaluate students' mastery of reasoning and preparing debate briefs. You may want students to turn in written evaluations or marked ballots for **Activity 7** so you can assess their understanding of the criteria for judging a debate.

Reteaching

Have students conduct a debate. The whole class will select a topic and develop a proposition. Give students time to gather evidence for and against the proposition. Then students will come to class with their evidence and draw to see which side they will be on. Half of the class will take the affirmative position and half will take the negative position. Then have students compile

Ongoing Assessment

Activity 4

Numbers 1–5 could be used for a problem-solution pattern, and numbers 6–8 could be used for a comparative advantages pattern. Here are some arguments against the reasons cited for the comparative advantages pattern.

1. Reducing commitments would not contribute to our meeting our foreign policy goals (refutes reason 6).
2. Reducing commitments would weaken ties with our traditional allies (refutes reason 7).
3. Reducing commitments would result in more problems than the present policy is causing (refutes reason 8).

Students should be able to defend their choices.

Teacher's Resource Binder

Skills for Success 3
Refuting an Argument

Activity 4

Selecting Reasons for Different Patterns of Argument

Imagine that you are on the affirmative side debating the policy proposition "*Resolved,* That the United States should substantially reduce its foreign policy commitments." In your research you have discovered the numbered reasons listed below. First, select the reasons you would choose for a problem-solution pattern. Next, select the reasons you would choose for a comparative advantages pattern. Finally, imagine that you are on the negative side and that you are using the straight refutation pattern. List the reasons you would use *against* the reasons you selected for the comparative advantages pattern.

1. Our foreign policy commitments have led to the loss of valuable friendships and prestige.
2. Our foreign policy commitments have significantly weakened the national defense.
3. Our foreign policy commitments have not significantly aided underdeveloped nations.
4. Our foreign policy commitments have not deterred aggression.
5. Our foreign policy commitments have weakened regional alliances.
6. Reducing commitments would better enable us to meet the goals of our foreign policy as set forth by the administration.
7. Reducing commitments would allow us to strengthen ties with traditional allies.
8. Reducing commitments would result in fewer problems than the present policy is causing.

Considering Refutation and Rebuttal

Refutation means attacking the argument of the opposition. **Rebuttal** means rebuilding your argument after it has been attacked.

Refutation

No matter which side you have taken in a debate, you may refute your opposition's quantity of evidence, quality of evidence, and reasoning from the evidence.

Quantity of Evidence. Any reason presented in a debate must be supported with evidence. Sometimes debaters give little or no supporting evidence. In such cases, the opposing team may simply refute an argument on that basis—lack of evidence.

their evidence and select one person to represent each side. Use the Lincoln-Douglas format and allow for group consultation. Require each person to create a brief. You can act as judge and provide an oral critique.

See p. 510 for **Extension, Enrichment,** and **Closure.**

Example: A debater gives little or no evidence to support the following reason: "Supreme Court decisions have unduly restricted law enforcement agencies." An opposing debater could refute by saying, "The affirmative has asserted that Supreme Court decisions have unduly restricted law enforcement agencies. We remind the affirmative that they have the burden of proof, and until we hear evidence to support the assertion, we need not reply to it."

Quality of Evidence. A more effective method of refutation is to attack the quality of the evidence presented. If sheer number of evidence cards were most important, judges would need only to count cards and would not have to weigh arguments. One statement by a law enforcement officer about the effects of a court decision on crime could be worth far more than interviews with a dozen random citizens.

Reasoning from the Evidence. The most effective form of refutation is to attack the opposition's reasoning from the evidence. Each argument is composed of at least three elements: (1) evidence or data from which a conclusion is drawn, (2) the conclusion itself, and (3) the reasoning that links the evidence and the conclusion. Most debates involve four common types of reasoning: generalization, causation, analogy, and sign.

PEANUTS reprinted by permission of UFS, Inc.

1. Generalization. A **generalization** is a conclusion based on one or more specific instances.

Examples:

- You noticed in your math class that Heather had a pocket calculator, Tim had a pocket calculator, and Tanya had a pocket calculator. If you concluded from these instances that all your classmates had pocket calculators, you would be reasoning by generalization.
- In the debate about giving law enforcement agencies more freedom, your opponent might argue that for the past twenty-five years most Supreme Court decisions related to

Critical Thinking

Analysis

Have students bring to class recent newspapers and magazines. Then have students work in small groups to locate five fallacies in the editorial, opinion, or news sections of the publications. The groups should also locate five fallacies in the advertisements. You may want to have students review the section on faulty reasoning in **Chapter 5: "Analyzing Yourself as a Communicator"** as they work. Each group can share its discoveries with the other groups.

investigation and prosecution of crime have restricted law enforcement agencies. He or she might cite three examples: the Mapp decision, the Mallory decision, and the Miranda decision. Thus, your opponent would be generalizing, using specific instances as the basis for a conclusion: that most Supreme Court decisions have restricted law enforcement agencies.

You can refute such a generalization by asking the following three questions:

- **Are enough instances cited?** Two or three examples are seldom enough to draw a generalization.
- **Are the specific instances typical of all possible instances?** If examples are very unusual, they do not provide a sound basis for a generalization. Other people will discount or dismiss such unusual examples.
- **Are there any negative instances, or instances that prove the opposite?** If negative instances can be found, they may disprove the generalization.

2. Causation. A **causation argument** provides a conclusion that is a direct result or a direct effect of one or more particular sources or conditions.

EXAMPLES:

- Your friend Heather told you that she studies math at least one hour a night. If you concluded that Heather will get a good grade in math, you would be reasoning by causation. Your reasoning is probably sound: Studying at least one hour a night often helps to produce good grades.

- Your opponent might argue that the crime rate has risen dramatically as a direct result of Supreme Court decisions restricting law enforcement agencies. Thus, your opponent would be presuming a causal relationship between Supreme Court actions and the crime rate. However, a rise in the crime rate does not necessarily mean that there is a causal relationship between that rise and the Supreme Court decisions.

To refute a causal relationship, ask the following two questions:

- **Are the items of evidence important enough to lead to the conclusion?** If the effect can be explained without the information being cited as evidence, then that information does not describe an important cause.
- **Do other factors really cause the effect?** If other sources or conditions seem more important in bringing about the effect, then you can question the causal relationship in the information presented as evidence.

3. Analogy. An argument can be based on an **analogy,** which is a comparison of something with a similar event, state, or set of circumstances.

EXAMPLES:

- A classmate, Jorge, has been elected to the National Honor Society. You recall that he is a junior, has a B average, and is active both in Glee Club and on the school newspaper. If you concluded that another classmate, Arletha, ought to have been elected to the National Honor Society because her background is similar to Jorge's, you would be reasoning by analogy.
- During a debate on crime, your opponent might argue that when law enforcement agencies in another country similar to ours (perhaps England or Canada) were given increased freedom, the crime rate there went down. If your opponent reasoned that the United States should give increased freedom to law enforcement agencies because the crime rate decreased when England or Canada relaxed controls over its law enforcement agencies, your opponent would be reasoning by analogy.

To refute an analogy, ask the following two questions:

- **Are the subjects that are being compared similar in all important ways?** Are criminal activity and the legal system in the United States similar to those in England or Canada? If subjects do not have significant similarities, then they are not really comparable.

Making Connections

Government

Students might find out what bills are currently being debated in Congress and study the arguments being used by the negative speakers against the bills. Students should consider the types of cases and the issues the negative sides are developing. Social studies teachers might be valuable resources for this exercise.

- **Are any of the differences between the two subjects important to the conclusion?** Do the crime rate and legal system in the United States differ in important ways from those in England or Canada? If so, then an analogy drawn between the United States and either of the other two countries may not be sound.

4. Sign. A **sign argument** draws a conclusion based on certain signs or indicators.

EXAMPLES:

- You see that your brother's eyes are watering and that his nose is running. If you concluded that he has a cold, you would be reasoning by sign.
- Your opponent might argue that the steady increase in the percentage of unsolved crimes is a sign of undue restrictions on law enforcement agencies.

To refute a sign argument, ask the following questions:

- **Do the signs given as evidence always indicate the conclusion?** Do watering eyes and a runny nose always indicate a cold? If not, they are not reliable indicators of the conclusion.
- **Are enough signs present?** Are the two signs, watering eyes and a runny nose, enough to indicate a cold? If not, the presence of the signs does not necessarily imply the conclusion.
- **Are there contradictory signs?** Is your brother alert and energetic? If so, he may not have a cold.

HOW TO *Refute an Argument*

1. **State clearly and concisely the argument you are going to refute.** For example, you might say, "The affirmative has argued that Supreme Court decisions have unduly restricted law enforcement agencies in the investigation of crime."
2. **State what you will prove.** Tell the audience how you plan to proceed so that they can follow your thinking. For example, you might say, "We on the negative side are going to argue that although law enforcement agencies are indeed restricted, there is no reason to believe that the restrictions are either undue or unnecessary."
3. **Present the proof completely with documented evidence.** For example, you might present facts, statistics, and quotations to back up your assertion that the restrictions are neither undue nor unnecessary.
4. **Draw a conclusion.** You cannot rely on the audience or the judge to draw the proper conclusion for you. Do not go on to another argument until you have drawn your conclusion. For example, you might say, "Therefore, we can see that although the police are restricted, the restrictions can hardly be labeled undue or unnecessary. Until the affirmative team can offer more evidence, we are going to have to conclude that these needed restrictions do not hamper law enforcement agencies."

ACTIVITY 5 Identifying Arguments and Questioning Their Reasoning

Identify the following arguments as generalization, causation, analogy, or sign. Then, for each of the six arguments, write two questions that you need to ask about that kind of reasoning.

1. After our neighbor painted his house, the leaves on the tree in front of our house started to turn brown. The paint must have had some poison in it.
2. Most of us got our lowest golf scores on the fifth hole. The fifth hole must be the easiest.
3. We think it's the measles. He has a fever and has broken out in a rash.
4. The plan worked well for North High's junior class. It will probably work for our junior class.
5. We're probably going to have a bad storm. The sky has filled with very dark clouds, the wind has started to blow, and lightning is flashing.
6. Each of the drivers got a flat tire at the intersection of Main Street and West Avenue. There must be something hazardous on the road.

Activity 5

Answers may vary. Most students will probably suggest the following answers:

1. causation
2. generalization
3. sign
4. analogy
5. sign
6. generalization

Students' questions should reflect those questions discussed in the text for each type of argument.

WRITING TO LEARN

Students can write letters to the editor of the local newspaper to refute an editorial, an opinion expressed in a column, or another letter to the editor. If their letters are well written and brief, encourage students to send their letters in. Maybe some will be published.

Rebuttal

Whereas *refutation* means attacking an argument, *rebuttal* means rebuilding an argument. Both sides have a chance to rescue points from their original arguments that have been attacked. Rebuttal is very similar to refutation in form.

HOW TO *Develop a Rebuttal*

1. **Restate the argument you made originally.** You might say, "We first argued that Supreme Court decisions have unduly restricted law enforcement agencies."
2. **State what your opponent said against your original point.** For example, you might say, "The negative argued that although law enforcement agencies are indeed restricted, there is no reason to believe that the restrictions are either undue or unnecessary."
3. **State your position on your opponent's attack.** You might say, "You will see that the negative side's evidence is far outweighed by evidence from all over the country."
4. **Present the proof completely, with documented evidence.** Use facts, statistics, examples, details, and quotations to support statements you make in rebuttal. For example, you might give a recent quotation from a police commissioner stating that court decisions have hampered efforts to indict and prosecute felons.
5. **Draw a conclusion.** You might say, "Therefore, we can see that even though the negative presented some isolated evidence in support of its attack, the bulk of the evidence supports our point that court decisions have unduly restricted law enforcement agencies."

TEACHER'S RESOURCE BINDER

Skills for Success 4
Developing a Rebuttal

Communication Journal

In your communication journal, keep a list of ideas that you might develop into debate topics. Some ideas for topics may spring to mind immediately, but others may occur to you as you attend class, talk with friends or relatives, listen to the news on television or radio, or read newspaper or magazine articles. When you have accumulated several good ideas, state each of them as debate propositions. Practice writing all three types: propositions of fact, propositions of value, and propositions of policy.

Shoe, by Jeff MacNelly, reprinted by permission: Tribune Media Services.

Creating a Flow Sheet

Listening is a critical debate skill. Your ability to debate effectively depends on your immediate understanding of each speech. To keep track of the flow, or progress, of arguments, take notes on each speech and, in parentheses, remind yourself how you will respond to each of the opposition's points. [For more on critical-listening skills, see pages 84–87 of Chapter 4.]

Make careful outline notes of each speech on a **flow sheet,** a record of the progress of arguments. Use an 8-1/2 × 14-inch legal pad turned sideways. Draw eight columns on the page. Then take notes on each speech as it is given. Accurately write each of the reasons presented, and include an abbreviated sketch of the evidence. Getting each speech down on paper in a separate column will help you to see the flow of the major arguments throughout the debate. This can help you to plan an effective strategy.

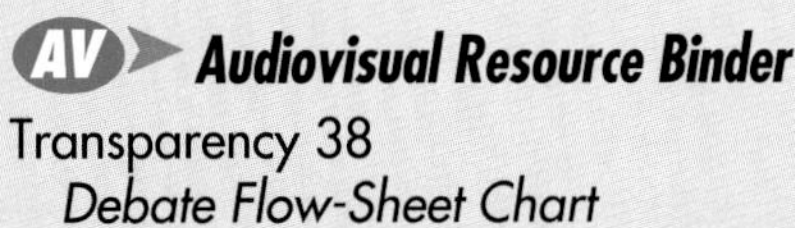

AV **Audiovisual Resource Binder**

Transparency 38

Debate Flow-Sheet Chart

USING THE CHART

To show students exactly how a flow sheet works, invite members of your school debate team to present a debate to the class after you have discussed the **Sample Flow Sheet** that is based on the national debate question of 1965. While listening to the debate, students can create flow sheets using the sample as a guide. Afterward, the debaters can explain informally how they build a case and prepare for a tournament, and students can compare their flow sheets with those of the debaters.

SAMPLE FLOW SHEET

PROPOSITION: *Resolved,* That law enforcement agencies should be given greater freedom in investigating and prosecuting crime.

1st Aff. Constructive	1st Neg. Constructive	2nd Aff. Constructive	2nd Neg. Constructive
I. Restrictive Supr. Court rulings on law enforcement have resulted in continued increase of major crime. →	Status quo is okay. →	Supr. Court rulings show status quo not effective. →	Aff. plan is not effective. Disadvantages: **1.** Reduce individual freedom.
A. Violent crime up 200% since 1961. →	**1.** Rise in crime rate not linked to Supr. Court rulings. →	**1.** Supr. Court rulings linked directly to 200% increase in crime rate.	**2.** Threaten civil liberties.
B. Crime up 25% in past 5 years. →	**2.** Rise in crime rate due to increase in population. →	**2.** Crime rate has grown 8 times faster than population.	**3.** Increase court backlog. Disadvantages 1, 2, and 3 outweigh the possible decrease in street crime.
II. Giving greater freedom would solve these problems.			
A. Police can work more effectively with fewer restrictions. →	**1.** Police will be tempted to abuse authority. →	**1.** Police work better without Supr. Court rulings.	
B. Crime rate will decrease. →	**2.** Crime rate will increase due to more arrests for minor crimes. →	**2.** Crime rate will fall: no link with number of arrests.	
III. Giving greater freedom would be the best solution to the problem.			
A. It would reduce street crime. →	Citizens' crime watch would be better solution. →	**1.** Crime watch is not enough.	
B. It would reduce the number of victims. →	∅ →	**2.** Argument for reduced number of victims—dropped.	

1st Neg. Rebuttal	1st Aff. Rebuttal	2nd Neg. Rebuttal	2nd Aff. Rebuttal
→ Status quo is okay. →	Status quo is not working. →	Status quo is okay. →	Increase in crime means status quo is not okay.
	Aff. plan will not create disadvantages.		
→	**1.** Will not reduce individual freedom; instead will protect.	Disadvantages 1 and 2: will reduce freedom and cause loss of civil liberties. →	Only affects criminals; does not harm individual civil liberties.
→	**2.** Hurts only criminal; helps victim & society.		
→	**3.** Backlog already exists. →	→ ∅ →	Disadvantage 3 dropped.
→ Population growth does not accurately reflect crime rate. →	Crime rate increase of 25% in past 5 yrs. must be considered.		
→ ∅ →	Neg. argument dropped on Point II. →	→ ∅ →	Aff. wins Point II.
→ ∅ →	Aff. proves that greater freedom is a solution. →	→	Greater freedom from Supr. Court rulings will solve problems.
→ Alternate solutions to giving police more power: Citizens' groups can work if crime decreases. →	Aff. plan is best method.		
→ Number of victims is not an issue →	Citizens' groups can't eliminate crime and can't aid victims. →	→ ∅ →	Point III dropped. Increased freedom is best way to solve problem and reduce crime rate.

Preparing the Debate Brief

The **debate brief** is a complete outline of the affirmative and negative cases. It is written before the debate and includes each side's reasons with an outline of the evidence to support each reason. Each item in the outline is written as a complete sentence.

Resolved, That law enforcement agencies should be given greater freedom in investigating and prosecuting crime.

Affirmative

I. Restrictive Supreme Court rulings on law enforcement have resulted in continued increase of major crime.

A. Violent crime has increased; it has shown an increase of 200% since 1961.

B. The general crime rate has increased by 25% during the last 5 years, an increase that was considerably greater than the increase in population over the same period of time.

II. Removing the restrictions on law enforcement agencies would improve protection for all citizens.

A. Law enforcement officials would be free to perform their work more effectively.

B. Because they will be able to work with fewer restrictions, law enforcement officials will be able to collect more evidence and solve more crimes.

C. The crime rate will decrease as people recognize that they do not have the legal loopholes to escape the law.

III. Giving law enforcement agencies greater freedom is the best solution to the problem of crime in the United States.

A. Other solutions, like citizens' crime watches, are only partially effective. Law enforcement agencies still have to have the freedom to investigate and prosecute.

B. It would reduce crime, and because fewer crimes would be committed, it would reduce the number of victims.

Negative

I. The current restrictions are not necessarily the cause of the increase in the crime rate.

A. There is no evidence of a direct link between the rulings of the Supreme Court and an increase in crime.

B. The rise in the crime rate is directly related to an increase in population.

II. Giving greater freedom to law enforcement agencies would not improve the protections for citizens.

A. Removal of safeguards to citizens will lead to abuse of authority.

B. Rather than decreasing, the crime rate would increase as more people are arrested for minor infractions.

III. Giving greater freedom to law enforcement agencies is not the best solution to the problem of the growing crime rate because it would create other problems.

A. It would lead to a loss of civil liberties and threaten every citizen's right to freedom from harassment.

B. The increase in arrests for minor crimes would increase the backlog in the court system.

Writing a Debate Brief

Choose a format for a debate. Decide on a proposition. Establish the affirmative and negative sides; then write a debate brief that identifies the specific arguments each side would present.

Judging Debates

A debate is not like a soccer game in which each goal made leads to a point scored. Debate is more like skating or gymnastics, in which each judge estimates how well each performer met a standard. Criteria for judging are fairly uniform, but applying the criteria is difficult, and two or more judges may disagree in their decisions. The following chart presents criteria for judging a policy debate using the traditional or cross-examination format.

Judging a Policy Debate

Pattern	Affirmative Must Prove	Negative Must Prove
Problem-Solution	**1.** that there is a significant problem **2.** that its proposition will solve the problem **3.** that its proposition offers the best solution	**1.** that no problem exists **2.** that the affirmative's proposition would not solve the problem **3.** that the affirmative's proposition either is not the best way to solve the problem or will cause new problems [**Note:** The negative needs to defeat only one of the affirmative's three issues.]
Comparative Advantages	**1.** that its proposition offers significant advantages over the status quo **2.** that its proposition will not create significant problems when implemented	**1.** that the advantages are not significant **2.** that significant disadvantages will result [**Note:** The negative needs to defeat only one of the affirmative's two issues.]

Ongoing Assessment

Activity 6

Briefs should contain properly worded propositions with detailed arguments and evidence for both the affirmative and the negative sides. The briefs should follow the format of the example on p. 508. Students will need library time to prepare their briefs.

EXTENSION

Have students bring to class examples in recent newspapers and magazines of the four types of reasoning discussed in this chapter. Students can show their examples to the class, explain how they would examine the arguments, and tell whether the reasoning is sound or faulty.

ADDITIONAL ACTIVITY

As a class, students can choose a debatable proposition and conduct a brief debate in the Lincoln-Douglas format. Each student will debate two rounds, one affirmative and one negative. Students can also serve as judges, or you might arrange for a judge who will decide the winners in each round. Undefeated debaters will meet other undefeated debaters. Eliminations will continue until two debaters remain. The debate between these two individuals will determine the class champion.

In many close debates, neither side actually wins an issue. Instead, the debate is decided by determining which side demonstrated superior skill in several possible areas: analysis, evidence, reasoning, organization, refutation, and presentation (expression, delivery, and rate). If no issues are decisively won or lost, the side with the most speaker's points is judged the winner.

For each debate, the judge completes a ballot. A ballot usually provides a place to insert speaker's points. It also contains sufficient space for comments about each speaker and a place to indicate who won. No one standard ballot exists for all high school debates, but the examples shown below are representative models.

Lincoln-Douglas debates are judged in much the same way that traditional and cross-examination debates are. The winner in a Lincoln-Douglas debate is the speaker who earns more points in organization, reasoning, delivery, supporting evidence, and persuasive argumentation of values. The ballot for a Lincoln-Douglas debate is shown below.

DEBATE BALLOT

University Interscholastic League

Conference: ______ Date: ______ Judge: ______ Room: ______ Round: ______

Affirmative Team #______ Negative Team #______

Circle the number on each category below representing your evaluation of each speaker:

1—Below Average 2—Average

1st Aff. Speaker	2nd Aff. Speaker	*Voting Criteria*
1 2 3 4	1 2 3 4	Analysis
1 2 3 4	1 2 3 4	Organization
1 2 3 4	1 2 3 4	Refutation
1 2 3 4	1 2 3 4	Oral Style
1 2 3 4	1 2 3 4	Speed of Delive
Total Points ____	Total Points ____	

AFFIRMATIVE CRITICISM: **NE**

Rank each debater in order of excellence (1st for best, 2

1st Aff. (Name) Rank (______) 1st

2nd Aff. (Name) Rank (______) 2nd

The significant clash(es)/issue(s) used as the basis for my

In my judgment, the ______

(Affirmative or Negative)

LINCOLN-DOUGLAS DEBATE BALLOT

University Interscholastic League

Conference: ______ Date: ______ Judge: ______ Room: ______ Round: ______

Affirmative #: ______ Negative #: ______

Circle the one number representing your evaluation of each speaker:

	Superior	Excellent	Good	Average
Affirmative	25 24 23 22 21	20 19 18 17 16	15 14 13 12 11	10 9 8 7 6
Negative	25 24 23 22 21	20 19 18 17 16	15 14 13 12 11	10 9 8 7 6

AFFIRMATIVE	**NEGATIVE**
Analysis:	Analysis:
Argumentation:	Argumentation:
Presentation:	Presentation:

Reason for Decision:

In my judgment, ______ debater # ______ won the debate.
(affirmative or negative)

Judge's Signature

Enrichment

Encourage students to watch a television news broadcast such as *Meet the Press* that presents two sides of an issue. Students can take notes using the format of the **Sample Flow Sheet** on pp. 506–507. Then students can evaluate the effectiveness of each position and share their ideas with the class. They might also offer suggestions for how these shows can be improved.

Closure

Write the categories of this segment on the chalkboard: affirmative case, negative case, refutation, rebuttal, flow sheet, brief, and judging. Then ask students to define each term while you list the responses under the headings.

Activity 7: Judging a Debate

Imagine that you are judging a debate. What issues would the affirmative side have to win in order to win the debate? What issues would the negative side have to win? Listen to a classroom debate and decide who won the issues. Also, give your evaluation of how each speaker performed in analysis, evidence, reasoning, organization, refutation, and presentation.

GUIDELINES for Participating in Debate

- Do I understand the debate proposition?
- Have I determined the key issues for the debate?
- Have I researched the topic carefully to develop reasons and evidence?
- Have I developed a case that is consistent with the material?
- Have I prepared a brief of my case?
- Have I anticipated the arguments of my opponent?
- Am I prepared to refute the arguments of my opponent?
- Am I prepared to rebuild the arguments my opponent attacks?
- Have I practiced?

Ongoing Assessment

Activity 7

Responses might go in students' communication journals and should contain specific details to support students' opinions and ideas. You could take up the journals, give them a quick check, and provide input. You might make copies of debate ballots for students to use for their evaluations.

Meeting Individual Needs

Linguistically Diverse Students

To review chapter concepts, show a videotape of one of the 1992 presidential debates. The debates will likely open windows for nonnative students through which important cultural information is conveyed. Although the format of these debates may not exactly parallel that of those mentioned in the text, elements of all three are implemented. After showing the videotape, encourage classroom discussion in which the debate is judged. Encourage students to give the same kind of evaluation described in **Activity 7.**

◆ Profiles in Communication

Performance Objective

- To observe and judge a debate

Teaching the Feature

Have a volunteer read aloud the profile of Chief Wilma Mankiller. Ask students what they think the personal qualities might be of a person who practices debate in his or her career. [Students may mention a logical mind and good verbal skills.]

Point out to students that formal debate is used mainly by people in law and government, but the skills of logic and reason developed in practicing debate are useful in many areas of life.

Activity Note

You may want to have students work together to develop a debate ballot for evaluating the debates in this activity. You could have the whole class watch the same debate and have a class discussion after student pairs or groups have formed their judgments; or as the textbook suggests, you could have pairs or groups work on their own and report to the class.

PROFILES IN COMMUNICATION

Wilma Mankiller, principal chief of the second largest Indian nation in the United States, learned to debate political issues as a teenager. In her home, she recalls, "arguments were never personal but were about some social or political idea. That stimulating atmosphere of reading and debating set the framework for me."

Ms. Mankiller has improved the lives of the more than 140,000 Cherokees she represents. She began her public service career doing volunteer work in San Francisco. As she studied tribal governance, sociology, and the history of the Cherokee people, she became angry at the injustices suffered by her people and committed to helping them regain their self-reliance. When she moved back to Oklahoma in 1977, she saw the tribe's great need for adequate housing, health care, and employment, and set out to provide needed services.

The communication skills nurtured in Wilma Mankiller around the kitchen table in her childhood home have been essential to her success. During her fourteen-hour workdays, she represents her people's interests in intense discussions with colleagues, investors, and local, state, and federal officials.

ACTIVITY

Working with one or more classmates, watch a debate. Watch a live debate or locate a videotape or a cassette recording of a debate through the media center.

Take notes, using the criteria given in this chapter to evaluate the performance of each participant. Keep in mind that you may not necessarily agree with the winner's opinion: You are simply evaluating his or her methods of debating the issue.

Decide, based on your notes on the participants' effectiveness in the debate, which side was the winner. Discuss your decision with your classmates, and explain your reasons for your choice.

S•U•M•M•A•R•Y

DEBATE is a form of decision making in which two or more people present speeches on opposing sides—the affirmative and the negative—of a public issue.

- **A debate centers on a proposition,** which clearly states a position on a specific topic. Propositions give the burden of proof to the affirmative side. They should be clearly worded and should deal with only one controversial topic.
- **Debate can follow any number of formats.** The most common formats are traditional, cross-examination, and Lincoln-Douglas.
- **A case** consists of the reasons and evidence that a side uses as a foundation for its position.
- **Constructive speeches** build arguments on both sides of the proposition. Depending on the type of proposition, both the affirmative and negative sides select patterns for organizing their arguments.
- **Refutation** is the attacking of ideas. Refutation may be based on the amount, the quality, or the reasoning of the evidence. **Rebuttal** is the rebuilding of an argument.
- **A debate brief** is an outline of the affirmative case, the negative case, or both. The debate brief includes all the reasons given for the case and key evidence that supports the reasons.
- **Debates are judged on two criteria:** which side gave the best argument concerning the issues and which side did the better job of debating.

CHAPTER **18**

Vocabulary

Find the meaning of each of the following terms. Write each term and its meaning in your communication journal.

affirmative case, *p. 494*
analogy, *p. 501*
burden of proof, *p. 481*
case, *p. 494*
causation argument, *p. 500*
comparative advantages pattern, *p. 495*
constructive speech, *p. 481*
counterplan, *p. 497*
cross-examination debate, *p. 485*
debate, *p. 479*
debate brief, *p. 508*
evidence, *p. 492*
flow sheet, *p. 505*
generalization, *p. 499*
key issues, *p. 488*
Lincoln-Douglas debate, *p. 486*
negative case, *p. 496*
prima facie* case, *p. 494
problem-solution pattern, *p. 495*
proof, *p. 490*
proposition, *p. 480*
propositions of fact, *p. 482*
propositions of policy, *p. 483*
propositions of value, *p. 483*
reasons, *p. 491*
rebuttal, *p. 498*
rebuttal speech, *p. 481*
refutation, *p. 498*
sign argument, *p. 502*
status quo, *p. 481*
stock issues, *p. 488*
straight refutation, *p. 496*
traditional debate (or **formal debate), *p. 485***

TEACHER'S RESOURCE BINDER

- Chapter 18 Vocabulary

REVIEW QUESTIONS

Answers

1. fact: Chris Smith is guilty; value: Compulsory national service for all qualified citizens is desirable; policy: Main Street should be made wider.
2. traditional, cross-examination, and Lincoln-Douglas; Traditional and cross-examination debates involve two affirmative speakers and two negative speakers and argue a proposition of policy. The time schedules are different, and in cross-examination the participants question their opponents. Lincoln-Douglas debate involves one affirmative and one negative speaker who argue a proposition of value; this format also includes cross-examination.
3. proposition of policy: ill, blame, cure, and cost; proposition of value: determine the criteria or standards of judgment for evaluation and determine whether the case meets the criteria

DISCUSSION QUESTIONS

Guidelines for Assessment

Student responses may vary.

1. The affirmative side goes first because debates begin with the assumption that the status quo is satisfactory until proven otherwise.
2. Cross-examination involves two affirmative and two negative speakers while Lincoln-Douglas has only one speaker to represent each opposing side and debates only propositions of value. The time schedules also differ. The Lincoln-Douglas format might be useful in loosely structured settings such as the workplace, where employees must research solutions to problems and present their plans. Cross-examination or traditional debate is used in more formal situations such as trials or public forums.
3. Pascal is possibly referring to the need to understand the opponent's point of view before a person can successfully argue against that point of view. In debate, the speaker can more easily demonstrate the invalidity of the opposite argument if he or she understands what makes the opponent's argument seem true.
4. In addition to building a sound case, an effective debater must use good analysis, reasoning, listening, and delivery skills that include vocal and facial expression, gestures, and eye contact.
5. Fuller may be saying that no matter how strong the argument, it is unlikely that a person will be convinced to accept a view that is against his or her principles or preferences. Applied to debate,

CHAPTER 18

Review Questions

1. Give an example of each of the three types of debate propositions: propositions of fact, propositions of value, and propositions of policy.
2. List the three standard debate formats and explain how they are alike and how they differ.
3. What are the stock issues for a proposition of policy? What are the stock issues for a proposition of value?
4. One way to organize the affirmative case for a proposition of policy is to use the problem-solution pattern. What is another way to organize the affirmative case?
5. One way to organize a negative case is to use the straight refutation approach. What are two other ways that a negative case can be organized?
6. What is a weakness of defending the status quo in the negative case?
7. Explain the difference between refutation and rebuttal and give at least one example of each.
8. One basis for refutation is the opposition's insufficient quantity of evidence. What are two other grounds for refuting the opposition's arguments?
9. One common type of reasoning is generalization. What are three other types of reasoning from the evidence?
10. What is the purpose of the flow sheet? of the debate brief?

Discussion Questions

1. Discuss some possible reasons why the tradition developed that the affirmative side always presents its case before the negative side in a debate.
2. Identify the major differences between a traditional or a cross-examination debate and a Lincoln-Douglas debate. Then, discuss cases in which each of these debate formats would be most appropriate.
3. The French mathematician and philosopher Blaise Pascal wrote, "When we wish to correct with advantage, and to show another that he errs, we must notice from what side he views the matter, for on that side it is usually true." First, discuss the meaning of this quotation. Then, discuss how it relates to the issues of refutation and rebuttal in debate.
4. Discuss why effective debating involves more than building solid arguments on the issues.
5. The famous English physician and writer Thomas Fuller wrote, "Argument seldom convinces anyone contrary to his inclinations." First, discuss the meaning of this quotation. Then, discuss how it relates to debate.

4. comparative advantage
5. defend status quo or offer counterplan
6. requires negative side to construct two arguments
7. In refutation, the speaker attacks the opponent's plan; in rebuttal, the speaker rebuilds his or her own case. Example arguments should be worded as a debater would state them.
8. the quality of evidence and reasoning from the evidence
9. causation, analogy, and sign
10. A flow sheet allows debaters to keep track of the progress of arguments during each phase of a debate; debate briefs allow debaters to organize arguments before a debate.

ACTIVITIES

1. Revising the Wording of Propositions. Rewrite the following propositions to meet the three guidelines for wording a proposition given on page 484.

a. All American auto makers should be required to install both driver's and passenger's side air bags on all models of their automobiles.

b. The system of funding public elementary education through property taxes should be reconsidered.

c. An equal rights amendment should not be adopted.

d. The current method for responding to stated complaints by customers interacting with personnel in both retail sales and in customer service should be altered in favor of customer satisfaction.

e. Motorcycle manufacturers should be permitted to produce for private ownership motorcycles that can exceed the legal speed limit by more than ten miles an hour.

2. Organizing Support for an Issue.

A. Select a stock issue on a policy of your own choice. Then, write the affirmative and the negative reasons that make up the proof for this issue. Finally, find three pieces of evidence to support each reason. Be prepared to discuss why the evidence that you have found through your research provides convincing support for the affirmative position and negative position.

B. Use either a problem-solution pattern or a comparative advantages pattern to organize the reasons and evidence you have gathered for Part A. Be sure that you have identified the status quo clearly, and be specific about how your reasons and evidence resolve the issue.

3. Understanding the Importance of a Historical Debate. Prepare an informative speech on one of the presidential election-year debates shown below or on another famous debate or series of presidential debates of your own choice. Identify, if possible, the most significant issue about which the participants disagreed. In proposition form, state each candidate's position on this issue.

As you investigate your topic, research the effects that this particular debate or series of debates had on the outcome of the election. Also, analyze and briefly explain how these results affected (or are likely to affect) subsequent political campaigns.

a. The Jimmy Carter-Ronald Reagan debates in 1980

b. The George Bush-Bill Clinton-Ross Perot debates in 1992

Fuller's statement suggests that debate will rarely change the ideas of someone who has already thought the matter through and come to a conclusion.

ACTIVITIES

Guidelines for Assessment

1. Responses will vary but should restate propositions to correct the following weaknesses:
   a. must contain only one topic
   b. *reconsidered* is unclear
   c. negative has burden of proof
   d. no specific plan of action; unclear wording
   e. "more than ten" not specific enough
2. A. Students should state their propositions clearly, and their stock issues should reflect the criteria in the chapter. You may want to have small groups of students evaluate each other's issues, reasons, and evidence.
   B. Students could prepare brief outlines like those on p. 495.
3. You may wish to refer students to **Chapter 14: "Speaking to Inform"** to review the features of an informative speech. Assess speeches on organization and delivery.

Summative Evaluation

Your **Teacher's Resource Binder** contains a reproducible **Chapter 18 Test** that may be used to assess students' mastery of the concepts presented in this chapter.

Portfolio Assessment

For future reference and evaluation you may want to have students keep in their portfolios any skill sheets or evaluation forms that you have used with this chapter along with any other recorded or written materials that students have created.

4. Propositions should reflect the criteria for each type as discussed in the chapter. Students might share their lists with the class for peer feedback.

5. Students' plans should include clearly stated propositions, the key issues, and well-developed reasons and evidence. You may want students to turn in their outlines and evidence cards or to present their cases to the class.

6. Students' responses need sound propositions and clearly stated issues supported by specific reasons and adequate evidence. Students can turn in their evidence cards, predictions of the opposition's arguments, and outlines in which they identify the patterns of cases. Or students could work in groups of four with one pair taking the affirmative side and the other pair taking the negative to present actual debates for the class.

4. Choosing Topics and Propositions for Debate. List three topics that you believe are worthy of debate. For each topic, write three debate propositions: a proposition of fact, a proposition of value, and a proposition of policy. Then list each set of propositions in your order of preference, giving the one you would most enjoy debating first.

5. Preparing for a Values Debate.

A. Select one of the following propositions of value or a proposition of your own choice for debate. Then list the key issues for the proposition that you selected.

1. *Resolved,* That the spirit of the law is more important than the letter of the law.
2. *Resolved,* That American presidential campaigns are too long.
3. *Resolved,* That plagiarism is morally wrong.

B. Select a partner, choose a side, and prepare to debate the proposition you selected in Part A. Identify the stock issues for the proposition, and develop reasons and evidence to support them. Prepare a file of evidence cards to use as you develop your case. Predict your opponent's arguments, and be prepared to discuss why your arguments are sound.

6. Preparing for a Policy Debate.

A. Select one of the following propositions of policy or a proposition of your own choice for debate. Then list the key issues for the proposition that you selected.

1. *Resolved,* That the minimum age to obtain a driver's license should be raised to eighteen.
2. *Resolved,* That all fifty states should follow the same yearly schedule for public schooling.
3. *Resolved,* That cat owners should be required to keep their pets on a leash.

B. Select a partner, choose a side, and prepare to debate the proposition you chose for Part A. Make sure that your issues can be supported by specific reasons. Prepare a file of evidence cards that you can use in developing your case. Identify the pattern or approach you will use to organize your evidence. Predict your opposition's likely arguments for the constructive speeches and for rebuttal and refutation. Be prepared to discuss why your position is more sound and more convincing than the opposing position.

◆ Real-Life Speaking Situations

PERFORMANCE OBJECTIVES

- To judge and write an evaluation of a debate
- To deliver a speech presenting a case for an imaginary legal case

REAL LIFE Speaking Situations

1 Decision makers in a democratic society—presidential candidates, members of Congress, local leaders—use debate to resolve opposing views. Many controversial topics that have a direct bearing on your life are discussed in these debates.

Attend a debate concerning a controversial topic that interests you. If you are unable to attend a live debate, you might watch one on television or watch a video recording of a presidential debate. Listen to the debate as carefully as you can, and chart it on a flow sheet. Judge the debate. (As a matter of fact, you will be a judge when you become a voter and cast your ballot on debated issues.)

Write a brief report on the main features of the debate—the proposition, the affirmative and negative cases, the issues, any refutation or rebuttal, and the outcome. Finally, give your evaluation of the debate. Who do you think won? Why? What were the strong points and weak points of the opposing arguments? Be prepared to give your report in class and to conduct a question-and-answer session afterward.

2 Attorneys practice debate as a profession. Laws and regulations establish the legal status quo. Cases involving these laws and regulations test them through debate. Opposing attorneys present the affirmative and negative arguments on how legal standards are specifically applied in each case. A judge or jury then evaluates the attorneys' arguments and decides which is stronger.

You are an attorney preparing the argument for your next case. First define your position and note the specifics of the case. Will you present the affirmative or the negative side—that is, are you the attorney for the defense or for the prosecution? What legal issues will you debate? Who is your client? What arguments will you offer to support your position?

Write a brief speech presenting your case. Be prepared to deliver your speech in class and to conduct a question-and-answer session in which you defend your position against issues and arguments offered by your classmates. Ask your teacher or classmates to evaluate your presentation according to the guidelines on page 511.

ASSESSMENT GUIDELINES

1. Reports should include the time and place of the debate and the names of the participants. Reports should also include specific details to support students' ideas and evaluations. When presenting their reports to the class, students might use extemporaneous delivery with note cards (the style often preferred by debaters).
2. You might encourage students to examine recent newspapers and magazines for possible scenarios in preparing their cases. Students can use some of the actual evidence and testimony as reported in these periodicals. To present their speeches to the class, students might want to speak extemporaneously as lawyers do during trials.

Chapter 19
Parliamentary Procedure
pp. 518–549

Chapter Overview

This chapter presents the principles of parliamentary procedure and discusses how this system for conducting orderly meetings operates. The information includes the rules for running a meeting and the duties of the officers. Also provided is a thorough explanation of the classification of motions and how they are used, changed, and voted on.

Teacher's Resource Binder

The following materials are identified at their point of use in this chapter:

- Skills for Success
  1 *Planning an Agenda*
  2 *Writing Minutes for a Meeting*
  3 *Understanding the Precedence of Motions*
  4 *Using Motions to Conduct Business*
- Chapter 19 Vocabulary
- Chapter 19 Test/Answer Key

AV Audiovisual Resource Binder

The following materials are identified at their point of use in this chapter:

- Transparency 39
  Understanding Motions

Introducing the Chapter

Some students may belong to school organizations that do not use parliamentary procedure. These students may recall occasions when they attended meetings that were so disorganized that nothing was accomplished. Or they may feel that a vocal minority usually runs the meetings or makes the decisions. Tell students that this chapter will provide them with the tools for conducting orderly meetings and establishing procedures for better decision making.

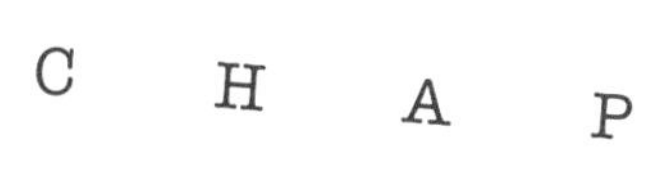

CHAPTER 19

Parliamentary Procedure

OBJECTIVES

After studying this chapter, you should be able to

1. Explain the principles of parliamentary procedure.
2. Explain the procedures for running a meeting.
3. Name the key officers of parliamentary organizations and describe the responsibilities of each.
4. Explain the five classifications of motions: main, subsidiary, privileged, incidental, and renewal.
5. Identify the traits and uses of parliamentary motions.
6. Identify the procedures for calling and completing a vote.

What Is Parliamentary Procedure?

Members of the prom committee are meeting to decide on the entertainment, and opinions differ as to what type of band should be hired. Committee members are shouting out their opinions to be heard by the group. One student, who strongly supports a rock-and-roll band, is arguing with another student, who prefers a rap band for the occasion. Several students believe that they have a majority in favor of hiring a jazz band, but they cannot get the group's attention in order to call a vote.

Without a system for an efficient and productive exchange of ideas, people with differing opinions are likely to spend long hours in heated debate that may never lead to a satisfactory resolution. **Parliamentary procedure,** a set of rules for conducting orderly meetings, was developed to prevent such inefficiency. The three major functions of parliamentary procedure are to ensure that meetings run smoothly, to help a group focus on the issues that are most important to the entire membership, and to ensure that meetings are run according to democratic principles.

Bibliography of Additional Materials

Professional Readings

- Jones, Garfield. ***Parliamentary Procedure at a Glance.*** New York: Viking Penguin.
- Ryan, Stanley. ***Parliamentary Procedure: Essential Principles.*** Cranbury, NJ: Associated University Presses.

Audiovisuals

- ***Parliamentary Procedure in Action***—Coronet/MTI Film & Video, Deerfield, IL (videocassette, 16 min.)
- ***Parliamentary Procedure in Action, Program 1: Order of Business***—Educational Video Network, Huntsville, TX (videocassette, 45 min.)
- ***Parliamentary Procedure in Action, Program 2: Introduction of New Business and Committees***—Educational Video Network, Huntsville, TX (videocassette, 45 min.)
- ***Parliamentary Procedure in Action, Program 3: Amendments, Point of Order, Appeal and Nominations***—Educational Video Network, Huntsville, TX (videocassette, 45 min.)

Segment 1 *pp. 520–526*

- **Understanding the Principles of Parliamentary Procedure**
- **Running a Meeting**
- **Understanding the Duties of Officers**

Performance Objectives

- To analyze a group meeting in terms of parliamentary procedure
- To investigate quorum requirements
- To write an agenda for a group meeting
- To evaluate the performance of officers in a group that uses parliamentary procedure
- To determine one's suitability to be an officer of an organization

Making Connections

Technology

Obtain permission to record on audiotape or videotape a general session of a parliamentary group such as the city council. Edit the tape to use only significant portions that illustrate procedures addressed in this chapter such as calling a meeting to order or beginning a new step in the order of business. You could use this edited tape in several ways: as preparatory material before a lesson, as a source of dynamic examples during a lesson, or as a review following a lesson.

Teaching Note

The best way to learn parliamentary procedure is to use it in an organized group that operates by the rules of parliamentary procedure. Turn the class into a parliamentary body, elect officers, and conduct the class as a meeting, with class decisions made according to the rules of parliamentary procedure.

Understanding the Principles of Parliamentary Procedure

Many groups—governmental, business, educational, and social—conduct their business at meetings to which all members are invited. Based on the rules and customs of the early British Parliament, the set of rules for conducting meetings is called **parliamentary procedure.**

To maintain order, group meetings are generally conducted according to the following five principles of parliamentary procedure.

Principles of Parliamentary Procedure*

Principle	Explanation	Advantage
Only One Item at a Time	Only one matter of business may be considered at a time.	helps to maintain order
Open Discussion	Everyone has a right to express an opinion, and each opinion is treated as valuable.	enables the group to come to an informed decision
Equality of Voting Rights	Every member has the right to vote, and each vote is counted as equal.	ensures a fair vote
The Majority Rules	The minority agrees to accept the decisions of the majority. Most votes require a **simple majority,** which consists of at least one more than half of those voting. Special situations need a two-thirds majority.	assures that the collective judgment of the group prevails; saves time
Protection of Minority Rights	• When any motion infringes on personal rights, at least two thirds of those present and voting must affirm that motion for it to pass. • Rules give minority opinion an equal right to be heard on all motions.	assures that each motion is carefully considered from all viewpoints

* For a complete discussion of parliamentary procedure, consult *Robert's Rules of Order, Newly Revised.*

Motivation

Begin the lesson by asking students to list all the organizations they belong to. Then ask students to discuss how these organizations conduct their meetings and business. Write the following questions on the chalkboard and have students refer to them in the discussion: How and when are meetings called? What order do the meetings follow? Who are the officers and what are their responsibilities? How are decisions made? Does a minority or the majority rule?

After the discussion, tell students that in this segment they will learn the principles and procedures of conducting an orderly meeting. They will also be able to determine whether their organizations follow these principles and procedures.

Public Record

All proceedings included in a meeting are considered to be a matter of public record. The group's secretary takes **minutes,** a written and official record of the meeting's proceedings. These minutes are read and presented for an approval vote at the next scheduled meeting. They are kept in the official files of the organization.

ACTIVITY 1 **Analyzing a Group Meeting**

Plan with a classmate to attend a meeting of a formal group, such as a town council. Note when the group used parliamentary procedure. How were the rights of individuals protected? How did the members benefit from observing the principles of parliamentary procedure? Discuss these questions with your classmate.

Running a Meeting

The rules of parliamentary procedure cover almost all situations that might arise during a meeting: the writing of the constitution and bylaws, the duties of officers, and the specific rules governing debate. An organization can also create its own set of rules, to be included in the organization's constitution and bylaws.

MEETING INDIVIDUAL NEEDS

Cultural Diversity

Activity 1 suggests that each student plan with a classmate to attend a meeting of a formal group. Because some of your students may be new to this country (and therefore to the school and community), they may feel shy about approaching fellow classmates. Assign groups of two or three students to attend specific meetings. (A city council meeting is ideal.) Make sure that transportation is not a problem. Ensuring that students participate in the activity can be advantageous in two ways: Students can learn important cultural and social information from the experience, and they will have opportunities for shared peer activities.

ONGOING ASSESSMENT

Activity 1

Students can present their observations informally for the class. They should discuss how the group they observed used the principles of parliamentary procedure, and they should note specific details to support their opinions.

TEACHING THE LESSON

To begin the lesson, invite students to examine the **Principles of Parliamentary Procedure** chart on p. 520 and **Running a Meeting** and **Understanding the Duties of Officers** on pp. 521–526. Discuss the advantages of parliamentary procedure briefly, and ask students to brainstorm and list on the chalkboard organizations that use parliamentary procedure. Then ask students to list any organizations that might not benefit from using parliamentary procedure. Compare the two lists of organizations and discuss the criteria that might be used to determine whether a group would find parliamentary procedure effective for meetings. (For example, size of group, formality, kind of business, and regularity of meetings could be considered.)

Before assigning **Activities 1, 2,** and **4** as independent practice, help students research

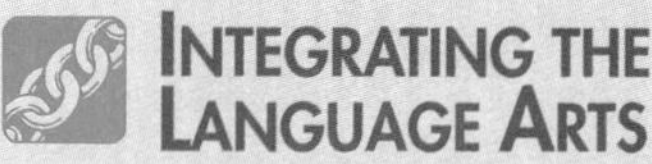

INTEGRATING THE LANGUAGE ARTS

Research Link

Students might use their library skills to find *Robert's Rules of Order* and other books that address topics such as the origins of parliamentary procedure. Working in small groups, students can present their discoveries to the class in a symposium or a panel-discussion format.

ONGOING ASSESSMENT

Activity 2

Students can present their investigations informally to the class. In determining the quorum, each student should be able to support his or her opinion with specific reasons.

Although all of these rules and procedures are important, the ones that are most vital to you in your role as a potential leader or member of an organization are those that deal directly with running a meeting.

Calling a Meeting

When a meeting is planned, members must be given notice, usually ten days in advance, that the group will assemble. Notice should be provided to members in writing, and commonly an **agenda,** a short list of items to be discussed, is included. This practice ensures that all members are aware of the group's planned activity and have an opportunity to participate.

Advance notice is important for special meetings or meetings for a group that does not meet on a regular basis. If officers fail to give members advance notice, any business conducted at a meeting can be nullified. In addition, if it can be proved that officers planned to hold a secret meeting, they can be removed from office.

The Quorum

At the beginning of a meeting, the chairperson must always make sure that a quorum is present. A **quorum** is the minimum number of members that must be present for the group to conduct business. A quorum can be set at any number. For most groups, the quorum is set at 40 to 60 percent of the membership. For very large organizations, 20 percent of the membership often constitutes a quorum. If no number is set by an organization, then the quorum is one person more than 50 percent of the membership.

The quorum should be high enough that the business conducted represents the thinking of the organization as a whole. However, it must be low enough that a reasonably well attended meeting is likely to have enough members to conduct business.

Setting a Quorum

Investigate the quorum requirements of two groups that meet on your school campus or in your community. Ask the officers or members of each group why they chose high or low quorum requirements, and report your findings to the class. Suppose that your class were going to function as an organization. What number would you suggest as a quorum? Why?

school and community groups, and then post a list of possible meetings that the students can visit. Be sure to model an effective analysis of a meeting before students go to one. Students should report their findings to the class.

Students might work in small groups to complete **Activity 3** and then compare their agendas and get comments from their classmates.

ASSESSMENT

By observing how well students analyze group meetings and plan imaginary agendas in **Activities 1–4,** you can assess students' understanding of this segment. If you feel students need to commit the material to memory, you might give a brief quiz over the information.

Order of Business

The order of business for a meeting involves the sequence of items on the agenda. Most formal organizations use the following standard items, which are suggested in *Robert's Rules of Order.*

1. Call to order
2. Reading and approval of minutes from previous meeting
3. Officers' reports
4. Standing committee reports
5. Special committee reports
6. Old business
7. New business
8. Announcements
9. Adjournment

A group can follow this standard order of business or set its own order of business in its bylaws. Even when an order is set, items can be shifted with the consent of the group.

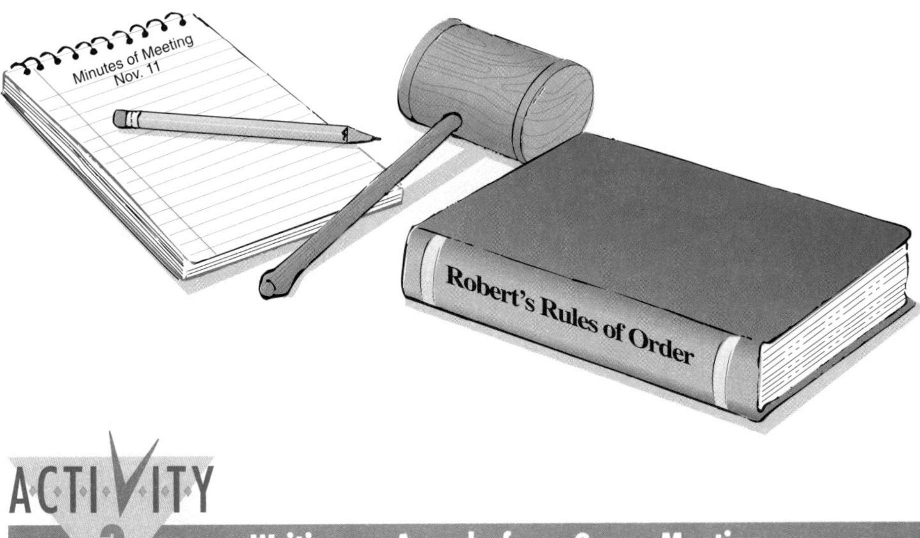

ACTIVITY 3

Writing an Agenda for a Group Meeting

Imagine that your class functions as an organization. At the last meeting the group members elected class officers for the year, and at the upcoming meeting they will begin to consider new business. Write an agenda that could be used for that meeting. Be creative, but make sure that you include the standard items listed under "Order of Business." Then share your agenda with your classmates and respond to feedback from them.

ONGOING ASSESSMENT

Activity 3

Students might include in their communication journals the agendas they propose. After students have shared with the class, they can turn their journals in to you for a quick check. Their agendas should reflect the standard sequence listed on this page.

TEACHER'S RESOURCE BINDER

Skills for Success 1
Planning an Agenda

RETEACHING

Divide the class into three or four groups and ask each group to set up a mock organization that is to hold a meeting. Each group should select officers, establish a meeting time, and determine an agenda. Ask each group to explain the process followed and to determine the responsibilities of the officers.

An Alternative Approach

Be prepared to give students prompts as they make their first efforts with parliamentary procedure. Often it is the chairperson's duty to prompt members; however, you will likely need to assume this duty unless one of the students is very knowledgeable about parliamentary procedure and can act as a qualified chair. As you prompt students, remind them repeatedly that you know they are novices so that they do not become overanxious or hesitant to participate.

Understanding the Duties of Officers

Parliamentary organizations have at least three key officers. The chairperson presides, or exercises control, over meetings. When the chairperson is absent, the vice-chairperson presides. The secretary keeps an accurate, official record of each meeting, the minutes.

The Chairperson

The **chairperson,** or chair, is responsible for running pleasant, efficient meetings and for protecting the rights of everyone at the meetings. To do so, the chairperson should have a mastery of parliamentary procedure. The chairperson should

- govern the group by parliamentary procedure, an established organizational pattern that members can agree on
- educate the members of the organization by explaining procedures whenever necessary, so that everyone understands what is taking place and why it is taking place
- maintain order by insisting that all members follow parliamentary procedure during meetings
- be fair in recognizing members to speak

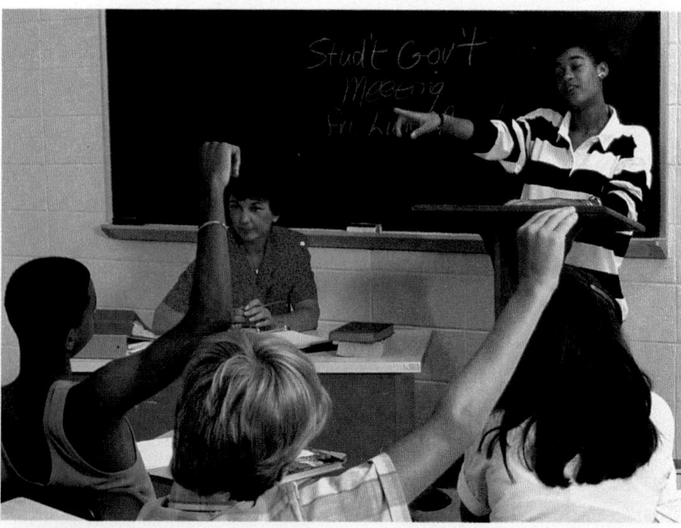

Procedure calls for a member to raise one hand (or to stand at large meetings) to be recognized. In small groups, people may just speak out. Effective chairpersons try to ensure fair speaking order, to avoid having especially outspoken people dominate the meeting.

EXTENSION

Have each student interview at least one member of an organization that uses parliamentary procedure. Students should ask some of the following questions:

1. How does parliamentary procedure help get business done?
2. How does it permit the participation of all members?
3. How does it allow the minority to be heard?
4. How does it save time?
5. What personal characteristics are necessary for a person to serve competently as an officer?

Students should report the results to the class.

HOW TO *Ensure Fair Speaking Order*

1. Give the person who made the motion the right to speak first.
2. Call on each person by name.
3. If possible, try to alternate speakers so that the different sides of an issue are presented in a balanced discussion.
4. Be sure that everyone has a chance to speak once before anyone gets the chance to speak for a second time.
5. Maintain good eye contact with the whole group. The chair should not always look at the same section of the group or at the same person whenever a debate begins.

The Vice-Chairperson

The **vice-chairperson** assumes the duties of the chair when the chair is unable to do so. The vice-chair also assumes the duties of the chair when the chair steps down to debate a motion. Once a chair steps down, he or she cannot resume the role of chair until that particular motion is voted upon.

The Secretary

The **secretary,** the major recording officer and keeper of records, must be trustworthy and accurate. The primary role of the secretary during a meeting is to take the minutes. Policy demands that proceedings be a matter of public record. Therefore, the minutes are kept on file.

A secretary can keep an official record of a meeting with handwritten notes and electronic devices.

COOPERATIVE LEARNING

After students have read and discussed the responsibilities of each officer in a parliamentary organization, form groups of three or four students and assign each group one office. In their groups, students should brainstorm all the qualities a person might need to be effective in that particular office. Then each group should share the list they generated with the class. Allow time for students to compare their lists.

TEACHER'S RESOURCE BINDER

Skills for Success 2
Writing Minutes for a Meeting

Enrichment

Have students create cue cards to use during meetings that are conducted using parliamentary procedure. Students might make cards covering guidelines for running a meeting, duties of officers, items to include in minutes, and order of business.

Closure

Ask students to close their books and to recall the elements of parliamentary procedure they have learned so far. After they have exhausted the ideas, ask them to refer to their textbooks for anything they may have forgotten.

Writing to Learn

Ask each student to write an account of a meeting of a group to which the student belongs (or an account of a fictitious meeting). The account should follow the order of business listed on p. 523. Descriptions of reports and of new and unfinished business should be given.

Ongoing Assessment

Activity 4

Students might present their reports informally for the class. Students' descriptions of how the officers perform their duties should include specific details.

What to Include in the Minutes

1. The kind of meeting (regular or special)
2. The name of the organization
3. The date, hour, and place of the meeting
4. The name of the presiding officer
5. The number of members present and the names of absentees
6. The action taken on minutes of the previous meeting
7. Committee reports
8. Each main motion, the name of the person introducing it, and the action taken
9. Points of order and appeals
10. Any material that in the future may be helpful in explaining what was done at the meeting
11. The program, if any, such as a special presentation, speech, ceremony, or entertainment
12. The time of adjournment

Evaluating the Performance of Officers

Attend a meeting of a group in your school or community that uses parliamentary procedure. Note how each of the club officers performs his or her duties. Be especially aware of how the chairperson ensures that everyone's rights are protected during debate on any motions that are presented. How well does the chair maintain order? How does the chair maintain fairness in recognizing members to speak? Comment on any failures you note during the proceedings, and suggest ways that they could have been avoided by adhering to parliamentary procedure.

Do you think that you would like to be an officer of an organization? If so, which office most appeals to you? In your journal, list the responsibilities of that office. Then examine your character traits, your strengths and weaknesses, and your likes and dislikes. Evaluate whether or not you would be a good candidate for the office.

Segment 2 *pp. 527–543*

- **Understanding Motions**
- **Using Motions**
- **Voting on a Motion**

Performance Objectives

- To apply the rules governing motions to specific situations
- To demonstrate knowledge of how to make and amend a motion
- To observe televised proceedings of a legislative body and to report on voting procedures

Understanding Motions

In a parliamentary organization, all of the business in a meeting is handled through the making of motions. A **motion** is a proposal for action made by a member. There can be no discussion unless there is a motion before the members. Once a motion is made, the members must act on it in some way.

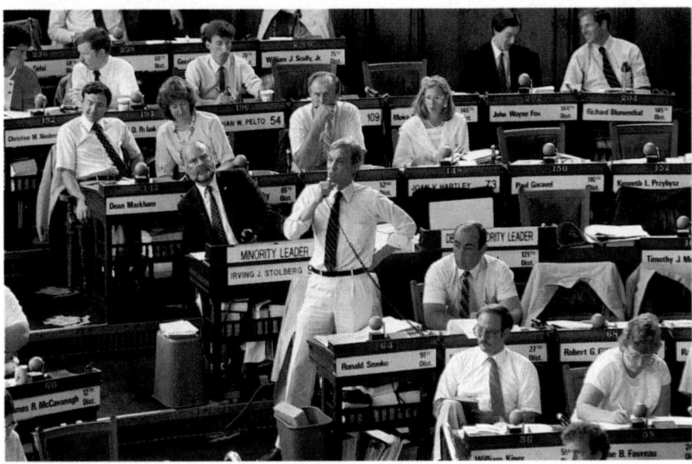

Classification of Motions

In most groups you will use five classifications of motions:

- main
- subsidiary
- privileged
- incidental
- renewal

Main Motions. **Main motions** are those that set forth new items of business to be considered. Ordinarily, they must be made first; many of the motions in the other classifications are used in response to main motions. There can be only one main motion on the floor at a time.

EXAMPLES:

- I move that club members actively participate in the drive to eradicate illiteracy.
- I move that we hold a Valentine's dance on February 14.
- I move that club members volunteer to work one hour a week at the local day-care center.

Meeting Individual Needs

Linguistically Diverse Students

The terminology in this segment may be difficult for nonnative speakers to learn because of the number and similarity of terms. You may want to suggest that students make frequent journal entries of unfamiliar vocabulary words.

As often as possible, give simple definitions of key vocabulary items and model ways of using the words in simple, informal sentences. For example, define *agenda* as "list" or "program." Then use it in an expression to clarify the meaning. "What's on the agenda?" might mean "What are you planning to do today?" Write the terms, definitions, and sentences on the chalkboard and have students copy the information in their journals.

The vocabulary study might include the following terms: *agenda, quorum, preside, assume, resume, minutes, postpone, amend, adjourn, recess, incidental, rescind, withdraw, precedence,* and *debatable.* Make these abstract terms as concrete as possible to enhance students' understanding and interest.

Motivation

Present several scenarios of formal business meetings to the class. Stop your descriptions at the point at which a particular motion would be appropriate. Ask students to speculate as to what event might happen next and list ideas on the chalkboard. Some students will probably know a little about motions, and they may suggest a motion during the class discussion. Tell students that in this segment they will learn about the categories of motions and how to use the motions.

MEETING INDIVIDUAL NEEDS

An Alternative Approach

Ask students who are adept at using parliamentary procedure (perhaps those who have served as chairpersons) to lead class activities. You might devise a tutorial plan that allows the more experienced students to work with the less experienced students during class activities.

Subsidiary Motions. **Subsidiary motions** allow members to change or dispose of a main motion that is being discussed.

1. The motion to **lay on the table** calls for a temporary postponement of action until someone makes a motion to remove the original motion from the table.
2. The motion to move the **previous question** calls for a vote to stop discussion on a motion.
3. The motion to **limit debate** calls for a time limit on individual speeches or on the entire debate; the motion to **extend debate** moves that debate be extended to allow more complete discussion of the issue.
4. The motion to **postpone to a definite time** calls for a postponement of action until a particular time set by the person making the motion.
5. The motion to **refer to a committee** calls for shifting discussion of the matter at hand to a smaller group meeting at some other time.
6. The motion to **amend** calls for an alteration in the wording of a motion.
7. The motion to **postpone indefinitely** calls for a postponement of discussion for that session and thus prevents the main motion from coming to a vote.

Privileged Motions. **Privileged motions** concern the running of the meeting itself. Because of their urgent nature, they take precedence over all other classes of motions.

1. The motion to **adjourn** calls for the meeting to close.
2. The motion to **recess** calls for a break during the meeting.
3. The motion **question of privilege** calls for immediate action on such things as heating, lighting, ventilation, and disturbances.

Teaching the Lesson

The class might benefit by having several volunteers read aloud the information in the chapter. You should periodically stop to clarify any terms and to answer any questions. The **Table of Parliamentary Motions** on p. 533 will prove valuable, but students will probably need much practice before they are able to understand and use the various motions.

To provide guided practice, call out a motion listed in the **Table of Parliamentary Motions** and have students answer one or more of the following questions: Does the motion require a second? Is it debatable? What vote does it require? What motion is directly above it in the order of precedence?

Drill the class in this manner for a while and provide oral prompts when needed. After the class seems comfortable with the various

4. The motion **call for the orders of the day** alerts the chairperson that a scheduled event has been overlooked.

Incidental Motions. The motions that relate to questions of procedure arising out of the discussion are called **incidental motions.** There are a number of these incidental motions that are commonly used.

1. The motion to **appeal** is used to force the chairperson to submit a disputed ruling made by the chairperson to a vote by the entire group.
2. The motion to **close nominations** calls for an end to the process of nominating persons for offices.
3. The motion **division of assembly** requires the chairperson to call for a second vote. This second vote will preferably be conducted by a method other than the method used to conduct the first vote.
4. The motion **division of question** requires the chairperson to divide a motion with more than one part into its various parts. Dividing a question allows each part to be discussed and voted on separately.
5. The motion to raise a question of **parliamentary inquiry** is made to request information about whether making a motion would be in order. This motion is always made to the chair.
6. The motion **object to consideration** allows the group to dismiss a main motion that is irrelevant, that is considered inappropriate, or that is for some other reason deemed undesirable. Objections to consideration must be made before any debate of the main motion begins and before any subsidiary motions are made.

motions, you can develop a game organized like a spelling bee.

After the class becomes familiar with the parliamentary motions, students can proceed to **Activity 5** on p. 534, which they might do with partners. Before you assign **Activity 6** on p. 537, model the proper wording for making and amending motions. If your community is small or if your television listings are limited, you may want to provide an alternative activity so students can observe voting procedures for **Activity 7** on p. 543.

7. A motion to **reopen nominations** is made to allow more nominations to be made after nominations have been closed.
8. A motion to **suspend the rules** calls for the suspension, during the current meeting, of any standing rule that the organization may have. Such suspensions are generally intended to allow members to do something not normally allowed by the rules.
9. A motion to **establish the method of voting** calls for the chairperson to take the vote in the manner stated in the motion (for instance, by secret ballot or by a show of hands).
10. A move to **withdraw a motion** gives the person who made the motion permission to remove it from consideration.
11. The motion **point of order** calls attention to a violation of parliamentary procedure.

"You can't move we adjourn, Wilson. We just started."

Renewal Motions. **Renewal motions** get discussion reopened on decisions that have already been made. There are three renewal motions that you will use.

1. The motion to **reconsider** calls for discussion of a motion that has already been passed.
2. The motion to **rescind** calls for the cancellation of action taken on a previous motion.
3. The motion to **take from the table** calls for reopening discussion of a motion that had earlier been laid on the table by a subsidiary motion.

Assessment

By checking **Activities 5** and **6,** you can assess students' mastery of the skills covered in this segment. Again, a few short quizzes might also isolate areas that need reteaching.

Reteaching

With your class, set up an imaginary club or governmental body and conduct a meeting. Begin by establishing an agenda. Have students form two groups with different ideas about the agenda. One group wishes to pass as many motions as possible; the other group wishes to postpone action on as many motions as possible. Elect a chair and begin the meeting. You may 

Making Connections

Community Involvement

Invite a public official such as a city council member, a school board member, or a local legislator to your class to speak about real-life situations in which participants need to know and use parliamentary procedure. Ask the speaker to prepare several examples that show how formal rules have saved the day in meetings. Provide for a question-and-answer period.

Business in a formal parliamentary body, whether large or small, is conducted through *motions.*

Precedence of Motions

Perhaps the main appeal of parliamentary procedure is its orderliness. The motions that are listed on pages 527–530 are presented in the order in which they can be introduced. The order in which the motions must be voted on or acted upon is called the **order of precedence.** Privileged and subsidiary motions are ranked above main motions in the following order.

Privileged Motions	**1.** Adjourn **2.** Recess **3.** Question of privilege **4.** Call for the orders of the day
Subsidiary Motions	**5.** Lay on the table **6.** Previous question **7.** Limit debate or extend debate **8.** Postpone to a definite time **9.** Refer to a committee **10.** Amend **11.** Postpone indefinitely
Main Motions	**12.** Any main motion

Teacher's Resource Binder

Skills for Success 3
Understanding the Precedence of Motions

want to act as parliamentarian. After adjourning, discuss the experience with students.

See p. 541 for **EXTENSION, ENRICHMENT,** and **CLOSURE.**

A motion of higher precedence is in order when a motion of lower precedence is on the floor.

EXAMPLE: Suppose that the main motion before a student council meeting is "to hold a dance in the school gym on Saturday, March 15, beginning at 8:00 P.M." If while the motion is being debated someone moves "to lay the motion on the table" (number 5 in precedence), this motion takes precedence over the main motion (number 12). If after the motion "to lay on the table" is seconded, or supported by another person, someone else moves "to postpone discussion of the main motion until the next meeting" (number 8), this motion is out of order because "lay on the table" (number 5) is of higher precedence than "postpone to a definite time" (number 8).

Note that incidental motions and renewal motions are not ranked in order of precedence. They are dealt with as they are made rather than in a sequential order of preference.

Table of Parliamentary Motions

The following table gives a concise overview of the rules governing motions. The first column, labeled "Rank," gives the order of preference. Needing a **second** means that a person other than the person making the motion must indicate that he or she is willing to have the group consider the motion. **Debatable** refers to whether that motion can be discussed by the group before it is voted upon. **Amendable** refers to whether any changes in the motion are allowed.

TABLE OF PARLIAMENTARY MOTIONS

Privileged, Subsidiary, and Main Motions

Rank	Name of Motion	Interrupt a Speaker?	Need a Second?	Debatable?	Amendable?	Vote
1.	Adjourn	no	yes	no	no	maj.
2.	Recess	no	yes	yes	yes	maj.
3.	Question of privilege	yes	no	no	no	none
4.	Call for the orders of the day	yes	no	no	no	none
5.	Lay on the table	no	yes	no	no	maj.
6.	Previous question	no	yes	no	no	2/3
7.	Limit or extend debate	no	yes	yes	yes	2/3
8.	Postpone to a definite time	no	yes	yes	yes	maj.
9.	Refer to a committee	no	yes	yes	yes	maj.
10.	Amend	no	yes	yes	yes	maj.
11.	Postpone indefinitely	no	yes	yes	no	maj.
12.	Any main motion	no	yes	yes	yes	maj.

Incidental Motions

Name of Motion	Interrupt a Speaker?	Need a Second?	Debatable?	Amendable?	Vote
Appeal	yes	yes	yes	no	maj.
Close nominations	no	yes	no	yes	2/3
Division of assembly	yes	no	no	no	none
Division of question	yes	no	no	yes	none
Parliamentary inquiry	yes	no	no	no	none
Point of order	yes	no	no	no	none
Object to consideration	yes	no	no	no	2/3
Reopen nominations	no	yes	no	yes	maj.
Suspend the rules	no	yes	no	no	2/3
Voting, motions relating to	no	yes	no	yes	maj.
Withdraw a motion, leave to	yes	no	no	no	maj.

Renewal Motions

Name of Motion	Interrupt a Speaker?	Need a Second?	Debatable?	Amendable?	Vote
Reconsider	no	yes	yes	no	maj.
Rescind	no	yes	yes	yes	2/3
Take from the table	no	yes	no	no	maj.

USING THE CHART

You may want students to keep the **Table of Parliamentary Motions** handy as they work through this segment. They might even work with partners to memorize the information. The ability to recall quickly the types of motions and to know how to use them will make participation in class activities for this chapter easier for students.

Transparency 39
Understanding Motions

Ongoing Assessment

Activity 5

Students can turn in this activity to you for a quick check.

1. a. yes d. yes
b. yes e. no
c. no

2. a. no vote
b. 2/3 majority
c. simple majority
d. 2/3 majority
e. simple majority

3. a. yes d. yes
b. no e. yes
c. yes

MEETING **INDIVIDUAL** NEEDS

Students with Special Needs

Students with learning disabilities need as much structure in their assignments as possible. To help students complete question 3 in **Activity 5,** provide the following list of steps:

1. Use a straightedge to help read the lines.
2. Underline the two motions.
3. Decide what the rank of motion 1 is. What is the rank of motion 2?
4. Evaluate. Is the rank of motion 2 lower than that of motion 1? Then motion 2 is in order. Is the rank of motion 2 greater than that of motion 1? Then motion 2 is out of order.

ACTIVITY 5 Understanding Motions

The key to understanding and using motions is to know when a motion is in order, whether it is debatable or amendable, and what vote it requires to pass. Use the table on page 533 to help you complete the following activities.

1. Indicate whether each of the following motions is amendable.
a. Take a recess
b. Main motion
c. Lay on the table
d. Postpone to a definite time
e. Adjourn

2. Indicate what vote (no vote, simple majority, or two-thirds majority) each of the following motions requires to pass.
a. Call for the orders of the day
b. Close nominations
c. Take from the table
d. Previous question
e. Amend

3. For each of the following situations, indicate whether the second motion is in order.
a. Diego moves to have a party. Paul moves to amend the motion.
b. Ella moves to take a recess. Wenona moves to lay on the table the motion about having a party.
c. Heather moves to postpone the motion until the next meeting. Tyrone moves to adjourn.
d. Juan moves to redecorate the meeting room. Joan moves to refer the motion to a committee.
e. Tanya moves to amend the motion to redecorate the meeting room. Sylvia moves the previous question.

Using Motions

Each parliamentary motion has its own specific characteristics and uses. Each has its own particular function in parliamentary proceedings.

Getting a Motion on the Floor

According to the rules of parliamentary procedure, no discussion is in order unless a motion is on the floor. The procedure for making a motion involves the following steps.

1. The chairperson grants the floor by stating the member's name, for example, "Tom" or "Mrs. Lopez."
2. The person makes a motion, such as "I move that the annual dance be held at 8:00 P.M., Saturday, June 4, at the Topper Club."
3. Another member then seconds the motion by calling out, "I second the motion" or simply "Second." The member who seconds does not have to be recognized. Since seconding only indicates willingness to have the motion discussed, the seconder need not be in favor of the motion. If no one calls out a second, the chair asks, "Is there a second?"
4. If the chair does not hear a second, he or she says, "The motion fails for lack of a second. Is there further business?" If the chair does hear a second, the chair says, "It has been moved and seconded that the annual dance be held at 8:00 P.M., Saturday, June 4, at the Topper Club. Is there any discussion?"
5. After discussion of a main motion (or immediately in cases when no discussion is allowed), the chair calls for a vote.

WIZARD OF ID by permission of Johnny Hart and Creators Syndicate, Inc.

Changing the Motion

A main motion can be changed in several ways during the discussion preceding the vote. It can be withdrawn or amended.

Withdraw the Motion. If a motion is so poorly phrased that it is difficult to understand, the person who made the motion can ask to withdraw it. Usually, the motion is withdrawn if the person who

TEACHER'S RESOURCE BINDER

Skills for Success 4
Using Motions to Conduct Business

Critical Thinking

Synthesis

Have students imagine that the class is a parliamentary organization. Select one person to act as chair. Have that person hold a meeting.

During the meeting, members of the class should practice using various parliamentary motions. When someone in class does not understand what has happened, or if someone makes a mistake in procedure, the class should stop and discuss the point. Each student should keep minutes of the meeting. Then ask students to compare their minutes with their classmates' minutes.

originally seconded it gives permission. However, the chair must get the consent of the group. If someone objects, a vote is taken. If a majority favors withdrawing, the motion may be withdrawn.

Amend the Motion. At any time during discussion of a motion, any member can move to amend or change the wording of a motion. The following rules govern the amending of a motion.

1. An amendment must be specific when it is put before a group. The following chart outlines the five different ways to amend the motion "I move to hold the annual Spring Dance at 8:00 P.M., Saturday, June 4, at the Topper Club."

Way to Amend	Example of Motion to Amend
Inserting	"I move to amend the motion by inserting the word *Formal* after *Spring*."
Adding	"I move to amend the motion by adding the words *Lower Pavilion* after *Club*."
Striking out	"I move to amend the motion by striking out the word *annual*."
Striking out and inserting	"I move to amend the motion by striking out *8* and inserting *9*."
Substituting	"I move to amend the motion by substituting for it the following motion: To hold a picnic at 2:00 P.M., June 4, at Parker Field."

2. Only one primary amendment and one secondary amendment may be considered at a time. A **primary amendment** is an amendment of the main motion. A **secondary amendment** is an amendment of a primary amendment.
3. An amendment must be germane to a motion. To be **germane** means that the amendment must in some way relate to the issue of the original motion.

   EXAMPLE: If a member moved to amend the annual dance motion by adding "and that eating shall be allowed at group meetings," the amendment would not be germane.
4. An amendment cannot be made by inserting the word *not* into the main motion.

Making and Amending Motions

Suppose you belong to an organization and want to propose buying a lectern for the meeting room. Write down the steps you will follow to get the motion before the group. Practice saying the steps aloud. Next, amend the motion to propose buying a gavel instead of a lectern. Write how you will make such an amendment. Practice the wording aloud.

Activity 6

Students might write their motions and amendments in their communication journals to turn in to you for brief evaluations. Or students might come up with additional lists of items for motions and amendments, write them down, and then share them with the class for your assessment.

Putting Off Discussion

There are several parliamentary procedures available to group members when they wish to delay discussion of a motion either temporarily or permanently.

1. If a certain motion seems inappropriate for the group's consideration, a member can **object to consideration.** This motion is in order before any debate on the motion occurs.

   EXAMPLE: If at the meeting of the junior class one student moved "to ask the principal to purchase supplies for Mrs. Kwan's tenth-grade homeroom," another student could object to consideration of the question on the grounds that it is irrelevant to the ordinary business of the group since that business is supposed to pertain to eleventh-grade issues.
2. If a member believes that group discussion of a subject would be more appropriate either later in the meeting or

at a different meeting, he or she can move to **postpone to a definite time.** This is a motion to defer the group's action temporarily.

EXAMPLE: If a motion requiring data about finances is before the group and the class treasurer has not yet arrived, a member can move to delay consideration of the subject until the treasurer gets to the meeting.

3. If a member believes that a motion should be delayed but is not sure exactly when would be the best time to return to it, he or she can move "to lay the motion on the table." This motion places the main motion on the secretary's table, where it stays until someone moves to take it from the table.

   To **lay on the table** is probably the best known of the delaying motions, but it is also the most abused. The most frequent misuse is in specifying a time.

   EXAMPLE: The wording "I move to lay the motion on the table until next week" is improper since the motion to lay on the table cannot specify any time limit. If a member wants the motion set aside at this meeting but brought up at the next meeting, then he or she should move to postpone it, not to lay it on the table.

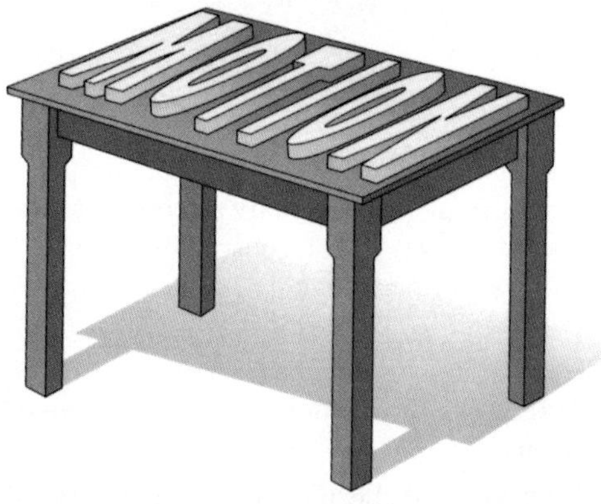

Expressing Disagreement

Even when parliamentary procedure is used to govern the proceedings of a meeting, situations that are out of order may occasionally arise. If a member believes that the rules of parliamentary procedure have been violated, there are two courses of action.

1. A member can rise to a **point of order** at any time. When someone stands and says, "Point of order," the chair will ask that person to state the point (even if doing so interrupts another speaker). If the speaker is correct, the chair will change the procedure accordingly.
2. A member can **appeal** the decision of the chair. If a member believes that the chair has made a decision that does not seem in keeping with the parliamentary rules used by the group, that member can appeal the decision. With this motion a member calls upon the chair to open discussion on the merits of the judgment and then to put the question to a vote. If a majority of those voting support the person making the appeal, then the chair's decision is reversed.

Dealing with Complicated or Time-Consuming Subjects

When a member thinks that the subject under discussion is too complicated or too time-consuming for the group to consider, he or she can refer the motion to a committee. The purpose of this motion is to have a smaller group consider the matter in detail to save time for the larger group. Many organizations run almost entirely under a committee structure by requiring that every motion come through a committee before it can be debated on the floor. Most organizations have at least a few standing committees, each considering a certain type of question, so that most business is reviewed by a committee before being sent to the entire organization for consideration.

Additional Activity

Sometimes parliamentary procedure is used to confuse and delay debate rather than to make it more efficient. To illustrate this problem, ask several students who are very familiar with parliamentary procedure to demonstrate techniques such as filibustering and extending or postponing motions to kill an action they wish to defeat. Afterwards, discuss the effects such delaying techniques have on meetings.

A member who makes a motion to **refer to committee** may wish to designate the makeup of the committee and its authority.

EXAMPLE: Someone might say, "I move to refer the motion to a committee of three members appointed by the chair with instructions to report back to this group at our next regular meeting."

Controlling Length of Debate

Before debate begins on any issue, or even during the debate itself, a member can move to **limit** or to **extend debate.**

EXAMPLE: If, in today's debate, you fear that everyone might want to speak at great length, you might say, "I move to limit speeches to three minutes each" or "I move to limit the total discussion to one hour."

If a member wishes not just to control the length of speeches or the debate but to stop the meeting completely, he or she can move to **recess,** which will stop the meeting for a few minutes, or move to **adjourn,** which will end the meeting for the day.

Voting on a Motion

After discussion of a main motion (or immediately in cases when no discussion is allowed), the chair calls for a vote. Ordinarily an oral vote is taken, with members saying either "aye," "no," or "abstain" aloud. A vote to **abstain** indicates that the member does not wish to support or to oppose a motion that is being voted upon. If a member of the group wishes to vote by some other method, a motion about how to vote is always in order. Voting may be done by a show of hands, by standing, by secret ballot, or by **roll-call vote,** in which the secretary calls out each member's name and records his or her response. Votes are counted by the chairperson or the secretary or sometimes by both. Except when a two-thirds majority is required, all motions require a simple majority vote.

Extension

Have the class develop a list of problems that might arise during a meeting and that the chair would have to deal with. These problems might include personal attacks, unruly behavior, inappropriate motions, and uncertain voice votes. Then let students meet in small groups to take turns acting as chair while other group members act out the problem situations. Have students assess how well the chairs handled the difficulties.

When the Vote Is Too Close to Call

When a vote is taken and the outcome is too close to call either way, the group always has the right to assure itself that the votes are counted correctly. The motion **division of assembly** requires the chairperson to call for a second vote. By using this motion (or by just calling out, "Division"), a member can indicate his or her opinion that the vote is close enough to require a recount. It is preferable that the second vote be conducted by another method. For example, if the first vote was taken by voice, the second count will be taken by show of hands or by standing.

"All who thought my little joke very funny say 'Aye.'"

Drawing by Joe Mirachi; © 1979 The New Yorker Magazine, Inc.

Breaking a Tie

One of the chair's most important rights is the right to vote to break a tie. Therefore, if a motion requiring a majority has fifteen aye votes and fifteen no votes, the chair may vote. However, the chair can never be forced to vote. If the chair refuses to vote when there is a tie, the motion fails for lack of a majority. Breaking a tie is not the chair's only opportunity to vote. The chair may vote any time that his or her vote will affect the outcome.

Cooperative Learning

Have small groups of students discuss the contributions of parliamentary procedure to the function of a democracy. Have them consider governmental bodies such as the U.S. Senate and the House of Representatives. Could a democracy function without parliamentary procedure? How productive would legislative groups be without parliamentary procedure? Also, ask students to consider nongovernmental organizations and students' personal experiences. Each group should come to a consensus and share its ideas with the other groups.

ENRICHMENT

Have your class imagine that it is a state legislative body. Ask students to decide on three laws that will be debated during a meeting. Establish an agenda and elect a chair. During the meeting, have students attempt to use as many types of motions as possible. You may want to appoint a committee to write the proposed laws and established agendas beforehand. Students might use this activity in conjunction with their social studies classes.

Changing the Outcome After the Vote

Parliamentary procedure allows for people to change their minds on an issue. Any time after a motion has been passed, a member of the group may move to **rescind** it. To rescind means to cancel the action taken on a previous motion.

A member may also move to **reconsider** a motion any time within the same meeting or at the next meeting. This motion means that a member is asking the group for permission to reopen discussion on the question. If the motion to reconsider passes, then discussion is reopened, and eventually another vote will be taken. If the motion to reconsider fails, then the group moves on to other business.

In order to prevent abuse of the motion to reconsider, parliamentary law requires the member calling for reconsideration to have voted on the winning side. This ensures that a member who voted on the losing side does not use this motion to delay the proceedings or to obstruct the will of the majority.

Bringing a Motion to a Vote

There are two ways to bring a motion to a vote.

1. Informally, a member simply calls out, "Question." Although anyone who wishes to discuss the motion further has the right to do so, the knowledge that at least one person wants to get on to the vote may lead others to show a similar feeling. Also, a chairperson may say, "It sounds as if some of you believe we have exhausted meaningful discussion. Are we ready to get on to the vote?"
2. More formally, a member who is ready to vote raises one hand to be recognized. When called on by the chair, he or she makes the motion "to move the previous question" to see whether the group wants to stop discussion and vote on the motion. A positive vote on the motion to move the previous question means

CLOSURE

Ask students to create a few questions that they think a teacher might ask while covering the information in this segment. Then students can ask each other their questions for a quick review.

that no further discussion of the current motion is allowed. The chair subsequently calls for a vote on the main motion before the group.

Observing Voting Procedures

Some television channels carry the proceedings of local legislative bodies. Check your local TV listings to see if any program like this is available to you. If so, follow the proceedings and pay particular attention to the voting procedures. Report your findings to your class.

GUIDELINES for Using Parliamentary Procedure

- Do I know the duties of the chairperson, the vice-chairperson, and the secretary?
- Do I know the meanings and uses of parliamentary motions?
- Do I understand when a motion is in order?
- Do I know how to make commonly used motions?
- Do I know how to change a motion?
- Do I know how to express disagreement?
- Do I know what motions relate to voting?

ONGOING ASSESSMENT

Activity 7

If they are able to follow the proceedings of local legislative bodies, students should include the dates of the meetings and the issues discussed. They should use specific details to illustrate their reports and should include particular voting procedures.

BUILDING A PORTFOLIO

Ask students to write out answers to the questions in **Guidelines for Using Parliamentary Procedure** and to save the answers in their portfolios. Later in the term, they could check their responses to see if their level of mastery has increased.

◆ Profiles in Communication

Performance Objective

- To attend and analyze a meeting of a group that uses parliamentary procedure

Teaching the Feature

Have students read the profile of Senator Gonzalo Barrientos. Ask students if they can think of other professions in which knowledge of parliamentary procedure would be useful. Lead the class to discover that parliamentary procedure is used in most situations in which a fairly large number of people need to conduct a meeting. For many people, such situations arise in their lives outside of work rather than at their jobs.

Activity Note

If the groups visited allow it, students might want to tape-record the proceedings they observe. You could have students do this activity with partners or in small groups. Then the pairs or partners could prepare their findings and present the reports to the class.

PROFILES IN COMMUNICATION

Gonzalo Barrientos

To Gonzalo Barrientos, Texas state senator, speech communication skills are the key to success as a legislator, and mastering parliamentary procedure is especially important. The Texas Senate uses *Robert's Rules of Order,* but there are also many special senate rules. What is Senator Barrientos's advice to a new member of the senate? "Study the *Senate Rules Book,* because parliamentary procedure can be a powerful instrument to accomplish what you want—or to dissuade an opponent."

Simply learning the rules isn't enough, he cautions; senators must constantly review them, and they are always sending staff members to consult the rule book. "People who have been legislators for twenty or thirty years still have to brush up on the subtleties," he adds. "Precedents are always being set, and there's always some new interpretation that the president of the senate can put on a rule." If a disagreement arises, there is an official referee: the senate's parliamentarian, a member of the lieutenant governor's staff. However, the president of the senate has the final say and may not always agree with the parliamentarian.

Each day, Senator Barrientos attends as many as fifteen meetings and functions, and often he is asked to give speeches before different groups. "Because I represent the state capital area, I'm in greater demand as a speaker than other state senators," he says. "So it's a good thing I enjoy public speaking."

Attend a meeting of a local group that conducts its official business according to the principles of parliamentary procedure. For example, you might attend a meeting of your school board. As you listen, pay close attention to how the rules of parliamentary procedure affect how group members speak and reach decisions. If the group departs from what this chapter outlines, make note of it. After the meeting, try to obtain a copy of the minutes and review them to confirm your observations. Be prepared to discuss your findings with your classmates.

S☆U☆M☆M☆A☆R☆Y

PARLIAMENTARY PROCEDURE, a set of rules for conducting meetings, is designed to allow free debate among members while maintaining order and ensuring that all members have an opportunity to be heard.

- **Understand the principles of parliamentary procedure,** which follow certain basic ideas: only one item may be considered at a time; everyone has a right to express an opinion, and each opinion is valued; every member has a right to vote, and each vote is counted as equal; the group always follows the opinion of the majority; minority rights are protected; and the minutes of the meetings are public record.
- **Run meetings** by using rules of parliamentary procedure that cover calling meetings, setting the quorum, and establishing the order of business.
- **Understand the duties of officers** and their responsibilities. The chairperson runs the meeting; the vice-chairperson assumes the duties of the chair when the chair is unable to do so; and the secretary keeps the minutes.
- **Understand motions,** proposals for action made by a member. Once a motion is made, members must act on it in some way. Motions are classified as main, subsidiary, privileged, incidental, and renewal. The motions in each classification have specific characteristics, ranks, and uses, and are governed by specific rules.
- **Use motions** to initiate action.
- **Vote on a motion** with a method that allows members to express their opinions clearly. Voting is usually done by voice or by hand, but it can also be done by ballot or roll call.

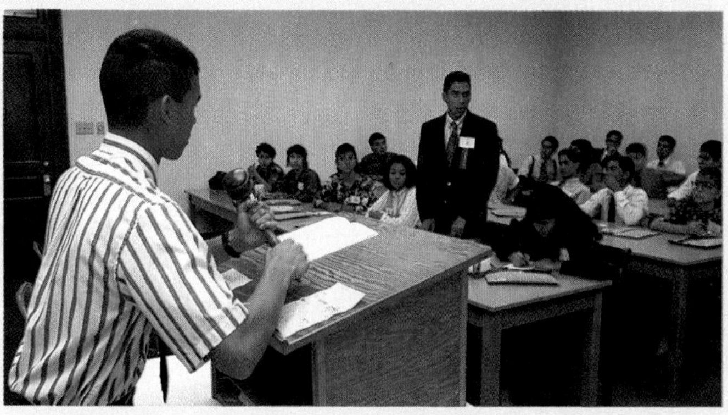

CHAPTER **19**

Vocabulary

Write each term and its meaning.

abstain, *p. 540*
adjourn, *p. 528*
agenda, *p. 522*
amend, *p. 528*
amendable, *p. 532*
appeal, *p. 529*
call for the orders of the day, *p. 529*
chairperson, *p. 524*
close nominations, *p. 529*
debatable, *p. 532*
division of assembly, *p. 529*
division of question, *p. 529*
establish the method of voting, *p. 530*
germane, *p. 537*
incidental motions, *p. 529*
lay on the table, *p. 528*
limit or extend debate, *p. 528*
main motions, *p. 527*
minutes, *p. 521*
motion, *p. 527*
object to consideration, *p. 529*
order of precedence, *p. 531*
parliamentary inquiry, *p. 529*
parliamentary procedure, *p. 519*
point of order, *p. 530*
postpone, *p. 528*
previous question, *p. 528*
primary amendment, *p. 537*
privileged motions, *p. 528*
question of privilege, *p. 528*
quorum, *p. 522*
recess, *p. 528*
reconsider, *p. 530*
refer to a committee, *p. 528*
renewal motions, *p. 530*
reopen nominations, *p. 530*
rescind, *p. 530*
roll-call vote, *p. 540*
second, *p. 532*
secondary amendment, *p. 537*
secretary, *p. 525*
simple majority, *p. 520*
subsidiary motions, *p. 528*
suspend the rules, *p. 530*
take from the table, *p. 530*
vice-chairperson, *p. 525*
withdraw a motion, *p. 530*

TEACHER'S RESOURCE BINDER

- Chapter 19 Vocabulary

Review Questions

Answers

1. to help a group focus on issues important to the entire group; to ensure that meetings are run according to democratic principles
2. one item of business at a time; open discussion; equality of voting rights; majority rules; protection of minority rights
3. chair: governs group according to parliamentary procedure, educates members in parliamentary rules, recognizes members, maintains order; vice-chair: assumes duties of chair when chair is unable; secretary: takes minutes
4. motions already being discussed
5. reopen discussion on decision already made
6. privileged: adjourn, recess, question of privilege, call for the orders of the day; subsidiary: lay on table, previous question, limit or extend

Discussion Questions

Guidelines for Assessment

Student responses may vary.

1. Minority and majority rights are both protected by allowing everyone to present and to discuss ideas. A disadvantage to majority rule, when the number of votes is close, is that the entire organization is bound by majority rule when many people disagree with the vote. To ensure that everyone's rights are protected, the record of each meeting is made public so that the group's actions are open to scrutiny by all members.
2. Parliamentary procedure is not appropriate with very informal gatherings. Parliamentary procedure is useful in business or official meetings involving groups of people who do not have an informal network of communication established among themselves. Parliamentary procedure is also invaluable in meetings in which disagreement is heated and intense.
3. A motion to postpone is usually used when a specific reason exists to reschedule the discussion. To move to lay a motion on the table is useful when the issue seems untimely and no one is sure when the circumstances will be better for discussion or if the issue will be more pertinent at another date.
4. Generally speaking, a motion that can infringe on a person's freedom such as the right to speak to the group requires a two-thirds vote to pass. Most motions require only a majority of the quorum to pass.

CHAPTER **19**

Review Questions

1. One function of parliamentary procedure is to ensure that meetings run smoothly. What are the other functions of parliamentary procedure?
2. Parliamentary procedure is based on five principles. What are they?
3. What are the duties of the chairperson, the vice-chairperson, and the secretary?
4. Privileged motions have to do with the conduct of meetings. With what are subsidiary motions concerned?
5. Incidental motions relate to questions of procedure that arise from debate. What is the purpose of renewal motions?
6. *Precedence* refers to the ordering or ranking of motions. List privileged motions and subsidiary motions in order of precedence.
7. What are the five steps for getting a motion on the floor?
8. One way of changing the wording of a motion is by amendment. In what five ways may an amendment be put before a group?
9. What are the ways of delaying a discussion or a vote on a motion?
10. After a main motion has been discussed, the chair calls for a vote. What methods may be used for voting?

Discussion Questions

1. Discuss parliamentary procedure as a democratic process. To what extent are the rights of the minority protected? To what extent are the rights of the majority protected? What are the pros and cons of majority rule? In addition to voting, what other aspects of parliamentary procedure promote democratic processes?
2. Discuss whether parliamentary procedure can be used at every kind of meeting. For what types of meetings is it most appropriate? Are there any types of meetings in which parliamentary procedure is not appropriate?
3. Discuss the circumstances under which it is better to postpone a motion to a definite time rather than to lay it on the table.
4. Discuss the reasons why some motions take a two-thirds vote to pass, while others take only a simple majority.
5. Henry David Thoreau wrote, "A wise man will not leave the right to the mercy of chance, nor wish it to prevail through the power of the majority. There is but little virtue in the action of masses of men." First discuss the meaning of the quotation. Can you think of any historical instances in which Thoreau's quotation proved true? How can a minority gain power over a majority? Then discuss what the chair can do in situations when a small minority dominates the meeting.

debate, postpone to definite time, refer to committee, amend, postpone indefinitely

7. Chair grants floor to member; member makes motion; another member seconds motion; if no second, the chair says motion fails for lack of second; if motion seconded, chair calls for discussion; after discussion, chair calls for vote.
8. inserting, adding, striking out, striking out and inserting, substituting
9. object to consideration, postpone to a definite time, lay on the table
10. voice vote, show of hands, standing vote, secret ballot, or roll-call vote

ACTIVITIES

1. Explaining How and Why Parliamentary Procedure Is Used.

A. Prepare a short informative speech explaining the rules governing the precedence of motions. After your speech, ask your classmates for oral critiques of your speech.

B. Prepare a persuasive speech telling why meetings should be held according to the rules of parliamentary procedure.

2. Dealing with Disagreement in a Meeting. The picture below illustrates what can happen in even the most formal and orderly meetings when debate becomes heated.

A. Working with a group of classmates, imagine yourselves in such a situation. What can be done to restore order when a disagreement arises?

B. With your classmates, choose a topic for debate and have two members or two factions take opposing sides on the issue. As the debate gets more heated, have each other member of the class act as chairperson and try to settle the conflict.

C. With a small group, think of some ways to prevent an outburst like the one shown below. How might the chairperson take the group's emotional "temperature"? What could he or she do to keep the meeting orderly? In what ways might the protection of minority rights help to ensure that a meeting runs smoothly?

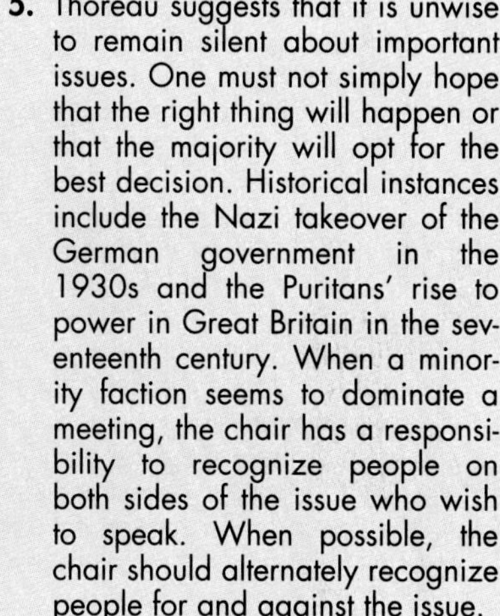

5. Thoreau suggests that it is unwise to remain silent about important issues. One must not simply hope that the right thing will happen or that the majority will opt for the best decision. Historical instances include the Nazi takeover of the German government in the 1930s and the Puritans' rise to power in Great Britain in the seventeenth century. When a minority faction seems to dominate a meeting, the chair has a responsibility to recognize people on both sides of the issue who wish to speak. When possible, the chair should alternately recognize people for and against the issue.

ACTIVITIES

Guidelines for Assessment

1. A. Students will need to review **Chapter 14: "Speaking to Inform."** They might want to include visuals to enhance their speeches.
   B. **Chapter 15: "Speaking to Persuade"** will be useful for this activity. Encourage students to use concrete details and examples to support their opinions.
2. A. Encourage students to refer to **Chapter 17: "Group Discussion"** (which discusses dealing with disagreement) as they discuss this question. Groups can present their solutions to the class.
   B. This is an excellent opportunity for students to practice parliamentary procedure. Each member of the groups should play a role.

SUMMATIVE EVALUATION

Your **Teacher's Resource Binder** contains a reproducible **Chapter 19 Test** that may be used to assess students' mastery of the concepts presented in this chapter.

PORTFOLIO ASSESSMENT

For future reference and evaluation you may want to have students keep in their portfolios any skill sheets or evaluation forms that you have used with this chapter along with any other recorded or written materials that students have created.

C. Students might benefit from reviewing **Chapter 17: "Group Discussion."** The information on leading group discussions may be especially helpful. Students should have specific methods for preventing unnecessary conflict.

3. a. yes
b. yes
c. yes
d. The motion first needs a second. If there is no second, Pat is out of order. After receiving a second, the motion to limit the speeches can be debated.
e. no, just a simple majority

4. You may want to combine the various parts of this activity. Set up the meeting as required in part A. Then proceed with the meeting and allow the members of the class to act as chair at various points during the meeting as suggested in part B; then take votes in the multiple ways stated in part C. You may need to act as parliamentarian by occasionally providing prompts to keep the meeting on track.

3. Understanding Motions. You are the parliamentarian of the student council. Answer each of the following questions according to the rules of parliamentary procedure.

a. The nomination of new officers to the student council was discussed at last week's meeting. Carla moves to reopen nominations this week. Does she need a second?
b. Brandon is reading the minutes of last week's meeting. Amy interrupts him and moves to postpone indefinitely the reading of the minutes. Is Amy out of order?
c. Maxine moves to postpone debate on fund-raising activities until next week's meeting at 3:30 P.M. on Tuesday. Jesse moves to amend Maxine's motion by striking *3:30* and inserting *3:45.* Is Jesse allowed to make this motion for amendment?
d. Because there are many items on the agenda, Reggie moves to save time by limiting individual speeches on each item to two minutes. Pat, the chairperson, opens this motion to debate. Is Pat out of order?
e. Karl's motion to adjourn has been seconded and is now put to the vote. Does the motion require a two-thirds majority in favor of it to pass?

4. Running a Meeting According to Parliamentary Procedure.

A. Run a meeting according to parliamentary procedure. Plan to have each member of the class submit a motion (such as "I move that *Oklahoma!* be selected as the junior class musical this year"). Before the meeting, have an agenda committee composed of three members of the class word the motions and set up an agenda. Have a second committee of three members set up rules to govern discussion. Make sure that these rules cover maximum length of speeches, number of times a person may speak on one motion, and method of determining the chairperson for each debate.

Each member of the class should be prepared to present a short speech supporting the motion he or she submits. Discuss each motion until it is passed, defeated, or delayed.

B. Have each member of the class act as chair in a discussion of a motion. Other class members should contribute to the discussion by making privileged, subsidiary, or incidental motions. The chair will rule on each motion and will conduct the discussion until the motion is passed, defeated, or delayed by passage of some other motion. First, have a short practice round in which mistakes are called to the chair's attention so that the chair can correct them. In a second round, have the chair step down when he or she makes a mistake, and have another student take over as chair. The goal is for the chair to get through an entire motion without making a procedural mistake.

C. Practice voting by voice, by show of hands, by rising, by roll call, and by written ballot on such things as appointing a committee, changing the time or place meetings will be held, and other actions that might be proposed as motions in a meeting.

◆ Real-Life Speaking Situations

PERFORMANCE OBJECTIVES

- To write and present an informative speech as part of the parliamentary process used in a nongovernmental group
- To write and present a dialogue involving parliamentary procedure in a governmental organization
- To conduct a question-and-answer session

REAL LIFE Speaking Situations

1 Neighbors often form homeowners' (or renters') associations, crime-watch committees, and community councils to deal with local issues. The group usually establishes guidelines for conducting business, often adhering to parliamentary procedure.

You have recently moved into your first house or apartment. You read in a newsletter from your homeowners' or renters' association that a regulation you oppose will be discussed at the next meeting, so you decide to attend to express your opinion. Assuming that the meeting is to be conducted according to parliamentary procedure, how will you present your views? Begin by defining the regulation. How will it affect you? Why do you oppose it? Next, identify how others at the meeting feel about the regulation. How many are for it? How many are opposed? Would you be more willing to support the regulation if it were amended?

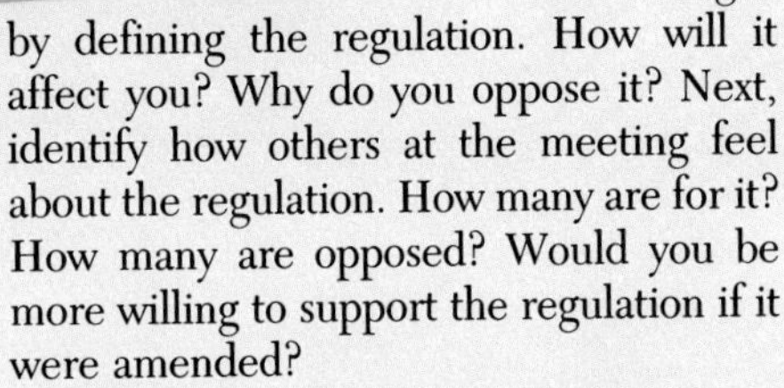

Write a two- or three-page informative speech narrating what you would do. Be prepared to present your speech and to respond to feedback from your classmates.

2 All businesses in our country are subject to government regulation. In many cases government agencies hold open meetings in which business people and others can present their views on these regulations. Such meetings generally follow parliamentary procedure.

Imagine that you are in business and are attending a meeting of a governmental body to oppose a regulation that affects your company. How will you present your views? Begin by defining your company and the governmental body. Do you work for a large corporation, for a regional firm, or for yourself? Are you addressing a federal, state, or local municipal agency? Next, identify the regulation. What will it govern? Why is it being enacted? Finally, specify your arguments against the regulation. Why exactly do you oppose it?

Write a three- or four-page dialogue of an open meeting in which you present your views. Use at least three parliamentary motions. Present your dialogue in class, and conduct a question-and-answer session on your use of parliamentary procedure.

ASSESSMENT GUIDELINES

1. Students should follow the organizational strategy as outlined in the activity. Encourage students to use their imaginations and to be specific. They might even interview parents or neighbors as an aid to defining a regulation.
2. You may want students to work in pairs to create this situation. The partners can present their dialogues in class and then hold their question-and-answer sessions. Tell students they need to be able to explain their use of parliamentary procedure.

PARLIAMENTARY PROCEDURE 549

Unit 6 • Performing Arts

Performing Arts

Chapter 20
Oral Interpretation
pp. 552–587

Chapter Overview

This chapter introduces students to oral interpretation of prose, poetry, and drama. In the first segment, students are taught to evaluate material and to understand selections. In the second segment, students prepare introductions, prepare manuscripts, and practice delivery.

Then the chapter covers how to determine point of view; how to condense material for

Teacher's Resource Binder

The following materials are identified at their point of use in this chapter:

- Skills for Success
  1. *Analyzing a Prose Selection*
  2. *Analyzing a Poetry Selection*
  3. *Introducing an Oral Interpretation*
  4. *Preparing an Oral Interpretation Manuscript*
- Chapter 20 Vocabulary
- Chapter 20 Test/Answer Key

An Oral Interpretation supplement provides additional instructional material and activities for this chapter.

AV Audiovisual Resource Binder

The following materials are identified at their point of use in this chapter:

- Transparency 40 *Analyzing a Selection*
- Transparency 41 *Evaluating an Oral Interpretation*
- Audiotape 1 includes readings of poetry, prose and drama that may be used as models of effective oral interpretation. You may find it helpful to play these selections before or during your discussion of the related textbook material.

prose works; how to use rhythm, repeated sounds, and choral speaking for performing poetry; and how to interpret characters and use physical action in reading drama. Techniques for reader's theater are presented, and finally, students are asked to prepare stories to read to children and to prepare selections of nonfiction for an audiotape.

Introducing the Chapter

Students who enjoy literature often enjoy hearing it read aloud. Tell students that this chapter will help them acquire interpretive skills so that they can entertain audiences.

CHAPTER 20

Oral Interpretation

After studying this chapter, you should be able to

1. Select a work of literature for oral interpretation.
2. Analyze the literature to determine its meaning and mood.
3. Prepare and present an oral interpretation of a piece of literature.
4. Participate in a choral speaking performance.
5. Participate in reader's theater.

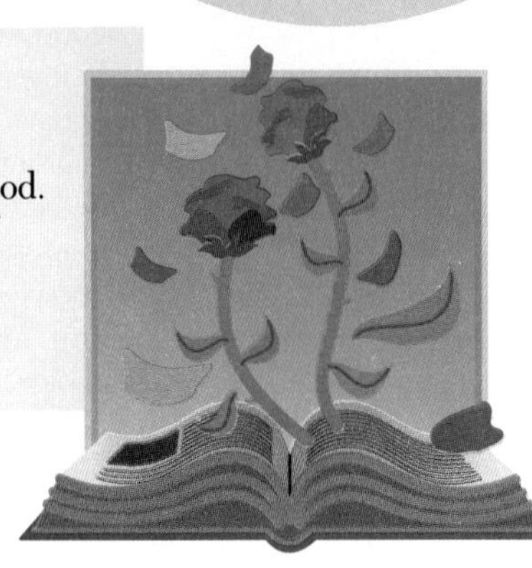

What Is Oral Interpretation?

Oral interpretation is a performance art. The speaker attempts to communicate his or her sense of the meaning and beauty of a work of literature by reading it aloud to an audience. An oral interpretation is generally thought of as a reading performance by a single interpreter. Two related forms are

- *choral speaking,* in which a group of people combine their voices in a group reading of a poem
- *reader's theater,* in which a group of people read and interpret a play

Both the interpreter and the audience benefit from the oral performance. By experimenting with the use of voice, facial expression, and gesture, the interpreter learns more about the piece of literature as he or she studies and prepares to interpret it. Through the reading performance, the listener sees a work of literature come alive. In fact, some people enjoy a work of literature when it is interpreted aloud much more than when it is read silently.

In this chapter, you will learn how to perform an oral interpretation, how to speak in a choral group, and how to perform in a reader's theater.

Bibliography of Additional Materials

Professional Readings

- Krider, Ruby. ***Creative Drama.*** Grandview, MO: Dale Publishing Company.
- Lee, Charlotte I., and Timothy Gura. ***Oral Interpretation.*** Boston: Houghton Mifflin Company.
- McGraw, Charles, and Larry D. Clark. ***Acting Is Believing: A Basic Method.*** Fort Worth: Harcourt Brace Jovanovich.

Audiovisuals

- ***Poetry in Motion***—Voyager Company, Santa Monica, CA (videodisc, 90 min.)
- ***A Storyteller's Story***—Kinetic Film Enterprises, Ltd., Buffalo, NY (videotape, 27 min.)
- ***Whispers on the Wind***—Monterey Home Video, Agoura Hills, CA (videocassette, 45 min.)
- ***With a Feminine Touch***—Monterey Home Video, Agoura Hills, CA (videocassette, 45 min.)

Segment 1 *pp. 554–563*

- **Choosing Literature for Interpretation**
- **Understanding Your Selection**

Performance Objectives

- To list in a communication journal selections appropriate for oral interpretation
- To evaluate the appropriateness of literary selections for oral interpretation
- To evaluate the appeal of a literary selection and to analyze how speaker, audience, meaning, and mood affect its interpretation

Writing to Learn

To help students identify the kinds of selections they would enjoy and want to share with others, write the following list on the chalkboard:

1. people that I admire
2. emotions that stir me
3. mysteries that intrigue me
4. stories or events that sadden me
5. relationships that interest me

Have students freewrite about any or all of these ideas in their journals. Encourage students to write honestly and openly as they free-associate about these topics. Tell them the objective is to get to know themselves and their interests better. Ask a few volunteers to share some of their writing with the class.

Choosing Literature for Interpretation

An **oral interpretation** involves the presentation of a work of literature to a group of listeners in order to express the meaning contained in the literary work. Therefore, an oral interpretation is only as good as the literature being interpreted. Your choice of a selection for your interpretation should be based not only on your interests but also on your knowledge of literature. You may find suitable choices among a variety of types of literature.

Recognizing Types of Literature

What is **literature?** It is writing as an art form. Literature expresses ideas of permanent or universal interest, and it is characterized by excellence of form or expression.

Prose. Prose is writing that corresponds to everyday patterns of speech. It is usually divided into nonfiction and fiction.

- **Nonfiction** tells about real people and real events. It is the truth as the author understands it. A *biography*, for example, is an account of a person's life written by someone else. An *autobiography*, in contrast, is an account of the writer's own life. Another popular form of nonfiction is the essay, a short piece of writing that presents an author's thoughts or feelings on some subject. A *personal essay* usually focuses on the writer's feelings and responses to an experience. A *formal essay* attempts to analyze a topic from a more objective point of view.
- **Fiction** is writing drawn from the writer's imagination. Although fiction may be based on actual events or real people, the facts merely serve as a starting point for the author's imagination. Two of the most common forms of fiction are the *novel* and the *short story*.

Motivation

Ask students if they can remember having stories read to them when they were children. Have them list the interpretive elements that made these readings memorable (pauses, hushed tones, gestures, facial expressions, loud exclamations, etc.). Explain that the readers who entertained them were practicing oral interpretation, a subject they will be studying in this unit.

Teaching the Lesson

Have a volunteer read aloud the introductory material on oral interpretation. Discuss with students the material in **Recognizing Types of Literature** and **Identifying Suitable Selections.** Then guide students as they evaluate the appropriateness for oral interpretation of the poems by Hughes and Cisneros, pp. 556 and 557. Assign **Activity 1** on p. 558 as independent

Poetry. Poetry appeals to emotion and imagination through the creative arrangement of words for their sounds and meanings. In contrast to the everyday speech patterns of prose, poetry is compressed, musical language.

Poetry is a natural form for oral interpretation because it has its roots in the oral tradition. When written language was unavailable and all stories had to be passed along orally, the rhythms and rhymes of poetry helped people to remember the words. Although many modern poets write in free verse, which does not have a regular rhythm or rhyme scheme, they use other sound effects that enhance an oral reading.

Drama. A drama is a story that is written to be acted out for an audience. Like short stories and novels, drama focuses on character and conflict, developed by the use of dialogue. Although most drama is prose, you will find some plays—Shakespeare's plays, for example—that are written in poetry.

As you read textbooks for other classes, or as you read magazines, newspapers, or books, you may come across items that you would like to share with others in an oral interpretation. Keep a list of these items in your communication journal. When you need material for oral interpretation, this list will be a valuable source. You might also make notes about what parts of the pieces you would like to emphasize.

Identifying Suitable Selections

Whether you choose prose, poetry, or drama for oral interpretation, your first consideration should be your own interests. If you don't enjoy and appreciate the selection yourself, there is no point in sharing it with others.

In addition to your own interests, here are some other factors to consider as you make your choice.

Universal Appeal. One characteristic of good literature is that it has **universal appeal**—relevance, or relationship, to the experience of all human beings. This does not mean that everyone will like the selection, but it does mean that it will be of interest to most people. The following poem is an example of a piece of literature with universal appeal.

practice. Circulate around the room to give support and guidance as needed.

Read and discuss the material on **Understanding Your Selection,** pp. 558–563. To prepare students for **Activity 2** on p. 563, you might use a selection such as Robert Frost's poem "Stopping by Woods on a Snowy Evening." Write the poem on the chalkboard and model applying the seven steps in **How to Analyze a Selection** on p. 560. Then guide students through the five questions in **Activity 2** as applied to the Frost poem. Finally, conclude this segment by assigning **Activity 2** as independent practice.

CRITICAL THINKING

Synthesis

You may want to deepen students' understanding of Langston Hughes's poem "Dreams" by involving the class in a brainstorming session about dreams and aspirations. Place the following idea web on the chalkboard:

Using the web as a starting point, ask each student to list at least three dreams or aspirations a young person might have. Have the student write next to each dream an occurrence that might cause a person to become discouraged and doubt a dream. (For example, a person might dream of becoming an actor, but despite hard work and effort, the person does not win a part in a play.) Conclude with a discussion of the poem's essential message.

Dreams

Hold fast to dreams
For if dreams die
Life is a broken-winged bird
That cannot fly.

Hold fast to dreams
For when dreams go
Life is a barren field
Frozen with snow.

—Langston Hughes

Why does this poem have universal appeal? It deals with a subject that most of us experience in one way or another: We discover that our dreams are fading and we don't know what to do about it. For an oral interpretation, a selection with universal appeal has the advantage of being likely to interest the audience.

Ideas and Insights. Most good literature offers readers **insight,** or important ideas or new perceptions of life. Sometimes the writers are merely putting into words the ideas and insights that we have not been able to express for ourselves. For example, when Langston Hughes calls life without dreams "a barren field / Frozen with snow," he gives us an insight into what our own lives might be like if we gave up our dreams. Selecting a piece of literature that offers new ideas or insights is another way of ensuring that your audience will be interested in your interpretation.

Emotional Appeal. Another factor to consider in choosing a selection is its **emotional appeal** to your audience. Most good literature appeals to the emotions and to feelings, as well as to the mind. Sometimes the emotional appeal is a result of the ideas in the

Assessment

Evaluate work on **Activities 1** and **2** to assess students' abilities to identify literary selections for oral interpretation and to understand literary works.

Reteaching

Students who have difficulty grasping the meaning of *universal appeal* might benefit from the following activity: List on the chalkboard titles of movies and television shows that have won high ratings. Underneath, list the following kinds of people: (1) elderly people, (2) married people, (3) career people, (4) children, (5) teenagers, and (6) people from different cultures.

literature, and sometimes it is a result of the language itself. In this poem by Sandra Cisneros, the emotional appeal is a result of both the subject of the poem and the language the poet uses.

Abuelito Who

Abuelito who throws coins like rain
and asks who loves him
who is dough and feathers
who is a watch and glass of water
whose hair is made of fur
is too sad to come downstairs today
who tells me in Spanish you are my diamond
who tells me in English you are my sky
whose little eyes are string
can't come out to play
sleeps in his little room all night and day
who used to laugh like the letter k
is sick
is a doorknob tied to a sour stick
is tired shut the door
doesn't live here anymore
is hiding underneath the bed
who talks to me inside my head
is blankets and spoons and big brown shoes
who snores up and down up and down
up and down again
is the rain on the roof that falls like coins
asking who loves him
who loves him who?

—Sandra Cisneros

The subject of this poem, a child's sadness and sense of loss in the face of an elder's declining health, arouses our feelings of

Teaching Note

You may want to offer students some background material on the poet. Born in 1954, Sandra Cisneros often writes about the poverty and feelings of instability she faced as a child growing up in inner-city Chicago. She writes to share her Latino culture with the people of other cultures. Her unique style of writing blends the working-class English of her mother with the elegant Spanish of her father. She has written one novel and more than thirty-nine other works and has received international acclaim.

Meeting Individual Needs

Cultural Diversity

If possible, ask members of different cultural groups to share poems, stories, or songs recited or sung at family celebrations—baptismal ceremonies, bar and bat mitzvahs, graduations, weddings, birthdays, anniversaries, and so on. Have students explain the sentiments expressed in these selections—praise, love, appreciation, happiness, etc.

Ask students to imagine all these people watching the highly rated shows. What aspects of the shows would appeal to most of the groups? Discuss specific settings, characters, humor, conflicts, family situations, etc. Develop with students a rough list of some of the things that create universal appeal (common experiences, common problems, a common dilemma, questions that concern most people, etc.).

See p. 561 for **EXTENSION, ENRICHMENT,** and **CLOSURE.**

sympathy. But the language tugs at our emotions as well. Notice the childlike words and phrases and the repetition of the word *who*, which becomes a sorrowful refrain.

Technical Quality. Not all literature is equally well written. Choose a work that has **technical quality,** meaning that it is constructed well. Are the ideas expressed clearly? Is the language precise and vivid? As a rule, the better a work is written, the easier it is to read aloud.

Appropriateness for the Occasion. In addition to being a great piece of literature, the work you choose must be appropriate for your purpose and occasion. First, the ideas and the tone should be appropriate. For example, to celebrate your grandmother's birthday, you might choose a selection that praises a grandmother; for an engagement party or wedding, you might choose a love poem.

Second, the length must be appropriate. For example, if you have a time limit of five minutes for your performance, you cannot read a twenty-page short story. You may have to use an excerpt or a shorter work.

Activity 1

Students should be able to support their final choices with specific reasons. Ask students to explain why the selections they chose would make effective oral interpretations.

ACTIVITY 1

Identifying a Selection for Oral Interpretation

Refer to your communication journal or do some reading, and prepare a list of three or four of your favorite works of literature. Evaluate the appropriateness of each work for an oral interpretation by considering whether the selection has (1) universal appeal, (2) ideas and insights, (3) emotional appeal, (4) technical quality, and (5) appropriateness for a class reading. Identify, from your list, your choice of a selection that you think would work best for an oral interpretation.

Understanding Your Selection

Before you can interpret a selection for other people, you must have a good understanding of it yourself. You need to have a good sense of what the writer tried to accomplish, as well as what the writer did accomplish.

You should keep in mind, however, that there may be more than one way to interpret a piece of literature. Just as no two people bring identical interests and needs to a reading, no two people will respond to the literature and interpret it in exactly the same way. Nevertheless, to prepare a good oral interpretation, you should learn as much as you can about your selection.

TEACHER'S RESOURCE BINDER

Skills for Success 1
Analyzing a Prose Selection

Skills for Success 2
Analyzing a Poetry Selection

Meaning

In your interpretation you will be attempting to convey the main idea of the selection. To do that, you have to think about the meaning of the individual words as well as the meaning of the work as a whole. What does this word mean and why does the author use it here? What does it all add up to? What's the point?

As you read the following poem, think about the meaning of the individual words, as well as the meaning of the entire poem.

Grass

Pile the bodies high at Austerlitz
and Waterloo.
Shovel them under and let me work—
I am the grass; I cover all.

And pile them high at Gettysburg
And pile them high at Ypres and Verdun.
Shovel them under and let me work.
Two years, ten years, and passengers
ask the conductor:
What place is this?
Where are we now?

I am the grass.
Let me work.

—Carl Sandburg

Since the vocabulary of this poem is simple, you probably would not have to look up word meanings as such, but you might need to check specific references. If you looked up *Austerlitz, Waterloo, Gettysburg, Ypres,* and *Verdun,* for example, you would learn that they are all sites of famous battles, battles that together took the lives of millions of men. With this knowledge, it becomes easy to understand the other references to "piling bodies high."

Critical Thinking

Analysis

One way to understand whether a writer has accomplished what he or she wanted to in a piece is to study the selection from a historical perspective. Illustrate this point by delving into the history of the Gettysburg Address (included on p. 683 in the **Appendix of Speeches**). Have students work in groups to research the Battle of Gettysburg—the losses suffered and the effect the battle had on morale in the Union States. Ask students to consider Lincoln's perspective a few months after the battle as he faced a grieving crowd. Then have each group answer the following questions: Why does Lincoln refer to the war as a test? Why does he say he cannot dedicate the field? Why does he say the field is already consecrated? Why does he urge the people to resolve "that government of the people, by the people, and for the people shall not perish . . ."? You could circulate around the room and monitor the group discussions. Ask each group to assess how their discussion enhanced their understanding and to appoint a spokesperson to report that information to the class.

INTEGRATING THE LANGUAGE ARTS

Library Link

To help students analyze selections effectively, make sure the class knows where reference books are in the library. Are references in a separate room or in a separate section of the library? How are they marked? [Either *R* or *REF* is marked above the call number on the spine of the book.] You might ask students to report on which of the following resources can be found in their library: dictionaries, thesauruses, encyclopedias, almanacs and yearbooks, biographical references, and literary reference books. In their reports, students should briefly explain what can be found in each reference source.

AV Audiovisual Resource Binder

Transparency 40
Analyzing a Selection

HOW TO *Analyze a Selection*

1. **Look up the meanings of unfamiliar words.** Find the definitions of words you do not know in a good dictionary.
2. **Pay attention to denotations and connotations of words.** In addition to the dictionary definition, or denotation, of the word, pay attention to its connotation, the feelings it arouses.
3. **Look up specific references to places, people, and events.** You might consult encyclopedias, biographies, or textbooks.
4. **Find information about the author and this particular work.** Study the author's background to find out why, when, and where the piece was written.
5. **Think about the writer's choice of words.** Why was one word chosen over another?
6. **Look up the pronunciation of any word you are unsure of.** Correct pronunciation will be very important when you perform your oral reading.
7. **Paraphrase the work.** Try to put the work into your own words to be sure you understand its meaning.

The Speaker

Before you can orally interpret a piece of literature, you need to know who is speaking. Sometimes, particularly in prose, the author speaks directly to the reader. At other times, the author speaks to the reader indirectly, through the voice of a character or a role the author has assumed. In fiction, a fictional **speaker** or narrator is often a character in the story or novel. To adequately interpret a piece of literature, you will have to stand in the speaker's shoes and assume his or her voice.

Extension

Have students meet in small groups and have each group select from their literature textbooks a short story or poem that is suitable for an oral presentation. Have each group edit its selection so that the presentation takes less than five minutes. Then have students work together to mark the piece for pauses and emphasis. Ask the group to select one person to present the piece to the class. Allow time for the chosen speaker to rehearse the presentation with the group. When the speakers are finished, ask the class to comment on the strengths of each presentation.

The character speaking in Edgar Allan Poe's short story "The Cask of Amontillado" is the voice of Montresor, a madman. In the following excerpt, Montresor is explaining how he planned his revenge on Fortunato. To interpret this story successfully, you would have to tell the story as if you were this madman.

The thousand injuries of Fortunato I had borne as I best could; but when he ventured upon insult, I vowed revenge. You, who so well know the nature of my soul, will not suppose, however, that I gave utterance to a threat.* At length *I would be avenged; this was a point definitively settled—but the very definitiveness with which it was resolved, precluded the idea of risk. I must not only punish, but punish with impunity. A wrong is unredressed when retribution overtakes its redresser. It is equally unredressed when the avenger fails to make himself felt as such to him who has done the wrong.

It must be understood, that neither by word nor deed had I given Fortunato cause to doubt my good-will. I continued, as was my wont, to smile in his face, and he did not perceive that my smile* now *was at the thought of his immolation.

The Audience

Another key to a good interpretation is knowing the audience that the author or the speaker is addressing. The way that people speak to an audience is directly affected by their relationship to the audience.

For example, most literary selections do not have a narrator. However, in some selections the speaker reveals his or her feelings directly to the audience and may, in some instances, address the audience as if the individual readers were close friends.

Integrating the Language Arts

Literature Link

Students can gain a deeper understanding of the speaker in "The Cask of Amontillado" by listening to other stories and poems in which a madman is the speaker. Choose selections such as Poe's "The Tell-Tale Heart," Browning's "Porphyria's Lover," or Shakespeare's *Macbeth,* if these selections are available in your library or in a literature textbook. Read these selections aloud to the class and ask students to listen for signs of distorted thinking, obsession with real or imaginary insults, and desire to feign affection for the antagonist.

Enrichment

Students may enjoy choosing favorite Shakespearean scenes for special study: the balcony scene in *Romeo and Juliet,* Mark Antony's speech over Caesar's body, or Hamlet's soliloquy that begins with "To be, or not to be." Encourage students to scour recording libraries and video outlets to obtain interpretations of the same speeches by different actors. As they review the presentations, let students pretend they are casting directors auditioning each of the actors. Which actor gives the best overall interpretation? Why? Divide the class into groups of three or four and have each student briefly report on his or her experience and findings.

Additional Activity

As you discuss the **Audience/Relationships** chart, point out that in an oral interpretation the speaker often addresses the actual audience as if it were a fictional audience. For example, when giving an oral interpretation of "The Cask of Amontillado," the speaker talks to the audience as if they were medieval jesters or servants in a castle. Have students brainstorm strategies that performers might use to achieve this transformation. Possibilities are immersing themselves in the character's personality, visualizing the auditorium as a dungeon, or wearing something archaic (jewelry, a scarf) as a reminder that they are in an earlier time and place.

Audience	Relationships
General readers	• relatively distant because the author/speaker does not know the individuals in the audience; most literature written for this audience
The writer himself or herself	• personal, private writing such as that found in diaries and journals
A character within the story or poem	• personal address that is affected by the fictional relationship between the speaker and the character; may be friendly, hostile, or loving, and so forth; listener may be superior or inferior in status to speaker

In the following excerpt from Robert Browning's poem "My Last Duchess," the speaker is the Duke of Ferrara, a fictional Renaissance nobleman. What can you tell about the audience he is speaking to?

That's my last Duchess painted on the wall,
Looking as if she were alive. I call
That piece a wonder, now: Frà Pandolf's[1] hands
Worked busily a day, and there she stands.
Will 't please you sit and look at her? . . .

You can tell the Duke is speaking to a character in the poem because of the last line. He asks the other character, an envoy who is of inferior rank to the Duke, to sit down and look at a picture of his last Duchess. If you were interpreting this poem, you would read it as though you were talking to a single person alone in a room, and you would try to reflect the personal relationship between the Duke and the envoy.

Mood

The **mood** of a piece of literature is the emotional tone it exhibits. Although emotional tone is not equally strong in all works of literature, recognizing the tone or mood will help you with your

[1]**Frà Pandolf:** an imaginary monk and painter of the Italian Renaissance period. *Frà* means "Brother."

Closure

To close the lesson, ask students to identify three different types of literature. Then ask several students to name factors in identifying and understanding a literary selection for oral interpretation.

interpretation. If the mood is somber or sad, for example, you wouldn't want to read the piece in a happy, lively voice. Writers convey mood through the words they choose, through rhythm, and through setting. Think about the plaintive repetition of *who* in "Abuelito Who" and the setting of "The Cask of Amontillado" in dark, eerie, empty catacombs.

Activity 2

Understanding a Literary Work

Choose a selection that you believe is appropriate for an oral interpretation. It may be the selection you identified in Activity 1 on page 558. Use these questions to develop your understanding of the work.

1. Do you think this work has universal appeal? If so, what is that appeal?
2. What is the central meaning of this piece of literature?
3. Who is the speaker, and how would an understanding of that speaker's characteristics affect an interpretation of the work?
4. What audience is the speaker addressing, and how would the relationship between the speaker and the audience affect an interpretation of the work?
5. What is the mood of this work? How do you know, and how would it affect your interpretation?

Making Connections

Mass Media

Select a videotape of a classic movie in which a character's performance sustains the mood of the film. Consider Gene Kelly's optimism in *Singin' in the Rain,* Michael Douglas's rage toward Charlie Sheen in *Wall Street,* or Audrey Hepburn's terror in *Wait Until Dark.* Show selected scenes from these videos with the sound turned off, and ask students to focus on facial expressions and body language. Discuss how each actor's performance contributes to the mood of the film.

Ongoing Assessment

Activity 2

Students should be able to support their answers to show true understanding of the literary selections. Evaluate students' responses and keep a record of your evaluations for future assessment.

Segment 2 *pp. 564–581*

- **Preparing Your Presentation**
- **Interpreting Literary Selections**
- **Participating in Reader's Theater**

PERFORMANCE OBJECTIVES

- To practice reading a selection and to evaluate one's own and a partner's delivery on the basis of emphasis, rate, and voice quality
- To give an oral interpretation of a prose selection
- To prepare a choral presentation of a poem

COMMON ERROR

Problem. Students may confuse an introduction to an oral interpretation with an introduction to a speech.

Solution. Explain to students that an introduction to an oral interpretation is like a warm-up. It precedes the oral interpretation and helps the audience become familiar with the speaker and with the piece they are about to hear.

In a speech, the introduction is part of the speech and often provides the thesis statement. It sets up the main points that will follow.

TEACHER'S RESOURCE BINDER

Skills for Success 3
Introducing an Oral Interpretation

Preparing Your Presentation

Your oral interpretation will consist of two parts: an introduction to the material and the reading itself. Both must be planned and rehearsed before you perform.

Preparing an Introduction

The purpose of your introduction is to gain the interest of your audience and to provide information they will need in order to understand and enjoy your presentation. The following suggestions will help you identify information you may wish to include in your introduction.

1. Give your reasons for choosing the particular selection you are presenting.
2. Identify the author and the title of the selection.
3. Provide background information about the author or the selection. For example, explain the author's reasons for writing this piece or tell when and where it was written.
4. If you are using a portion of a play or story, review the action that precedes the passage and introduce any characters involved with it.
5. Describe any special features of the setting.
6. Be brief. The most important part of the presentation is the oral interpretation of the selection itself.

- To prepare an oral interpretation of a dramatic passage
- To read a scene from a play in a reader's theater

MOTIVATION

While they may not have experienced oral interpretation, many students will have seen musicians perform. Ask students whether they have seen a musician talk to the audience to introduce a piece. Have volunteers share what they remember about such introductions.

Then ask students why singers talk to audiences before starting to sing. Lead students to 

Considering Punctuation and Word Groupings

In silent reading, punctuation serves as a guide to accurate understanding. However, in oral reading, you need to vary your vocalization, articulation, pauses, and gestures to punctuate words and sentences and to group ideas. The following chart outlines some of the techniques that you can use to indicate punctuation and word groups in an oral reading.

Punctuation Appearing in the Selection	Oral Technique Used in Interpreting the Selection	Marks Made to Prepare the Reading Manuscript
Commas, semicolons, colons, dashes, and periods	Use pauses of varying lengths.	Use a slash (/) to indicate short pauses, a double slash (//) for longer pauses.
Words in parentheses	Pause and lower volume.	Mark parentheses or highlight in color.
Italicized or underlined words	Use louder volume, with stress placed on the words for emphasis.	Highlight italicized or underscored words.
Words inside quotation marks	Use a variety of changes in voice, such as changes in volume, quality, rate, and use of accents.	Underscore, mark pauses, or use colored highlights to indicate treatment of different characters.
Question marks	Use a rising inflection.	Mark an arrow with rising curve.
Meaningful word groups such as clauses and phrases	Emphasize meaning by using a variety of changes in voice quality, volume, or rate.	Mark specific word groups, underscore for emphasis, or use colored highlights.

Preparing a Manuscript

Even if you are planning to interpret a selection from memory, it is still a good idea to have the manuscript in view. In most cases, the manuscript should be typed (double-spaced) and marked in ways that will help you with your reading. For example, you might highlight or underline words you want to emphasize, or you might provide phonetic spellings for words you have difficulty pronouncing. On the next page, you will see an example of a manuscript that has been marked for an oral interpretation.

USING THE CHART

If it is available, copy Langston Hughes's short poem "Harlem" on the chalkboard. Have students note the question marks, dashes, and italicized words. Work with the class to mark the poem according to the directives on the **Considering Punctuation and Word Groupings** chart. Then have volunteers use these marks as an aid for giving oral interpretations.

understand that performers try to connect with audiences by introducing themselves, by talking about their music, or by setting a certain mood. Speakers must also win over audiences before beginning speeches.

TEACHING THE LESSON

Lead into the lesson by reviewing the **Preparing an Introduction** checklist on p. 564. Point out that the six points are only suggestions; the goal of an introduction is to establish rapport with an audience.

Help students to see that preparing the manuscript and practicing the delivery go hand in

How do I love thee? Let me count the ways./
I love thee to the depth and breadth and height
My soul can reach,/when feeling out of sight
For the ends of Being and ideal Grace.//
I love thee to the level of every day's
Most quiet need, by sun and candlelight.
I love thee freely, as men strive for Right;/
I love thee purely, as they turn from Praise.//
I love thee with the passion put to use
In my old griefs,/and with my childhood's faith.//
I love thee with a love I seemed to lose
With my lost saints/— I love thee with the breath,
Smiles, tears, of all my life!//and, (if God choose,)
I shall but love thee better after death.//

Elizabeth Barrett Browning, "Sonnet 43"

Practicing Your Delivery

For a good performance, you must practice. Remember that an oral interpretation is more than just sight reading. Here are some general guidelines that you can follow during practice sessions to help you sharpen your presentation.

1. Record your practice sessions on audiotape or videotape, and then carefully evaluate your presentation. Make any necessary changes.
2. Experiment with different ways of expressing ideas or lines or words.
3. Practice reading the work several times, until you are convinced that your interpretation is as effective as you can make it.
4. Practice the gestures and facial expressions you will use. Make sure that they help to express the meaning and the mood of the material.

As you practice your reading, remember that the success of an oral interpretation is in part due to the effective use of emphasis, rate of speaking, and vocal quality and tone.

TEACHER'S RESOURCE BINDER

Skills for Success 4
Preparing an Oral Interpretation Manuscript

hand; something that seemed like a good idea may fall flat when one practices it.

To prepare students for **Activity 4,** use **Activity 3** on p. 568 as guided practice. Present an oral interpretation of a short story, and guide students in evaluating your presentation. Then, as students work with partners on **Activity 3,** you can give suggestions if needed.

As you finish the segment, have students pay special attention to the guidelines on p. 570 for condensing prose. You could model the process by condensing a short story. Then assign **Activity 4** on p. 570 as independent practice.

As you present the material on poetry, have volunteers read aloud the poetry in the textbook. After covering all the concepts in this section, you could work with the class to analyze a poem. Look for rhythm, repeated sounds, figures of speech, and sensory images. To prepare students for their choral presentations, use the poem

Additional Activity

You may want to invite a local actor or director to speak to the class on the ways actors prepare for performances. Prior to the guest's visit, have the students brainstorm about acting techniques they have heard about. Encourage your guest to share anecdotes that might help students improve their oral interpretations.

Emphasis. The **emphasis** you place on a word or phrase influences the meaning you communicate to your audience. You can use both stress and pauses to emphasize.

Rate. Changes in **rate** also affect meaning and mood. For example, a slower rate is usually more appropriate for a selection that is sad or serious. A lighter, faster rate may suggest happiness and joy, or it may suggest excitement and fear. When reading a poem, pay close attention to the rhythm the poet has created, and try to adjust your reading rate to that rhythm. Finally, remember that most selections should be read at a moderate rate, neither too fast nor too slow. Don't rush through your presentation.

Voice Quality and Tone. Your voice quality and your tone can also reflect meaning and mood. Think about the way your voice sounds when you say "No!" in a happy, excited way as opposed to the way you say it when you are angry. With practice, you can control the quality and tone of your voice to reflect the meaning and mood of the selection you are reading.

to model the steps of preparing a script. Then assign **Activity 5** on p. 576 as cooperative learning. Students may find it difficult to pause according to punctuation marks because most students automatically pause at the end of each line. Point out that they can write their own copies of poems to change the line breaks and make the oral readings easier.

Have a student volunteer read aloud **Drama,** pp. 577–578. Choose a short passage from a play and work with the class to prepare the passage for oral interpretation. Then divide the class into pairs and assign **Activity 6** on p. 578 as independent practice.

Conclude the lesson with material on reader's theater. Point out to students that reader's theater is an excellent way to enjoy theater because it

Ongoing Assessment

Activity 3

Because this activity requires self-evaluation, you may want to have a short conference with each student to discuss his or her evaluation. Keep records for your files.

ACTIVITY 3

Practicing Your Delivery

With a partner, practice reading the following excerpt from Gary Soto's short story "The Jacket," which is about a boy who is humiliated by the ugly jacket his mother has bought for him. Take turns reading the selection and evaluating your delivery on the basis of (1) emphasis, (2) rate, and (3) voice quality.

> That was the first afternoon with my new jacket. The next day I wore it to sixth grade and got a D on a math quiz. During the morning recess Frankie T., the playground terrorist, pushed me to the ground and told me to stay there until recess was over. My best friend, Steve Negrete, ate an apple while looking at me, and the girls turned away to whisper on the monkey bars. The teachers were no help: they looked my way and talked about how foolish I looked in my new jacket. I saw their heads bob with laughter, their hands half-covering their mouths.
>
> Even though it was cold, I took off the jacket during lunch and played kickball in a thin shirt, my arms feeling like braille from goose bumps. But when I returned to class I slipped the jacket on and shivered until I was warm. I sat on my hands, heating them up, while my teeth chattered like a cup of crooked dice. Finally warm, I slid out of the jacket but a few minutes later put it back on when the fire bell rang. We paraded out into the yard where we, the sixth graders, walked past all the other grades to stand against the back fence. Everybody saw me. Although they didn't say out loud, "Man, that's ugly," I heard the buzz-buzz of gossip and even laughter that I knew was meant for me.

Interpreting Literary Selections

Prose

Prose is the normal form of written or spoken language; it is any type of speech or writing that is not poetry. Examples of prose writing include works of fiction, such as short stories and novels, and works of nonfiction, such as essays and biographies. Fiction works generally include certain literary elements, such as characters, setting, plot, and theme, that you will need to consider when you are adapting a selection for an oral interpretation. Other concerns that you will need to address are the point of view expressed, the length of the selection, and the process of condensing the material.

Point of View. The **point of view** refers to who is telling the story. You will need to consider the point of view to determine the voice to use when you are reading aloud.

focuses entirely on the interpretation; no time or money is spent on costumes or sets.

Read aloud the material on reader's theater, pp. 580–581. For guided practice, model the process of selecting a scene, blocking the movements, and reading the parts. If a videotape of a reader's theater presentation is available, you could show it to the class. Then assign **Activity 7** on p. 581 as independent practice.

Assessment

Use **Activities 4–7** to assess the following skills: emphasis, rate, and voice quality in an oral interpretation of a prose selection; condensing prose; choral presentation; oral interpretation of a dramatic passage; and reading in a reader's theater.

Point of View

Type	Interpretation	Example
First Person, Main Character: speaker has a primary role in story; referred to with pronoun *I*	Reader adopts a voice to suit the personality and vocal qualities of this main character, a character who has a personal stake in what happens.	"I left the woods for as good a reason as I went there. Perhaps it seemed to me that I had several more lives to live, and could not spare any more time for that one." —Henry David Thoreau, from *Walden*
First Person, Observer: speaker is only indirectly involved in the conflict of the story; referred to with pronoun *I*	Reader takes on the vocal qualities of this observer, a character who can be relatively objective because he or she often watches instead of participating in the action of the story.	"One confidential evening, not three months ago, Lionel Wallace told me this story of the Door in the Wall. And at the time I thought that so far as he was concerned it was a true story." —H. G. Wells, from "The Door in the Wall"
Third Person, Limited or Omniscient: speaker is outside the story; uses third-person pronouns—*he, she, they*	Reader retains his or her own vocal qualities; thus, reader narrates the story objectively, as a commentator rather than a participant in the action of the story.	"Granny wished the old days were back again with the children young and everything to be done over. It had been a hard pull, but not too much for her. When she thought of all the food she had cooked, and all the clothes she had cut and sewed, and all the gardens she had made—well, the children showed it. There they were, made out of her, and they couldn't get away from that." —Katherine Anne Porter, from "The Jilting of Granny Weatherall"

Length. Since most prose pieces—short stories, novels, and essays—are fairly long, you may not have time to read the entire piece aloud. In some works, you might be able to find a part that will stand on its own well enough to be read by itself. For example, a description or a bit of dialogue might work well for oral interpretation.

At other times you may need to **condense,** or cut, the work. Such cuts can be used not only to shorten a work, but also to remove portions that are inappropriate for the audience or that do not lend themselves to oral presentation.

RETEACHING

If students have poor delivery skills, have the students tell informal anecdotes or personal stories (even jokes) rather than prepare more formal pieces. Allowing students to use material that is either humorous or very contemporary and relevant to their lives may also be useful.

See p. 579 for **EXTENSION, ENRICHMENT,** and **CLOSURE.**

MEETING INDIVIDUAL NEEDS

Cultural Diversity

For **Activity 4**—and for subsequent activities—encourage students to present selections by poets and writers from the students' own cultures. Suggest that students who speak languages other than English might want to present oral interpretations both in English and in their native languages.

ONGOING ASSESSMENT

Activity 4

Students should demonstrate knowledge of how to select prose pieces and how to condense the pieces if necessary. Make notes as you listen to each student's interpretation. You may want to have students do self-evaluations. Remind students to list the strong points of their presentations as well as their criticisms.

HOW TO Condense Prose

1. Cut descriptive and narrative passages that are not essential to the story line.
2. Eliminate or condense flashbacks.
3. Cut quotation tags, such as "he said" or "Mary replied," as well as descriptions of the way each character speaks.
4. Eliminate repetitive material that is not essential to the story or essay.
5. Cut references to events or characters not directly involved in the portion of the work you are reading.

ACTIVITY 4 Giving an Oral Interpretation of a Prose Selection

Choose a work of prose you would like to share with your classmates. Study it carefully to make sure you understand its meaning, point of view, and mood. If you need to, condense it using the guidelines at the top of this page. Practice your delivery, and then give an oral interpretation for your classmates.

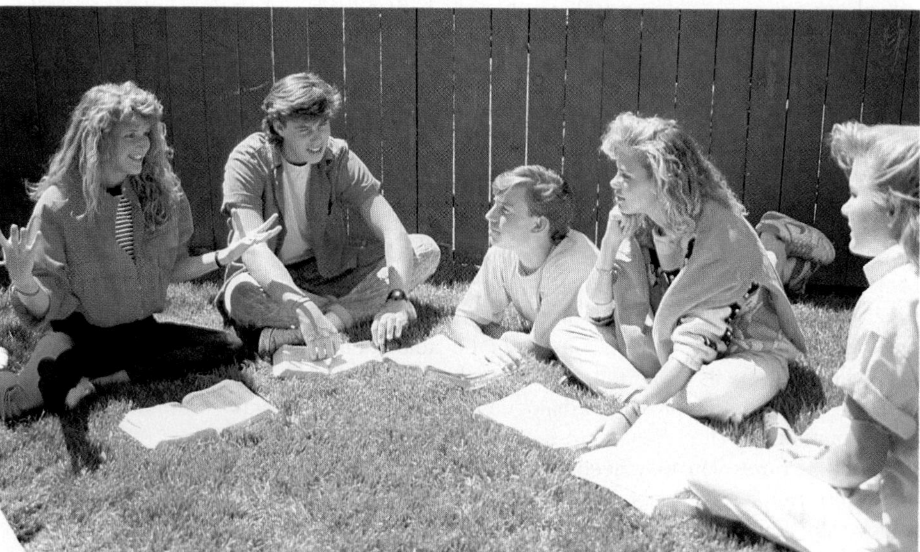

Poetry

Poetry is compressed, highly charged language that appeals to our emotions and imaginations. Usually, a poem is arranged in lines with a regular rhythm and often with a definite rhyme scheme. Poets often use various other literary elements, including figurative language, imagery, and repetition, to heighten feeling and suggest meaning.

Rhythm. **Rhythm,** a rise and fall of the voice created by the flow of stressed and unstressed syllables, is far more important in poetry than in prose. Although it occurs in all speech, it is deliberately used by poets to create a musical quality, as well as to bring out the meaning of the poem.

In an oral interpretation of a poem, you can use your awareness of the pattern of stressed and unstressed syllables to bring out the poem's music and meaning. Notice the rocking, lilting rhythm in the following stanza from the poem "Recuerdo." (*Recuerdo* is a Spanish word meaning "remembrance" or "souvenir.")

If you were to read the following stanza aloud, you would want to use the rhythm of the syllables to express the happiness of the speaker's memories. As shown above the first line, the symbol (ʹ) is used to identify stressed syllables, and the symbol (˘) is used to identify unstressed syllables.

from **Recuerdo**

We were very tired, we were very merry—
We had gone back and forth all night on the ferry.
It was bare and bright, and smelled like a stable—
But we looked into a fire, we leaned across a table,
We lay on a hill-top underneath the moon;
And the whistles kept blowing, and the dawn came soon.

—Edna St. Vincent Millay

As another example, read the following excerpt from Alfred, Lord Tennyson's poem "The Charge of the Light Brigade," a poem about a cavalry brigade that was sent into a battle impossible to win. Notice, as you read the stanza on page 572, how the rhythm in the poem captures the onrushing doom of the galloping cavalry.

Additional Activity

For students who want more practice reading free verse, the following poems are good selections: "Women" by Alice Walker; "In a Mirror" by Marcia Stubbs; "Poem to Be Read at 3 A.M." by Donald Justice; and "If the Owl Calls Again" by John Haines. If these poems are available, have students read the poems naturally. Students should incorporate the musical rhythms.

"Fórwárd, the Light Brigáde!"
Was there a man dismayed?
Not though the soldier knew
Someone had blundered.
Theirs not to make reply,
Theirs not to reason why,
Theirs but to do and die,
Into the valley of Death
Rode the six hundred.

If the poem you are reading is written in **free verse,** as is most modern poetry, you will not find regular rhythmic patterns. Instead, you will find rhythms more like that of natural speech. Rhythm is still used to create a musical quality, however, as you can see in the following free verse poem.

The Time We Climbed Snake Mountain

seeing good places
for my hands
I grab the warm parts of the cliff
and I feel the mountain as I climb.
somewhere around here
yellow spotted snake is sleeping
on his rock
in the sun.

so please
I tell them,
watch out,
don't step on yellow spotted snake,
he lives here.
The mountain is his.

—Leslie Marmon Silko

Repeated Sounds. In addition to rhythm, another way that a writer can add a musical quality to a poem is by **repetition,** or repeated sounds. Such deliberately duplicated sounds may affect your interpretation of a poem in two ways.

1. You should be aware of repeated sounds because they may highlight meaning. For example, if a word or a phrase is repeated throughout the poem, this emphasis usually indicates that the word or phrase is important to the meaning or the mood of the poem.
2. You should be aware of repeated sounds as you read so that you give them neither more nor less emphasis than they deserve. For example, the rhymed words at the ends of lines of poetry are not always the most important ones in a line or a stanza.

Some Types of Repeated Sounds

Form of Repetition	Example
Repetition of words or phrases	who is dough and feathers who is a watch and glass of water —Sandra Cisneros, from "Abuelito Who"
Repetition of consonant sounds, usually at the beginning of words: alliteration	somewhere around here yellow spotted snake is sleeping —Leslie Marmon Silko, from "The Time We Climbed Snake Mountain"
Repetition of sound in two or more words that appear close together: rhyme	Theirs not to make reply, Theirs not to reason why, Theirs but to do and die: —Alfred, Lord Tennyson, from "The Charge of the Light Brigade"

Punctuation and Line Length. Because poetry is written in lines, it is tempting to pause at the end of each one. As in prose, however, the meaningful unit of a poem is the sentence. When you read a poem, use the punctuation marks—commas, periods, and so forth—to determine when to pause. Otherwise your reading will emphasize words and ideas that the poet did not intend to emphasize so explicitly. To see what a difference this makes, reread "The Time We Climbed Snake Mountain" on page 572. In the first reading, stop at the end of every line. In the second reading, follow the punctuation.

MEETING INDIVIDUAL NEEDS

An Alternative Approach

After discussing the **Some Types of Repeated Sounds** chart, students might benefit from a closer study of repetition. Ask students to look up definitions of *alliteration, assonance,* and *dissonance* and to copy the definitions in their journals. Ask them to find examples of poems that use these literary devices and to copy the poems in their journals. Have them underline or circle the words or phrases that demonstrate the devices.

Figures of Speech and Sensory Images. Although both prose and poetry may contain figures of speech and sensory images, they are far more important in poetry. **Figures of speech** are words and phrases that compare two things that are basically very dissimilar. They are not meant to be taken literally.

For example, in his poem "Fog," Carl Sandburg describes the fog coming in "on little cat feet." Understanding that figure of speech will help you see how the fog creeps in silently, and it would probably affect your oral reading of the poem.

Sensory images are words and phrases that evoke mental pictures by appealing to the senses—sight, hearing, smell, taste, or touch. To interpret a poem, you need to be aware of these images. Leslie Marmon Silko uses an image to appeal to the sense of touch in the lines "I grab the warm parts of the cliff / and I feel the mountain as I climb." Silko's image is a pleasant image, but compare it to the following image from Carl Sandburg's "Grass" (page 559):

Shovel them under and let me work—
I am the grass; I cover all.

This visual image creates a mental picture of a grave, a picture that would shape your interpretation of the poem.

Choral Speaking. Poetry is often performed for an audience through **choral speaking,** an oral interpretation in which several voices speak together in a group. Choral speaking works well with poetry because of poetry's tight structure and musical sounds.

The goal in choral work is to maintain a coordinated ensemble sound, a sound that may include solo voices as well as group voices. A choral reading group is often put together in an arrangement of voices similar to that of a singing chorus: soprano, alto, tenor, and bass. Combinations of voices are then used to create special effects. For example, the soprano and tenor voices speaking in unison will give an effect different from the effect of the alto and bass voices together.

In planning a group oral interpretation, keep the following suggestions in mind.

1. Each reader should have a copy of the script and should highlight or underline the lines he or she will be reading.
2. Readers should learn the rhythm of the work and practice starting and stopping at the same time.
3. Although there is little movement in choral speaking, some coordinated movements may be planned. Such movements might include turning or bowing heads, raising a hand or an arm, or swaying from side to side.

Today, choral speaking is used in some plays to represent an entire group of people or some nonhuman force. Especially with a complex poem, a choral reading can add power and heighten the emotional impact of the reading.

Making Connections

Music Link

Show a videotape of a performance by a professional chorus. Help students identify individuals or groups singing soprano, alto, tenor, and bass. Have students watch the conductor increase and decrease the volume and tempo to create different moods and tones.

Tell students that choral speaking is based on the same principles as choral singing. It can be presented on a stage with costumes and a set or combined with dance and music.

Ongoing Assessment

Activity 5

Have the class create a checklist for evaluation. Advise students to consider factors such as articulation, unity, and pitch. Ask each group to evaluate its reading and to share the evaluation with the class.

Teaching Note

You may want to point out that Sandburg's poem is about Chicago during the period from about 1912 to the mid-1920s, when Chicago was a highly industrialized, smoky, crowded city. Although still a major center of industry, today's Chicago is a beautiful city with one of the world's most extraordinary lakefronts, an excellent symphony, and well-endowed museums of art, history, and science.

ACTIVITY 5

Preparing a Choral Presentation of a Poem

Work with a group of eight students whose voices can be divided into four pairs: two sopranos, two tenors, two altos, and two basses. Prepare a reading of Carl Sandburg's poem "Chicago," which is given below.

First analyze the poem, then decide which passages will be read by each vocal pair. For example, for the five lines that open the poem, the altos might read the first line, the tenors the second, the sopranos the third, and the basses the fourth. The entire group could read the fifth line. Practice your presentation and perform it for your class.

Hog Butcher for the World,
Toolmaker, Stacker of Wheat,
Player with Railroads and the Nation's Freight Handler;
Stormy, husky, brawling
City of the Big Shoulders:

They tell me you are wicked and I believe them, for I have seen your
painted women under the gas lamps luring the farm boys.
And they tell me you are crooked and I answer: Yes, it is true I have
seen the gunman kill and go free to kill again.
And they tell me you are brutal and my reply is: On the faces of women
and children I have seen the marks of wanton hunger.
And having answered so I turn once more to those who sneer at this my
city, and I give them back the sneer and say to them:
Come and show me another city with lifted head singing so proud to be
alive and coarse and strong and cunning.
Flinging magnetic curses amid the toil of piling job on job, here is a
tall bold slugger set vivid against the little soft cities;
Fierce as a dog with tongue lapping for action, cunning as a savage pitted
against the wilderness,
Bareheaded,
Shoveling,
Wrecking,
Planning,
Building, breaking, rebuilding
Under the smoke, dust all over his mouth, laughing with white teeth,
Under the terrible burden of destiny laughing as a young man laughs,
Laughing even as an ignorant fighter laughs who has never lost a battle,
Bragging and laughing that under his wrist is the pulse, and under his
ribs the heart of the people,
Laughing!
Laughing the stormy, husky, brawling laughter of Youth, half-naked,
sweating, proud to be Hog Butcher, Toolmaker, Stacker of Wheat,
Player with Railroads and Freight Handler to the Nation.

Drama

A **drama** is a story that is written to be acted out on a stage. The playwright usually emphasizes literary elements such as character, conflict, and action, which are developed in a play by the use of dialogue and action. Since dramas are meant to be performed, they often make excellent material for oral interpretation.

Characters. The fact that a play is meant to be performed on a stage with different characters talking to one another presents a difficult problem for the single oral interpreter. How do you show a difference between the characters? The following suggestions may help you to solve this problem.

1. So that you won't have to read for several different characters, select a scene or portion of the play that has only one or two characters.
2. Use different vocal characteristics for each character. For example, you might change your rate, pitch, or accent when you switch from one character to another.
3. Employ different body language and posture for each character.

Physical Action. While performers in a play are free to use their entire bodies and the entire stage to play their parts, you do not act out an oral interpretation. Your actions should be limited to small, subtle movements. For example, you could turn your head in a different direction to indicate where your characters are. If you feel the audience needs to know something about the action, you may describe it briefly in your introduction.

Making Connections

Mass Media

One way for students to develop vocal skill and flexibility is to imitate professional speakers' voices. If possible, have students tape presentations by favorite newscasters, sportscasters, or actors. Then have the students work to match the pitch, pace, and timbre of these professionals. This exercise will help to show students their real speaking potential and the vast repertoire of pitch and tone they possess. Encourage students to practice using different voices and vocal styles.

Ongoing Assessment

Activity 6

Have students choose partners to rehearse the passage before they give their oral readings. This long passage provides a good opportunity to assess students' understanding of the material in this chapter.

Teaching Note

Jean Anouilh (1910–1987) was a popular French playwright who developed sensitive, emotional characters in his many plays. His portrait of Antigone, based on the classical myth, shows us a courageous young woman who goes to extremes to follow the dictates of her heart. She is thoroughly modern in her search for the right thing to do.

Length. The guidelines for condensing prose (page 570) apply to drama as well, but here are some additional points to keep in mind when you need to condense a section from a dramatic work when preparing it for an oral interpretation.

1. Cut characters that are not essential to the major action of the play.
2. Cut material from the passage that comments on action that has taken place earlier in the play.
3. Cut or condense parts that involve a great deal of stage action but have little or no dialogue.

Activity 6: Preparing an Oral Interpretation of a Dramatic Passage

Prepare an oral reading of the following passage from the play *Antigone* by Jean Anouilh.

In this scene the young woman Antigone confronts her uncle, Creon, the king of Thebes. Antigone's brother Polyneices has rebelled against the state and has been killed in battle. As an example to other would-be rebels, Creon has decreed that Polyneices' body be left in the open to rot. However, to leave a body unburied is profoundly against Greek religion. Antigone, who feels that her duty to her brother must be honored, has defied Creon's order by attempting to bury Polyneices, even though she knows the penalty for her disobedience is death. As the scene opens, Antigone has just been caught and brought before her uncle, Creon, the king.

CREON. Had you told anybody what you meant to do?

ANTIGONE. No.

CREON. Did you meet anyone on your way—coming or going?

ANTIGONE. No, nobody.

CREON. Sure of that, are you?

ANTIGONE. Perfectly sure.

CREON. Very well. Now listen to me. You will go straight to your room. When you get there, you will go to bed. You will say that you are not well and that you have not been out since yesterday. Your nurse will tell the same story. [*He looks toward arch, through which the* GUARDS *have exited.*] And I'll dispose of those three men.

ANTIGONE. Uncle Creon, you are going to a lot of trouble for no good reason. You must know that I'll do it all over again tonight.

Extension

Give students an opportunity to listen to outstanding performers read poetry. You might begin with recordings of Emily Dickinson poems read by Julie Harris. These readings are available at most libraries.

Ask what a professional does that the students have perhaps not thought to do. Lead students to identify Harris's crisp pronunciation of consonants, her deliberate lowering and raising of the voice, and her assumption of the proper voice of a minister's daughter.

[*A pause. They look one another in the eye.*]

Creon. Why did you try to bury your brother?

Antigone. I owed it to him.

Creon. I had forbidden it.

Antigone. I owed it to him. Those who are not buried wander eternally and find no rest. Everybody knows that. I owe it to my brother to unlock the house of the dead in which my father and my mother are waiting to welcome him. Polyneices has earned his rest.

Creon. Polyneices was a rebel and a traitor, and you know it.

Antigone. He was my brother, and he was a human being. Who, except you, wants my brother's body to rot in a field? Does God want that? Do the people want it?

Creon. God and the people of Thebes are not concerned in this. You heard my edict. It was proclaimed throughout Thebes. You read my edict. It was posted up on the city walls.

Antigone. Of course I did.

Creon. You knew the punishment I decreed for any person who attempted to give him burial.

Antigone. Yes, I knew the punishment.

Creon. Did you by any chance act on the assumption that a daughter of Oedipus, a daughter of Oedipus' stubborn pride, was above the law?

Antigone. No, I did not act on that assumption.

Creon. Because if you had acted on that assumption, Antigone, you would have been deeply wrong. Nobody has a more sacred obligation to obey the law than those who make the law. You are a daughter of lawmakers, a daughter of kings, Antigone. You must observe the law.

Antigone. Had I been a scullery maid washing my dishes when that law was read aloud to me, I should have scrubbed the greasy water from my arms and gone out in my apron to bury my brother.

Creon. What nonsense! If you had been a scullery maid, there would have been no doubt in your mind about the seriousness of that edict. You would have known that it meant death; and you would have been satisfied to weep for your brother in your kitchen. But you! You thought that because you come of the royal line, because you were my niece and were going to marry my son, I shouldn't dare have you killed.

Antigone. You are mistaken. Quite the contrary. I never doubted for an instant that you would have me put to death.

ENRICHMENT

You may want to have students set up a reader's theater notebook. Have them work together to review well-known plays by contemporary playwrights and to select scenes that would make effective reader's theater presentations. Suggest a review of plays by playwrights such as Arthur Miller, Tennessee Williams, and Lorraine Hansberry. To make the notebook, students could copy the scenes and put them in a binder. Throughout the year, interested students could be invited to use the notebook to plan performances for the class.

MEETING **INDIVIDUAL** NEEDS

An Alternative Approach

Encourage students who like to be challenged to form a reader's theater club outside of class. Such a club is an excellent way to grow in interpretive skill and to study many classical and modern dramas. Like a book club, a reader's theater club exists for the pleasure and growth of its members.

Participating in Reader's Theater

A popular form of oral interpretation is known as **reader's theater.** It can take many forms. At its simplest, a group of readers sits in a circle and reads a play aloud. Each person reads one or more parts, and the group is its own audience. While an individual can enjoy reading a play silently, the conflict and excitement of a drama is much more apparent in a group oral reading.

More often, reader's theater is performed for an audience. The readers sit or stand facing the audience and read the roles they have been assigned. In contrast to a play, in which the actors talk directly to each other and appear to ignore the audience, in reader's theater the performers acknowledge the presence of the audience and read toward them. A narrator may be used to describe the setting of the play and the physical appearance of the characters, and, where a cut version of a play is being presented, give needed background information.

Techniques for Reader's Theater

1. Readers can stand or sit. They may sit when they are not in a scene and rise as their characters enter.
2. A character who is in a scene but is silent or uninvolved may stand with his or her back to the audience.
3. Scripts may be carried by hand, or stands may be used.
4. Everyone may dress in clothes of a similar design and color, or items of clothing may be used as clues to character.
5. Movements and gestures are suggested or symbolic. Two characters who share a scene, for example, may move forward to be in front of the group.

CLOSURE

Since different people have different styles of interpretation, ask students what they have learned from observing their classmates' presentations.

Selecting Material

Some plays are more suitable than others for reader's theater. Comedies that have knockabout action lose much of their appeal when this is omitted. Plays presented directly to an audience are especially effective as reader's theater. These include Greek tragedies, such as Sophocles' *Antigone,* and twentieth-century plays, such as Thornton Wilder's *Our Town.*

Reader's theater need not be confined to plays. Poems, stories, myths, and sections of novels can be adapted for use in an effective program that an audience will enjoy.

ACTIVITY 7 Reading a Scene from a Play

With two or three of your classmates, select a scene from a play to perform in a reader's theater. Be sure that it is a scene that has no more than three or four characters. Decide who will read each part, and then practice together. Concentrate on oral expression, and allow yourselves only a few subtle gestures and movements. Decide how you will dress and whether you will sit or stand as you are reading. Finally, perform the scene for the entire class.

GUIDELINES for Giving an Oral Interpretation

- Does my selection have the characteristics of good literature?
- Do I understand the meaning and the mood of the work?
- Have I prepared an effective introduction to the selection?
- Have I prepared a manuscript to guide my delivery?
- Have I practiced my reading thoroughly?
- Have I taken into consideration the special features of the form—prose, poetry, or drama—that I am interpreting?
- Do I use my voice to punctuate and group ideas?
- Do I use both stress and pauses to emphasize important words and ideas?
- Do I control my rate of speaking to reflect meaning and mood?
- Do I control my voice quality and tone to reflect meaning and mood?

ONGOING ASSESSMENT

Activity 7

Evaluate students' readings by considering each of the following aspects: scene selection, casting, oral expression, gestures, movements, and dress.

ADDITIONAL ACTIVITY

Encourage students to study the **Guidelines for Giving an Oral Interpretation** and ask each student to select five or six items to focus on. Have students copy these specific guidelines in their journals. Encourage students to write any additional guidelines they feel they need to consider when making oral presentations.

BUILDING A PORTFOLIO

Have students write responses to the questions in **Guidelines for Giving an Oral Interpretation.** Students could keep their responses in their assessment portfolios and check later in the year to see if their levels of mastery have increased.

AV *Audiovisual Resource Binder*

Transparency 41

Evaluating an Oral Interpretation

◆ Profiles in Communication

Performance Objectives

- To prepare and present an oral interpretation of a children's story with a message
- To evaluate classmates' oral interpretations

Teaching the Feature

Have a volunteer read aloud the profile of Colonel Lorraine K. Potter. Ask students to list the qualities of a good inspirational oral interpretation. Lead them to see that these qualities are the same qualities used for other types of oral interpretation. Whether the selection is inspirational or not, the speaker always wants to have an emotional impact on the audience.

Activity Note

You may want to have students make a trip to a library to choose selections. Students could consult with the children's librarian if they have trouble finding suitable stories. You could have students work with partners to practice delivery. Remind them that when they give feedback, it's useful to start with something positive about the delivery.

PROFILES IN COMMUNICATION

Lorraine K. Potter

Interpretive reading is an essential part of the duties of Lorraine K. Potter, Chaplain, Colonel, United States Air Force. Typically, she includes an inspirational passage as part of the Sunday services. "I read the passage aloud at least three or four times that first morning," she says, "and then it stays on my desk all week. During the week I practice several times every day, deciding which words to stress, where to pause for emphasis, what gestures to use, and so on." She visualizes the people and events in the passage in her mind as she reads, and tries to evoke the same picture for her listeners.

Chaplain Potter personally selects interpretive readings for many other rituals and occasions, such as weddings and funerals. She feels that when choosing a passage to read aloud, it is important to be sensitive to the age and emotional state of one's listeners. "It's best to choose a brief selection with only one or two main points, so that people will remember the thoughts you want to leave them with."

"Choosing our words is only one part of oral communication," concludes Chaplain Potter. "Just as important is speaking those words skillfully to express human thoughts and feelings—hope, fear, sorrow, wonder, and joy. And the only way to become a skilled speaker is to practice, practice, practice."

Choose a children's story—perhaps one of Aesop's fables—that illustrates an important truth about life. When reading the dialogue you can use paralanguage cues, such as tone of voice and rate of speech, to bring the story's characters to life. Once you are familiar with the story, practice your delivery using a mirror to check your use of facial expressions, body language, and gestures. Finally, present your interpretation to the class. Ask your classmates how they think a young child would respond to your reading.

S·U·M·M·A·R·Y

ORAL INTERPRETATION is a performance art in which the speaker communicates his or her sense of the meaning and beauty of a work of literature by reading it aloud. Two related performing arts are choral speaking and reader's theater. In choral speaking, a group of people combine their voices to read a poem. In reader's theater, a group of people interpret a play by reading it aloud, rather than acting it out. Keep the following points in mind as you practice the art of oral interpretation:

- **Select literature** that interests you and that has universal appeal, ideas and insights about life, emotional appeal, and good technical quality.
- **Develop an understanding** of a piece of literature by identifying the central meaning of the work, the speaker and his or her relationship to the audience, and the mood.
- **Consider the special characteristics** of a work when preparing an interpretation. With prose, consider point of view and length. With poetry, consider rhythm, line length and punctuation, sounds, figures of speech, and sensory images. With drama, consider character development, physical action, and length.
- **Use changes in voice** such as volume, rate, inflection, stress, pauses, and accents to reflect the meaning and mood of the work being interpreted.
- **Coordinate your rhythm, timing, and movements** with other performers in a choral speaking performance.
- **Use reader's theater** to communicate the meaning and mood of a play without physical action, scenery, or complicated sets.

CHAPTER 20

Vocabulary

Look back through this chapter to find the meaning of each of the following terms. Write each term and its meaning in your communication journal.

choral speaking, *p. 575*
condense, *p. 569*
drama, *p. 577*
emotional appeal, *p. 556*
emphasis, *p. 567*
fiction, *p. 554*
figures of speech, *p. 574*
free verse, *p. 572*
insight, *p. 556*
literature, *p. 554*
mood, *p. 562*
nonfiction, *p. 554*
oral interpretation, *p. 554*
poetry, *p. 571*
point of view, *p. 568*
prose, *p. 568*
rate, *p. 567*
reader's theater, *p. 580*
repetition, *p. 573*
rhythm, *p. 571*
sensory images, *p. 574*
speaker, *p. 560*
technical quality, *p. 558*
universal appeal, *p. 555*

TEACHER'S RESOURCE BINDER

- Chapter 20 Vocabulary

Review Questions

Answers

1. the art of communicating the sense of meaning and beauty of a work of literature by reading it aloud to an audience
2. prose, poetry, and drama
3. ideas and insights, emotional appeal, technical quality, and appropriateness for the occasion
4. the speaker, the audience, and the mood
5. your reason for choosing selection, author's name, title of piece, background information, and brief description of setting
6. In first-person narration, the narrator is also a character in the story and uses the pronoun *I*. In third-person narration, the speaker is outside the story and uses third-person pronouns. In third-person point of view, the story is usually read primarily in the reader's own voice. In first-person point of view, the reader must

Discussion Questions

Guidelines for Assessment

Student responses may vary.

1. An oral reader must interpret and communicate material that someone else has written; preparation for a speech involves writing the speech.
2. with works that can be divided into parts and that are rhythmic, dramatic, and emotional; Martin Luther King, Jr.'s speech "I Have a Dream"; Walt Whitman's poem "I Hear America Singing," T. S. Eliot's poem "The Rum Tum Tugger," and most ballads
3. The literature must have strong language, universal appeal, and insight. The interpreter must understand the author's message and communicate that message to an audience. The audience must be participatory in the sense that listeners are willing to appreciate the selection.
4. Costumes, movements, and other visual cues can draw attention away from the language and sound. Listening to a radio drama as compared with watching a drama on television illustrates this point. In oral interpretation, the sound of the language should generally be at the center of the performance, and movement should be minimal.

CHAPTER **20**

Review Questions

1. What is oral interpretation?
2. List three kinds of literature that are appropriate for an oral reading.
3. Universal appeal is one factor to consider when you are choosing a literary selection to interpret. What are four other factors that you should consider?
4. Understanding meaning is one aspect of understanding a work of literature. What are three other elements that you should understand before you interpret a selection for other people?
5. What kinds of information about a selection and its author might you include in an introduction?
6. Explain the difference between first-person narration and third-person narration, and list some ways in which each type of narration affects oral interpretation.
7. What distinguishes poetry from prose?
8. How is choral speaking both similar to and different from an individual interpretation?
9. In an oral reading of drama, how could you show where the characters are?
10. If you were participating in a reader's theater presentation, how could you show that your character was not a participant in the scene at the moment?

Discussion Questions

1. Discuss the ways in which preparation for an oral reading differs from preparation for a speech.
2. Discuss the circumstances under which choral speaking should be considered for oral interpretation, and list at least three works of literature that lend themselves to choral speaking.
3. Three elements contribute to a successful oral interpretation—the quality of the material, the preparation of the interpreter, and the goodwill of the audience. Discuss the role of each of these elements.
4. American playwright Thornton Wilder once wrote, "The less seen, the more heard." First, discuss the meaning of this quotation. Think of some examples that illustrate this idea. Then explain how this quotation relates to oral interpretation.
5. The Greek philosopher Epictetus once wrote, "First learn the meaning of what you say, and then speak." First, discuss the meaning of this quotation. Do you agree or disagree with the philosopher's statement? Think of specific examples that can be used to support your opinion. Then discuss whether this quotation applies to oral interpretation.

adopt the vocal qualities of the narrator of the story.

7. Poetry is expressed in highly charged language usually arranged in lines with a regular rhythm and a definite rhyme scheme. Prose is expressed in standard sentences without regular rhyme or rhythm.
8. Preparation and delivery involve the same processes, except that readers need to learn to speak in unison for choral reading.
9. by turning your head in different directions
10. by standing with your back to the audience

ACTIVITIES

1. **Choosing a Selection That Suits a Particular Audience.** Imagine that you have been asked to present an oral interpretation in each of the situations that are pictured below. Working with a partner, choose a piece of literature that is appropriate for each occasion. Consider selections that might amuse, teach, or otherwise entertain the audience as well as selections that might inspire or uplift your listeners. Compare your selections with those of the rest of the class.

2. **Analyzing Oral Reading.** Stop for a few minutes to think about the number and kinds of situations during the past few days in which someone has read material to you. The situation might involve someone reading to you either in person or on television or on the radio. Would any of these readings be called "oral interpretation"? Why or why not?

3. **Reading and Analyzing Poetry.**

A. First, practice reading the following poems aloud. In your reading, try to discover and follow the rhythm intended by the poet. Then, identify examples of figurative language and sensory images in the two poems. With your classmates, discuss how the rhythm, figurative language, and sensory images affect the meaning and mood of the poem.

1. ***I've got the children to tend***
The clothes to mend
The floor to mop
The food to shop
Then the chicken to fry
The baby to dry
I got company to feed
The garden to weed
I've got the shirts to press
The tots to dress
The cane to be cut
I gotta clean up this hut
Then see about the sick
And the cotton to pick

Shine on me, sunshine
Rain on me, rain
Fall softly, dewdrops
And cool my brow again.

Storm, blow me from here
With your fiercest wind
Let me float across the sky
'Til I can rest again.

Fall gently, snowflakes
Cover me with white
Cold icy kisses and
Let me rest tonight.

Sun, rain, curving sky
Mountain, oceans, leaf and stone
Star shine, moon glow
You're all that I can call my own.

—Maya Angelou, "Woman Work"

5. Speaking about something one does not understand sometimes betrays either ignorance or arrogance, and Epictetus is probably warning speakers against these pitfalls. Most students will probably agree. One example is someone giving an analysis that is not well thought out. The quotation applies to oral interpretation in that a speaker must study and understand the material to present it effectively.

ACTIVITIES

Guidelines for Assessment

1. Students should be able to support their choices by explaining why each selection is appropriate for the occasion.
2. Students should give reasons that support their opinions. Have students evaluate a reading by finishing the following sentence:
I felt that the reading was (or was not) an oral interpretation because ____.

   Evaluate the responses. Are the reasons given suitable as criteria for oral interpretation?
3. A. Have students make charts to show examples of figurative language and sensory images in the poems. Challenge students to find where the mood of each poem changes.

Summative Evaluation

Your **Teacher's Resource Binder** contains a reproducible **Chapter 20 Test** that may be used to assess students' mastery of the concepts presented in this chapter.

Portfolio Assessment

For future reference and evaluation you may want to have students keep in their portfolios any skill sheets or evaluation forms that you have used with this chapter along with any other recorded or written materials that students have created.

B. Have students add to their charts from part A examples of the repeated sounds in these poems. Listen to the discussion to determine whether students are on target with their comments.

The word *checks* in the last line of Dickinson's poem refers to railway tickets that were given to passengers to assure the conductor that the passengers were headed in the right direction.

4. Students should demonstrate a working knowledge of how to select a literary piece suitable for an oral interpretation. They should be able to support their decisions based on the material in this chapter.

5. A. Evaluate students' use of vocal punctuation. Have students explain why they paused and how they think pauses affect the moods of the works.

B. Have students give reasons for their decisions.

6. Students should demonstrate an understanding of the material covered in this chapter.

2. ***I wandered lonely as a cloud***
That floats on high o'er vales and hills,
When all at once I saw a crowd,
A host, of golden daffodils;
Beside the lake, beneath the trees,
Fluttering and dancing in the breeze.

—William Wordsworth, from "I Wandered Lonely as a Cloud"

B. Identify the repeated sounds in each of the following poems. Then read the poems aloud and discuss with your classmates how reading aloud helps communicate the meanings of specific words and the meaning of the total poem.

1. ***It is blue-butterfly day here in spring,***
And with these sky-flakes down in flurry on flurry
There is more unmixed color on the wing
Than flowers will show for days unless they hurry.

But these are flowers that fly and all but sing:
And now from having ridden out desire
They lie closed over in the wind and cling
Where wheels have freshly sliced the April mire.

—Robert Frost, "Blue-Butterfly Day"

2. ***I never saw a moor—***
I never saw the sea—
Yet know I how the heather looks
And what a billow be.

I never spoke with God
Nor visited in Heaven—
Yet certain am I of the spot
As if the checks were given.

—Emily Dickinson, "I Never Saw a Moor"

4. Choosing Selections for Oral Interpretation.

A. Working in a group, list the types of literature and the specific selections that are enjoyed most by each person in the group. Then study the list to determine which selections would be suited to oral interpretation.

B. Using an anthology of literature, choose one example of each of the major types of literature (prose, poetry, drama) that you think would be a good selection for an oral reading. Be prepared to discuss why you made each selection.

5. Using Vocal Techniques to Communicate Meaning and Mood.

A. Select a short work and read it aloud to show how vocal punctuation can be used to change the meanings of words and ideas. Discuss your reading with your classmates after you have finished.

B. Select two poems that are totally different in mood. Explain how you would read each poem to show the differences in mood between them.

6. Reading a Prose Selection Aloud. Bring a favorite story to class and read it (or a portion) aloud. Be sure that you understand the story. Consider the speaker and the point of view. Prepare an introduction and a manuscript for your reading. Use your vocal skills to express the meaning and mood. When you finish your reading, briefly discuss the story's meaning and conduct a question-and-answer session.

◆ Real-Life Speaking Situations

Performance Objectives

- To prepare an oral interpretation for small children
- To select a nonfiction book or story suitable for a reading on audiotape
- To prepare an introduction for an audiotape
- To prepare an audiotape reading of a nonfiction selection

REAL LIFE Speaking Situations

1 At some time in your life, you will probably find yourself taking care of a younger child—perhaps your brother or sister, a niece or nephew, or the son or daughter of a neighbor. Remember that children like to be entertained. No matter how many toys they have or how much they enjoy playing games, children still get bored. What can you do to keep them occupied once they have tired of their toys? You can read them stories.

Imagine that you are on a camping trip with a group of young children. You have just promised that you will read to them by the campfire. Think. What story would you read to them? How would you present it? What gestures, if any, would you use to enliven your reading?

First, identify the ages of the children, and then select a story appropriate for that age group. Make sure the story is one that you can read in less than ten minutes; otherwise the children may become bored. Practice reading the story in a way that will make it entertaining and interesting for young children. If possible, try your reading out on some children, and then read your story to your class.

2 At one time, books were available only in print. With the advent of phonograph records and tape recordings, however, books have also gone audio.

Imagine that you are working for a company that produces audiotapes of books and stories. Your assignment is to identify a nonfiction book, either autobiography or biography, that you could record. Then it will be manufactured and distributed by your company. What book do you select? How will you make an interesting recording?

First, do some research in the library to find a good biography or autobiography. If you cannot find one that interests you right away, ask your English teacher or librarian for recommendations. Read or skim the book, and select a portion that you could read aloud in five or ten minutes. Prepare an introduction and practice reading the selection. If you think background music would be helpful, select something appropriate. Then prepare an audiotape. Play the tape for some of your classmates, and then lead a discussion about the advantages and disadvantages of books on tape.

Assessment Guidelines

1. Students should demonstrate mastery of the criteria for identifying a suitable selection for an oral reading and should prepare lively, entertaining presentations.
2. You might wish to have students evaluate themselves. Using the **Guidelines for Giving an Oral Interpretation** on p. 581, have students rate their audiotapes as good, fair, or excellent on each question.

Chapter 21
Theater
pp. 588–627

Chapter Overview

This chapter acquaints students with the history of theater and with the primary components of a theatrical production. Students will examine varied aspects of formal theater from auditioning, casting, and rehearsing to preparing to act in a play. Additionally, students will explore the non-acting roles that are necessary to present formal theater productions. This chapter also presents

Teacher's Resource Binder

The following materials are identified at their point of use in this chapter:

- Skills for Success
  1 *Analyzing Characters*
  2 *Learning Movement*
  3 *Analyzing a Formal Play*
  4 *Pantomiming*
  5 *Improvising*
  6 *Storytelling*
- Chapter 21 Vocabulary
- Chapter 21 Test/Answer Key

A Theater supplement provides additional instructional material and activities for this chapter.

AV Audiovisual Resource Binder

The following materials are identified at their point of use in this chapter:

- Transparency 42
  Evaluation Checklist for Taking Part in a Play
- Transparency 43
  Evaluation Checklist for Pantomime

instruction for three forms of informal theater—pantomime, improvisation, and storytelling.

Introducing the Chapter

Consider introducing this unit with a guided tour of the theater production area in your school. Whether it is small or sophisticated, students can envision the behind-the-scenes aspects that are involved in student productions. Ask the faculty member who directs plays to act as tour guide. If possible, take your class on tour when a rehearsal or another production activity is taking place so that your students can see the activity.

CHAPTER 21

Theater

OBJECTIVES

After studying this chapter, you should be able to

1. Trace the historical development of drama.
2. Explain the difference between formal and informal theater.
3. Prepare yourself to act in a play.
4. Contribute to the production of a play in a nonacting role.
5. Participate in an informal theater performance.

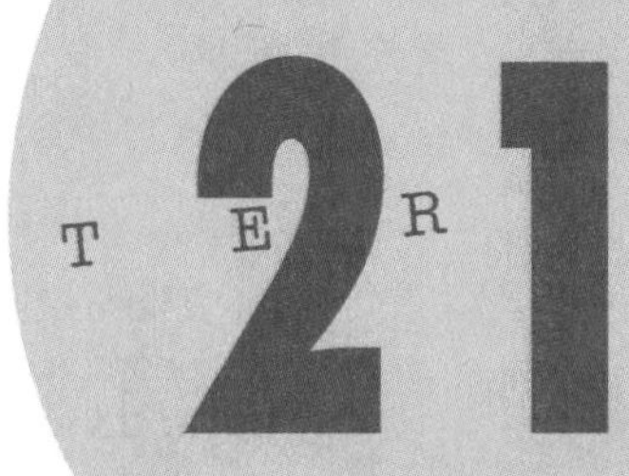

What Is Drama?

Drama is an art form in which a story dealing with a human conflict is acted out on a stage. Unlike other art forms, such as music, sculpture, and dance, drama often incorporates all the other art forms. The excitement of theater is created by the interaction of performers playing their parts and an audience reacting to them.

The two basic types of drama are

- **formal theater,** in which the actors follow a script for the dialogue and the actions of the play
- **informal theater,** in which the actors rely on their imaginations to generate the story, dialogue, and movement

Some examples of formal theater include school plays, Broadway plays, and repertory theater. Movies and television dramas have much in common with formal theater, with the major difference being that movies and television dramas are not performed for a live audience. Because acting is performed for a camera, actions, gestures, and voice must be more natural. Some examples of informal theater are the mime who performs at a street festival and the person who tells stories around the campfire at a summer camp.

In this chapter you will learn how to participate in both formal and informal theater.

Bibliography of Additional Materials

Professional Readings

- Aaron, Stephen. ***Stage Fright: Its Role in Acting.*** Chicago: University of Chicago Press.
- Dean, Alexander, and Lawrence Carra. ***Fundamentals of Play Directing.*** Fort Worth: Harcourt Brace Jovanovich.
- Olfson, Lewy. ***Fifty Great Scenes for Student Actors.*** New York: Bantam Books.
- Tanner, Fran Averett. ***Basic Drama Projects.*** Topeka, KS: Clark Publishing.

Audiovisuals

- ***Drama: Play, Performance, Perception, Programs 1–4***—Films, Inc., Chicago, IL (videocassettes, 60 min. each)
- ***John Houseman's Introduction to Theatre***—FMS Productions, Santa Barbara, CA (videocassette, 31 min.)
- ***The Theatre: One of the Humanities***—Britannica Films, Chicago, IL (videocassette, 30 min.)
- ***Walter Kerr on Theater***—Coronet/MTI Film & Video, Deerfield, IL (videocassette, 26 min.)

Segment 1 *pp. 590–594*

- **Understanding the Development of the Theater**

PERFORMANCE OBJECTIVE

- To make lists of favorite comedies and tragedies to share with classmates

MAKING CONNECTIONS

Community Involvement

Have students investigate any theatrical productions currently running in your community. Post a list of these productions in the classroom and encourage each student to attend at least one production. You might give students extra credit for attending or you might require students to write critical reviews of a production.

Understanding the Development of the Theater

The roots of theater are deep. It is likely that in prehistoric times, people acted out scenes as part of religious ritual. In these scenes myths might have been acted out and heroic deeds re-created. Such scenes probably included choral chants, singing, mime, and dance.

A Brief History

Greek Theater. Formal theater began in ancient Greece as a religious celebration associated with the worship of Dionysus, the god of wine. These festivals lasted five or six days, with the final three days devoted to dramas that competed for annual prizes. Records dating from about 534 B.C. show that the actor and dramatist Thespis won the first contest. The word ***thespian,*** meaning "actor," comes from his name.

The first formal theater was founded in Athens in the fifth century B.C. The plays were presented with one, two, or three actors playing all the parts and with a **chorus** that gave background information and commented on the action. All participants wore masks, and all parts were played by men.

Greek dramas were presented in an amphitheater setting that had a round playing area with an altar, a building or scene house used for changing, and seats most of the way around the playing area. There was no raised stage with a framing arch as there is in most modern theaters.

Motivation

Introduce the chapter by asking students to list plays they have read or seen or possibly acted in. As volunteers share their lists with the class, engage in a brief discussion of what kinds of plays these are and, if known, when the plays were written. Students might also tell something about the plays they have listed.

Teaching the Lesson

You may wish to begin the lesson by having students read **A Brief History** on pp. 590–593. They can read this information silently in class before class discussion. Then students can work in small groups on **Activity 1** on p. 594. Model making your own lists of comedies and tragedies before students begin. Each group might share

Greek drama followed certain principles.

- The drama was designed to bring about a catharsis, a release of emotions, in the audience.
- The main characters in the drama were of noble birth. In tragedies the main character suffered a fall from grace, usually as a result of a tragic flaw in his or her nature.
- The drama was written in poetic language.

Roman Theater. About 200 B.C., Rome overtook Athens as the cultural center for drama. Surviving Roman dramas are considered inferior to the Greek dramas they imitated. However, the Romans made major contributions to the theater's physical setting by developing a more modern elevated stage.

Theater in the Middle Ages. With the decline and fall of Rome, formal theater disappeared for centuries. Beginning in the tenth century, the Church began giving presentations dealing with biblical events and parables. These continued through the Middle Ages until the sixteenth century. In England groups of players constructed pageant wagons, providing a movable stage for acting out religious stories or events. Each scene of their dramas was presented at a different place in town, with the crowd of spectators following in a sort of miniature pilgrimage. Three types of plays were developed during this period.

- **Miracle plays** dramatized events from the Bible.
- **Mystery plays** presented events from the saints' lives.
- **Morality plays** presented allegorical stories in which characters personified religious or moral abstractions.

Renaissance Theater. From about 1300 to 1600, an era called the Renaissance (literally, "rebirth") brought renewed interest in Greek and Roman plays. In addition, original comedies, tragedies,

Integrating the Language Arts

Literature Link

Students might bring literature textbooks to class and find the plays published in them. Students can analyze and discuss the historical periods in which the plays were written, the notable characteristics of each period, and the types of plays. Students might also consider why certain plays are included at particular grade levels.

Teaching Note

Depending on the time available and on your class's needs, you may have to determine how much theater history to study with your classes. You may wish merely to have your students read the historical information and work **Activity 1** so you can move on to the performance activities.

its list and discuss the plays students have seen and enjoyed.

Then you might assign the first discussion question on p. 624 so students can do independent research on the historical periods. You could allow students a day in the library to work in their groups. Afterward, they can present their research, including titles of both comedies and tragedies.

Assessment

To assess understanding of the historical periods and types of drama, create a holistic scoring guide for students' oral presentations and have students evaluate their presentations by writing what they learned about each period. Students can turn in their lists from **Activity 1** along with their evaluations.

MEETING **INDIVIDUAL** NEEDS

Learning Styles

Visual and Kinetic Learners. Collect professional or community theater memorabilia such as theater playbills, ticket stubs, newspaper reviews, or photographs of productions for students to examine. Students might be interested in combining the material to create a bulletin board depicting the various aspects of theater.

Some students might also enjoy researching the construction of historical theaters. Students might be able to locate diagrams of period theaters and to construct models for your classroom.

and **pastoral plays** (love stories in idealized woodland settings) were created and performed. A major contribution was Italy's **commedia dell'arte,** popular comedy in which professional actors improvised, or made up, their roles as stock characters in humorous, standardized situations.

English Renaissance drama flourished between 1590 and 1630. Three events in this period brought about the development of the English theater: the development of secular (nonreligious) themes, the rise of professionalism in both acting and play writing, and the performance of plays in English rather than in Latin.

A conjectural reconstruction of the Globe Theater (1599–1613)

Globe Playhouse (c. 1599–1613). Reconstruction drawing by C. Walter Hodges.

The Elizabethan theater period was named for Elizabeth I (1533–1603), queen of England from 1558 to 1603. William Shakespeare (1564–1616), regarded as one of the world's greatest playwrights, wrote and performed during this age. His plays include tragedies, comedies, and histories (dramas based on historical events).

The French theater blossomed at the end of the Renaissance with the works of Molière (1622–1673), considered a comic genius. His plays ridicule people, ideas, hypocrisy, medicine, and forced marriages.

Restoration Theater. After 1660, a new era of drama began in England. This period, called the Restoration after the restoration of the royal family of Stuart to the throne in 1660, continued until 1700. Restoration comedy, also called **comedy of manners,** satirizes social customs. During this period, women were allowed to appear on stage for the first time in England.

Nineteenth-Century Theater. During the nineteenth century, Romanticism flourished throughout Europe. In general, during the Romantic Period, the belief in the reliance on reason was replaced by the belief that human beings should be guided by feelings and emotions. Playwrights during this period experimented with a great variety of new themes and characterizations. Many plays were made into operas, an elaborate form of musical theater still performed today.

Reteaching

You might show several clips from videotaped plays and ask students to identify what type of play each is and to name characteristics of its historical period.

Extension

Ask students to imagine being actors in the periods the class has just studied. Have each student write a monologue from the perspective of an actor in a selected time period. Would the performer have been a comedian or a tragedian or able to act in both types of plays? Students can share their monologues orally with the class.

Late in the nineteenth century, **modern drama** was born with the works of such dramatists as Henrik Ibsen (1828–1906) in Norway, August Strindberg (1849–1912) in Sweden, Anton Chekhov (1860–1904) in Russia, and John Galsworthy (1867–1933) and Bernard Shaw (1856–1950) in Great Britain. This early modern period was marked by realism, a movement to portray people and situations as they really are in everyday life.

Contemporary Theater. During the past few decades playwrights have experimented with many styles of theater. One of the most interesting styles to emerge has been the **theater of the absurd.** In this style, life is viewed as meaningless and people's strivings as absurd, since they cannot do anything to improve the human lot.

Today, many different styles of theater coexist, with no one style dominating. Revivals provide opportunities to see the styles of the past, while experimental theater presentations allow us to watch new theatrical styles emerging.

Understanding the Characteristics and Types of Drama

The most important characteristics of drama are (1) that it tells a story, and (2) that performers interact with a live audience.

In formal theater the actors follow a complete script, which provides both the dialogue and directions for the action in the play. Formal plays are traditionally classified as either comedy or tragedy. These two forms are often defined by how they end—a **comedy** has a happy ending and a **tragedy** has a sad or disastrous ending. Comedy is also often characterized by exaggerated or eccentric behavior. Its primary goal is to entertain people and to

MEETING **INDIVIDUAL** NEEDS

An Alternative Approach

Students who are well versed in the historical periods of theater might be interested in focusing on the work of a specific playwright from a given period—Sophocles, Shakespeare, or Neil Simon, for example—instead of sampling dramatic literature throughout the ages.

Encourage any interested student to select a favored playwright from any era, to scan through a representative sampling of plays, and to make an informal report to the class. A student might be interested enough to use a selected playwright as the topic for an informative speech.

- To gather information about auditions and rehearsals
- To explore and select a nonacting role of personal interest
- To record information in a journal to chart progress in rehearsals or work sessions

MOTIVATION

Ask students to think about the television shows, movies, or live plays they have seen lately. They might want to refer to their lists from **Activity 1** for ideas. Have students imagine what kind of process is involved in producing such a show. Students might brainstorm for ideas about what they think goes on before an audience sees a production. Have a volunteer write the ideas on

Students with Special Needs

Students with learning disabilities may need visual reminders to help them listen carefully during early rehearsals. You may want to write a list of cues students should listen for to be prepared for their parts. Discuss any background knowledge they may be lacking to help provide them with a clear understanding of their roles.

TEACHER'S RESOURCE BINDER

Skills for Success 1
Analyzing Characters

Occasionally a director asks people to read a part "cold," without having had a chance to practice. When that happens, you should still try to concentrate on the way the character should look and sound, and move into that role.

Attending Rehearsals. When you accept a part in a play, you become a member of the **cast,** the ensemble of actors. Becoming a cast member means that you agree to attend all rehearsals and performances. Even people with the smallest parts are expected to attend all rehearsals unless they are specifically excused by the director. If you know you will be late to a rehearsal, you must notify your director in advance.

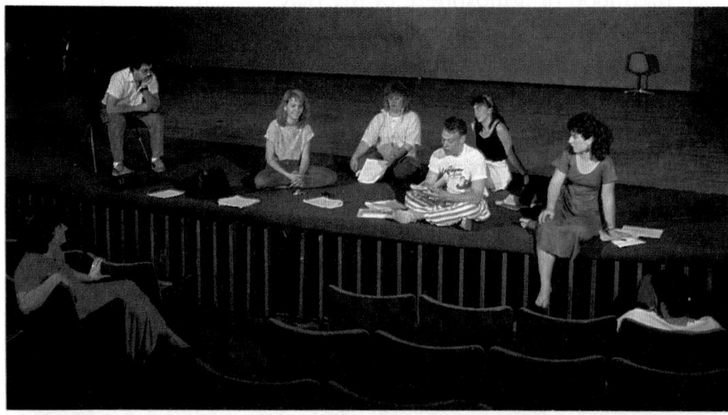

Analyzing a Character

By studying the script carefully, you can begin to understand your character's motivations, why the character acts as he or she does. An author may reveal the motivations and personality of a character through

- stage directions that say what the character looks and sounds like
- what the character says and does
- what other characters say

Another way of getting insight into your character is to observe how real people behave when they are in situations like those being portrayed in the play. An accomplished actor is a keen observer of human nature. You may also use your own experience. If your character, for example, has to make an agonizing choice, you might try to remember how you felt when you yourself had to make a difficult decision.

the chalkboard as the class discusses aspects of the production.

Teaching the Lesson

Ask students to read the first part of the segment to learn about the roles that the script, the audition, and the rehearsal take in a formal play. Then direct students' attention to the information concerning analyzing character. Student volunteers might read this material aloud as you stop them periodically to discuss and clarify terms.

After you understand why your character behaves as he or she does, you can begin to explore how you will portray that behavior. You will decide how the character walks (quickly or slowly), stands (upright, stooped, slouched), sounds (soft-spoken, abrasive, boisterous), and acts (angry, nervous, happy) in various situations.

Of course, any of the decisions you make may be changed as you practice your part and as other actors develop their characters. There is rarely one "right" way to play a character. Inevitably, different actors will find different facets of a character to emphasize.

It is important to remember that, although some behavior is virtually universal, a good actor goes beyond trite, conventional responses. For example, in the play *The Diary of Anne Frank*, Anne Frank is a thirteen-year-old girl. An actress could play the part simply by thinking of how any girl that age behaves. However, to portray Anne successfully, a performer must be sensitive to the girl's peculiar situation. In other words, an actress would need to get beyond the stereotype to uncover what makes Anne special. Playing her as a typical thirteen-year-old girl would not work well because Anne's circumstances made her life and her actions unique. Even when a character lives a fairly normal life, unlike Anne's, you should always work on portraying those special traits and features that make the character special.

Although stereotypes help us identify common or average human traits, the effective performer must go beyond the stereotypes. Perhaps the most important task an actor faces in playing a role is creating a unique individual on the stage.

Teaching Note

A different approach to giving students experience in acting in and producing a formal play is to find several one-act plays and to allow the students to present them according to the guidelines in the textbook. Students who want to direct a production might do so. They can hold auditions and rehearse in class. Perhaps they will need to double up on acting and nonacting roles. You can decide how sophisticated they need to get with scenery, props, and costumes. After the performances, each director, cast, and crew can report on the problems and successes of their plays.

Once students understand how to analyze the writer's interpretation of character and the methods an actor uses to develop character, you might show a clip of a film or a play and have students do **Activity 2.** You could choose an actor to analyze yourself and model for students how to use the questions to examine an actor's characterization. Students can write their analyses in their communication journals and then share their ideas with the class.

Guide students through the strategies for learning lines and movement so that students will be prepared to practice their speaking roles in **Activity 3.** They might add the analysis from this activity to their communication journals also. Then students can present their interpretations for the class.

Before assigning **Activities 4, 5,** and **6,** ask each student to choose a play from one of the lists on p. 605. You might need to guide students in

Understanding Relationships Among Characters

Since your character is not alone on the stage, you must study the other characters and their relationships to the character you are playing. Ask yourself the following questions.

- What is your character's place in the total play? Is he or she the **protagonist,** the main character, in the play? Or is he or she the **antagonist,** the main opponent of the protagonist?
- If your character is neither the protagonist nor the antagonist, what is his or her relationship to these characters?
- What is your character's relationship to minor characters in the play?
- If there are family relationships, what are they like? Are they tense and distrustful? supportive?
- What is the background of these characters' relationships? Why do they like or dislike one another?

Once you understand the relationships among the characters, you can adapt your behavior—the way you look at another character, your gestures, your tone of voice—to illustrate those relationships.

Developing a Character's Voice

The character's voice is as important as his or her dialogue and actions. By concentrating on projection, rate, and volume, you can create a voice that is interesting as well as one that helps to reveal the character and his or her motivations.

their selections by making sure that students can find these plays or by having copies of a few available for class. Students should work in groups of three or four for these activities. After they have read the play and organized auditions and rehearsals, each group should report to the class their plans for the play they chose.

Finally, students can consider the nonacting aspects of a play by reading the information on pp. 608–613 about production work. For **Activity 7** on p. 613, you might have each student choose one of the nonacting roles and then have students write about their preferences, talents, and skills in their communication journals; they can share in small groups or with the whole class. Or you might let students assemble in groups according to their preferences to see which are the most popular production jobs.

Projection. Since theaters and auditoriums may not have public-address systems, voice projection—the volume and force of the voice—is extremely important. You will need to practice projecting your voice so that it can be heard in the back of the auditorium. Since it is difficult to do this while controlling your voice so that it doesn't become harsh or indistinct, you will probably need to practice the technique.

Rate. A good actor controls the rate of his or her speech to suggest emotions or feelings. For example, you might speak quickly if your character is excited but slow down your speech if your character is feeling lonely or depressed.

Pitch. You can use pitch—the highness or lowness of your voice—to suggest the feelings and tensions of your character. Remember that rising inflections communicate uncertainty and surprise and that falling inflections communicate certainty and the completion of a thought.

ACTIVITY 2 Analyzing a Characterization

Watch a film or a play of your choice. As you are viewing the film or play, choose one actor to study. Use these questions to analyze how the actor develops the character he or she is playing.

1. How does the way the actor talks—rate, pitch, inflections, accents—reflect the personality of the character he or she is playing?
2. How do the movements and nonverbal behaviors of the actor reflect the personality of the character?
3. Does the actor present a fully developed character or a stereotype?
4. What are the relationships between this character and the other characters in the play or film? How do the actor's nonverbal behaviors suggest those relationships?

ONGOING ASSESSMENT

Activity 2

You may want to have students turn in their written analyses for your comments on how well the students used the questions in the text to analyze the actors' characterization.

Assessment

You might want to have students share their analyses in **Activity 2.** Then you can briefly make comments about their examinations. By observing the performances in **Activity 3** on p. 603, you can tell if students understand the steps in practicing a speaking role.

From the group presentations for **Activities 4, 5, 6,** and **7,** you can evaluate students' understanding of the process of selecting, auditioning, and rehearsing a play, as well as their understanding of production roles. Students might turn in written proposals for a quick check.

MEETING **INDIVIDUAL** NEEDS

Students with Special Needs

You may have learning disabled students in your classes who are eager, expressive actors but who are not good readers. They will probably need more time to prepare for their parts and more help in learning their lines.

Many learning disabled students are good with auditory-memory skills, so once they hear a play read, they will begin to remember lines. Suggest that students work with partners to learn lines so that reading disabilities do not thwart their enthusiasm. Or try tape-recording the script so that students can follow along and tap their auditory-memory skills.

After students have had initial help in reading the play, the ideas in **How to Learn Lines** may be especially helpful to them.

Teacher's Resource Binder

Skills for Success 2
Learning Movement

Memorizing Lines

Some people have more trouble than others do in learning lines. Nevertheless, at some point in the rehearsal schedule, performers are expected to be "off book," that is, to have mastered their lines so that they can concentrate on character development. Remember that in addition to learning your lines, you must also know your cues. There are several traditional methods for learning lines. Use one or all of them.

HOW TO *Learn Lines*

1. **Ask another person to cue you.** Get another person to speak your cues to you and then, script in hand, follow along to make sure you are saying your lines correctly.
2. **Using a blank piece of paper, cover your lines so that you can only see your cue.** Say your lines to yourself; then uncover the lines to see if you were correct.
3. **Read your cues into a tape recorder.** Leave pauses so that when you play the tape, you can say your lines in between the cues.
4. **Run lines as frequently as possible.** Use time when you are not on stage to practice lines with other actors.
5. **Associate lines with movement.** As you learn your lines, walk through the acting you will perform, including movements such as walking, sitting, turning, or handling props.

Learning Movement

One of the major questions that beginning performers have is what to do with their bodies while on stage. Most play scripts provide each actor with general directions, which are often enclosed in parentheses or brackets. For example, the script will specify when to come on stage and when to leave. However, stage directions may be less specific about how and where a performer should move while on stage.

The director plans the movements of all the actors on the stage. The overall plan for actor movement is called **blocking.**

A theatrical stage is divided into nine parts [see the diagram on page 601]. *Upstage* is farthest from the audience; *downstage* is closest to the audience. These terms were inherited from old theaters, where the stage floor slanted downward, or "raked," so that people sitting in the audience could see better. In modern theaters the stage is flat, and the auditorium seating is slanted.

Reteaching

Provide copies of a short story and tell students to turn the story into play form. Working in small groups, students should create a play from the story and determine how they would audition and rehearse it. What acting roles and nonacting roles will they need? Then each person in the group should analyze one character. Each group can present its version for the class and explain the processes of auditioning and rehearsing. Groups should also describe methods for production work.

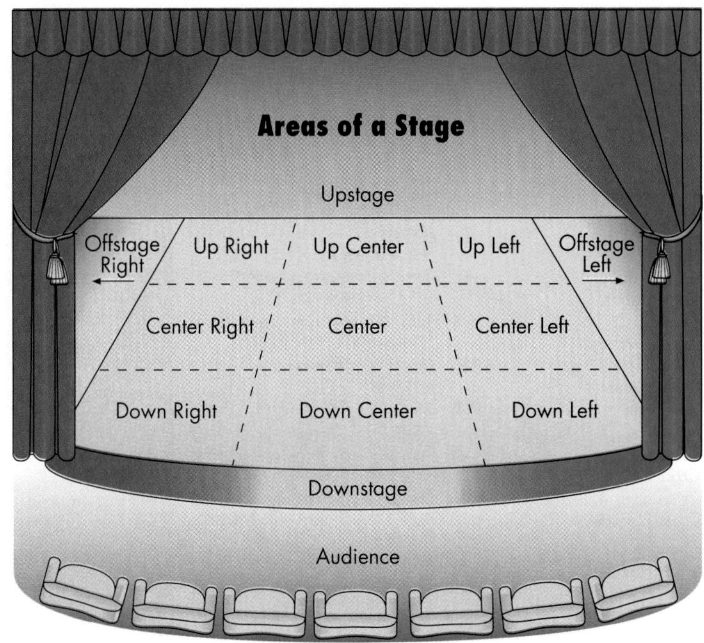

Stage directions are given from the vantage point of the actor as he or she faces the audience. Thus, "stage right" will refer to your right, not the audience's right. During early rehearsals the director will work through each scene in the play, giving each actor his or her blocking. For example, as you deliver a line of dialogue, you may need to move from a chair at downstage left and walk behind a sofa as another character replies. When the director gives you your blocking, be sure to write it down. Use a pencil (blocking may be changed later), and save time by using the simple abbreviations given on the next page.

Stage movement always has a purpose. Sometimes it is simply to get the actor from one place to another. Mostly, however, movement occurs for dramatic effect; that is, movement is motivated by what the character is saying or thinking. In general, characters move when they say their own lines and are still when others are speaking. Sometimes, to create a particular effect, this general rule is broken.

A good director will maintain visual balance throughout the play by coordinating the actors' movements so that the actors are in complementary areas of the stage. Thus, sometimes actors may be moved into specific positions so that they contribute to the complete stage picture.

Additional Activity

Invite the director of school productions to speak to your class about the various elements of school play production, from selecting the literature to striking the set after the final curtain call on closing night. If possible, invite several student actors to share in this presentation and discussion.

See p. 611 for **EXTENSION, ENRICHMENT,** and **CLOSURE.**

An Alternative Approach

Urge students who display a keen interest in theater to consider auditioning for a role in a school or community production. Encourage those who seem inhibited by acting but who enjoy being involved to take on nonacting roles. You might give students who participate in any capacity extra credit if they report to the class about their experiences.

Abbreviations for Stage Directions

UR	Upper Right	↑	Voice up
UC	Upper Center	↓	Voice down
UL	Upper Left	**¼ L**	Turn ¼ away from center front toward stage left
CR	Center Right		
C	Center	**¼ R**	Turn ¼ away from center front toward stage right
CL	Center Left		
LR	Lower Right	**PSL**	Stand in profile toward stage left
LC	Lower Center		
LL	Lower Left	**PSR**	Stand in profile toward stage right
D	Downstage		
U	Upstage	**¾ USL**	Turn ¾ away from facing center front toward upper stage left
XC	Cross Center Stage		
XSL	Cross Stage Left	**¾ USR**	Turn ¾ away from facing center front toward upper stage right
XSR	Cross Stage Right		
XDR	Cross Down Right	**( )**	Stage directions, usually enclosed in parentheses
XUR	Cross Up Right		
XDL	Cross Down Left	______	Underline words which are to be emphasized
XUL	Cross Up Left		
(X)	Cross on curved line	><	Cut

Samples of Script Marked with Stage Directions
Scene from Act 1 of
THE DIARY OF ANNE FRANK

Ⓟ Peter Van Daan
Ⓚ Mrs. Van Daan
Ⓥ Mr. Van Daan

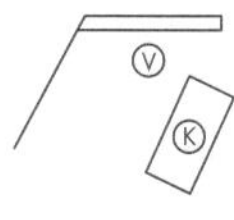

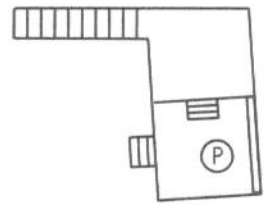

Peter Van Daan *is standing at the window of the room on the right.* [PDSL]

Mrs. Van Daan *(rising, nervous, excited).* Something's happened to them! [XCL] I know it!

Mr. Van Daan. Now, Kerli! [XUC]

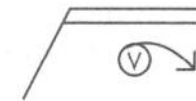

Mrs. Van Daan. Mr. Frank said they'd be here at seven o'clock. [¼ L] He said . . .

Mr. Van Daan. They have two miles to walk. You can't [XDC] expect . . .

Mrs. Van Daan. They've been picked up. [XDR] That's what's happened. They've been taken.

Mr. Van Daan *(indicates [PSL] that he hears someone coming).* You see? [↑]

Peter Van Daan *(takes up his carrier and his schoolbag, etc., and goes into the main room as Mr. Frank comes up the stairwell from below).* [move UC and down stairs, XC]

Maintaining Intensity

Intensity is the depth of feeling a performer has for a part. Whether or not you have been able to bring a character to life at every rehearsal, you must do so when the curtain goes up. Act as if the dramatic action is happening for the very first time. You must respond on stage with the energy that a real person would show if he or she were in the character's circumstances in real life. In a way, you must be more real than life.

HOW TO *Prepare to Act a Role*

1. **Understand the script.** Read the script carefully and be sure that you have a clear idea of the meaning of the play.
2. **Analyze the characters.** You should be aware of what motivates your character and why this person acts and speaks the way he or she does in the course of the play. In addition, you will need to understand the relationships between your character and the other characters in the play.
3. **Develop a fully rounded portrayal of the character you play.** As you rehearse, you learn the words your character speaks. At the same time, practice using your voice, your movements on stage, and your gestures to express the character you are playing.
4. **"Become" your character.** When you are on stage, your words and movements must be consistent with the character you are playing.

Practicing a Speaking Role

Follow these steps to practice a speaking role in the excerpt from *The Diary of Anne Frank* on the next page.

1. Using some or all of the strategies listed on page 600, memorize Mrs. Van Daan's or Mr. Frank's lines.
2. Outline the character's movement on the stage.
3. Analyze the relationships among the characters, and identify verbal and nonverbal behavior you could use to show those relationships.
4. As other students read their parts, perform the role you have studied.

Activity 3

Allow students to peer evaluate each other's performances as they present their scenes from *The Diary of Anne Frank.* You might create an analytic scale for students to use. The scale should be based on the steps for practicing a speaking role.

AV Audiovisual Resource Binder

Transparency 42
Evaluation Checklist for Taking Part in a Play

Critical Thinking

Analysis

To make students aware of how everything a character does on stage must be meaningful to the character's motivation, have students develop interior monologues (also called subtext) for the dialogue, movement, and business in this scene from *The Diary of Anne Frank.* Put students in groups of three or four and have the groups decide what the characters are thinking as they speak and move and do other business as indicated in the stage directions.

Students might then perform the scene twice—first with interior monologues so that they can hear what the characters are thinking and then as it is written. Afterwards, students can analyze how having an interior monologue helps an actor to develop characterization and to concentrate on the scene.

The Diary of Anne Frank

by Frances Goodrich and Albert Hackett

Act One, Scene 2

It is early morning, July, 1942. Mr. Van Daan, *a tall, portly man in his late forties, is in the main room, pacing up and down, nervously smoking a cigarette. His clothes and overcoat are expensive and well cut.* Mrs. Van Daan *sits on the couch, clutching her possessions—a hatbox, bags, etc. She is a pretty woman in her early forties. She wears a fur coat over her other clothes.* Peter Van Daan *is standing at the window of the room on the right, looking down at the street below. He is a shy, awkward boy of sixteen. He wears a cap, a raincoat, and long Dutch trousers, like "plus fours."*[1] *At his feet is a black case, a carrier for his cat. The yellow Star of David*[2] *is conspicuous on all of their clothes.*

Mrs. Van Daan *(rising, nervous, excited).* Something's happened to them! I know it!

Mr. Van Daan. Now, Kerli!

Mrs. Van Daan. Mr. Frank said they'd be here at seven o'clock. He said...

Mr. Van Daan. They have two miles to walk. You can't expect...

Mrs. Van Daan. They've been picked up. That's what happened. They've been taken...

[Mr. Van Daan *indicates that he hears someone coming.*]

Mr. Van Daan. You see?

[Peter *takes up his carrier and his schoolbag, etc., and goes into the main room as* Mr. Frank *comes up the stairwell from below. His movements are brisk, his manner confident. He wears an overcoat and carries his hat and a small cardboard box. He crosses to the* Van Daans, *shaking hands with each of them.*]

Mr. Frank. Mrs. Van Daan, Mr. Van Daan, Peter. [*Then in explanation of their lateness*] There were too many of the Green Police[3] on the streets... we had to take the long way around.

[*Up the steps come* Margot Frank, Mrs. Frank, Miep *(not pregnant now), and* Mr. Kraler. *All of them carry bags, packages, and so forth. The Star of David is conspicuous on all of the* Franks' *clothing.* Margot *is eighteen, beautiful, quiet, shy.* Mrs. Frank *is a young mother, gently bred, reserved. She, like* Mr. Frank, *has a slight German accent.* Mr. Kraler *is a Dutchman, dependable, kindly.*

As Mr. Kraler *and* Miep *go upstage to put down their parcels,* Mrs. Frank *turns back to call* Anne.]

Mrs. Frank. Anne?

[Anne *comes running up the stairs. She is thirteen, quick in her movements, interested in everything, mercurial*[4] *in her emotions. She wears a cape, long wool socks, and carries a schoolbag.*]

Mr. Frank *(introducing them).* My wife, Edith. Mr. and Mrs. Van Daan [Mrs. Frank *hurries over, shaking hands with them.*]...their son, Peter...my daughters, Margot and Anne. [Anne *gives a polite little curtsy as she shakes* Mr. Van Daan's *hand.*]

[1] **"plus fours":** baggy trousers gathered under the knee; also called *knickers.*
[2] **Star of David:** a six-pointed star, a symbol of Judaism that Nazis required Jews to sew on all their clothing for identification as Jews.
[3] **Green Police:** Nazi police who wore green uniforms.
[4] **mercurial:** quickly changeable.

Producing a Formal Play

A play is more than just actors on stage. What goes on behind the scenes? Who pulls it all together?

Many people with a variety of responsibilities take part in producing a play. You will have a greater understanding and appreciation of drama if you understand more about the complete process of producing a play.

Selecting a Play

Before the producer or director can do anything else, a play must be selected. Some make the choice without any advisors; others use a play-reading committee. No matter who makes the decision, however, the following questions should be answered satisfactorily.

- How large is the cast? Do we have enough actors for all of the parts?
- What is the composition of the cast? How many males and how many females are there? What special skills are needed?
- What are the technical requirements? Is our stage large enough? Do we have the budget for lighting and costumes? Can we build the sets or are they too complicated?
- Is the play appropriate for our audience? Is it both emotionally and intellectually suitable? Will our audience enjoy this play?
- How much is the royalty, the payment of money for the right to produce the show? Can we afford it?

To find plays, you could start with drama anthologies in your school or city library. You also could consult the publication *Dramatics,* which lists and reviews plays. The following list identifies several frequently performed plays.

Musicals: *The Music Man, Little Mary Sunshine, Carousel, Oliver!, The Wiz, The King and I, West Side Story*

Comedies: *Auntie Mame, The Boy Friend, Charley's Aunt, Arsenic and Old Lace, Harvey, Life with Father, Blithe Spirit*

Dramas: *Our Town, A Streetcar Named Desire, A Raisin in the Sun, Dark of the Moon, I Remember Mama, The Diary of Anne Frank*

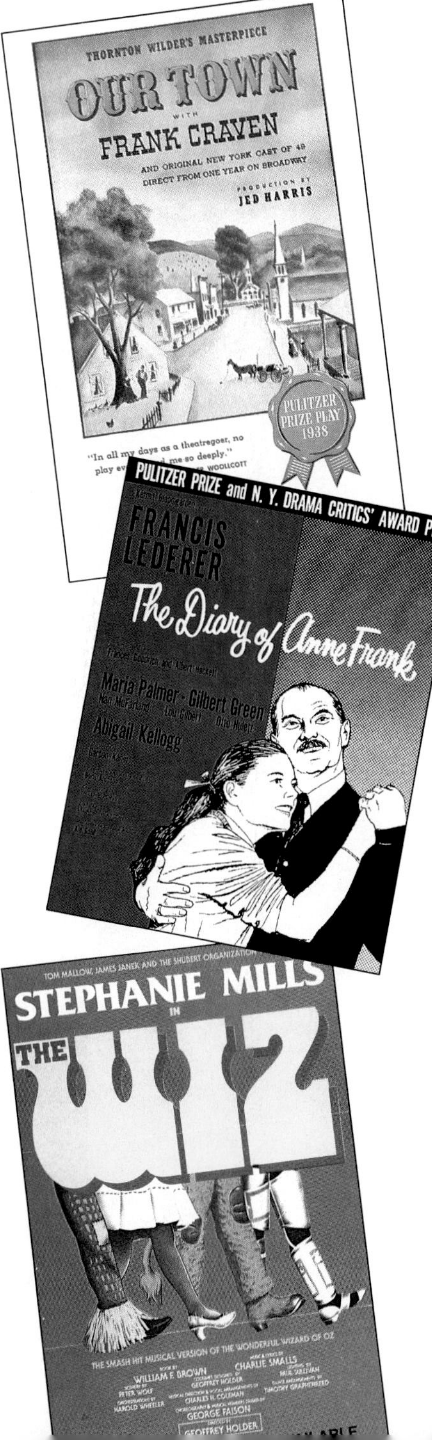

Making Connections

Technology

If possible, be sure to videotape your students as they perform any scenes they prepare. Also, give students the experience of videotaping each other so that they can become comfortable using a videocamera.

Teacher's Resource Binder

Skills for Success 3
Analyzing a Formal Play

Activity 4

To assess students' understanding of the process of play selection, be sure the responses reflect consideration of the questions listed in **Selecting a Play** on p. 605.

ACTIVITY 4

Selecting a Play for Production

Working in a group, select one of the plays listed at the bottom of the previous page. Read the play and then use the questions given above the list to decide whether you could produce this play in your high school.

Organizing Auditions

The Structure of the Audition. Most high school and college plays are cast through **auditions**—formal tryouts in which people have a chance to show their abilities. Usually these auditions are open to anyone who wishes to try out for a part. A director who has a particular person in mind for a part may give that person an audition before the open auditions. Many professional shows are cast in this way. At times, auditions are closed, which means that only those who meet specific conditions are allowed to try out. For example, tryouts may be open only to people with singing or dancing experience in shows or only to students in the junior class.

Sometimes a separate audition is held for each type of part. For example, auditions for singers may be held one day, auditions for lead speaking parts a second day, and auditions for all other parts a third day.

At the beginning of auditions, the director usually asks everyone to fill out an audition form. An audition form asks for previous productions, personal information such as weight and height, any roles played, and identification of possible conflicts with the proposed rehearsal schedule.

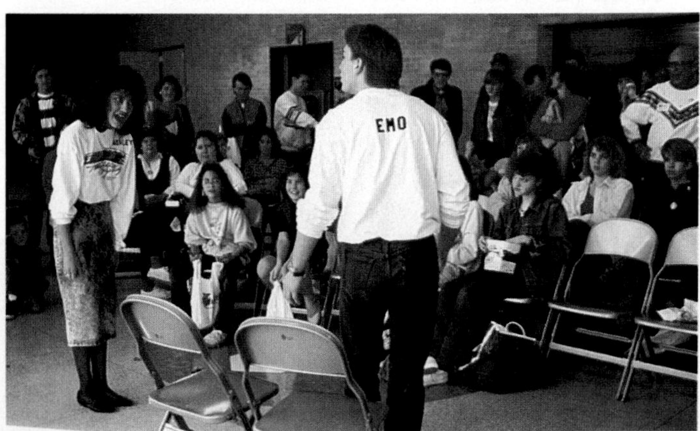

Casting. Ordinarily, the director decides who will be in the cast after he or she has heard everyone audition. During auditions the director looks for specific characteristics from the actors trying out for the parts. These characteristics may include an actor's experience, physical build, or vocal qualities. A director may also consider other qualities needed to portray a particular character.

During the audition period, the director will also be selecting people to work on the various backstage crews. Remember that you can show your interest and learn something about the theater by volunteering to become a member of the stage crew.

ACTIVITY 5

Organizing an Audition

With a partner, select a play with which you are both familiar. If you wish, you may use the play you selected and read for Activity 4 on page 606. Then develop a plan for auditioning and selecting cast members for the play. Decide whether you would have open or closed auditions, whether you would have a separate audition for each type of part, and what information you would ask for on an audition form. After you have finished your audition plan, be prepared to explain your decisions to other members of your class.

Activity 5

Students' plans for auditioning and selecting cast members should be feasible for the plays chosen. Also, students should be specific as to the types of auditions they will hold—open or closed. They might even prepare an audition form to turn in for evaluation.

Structuring Rehearsals

Rehearsals, or practice sessions, may be conducted for a period of from two to ten weeks, depending upon the experience of the cast and the complexity of the play. Musicals, for example, demand more rehearsal time.

Early in the rehearsal schedule, the performers usually practice scene by scene. For example, one entire rehearsal might be devoted to one complicated scene. As performance time nears, more of the play is covered at every rehearsal. Often, during the last ten rehearsals, the entire play may be rehearsed. At any stage of a rehearsal, the director may make suggestions to the actors as they are working. At the end of each rehearsal, the director gives the cast feedback about the portion rehearsed.

During the last week or so of rehearsals, the technical aspects of the show are added. Scenery is finished and lighting is coordinated. In the last two or three rehearsals, called **dress rehearsals,** every aspect of the show is rehearsed just as it will be done at the time of performance. Often, a small audience is invited to attend.

Ongoing Assessment

Activity 6

This assignment can possibly be fulfilled by having the theater director come to the classroom as a guest speaker to address the class concerning the questions covered in the activity. A quick quiz afterward could determine students' comprehension.

Activity 6: Gathering Information About Auditions and Rehearsals

Meet with someone who is directing an upcoming play, such as a teacher in your school or a director for a community theater in your area. Ask the following questions concerning auditions and the rehearsal schedule, and report your findings to your classmates.

1. How many parts are in the play?
2. What are the parts in the play?
3. Will those who try out need to be familiar with the play?
4. Will those who try out need to have any special skills, such as singing or dancing ability?
5. How long a period is scheduled for rehearsals?
6. How long will each rehearsal be?
7. What time do rehearsals begin and what time do they end?
8. Which days of the week will rehearsals be held?
9. When will all actors need to know all their lines?
10. When are dress rehearsals scheduled?

Working in Nonacting Roles

There are many nonacting roles that are essential to a successful theater production, and many people enjoy working in these areas. Some people prefer to work in one of the technical or production aspects of a play rather than to act a role on stage. Nonacting roles include responsibilities such as directing or producing the play, building and painting the set, finding or making props, making or preparing costumes, running lights or sound during the play, and selling tickets or seating patrons.

Nonacting roles not only are necessary to the production of a play, but also are fun to accomplish. Following are some of the important roles in production.

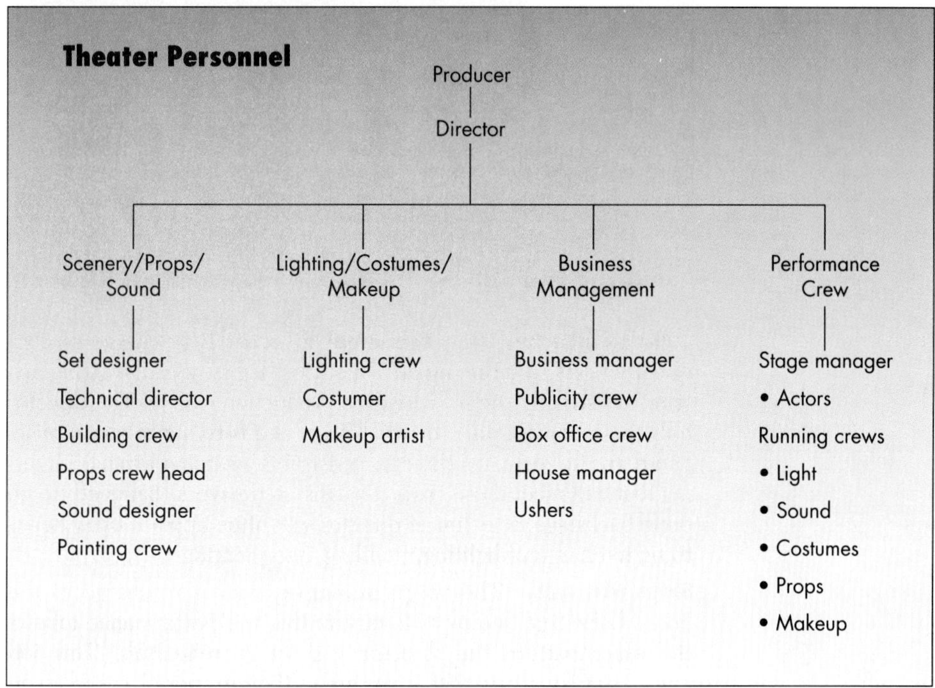

Producer. As the head administrator of a dramatic production, the **producer** is the person who is responsible for bringing together the script, the theater, and the director. In professional theater, the producer also arranges the financing for a show. Although the role of producer is separate from the role of director in professional theater, in high school theater the producer is usually also the director.

Director. The **director** is in charge of selecting the play, casting the parts, coaching the actors, and coordinating the work of the set designer and the costumer. Although the teacher in charge of drama will most likely direct the major productions, students often are able to gain experience in directing scenes, one-act plays, and

An Alternative Approach

You may have students in your class who need more self-confidence in their acting ability before they perform before an audience. Help them to understand the integral part each of the nonacting roles plays in producing a play and encourage them to work in nonacting roles first so they can gain theater experience and confidence before they take on acting roles.

other short productions. If you are interested in directing, you may be able to assist the teacher or the director in carrying out the many tasks a director must do.

Technical Director. The **technical director** is in charge of constructing sets, positioning and operating lights, managing the curtain, and striking the set when the production is over. The director tells the technical director what he or she is trying to accomplish, and then the technical director constructs a set and arranges lighting that will meet those goals. To assist in the work that needs to be done backstage, a technical director will often appoint crew heads to be in charge of lighting, building, and painting.

Stage Manager. The **stage manager,** who is in charge of the entire backstage, attempts to ensure that the performance follows the exact pattern the director has set in rehearsals. This job involves making sure that actors are in their proper places to go on stage, cuing actors (helping them learn when they go on and when they speak), prompting when necessary, and in general helping rehearsals run smoothly. The stage manager records all of the director's instructions about blocking, cues, and sound effects in a master prompt book so that anyone at any time can see the movement of a scene. Once the production begins, the stage manager takes over many of the director's chores, such as managing the actors and the overall production of the show.

Set Designer. The **set designer** is responsible for designing all visual elements, including stage sets and lighting, that will be used for the production. The set designer works closely with the director to design a set and lighting that will create the proper atmosphere

Extension

Ask each student to choose a monologue, to analyze the character, to add blocking notes, and to perform the monologue for the class. After the performances, students might explain the processes of selection and rehearsal and then ask for and respond to comments from classmates.

for the play. A successful set will create a mood that will help the audience to better understand the meaning and intent of the show. For instance, cheerful colors will usually be used for a comedy or a musical, while the set for a serious drama will commonly employ darker, more somber tones.

After the designer has a basic concept of how the set will look, he or she creates a **floor plan,** which is a diagram that shows the positions of walls, entrances, and furnishings on the stage. The set designer draws separate designs for each of the different settings in a particular play. Although some plays, such as *The Diary of Anne Frank,* have only one set for the entire production, other plays have two, three, or even more different sets. Below is an example of a floor plan.

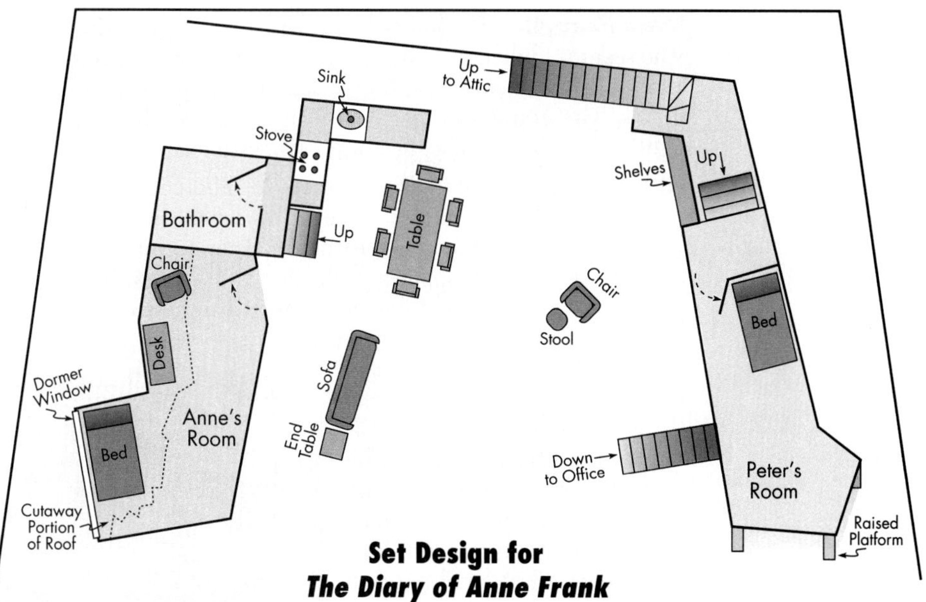

Set Design for *The Diary of Anne Frank*

Costumer. The **costumer** is in charge of the performers' attire. Costumes must reflect the period in which the play is set, and they may also reveal aspects of a character's age, personality, job, and social standing. For contemporary plays, the costumer may be limited to simply offering ideas about what each of the actors may wear. Some plays, however, make special demands. For example, when a theater group produces a historical play or a play set in an exotic or a fantasy location, the costumer will have to make or rent appropriate costumes.

Making Connections

Art and Design

Students who are interested in set or costume design might want to investigate a selected play to make suggestions for appropriate costumes, sets, or props that achieve the desired mood, time frame, and backdrop for the characters.

If they select historical plays, students can research the appropriate costumes and interior design styles for the era. If they choose contemporary plays, students can emphasize creating the mood they wish to achieve. Have students share their reports with the class.

Enrichment

Students might attend a performance of a play in school or the community. They could interview a person involved in the play (in either an acting or a nonacting capacity) and write about the person's process in preparing for the production. Students should share their interviews with the class.

Closure

Ask students to review the questioning processes for developing characterization, selecting a play for production, and organizing auditions and rehearsals. Then have students explain how non-acting roles are important to play production.

Teaching Note

If you don't plan on giving elaborate productions but do want students to practice all aspects of theater production, you might suggest that students create a few props and costume changes for their plays. You could use a portable clothes rack to hold a few wardrobe items to suggest each character's traits and a few props to suggest the appropriate setting or mood.

Making Connections

Technology

Students who are familiar with desktop-publishing applications on computers may want to design and print programs or publicity fliers to advertise their productions.

Business Manager. The **business manager** takes care of the financial matters that relate to the production—paying bills, issuing and keeping track of tickets, filing receipts, and keeping good records. The business manager may also be responsible for printing programs. A program includes listings of the cast in order of appearance, of the production staff, and of committees and crews. Programs also carry "acknowledgments" for those who lent assistance. For example, if a florist donated the plants for a wedding scene, the florist's name would be acknowledged on the program.

The business manager is also likely to be in charge of publicity for the show. Publicity may involve making posters, submitting articles about the show to the school or local newspaper, and writing press releases for local radio or television stations.

House Manager. The **house manager** is in charge of the ushers, who seat the audience. Being house manager involves selecting the ushers, coordinating their dress, and supplying them with programs. The house manager is also in charge of checking house lighting, air conditioning, heating, and ventilation.

Makeup Artist. Since stage makeup is different from regular makeup, productions assign someone to be the **makeup artist** responsible for using special theatrical makeup techniques. After a foundation has been applied, highlights and shadow are used to suggest age and character. Sometimes wigs, hairpieces, beards, and mustaches are made. The makeup artist sometimes uses latex to create three-dimensional skin textures or to give a young actor the look of old age. In large productions a makeup crew will be used. Actors may assist in doing their makeup. For example, they may do the basic makeup, with a makeup artist applying the finishing touches.

Property Crew Head. Properties (or "props") consist of furniture and items such as pictures, bookcases, and carpets. They also include hand props, such as swords, crockery, and walking sticks. The **property crew head** is responsible for collecting these items and making them available during rehearsals and performances.

Segment 3 *pp. 613–621*

• Participating in Informal Theater

PERFORMANCE OBJECTIVES

- To select a situation and to perform a pantomime
- To develop a situation into an improvisation
- To select and tell an entertaining story

ACTIVITY 7

Choosing Production Roles

Review the explanation of nonacting production work (pages 608–612), and think about your special skills or talents and how they would be useful in taking on the various responsibilities that are involved in producing a play. Then choose the nonacting role you would be most interested in. Finally, get together with a group of three or four classmates to discuss your preferences as well as your reasons for those preferences.

ONGOING ASSESSMENT

Activity 7

You might want to walk around from group to group to listen to students' discussions. Be sure students have provided specific reasons for their choices of nonacting roles.

After each rehearsal, if you have a role in a play, or after each work session, if you have a backstage job, record in your journal exactly what happened during the day's session. Later, when you go back and reread your entries, you will probably be surprised to discover that while little progress seems to be made in each daily session, great strides have been made over the course of five or six sessions.

CRITICAL THINKING

Analysis

If you can find a videotape or a film of a professional mime in action, view the production with the class. Have students analyze the movements to determine the basic, minimal movements that create communication. The class could categorize the mime's movements as facial expression, gesture, or locomotion.

Participating in Informal Theater

Participating in informal theater can be very rewarding. Informal theater gives a performer the opportunity to gain theatrical experience without requiring the time, expense, or other complications of being involved in a formal production.

Pantomiming

Pantomime is dramatic communication performed entirely without words. Do you remember times when you silently mimicked the way a person put on makeup or answered the telephone? Such mimicry is an example of pantomime.

Professional mimes (pantomimists), like the world-famous French master mime Marcel Marceau, frequently amaze audiences with their ability to communicate using no words at all. Mimes rely entirely on gesture, facial expression, and movement to represent action and express meaning. Every action performed by a mime—even the smallest movement of a finger or the slightest change of expression—is designed to carry meaning.

MOTIVATION

Ask several volunteers to go to the front of the room. Tell each student to choose a place where a person might be trapped—a pit, a cave, an elevator, a closet. Suggest that the student visualize the size, the shape, and the position of the chosen place. Then have students individually pantomime their efforts to escape until you call "cut." Have the class discuss where they think each student was trapped and how believable the actions were.

Pantomiming is an art form itself, but it is also good practice for learning to express physical and mental states. For example, trying to pantomime such actions as picking a flower, meeting a new friend, catching a ball, polishing a car, or digging a ditch can help you develop a heightened awareness of the feelings associated with those actions and can prepare you for other, more formal, acting experiences.

Identifying a Situation. When you are trying to decide on the subject of a pantomime, think of a situation, a little story. For example, you might think of a pitcher trying to strike out a batter, a person pestered by ants at a picnic, a child trying to tie her shoe, or a teenager who has locked himself out of his car. Notice how each of these situations has the potential for some conflict and suspense. Once you have thought of a good situation, you can begin to think of the character and how you will show his or her actions and feelings.

Observing People. One of the keys to a good pantomime is accuracy of detail. The audience has to be able to recognize the process that the movements are suggesting. The best way of identifying those details is by observing other people as they go through similar situations.

For example, if you were going to pantomime someone trying to carry an awkward armload of packages, it would probably be a good idea to watch someone who is trying to handle an actual stack of packages. Here are some examples of the kinds of questions you might ask yourself to guide your observation.

- *Is there a conflict in this situation?* What does the person do when he or she first becomes frustrated or realizes there is a problem? For example, what does the person do when he or she first discovers that the packages are awkward to carry?
- *What kinds of expressions do you see on the person's face?* Do the person's lips pucker or do the corners of the person's mouth turn down?
- *What happens with the rest of the person's body?* Does the person contort his or her body to try to hold the packages and keep them balanced?
- *What is the sequence of actions?* Step by step, what actions does the person take in trying to resolve the problem? How do the person's emotions build?
- *How does the person solve the problem?* Does the person manage to balance the packages, drop them all and stomp on them, or find someone to help carry some of the load?

TEACHER'S RESOURCE BINDER

Skills for Success 4
Pantomiming

AV ➤ Audiovisual Resource Binder

Transparency 43
Evaluation Checklist for Pantomime

TEACHING THE LESSON

Guide students through the information about pantomiming and improvising and stress the importance of characterization and action in these types of performances. When you assign **Activity 8** on p. 618, you might have students work in small groups for the pantomimes as you monitor their acting skills. Then students can proceed to the second part of **Activity 8**—developing the situations into improvisations. Students can work independently in pairs for a brief time and then perform their improvisations for the class.

As you move on to **Storytelling** on p. 618, make students aware that this art form often uses pantomime and improvisation also. A few volunteers might read the material aloud. It might be helpful for you to select a short anecdote to model how to tell a story effectively. Then give students time to practice on their own before they

Practicing. Pantomiming is like formal acting in the sense that much practice is necessary for a good performance, and the best way to practice pantomiming is to watch yourself in a mirror. For example, suppose you are going to pantomime the situation in which the small child is trying to tie a shoelace, and you have begun your preparation by observing such a child.

You could try mimicking the child's behavior while you watch yourself in a mirror. Observing yourself, you might decide that your pantomime is not dramatic enough and might try to think of something to improve it. Perhaps just as you have finally succeeded in forming a bow, you tug on the shoelaces to tighten the knot and one of the laces breaks. You could then try out that action in front of the mirror to see if it would make your performance more dramatic.

Joining a Group. Eventually you may want to work with others to create more complicated scenes. Suppose, for example, you wanted to pantomime a crowd reacting to a football play that resulted in the winning touchdown being scored in a tense, hotly contested game. You and one, two, or three others could sit on a bench facing an audience of classmates. Then each of you could act out various kinds of behavior, such as jumping up and down or hugging each other.

Performing. As with any other performance art, a successful pantomime depends on your ability to create a complete experience for your audience. The following list identifies some of the things you can do to create that experience.

1. Do not use a verbal introduction. Let the pantomime speak for itself.
2. Remain in character from the time you appear before the audience until you leave.
3. As you perform, keep in mind what the person would be thinking. It will help you to focus your emotions and your actions. Also, if your actions have no thought behind them, they will seem unnatural.

MEETING INDIVIDUAL NEEDS

An Alternative Approach

For students who have difficulty concentrating and making their movements clear in pantomiming, suggest that they create subtext, or internal monologues. They might write down what they would think while performing the movements. Then they can practice the movements by first saying aloud what they are thinking and then by performing the movement as they concentrate on the internal monologue. This strategy will help them remember what they are doing and will make the movement more believable.

tell their stories to the class. You might allow class time for evaluation of the storytellers' techniques.

Assessment

By watching the performances in pantomime, improvisation, and storytelling, you can assess students' mastery of these art forms. Also, students might benefit from self-evaluations of their performances.

Additional Activity

To help students relax, have them play charades in class. Start with a review of traditional signals such as a tug on the ear for "sounds like." Then develop a list of famous sayings, quotations, and titles. Call on volunteers to pantomime each for the class. When students have had some practice with pantomime, let them play charades in teams.

Cooperative Learning

Have the class divide into four performance groups with the groups balanced as to students' acting abilities. Have each group write three situations on slips of paper for the other groups to improvise. Have groups exchange slips and then let groups improvise the situations they have been assigned. You might make suggestions about activities such as solving crises or planning group projects.

Teacher's Resource Binder

Skills for Success 5
Improvising

4. Remember to use your eyes, your mouth, and subtle movements of your hands and arms to suggest your thoughts and feelings.
5. Exaggerate your gestures slightly so that the audience can see them and recognize what they mean.
6. Use sound effects—squeaks, groans, clicks, and so forth—only if they are critical to setting up the situation.

Improvising

Improvisation is a form of drama that is spontaneous rather than planned. It is performed without scripts or rehearsal. One important difference between improvisation and pantomime is that the former includes speech as well as action. Like a formal play, improvisation includes at least the following three basic elements: a dramatic situation, dialogue, and characterization.

A Dramatic Situation. Although life itself may be viewed as drama, just showing life as it occurs would not be very effective as theater. Whether you are doing improvisation or creating a play, your situation must be dramatic. A **dramatic situation** is one in which the characters are facing a situation that forces them to act. Whatever they choose to do, or not do, will have consequences.

Without a dramatic situation, an improvisation is unlikely to hold an audience's interest. For example, an audience would soon lose interest in a dialogue between you and your partner in which the two of you chatted aimlessly about the weather. If, on the other

RETEACHING

Have someone start a pantomime that could involve group activity such as painting a house. Once the student has established the scene, invite others to join the pantomime and interact in the activity, one at a time. After several people have entered and become part of the pantomime, call "cut." Ask students to tell what the performers were doing and then discuss what about performing the scene was characteristic of both pantomime and improvisation.

You can reteach storytelling in a similar fashion. Bring five students to the front of the room and have one student begin improvising a story for several seconds. Stop the student with a signal, and have the next student pick up the story. Continue until the last person finishes the story.

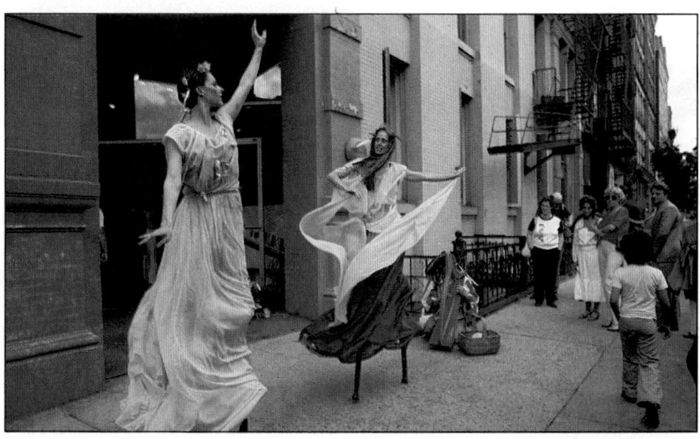

hand, you play a student who has been wrongly accused by a teacher of cheating on an important exam, your solution to this problem could provide dramatic interest.

Dialogue. **Dialogue** is the conversation that occurs between two or more characters in a drama. Although dialogue originally applied to conversation between just two people (*di-* is a Greek prefix meaning "two"), it is now used to apply to all conversation in a play. The term **monologue** refers to an extended speech by one person.

There is a major difference between dialogue in a formal play and dialogue in an improvisation, however. Improvisation has no scripts. The actors know the situation and they make up the dialogue as they go along. The only requirement is that they try to be true to the situation and maintain their characters.

Characterization. **Characterization** means the portrayal of the physical, intellectual, and emotional traits of each character. During rehearsals for a formal play, you have many opportunities to think about how you will portray a character. [See pages 596–599.] But during an improvisation, you will have to react spontaneously. Still, the nature of the situation will help you determine what you will say. For example, if you were portraying one person as a spoiled brat, you would want to exhibit the kinds of behavior that you would expect from such a person in such circumstances. You would be quick to anger, and perhaps you would whine and cry.

Whatever type of character you decide to develop, be consistent throughout the improvisation, whether it is supposed to last for one minute or for ten minutes. In addition, never stop acting in the middle of an improvisation. Keep in mind that you are creating an illusion. To do so, you must be consistent and stay in character.

CRITICAL THINKING

Evaluation

Record either on videotape or on audiocassette several improvisations that students present so that you can play the dialogue back. Ask students to compare their impromptu dialogues with dialogues from a written script. Students might then rewrite their dialogues and discuss which versions are better and what makes these versions better.

See p. 620 for **Extension, Enrichment,** and **Closure.**

ACTIVITY 8

Pantomiming and Improvising

First, pantomime one of the following situations. Then, working with a partner, develop one of the situations into an improvisation.

1. You walk by a pet shop, see a dog in the window, go into the shop to ask about the dog, and are so taken with it that you buy it.
2. You order a sandwich and a glass of milk, and you get a bowl of soup and a glass of soda water.
3. You ask a person you do not know very well out on a date for the first time.
4. You walk into a china shop carrying a large package.
5. You are watching a sporting event on television, and your favorite team is losing.

Ongoing Assessment

Activity 8

Create a scale for pantomime and improvisation presentations based on descriptions of good dramatic portrayals. Be sure the scale includes the criteria covered in the text.

Teacher's Resource Binder

Skills for Success 6
Storytelling

Storytelling

The History of Storytelling. Human beings have always been storytellers: Our ancestors told stories in their caves, in their tents, and in their huts. Before there was a written language, people told stories to pass along their heritage and traditions, as well as to entertain. Storytelling did not die when the printing press was invented. It is still alive and well, and it is an art you can learn and use.

Identifying a Good Story. You can find ideas for a story almost anywhere. You may think of a story one of your grandparents told you, or you may remember something that happened to you. You can even pick up ideas from newspapers and television news programs.

Your story can be based on fact, or it can be totally imaginary. The important thing is that your story be entertaining. Here are some guidelines for thinking of a good story.

1. To flesh out the ideas for your story, answer the questions *Who? What? Where? When? Why?* and *How?*
2. Be sure there is some kind of conflict and suspense. You want your audience to be eager to find out what happens next.
3. Your story should build up to a high point of tension or interest, and the ending should resolve the conflict and end the suspense.
4. You should include details drawn from your senses of sight, hearing, touch, taste, and smell. Sensory details will help your readers to picture the scene and actions in their own minds.
5. If you have a point to make in your story, let the outcome or resolution make it for you. Do not say "and the moral is" or "and that's why this story is important."

Telling the Story. The act of storytelling is mostly verbal, but a good storyteller does not rely on words alone. Facial expressions, gestures, and other movements help to create the complete performance. For example, if you were telling a story about a ghost, you might jump and throw your hands in the air as if frightened when telling about the ghost's surprising appearance.

MEETING INDIVIDUAL NEEDS

Cultural Diversity

Ask students from other countries or with different cultural backgrounds to recall favorite tales or myths that originate with the students' native cultures. If students prefer, have them write these stories first in their native languages and with as much detail as possible. Then have them rewrite the stories in English. Encourage them to use their imaginations to fill in any gaps. After telling the stories, students should be prepared to answer questions from classmates.

EXTENSION

Create sets of note cards on which are written names of types of characters or occupations, settings, and emotions. Have students choose any combination of cards. Then students can work with partners to create improvisational scenes based on the people, settings, and emotions they have selected. They should make it clear who they are, where they are, and how they feel without directly telling the audience—students should show, not tell. The audience can guess the characters and situations.

INTEGRATING THE LANGUAGE ARTS

Literature Link

Students might research children's stories such as fairy tales and legends to use for their storytelling activities. After students have practiced and performed their stories for the class, you might arrange for some students to go to a local elementary school to tell their stories.

ONGOING ASSESSMENT

Activity 9

Create a numerical scale based on the five guidelines for a good story on p. 619. Be sure your scale includes the storyteller's use of facial expressions, gestures, and other movements as well as vocal techniques.

In storytelling, however, the voice is the primary instrument of performing. To make a story come to life for your audience, you need to make use of these vocal techniques.

- Remember that inflections—upward or downward glides of pitch—communicate feelings. Change the pitch of your voice to suggest strong feelings or tensions, or to suggest that another character is speaking.
- Control the volume of your voice to heighten the suspense of the story, as well as to make sure that everyone in your audience can hear you.
- Control the rate of your speech. You can speed up a little or slow down slightly to reflect the pace of the action, but be careful not to talk so quickly that you lose your audience.

ACTIVITY 9 Telling a Story

Select a story that you can tell to students your own age. It can be one you have heard from someone else or one you create yourself, but it should have conflict and suspense. Practice telling the story in an entertaining way. You might videotape yourself or ask a friend to be your audience and critique your performance. Be sure you are using your voice as well as facial expressions and gestures to make the story more interesting. After you have practiced thoroughly, tell the story to your entire class.

ENRICHMENT

You might hold an evening or Sunday afternoon drama presentation of pantomimes, improvisations, and storytelling and give students an opportunity to perform for family and friends. You might even include audience participation with improvisations from the attendees.

CLOSURE

Ask students to write in their communication journals the activities they enjoyed the most and feel that they have a talent for. Then have them explain why. Some students might share their responses.

GUIDELINES

for Taking Part in a Play

- Have I analyzed the play completely?
- Do I understand the motivations behind my character's actions?
- Do I understand the other characters in the play?
- Have I chosen the gestures, movements, and voice that best portray my character?
- Have I taken advantage of my own powers of observation to bring truth to the character?
- Have I relied on stereotyped reactions, or have I created uniquely appropriate, fully rounded human responses for my character?
- Have I memorized my lines?
- Can I bring intensity to the performance?
- Do I play the role with enough diversity?
- Is my portrayal true to the character?

REVIEW QUESTIONS

Answers

1. formal theater—actors follow a script; informal theater—actors rely on their imaginations to generate story, dialogue, and movement
2. Thespis was an actor and dramatist who won the first Greek drama prize in 534 B.C. The word *thespian* for "actor" comes from his name.
3. Cover your lines so that you can see only your cue; read cues into a tape recorder; run lines as frequently as possible with other actors; and associate lines with movement.
4. the actor's right as he or she faces the audience
5. When the director blocks the movement on stage, the actors have an overall plan for movement and can discuss the blocking to determine the best individual movements for each actor.
6. Consider the technical requirements for the play, the size of the cast, and the composition of the cast.

DISCUSSION QUESTIONS

Guidelines for Assessment

Student responses may vary.

1. Encourage students not to tell everything about the periods they select, but to choose a few important details or to expand on what is in the textbook. To help students discover the transitional aspects of the periods they select, discuss the periods in chronological order and discuss similarities between periods.
2. Students should identify the director as the controlling creative force in the production who bears the final word in every decision on and off stage. In an amateur production, the director usually fulfills some of the duties of the producer, such as bringing together the script, theater, and cast. The director in an amateur production may also let others try directing.
3. Actors should be prepared to show their flexibility as performers during auditions by trying everything the director asks of them. After the director casts the play, the actors must be prepared to work with the director as each scene is blocked and to listen to comments from the director during the rehearsal period.
4. In formal theater, actors work with prepared scripts that may require them to use their voices in particular ways, and they use the stage directions or director's blocking for their movements. In informal theater, actors can be more imaginative with their voices and physical movement, since they often are creating as they go along.

CHAPTER 21

Review Questions

1. What is the difference between formal and informal theater?
2. Formal drama began in ancient Greece as part of religious ceremonies. Part of the ceremony was devoted to annual theatrical competitions. Who was Thespis?
3. One method for learning lines is to ask another person to cue you. What are four other methods for learning lines?
4. Stage directions that appear in the script or that are given by the director tell the actors where and how to move on the stage. What is meant by "stage right"?
5. How does blocking help the actors determine their movements on the stage?
6. One factor to consider when deciding whether a play is worth producing is the interest of your audience. What are two other factors to consider?
7. Opening night is preceded by many rehearsals. What is the purpose of a dress rehearsal?
8. An actor is responsible for "creating" a believable character that works in the context of a particular play. What are the responsibilities of a director?
9. Many people work behind the scenes to make a theatrical production a success. What are the responsibilities of a stage manager?
10. Both pantomime and improvisation are types of informal theater. How does improvisation differ from pantomime?

Discussion Questions

1. Research and prepare a three- to five-minute oral report on one of the following periods of drama: Greek, Roman, Medieval, Renaissance, Elizabethan, Restoration, Romantic, Realistic. Consider what influence the style of this period had on the dramatic periods that followed it. List the period's leading playwrights and the titles of their most famous works. Then, discuss each of these periods with your classmates.
2. Discuss the role of the director in bringing a play to the stage. How does the director's role in an amateur company differ from that in a professional company?
3. Discuss the responsibilities of the actor during auditions and rehearsals versus the responsibilities of the director.
4. Discuss and give several examples of the actor's use of voice and physical movement in both formal theater and informal theater.
5. The poet and literary critic T. S. Eliot was quoted in the *New York Post* (Sept. 22, 1963) as saying, "A play should give you something to think about. When I see a play and understand it the first time, then I know it can't be much good." First, discuss the meaning of this quotation. Then, discuss whether or not you agree with it.

7. All the elements of the production come together as they will on opening night; it serves as a check for any forgotten details.
8. selecting the play, casting the parts, blocking, coaching the actors, and possibly making final technical and production decisions
9. The stage manager is in charge of the entire backstage. He or she makes sure that the performance follows the pattern established by the director during rehearsal; cues actors and ensures they are in their places; and records all the director's instructions about blocking, cues, and technical effects in a master prompt book.
10. Pantomime is nonverbal and is rehearsed; improvisation is verbal and uses little or no rehearsal.

ACTIVITIES

1. **Reporting on Nonacting Areas of a Production.** Watch a community theater or professional theater production. Then prepare and give an extemporaneous oral report discussing the costumes, scenery, and lighting for the play. How appropriate were they to the action and meaning of the play? Can you think of any changes that would have made them better?

2. **Presenting a Dramatic Scene.** Working with three or four of your classmates, select a scene from a play that you could perform. Choose one group member to direct the scene, and divide the acting roles among the other members of your group. Memorize lines, block movements, and rehearse your scene before presenting it to the class. After you have completed the performance, discuss with the class what you have learned about characterization and movement.

3. **Participating in Pantomime.**
   A. Working in a group, identify the kinds of gestures, facial expressions, and movements that would be needed to pantomime the following situations:
      1. Dealing with a vending machine that has taken your money without giving you the merchandise you wanted
      2. Trying to keep a kite in the air
      3. Walking barefoot across hot sand or a hot street
      4. Carrying a large box down a flight of stairs
      5. Planting a garden

   B. Pantomime actions that would be characteristic of the following things:
      1. A photocopy machine making a copy
      2. A dog begging for a treat
      3. A tree in a spring breeze
      4. A bird preening itself
      5. A balloon slowly deflating

4. **Presenting an Improvisation.** Working with a partner, improvise one of the situations shown in the following pictures or another situation of your own choosing. Act out your improvisation. Then ask your classmates to identify the situation you portrayed.

5. Many students may suggest that Eliot refers to the layers of meaning open to interpretation in a complex piece of literature. They might also point out that appreciation of any literary work is subjective and open to interpretation. Those who disagree might say that some people always try to dig too deep when there is little reason to.

ACTIVITIES

Guidelines for Assessment

1. You might want to refer students to **Chapter 13: "Presenting Your Speech"** and pp. 319–320 on extemporaneous speaking before their presentations. Students might prepare outlines of the various nonacting areas they wish to address and turn them in for your evaluation.
2. Encourage students to choose scenes that are within their ability ranges to perform. They might choose from the historical periods they have studied or from the plays listed in the textbook. Have students create a checklist to use for self-evaluation.
3. A. You may want to assign a group of four or five students to each of the five situations and then have each group present their list of gestures, facial expressions, and movements to the class. They might demonstrate several ways to pantomime the situation. Some peer evaluation might be suitable as commentary for groups' actions.
   B. Pantomimes should be evaluated on how well students

SUMMATIVE EVALUATION

Your **Teacher's Resource Binder** contains a reproducible **Chapter 21 Test** that may be used to assess students' mastery of the concepts presented in this chapter.

PORTFOLIO ASSESSMENT

For future reference and evaluation you may want to have students keep in their portfolios any skill sheets or evaluation forms that you have used with this chapter along with any other recorded or written materials that students have created.

adapt these nonhuman actions to human motions—gestures, facial expressions, and other movements.

4. Improvisations should clearly establish the conflict or relationships between characters, and the scene should develop through appropriate dialogue and character motivation. You might write the scenarios on slips of paper for students to draw and then have the students perform the improvisations.

5. Before they report to the class, students can prepare outlines of their findings about auditions they have attended. Students should turn in their outlines.

6. Students' interpretations of the roles will vary. Invite students to explain how they made their decisions about the characters in the script after several pairs have presented their dialogues to the class.

7. Help students become aware of how actors can use subtle actions to show character by having several students demonstrate the characteristics they observed. Then show how the characteristics, taken as a whole, can create compelling and unique characterizations.

8. Students should demonstrate an understanding of the scene, the characters, and their motivations by making appropriate suggestions for blocking the scene from *Antigone*. Students will also want to consider how to balance the stage. You might want to have students draw diagrams of the scene to turn in with the stage directions.

5. Reporting on an Audition. Attend an audition for a play—a school play, a neighborhood play, or a community theater play. Be prepared to tell the class how the audition was held. Where did the audition take place? Who was there? What did those who were auditioning have to do? Did the director indicate how he or she would decide whom to cast for specific roles?

6. Interpreting a Role in a Play. Working with a partner, decide how you will present the lines of dialogue given below. How will you interpret each role? Are the speakers acquaintances or co-workers? Do they feel friendly, neutral, or hostile toward each other? Is one speaker a man and the other a woman? Are they both men?

After you have determined who the speakers are and what the relationship between them is, think of ways to portray each character. Present your dialogue to the class. Then, compare your interpretation with those of your classmates.

Speaker #1: Hey, over here.
Speaker #2: There you are!
Speaker #1: Great weather we're having today!
Speaker #2: Uh, huh. Have you been waiting long?
Speaker #1: Not very long. Please sit down.
Speaker #2: Thanks.
Speaker #1: So, what have you been up to?
Speaker #2: Nothing much. How about you?

7. Observing and Recording Mannerisms. Many of the very best actors are also keen observers of human nature. Such actors have a huge supply of observed gestures, accents, and mannerisms from which they can draw to create a new character.

Observe the mannerisms or actions of five people whom you know well or whom you see on a regular basis, such as your lab partner in science or the school bus driver. Record these observations in your communication journal. Then, list at least five specific mannerisms or actions that you would adopt to characterize each person you observed.

8. Giving Stage Directions.

A. Familiarize yourself with the scene from *Antigone* on pages 578–579. As you read, imagine that you are a director blocking this scene. How might you use stage movement to heighten the dramatic effect of the scene? What movements would be appropriate for Creon? for Antigone? How would you make sure the stage appeared balanced?

B. Working with several of your classmates, block the scene from *Antigone*. As you decide which movements work best, mark a copy of the script with specific stage directions. [Use the chart and the example on page 602 as a model.] Compare your group's blocking of the scene with that of another group in the class.

◆ Real-Life Speaking Situations

Performance Objectives

- To present a lesson teaching someone how to successfully perform a service-industry job
- To write a review of a play

REAL LIFE Speaking Situations

1 Some jobs involve role-playing that has all the elements of theater. For example, in many restaurants employees are required to wear costumes and are given specific direction on how to act. In many cases, retail clerks, parking valets, and others who greet the public are even given particular lines to say.

You have been asked to train the new employees who will work at the counter of a health-food restaurant. As employees who must meet the public and represent the company, they are required to play a specific role. What will you include in your training session?

First, you will need to address the issue of costumes (uniforms) and how they are to be worn. You will also need to provide scripts (precise words and lines) for greeting customers, taking orders, and handling complaints. Finally, you will have to instruct the employees in using specific nonverbal behaviors and physical actions that are appropriate for the job.

Prepare a five- to ten-minute portion of a training session in which you teach someone how to do this job. Present the lesson to your class.

2 Your boss, the editor of the local newspaper, has asked you to write a review of the community theater's new play. You want to give a fair review that identifies strengths as well as weaknesses of the production. What will you say about the actors' performances? What about set design and lighting? Do you have any comments to make about the appropriateness of the play for the audience? You might even comment on ticket prices or the helpfulness of ushers.

First, you will need to see a production on which to base your review. If at all possible, attend a local theatrical production by a school or a community theater group. Otherwise, view a video recording of a stage production that interests you. Try to jot down your impressions as you watch the performance or as soon after it as you can. Also, you may want to find out what other critics have said about this play or these performers.

Write a one- to two-page review giving your opinion of the performance and identifying some of its specific strengths and weaknesses. Share your review with your classmates.

Assessment Guidelines

1. Students might take on the role of trainer and present their lessons as if they were speaking to a class of potential trainees. The trainees then might evaluate whether the trainer made their job expectations clear.
2. Students will need to attend a local production to write this review, or if this is not possible, they might base their reviews on a televised drama and use their imaginations to create this review. Reviews should include specific details, even if the details are made up.

Chapter 22
Radio and Television
pp. 628–657

Chapter Overview

This chapter begins with a segment on the development of radio and television. A segment on planning and producing a radio talk show and a radio drama follows. Next, a segment on planning and producing a television news show and a public service announcement is presented.

Teacher's Resource Binder

The following materials are identified at their point of use in this chapter:

- Skills for Success
  1. *Comparing News Coverage in Print and on the Radio*
  2. *Analyzing Your Prime-Time Viewing Habits*
  3. *Preparing a Radio Talk Show*
  4. *Analyzing Your Radio-Listening Habits*
  5. *Preparing a Public Service Announcement for Television*
  6. *Evaluating Radio and Television Presentations*
- Chapter 22 Vocabulary
- Chapter 22 Test/Answer Key

AV Audiovisual Resource Binder

The following materials are identified at their point of use in this chapter:

- Transparency 44
  Evaluating Radio and Television
- Audiotape 1, Lesson 10
  How to Perform on Radio and Television

Introducing the Chapter

Radio and television are cultural fixtures that many high school students take for granted, but these media have histories and have significant impact on what students know and value. This chapter provides a chance to explore how these media developed and how their major program formats are produced.

The first part of the chapter considers the media as factors in American culture. The second and third segments deal with the practical concerns of planning and producing radio and television shows. You can point out that knowledge of how the media work can make students more appreciative consumers. Some students may even be stimulated to consider careers in radio and television.

CHAPTER 22

Radio and Television

OBJECTIVES

After studying this chapter, you should be able to

1. Summarize the history of radio and television and describe current trends in both fields.
2. Explain and give examples of how the mass media, including radio and television, affect culture.
3. Plan and produce a mock radio talk show.
4. Plan and produce a radio drama.
5. Plan and produce a mock television news story.
6. Prepare a public service announcement.

What Are Radio and Television?

Radio and television are two forms of electronic mass media. Because they deal in oral and visual messages, they involve speaking and listening skills.

Four common forms of radio and television presentations are

- the **radio talk show,** in which a moderator and one or more guests discuss a topic
- the **radio drama,** in which actors present an oral performance of a play or radio script
- the **television news story,** in which a reporter or newscaster uses videotape to illustrate a current news event
- the **public service announcement (PSA),** in which a brief persuasive message is presented

These presentations cover all types of subjects and issues. For example, on a radio talk show the moderator and guests might discuss a current controversy over the lack of new textbooks in local schools. A television station might carry a public service announcement urging people to register to vote.

Bibliography of Additional Materials

Professional Readings

- Brown, Les. ***Les Brown's Encyclopedia of Television.*** Detroit: Gale Research.
- Sloan, Wm. David. ***Perspectives on Mass Communication History.*** Hillsdale, NJ: Lawrence Erlbaum Associates, Publishers.
- Zettl, Herbert. ***Television Production Handbook.*** White Plains, NY: Knowledge Industry Publications.

Audiovisuals

- ***The Impact of Television***—Britannica Films, Chicago, IL (videocassette, 20 min.)
- ***Radio and Television Production***—Morris Video, Torrance, CA (videocassette, 15 min.)
- ***Radio Drama: Life and Rebirth***—Michigan Media, Ann Arbor, MI (videocassette, 29 min.)
- ***Television and Human Behavior***—The Learning Seed, Lake Zurich, IL (videocassette, 26 min.)

Segment 1 pp. 630–637

- **Tracing the Development of Radio and Television**

PERFORMANCE OBJECTIVES

- To compare local radio and television programming
- To create an inventory of personal media usage

MEETING INDIVIDUAL NEEDS

An Alternative Approach

Have interested students research some of the people who have contributed significantly to the development of the mass media and then have the students report to the class on their findings. Some people to consider include Johannes Gutenberg, William Caxton, Guglielmo Marconi, V. K. Zworykin, Philo Farnsworth, and Allen B. Dumont.

USING THE CHART

Some of the kinds of programs listed in the chart showing the milestones in the development of radio can still be found on radio and television. Ask students to identify these programs and discuss why they are still popular.

Tracing the Development of Radio and Television

The printing press, invented by Johannes Gutenberg in the 1430s, was the first example of **mass media**—practical methods for communicating with a mass, or large group, of people. Before Gutenberg, books were extremely difficult to make and therefore too costly to be widely distributed. After Gutenberg, books began to be mass-produced, and an explosion of literacy occurred.

Since the time of Gutenberg, many other mass media have appeared, including newspapers, magazines, films, and billboards. The most influential mass media in our time are radio and television.

The Origins of Radio and Television

The Emergence of Radio. In the late 1800s, people had two means of long-distance communication—the telegraph and the telephone. In 1895, Guglielmo Marconi, an Italian inventor, created the first radio communication. By 1901, Marconi's equipment was sending signals across the Atlantic Ocean. The following chart shows some of the major events in radio's early history.

Date	Event
1910	Lee De Forest produces a program starring tenor Enrico Caruso singing from New York's Metropolitan Opera House.
1916	First experimental programs are broadcast.
1920	KDKA, first professional station, broadcasts election of President Warren G. Harding.
1925–26	Radio's Golden Age begins: Soap operas, afternoon children's serials, and nighttime comedies and dramas become popular.
1926	NBC, first permanent national network, is created.
1941–45	President Franklin Roosevelt uses "fireside chats" to rally people to support World War II.
1950	Radio's Golden Age ends as television challenges radio's popularity.

Motivation

Ask students to volunteer answers to the following questions: Which came first, television or radio? What years were radio and television invented?

Discuss the range of years students suggest. Tell them this segment will give the answers to these questions.

Teaching the Lesson

Much of the information in this segment is historical and technical data and you may want students to preview the information before you discuss the material in class. You might ask students to read **Tracing the Development of Radio and Television** as homework and to be prepared for a class discussion. Have students quiz their older family members or neighbors to see if

The Emergence of Television. The groundwork for television was laid in the 1870s when it was discovered that there was a way to transform light variations into electrical signals. Both a mechanical scanning disc and the first photoelectric cells were designed just a few years later. However, it was not until 1923—when V. K. Zworykin applied for a patent on the iconoscope, an all-electric television tube—that the development of television broadcasting became possible.

By the late 1920s, the technology for sending and receiving television signals had been invented, and in the 1930s the first television broadcasts began. However, the cost of television and the coming of World War II delayed until the late 1940s the emergence of television as an important communication medium. By the 1950s, television had become popular enough to challenge radio. Some people even predicted that radio would disappear altogether. In 1950, only 9 percent of U.S. households had television sets, but just fifteen years later, in 1965, 95 percent of households had at least one set. In a short period of about forty years, television had become a fixture in almost every household in the United States.

Radio's Response to Television. Radio stayed alive despite the success of television by adopting new formats. A **format** is a particular combination of content and style. Increasingly, radio stations began concentrating on music, news, and talk formats and left comedic and dramatic programming to the visual medium of television.

Critical Thinking

Analysis

Show videotapes of one or two episodes of a 1950s situation comedy such as *I Married Joan, The Adventures of Ozzie and Harriet,* or *I Love Lucy.* Ask students to compare the 1950s show to a situation comedy of today. What similarities and differences do they notice?

Cooperative Learning

Ask groups of four students to analyze the formats used by local radio stations and to report to the class on their findings. Each group might analyze a different radio station's format. The first meeting might be devoted to planning the group's research, which will probably have to be done outside of class. Subsequent meetings in class can be used to analyze findings and to prepare the report for the class.

anyone remembers the days of television's infancy or recalls early radio dramas.

As you discuss this segment, have students compare any information they have gleaned about early media days to their knowledge of radio and television today. As you discuss future trends, encourage students to make projections for future technologies.

After students have discussed the material, have them examine a weekly television schedule in a newspaper or other publication to group programs into categories like sports, news, situation comedies, and specials. Then have students do the same for local radio schedules. (You may have to call radio stations for copies of these.) Students should then be ready to do **Activity 1** on p. 634.

As you discuss **The Effects of Radio and Television** on pp. 635–637, allow students to comment on any events or examples that they

MEETING **INDIVIDUAL** NEEDS

Cultural Diversity

Ask students to report to the class on the radio stations in your area that target audiences of particular cultural or linguistic backgrounds. Students can focus on the language(s) used for broadcasts, the programming, the advertising, and the estimated audience size.

Students with Special Needs

It can be helpful to be aware of the particular learning styles of special-needs students. Developing their strengths can help them gain self-confidence.

If a student is primarily an auditory learner, you may want to have the student focus on the radio sections of the chapter. If a student is a visual learner, focus on the television and film sections of the chapter. If you have kinesthetic learners, you may want to have them work on sound effects or other technical aspects of radio or television.

Radio and Television Today

Radio Today. Far from disappearing, radio is more popular than ever before. There are now more than ten thousand radio stations in the United States, and in 1990 alone, more than twenty-one million radio sets were sold.

The popularity of modern radio is partly due to the development of portable receiving devices. Millions of people listen to radios in their cars, at work, and at play—places where television sets are not commonly found. Another reason for the continued popularity of radio is its ability to be audience specific. Being small, most radio stations can target their programming and advertising to specific audiences. As a result, whoever you are, you can probably find a radio station with a format tailored to your interests.

Although music stations are by far the most common type of radio station today, news and talk radio stations are becoming increasingly popular. A talk radio station typically mixes news reports with moderated, live "call-in" programs in which listeners express their opinions on various topics.

Independent college radio stations are often nontraditional types of radio stations. College radio stations are often very small and are frequently staffed by nonprofessionals—students who are learning about broadcasting. Because they often do not have to earn profits and are usually staffed by students, college radio stations are often creative in their programming. They may play avant-garde music or hold discussions of controversial subjects. They have returned to radio some of the excitement (and some of the pitfalls) of the days of live radio programming.

found particularly interesting or pertinent. You may want to model the **Communication Journal** assignment on p. 637 by sharing with students notes you have taken concerning one day's television and radio exposure.

Assessment

You can evaluate students' performance on **Activity 1** and the **Communication Journal** assignment in this segment to assess students' mastery of the material on the development of radio and television.

Television Today. No one would dispute the importance and popularity of television today. Nearly every home in America has at least one television set, and by the time the average American reaches the age of thirty, he or she has logged over thirty-five thousand hours in front of the television.

Although most early television programs were **live** (transmitted as they occurred), most of today's programs are **prerecorded** (recorded earlier for later broadcast). The exceptions are generally newscasts, most of which are live, and some talk and interview shows.

In the United States, there are two kinds of television stations: commercial stations and noncommercial, or educational, stations. The commercial stations are funded by advertisers. The noncommercial stations are funded by a combination of government money, private donations, and subscriptions. Noncommercial stations typically air children's shows, news programs, nature studies, classic films, biographies, political or social documentaries, and science and arts programming. Commercial stations also show some of the same types of programs, but they are largely dominated by situation comedies, dramas, and talk shows.

In recent years cable television and home satellite dishes have had a tremendous effect on the quality of reception and variety of programs available to Americans. **Cable television** brings programs over cables into people's homes, while home satellite dishes pick up signals from the commercial satellites used by the networks and television stations. **Pay television** is a type of cable television in which people pay a fee to watch a particular program, usually a movie, a sports event, or a concert. **Pay-cable television** is a regular subscription service that brings a variety of programs into the home on one channel in exchange for a monthly fee.

In the United States, the three major television networks saw their markets erode during the 1980s and early 1990s as a result of the viewing options made possible by means of cable and satellite. During the 1980s the number of cable television subscribers jumped from a little over fifteen million to more than fifty million. Several pay-cable channels emerged during this period, including Home Box Office, The Disney Channel, The Movie Channel, The Learning Channel, and Bravo! Many of these pay-cable channels develop their own programs.

Critical Thinking

Analysis and Synthesis

While people of all ages watch television, people in some age groups watch more television than people in other age groups. Divide the class into research teams and have each team survey members of a particular age group (for example, preschoolers, retired people, and so on) to find out the average amount of time each group watches television every week. Then construct a graph of the averages. Ask students to draw conclusions and to suggest possible reasons for age-group differences.

Cooperative Learning

Have students bring television listings to class. Working in groups of four, students can analyze the kinds of shows available in your area. How do commercial and noncommercial offerings differ? How do cable channels differ in their shows from network channels?

RETEACHING

For students who need reteaching, you can use sample schedules from a radio station and a television station to compare and contrast programming. If the categories students use are too specific, encourage students to be more general (for example, *sports* instead of *football*).

See p. 636 for **EXTENSION, ENRICHMENT,** and **CLOSURE.**

ONGOING ASSESSMENT

Activity 1

Students can limit their analyses to a single day for only one major radio and one major television station. Their answers to the questions should include examples to support their points. Answers should reflect an awareness of differences in audiences at different times of the day.

USING THE CHART

Ask students to obtain more information about the emerging technologies listed in the **Emerging Audio and Video Technologies** chart and to report to the class on their findings. The reports should emphasize nontechnical information, with special emphasis on how each new technology will affect television viewing.

ACTIVITY 1

Comparing Radio and Television Programming

With a partner, survey the radio and television programming available in your community. Gather your information by listening and viewing as well as by studying program guides and listings. How does the radio programming differ from the television programming? How are the radio and television progamming alike? How does the programming vary according to time of day or evening? What do these differences indicate about the reasons people listen to the radio or watch television? Share your findings in a class discussion.

Trends for the Future

Predicting the future of any technology is a risky business. There was a time, for example, when popular storytellers predicted travel to the moon in hot-air balloons! However, there are some emerging technologies and trends in the television and radio industries that bear watching.

Emerging Audio and Video Technologies

High-Definition Television (HDTV)	creates a sharper image due to its higher **resolution,** (a more detailed definition of an image achieved by using a greater number of picture cells, or pixels, to create the image)
Digital Recording	a technique that converts sounds or images into groups of electronic bits and stores them on a specific medium; during playback, the recorded bits are read electronically, often by means of a laser beam
Information Network	single machine (combination telephone, computer, compact disc player, television, radio, and electronic newspaper) in the home connected by fiber-optic cables to a nationwide or worldwide information network
Interactive Television	system that allows the viewer to interact with and respond to what is seen on the television screen, using one or more special communication devices

The Effects of Radio and Television

The mass media are powerful communication tools because they reach so many people. With the mass production of newspapers, magazines, and books in the nineteenth century, people came to be influenced by what they read as well as by those around them. When radio, and then television, came along, these media were even more influential because they reached more people more quickly.

The Power of Electronic Media. In 1938, Orson Welles dramatically demonstrated the power of radio by presenting a story about an invasion from Mars as though it were a series of news bulletins. Thousands of people panicked, believing that the United States was being attacked by Martians.

In the 1950s and 1960s, the commercial side of television helped to produce the world's first mass consumer economy. A large and powerful advertising industry grew up around television, and enormous sums of money were spent convincing viewers to buy everything from automobiles to cereal. In 1960, the power of television was demonstrated when a little-known senator named John Kennedy challenged a well-known, popular vice-president, Richard Nixon, in a series of televised debates. Kennedy won both the debate and the presidential election.

Today, a presidential election can be influenced by a single statement broadcast on the evening news. In addition, images from across the globe of wars, floods, and famines come directly into our living rooms and arouse our sympathy or our wrath. People all over the world watch American television programs. Advertisers influence how viewers spend their money and how they think of themselves. In short, life in the twentieth century has been powerfully influenced by the broadcast media.

MEETING INDIVIDUAL NEEDS

An Alternative Approach

Interested students can research the panic that Orson Welles's 1938 broadcast of *The War of the Worlds* caused. Besides conventional library research, students may want to interview any people in the community who heard the original broadcast to find out what their reactions were.

Writing to Learn

Have students write compositions about the ways in which television's portrayal of American life differs from life as they know it. Students can discuss why these differences exist and what effects they may have on viewers of different ages. Let a few volunteers read their compositions to the class.

Building a Portfolio

Students can include their compositions from the above **Writing to Learn** feature in their portfolios.

Teacher's Resource Binder

Skills for Success 1
Comparing News Coverage in Print and on the Radio

EXTENSION

Have students listen to a radio talk show for a week and compare and contrast the topics discussed to the topics discussed on a television talk show during the same week. How do the topics differ? Why?

MEETING INDIVIDUAL NEEDS

Cultural Diversity

Class discussion of the value of television in the world today is an ideal way to get students from other countries to communicate their beliefs and opinions. Ask students new to the United States about the prevalence of television in their native countries.

Did the students' families watch television as the students were growing up? If so, how frequently? Were there public broadcasting systems in their countries? Did television play an important part in presenting cultural and political events in their countries? Was television chiefly regarded as an entertainment medium? Was news broadcasting impartial or sensational?

TEACHER'S RESOURCE BINDER

Skills for Success 2
Analyzing Your Prime-Time Viewing Habits

The Values Presented in the Electronic Media. Unfortunately, the values that the media teach may not always be the values that are in the best interests of society. Radio and television advertising, for example, has been criticized for presenting a view of the world in which happiness seems to be a result of what people have and what they can buy.

Calvin and Hobbes **by Bill Watterson**

Commercial television has drawn fire in recent years for its violence, its promotion through advertising of materialistic values and waste, and its tendency to stereotype women, minorities, teenagers, elderly people, and just about everyone else. In addition, commercial news programs have been criticized for oversimplifying issues. For example, the broadcast news has been criticized for providing one- or two-second statements, called **sound bites,** instead of in-depth analyses.

Finally, commercial television is often attacked for sensationalizing the news and for concentrating on negative aspects of social and political life. It has been shown, for example, that the more television people watch, the more violent and dangerous they believe the world to be.

On the positive side, both commercial and noncommercial television serve necessary functions: They draw together people from diverse backgrounds and give them a shared culture, and they expose people to information and issues about which they might otherwise have been unaware.

The Critical Audience. The power and influence of the media and its potential to affect the audience make it essential that we all become critical viewers and listeners. When you listen to the radio or television, be aware of the purposes of the programming. Is the program attempting to entertain, to inform, or to persuade you to

ENRICHMENT

Arrange a field trip to a local radio or television station so students can see what goes on during broadcasts. If possible, ask staff members of the station to explain their jobs to students. You might also arrange for a question-and-answer session to follow.

CLOSURE

Review the information in the segment by constructing on the chalkboard a chart of the milestones in the history of radio and television. Ask students to speculate about when new developments in radio and television will occur.

buy something? Analyzing the program's basic purpose will enable you to make the first step toward controlling the effects that the media may have on you.

HOW TO *View and Listen Critically*

1. **Identify the purpose of the program.** Try to analyze the aim or goal of what you are listening to or viewing. Is the program attempting to entertain you, to inform you, or to persuade you?
2. **Analyze the values or assumptions that the program represents.** What ideas does the program take for granted? For example, if the purpose of the program is to entertain, determine whether the humorous portions of the program could be considered derogatory or insulting to any group of people. If the purpose of the program is to inform or to persuade, be sure to think about the information presented to distinguish between actual, provable facts and someone's preferences or opinions. [See pages 228–229 for more on facts and opinions.] You will need to think carefully about the information presented to identify the sources of information, their reliability, and any biases they might have. You should be able to verify the accuracy of facts and statistics.
3. **Make your own judgment.** Remember that information that is presented to you through the mass media often represents someone else's opinion or point of view. Even seemingly objective images and pictures may distort reality. If you listen and observe carefully and evaluate media presentations critically, you will become an informed, intelligent listener or viewer.

COMMUNICATION JOURNAL

For a period of one week, keep a record in your communication journal of everything you listen to on the radio or watch on television. Note all commercials, songs, and news stories that you are exposed to and every instance of stereotyping or violence that you encounter. At the end of the week, look over your notes and ask yourself these questions: What messages am I exposed to in the media? What are advertisers telling me that I need? What stereotypes have been reinforced by my media usage this week? How much violence did I hear about or watch each day? What, if anything, did I learn from the media during the week? After you have completed your inventory, compare your findings with those of your classmates.

HOW TO VIEW AND LISTEN CRITICALLY

Ask students to use the "**How to**" suggestions to devise a checklist that people could use as they view or listen to television or radio. Have students field-test their checklists in a real viewing or listening situation and have them make any changes in their checklists they think are necessary.

BUILDING A PORTFOLIO

Students can include the checklists they develop from the "**How to**" guidelines in their portfolios for future use.

Segment 2 *pp. 638–644*

- **Preparing a Radio Talk Show**
- **Preparing a Radio Drama**

Performance Objectives

- To plan and produce a radio talk show
- To plan and produce a radio drama

Cooperative Learning

Have students work in pairs to create lists of topics that would be appropriate for a local radio talk show. You can allow students to use newspapers and current national news magazines for ideas.

Teacher's Resource Binder

Skills for Success 3
Preparing a Radio Talk Show
Skills for Success 4
Analyzing Your Radio-Listening Habits

AV *Audiovisual Resource Binder*

Audiotape 1, Lesson 10
How to Perform on Radio and Television

Preparing a Radio Talk Show

The Format of a Talk Show

Talk radio is one of the most rapidly growing forms of radio programming today. Formats for talk radio programs differ considerably, but a common format runs like this:

- A host, or moderator, appears in a regular time slot—fifteen minutes to an hour each day.
- At the beginning of the show, the host introduces some issue that will be of interest to many listeners. Often this is an issue raised by some recent news event that is summarized by the host.
- Then the host introduces a guest or a panel of guests to discuss the issue.

Generally, the guest or guests on radio talk shows are celebrities, politicians, authors, or journalists. In addition there are sometimes knowledgeable commentators, or pundits, who appear regularly with the host and his or her guests. After an open discussion in which the host, the guests, and the pundits address the issue, the host then takes telephone calls from listeners, who are invited to ask questions or to comment on the issue.

Skills Needed for a Talk Show

There are only two roles in a radio talk show—host or guest. Although the speaking and listening skills needed on a radio talk show are similar to those needed in other speech situations, remembering the following guidelines will help you prepare for any talk show appearance.

MOTIVATION

Play a tape of a portion of a radio drama and ask students if they've ever heard anything like this. Tell them radio dramas used to be extremely popular and point out that they will learn how to plan and produce one in this segment.

TEACHING THE LESSON

After you interest students in radio programming, encourage them to discuss the formats and types of participation in talk shows. Students may have favorites that they listen to regularly and have anecdotes to share. Discuss the guidelines in **How to Participate in a Radio Talk Show** so that students will be prepared for **Activity 2.**

HOW TO *Participate in a Radio Talk Show*

1. **Use your voice effectively.** Remember to control the volume, rate, and pitch of your voice to create interest and to communicate clearly. [See pages 53–73 for more about using your voice.] Be sure you are familiar with the type of microphone being used, and take care with plosives (*p, b, d, t, k, g*), sounds that can be distorted by microphones. [See pages 333–335.]
2. **If you are the host, you should lead the discussion and keep it moving.** Before the show, prepare by identifying an issue or topic that will be of interest to your listening audience. Look for current issues in the news or current topics of discussion in the community. As the program begins, introduce your guests and refer to them by name when asking them questions or commenting on their responses. As the program proceeds, use three types of questions to stimulate discussion: questions that request information, questions that probe deeper, and questions that check your understanding. [See pages 173–176 for more information about conversational skills and pages 196–198 for more about being an effective interviewer.] Remember to demonstrate respect for the opinions of others. [See pages 141–143.]
3. **If you are the guest, you should speak up to express your ideas and opinions.** A talk show, by definition, requires its participants to communicate their ideas. [See page 638.] Participants should use questioning and paraphrasing to clarify ideas and shared perceptions. [See pages 144–145.] Talk show guests should respect the opinions of other guests and of the host, and take turns in the discussion. A talk show guest should speak up about his or her ideas, but he or she should also remember that he or she may politely refuse to discuss topics that he or she feels are too private or not appropriate for the discussion. [See pages 146–149.]

ACTIVITY 2 Planning and Producing a Radio Talk Show

Work with a small group of classmates to plan your own fifteen-minute radio talk show. Choose one person to act as the host while the others in the group act as guests. Identify an issue that members of the group care about deeply—one that is likely to get a response from them. Plan an opening, or introductory, statement by the host as well as the questions that the host will ask the guests. Present your radio talk show to your class, allowing a five-minute period in which you will take questions or comments from your "listeners"—the other members of your class who are not in your group. If you have facilities available to do so, perform your talk show using microphones and a tape recorder.

HOW TO PARTICIPATE IN A RADIO TALK SHOW

You may want to have students use the "**How to**" suggestions to make a checklist that they can use when they do **Activity 2.** The checklist can be a reminder of how to perform on a radio talk show, and it can also serve as guidelines for assessment.

BUILDING A PORTFOLIO

Students can include their checklists based on **How to Participate in a Radio Talk Show** in their portfolios for later reference.

ONGOING ASSESSMENT

Activity 2

Students can work on this activity in groups of three. The topic chosen for discussion should be one of interest to students, and the moderator's questions should reflect the unique qualities of the two guests.

To get students interested in preparing their own radio dramas in **Activity 3** on p. 644, plan to listen to more of the radio drama you selected to motivate students. As you listen to the drama, point out the sound effects, the music, the dialogue, and the narration. Discuss any acting instructions you think may have been included in the script.

Let several students read the parts in the **Excerpt from a Radio Drama** (pp. 642–643) for the class. Ask the class if the format and plot catch their interest. What is it about the use of auditory messages alone that makes this possible? Before students begin **Activity 3,** read through **How to Participate in a Radio Drama** on p. 643.

INTEGRATING THE LANGUAGE ARTS

Literature Link

Locate a recording of a radio drama based on a short story such as "The Monkey's Paw" by W. W. Jacobs. Have students read the story and then have them listen to the recording. Ask students to discuss which version they liked better and why they preferred that version.

ADDITIONAL ACTIVITY

To illustrate how sound functions in television shows, play a portion of a videotape of a soap opera with the television screen covered. Ask students to discuss whether the sound alone sets the scene and establishes the mood as it does in a radio drama.

Preparing a Radio Drama

Radio's Golden Age was a time when hundreds of thousands of listeners regularly gathered around their radio sets to hear comedy sketches and radio dramas. Some of the dramas produced on radio, like Lucille Fletcher's *The Hitchhiker,* Orson Welles's version of *The War of the Worlds,* and W. W. Jacobs's *The Monkey's Paw,* have become classics. Many people who remember radio dramas from their childhoods consider this medium to be the most moving of all theatrical forms—more so than live theater or television or film.

The power of radio drama lies in its appeal to the imagination. Viewers of live theater, television, or film are limited by what the visual medium actually shows them. Listeners to a radio drama, on the other hand, are limited only by their imaginations. When a radio program's narrator describes a ghostly figure standing by a roadside, the listener is invited to reach inside himself or herself and to conjure up a figure more ghastly than any actual picture might be.

Orson Welles is shown here during the radio broadcast of *The War of the Worlds.* At the time, he was unaware of the panic that his radio play was causing among thousands of his listeners.

The Format of a Radio Drama

The script of a radio drama contains sound effects, music, dialogue, acting instructions, and narration.

Sound Effects. In a radio script, the abbreviation SFX stands for "sound effects." To a great extent, sound effects play the same role in radio drama that pictures play in television drama. Sound effects help to set the scene and to establish the mood, or atmosphere. They also help to reveal the actions taking place. For example, the sound of a doorbell lets the audience know that someone is at the door.

Assessment

The finished product of each activity can serve as the basis for assessment. If you need additional assessment procedures, have students write brief descriptions of what they did to plan and produce the radio talk show and the radio drama.

Reteaching

You can reteach the material in this segment by working through the process of producing both kinds of radio programs with the whole class. The programs created under your direct guidance can then serve as models.

Music. Music is an important part of most radio, television, and film drama. In television and film, music often plays continuously under the action and mirrors in its emotional quality the emotions that the director wants the audience to feel. For example, a chase scene might be accompanied by fast-paced music, and a tender scene between a child and his father might be accompanied by a soft children's melody.

In radio dramas, music rarely plays continuously in the background. Instead, musical cues are used to open and to close scenes. These cues act as transitions to move the audience from one scene to another. The chart below shows some instructions that are commonly used for music.

Audio Script Terminology	
GOES UNDER	The music is heard quietly in the background and fades as someone begins to speak.
UP AND OUT	The music returns to its full volume at the end of a scene.
UP AND OVER	The music rises in volume until it drowns out the voices.
UP TO ESTABLISH	Music is played at full volume at the beginning of a scene.

Dialogue. The words actually spoken by the characters in a radio play are referred to as **dialogue.** Obviously, most of the work in a radio drama is done by the dialogue. The audience cannot see the setting or the costumes or the expressions on actors' faces, so dialogue, music, and sound effects must convey all of those things.

Using the Chart

Play a recording of a portion of a radio drama and have students identify the use of music by applying the terms in the chart to the variations in the music they hear.

EXTENSION

Ask your students to bring their literature textbooks to class and to find a short story or a narrative poem they think would make a good radio drama. After they have identified a literary work, ask them to discuss the elements of the work that make it suited for production as a radio drama.

ENRICHMENT

Invite a local radio personality to class to discuss the work he or she does. Ask the person to explain the kind of training required, the licensing requirements in your state, and the rules the FCC imposes on radio stations.

INTEGRATING THE LANGUAGE ARTS

Dictionary Link

The supporting characters in radio dramas are often stock characters, that is, characters who fit types that tend to remain the same from one drama to another. Have students look up the following terms for common stock characters in a dictionary. Then have them write the definitions in their communication journals.

1. dowager [rich elderly woman]
2. fop [dandy overly concerned with appearance]
3. ingénue [romantic female lead]
4. pedant [know-it-all]
5. rogue [fun-loving rascal]
6. villain [wicked person]

WRITING TO LEARN

After students have read the portion of the radio drama in the textbook, ask them each to write a paragraph describing what might happen in the rest of the drama. The scenarios can be quite creative, but they should reflect an awareness of the setting, characters, and other information given in the script.

Acting Instructions. Some scripts for radio dramas include acting instructions that are embedded in the lines of dialogue. These acting instructions often appear in parentheses and in italics; they tell how the characters are feeling or describe how the characters' lines are to be delivered. In well-written radio dramas, acting instructions are usually unnecessary because the characters' emotions or tones of voice are clear from the situation and from what is being said.

Narration. Many radio dramas include a **narrator** or announcer whose job it is to introduce the scenes, to provide transitions, and to conclude the program. The words spoken by the narrator or announcer are called **narration.**

Excerpt from a Radio Drama

SFX: WIND AND SEA. FOGHORN IN DISTANCE.

MUSIC: TIN WHISTLE PLAYS "THE GREAT SILKIE," GOES UNDER.

NARRATOR: Ten miles off the Welsh coast, a fishing boat, the *Swansea*, casts its nets into dark, churning waters. It's an ancient act, casting nets upon the sea, an act that, for all its familiarity, remains mysterious. One never knows what the abyss will yield up to the world of sunlight and air.

MATE: Captain, you'd better have a look at this. There's something strange caught in our nets, abeam, port side.

CAPTAIN O'DONNELL: *(Annoyed)* What do you mean, something strange?

MATE: I don't know . . . something.

CAPTAIN: Well, clear the net and get on with your fishing. What's the matter with you?

MATE: I think you'd better go above and have a look for yourself.

SFX: FOOTSTEPS OF CAPTAIN AND MATE UP LADDER AND ACROSS THE DECK. GULLS CRYING.

CAPTAIN: You called me on deck for this? Come on, lad, are you daft? You'd think you'd never seen a dead seal before.

MATE: Captain, that's not a dead seal. It's, it's . . . I don't know what it is.

CAPTAIN: Well, haul it up an' let's have a look.

SFX: WATER SLOSHING. HEAVY WEIGHT BEING LIFTED. EXCLAMATIONS OF SURPRISE FROM THE SAILORS.

CLOSURE

Review the processes of creating radio talk shows and radio dramas by asking students to volunteer information about the steps needed to produce these programs. You can summarize the steps in a chart on the chalkboard or on a poster for display in the classroom.

> **MATE:** What do you make of it?
> **SAILOR:** Some sort of monster if you ask me.
> **MATE:** Ever seen the like?
> **CAPTAIN:** Not while awake I haven't.
> **MATE:** Me neither. Looks almost human, doesn't it?
> **CAPTAIN:** Never seen the like of it.
> **SAILOR:** Some sort of monster.
> **MATE:** Almost like . . . a girl.
> *SFX: WIND AND SEA. MUSIC: "THE GREAT SILKIE" UP AND OUT.*

The Literary Elements of a Radio Drama

A radio drama contains elements that are common to all works of literature, such as setting, mood, characters, conflict, and plot. [See pages 558–563 and pages 596–599 for information about how these elements are handled in adaptations of literary works.] For radio dramas, these literary elements are handled in specific ways. For example, the mood may be established by music or the setting may be explained by the narrator.

Skills Needed to Perform in a Radio Drama

Since actors in a radio drama cannot be seen by the audience, scripts can be read rather than memorized. Actors also do not have to worry about physical actions. However, the absence of visual cues makes an actor's voice crucial to the success of a radio drama.

HOW TO *Participate in a Radio Drama*

1. **Use your voice effectively.** Vary the pitch, rate, and volume of your voice to convey the emotions of the character. [See pages 596–599.]
2. **Prepare a reading script.** Mark a copy of your script so that you can see where you need to use changes in pitch, rate, volume, and stress. [See pages 565–566.]
3. **Use the microphone correctly.** Before the performance, practice using the microphone. [See pages 333–335.] During the performance, hold your script carefully to avoid making noise with the paper.

HOW TO PARTICIPATE IN A RADIO DRAMA

Encourage students to refer to the "**How to**" information as they do **Activity 3** on p. 644.

Segment 3 pp. 644–651

- **Preparing a Television News Story**
- **Preparing a Public Service Announcement for Television**
- **Evaluating Radio and Television Presentations**

PERFORMANCE OBJECTIVES

- To write and present a television news story
- To prepare a public service announcement

ONGOING ASSESSMENT

Activity 3

Students can work in groups of six on this activity. The radio drama can be based on a short story, a one-act play, or a plot of the students' creation. Allow students to tape-record their dramas to play to the class and to keep on file for use as models in the years to come. The radio dramas should use music, sound effects, and acting skills to create their effects.

MEETING INDIVIDUAL NEEDS

An Alternative Approach

Students who are interested in possible careers in journalism can write to the Cable News Network for brochures and other information about the network's size, its budget, and its organization. These students can prepare a report on CNN and present it to the class.

ACTIVITY 3 Planning and Producing a Radio Drama

Work together with a group of classmates to write and produce your own radio drama. You can create an original script or adapt a published story. Work out a plan for sound effects and music to establish the settings and to create the moods. Write a script for your radio play. Follow the format of the sample on pages 642–643. After you have completed the script, assign parts and present the radio play in front of the class (or record it for playback in class). If possible, include appropriate sound effects in your presentation.

Preparing a Television News Story

Television news programs have a large impact on public opinion. The creation and presentation of a television news story involve three areas of responsibility: script preparation, technical production, and on-air performance.

Script Preparation

A television script has two parts—a **video,** or picture, section and an **audio,** or sound, section. The video section describes the video footage and sound effects in the script. The audio section presents the words to be spoken. The following chart identifies some of the terms used in the typical script on the next page.

Video Script Terminology	
COVER	videotape of scene used in conjunction with the anchor's or the reporter's voice
CU	close-up, a picture of something or someone taken at close range
OUT	last words of videotaped segment
SOT	sound on tape, a videotape clip containing sound
SUPER	superimposed letters or graphics, often used to identify persons appearing in newscasts
TIME	length of time, in seconds, of videotaped segment
TRACK UP	begin playing videotape
V/O	**voice-over,** a voice played without an accompanying picture of the speaker, usually over a film of some scene

MOTIVATION

Ask students to indicate by a show of hands how many read a newspaper every day. Then ask how many watch some portion of the television news on a daily basis. Finally, ask how many do both. Write the three figures on the chalkboard.

Lead the class in a discussion of why some people prefer television news. Ask students to describe the advantages and disadvantages of the ways the news is reported on television. Point out to students that this segment will give them information about how television news is prepared and presented.

Script for Television News Story

Video	Audio
Anchor lead-in	In a visit today to Diego Rivera High School, Governor Gonzales announced his new Computers for Kids program. Financed entirely by private contributions from individuals and businesses, Computers for Kids aims to provide computers for every elementary and secondary school classroom in the state by the year 2005.
SOT (CU of Gov. Gonzales) SUPER: Governor Gonzales	TRACK UP OUT: ". . . for the twenty-first century." TIME: 23
V/O transition COVER of students gathered around computer	Reaction from teachers and students has been largely enthusiastic. Students at Rivera High now typically wait in long lines to get access to computers, but that will soon be a thing of the past.
V/O Set-up shot of Myra Rodriguez	Of course, the introduction of computers into daily classroom instruction will require teachers to master this new technology.
SOT (CU of Ms. Rodriguez) SUPER: Myra Rodriguez, English Teacher	TRACK UP OUT: ". . . if only I had the time." TIME: 18
V/O Shot of school SUPER: 1–800–555–2343	Word processing, spreadsheets, databases, programming—providing classrooms with computers will open up a new world of learning to students at this high school and soon at every high school across the state. Within a few years, every elementary classroom will be provided with computers. Businesses and individuals interested in donating to Computers for Kids can call the governor's office at 1–800–555–2343.

On-Air Performance

Speaking skills, although important in all areas of television production, are of primary importance for the people who present the news. Because television is a visual medium, the presenters, like actors on stage or in films, must communicate nonverbally as well as verbally.

CRITICAL THINKING

Analysis

Have students compare the script for a television news story to a script for a stage play. How are the two scripts alike? How are they different? Then let students examine a stage script that has been marked for the lighting and sound technicians. How is this script similar to a television script?

USING THE CHART

After students have read the **Script for Television News Story** chart, ask students to describe what Governor Gonzales, the students gathered around the computer, and Myra Rodriguez might be doing in the video shots.

TEACHING THE LESSON

When students have read and discussed **Preparing a Television News Story** on pp. 644–647, you can prepare them for **Activity 4** by discussing possible topics for their news stories. You can also show videotapes of several real news stories from local television stations for students to use as models. You may want to stop the videotape from time to time to point out technical aspects of the camera and audio work.

You can help students with **Activity 5** on p. 651 by going over the guidelines in **How to Prepare a Public Service Announcement** on p. 650. It might also be a good idea to show videotapes of several PSAs to the class so students can have real-life models to focus on as they do the activity.

CRITICAL THINKING

Analysis

Ask students to watch a portion of a local television news show and have them identify the types of stories they find [news stories, human-interest stories, features]. Also, ask students to discuss the kinds of skills needed to be a news anchor, a news reporter, a features reporter, a weather reporter, and a sports reporter.

Types of News Talent. Not all performers on a television news show have the same responsibility. A newscaster or news **anchor** may be responsible for writing and editing news stories as well as for reading them accurately on the air. A reporter may be responsible for preparing stories for newscasters as well as for presenting live on-scene reports. A **commentator** may have responsibility for analysis of the news. Unlike the typical newswriter, who attempts to present an unbiased, factual report, a commentator often expresses his or her personal opinions about the news.

Skills Needed for On-Air Performance. Television **talent**—the performers who appear on camera—must be able to communicate well both verbally and nonverbally. In addition, television performers must understand the technical aspects of television production that affect their performance. For example, most television stations have a **teleprompter** that scrolls the script for performers to read. When using a teleprompter, performers have to avoid staring at it. They also have to be prepared to handle a script themselves if something goes wrong with the teleprompter.

In low-budget video productions, performers may need to read **cue cards**—large sheets of cardboard with handwritten script or notes. The danger of cue cards is that they may get mixed up; again, the performer has to be prepared to continue with the report if the cue cards are lost or out of order.

The guidelines on the following page identify other points that you will need to remember when you are preparing to perform in a television news show.

Assessment

The completed news stories and the public service announcements from the two activities in the segment can be used to assess students' progress. For further evaluation, you can have students write brief descriptions of the processes they used to create their new stories and public service announcements. Then appraise students' understanding from these descriptions.

Reteaching

You can reteach the material in this segment by using videotapes of news stories and PSAs from local television stations. Stop the tapes often to comment on aspects of the performances. Ask students to use **Guidelines for Radio and Television Presentations** on p. 651 as a guide in doing the activities.

HOW TO Perform for a Television Newscast

1. **Practice using a teleprompter or cue cards.** Rehearse several times in advance of a performance with the actual equipment you will use.
2. **Know the meaning of production cues.** Learn to respond to any hand signals used to relay the director's instructions for time cues, directional cues, and audio cues.
3. **Look into the camera.** When speaking directly to the video audience, look into whichever camera is on. The "on camera" is indicated by a red light. The only exception is that when you are talking to another person, you should maintain eye contact with that person, not with the camera.
4. **Look your best.** Recognize that your appearance—attire, hairstyle, and so forth—is important. It will create an image of you as a person and as a personality.

How to Perform for a Television Newscast

Encourage students to refer to the "**How to**" suggestions when they work on **Activity 4.**

ACTIVITY 4 Writing and Presenting a Television News Story

Work with two classmates to write and produce a television news story about an event at your school, such as a speech tournament, a drama club rehearsal, a football game, or a class activity. One person can perform as anchor or newscaster, one as field reporter, and one can prepare the scripts. You will need an introduction to the story, and you may need to interview a participant in the event. Present your story to your class. If you have access to a video camera, you can actually film footage to show as part of your news story.

Ongoing Assessment

Activity 4

Allow students to work in groups of three for this activity. The news stories they produce should be clear and concise, the video appropriate for the subject matter, and the scripts reflective of the terminology used in television scripts.

Preparing a Public Service Announcement for Television

A **public service announcement,** often called a **PSA,** communicates an informative or persuasive message that is in the community interest. For example, a museum might give information about a new exhibit, or a local charity might seek donations.

In terms of technical and artistic requirements, there is little difference between a PSA and an ad. Both are produced with careful attention to budgets, and both must fit into time slots of less than sixty seconds. The creator of a PSA, like the creator of an ad, will probably plan every aspect of the spot.

See p. 650 for **Extension, Enrichment,** and **Closure.**

The Storyboard

The tool most often used in planning all aspects of a video production, such as a PSA or a commercial production, is a **storyboard,** a layout that shows all of the pictures (usually shown in sketches), video, and audio cues that accompany the written script. The chart below defines some of the technical terms used to identify camera shots in television scripts.

The drawing at the left is a frame from an actual storyboard. The photograph at the right is a still shot showing this scene as it appeared in the film.

Using the Chart

Show videotapes of several public service announcements taken from local television stations and ask students to apply the terminology in the **Video Terminology** chart to the PSAs they watch.

Video Terminology	
INT	interior, inside
EXT	exterior, outside
CU	close-up
ECU	extreme close-up
Pull back	move camera away from subject
Zoom in	move camera toward subject
Angle on	shot that will include the subject
Cut to	abrupt change to a new picture
Pan	move camera from right to left or left to right
Point-of-view shot	view as seen by one of characters
Tight shot	view of subject and little, if anything, else

Using a storyboard, a director can work out exactly what he or she wants to say in dialogue, to show in pictures, and to express by using nonverbal cues such as music and sound effects. The more carefully a project is planned, the more likely that the production time and costs will be kept within acceptable limits.

PSA: "Computers for Kids"

	VIDEO	AUDIO
	OPEN ON ECU OF JOB AD IN NEWSPAPER, YOUNG MAN'S FINGER FOLLOWS TEXT AS HE READS.	V/O, YOUNG MAN: Good spelling and grammar. OK. Knowledge of bookkeeping. OK.
	PULL BACK TO REVEAL YOUNG MAN READING.	YOUNG MAN: Neat appearance. OK. Good interpersonal skills. OK.
	CU OF YOUNG MAN.	YOUNG MAN: Computer experience. Not OK.
	ANGLE ON YOUNG MAN AND FATHER AT BREAKFAST TABLE.	YOUNG MAN: How am I supposed to get any computer experience?
	CU OF YOUNG MAN.	I mean, we didn't even have computers at my school.
	CU OF FATHER.	FATHER: I know. I should have done something—complained, raised some money.
 1-800-555-KIDS	STILL OF "COMPUTERS FOR KIDS" LOGO. SUPER: 1-800-555-KIDS	V/O, NARRATOR: Help our children compete for jobs in the 21st century. Contribute to Computers for Kids. Call this number today for more information.
 1-800-555-KIDS	STILL OF CRUMPLED UP HELP-WANTED ADS. SUPER: 1-800-555-KIDS	V/O, FATHER: I should have done something. V/O: 1-800-555-KIDS MUSIC UP AND OUT

Extension

Have students write news stories that include audio and video scripts for events in history or in literary works. Students should indicate settings for the reports, the people that might be interviewed, and how the news stories would proceed. If time permits, some students could find costumes and videotape the news stories for the class to view.

Performance Skills

Acting in a public service announcement requires the same kinds of communication skills that are needed by performers in a television news show (pages 645–647).

- Speaking: Performers need to control the volume, rate, and pitch of their speaking voices. [See pages 53–73 for more about using your voice effectively.]
- Nonverbal communication: Performers need to control their gestures, posture, and movement. [See pages 36–37 and 600–603.]
- Technical understanding: Performers need to know how to respond to camera, use microphones, use scripts, and so forth.

FUNKY WINKERBEAN **BY TOM BATIUK**

WELL, HERE GOES MY FIRST ANNOUNCEMENT AS PRINCIPAL OF WESTVIEW HIGH!

How to Prepare a Public Service Announcement

Encourage students to use the "**How to**" suggestions when they work on **Activity 5.**

Teacher's Resource Binder

Skills for Success 5
Preparing a Public Service Announcement for Television

HOW TO *Prepare a Public Service Announcement*

1. **Identify the main idea.** Focus on the essential meaning of the informative or persuasive message you want to communicate. Decide what the audio portion will do and what the video portion of the message will do.
2. **Plan the audio and video portions of the presentation.** Create a storyboard that identifies the visuals or pictures, the video and audio cues, and the audio script. Use standard audio and video terminology on the storyboard. Use the storyboard as a guide for the production of the PSA. It will tell the director, the camera person, the audio person, and the actors what to do.
3. **Rehearse, then present, the PSA.** Practice and rehearse the announcement several times before recording or performing it.

Enrichment

Advertising agencies often work on public service announcements for worthy causes as a service to the organizations and to the community. Invite a representative of a local ad agency to class to discuss how his or her agency creates a PSA. If possible, ask the representative to bring a storyboard for the class to examine.

Closure

You can conduct a review of the main points of this segment by using the **"How to"** features on pp. 647 and 650. Read the guidelines and ask volunteers to explain what each one means.

Activity 5

Preparing a Public Service Announcement

Working with two or three classmates, choose an issue for a public service announcement. Select an issue from the following list or choose one of your own: air pollution, eating healthful foods, littering, recycling, staying in school, voting.

Plan a thirty-second PSA, and make a storyboard showing the video and audio portions. If possible, film your announcement with a video camera. If video equipment is unavailable, present your PSA to your class as a live performance.

Ongoing Assessment

Activity 5

The issues students feature in their public service announcements should be relevant to the audience and should employ appropriate persuasive techniques to convince an audience to act on the PSAs.

Evaluating Radio and Television Presentations

Because a media presentation has many elements, you will need to focus on specific aspects that you wish to analyze. Decide whether to analyze the program from the point of view of a viewer or from the vantage point of a performer or director. Use the following guidelines as a basis for your critique. [For information about giving oral or written critiques, see pages 96–98.]

Additional Activities

You may want to call students' attention to this checklist early in the chapter and encourage them to use it as they do the activities in segments 2 and 3. You can also use this checklist as the basis for your assessment of **Activities 2–5.**

GUIDELINES

for Radio and Television Presentations

- For a radio talk show, did the host identify an issue of interest to the listening audience and question the guests effectively? Did the guests express their ideas effectively while respecting the ideas of others? Did all participants use their voices and their microphones effectively?
- For a radio drama, was the presentation effective in telling a complete story? Did the sound effects and music set the mood and convey information about the action and the setting? Did the actors' voices convey emotions appropriately?
- For a television news story, to what extent did the reporter convey facts instead of opinion? Did the reporter or anchor use equipment, such as cameras and microphones, effectively? Did the video and audio portions work together well to tell the news story?
- For a public service announcement on television, did the announcement convey clear information or an effective persuasive message? Did the video and audio portions work together to convey the message?

Teacher's Resource Binder

Skills for Success 6
Evaluating Radio and Television Productions

Transparency 44
Evaluating Radio and Television

◆ Profiles in Communication

PERFORMANCE OBJECTIVES

- To write a news bulletin with an attention-getting lead and an effective conclusion
- To practice delivery and to present the news bulletin

TEACHING THE FEATURE

Ask students if any of them have considered careers in radio or television. Explain that many people in the media become interested in broadcasting when they are young, as the meteorologist in this profile, Don McNeely, did. Ask students to read the sketch of McNeely to decide whether forecasting weather in a community subject to severe storms seems like an interesting occupation.

ACTIVITY NOTE

During the presentations, you might want to use props to make the classroom simulate a newsroom desk. Encourage students to use the tone and demeanor of someone presenting the nightly news. Make sure students include the answers to the *5W-How?* questions in their presentations.

PROFILES IN COMMUNICATION

Don McNeely

Don McNeely is the chief meteorologist for KFVS-TV in Cape Girardeau, Missouri. He prepares three weather segments per day—for the 5:00, 6:00, and 10:00 P.M. news broadcasts—but it takes him all afternoon to study weather patterns and create the maps he will use on the air. To develop his graphics, Mr. McNeely consults up-to-the-minute information from the U.S. Weather Service. When his maps are complete, he loads them into the station's computer. Later, when he does his weather segment, he will really be pointing to a plain green panel. Each map he has created earlier is inserted electronically into the television transmission; to the viewer at home, it seems to be right behind him, but in fact he can see it only on a monitor off to one side.

Don McNeely recently celebrated his fiftieth year in broadcasting. "I got my first job as a radio announcer at the age of sixteen when one of my teachers recommended me," he explains, "and I've been on the air ever since."

"Spring is a particularly dangerous weather season in Southeastern Missouri," he says, "because of the likelihood of tornados and flash flooding." Mr. McNeely works closely with the National Weather Service to track tornados. He is authorized to issue his own warnings based on local eyewitness reports. This aspect of his broadcasting career has been especially gratifying, because his reports giving the location, direction, and speed of storms have often been instrumental in saving lives.

ACTIVITY

Write a news bulletin about a recent event that happened to you or someone you know. The event can be serious or funny, and it does not need to be of major importance. Plan an attention-getting lead-in and an effective conclusion. Practice delivering the bulletin until you feel that you sound like a newscaster. Finally, present your bulletin to the class. Did your classmates find your presentation authentic?

CHAPTER 22

S•U•M•M•A•R•Y

UNDERSTANDING RADIO AND TELEVISION is essential for anyone living in today's society. These media influence people's behavior and beliefs. You need to be a critical listener and viewer and to know how to use these common media to convey messages.

- **Understand developments** in technology that affect the ways radio and television have influenced society in the past and are likely to influence society in the future.
- **Listen and view critically,** with an understanding of both the negative and the positive effects of radio and television on individuals, on society, and on culture.
- **Prepare a radio talk show** by fitting the format, identifying and introducing an issue, and expressing opinions about the issue in a discussion.
- **Prepare a radio drama** by preparing a script that contains narration, acting, sound effects, and music. Then rehearse and present a convincing performance.
- **Prepare a television news story** by preparing a script that contains both audio and video cues.
- **Prepare a public service announcement (PSA)** by using a storyboard as a planning tool to anticipate all aspects of the video and audio portions of the presentation.
- **Evaluate radio and televison presentations** by identifying the purpose of the presentation and then analyzing how well the program achieved the purpose.

Vocabulary

Look back through this chapter to find the meaning of each of the following terms. Write each term and its meaning in your communication journal.

anchor, *p. 646*
audio, *p. 644*
cable television, *p. 633*
commentator, *p. 646*
cue cards, *p. 646*
dialogue, *p. 641*
digital recording, *p. 634*
format, *p. 631*
high-definition television (HDTV), *p. 634*
information network, *p. 634*
interactive television, *p. 634*
live, *p. 633*
mass media, *p. 630*
narration, *p. 642*
narrator, *p. 642*
pay-cable television, *p. 633*
pay television, *p. 633*
prerecorded, *p. 633*
public service announcement (PSA), *p. 647*
radio drama, *p. 629*
radio talk show, *p. 629*
resolution, *p. 634*
sound bites, *p. 636*
storyboard, *p. 648*
talent, *p. 646*
teleprompter, *p. 646*
television news story, *p. 629*
video, *p. 644*
voice-over, *p. 644*

TEACHER'S RESOURCE BINDER

- Chapter 22 Vocabulary

Review Questions

Answers

1. two forms of electronic mass media
2. practical methods for communicating with large groups or masses of people
3. by adopting new formats
4. Commercial stations are funded by advertisers; noncommercial stations are supported by public and private funds.
5. high-definition television, digital recording, information network, and interactive television
6. issues raised by recent news events
7. sound effects, music, and dialogue
8. Use your voice effectively and lead the discussion to keep it moving if you are the host or speak up to express your ideas and opinions if you are the guest.
9. verbal and nonverbal communication skills and knowledge of relevant technical aspects

Discussion Questions

Guidelines for Assessment

Student responses may vary.

1. Culture will probably become less homogeneous and more diverse.
2. Examples include recent elections and controversies about local and national issues such as the environment.
3. Radio talk shows are popular with voters. People can have direct access to leaders via telephone on call-in shows.
4. The diversity is shown in the wide variety of shows that appeal to people of various cultural backgrounds.
5. Children are more vulnerable than adults because children don't have the background and skills for critical listening and viewing.

CHAPTER 22

Review Questions

1. What are radio and television?
2. What are the *mass media?*
3. How did radio manage to survive despite the emergence of television?
4. What are the differences between commercial and noncommercial television stations?
5. What are four emerging technologies in the mass media today?
6. What kinds of subjects are generally discussed on radio talk shows?
7. What are three major means by which ideas and events are conveyed in a radio drama?
8. What are two of the skills needed by participants in a radio talk show?
9. What are two of the skills needed by the talent in television news shows?
10. What is the purpose of a storyboard, and what does it contain?

Discussion Questions

1. The mass media caused the emergence of a mass culture. Millions of people heard the same messages, adopted the same beliefs, and bought the same products because they were influenced by the same media. The technology of cable and the resulting emergence of numerous specialized channels may be changing all that. Instead of millions of people all tuning in to the same television network, individuals can now choose the programs that best suit them. What effect do you think this change might have on the culture of the United States?
2. Orson Welles's airing of *The War of the Worlds,* Roosevelt's "fireside chats," and the Nixon-Kennedy television debates all demonstrated the power of radio and television to sway people. Can you think of other examples in the present time period of the power of radio and television to sway public opinion or to bring about change in people's actions or beliefs? Explain your answer.
3. During the 1992 presidential election campaign, all the major candidates for president and vice-president were guests at least once on radio talk shows. What does this tell us about such shows? What role do you think such shows play in a democracy?
4. The United States is a diverse, or pluralistic, society. How is that diversity reflected in contemporary radio and television?
5. Advertisers on radio and television are often criticized for using unfair or misleading persuasive techniques. Review the discussion of these techniques on pages 92–95 of Chapter 4. Then discuss with your classmates the use of these techniques in popular radio and television advertisements. Are children especially vulnerable to misleading ads? Explain.

10. It identifies pictures and contains video and audio cues and the audio script.

ACTIVITIES

1. **Giving a Report on Radio or Television Production.** Visit a local radio or television station and watch a show being produced. Notice the use of microphones, cameras, cue cards, teleprompters or scripts, and hand signals. Prepare a three- to five-minute report with at least one visual aid. Rehearse your report and present it to your class. Leave time for a short question-and-answer session after your talk.
2. **Analyzing Current Technological Trends.** Research an emerging television or film technology such as fiber-optic cabling, interactive television, high-definition television, pay-cable television, digital editing, or virtual reality. Hold a class discussion in which each participant presents one new technology. Then, discuss the impact these new technologies might have on society.
3. **Understanding Television Genres.**
   A. Working with your classmates, identify as many different genres, or types, of television programs as you can. Some common genres include situation comedies, talk shows, game shows, soap operas, news programs, and mysteries. List the genres on a chalkboard or on an overhead transparency.

   B. Working with a small group of your classmates, choose one of the genres the class identified in Part A and analyze some of the genre's characteristics. One way to do this would be to select several representative shows within the genre and to determine what characteristics they have in common. Present your findings to the class. Be prepared to discuss television shows that seem to fit in more than one genre.
4. **Analyzing and Predicting Trends in Popular Television Programming.**
   A. Look at the following chart that lists the most popular television shows of the past four decades. What does this chart tell you about the television-viewing habits of people in the United States? What types of shows have been consistently popular? What do changes in the types of popular programming reflect about society's changing interests or needs? If you are not familiar with some of the shows mentioned, you can see reruns of many of them on cable TV. Or you can ask an older friend or family member who remembers the show to tell you what it was about. Working with a group of your classmates, prepare a short presentation about the television trends that you have identified.

MOST POPULAR TV SHOWS, BY DECADE

These charts are based on a show's average rating throughout each decade, and are thus an indication of both popularity and longevity.

Decade and program	Decade and program
1950–59	**1960–69**
1. *A. Godfrey's Talent Scouts*	1. *Bonanza*
2. *I Love Lucy*	2. *The Red Skelton Show*
3. *You Bet Your Life*	3. *The Andy Griffith Show*
4. *Dragnet*	4. *The Beverly Hillbillies*
5. *The Jack Benny Show*	5. *The Ed Sullivan Show*
6. *A. Godfrey and Friends*	6. *The Lucy Show/Here's Lucy*
7. *Gunsmoke*	7. *The Jackie Gleason Show*
8. *The Red Skelton Show*	8. *Bewitched*
9. *December Bride*	9. *Gomer Pyle*
10. *I've Got a Secret*	10. *Candid Camera*
1970–79	**1980–89**
1. *All in the Family*	1. *60 Minutes*
2. *M*A*S*H*	2. *Dallas*
3. *Hawaii Five-O*	3. *The Cosby Show*
4. *Happy Days*	4. *Dynasty*
5. *The Waltons*	5. *Knots Landing*
6. *The Mary Tyler Moore Show*	6. *Cheers*
7. *Sanford & Son*	7. *Magnum, P.I.*
8. *One Day at a Time*	8. *Murder, She Wrote*
9. *Three's Company*	9. *Who's the Boss?*
10. *60 Minutes*	10. *Family Ties*

ACTIVITIES

Guidelines for Assessment

1. The reports should be fluent, clear, well organized, and concise. They should deal with the aspects of production listed in the question.
2. More information may be readily available on some technologies than on others. Students may want to call local television stations for information. Also, some technologies will have a greater impact than others.
3. A. situation comedies, talk shows, game shows, news shows, mysteries, westerns, feature news shows, dramas, cooking shows, soap operas, variety shows, comedies, reality-based police shows, miniseries, music video shows, educational programming, nature shows, sports, feature sports, "how-to" shows, documentaries, and many others
   B. Characteristics will vary. Emphasize to students the explosion in types of programming and the difficulty in categorizing shows because of their varied formats.
4. A. Students may conclude that during the 1950s variety shows and comedies reigned, although westerns, game shows, and comedies were popular. In the 1960s, variety shows were still popular, but they were outranked by a profusion of comedies and situation comedies. In the 1970s, situation comedies were still the most popularly viewed shows, but dramas and feature news

SUMMATIVE EVALUATION

Your **Teacher's Resource Binder** contains a reproducible **Chapter 22 Test** that may be used to assess students' mastery of the concepts presented in this chapter.

PORTFOLIO ASSESSMENT

For future reference and evaluation you may want to have students keep in their portfolios any skill sheets or evaluation forms that you have used with this chapter along with any other recorded or written materials that students have created.

shows were also being viewed by large numbers of people. In the 1980s, *60 Minutes* became the most popular show. Situation comedies were still popular, as were soap operas and mystery or detective dramas.

B. Have students gather data like the data in the viewing chart before they make their predictions. Have them defend their predictions with statements about a future viewing public.

5. Lists will vary, but they should reflect stated or implied criteria for evaluation. The debate on the value of television should consider television's value to various audiences for various purposes (for example, entertainment or information).

6. The essay can be organized by the block method—consider each format completely before moving to the next, or by the point-by-point method—consider how each format is evaluated on each question. The essays should be clear and concise. The essays should convey familiarity with all three formats.

7. The questions on the surveys should be clear and free from ambiguity. The reports to the class should be interesting and obviously based on the data from the surveys.

B. Working with a partner, make some predictions about television-viewing trends of the 1990s. You may want to base your predictions on information in almanacs or on trends you have observed among your own family members, friends, and classmates. Compare your predictions with those of your classmates.

5. Evaluating the Quality of Television. Although many critics have panned television as being mindless or devoid of programs that enrich viewers' intelligence, others have praised television because it brings the whole world into viewers' living rooms. Prepare a list of programs that you feel are particularly mindless and a separate list of programs that you feel are particularly noteworthy. Present your lists to the class. Then debate the question "What is the value of television?"

6. Analyzing Television News Programs. Watch several television news programs with different formats, including local evening news programs, national evening news programs, and moderated news discussion programs. Compare and contrast the different formats. Which do the best job of presenting the issues in all their complexity? Which are the most in-depth? Which provide the most coverage of events? Which are the most interesting? Answer these questions in a comparison-and-contrast essay.

7. Analyzing Television and Radio Usage. Survey the students in your school to find out their habits of radio and television usage. Make up a questionnaire that deals with hours spent listening or viewing, preferred programming, parental guidance or lack thereof, differences between weekday and weekend listening and viewing, and other important information. Identify what you see as the most interesting or important results of your survey. Share your findings with your classmates in a class discussion. You may find it helpful to arrange your data in an expanded version of a chart like this one.

Categories of viewing	Freshmen	Sophomores	Juniors	Seniors
Average hours of viewing per week				
Hours watching news per week				
Hours watching comedies per week				
Hours watching dramas per week				
Hours watching talk shows or information programs				
Number of hours viewing with parent present				

◆ Real-Life Speaking Situations

Performance Objectives

- To produce a public service announcement
- To serve as a moderator of a radio talk show

REAL LIFE Speaking Situations

1 You have been working as a volunteer for the local humane society, and your supervisor has decided to promote an "Adopt a Pet" week. Your job is to write the script for and to produce a public service announcement to be aired on your local television station.

First, decide on your target audience. Next, think about what type of message or appeal would best suit this audience. Should your public service announcement be purely informative or should it also be persuasive? [For more information about persuasive techniques, see pages 387–396.] Then decide what your narrative (audio) will be, as well as what visuals or images you will show. Do you want to have a soundtrack of kittens meowing, the voice of an excited child, or a narrator reading the harsh statistics on abandoned animals? Identify images or scenes that will grab the audience's attention, and decide how the camera should focus on those images. Use the answers to your questions to create a storyboard. If possible, find some other students to help you videotape and produce your public service announcement for your class.

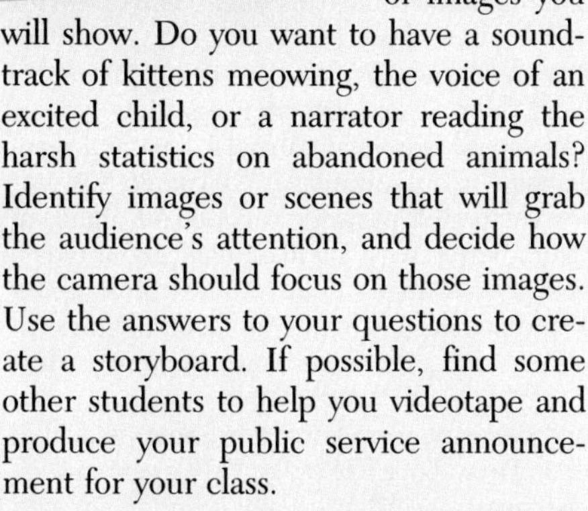

2 A television station in your community has decided to broadcast a new program targeted at teenagers. Designed to boost awareness of community issues, the program will invite teens to engage in on-air discussions of topics and events of local concern. You have been asked to be the guest moderator for the show. This week, you will invite one or two people from your community to talk with you about some local issue—the football team's losing season, the mayoral election, speeding on residential streets, the building of a new factory in town, the city council's proposal of a teen curfew.

Select an issue appropriate for one fifteen-minute program, and invite two other people to join you in a discussion of the issue. You might invite two classmates, or you might invite adults from your community who are particularly interested in the issue. [For more information about organizing and participating in a group discussion, see Chapter 17.]

Prepare the questions that you will ask, and schedule the session. Make an audiotape and play it for your classmates. Be prepared for a class discussion of how well you moderated the talk show.

Assessment Guidelines

1. Students should produce a storyboard like the model on p. 649. The PSAs should appeal to a broad general audience and they should leave the audience informed or persuaded to act.
2. The students' performances should follow the guidelines listed in **How to Participate in a Radio Talk Show** on p. 639.

• **Informative Speech: Expository Speech**

pp. 658–662

TEACHING STRATEGIES

These two speeches can be used with the chapters in Unit 3 on public speaking and with **Chapter 14: "Speaking to Inform."** Students might use the **Evaluation Checklist for Informative Speeches** on p. 375 in the chapter to evaluate this speech. They could give examples of each criterion.

Audiotape 2 in the *Audiovisual Resource Binder* contains a recording of Melodie Lancaster's speech.

EXPOSITORY SPEECH
by Melodie Lancaster

1
Ms. Lancaster's position as President of Lancaster Resources establishes her as a credible speaker. The audience can trust that she knows about succeeding in the business world.

2
The speaker uses this quotation to introduce the premise of her speech.

3
To illustrate dealing with the unexpected, the speaker compares the career journey to a flight plan. Referring to the pilot as *she* makes the comparison more personal for the audience of businesswomen.

4
The speaker states her specific purpose—the main idea of her speech.

5
The questions she poses involve her audience with the topic. The examples that follow relate the idea of change to the audience's experiences. The items listed are familiar to a majority of the audience.

APPENDIX OF SPEECHES

Note to the student: Keep in mind that speeches are created to be spoken. As you read the following speeches, try to say them aloud. Often, an oral reading will reveal facets of a speech, such as rhyme, alliteration, rhythm, and emphasis, that may go unnoticed in a silent reading.

INFORMATIVE SPEECH: EXPOSITORY SPEECH

"The Future We Predict Isn't Inevitable: Reframing Our Success in the Modern World"

Melodie Lancaster

1 *Melodie Lancaster, President of Lancaster Resources, presented this speech to the Symposium for the Houston Council of the American Business Women's Association in 1992. In her speech, Ms. Lancaster explains why working people need to come to a new understanding of "success in the modern world." She holds that, while change is inevitable, the future we plan for is not. Therefore, we must make plans that allow for change. A good informative speech presents new information to an audience in an interesting way. How well does this speech meet these criteria? What specific facts and details does Ms. Lancaster give to support her assertion that workers will need to be willing to change in order for them to succeed in the job market of the future?*

Thank you for the warm welcome. It's a privilege to take part in this program, to share the fellowship of this superb organization. I'd like to begin with a quote from Charles Handy's book, *The Age of Unreason,* which strikes at the heart of what I'd like you to remember today.

2 "The future we predict today isn't inevitable," he writes. "We can influence it if we know what we want it to be . . . We can take charge of our own destinies in a time of change." Is what Professor Handy is saying a contradiction? After all, change for most of us implies confusion, doubt, uneasiness. Control implies a firm grip.

3 To be in control is like the airline pilot who flies a flight plan to a certain city. She knows the route, but can't assume all will go smoothly. There could be storms, mechanical failure, and many other unforeseen problems. So, the pilot needs to be ready for all contingencies. This takes training and planning. If something unexpected happens, she has options: a change of course, a diversion for repairs, or an alternate destination.

You and I are much like that pilot. We are on a career journey. We also are facing an unpredictable working environment—unlike our parents and their parents experienced. How we see ourselves on this journey is really the key to success. We could fear what's ahead—a natural reac-
4 tion. But the wisest course is to take control, and use change to our advantage. We can do this provided we have the right information and act upon it. We can do this provided we open our minds to new ideas and new opportunities. How we get there from here is what I'd like to talk about today.

5 Do you like change? Do any of us really relish a dramatic change in our routine? Most would answer "no" even though we Americans are a very mobile people. It's human to feel a tightness in our bodies when we're facing some new adventure. There are some exceptions, of course. Slow change becomes part of our routine.

If you are 45 years old or older, all this has happened since you were born: television, penicillin, polio vaccine, xerox, plastic anything, frisbees and the Pill. How about FM radio, VCR's, computers, CD's, computer dating, electric typewriters, artificial hearts, word processors, and guys with earrings.

And ballpoint pens, air conditioning, drip-dry clothes, space walks, moon landings and Mars probes. Pancake make-up, microwave ovens, househusbands, weirdos, nerds, and McDonalds. Michael Jackson, Madonna and New Kids on the Block. Swing, rock, rap, and country.

6 Speaking of change, I remember the day when Neil Armstrong took that first step on the moon, and the thrill of accomplishment all of us felt. I don't believe anyone was really surprised we went to the moon. Science fiction writers and movies created moon travel long before the first rocket was on the pad. What no one predicted, and the most astonishing part of the trip, was we watched that step in our living rooms through the magic of television.

It took us ten years to get to the moon, and decades more preparing for it. That's why what has happened over the past five years is even more incredible. The social and political changes sweeping Eastern Europe still are unimaginable. Nothing in our memory compares to the end of the Cold War, and even more, the rise of enterprise from the ashes of communism.

7 What's even more unsettling is the vast social and political changes we've seen are compounded by equally jarring change in the business world. Suddenly, our companies are fighting for survival against foreign ones in our own backyard. Today's business fortunes also hinge on keeping products and services in tune with the vibrations of the consumer's ever changing tastes.

8 In this new world, we've even coined a brash new language. Restructuring, and downsizing, and outsourcing, and mergers, and sell offs. And to go with the new language we are seeing a different face to American business. A face that also keeps changing with the times. Corporations are shrinking, and I believe this trend will continue.

9 We also find the relationship between employers and employees decidedly different than just a few years ago. Twenty years ago, the average employee began and ended a career with the same company. He or she looked to the company for security, and expected the company to take charge of career development.

You won't find that kind of paternalism as much any more, just as you won't find the intense loyalty that employees used to give their corporations. What you will find is a much greater emphasis on decentral authority.

Decision making is now the province of "profit centers." Teamwork is stressed to improve efficiency and cut waste, and the key to success is individual achievement and accountability. The people who do the best will be the people who are the best prepared.

Going to work without knowing when the next shoe will fall isn't a pleasant experience for any-
10 body, but the uncertainty isn't likely to end. Our best hope is to accept change as the norm. We
need to begin reframing the challenge of career. The business climate isn't something to overcome.
11 Instead, it's a time to use change as an opportunity. So, I'd like to go over some trends and suggest how you might prepare yourselves to take advantage of them.

First, success in today's business world takes more knowledge. Most of us grew up during an age
when a strong back counted the most. Even nations achieved power because they had natural
12 resources and material wealth. Today, virtually every industry or business you can name is "knowledge intensive."

The image of the petroleum industry, for example, is more appropriately a computer than a roustabout on a drilling platform. Finding, producing and marketing petroleum can take dozens of disciplines—from political science, to environmental engineering, to law. It's not just the oil business. It's every business. Indeed, the main objective of business today is marshalling intellectual capital and making the most of it.

The shift to a knowledge base means you need more education and training to get a good job.
13 Even entry level people must have computer skills. As recently as the mid-1980s, 22 percent of the nation's jobs required a college degree. By the year 2000, half of all jobs will require education beyond high school. Most of them will be filled with college graduates.

We also know that 75 percent of the jobs created in Texas during the next decade will be in the

6
The speaker goes into greater detail and brings in personal feelings about change. Such methods help to hold the audience's attention.

7
After exploring everyday examples, the speaker focuses on change in business—the emphasis of the speech.

8
The technical language supports the speaker's point: Business is undergoing jarring changes. Ms. Lancaster lists examples of new language for impact; definitions are not necessary.

9
The use of transitions furthers the unity and cohesiveness of the speech.

10
The speaker reemphasizes the necessity for adapting to change—the main point of the speech.

11
The statement of intent lets the audience know that what follows will be important.

12
The speaker uses topical order as an organizational method.

13
Specific details add credibility to the thesis.

14
Enumerating the important points helps the audience follow the organizational pattern.

15
Using another familiar reference catches the audience's attention and prepares the listeners for a new focus.

16
The speaker uses quotations to illustrate a point.

service industries, which require technical skills.

14 *Second, as corporations shrink, the opportunities for entrepreneurship grow.* Restructuring often is seen as wholesale loss of jobs. However, just because a corporation is smaller, doesn't mean its responsibilities are fewer. Those tasks are now being contracted to consultants.

This is cost effective, because the company doesn't have to pay retirement, health and other large costs. There are other sound reasons: Consultants are focused on the job at hand. They are there when the company needs them, and are not caught up in company politics and turf battles. The temporary employee also is becoming a permanent fixture.

The Department of Labor estimates that by the year 2000, eighty percent of America's jobs will be in the service sector, which uses 75 percent of the nation's temporary employees. Temporaries are in demand because more and more people are interested in part-time work.

What's more, information technology innovation, such as computers and fax machines, have created an ideal marriage of suburbanites and their downtown counterparts. The company benefits from greater productivity.

The employee benefits because there are no traffic jams to fight and more time for family and other interests. In fact, the experts believe by the 21st century only half of all workers will be what we now call "full time." They will then join the ranks of a "new minority" in our country.

Third, our population is growing older, and the demand for older workers is also growing. In just eight years, the average employee will be 39 years old. As baby boomers reach middle age, I believe they will find their age a plus. This marks a move away from previous trends of hiring less experienced people, while providing on-the-job training. Even though corporations spent between $30 billion and $50 billion on training and remediation last year, companies were looking for experienced, seasoned people.

Fourth, the ability to communicate is essential—for people with jobs, those looking for jobs, and corporations seeking to reach the public. Ideas are driving the economy of the future. Communicating ideas is the fuel that makes the engine run. No company is insulated from public scrutiny, even those that do not sell directly to the public. Today, perception is reality for the bulk of the population—whether it's business practices or environmental sensitivity.

The need to communicate extends to everyone. With the need for greater personal accountability and responsibility comes the need to market ideas.

15 Which brings me to the "Dear Abby" part of my speech this afternoon—some advice based on my own experience talking with and working with thousands of people. I have three suggestions:

Ladies and gentlemen, learn to be properly selfish. In these times you and you alone must take charge of your career. Know the market, and understand the marketable skills that are needed, and develop them. Set firm goals, and have the conviction to go after them. By all means, don't waste your time blaming your problems on someone else.

Second, frame your career goals to reflect the modern business world. Some of you here will have "A" career in life. But the chances are good the average person will have three or more. Even more to the point, the career path you follow tomorrow may not even exist today.

Finally, never, ever believe this world is static. If people think it can be done, then the chances are it will be done.

16 Listen to these pearls of wisdom:

—In 1895 Lord Kelvin, a noted British physicist said: "Heavier than air flying machines are impossible."

—Here's one by the late Joseph Kennedy who declared: "I have no political ambitions for myself or my children."

—*Business Week* wrote this in 1979: "With over 50 foreign cars on sale here, the Japanese auto industry isn't likely to carve out a big slice of the U.S. market." And, as Admiral Frank Knox put it on December 5, 1941: "No matter what happens, the U.S. Navy is not going to be caught napping."

17 I say to you, "Don't dare get caught napping." Have courage. Have convictions, and do the very best you can. We recall the story of the three stonemasons who were asked what they were doing. The first said, "I am laying brick." The second replied, "I am making a foundation." And the third said: " I am building a cathedral." Let's you and I set our sights that high. Let's build cathedrals of success today, tomorrow and the day after tomorrow.

INFORMATIVE SPEECH: EXPOSITORY SPEECH

"The Green Mountain Boys"

W. Benson Chiles, student speaker

In this contest-winning speech, which placed first in the 1986 Texas State Competition, W. Benson Chiles sings the praises of the patriotic Americans known as the Green Mountain Boys. The goal of his speech is to paint a vivid picture of the role that the Green Mountain Boys played during the Revolutionary era. By outlining their valor and accomplishments, Mr. Chiles presents them as examples of all the heroes who have answered the call to defend their country. What does Chiles do to show that the acts of the Green Mountain Boys are the epitome of the spirit which brought freedom to our land? What elements does he use to inspire patriotism in the audience?

1 Ethan Allen, Seth Warner, Stephen Fay, Zadock Remington, Colonel James Easton, Major Brown, Captain Edward Mott, Captain Samuel Herrick. Gentlemen, our basic freedoms are in peril. The time has come to fight.

Almost ten years prior to the Revolutionary War, these men answered a roll call when they banded together in an effort to protect local property rights from royal decrees. Named after area mountains, the Green Mountain Boys played a substantial role in the American Revolution. Men like the Green Mountain Boys were the backbone for America during the Revolutionary era. Untrained and ununiformed, these men had a divine sense of righteousness and freedom when they volunteered for demanding military campaigns. This individualism and independence, which became so prevalent in the American militia of the time, provided the desire and commitment necessary to defeat such a world power as Britain. Nonconformity had grown in individuals from the
2 necessity to survive and the opportunity to prosper in the new land, America. The acts of the Green Mountain Boys are the epitome of the boldness of spirit which brought freedom to our land.

3 At the outset of the War when battles were fought at Lexington and Concord, Ethan Allen, the original leader of the Green Mountain Boys began collaborating with other area leaders to find ways to assist America in the War with their mother country. With some discussion, they agreed on an attack of Fort Ticonderoga, a vital British stronghold which contained many needed weapons. This fort was the main barrier between American and British Canadian colonies because of its strategic
4 location on Lake Champlain. On the night of May 9, 1775, after marching sixty miles and recruiting over two hundred Green Mountain Boys from cities along the way, Allen and his men stood at Hands Cove ready to cross the lake and attack the fort. With some difficulty they procured enough boats to make the crossing and just before dawn they stormed the fort and forced the British to surrender their valuable asset.

5 Americans gained three beneficial results from this victory. First, the Americans now controlled the route to Canada, allowing General Richard Montgomery's army to capture Montreal in the winter of 1775–1776. Second, it gave Americans confidence and courage to continue in the War. Third,

17
The speaker uses several concluding methods that end the speech on a high note. She summarizes the main point with a call to action and uses an anecdote to inspire the listeners.

Expository Speech
by W. Benson Chiles

1
The speaker's introduction contains pertinent historical background—a strategy for getting the audience's attention.

2
The clearly expressed thesis statement prepares the audience for the speaker's position.

3
Chronological order offers the best organization for the speaker's purpose and thesis.

4
The speaker uses factual details to support his thesis.

5
The speaker outlines the accomplishments of the Green Mountain Boys. He compares the Green Mountain Boys to later groups who also exhibited patriotic sacrifice and spirit.

• **Informative Speech: Process Speech** *pp. 662–664*

TEACHING STRATEGIES

This speech works well with **Chapter 14: "Speaking to Inform,"** which teaches how to give a process speech. Students might use the **Evaluation Checklist for Informative Speeches** on p. 375 in the chapter to evaluate this speech. They should give examples of each criterion.

Audiotape 2 in the *Audiovisual Resource Binder* contains a recording of this speech.

6
To inspire his audience, the speaker includes emotional appeals through the use of strong words and phrases: *flaming spirit, quest for freedom, spark,* and *fire.*

7
The conclusion is effective because it alerts the audience that the speaker is closing and leaves the audience with an idea to remember.

PROCESS SPEECH
by Monica Seebohm

1
The speaker has a twofold reason for presenting her speech: to help the audience better understand a half-time show at a football game and to show how valuable performances are so that audiences will appreciate them and be motivated to watch.

2
The speaker makes clear in her introduction that she is speaking to spectators who might pass up the half-time show.

the weapons confiscated from the fort were very instrumental in driving the British from the city of Boston later in the War.

But things did not continue to turn out so well for the Green Mountain Boys. Ethan Allen, being his usual brash self, made a premature attack on Montreal and was captured in the process, eliminating himself from the remainder of the War. Fortunately though, Seth Warner provided very capable leadership for the Green Mountain Boys who became a well-trained, disciplined fighting force.

When the British began sending reinforcements to Canada for full scale attack on America, the Green Mountain Boys again rose to the call and helped defend Fort Ticonderoga and added a decisive victory at Longueuil. But the most exciting and important victory for the Green Mountain Boys came at the Battle of Bennington, where they marched to the rescue of retreating American troops and defeated the army of Johnny Burgoyne.

6 The Green Mountain Boys, with their flaming spirit, gave America the winning edge over their redcoated foes of Britain by clearing a path to Canada. These men risked their lives for the freedoms which they held true, stated by Thomas Jefferson in the Declaration of Independence. The Green Mountain Boys, in their quest for freedom, began the spark and the fire which has historically remained as an ember capable of being rekindled during our country's time of need. As we know, this ember was rekindled in World War I when our young men left their farms to answer an overseas call to stop a wave of oppression that had developed in Europe. And again our patriots rekindled the fire in the early 1940's by openly enlisting in World War II to halt the onslaught of Hitler and his army. Even today, the flame of patriotism is there to be rekindled when called upon because of that small band of men, whose rough disposition and independent spirit helped lead us to victory and freedom.

7 So, when we think of the Green Mountain Boys' roll call, we will remember the heroes who answered roll in World War I and World War II and know that the future holds many more heroes who will also risk their lives to answer the roll call of freedom.

INFORMATIVE SPEECH: PROCESS SPEECH

"The Half-Time Show"

Monica Seebohm, student speaker

In this speech, student Monica Seebohm presents the steps involved in putting on a half-time show at a football game. The effectiveness of a process speech depends upon how clearly and thoroughly the steps of the process are presented and explained. After hearing a process speech, members of the audience should be able to list the steps of the process and either perform them to carry out the process or understand each of them clearly and thereby gain an understanding of the full process. How clearly has Ms. Seebohm stated the
1 *five steps of putting on a half-time show? Is her speech aimed at enabling her audience to perform or to understand the process she is presenting? Note how the introduction and the conclusion of the speech are tied together. How does linking the beginning and the ending of the speech in this way contribute to the effectiveness of the speech?*

2 Football is an American tradition. But when the half-time whistle blows, the spectators who rush out to get a snack are missing a second American tradition. This tradition is the half-time show. Millions of American high-school and college students are involved in marching band programs. But many of the fans don't appreciate or understand the time, the work, and the effort that goes into putting a half-time show on the field. For the next four minutes, I want to familiarize you with

the steps involved in putting on a half-time show.

3 The first step in putting on a half-time show is for the leader to plan the routines that the band will execute. Half-time shows are planned in the summertime, weeks before the first practice. The band director thinks of the various routines and sets them up on paper on grids like this one. This grid resembles a football field with each instrumental section of the band denoted by a different
4 symbol [visual aid 1]. Suppose that as a part of the show the director wanted the band to move in unison onto the field and then break into four blocks. He would draw the following grid [visual aid 2]. A complete half-time show might require twenty or thirty such grids, each indicating the number of steps and the direction.

The second step in putting on a half-time show is for the band leader to familiarize the section leaders with the formations he has planned. Section leaders meet with the band director once a week to discuss the drill. Each section leader is in charge of four or eight band members on the field, so if the band consists of eighty band members, the director would meet with ten to twenty section leaders. It is in these discussions that problems members may encounter are worked out. It's a lot easier to remedy a collision on paper than it is to remedy a collision on the football field. When the section leaders understand the movements of their units, they are ready to show members of their sections the various movements involved in each of the formations.

The third step in putting on a half-time show is for section leaders to work with their band members so that they can follow their various assignments.

5 There are six contemporary concepts of marching maneuvers: unison band, follow-the-leader, movable block, squad-four, step-two, and circular. Members of the band might learn some or all of these in order to carry out various maneuvers. This one example of a formation that might be used at the very beginning of the show illustrates a "movable block," a concept in which the band divides into symmetrical or asymmetrical units with each unit moving through the routine as a unit [visual aid 2 again].

The movements of a band are orchestrated to musical beats. And each move is organized to a count of eight. For example, it takes eight steps, or beats, to move five yards. This is what is referred to as marching "eight to five." When you watch a band on the football field and they march in straight lines, it is because all band members are taking the same size steps and are marching eight steps for each five-yard line [visual aid 3]. During a routine, squad members move to the command of military-like instructions from each squad leader. Key commands include "About face," which means you have to turn directly around; "Left face," which means you have to do a sharp turn to the left; and "Drag turn right," which means making a slow marching turn to the right [speaker demonstrates each command as she speaks].

As you march, you follow field markings to give you directions [visual aid 2 again]. Yard lines are your most important signposts; they let you know where you are as you march across the field. Hash marks are also very important, because they let you know how far off the sideline you are and how far from the middle of the field you are. And the press box can also be very important for you if you get mixed up and you are not quite sure of which side is the home side.

The next step in putting on a half-time show is to practice the drill. The entire band meets to work on drill together. The routine should flow as it did on the grid. The various squads should fit together to form the entire marching band. For instance, suppose at the start of the show, all the band is lined up on the sideline between the forty-yard lines, facing the playing field. To get started, the squad leader yells, "Forward march." Everyone in the band then marches out toward the sideline on the other side of the field. The first line members move "eight to five" until they reach their stopping point. Each of the next lines takes slightly shorter steps, being sure to stay in a straight line, until the band is properly spaced on the field [visual aid 4]. As soon as that point is reached, the squad leader says, "Left face." While members in Section C left face and march left as they learned in practice, section D marches right, and sections A and B continue forward. At that point the

3
The body of the speech is presented in chronological order. The speaker uses five main points with several subdivisions. This approach allows her audience to remember the principal steps easily.

4
The speaker begins her demonstration with visuals, which she uses throughout her speech.

5
In this complex step, the speaker provides one well-developed example as an illustration.

• Persuasive Speech

pp. 664–670

TEACHING STRATEGIES

These speeches can be used with **Chapter 15: "Speaking to Persuade."** Students can use the **Evaluation Checklist for Persuasive Speeches** on p. 409 to analyze the speeches and then present the analyses to the class. Or students can use the checklist and **The Written Critique** on p. 98 in **Chapter 4: "Listening and Evaluating"** to produce written critiques of any of the speeches. Other chapters in which the speeches might be incorporated are **Chapters 10** and **11** and especially **Chapter 12.**

Audiotape 2 in the *Audiovisual Resource Binder* contains recordings of these speeches.

6
In the conclusion, the speaker returns to the spectators in the audience when she suggests they skip the half-time snack and enjoy a well-planned performance, one they can better understand and appreciate after her speech.

PERSUASIVE SPEECH
by Susan B. Anthony

1
Susan B. Anthony delivered this speech before a hostile audience. She demonstrates her credibility and competence as a speaker through her knowledge of history and government philosophy. Her presentation is sincere and passionate.

2
To convince her hostile audience, Anthony uses the criteria-satisfaction method; she uses quotations from the Constitution as her criteria. She then proceeds with an inductive approach to show how she as a citizen of the United States meets the criteria.

3
To develop her beliefs, Anthony uses logical reasoning by interpreting the quotation through a definition of terms.

4
Emotional words such as *mockery, odious, hateful,* and *rebellion* strengthen her appeal.

5
Anthony uses ethical standards to persuade her audience. She has not resorted to manipulation.

leader says, "Continue for eight, about face and return for eight." At this time sections A and B move right face and left space respectively for sixteen steps [visual aid 5]. If every member of the band has moved properly, the entire band will have completed the first stage of a formation.

The final step in putting on a half-time show is completion of the show itself. Early the day of the game all the members assemble in uniform to polish each step. Five minutes before half time, the band assembles on the sideline. The half-time whistle blows and it's showtime. For the next ten minutes it is the band's responsibility to entertain that crowd.

6 At the end of the show, as band members march off the football field with pride in a job well done, they may forget the steps of planning, teaching leaders, teaching members, coordinating, and practice; but they will certainly remember the fun of the show itself. Next time you're at a football game and the half-time whistle blows, skip the snack and enjoy the performance.

PERSUASIVE SPEECH

"Woman's Right to the Suffrage"

Susan B. Anthony

1 *Susan B. Anthony, a leader in the women's rights movement during the late 1800's, was arrested and fined in Rochester, New York, for trying to vote in the 1872 presidential election (nearly fifty years before the passage of the women's suffrage amendment). This persuasive speech is her defense of her action. Notice how tightly she packages her argument in this short speech—every word is precisely chosen to fit into the line of defense she presents. What does she use as the basis for her justification of her action? What question does she see as the only relevant one in this case? What point or points do you find most convincing in her argument?*

2 Friends and Fellow Citizens: I stand before you tonight under indictment for the alleged crime of having voted at the last Presidential election, without having a lawful right to vote. It shall be my work this evening to prove to you that, in thus voting, I not only committed no crime, but instead, simply exercised my citizen's rights, guaranteed to me and all United States citizens by the national Constitution, beyond the power of any state to deny.

"We, the people of the United States, in order to form a more perfect union, establish justice, insure domestic tranquility, provide for the common defense, promote the general welfare, and secure the blessings of liberty to ourselves and our posterity, do ordain and establish this Constitution for the United States of America."°

3 It was we, the people; not we, the white male citizens; nor yet we, the male citizens; but we, the whole people who formed the Union. And we formed it, not to give the blessings of liberty, but to secure them; not to the half of ourselves and the half of our posterity, but to the whole people,
4 women as well as men. And it is a downright mockery to talk to women of their enjoyment of the blessings of liberty while they are denied the use of the only means of securing them provided by this democratic-republican government—the ballot.

5 For any state to make sex qualification that must ever result in the disfranchisement of one entire half of the people is to pass a bill of attainder, or an *ex post facto* law, and is therefore a violation of the supreme law of the land. By it the blessings of liberty are forever withheld from women and their female posterity. To them this government has no just powers derived from the consent of the governed. To them this government is not a democracy. It is not a republic. It is an odious

aristocracy; a hateful oligarchy of sex; the most hateful aristocracy ever established on the face of the globe. An oligarchy of wealth, where the rich govern the poor, or an oligarchy of learning, where the educated govern the ignorant, might be endured; but this oligarchy of sex, which makes father, brothers, husband, sons, the oligarchs over the mother and sisters, the wife and daughters of every household—which ordains all men sovereigns, all women subjects, carries dissension, discord, and rebellion into every home of the nation.

Webster, Worcester, and Bouvier all define a citizen to be a person in the United States, entitled to vote and hold office.

6 The only question left to be settled now is: Are women persons? And I hardly believe any of our opponents will have the hardihood to say they are not. Being persons, then, women are citizens; and no State has a right to make any law, or to enforce any old law, that shall abridge their privileges or immunities. Hence, every discrimination against women in the constitutions and laws of the several States is today null and void.

°The preamble to the Constitution.

6
Anthony's conclusion contains a proposition of belief.

PERSUASIVE SPEECH

from "An Indian's View of Indian Affairs"

Chief Joseph of the Nez Perce

Chief Joseph of the Nez Perce was an eloquent spokesman for the rights of his people. A brilliant tactician, Chief Joseph led his warriors in a prolonged conflict with the U.S. Army, but in 1877, he was forced to surrender. Two years later, Chief Joseph's views of Native American life were published in the North American Review. *His story moved many readers, and the public became increasingly aware of the plight of the Nez Perce. What are some of the logical and emotional appeals that Chief Joseph uses to persuade his audience to view Native Americans differently? What specific support does he give for his idea that his people should be free to go wherever they choose? Does Chief Joseph convince you that the government has treated the Nez Perce unfairly?*

1 . . . I have heard talk and talk, but nothing is done. Good words do not last long unless they amount to something. Words do not pay for my dead people. They do not pay for my country, now overrun by white men. They do not protect my father's grave. They do not pay for all my horses and cattle. Good words will not give me back my children. Good words will not make good the promise of your War chief General Miles. Good words will not give my people good health and stop them from dying. Good words will not get my people a home where they can live in peace and take care of themselves.

I am tired of talk that comes to nothing. It makes my heart sick when I remember all the good words and all the broken promises. There has been too much talking by men who had no right to talk. Too many misrepresentations have been made, too many misunderstandings have come up between the white men about the Indians.

2 If the white man wants to live in peace with the Indian he can live in peace. There need be no trouble. Treat all men alike. Give them the same law. Give them an even chance to live and grow. All men were made by the same Great Spirit Chief. They are all brothers. The earth is the mother of all people, and all people should have equal rights upon it.

3 You might as well expect the rivers to run backward as that any man who was born a free man should be contented when penned up and denied liberty to go where he pleases. If you tie a horse

PERSUASIVE SPEECH
by Chief Joseph

1
Chief Joseph uses repetition and parallelism to get his audience's attention.

2
Here is the speaker's main point—treat all men alike, including the Indian.

3
The speaker uses the problem-solution method, a deductive approach, to develop the body of his speech.

to a stake, do you expect he will grow fat? If you pen an Indian up on a small spot of earth, and compel him to stay there, he will not be contented, nor will he grow and prosper. I have asked some of the great white chiefs where they get their authority to say to the Indian that he shall stay in one place, while he sees white men going where they please. They cannot tell me.

I only ask of the government to be treated as all other men are treated. If I cannot go to my own home, let me have a home in some country where my people will not die so fast. . . .

When I think of our condition my heart is heavy. I see men of my race treated as outlaws and driven from country to country or shot down like animals.

I know that my race must change. We cannot hold our own with white men as we are. We ask only an even chance to live as other men live. We ask to be recognized as men. We ask that the same law shall work alike on all men. If the Indian breaks the law, punish him by the law. If the white man breaks the law, punish him also.

4 Let me be a free man—free to travel, free to stop, free to work, free to trade where I choose, free to choose my own teachers, free to follow the religion of my fathers, free to think and talk and act for myself—and I will obey every law, or submit to the penalty.

4
Interspersing his logical explanation with emotional appeals, Chief Joseph chooses specific words and images to convince his audience of the Indians' right to be free.

Whenever the white man treats an Indian as they treat each other, then we will have no more wars. We shall all be alike—brothers of one father and one mother, with one mother, with one sky above us and one country around us, and one government for all. Then the Great Spirit Chief who rules above will smile upon this land, and send rain to wash out the bloody spots made by brothers' hands from the face of the earth.

For this time the Indian race are waiting and praying. I hope that no more groans of wounded men and women will ever go to the ear of the Great Spirit Chief above, and that all people may be one people.

PERSUASIVE SPEECH

"Fat Chance"

Jennifer Cober, student speaker

In this contest-winning speech, Jennifer Cober makes an engaging appeal for people to evaluate others based on an appreciation of who they are inside, not based on what they look like on the outside. She advances her argument effectively, using touches of humor to remind her listeners of the sympathy toward others that all people should share. In her conclusion, she cites a personal incident to support her main point. What methods does she use in her introduction that make her audience trust and like her as a speaker? Which points do you find most convincing or memorable?

Persuasive Speech
by Jennifer Cober

1
The speaker uses the Monroe motivated sequence. She first gets the audience's attention by using ironic humor—she says one thing but means another. The audience can appreciate the speaker's situation.

2
Cober adds to her humor through the use of puns—she uses wordplay on the titles to which she alludes.

1 All right. I know what you're thinking. You're looking at me and you're saying to yourself, "Who is this play-bunny pinup,—this fine and feminine machine, this love goddess from above?" And then, of course, your next question is, "When did she realize she didn't quite have that perfect body she'd always dreamed of?" Well, maybe it was when my speech coach entered me into a reading . . . by myself. Or maybe it has to do with the fact that when a salesman tells me a pair of shoes look good on my feet, I have to take his word for it. Or maybe it has to do with the fact that I needed a nap after climbing a flight of stairs.

2 You see my problem is, I think about food all day long. Once, I tried to forget about food and just read a book, but all I could find was *The Grapes of Wrath* and *Goodbye, Mr. Chips.* So I turned on

the television set. It was the *Fortune Cookie,* starring Jack Lemmon. I was frustrated and upset, so I went to see my doctor. I told him I felt fine, but every time I looked in the a mirror, I wanted to throw up. He said he didn't know what was wrong with me, but he was sure I had no visual problems. He suggested that I start an exercise program and that's exactly what I did. But, I was unenthusiastic about the task that lay before me—of exercise. But all that changed when I met Biff—two *f*s.

3 He was my aerobics instructor and he had a body that just didn't stop. I pictured myself walking into my aerobics class like Jamie Lee Curtis in the movie *Perfect,* surrounded by hard-bodied, sweaty men in spandex. Instead, I felt more like Hoss on *Bonanza.* I was surrounded by three old men and a herd of cattle. I mean, I knew exercise would be bad, but I hadn't expected this. I had been misled.

4 Anyone that tells you that losing weight is a simple problem with a simple solution is either (A) lying, (B) badly misinformed, or (C) a cheerleader. The same goes for anyone that tells you that all you need to be thin for life is a little gumption and a strict diet. The truth is that an estimated 80 million Americans are overweight; 15 percent are under the age of thirty. According to Weight Watchers, a national weight-loss and health organization, overweight people have a disease, like alcoholism. They're literally addicted to food. With some 57 percent of our population over their ideal weight, we are right to be concerned and even alarmed at this problem.

5 But why do so many overweight people see the word *diet* and run? Well, maybe it's because the first three letters of the word spell *die.* It's not that fat people aren't trying to lose weight—we are. Fat people enrich the promoters of the weight-loss industry to the tune of some 10 billion dollars a year. This money goes toward diet books, diet pills, doctors' fees, health clubs and spas, and a variety of other gimmicks that couldn't possibly reduce anything except maybe your bank account. The extent to which this nonsense is believed shows today's extreme passion for slimness.

You know, many of us were brought up on the idea that there's something wrong with hungers of the flesh, that the body should be treated like a temple. Well now we're subscribing to new ideas—a new religion if you will—the religion of weight loss. *Slenderness* and *fitness* are watchwords of this new religion. Physical perfection is now a form of eternal salvation and diet messiahs abound, each propounding the virtues of his or her system with the passions of a tent preacher seeking converts. Each has his or her own faithful disciples spreading the gospel to every heathen, tellin' them to forsake of their fatness, and repent their high-calorie ways.

Now being thin isn't only fashionable, it's righteous. As a result, Americans are in a frenzy to be thin and they seem willing to try almost anything to get that way. One report in a bulletin sent to the American Heart Association states that there is now a tablet on the market that when taken releases a hormone in the body similar to that of the hormone released during exercise. It actually makes your body think it's working out. It's called passive exercise and it gives a whole new meaning to the phrase, "I'm on the pill." While this example may be funny, there are plenty that aren't.

This growing and spreading social malady has claimed such victims as a college co-ed who, convinced that he was just too fat, starved himself to death. A young woman suffering from a host of illnesses, who finally confesses to her doctor that she's been taking forty laxatives a day, every day, to control her weight. These are not isolated cases. They represent the hundreds of thousands of Americans that have fallen prey to the idea that in order to be successful, in order to fit in, in order to win, we have to be thin.

6 There are no easy answers to losing weight. If you are looking for one, then you're listening to the wrong person. What I will give you is the truth. It is possible to get thin and to stay that way. According to Dr. Alvin Feinstein of Yale University, the key to losing weight is to lose it gradually. His studies show that an overwhelming majority of those who have successfully lost weight quickly will regain their lost weight plus an additional fifteen to twenty pounds within six months.

7 Let's face it. Who am I to tell you to lose weight? I mean I am eighteen years old and my mother still gets morning sickness. Last week, a peeping Tom actually booed me. Why should you listen to me? Well, I'll tell you. Last summer I lost fifty pounds. I was happier, healthier, and most of all, I

3

The use of the analogy enhances the description that the speaker uses throughout the speech.

4

The speaker uses statistics, examples, and causal reasoning to show that action is required—the *need* step.

5

The speaker develops an emotional appeal with vivid language and explicit detail.

6

In the satisfaction step, the speaker tells the audience how to eliminate or reduce the behavior that needs changing. Included here is a proposition of value: It is possible to lose weight and stay thin.

7

The speaker helps establish her credibility with a personal anecdote.

8
The visualization step helps the listener see how the solution works. Often, visualization includes an analogy that describes how a given solution has worked in similar instances, thereby showing the audience members that the solution can work for them.

9
The speaker uses topical order to organize the main points of this section of the speech.

10
In the final step, action, the speaker encourages the listeners to implement the solution. The action step provides a way for the audience members to carry out the solution. They must personally believe they can do something about the problem.

PERSUASIVE SPEECH
by Brian Eanes

1
This contest speech follows the problem-solution pattern of organization.

was thinner. I ate a lot of lettuce and lean chicken breasts, drank a lot of tea and coffee, and I was losing weight. I thought I was doing myself a favor; that is, until the night of October twelfth when I found myself lying on my back and facing a bright light. I was having emergency surgery to remove my gallbladder. My yo-yo dieting had caused me a serious health problem that I could no longer ignore. All of a sudden, being fat wasn't funny any more. The jokes were old and the laughter had stopped.

Like so many other groups in American society, fat people are longing to find that magic bullet—the simpler the better—to cure their never ending problem. Every decade has had its own magical bullets. The '60s brought diet drinks; the '70s fad was low carbohydrates; the '80s brought us diet pills and walk-in diet clinics. And now in the '90s we have fat substitutes, which allow us to take in a greater amount of food with less fat and calorie content. But once these magic bullets have made their way through the American digestive system, fat people will be just as fat, if not fatter, and having failed again, they'll retreat back to their dandy excuses: "I'm not fat. I'm big boned." "I have a gland problem." "I'm just fat because it runs in my family." "I'm not overweight; I'm under tall."

8 A growing alternative to those of us that have tried to lose weight and failed seems to be the ever-popular Oprah Winfrey attitude, "I can't lose weight, so I'm just going to accept myself as I am." And, maybe a small percentage of them *can* do this. A very small percentage. A tiny percentage. All right, four people who've never left their dairy farm in Wisconsin. The point is, no one who's invested time and energy into losing weight will ever be truly happy with themselves fat. According to Dr. Gabe Mirkin's book *Getting Thin,* he tells us there are three key things that overweight people must realize. First of all, dieting may not be only a matter of what you eat, but in what amount. A balanced diet can include some of your favorite foods—eaten in moderation. Dieting doesn't have to be all raw fruits and vegetables, but you have to eat in portions that are adequate to your particular weight-loss needs.

9 Secondly, Dr. Mirkin tells us that not all fat is bad. He says that while having too much body fat is hazardous to your health, the storage of fat is vital to our very existence. Without body fat, camels couldn't cross the desert; seals couldn't reproduce; birds couldn't migrate; bears couldn't survive long winters, and Roseanne Barr just wouldn't be funny. You see society must stop viewing fat as the enemy and realize its assets to the human body. It can be a great source of energy and warmth.

Finally, Dr. Mirkin suggests an exercise program. He suggests aerobic exercise for overweight people because it raises the heart level without straining the heart beyond its capacity. According to Dr. Kenneth H. Cooper, aerobics is the most widely accepted form of exercise, endured by more people in more different forms than any other type. It's so efficient. It is the official form of exercise of the United States Air Force. And don't those guys look good?

10 My aerobic class is going really great. I'm under a physician's care now; I'm eating right; and most of all I'm exercising. You see, if we can all just forget the magic bullets and the excuses, we can realize that our fate, as a healthier and more aware nation, is much more than just a fat chance.

PERSUASIVE SPEECH

"With Rest, You Get Noise"

Brian Eanes, student speaker

1 *In this contest-winning speech, Brian Eanes tries to persuade his listeners to accept the relationship between hard work and top-quality results. He cites the positive value of working hard in order to achieve excellence, contending that too many people in our society are*

willing to accept and to give less than the best. However, he does not suggest that we exhaust ourselves, only that we commit ourselves fully to achieving all that we are capable of achieving and that we always strive to do the best we can in all our endeavors.

2 At the age of eight, Arnold Schwarzenegger looked—just like I look. Well, can you see it? I'll grant it I am a bit older than eight, and Arnold does have a slight head start on me at the moment, but it could happen. Me and a two-handed broadsword and Conan the well muscled, and all it would take is . . . a miracle!

3 Well, fortunately for me and for the Schwarzeneggers of the past, Robert Penn Warren contends that *work* is a four-letter word for *miracle.* Arnold Schwarzenegger seemed to sense the truth of this observation. He knew the price he'd have to pay to achieve the body of a modern Adonis, and he decided that he was willing to make the payment. He struggled through years of pain and hard work to improve his physique and to reach his ultimate goal—to be . . . an actor. Well, anyway his effort allowed him to accomplish things that no one would have believed of him at the age of eight.

Pablo Casals, world's renowned cellist, also achieved his status through struggle and hard work. Once when Casals was touring, his traveling companion noticed that the maestro continually practiced, until his hands literally hurt. Now, since Casals was in his 70s, and well in control of his talent, the young friend suggested that the cellist rest. But Casals exploded. He pounded his fist against the
4 arms of his chair and said, "Rest, never! With rest, you get noise. It takes pain to make music."

Life is a struggle. And yes, to make beautiful music it will probably hurt, somewhere along the line, but to understand the kind of hurt, we first need to understand what Casals might have meant by "pain." Now pain is not always physical. Hurt—"I want to make music." And, even if it is physical, it may not be the result of some external blow. Rather the pain of the struggle could emerge from the inner turmoil of having to make a difficult decision, or from long practicing to improve a talent, or perhaps from the simple business of daily survival. So the pain is the struggle itself. And according to Perry Pascarella in his book, *The New Achievers,* we are no longer willing to struggle unless the reward-to-effort ratio is greatly in favor of the payback. Honest effort it seems has become passé and therein lies the problem. We are afraid of the pain involved in the struggle to achieve. Now as a result of this negative view, life can become stale, and people will stagnate.

5 Frederick Douglass, a man who escaped slavery and then struggled to secure freedom for others, states in his autobiography, *Narrative of the Life,* "If there is no pain, there is no progress. Those who demand one without the other are men who want crops without plowing up the ground. They want rain without thunder. They want the ocean without the roar of its mighty waters." We can never further the world while we're unwilling to sacrifice and take part in individual struggles. Now this is not to say that all personal struggles have a great effect on the condition of the world, but they do have a great deal to do with our personal lives.

6 Nevertheless, the *Harvard Business Review* states that society today is suffering from a productivity panic caused by low commitment to work and effort. We want knowledge without study, success without sacrifice, responsibility without consequence. But commitment to an idea is as important, if not more so than the initial decision to commit. Robert Ard, the president of the Black Leadership Council, helps explain the difference between involvement and commitment when he says, "When you look at a plate of ham and eggs, you know that the chicken was involved, but the pig was committed."

Commitment is not something that can be sloughed off at the first sign of trouble. It is an absolute decision to follow through, come hell or high water. And most of the time you can count on both. Pain will occur, but the struggle to prevail will bring us into self-fulfillment unknown to the undecided and the lazy. As Shakespeare's King Lear agonizes, "Nothing can come of nothing."

7 A pearl is a beautiful example of growth through pain. The process begins when a single grain of sand slips into the shell of an oyster. The sand lies on the oyster irritating it, causing it to secrete a

2

Although the speaker gets the audience's attention with humor, the tone is sincere and concerned. It is indicative of the speaker's personal involvement in persuading his audience of the positive value of hard work.

3

The speech is laced with numerous anecdotes and quotations from authorities that support the speaker's viewpoint.

4

The speaker paraphrases and uses short, concise quotations to keep his audience interested and to allow listeners to easily follow the biographical accounts.

5

The colorful illustrations help the audience see the importance of struggle.

6

The transitional word *nevertheless* provides an effective contrast to lead the speaker to an emotional appeal. The speaker uses parallelism and repetition for emphasis.

7

To continue his emotional approach, the speaker uses a literal analogy.

healing liquid that surrounds the grain of sand. Now, this process continues until the sand is completely covered with a thick, solid layer of the healing enzymes, so that the oyster is no longer in pain. So you see, through the pain of the oyster, a pearl is created. Just as through our pain, our struggle, we produce valuable gems—those personal accomplishments we call our own.

8 Okay, so we know there's value in effort. Struggle matters. The problem is we have no guarantee of the outcome. It's a scary thought to work, to struggle, to suffer the pain, and then have nothing come of it. It's also frustrating, not to mention annoying, especially when we see others getting what we know we deserve. Somehow everything we've endured seems futile.

An old Burmese proverb defines *futility* as "playing a harp before a buffalo." And now, since there's no old Burmese here to explain, I'd like to take a stab. The point is that we won't get a positive reaction from plucking harp strings in front of a large, hairy beast. On top of that, buffalo are tone deaf. So all we're doing is wasting our time and annoying the buffalo.

But the value of struggle is not always the outcome. In his book *Man's Search for Meaning*, Viktor Frankl tells of his personal struggle to survive a Nazi concentration camp. Day after day, he saw men die. But day after day, he saw men give to one another. The meaning of their lives was in their struggle. That many died brutally was not as important as the fact that while they lived, they struggled grandly. As Frankl states, "Struggle has value. Victory is an aftertaste."

Now, in defense of victory, I'd like to say that the winning can certainly be fun. In our society it's hard to convince people otherwise. "Put forth effort and you'll be happy as a clam" just doesn't seem to cut it. But to be able to reflect on the struggle and say, "I tried" is a valuable thing. No struggle is futile. There is a victory whether we reach the goal or not.

9 So, how do we sell the idea of struggle? How do we convince people that suffering is good for them? Well, it's easy to explain, but difficult to carry out. It's simply a change in attitude. First, we
10 need to understand that to succeed and progress, we need struggle, and there will be pain. Pain of work, pain of disappointment, pain of endurance. Yes, to get the fruit, we've to climb the tree. We must be the pig and commit to our ideas and beliefs, for without commitment, it's too easy to jump back and say, "Well, uh, maybe not." And it's not good to leave an easy out. Too many times we choose to take it, rather than to stay the course.

Next, we need to remember that through the pain of the struggle, life can and will improve. There may be pain, but there will be progress, and life without either pain or progress is a life of boredom and stagnation.

Philosopher Arthur Schopenhauer puts it this way: "Life swings like a pendulum backward and forward, between pain and boredom." Struggle changes the color of an ordinarily gray world.

11 And last, don't fear futility. Since nowhere these struggles are futile, these fears are groundless. Not long before she died of cancer, Gilda Radner's autobiography appeared for the first time on the best-seller list. Entitled, *It's Always Something,* the book traces a variety of her struggles to achieve as a wife, an actress, a friend, a comedienne, a humanitarian. She had a great gift to make people laugh, a gift to bring joy. But, as she points out, laughter is born of pain. Her greatest struggle was for life and in the end, she lost a valiant battle. But the strength that she gave to others, the fun and the love she shared endured beyond the pain. An end will come to every struggle, and even if the outcome isn't positive, the struggle remains a learning, growing experience. Our resolve must be to endure despite the pain. If we begin to enjoy the struggle, we can begin to enjoy life. An old English proverb claims, "Nothing is got without pain, but dirt and long nails."

Let's struggle to extend our repertoire of accomplishments beyond these two, and remember, with rest you get noise. It takes pain to make a life.

8
Having explained the problem—that few people are willing to endure the sustained struggle in order to achieve excellence—the speaker now identifies the solution—a recognition that only through constant, dedicated effort is excellence achieved.

9
The speaker uses a question as an effective transition to his proposition of value.

10
The action step shows the audience how to implement the solution.

11
Eanes ends with a compassionate illustration as part of his emotional appeal.

• Special-Occasion Speech

pp. 671–683

TEACHING STRATEGIES

Students should understand that specialized speeches are those given in response to situations that occur frequently—awards and recognition occasions, ceremonies such as graduations and dedications, and contests. The speeches that follow can be used to teach specifically that type of speech or can be used in various chapters such as **Chapter 4** to evaluate listening skills or **Chapter 9** to analyze audience, occasion, and tone or to examine organization and transition.

Audiotape 2 in the *Audiovisual Resource Binder* contains recordings of these speeches.

SPECIAL-OCCASION SPEECH: GRADUATION SPEECH

University of Colorado School of Medicine Graduation

Antonia C. Novello, M.D., M.P.H.

In 1990, Antonia C. Novello was named Surgeon General of the United States—the first Hispanic and the first woman to be appointed to this position. Dr. Novello's own childhood health problems and her experiences as a public health physician make her uniquely qualified to address medical school graduates. As the main commencement speaker, Dr. Novello sets three goals for her speech: to congratulate, to counsel, and to challenge the graduates. How does she meet these goals? How does she offer optimistic and inspirational advice to the graduates?

1 Good morning, Dean Krugman, honored guests, members of the 1992 graduating class University of Colorado, esteemed faculty, parents, friends, ladies and gentlemen. I am honored that you have invited me here today to share this most significant day. You will come to think of this day as one of the proudest and most unforgettable days of your lives.

I am especially honored to be here because the University of Colorado School of Medicine is one of the jewels in the crown of American medicine. This excellent institution has it all—outstanding research, outstanding clinical training, and an outstanding faculty. It also has an outstanding history. As we stand here today, it is hard to imagine that the University of Colorado School of Medicine opened its doors in 1883 with two students and two senior faculty members. Today, the School of Medicine is the largest medical school in the Rocky Mountain Region.

2 But that growth tells only part of the story. This institution can be proud of the medical developments that have taken place here including the first totally man-made enzyme, the development of the first Child Health Associate Program in the country, and the identification of the "battered child" syndrome.

Also, your recruitment of women into medicine—44 percent of your graduating class today—is and has been exemplary. You members of the class of 1992 should feel proud to have attended a school with such credentials and such commitment to women and their careers.

I am also impressed by the scholarly dedication the 125 of you who are graduating today have shown to the profession of medicine in your years as students here at the University of Colorado. I have been told that one of you will graduate with both an M.D. and a Ph.D.; another of you will graduate with an M.D. and an M.P.H.; three of you have participated in the Public Health Service's COSTEP program; and some of you will stay behind to do work with the underserved.

I also understand you have shown an unusual amount of romantic commitment—six pairs of couples coming together in one class! This must be some sort of record for your school, or should I say, the weather!

But perhaps most impressive is the number of you who will enter the fields of Family Medicine, Internal Medicine, and Pediatrics, with one of you entering a combined Internal Medicine/Pediatrics program. When 50 percent of you are entering these fields, compared with the national average of 38 percent, this University should be proud of this accomplishment.

3 But truly, I am here because your class is small enough to be personal and large enough to be powerful! So what better than to have the first female Hispanic Surgeon General this country has ever had to address you this morning? My office, like your class, is small but powerful in messages and commitment.

This is why it is such a joy for me to join you today in celebrating this outstanding institution and to share your pride in these fine young men and women who will now carry your legacy into the future: your graduating class of 1992.

GRADUATION SPEECH
by Antonia C. Novello

1
In the lengthy introduction the speaker acknowledges the importance of the occasion, provides historical background, congratulates the graduates, and looks briefly at the graduates' futures.

2
The language of a commencement speech is usually formal.

3
Dr. Novello establishes credibility by explaining her qualifications as a speaker for such an occasion.

4
The speaker's purpose is clearly announced.

5
The body of the speech consists of three parts. In this part, Dr. Novello again congratulates the graduates and begins to develop the body of the speech by describing the challenges of the future.

6
The speaker reminds the graduates that their generation will continue the commitment to the medical field.

7
This second section of the speech contains the speaker's advice. She uses personal narration and description.

4 I stand before you today to do three things: to congratulate you, to counsel you, and to challenge you.

5 Congratulations. Just think of it—in one month you can finally start paying off your student loans. I do want to congratulate you on your entry into the profession of medicine. Yes, you are now back at the entry level.

As I'm sure you've heard from your previous high school and college commencement speakers, "Today marks not an end, but a beginning."

A cliché? Sure it is—but, like most clichés, it contains a kernel of wisdom, especially for physicians.

Think about it. Most of the science and technology you have learned will soon be obsolete. Even worse, in ten years you probably won't remember more than 10 percent of all the facts you have had crammed into your heads. While I doubt that this frightens you, I hope it will trouble you—trouble you enough that you will continue to learn.

It troubles me that so much of medical education must be spent in the drudgery of memorizing facts: the Krebs cycle, origins and insertions of obscure muscles, the pathophysiology of Tsutsugamushi fever, and so little time spent in the conceptual teachings of public health, prevention, and common sense.

Now of course, facts are necessary. They are the building blocks of our knowledge. Without them, scientific judgment is impossible, honesty is irrelevant, and compassion is fraudulent. However, facts change. That is why, for me, the true purpose of a medical education is not merely the accumulation of facts but the creating of a habit of mind, a way of being. By this I mean: The complete health professional must be humble in what facts he or she does not know.

Socrates said that if he was wiser than all the rest in Ancient Greece, it was only because he was aware of what he didn't know. That is why I prefer to evaluate health professionals not so much on the answers they give but on the questions they ask.

So while I congratulate you most warmly today, I urge you to embark upon a lifelong quest of learning, of healing, of caring . . . but, above all, of questioning. No matter what specific specialty path you choose, you will be at the center of ever more complex questions. Dealing with them will require that you maintain your curiosity and continue to study science and technology, balanced by a lifelong interest in the humanities and compassion for your fellow human beings.

6 You stand upon the shoulders of your faculty, just as they stood upon the shoulders of their predecessors. And, like them, you too will one day pass the torch to a new generation of professionals. It is important that you continue to question, to challenge ideas, and to test new ones, for this is truly how we learn and how life and science advance.

So my dear graduates, cherish and advance your profession. In the words of Hippocrates, "Whenever the art of medicine is loved, there also is love of humanity."

7 And now, my Counsel.

Sir William Osler, in his farewell address to American medical students, said, "To each one of you, the practice of medicine will be very much as you make it—to one a worry, a care, a perpetual annoyance; to another a daily joy and a life of as much happiness and usefulness as can well fall to the lot of man." And so I counsel you now to set your goals. After all, if you don't know where you're going, you're already there!

What kind of physician will you be? I want you to be known not only for your triumphs but also for your dreams. So plan thoughtfully and realistically, but dare to reach for the stars.

When I was a little girl growing up in Puerto Rico, I harbored a dream—a secret dream to become a doctor. Not just any kind of doctor—but a pediatrician. I dreamed only of caring for the children in my hometown of Fajardo.

After I completed my pediatric residency, I was drawn into a subspecialty, nephrology, largely because one of my aunts, really a second mother to me, had died of end-stage renal disease. Still later, I became interested in broader community-health issues, so I joined the Public Health Service and earned an M.P.H. degree. I have loved every step along the way. For me, my professional career has been a journey, not a destination.

That is why when Secretary Sullivan and President Bush asked me to become Surgeon General, I was stunned—stunned and honored. The first woman, and the first Hispanic, Surgeon General of the United States. And all of this the result of the secret, simple dream of a little girl whose only wish was to become a small-town pediatrician on a Caribbean island.

I share something of my own story with you not because I enjoy talking about myself. I don't. But the mere notion that I am the Surgeon General of this country today means that dreams do come true—sometimes in ways we never imagine. So I counsel all of you to dream and to think big. Don't listen to those who say that the American dream is dead. I stand before you as living proof that in this country anything is possible. Believe that you can and will make a difference, and be prepared for opportunities that will surely come your way.

It also helps, of course, to be lucky, but I'll tell you another secret: For me, luck is when preparation meets opportunity. Therefore, the harder I've worked, the luckier I seem to get.

We must also remember that our work as professionals defines us as human beings. As it has been said, “Much of the good and the bad you will ever do in this world will come through your work.”
8 How will you view your work? The author Robert Bella describes three types of work: First, there's the job where the goal is simply making money and supporting your family. Then there's the career where you trace your progress through various appointments and achievements. Finally, there's the calling—the ideal blending of activity and character that makes work inseparable from life.

My friends, I hope you are not just looking for a job. I hope you are not just planning a career. I hope each and every one of you has a calling—a physicianly calling.

I know that you will do well. Your faculty has seen to that. But I pray you will do good.
9 One word of caution, though, from one who sat where you are today twenty-two years ago—the world owes you nothing! To expect the world to treat you fairly because you're a good person and a graduate of this university is like expecting a raging bull not to charge you because you're a vegetarian!

The road to success has no short cuts or fast lanes. There can be no avoiding your responsibility to give something back to the community and to those responsible for you being here today.

So work hard, and avoid Kuschner's pillars of despair: complacency, mediocrity, and indifference. And beware those enemies of tranquility: avarice, ambition, envy, anger, and pride.

Will you be happy in your work? I hope so. But how will you do it? Riches, fame, and power will not make you happy. In fact, the happiest physicians and health-care professionals I know are those who go about their everyday lives doing good things for other people without asking, “What's in it for me?”

We must remember that service is the rent you pay for living—not only when you have reached your life's goal but also while working toward achieving it. After all, what you will be, you are now becoming.
10 The importance of this service attitude is painfully obvious in today's world. My friends, there is a spiritual vacuum in America's society today. There is too much of what-can-I-get, rather than what-can-I-give. It has been said that we are in need of a little more heart, a little more brotherhood, less personal greed, more personal good, more service to others. This is why, while I fervently wish you much happiness in your work, I caution you not to seek happiness for happiness sake. If you do good, happiness, believe me, will seek you. It will creep silently into your lives from many sources: the heartfelt “thank you” from a grateful patient, the quiet discovery in a laboratory, the well-crafted lecture, the scientific paper, the book, or the public policy that may affect the lives of millions. Medicine, you see, offers many paths to happiness. So I counsel you not to be good doctors or good health-care professionals only. First and foremost, be good men and good women.

Do not forget to put balance in your lives: family, friends, leisure time, hobbies, social causes,

8
The rhetorical questions involve the audience by getting them to think about work.

9
The speaker uses a startling statement to emphasize a point and to provide contrast to her earlier emphasis.

10
To sum up this part and to add emphasis to her word of caution, Dr. Novello uses parallelism.

in men, women, and children around the world. And by the end of the decade, it is expected that more than ten million children will be orphaned as their mothers or both parents die of AIDS—ten million orphaned children that will sadly have to bear the stigma of the disease, even when all of them won't harbor the virus.

With increasingly heterosexual transmission of the AIDS virus, the HIV epidemic will undoubtedly be the greatest challenge of your medical generation.

The urgency of reaching large numbers of persons in our communities who are not yet infected, but may be at high risk, will increasingly be a major challenge for all of us as health professionals. The knowledge and skill which will be required in the provision of the entire spectrum of health care for HIV will challenge all our creativity and imagination; and for this, we must be prepared. But please, I urge you to remember that behind each one of the AIDS statistics I have just mentioned, there is a human being in need of our compassion and care.

Challenge number eight is another that I have addressed as your Surgeon General: the challenge of violence in our society. Physicians are used to thinking that the issue of violence is the responsibility of other groups—the police, the courts, politicians, the media, the church. I would suggest, however, that this thinking needs revision. Violence is a legitimate public-health concern. It is your challenge—and mine.

Violence permeates every corner of our land—it destroys our cities, it destroys our communities, and it destroys our families. Homicidal violence is now a leading cause of death among our youth. The recent catastrophe in Los Angeles must stand as a grim reminder that America is divided against itself. We, as a society, must search for new solutions to preserve the unique vision of our great nation. If we are to remain a beacon to the world of freedom, justice, and equal opportunity, we must first deliver on those promises to our own citizens.

Physicians, as the guardians of lives, must speak up. We must get informed, get involved, and get in charge. Violence will stop when we stop accepting it as a way of life. We must insist—no more violence!

Challenge number nine is the challenge of working as a team with others. Physicians will not be able to solve the challenge of ravages like AIDS and violence on their own. You must learn to work effectively with other members of the health-care team as you will no longer be the sole proprietors of the state of America's health in the medical world you inherit. By this, I mean that you must work with other professionals who have expertise in their areas of competence, at least equal to your own: nurses, physician assistants, therapists of various types, dentists, engineers, researchers, pharmacists, administrators, police, judges, legislators—and yes, even lawyers.

My tenth and final challenge is the challenge of communication. As medical science becomes more complex, you will have to communicate effectively and become an educator of your community. This is crucial now, especially when the layperson is sometimes as knowledgeable as the provider. You will be a guide, a voice, an advisor, as well as a person of considerable power, in helping patients make correct decisions. If any of my previous nine challenges are to be overcome, they must be cogently and clearly addressed by sensible and sensitive communicators. In this effort, we physicians must be aware that our detached stance, so widely used to protect us from our own feelings, might prevent us from getting close to the people entrusted in our care.

So before you are tempted to astound your patients with your new knowledge, take a moment to listen. Believe me, if you want to develop better doctor-patient relationships, you will do it sooner by listening rather than talking. I urge you to bring empathy to your work—to see with your patient's eyes, to hear with your patient's ears, to feel with your patient's heart.

18
Even if the future does not seem bright, a commencement speaker is usually optimistic and reassuring.

18 So there you have it: a top-ten list of challenges from your Surgeon General. A "hit list" if you will, but of the healthiest variety. The going will be tough, but as I look out at the class of 1992, I am encouraged. Sitting before me I see our new generation of clinicians, teachers, researchers, communicators, administrators, and public-policy makers. I believe you are ready to meet these and all the other challenges that lurk in wait for you. Together, we can do what none of us can do alone.

19 In closing, I would like to pay special tribute to your families who have sacrificed to get you here and your faculty that has prepared you so well. The degrees you are receiving today testify to the support you have received from them along the way. As a matter of fact, this day is theirs every bit as much as yours. They are the bows from which you, as arrows, are sent forth. And as Gibran has written so eloquently, "Just as the Archer loves the arrow that flies, so too does he love the bow that gives them flight."

Today, it has been my distinct honor to congratulate, counsel, and challenge. The rest is up to you. May you seize this day and all others that are to follow to bring honor to your alma mater, joy to your family and friends, comfort to your patients, and true happiness to yourselves.

I pray that you do not lose your sense of who you really are, where your roots are, and who helped you in getting to this point. Most importantly, do not forget the impact of this great institution in molding your life and professional future. University of Colorado graduates of the Class of 1992, may you think clearly, act decisively, and care tenderly.

Thank you very much and God bless you.

19
Dr. Novello includes in her closing special congratulations to the families of the graduates.

SPECIAL-OCCASION SPEECH: SPEECH OF INTRODUCTION

Introduction of Gertrude Lawrence to the New York Advertising Club

G. Lynn Sumner, President of the New York Advertising Club

Often, the most difficult task in a speech of introduction is to praise the speaker without embarrassing him or her or setting expectations so high that they cannot possibly be met. In this introduction, G. Lynn Sumner does an excellent job of praising Gertrude Lawrence and getting the audience ready to listen to her speech. What means does Ms. Sumner use to build her credibility? What does she do to set the tone for her speech? In what ways does Ms. Sumner praise Gertrude Lawrence and build the audience's enthusiasm? If you had been in the audience, what would your reaction have been to this speech?

1 It is a traditional example of the busman's holiday that when a sailor gets a day's shore leave, he goes rowing in Central Park. And if you would know what advertising men are doing these autumn nights—well, they are flocking to the Morosco Theatre, where some aspects of the advertising business have been cleverly put into a play called *Skylark.* The scintillating star of that play—Miss Gertrude Lawrence—is our special guest of honor today. That is the reason why we had no trouble whatever getting a complete set of our vice presidents at the head table.

2 In *Skylark,* Miss Lawrence plays a familiar part—the neglected wife of an advertising agency executive who is so busy with his clients and his speculative plans for prospective clients that he too often forgets to come home. Of course this is just a play—just a comedy—all in fun—for I am very sure that if Miss Lawrence were *really* the wife of an advertising executive, his chief problem would be to keep his mind on his work.

3 From observation of her theatre audiences, supplemented by observations of this audience, Miss Lawrence has some observations of her own to make about advertising and advertising men. I hope she doesn't pull her punches. It is a great pleasure to present one of the most charming and talented actresses of the English and American stage—Miss Gertrude Lawrence.

SPEECH OF INTRODUCTION
by G. Lynn Sumner

1
The speaker begins with a short, pertinent anecdote to get her audience's attention. The anecdote sets a light tone for the occasion. A busman's holiday is a vacation in which a person engages in recreation similar to his or her usual work. Using this relevant analogy engages the audience's curiosity about the coming speaker.

2
Ms. Sumner establishes the speaker's credibility and builds the audience's enthusiasm by describing Miss Lawrence's experiences related to advertising.

3
Ms. Sumner announces the speaker's purpose.

SPECIAL-OCCASION SPEECH: SPEECH OF PRESENTATION

Presentation of Honorary Citizenship to Sir Winston Churchill

President John F. Kennedy

A speech of presentation is often given at a ceremony in which an honor, an award, a prize, or a gift is bestowed upon someone. Although a speech of presentation sometimes includes a long tribute to the recipient, for the most part it is a fairly short, formal statement of why the person is being recognized. At the very least, the speech of presentation should discuss the nature or importance of the award or gift and the accomplishments of the individual. In the following short speech, note how President Kennedy highlights why Winston Churchill had earned the honor he is being given. Why is this occasion a unique one in United States history? How does Kennedy justify bestowing this honor on Churchill?

Ladies and gentlemen, Members of Congress, Members of the Cabinet, His Excellency the British Ambassador, Ambassadors of the Commonwealth, old friends of Sir Winston led by Mr. Baruch, ladies and gentlemen: We gather today at a moment unique in the history of the United States.
1 This is the first time that the United States Congress has solemnly resolved that the President of the United States shall proclaim an honorary citizenship for the citizen of another country, and in joining me to perform this happy duty the Congress gives Sir Winston Churchill a distinction shared only with the Marquis de Lafayette.

In naming him an honorary citizen, I only propose a formal recognition of the place he has long since won in the history of freedom and in the affections of my, and now his, fellow countrymen.
2 Whenever and wherever tyranny threatened, he has always championed liberty. Facing firmly toward the future, he has never forgotten the past. Serving six monarchs of his native Great Britain, he has served all men's freedom and dignity.
3 In the dark days and darker nights when Britain stood alone—and most men save Englishmen despaired of England's life—he mobilized the English language and sent it into battle. The incandescent quality of his words illuminated the courage of his countrymen.

Indifferent himself to danger, he wept over the sorrows of others. A child of the House of Commons, he became in time its father. Accustomed to the hardships of battle, he has no distaste for pleasure.

Now his stately ship of life, having weathered the severest storms of a troubled century, is anchored in tranquil waters, proof that courage and faith and the zest for freedom are truly indestructible. The record of his triumphant passage will inspire free hearts all over the globe.
4 By adding his name to our rolls, we mean to honor him, but his acceptance honors us far more. For no statement or proclamation can enrich his name now; the name Sir Winston Churchill is already legend.

SPEECH OF PRESENTATION
by John F. Kennedy

1
Kennedy explains the uniqueness of the occasion as he announces the award and its recipient.

2
Kennedy outlines Churchill's qualifications for receiving honorary citizenship.

3
Kennedy uses a method of organization in which he first builds suspense and then announces the honoree at the end of the introduction.

4
To conclude, Kennedy expresses the appreciation of the group making the award.

SPECIAL-OCCASION SPEECH: SPEECH OF ACCEPTANCE

Nobel Peace Prize Speech of Acceptance

Elie Wiesel

1 *The purpose of a speech of acceptance is to express appreciation for receiving an award. Most speeches of acceptance include a brief thanks to those responsible for giving the award and, if appropriate, thanks to any who share in the honor. In the following speech,*

SPEECH OF ACCEPTANCE
by Elie Wiesel

1
Understanding the nature of the award, the speaker has chosen an appropriate topic—the struggle for peace for all persecuted people.

the writer Elie Wiesel, a survivor of the Nazi concentration camps, accepts the 1986 Nobel Prize for Peace. Seeking to avert new holocausts, Wiesel has worked to draw attention to the plight of Cambodians, Soviet Jews, South African blacks, and other victims of persecution throughout the world. In his speech, Wiesel accepts the prize not only for himself but also for the other survivors of the Holocaust and, by extension, all persecuted people. What light does the speech throw on Wiesel's past experiences and their effects on his present values and behavior? In what ways is this speech also a call to action?

2 It is with a profound sense of humility that I accept the honor you have chosen to bestow upon me. I know: your choice transcends me. This both frightens and pleases me.

It frightens me because I wonder: do I have the right to represent the multitudes who have perished? Do I have the right to accept this great honor on their behalf? I do not. That would be presumptuous. No one may speak for the dead, no one may interpret their mutilated dreams and visions.

It pleases me because I may say that this honor belongs to all the survivors and their children, and through us, to the Jewish people with whose destiny I have always been identified.

3 I remember: it happened yesterday or eternities ago. A young Jewish boy discovering the kingdom of night. I remember his bewilderment, I remember his anguish. It all happened so fast. The ghetto. The deportation. The sealed cattle car. The fiery altar upon which the history of our people and the future of mankind were meant to be sacrificed.

I remember: he asked his father: "Can this be true? This is the 20th century, not the Middle Ages. Who would allow such crimes to be committed? How could the world remain silent?"

And now the boy is turning to me: "Tell me," he asks. "What have you done with your life?"

And I tell him that I have tried. That I have tried to keep memory alive, that I have tried to fight those who would forget. Because if we forget, we are guilty, we are accomplices.

And then I explained to him how naive we were, that the world did know and remain silent. And that is why I swore never to be silent whenever and wherever human beings endure suffering and humiliation. We must always take sides. Neutrality helps the oppressor, never the victim. Silence encourages the tormentor, never the tormented.

4 Sometimes we must interfere. When human lives are endangered, when human dignity is in jeopardy, national borders and sensitivities become irrelevant. Wherever men or women are persecuted because of their race, religion or political views, that place must—at that moment—become the center of our universe.

Of course, since I am a Jew profoundly rooted in my people's memory and tradition, my first response is to Jewish fears, Jewish needs, Jewish crises. For I belong to a traumatized generation, one that experienced the abandonment and solitude of our people. It would be unnatural for me not to make Jewish priorities my own: Israel, Soviet Jewry, Jews in Arab lands.

5 But there are others as important to me. Apartheid is, in my view, as abhorrent as anti-Semitism. To me, Andrei Sakharov's isolation is as much a disgrace as Iosif Begun's imprisonment. As is the denial of Solidarity and its leader Lech Walesa's right to dissent. And Nelson Mandela's interminable imprisonment.

There is so much injustice and suffering crying out for our attention: victims of hunger, or racism and political persecution, writers and poets, prisoners in so many lands governed by the left and by the right. Human rights are being violated on every continent. More people are oppressed than free.

And then, too, there are the Palestinians to whose plight I am sensitive but whose methods I deplore. Violence and terrorism are not the answer. Something must be done about their suffering, and soon. I trust Israel, for I have faith in the Jewish people. Let Israel be given a chance, let hatred and danger be removed from her horizons, and there will be peace in and around the Holy Land.

2
Mr. Wiesel begins by thanking the committee for the prize and points out that he accepts the honor as a representative of many people with many visions.

3
The speaker uses a narrative approach to introduce his main point.

4
Wiesel clearly states his thesis—the world must interfere when human rights are abused.

5
To support his main idea, the speaker gives several specific examples.

6
The speaker takes a persuasive tone and calls on the audience to take action against future injustices.

7
Wiesel concludes his speech by reminding the audience of his earlier story and by restating his appreciation.

Yes, I have faith. Faith in God and even in His creation. Without it no action would be possible. And action is the only remedy to indifference: the most insidious danger of all. Isn't this the meaning of Alfred Nobel's legacy? Wasn't his fear of war a shield against war?

6 There is much to be done, there is much that can be done. One person—a Raoul Wallenberg, an Albert Schweitzer, one person of integrity, can make a difference, a difference of life and death. As long as one dissident is in prison, our freedom will not be true. As long as one child is hungry, our lives will be filled with anguish and shame.

What all these victims need above all is to know that they are not alone: that we are not forgetting them, that when their voices are stifled we shall lend them ours, that while their freedom depends on ours, the quality of our freedom depends on theirs.

7 That is what I say to the young Jewish boy wondering what I have done with his years. It is in his name that I speak to you and that I express to you my deepest gratitude. No one is as capable of gratitude as one who has emerged from the kingdom of night.

We know that every moment is a moment of grace, every hour an offering; not to share them would mean to betray them. Our lives no longer belong to us alone; they belong to all those who need us desperately.

Thank you Chairman Aarvik. Thank you members of the Nobel Committee. Thank you people of Norway, for declaring on this singular occasion that our survival has meaning for mankind.

COMMEMORATIVE SPEECH
by Dr. Martin Luther King, Jr.

1
Dr. King knew his audience and occasion and prepared his speech accordingly by choosing his language and ideas carefully.

2
Dr. King makes his audience aware of the setting and occasion by alluding figuratively to Abraham Lincoln's shadow, the Gettysburg Address, and the Emancipation Proclamation.

SPECIAL-OCCASION SPEECH: COMMEMORATIVE SPEECH

"I Have a Dream"

Dr. Martin Luther King, Jr.

1 *In August 1963, more than 200,000 people attended a rally in Washington, D.C., to focus attention on demands for equality in jobs and civil rights. For many people the high point of the day was the delivery of the famous "I Have a Dream" speech by Dr. Martin Luther King, Jr. A commemorative speech marks an important event. In his speech, Dr. King stresses that the time has come to pursue the group's goal of making racial justice a reality. In stirring language, he identifies the trials and tribulations of many in his audience; however, rather than allowing his audience to "wallow in the valley of despair," he outlines the challenge of the future—his dream for the people. The power, motivation, and inspiration of Dr. King's speech are developed through his skillful use of repetition, parallelism, and metaphor. Beginning in the fourth paragraph with his reference to "cashing a check," how does Dr. King use metaphor to heighten the impact of his message on his audience? What is the effect of repetition and parallelism in the "I have a dream" section in the latter part of the speech? In your opinion, what is the most inspirational passage in Dr. King's speech? How does Dr. King's use of language make this passage powerful?*

I am happy to join with you today in what will go down in history as the greatest demonstration for freedom in the history of our nation.

2 Five score years ago, a great American, in whose symbolic shadow we stand today, signed the Emancipation Proclamation. This momentous decree came as a great beacon light of hope to millions of Negro slaves, who had been seared in the flames of withering injustice. It came as a joyous daybreak to end the long night of their captivity.

But one hundred years later, the Negro is still not free. One hundred years later, the life of the Negro is still sadly crippled by the manacles of segregation and the chains of discrimination. One hundred years later, the Negro lives on a lonely island of poverty in the midst of a vast ocean of material prosperity. One hundred years later, the Negro is still languished in the corners of American society and finds himself an exile in his own land. So we have come here today to dramatize a shameful condition.

3 In a sense we've come to our nation's Capitol to cash a check. When the architects of our republic wrote the magnificent words of the Constitution and the Declaration of Independence, they were signing a promissory note to which every American was to fall heir. This note was a promise that all men—yes, black men as well as white men—would be guaranteed the unalienable rights of life, liberty, and the pursuit of happiness.

It is obvious today that America has defaulted on this promissory note insofar as her citizens of color are concerned. Instead of honoring this sacred obligation, America has given the Negro people a bad check; a check which has come back marked "insufficient funds." But we refuse to believe that the bank of justice is bankrupt. We refuse to believe that there are insufficient funds in the great vaults of opportunity of this nation. So we've come to cash this check—a check that will give us upon demand the riches of freedom and the security of justice. We have also come to this hallowed spot to remind America of the fierce urgency of *now.* This is no time to engage in the luxury of cooling off or to take the tranquilizing drug of gradualism. *Now is the time* to make real the
4 promises of Democracy. *Now is the time* to rise from the dark and desolate valley of segregation to the sunlight of racial justice. *Now is the time* to lift our nation from the quicksands of racial injustice to the solid rock of brotherhood. *Now is the time* to make justice a reality for all of God's children.

5 It would be fatal for the nation to overlook the urgency of the moment. This sweltering summer of the Negro's legitimate discontent will not pass until there is an invigorating autumn of freedom and equality. Nineteen sixty-three is not an end, but a beginning. Those who hope that the Negro needed to blow off steam and will now be content will have a rude awakening if the nation returns to business as usual. There will be neither rest nor tranquility in America until the Negro is granted his citizenship rights. The whirlwinds of revolt will continue to shake the foundations of our nation until the bright day of justice emerges.

But there is something that I must say to my people who stand on the warm threshold which leads into the palace of justice. In the process of gaining our rightful place we must not be guilty of wrongful deeds. Let us not seek to satisfy our thirst for freedom by drinking from the cup of bitterness and hatred.

We must forever conduct our struggle on the high plane of dignity and discipline. We must not allow our creative protest to degenerate into physical violence. Again and again we must rise to the majestic heights of meeting physical force with soul force. The marvelous new militancy which has engulfed the Negro community must not lead us to a distrust of all white people, for many of our white brothers, as evidenced by their presence here today, have come to realize that their destiny is tied up with our destiny. And they have come to realize that their freedom is inextricably bound to our freedom. We cannot walk alone.

And as we walk we must make the pledge that we shall always march ahead. We cannot turn back. There are those who ask the devotees of civil rights, "When will you be satisfied?"
6 We can never be satisfied as long as the Negro is the victim of the unspeakable horrors of police brutality. We can never be satisfied as long as our bodies, heavy with the fatigue of travel, cannot gain lodging in the motels of the highways and the hotels of the cities. We cannot be satisfied as long as the Negro's basic mobility is from a smaller ghetto to a larger one. We can never be satisfied as long as our children are stripped of their selfhood and robbed of their dignity by signs stating "For Whites Only." We cannot be satisfied as long as a Negro in Mississippi cannot vote and a Negro in New York believes he has nothing for which to vote. No, no, we are not satisfied, and we will not be satisfied until justice rolls down like waters and righteousness like a mighty stream.

3
Using this extended metaphor, Dr. King introduces the goal of the group being addressed.

4
This repetition prepares the audience for the urgency of Dr. King's message.

5
Dr. King establishes himself as a credible and knowledgeable speaker by using subtle allusions such as this line from Shakespeare's *Richard III.*

6
The parallelism used at the beginning of each sentence gives Dr. King's address added force.

7
Dr. King relates well to his audience through his use of personal pronouns *we* and *you*.

8
Dr. King uses emphasis through restatement and parallelism as he announces his main points.

9
The sensory images create vivid pictures for the audience and help to intensify the message.

10
Dr. King juxtaposes numerous contrasting words such as *despair* and *hope, jangling discord* and *beautiful sympathy, black* and *white, Jews* and *Gentiles,* and *Protestants* and *Catholics.* The contrasts add strong emotional appeal.

11
The specific locations enhance the universality of the message.

12
Although this speech could have had negative overtones, Dr. King maintains and builds a positive tone through his organizational strategies and choice of words. The speech ends with a stirring and passionate climax.

7 I am not unmindful that some of you have come here out of great trials and tribulations. Some of you have come fresh from narrow jail cells. Some of you have come from areas where your quest for freedom left you battered by the storms of persecution and staggered by the winds of police brutality. You have been the veterans of creative suffering. Continue to work with the faith that unearned suffering is redemptive.

Go back to Mississippi, go back to Alabama, go back to South Carolina, go back to Georgia, go back to Louisiana, go back to the slums and ghettos of our Northern cities knowing that somehow this situation can and will be changed. Let us not wallow in the valley of despair.

8 I say to you today, my friends, so even though we face the difficulties of today and tomorrow, I still have a dream. It is a dream deeply rooted in the American dream.

I have a dream that one day this nation will rise up and live out the true meaning of its creed: "We hold these truths to be self-evident; that all men are created equal."

9 I have a dream that one day on the red hills of Georgia the sons of former slaves and the sons of former slaveowners will be able to sit down together at the table of brotherhood; I have a dream—

That one day even the state of Mississippi, a state sweltering with the heat of injustice, sweltering with the heat of oppression, will be transformed into an oasis of freedom and justice; I have a dream—

That my four little children will one day live in a nation where they will not be judged by the color of their skin but by the content of their character; I have a dream today.

I have a dream that one day down in Alabama, with its vicious racists, with its governor having his lips dripping with the words of interposition and nullification, one day right there in Alabama little black boys and black girls will be able to join hands with little white boys and white girls as sisters and brothers; I have a dream today.

I have a dream that one day every valley shall be exalted, every hill and mountain shall be made low, and rough places will be made plane and crooked places will be made straight, and the glory of the Lord shall be revealed, and all flesh shall see it together.

This is our hope. This is the faith that I go back to the South with. With this faith we will be able
10 to hew out of the mountain of despair a stone of hope. With this faith we will be able to transform the jangling discords of our nation into a beautiful symphony of brotherhood. With this faith we will be able to work together, to pray together, to struggle together, to go to jail together, to stand up for freedom together, knowing that we will be free one day.

This will be the day . . . This will be the day when all of God's children will be able to sing with new meaning. "My country 'tis of thee, sweet land of liberty, of thee I sing. Land where my fathers died, land of the pilgrim's pride, from every mountainside, let freedom ring," and if America is to be a great nation—this must become true.

11 So let freedom ring—from the prodigious hilltops of New Hampshire, let freedom ring; from the mighty mountains of New York, let freedom ring—from the heightening Alleghenies of Pennsylvania!

Let freedom ring from the snowcapped Rockies of Colorado!

Let freedom ring from the curvaceous slopes of California!

But not only that; let freedom ring from Stone Mountain of Georgia!

Let freedom ring from Lookout Mountain of Tennessee!

Let freedom ring from every hill and molehill of Mississippi. From every mountainside, let freedom ring, and when this happens . . .

12 When we allow freedom to ring, when we let it ring from every village and every hamlet, from every state and every city, we will be able to speed up that day when all of God's children, black men and white men, Jews and Gentiles, Protestants and Catholics, will be able to join hands and sing in the words of the old Negro spiritual, "Free at last! free at last! thank God almighty, we are free at last!"

SPECIAL-OCCASION SPEECH: COMMEMORATIVE SPEECH

“The Gettysburg Address”

President Abraham Lincoln

A commemorative speech is given to dedicate a memorial, park, building, or some other place or thing for a particular purpose. On November 19, 1863, Abraham Lincoln presented a speech to dedicate the National Soldiers' Cemetery at Gettysburg, Pennsylvania. Before President Lincoln's speech, Edward Everett, president of Harvard, senator, and orator of the day, had delivered a two-hour analysis of the battles at Gettysburg. Following
1 *this lengthy tribute, President Lincoln presented his three-minute dedication. His speech has been hailed as the finest example of its kind—and is certainly the most widely quoted of American speeches. What does Lincoln do in the speech to build force behind the word* dedicated*? In your opinion, what qualities in the speech have caused it to endure as one of the world's great statements?*

2 Fourscore and seven years ago our fathers brought forth on this continent a new nation, conceived in liberty, and dedicated to the proposition that all men are created equal.

3 Now we are engaged in a great civil war, testing whether that nation, or any nation so conceived and so dedicated, can long endure. We are met on a great battlefield of that war. We have come to dedicate a portion of that field as a final resting-place for those who here gave their lives that that nation might live. It is altogether fitting and proper that we should do this.

4 But, in a larger sense, we cannot dedicate—we cannot consecrate—we cannot hallow—this ground. The brave men, living and dead, who struggled here, have consecrated it far above our poor power to add or detract. The world will little note nor long remember what we say here, but it can never forget what they did here. It is for us, the living, rather, to be dedicated here to the unfinished work which they who fought here have thus far so nobly advanced. It is rather for us to be here dedicated to the great task remaining before us—that from these honored dead we take increased devotion to that cause for which they gave the last full measure of devotion; that we here highly resolve that these dead shall not have died in vain; that this nation, under God, shall have a new birth of freedom; and that government of the people, by the people, for the people, shall not perish from the earth.

COMMEMORATIVE SPEECH
by Abraham Lincoln

1

Students should be aware that the length of a speech is not as important as what is said and how it is said.

2

Lincoln keeps his introduction short and focuses the audience's attention immediately on the topic.

3

Lincoln's choice of simple words and the use of careful phrasing have helped this speech to endure as a masterpiece.

4

To build force for the word *dedicated,* Lincoln uses transition from the past meaning of the word to implied future meanings and invokes the audience to be dedicated to the challenge of preserving the nation.

GLOSSARY

A

abstain a type of vote in a parliamentary meeting that indicates that a person does not wish to support or to oppose a motion that is being voted upon (p. 540)

abstract a brief statement of the key ideas of an article in a periodical (p. 253)

abstract words words that name things, such as ideas and beliefs, that cannot be perceived by the senses (p. 295)

acquaintances people that a person knows and talks with when he or she happens to meet them (p. 140)

ad hoc committee format a type of private group discussion in which a group is formed to study a single issue or to accomplish a single task (p. 452)

adjourn a privileged motion calling for the close of a meeting (p. 528)

affirmative case in debate, the reasons and evidence presented that support a proposition (p. 494)

"after-dinner" speech the featured entertainment at a meeting or at a special occasion (p. 433)

agenda a short list of items to be discussed at a group meeting (p. 522)

amend a subsidiary motion calling for an alteration in the wording of a motion (p. 528)

amendable refers to whether any changes in a motion are allowed (p. 532)

analogy a form of reasoning by comparison (p. 91; *also,* p. 501)

anchor a performer on a television news show who may be responsible for writing and editing news stories as well as for reading them accurately on the air (p. 646)

anecdote a brief, often amusing, story (p. 231)

announcement a statement of a speaker's evaluation of a point, given to emphasize that point (p. 301)

answering machine an independent mechanism hooked up to a telephone line that responds to calls with a tape-recorded or digitally reproduced message (p. 166)

antagonist the main opponent of the protagonist in a play (p. 598)

apathetic audience an audience in which a majority of listeners have no interest in the speaker's thesis (p. 399)

appeal an incidental motion used to force the chairperson to submit a disputed ruling made by the chairperson to a vote by the entire group (p. 529)

appearance how a speaker looks to his or her audience (p. 324)

articulation the shaping of distinct speech sounds into recognizable words (p. 59; *also,* p. 328)

assertiveness the practice of exercising one's personal rights (p. 148)

association the process of tying a behavior to some vivid mental image (p. 88)

attention sustained interest (p. 271)

attitudes organizations of beliefs that cause a person to respond in particular ways (p. 122)

audience the listeners or spectators attending a presentation or performance; the people who hear a speech (p. 11; *also,* p. 225)

audio the section of a television script that shows the words to be spoken (p. 644)

audiovisual materials resources that a speaker uses to clarify or to add to the verbal presentation of a speech (p. 335; *also,* p. 368)

audition a formal tryout in which people have a chance to show their abilities (p. 606)

authoritarian leadership a style of leadership in which responsibilities are given to one leader; also called *directive* (p. 459)

B

bandwagon a propaganda technique that encourages people to act because everyone else is doing it (p. 94)

begging the question assuming the truth of a statement before it is proven (p. 90)

blocking the overall plan for actor movement in a play (p. 600)

body the portion of a speech in which the main points are developed (p. 266)

body language the use of facial expression, eye contact, gestures, posture, and movement to communicate (p. 36)

brainstorming quickly listing possibilities about a topic without stopping to evaluate each one (p. 216)

breathiness a quality of voice that results from too much unvoiced air escaping through the vocal folds as a person is speaking (p. 68)

burden of proof the obligation of the affirmative team in a debate to present arguments for changing the status quo (p. 481)

business call a telephone call made to a company or organization to request information or help, to make a complaint, or to take care of some other business matter (p. 164)

business manager the person in charge of financial matters that relate to a dramatic production (p. 612)

C

cable television a television-distribution system that brings programs over cables into people's homes (p. 633)

call for the orders of the day a privileged motion that alerts the chairperson that a scheduled event has been overlooked (p. 529)

call number a number-and-letter code assigned to a book according to the classification system used to organize books in a library (p. 250)

card catalog a collection of cards arranged by subject, author, and title, listing all the books in a particular library (p. 249)

card-stacking a propaganda technique in which only partial information is presented so as to leave an inaccurate impression (p. 94)

case the reasons and evidence on which a debate team bases its position (p. 494)

cast an ensemble of actors (p. 596)

causation argument an argument in which the conclusion is a direct result or effect of one or more particular sources or conditions (p. 500)

cause-and-effect order an order in which information is arranged to show causes or conditions and the effects or results of those causes or conditions (p. 363)

cavity a partially enclosed area (p. 57)

chairperson in a parliamentary organization, the officer who is responsible for running pleasant, efficient meetings and for protecting the rights of everyone at the meetings; also called *chair* (p. 524)

channels the means for sending communication (p. 4)

characterization the portrayal of the traits of each character in a play (p. 617)

choral speaking an oral interpretation in which several voices speak together in a group (p. 575)

chorus in Greek theater, a group of people who gave background information and commented on the action (p. 590)

chronological order a pattern for arranging details or events according to the order in which they happen in time (p. 267; *also,* p. 359)

circumflex an up-and-down inflection (p. 64)

citation a statement giving credit to the source of quoted material (p. 257; *also,* p. 434)

clarity the clearness of expression (p. 291)

cliché a figurative expression that has been used so often that it has lost its power (p. 307)

climactic order a pattern of organization in which items are arranged according to their order of importance (p. 363)

closed questions questions that can be answered with *yes* or *no* or with only one or two words (p. 174; *also,* p. 202)

close nominations an incidental motion that calls for an end to the process of nominating persons for office (p. 529)

close relationship one in which people share their deepest feelings with each other (p. 140)

comedy drama that usually has a happy ending and that is often characterized by exaggerated or eccentric behavior (p. 593)

comedy of manners a form of drama, popular in England during the Restoration (1660–1700), that satirizes social customs (p. 592)

commedia dell'arte popular Italian Renaissance comedy in which professional actors improvised their roles as stock characters in humorous, standardized situations (p. 592)

commemorative speech a speech given to mark an important event or to honor a person (p. 432)

commentator a performer on a television news show who may have responsibility for analysis of the news, often expressing his or her personal opinions about the news (p. 646)

communication the process of sharing information by using symbols to send and receive messages (p. 3)

comparative advantage method a common deductive approach for presenting information in which each reason is presented as a benefit to the audience (p. 402)

comparative advantages pattern in debate, a pattern for organizing information to demonstrate that the proposal stated in the proposition would have significant advantages over the status quo (p. 495)

comparison a statement that shows the similarities between people, places, things, events, or ideas (p. 232)

comparison-and-contrast order a pattern of organization in which items of information are arranged to show the similarities and differences between them (p. 364)

competence the state of being well qualified (p. 394)

conclusion the final portion of a speech (p. 273)

concrete words words that name things that can be perceived by one or more of the five senses (p. 295)

condense to cut, or shorten, a work (p. 569)

conflict in group discussion, a form of disagreement (p. 466)

conflicting expression a facial appearance that does not match a speaker's words or actual feelings (p. 325)

connotation the hidden meaning of a word; the feelings and associations that a word evokes (p. 32; *also,* p. 95, p. 308, p. 560)

consensus a group decision that is worded in such a way that the entire group can agree on it (p. 469)

constructive criticism criticism that is beneficial and helpful rather than disapproving (p. 150)

constructive feedback the technique of evaluating a problem to negotiate a solution (p. 177)

constructive speech in debate, the speech that builds an argument (p. 481)

context the surrounding words and sentences (p. 85)

contrast a statement that highlights the differences between two things (p. 232)

conventional accepted by a large number of people (p. 29)

conversation the informal exchange of thoughts and feelings by two or more people (p. 173)

costumer the person in charge of the performers' attire in a theatrical production (p. 611)

counterplan in debate, the negative side's presentation of a solution that differs substantially from the affirmative side's proposition (p. 497)

credibility the amount of trust and belief the speaker inspires in an audience (p. 370); the quality of being believable (p. 394)

criteria-satisfaction method an inductive method for organizing information in which a speaker first gets the audience to agree with the soundness of certain criteria and then shows how the speaker's proposal will satisfy those criteria (p. 403)

critical listening comprehending what is being said while also testing the strength of the ideas (p. 84)

critique an analysis and evaluation (p. 96)

cross-examination debate a debate format that involves two affirmative and two negative speakers who argue a proposition of policy, but that includes brief cross-examination periods in which the participants question their opponents (p. 485)

cue cards large sheets of cardboard with handwritten script or notes that television performers read on the air (p. 646)

cues the signals of nonverbal communication, such as body language, appearance, and the sound of the voice (p. 28)

cultural characteristics a person's age, religion, and national and ethnic background (p. 14)

D

deadpan an expressionless facial appearance that never changes, regardless of what is being said (p. 325)

debatable refers to whether a motion can be discussed by the group before it is voted upon (p. 532)

debate formalized public speaking in which participants prepare and present speeches on opposite sides of an issue to determine which side has the stronger arguments (p. 479; *also,* p. 11)

debate brief a complete outline of the affirmative and the negative cases in a debate (p. 508)

decoding finding the meaning of verbal and nonverbal signals (p. 16)

decree a decision dictated by a group leader (p. 468)

deductive approach a method for organizing information in which the thesis is stated first and then reasons are presented to support it (p. 401)

definition an explanation of what a word or a concept means (p. 232)

democratic leadership a style of leadership in which the leader suggests procedures but also asks the other group members for ideas; also called *supportive* (p. 459)

demographic data the defining characteristics of an audience, such as average age, educational background, and cultural heritage (p. 225)

demonstration a procedure in which a speaker performs the steps of a process in order to help listeners understand it and learn how to perform it themselves (p. 368)

denotation the dictionary meaning of a word (p. 31; *also,* p. 95; p. 560)

description a word picture of a person, place, thing, or event (p. 232)

dialect a regional or cultural variety of language differing from standard American English in pronunciation, grammar, or word choice (p. 33)

dialogue the conversation that occurs between two or more characters in a drama (p. 617); the words actually spoken by the characters in a radio play (p. 641)

diaphragm a dome-shaped muscle at the base of the lungs (p. 54)

diction the words a speaker selects and the specific ways in which the speaker uses these words (p. 331)

digital recording a technique that converts sounds or images into groups of electronic bits and stores them on a specific medium; during playback, the recorded bits are read electronically, often by means of a laser beam (p. 634)

directions the instructions for finding a particular place (p. 160)

director the person in charge of selecting a play, casting the parts, coaching the actors, and coordinating the work of the set designer and the costumer (p. 609)

disagreement a difference of opinion among two or more people (p. 177)

discussion the process of talking through a problem, such as a disagreement, by following the problem-solving method (p. 177)

discussion format a public or private plan and procedure for conducting a group discussion (p. 451)

discussion outline an outline that usually consists of questions about the topic that the group members should address (p. 456)

division of assembly an incidental motion that requires the chairperson to call for a second vote, which will preferably be conducted by a method other than the method used to conduct the first vote (p. 529)

division of question an incidental motion that requires the chairperson to divide a motion with more than one part into its various parts (p. 529)

drama an artistic form of communication in which a story dealing with human conflict is acted out on a stage (p. 589; *also,* p. 11, p. 577)

dramatic situation in a play, an occasion in which the characters face a situation that forces them to act (p. 616)

dress rehearsals the last two or three practice sessions of a play in which every aspect of the show is rehearsed just as it will be done at the time of the performance (p. 607)

dynamism the quality of being energetic and enthusiastic (p. 395)

E

electronic communication forms of mass communication, including radio, television, and video (p. 12)

electronic databases extensive collections of information on computer (p. 254)

emotional appeals statements used to arouse emotional reactions (p. 95; *also,* p. 392, p. 556)

empathy an attempt to understand how another person feels (p. 141)

emphasis the force or special attention given to a particular word or point (p. 300; *also,* p. 567)

encoding the process of turning ideas and feelings into verbal and nonverbal symbols (p. 15)

enthusiasm the strong positive feeling speakers show for their topics (p. 327)

enunciation the distinctness of the sounds a speaker makes (p. 328)

environment all features of the immediate surroundings, including color, lighting, sound, and space (p. 41)

establish the method of voting an incidental motion that calls for the chairperson to take a vote in the manner stated in the motion (p. 530)

ethical standards society's guidelines for right, just, and moral behavior (p. 395)

eulogy a commemorative speech that honors a person who has recently died (p. 432)

euphemism a word or phrase that is used in place of words that are thought to be unpleasant or distasteful (p. 308)

evidence material that establishes the soundness of a reason (p. 388; *also,* p. 492)

exaggeration a form of figurative language that emphasizes or enlarges a description of actions, emotions, or other qualities (p. 298)

example a single instance that supports or develops a statement (p. 230)

expert opinion a statement of belief about a subject by a knowledgeable person recognized as an authority on that subject (p. 229; *also,* p. 390)

expository speech a speech which gives information about a specific subject (p. 355)

extemporaneous speech a speech that is fully outlined and practiced but not memorized (p. 319; *also,* p. 434)

extend debate (See *limit or extend debate.*)

extroverted describes social individuals who are relationship-oriented and responsive to the needs of others (p. 122)

eye contact a speaker's direct visual contact with the eyes of members of an audience (p. 325)

F

fact an item of information or a statement that can be proved, or verified, by testing, by observing, or by consulting reference materials (p. 228; *also,* p. 390)

false analogy an analogy that draws invalid conclusions from weak or often far-fetched comparisons (p. 91)

false consensus a group decision that does not reflect the actual views of group members (p. 469)

false premise a premise that is untrue or distorted (p. 91)

faulty reasoning a mistake in logic (p. 90)

favorable audience an audience in which the majority of listeners agree, from slightly to completely, with the speaker's thesis (p. 399)

feedback a return message (p. 4)

fiction writing drawn from the writer's imagination (p. 554)

figurative comparison a statement that imaginatively shows similarities between things that are essentially not alike (p. 232)

figurative language words and phrases that are not literally true, but that create a fresh, lively understanding of an idea (p. 296)

figures of speech words and phrases that compare two things that are basically very dissimilar (p. 574)

fixed-interval method a method of surveying in which the information-seeker asks questions of a specific proportion of people who pass by (p. 245)

floor plan a diagram that shows the positions of walls, entrances, and furnishings on a stage (p. 611)

flow sheet a record of the progress of arguments in a debate (p. 505)

follow-up questions questions that relate to the subject matter of an earlier question (p. 175; *also,* p. 202)

formal outline a short skeleton of a speech written in complete sentences (p. 275)

formal settings communication situations that people can prepare for ahead of time, such as interviews, group discussions, and debates (p. 9)

formal theater a type of drama in which the actors follow a script for the dialogue and the actions of a play (p. 589)

format a particular combination of content and style at a radio station (p. 631)

forum format a type of public group discussion in which a panel or a symposium is opened up to questions or comments from the audience (p. 451)

free-form format a type of private group discussion in which group members discuss a topic at will in no particular order (p. 452)

free verse a form of poetry that uses the rhythms of natural speech (p. 572)

fricatives the consonant sounds that make a friction-like noise (p. 61)

friendships mutually satisfying relationships (p. 140)

G

generalizations general conclusions or opinions drawn from particular observations (p. 90; *also,* p. 499)

generalize in language learning, to apply a rule of language to all cases (p. 30)

general purpose the overall intent of a speech (p. 220)

general words words that refer to an entire category of items (p. 294)

germane a requirement in parliamentary procedure that an amendment must in some way relate to the issue of the original motion (p. 537)

glides the sounds that result from the gliding movements of the articulators (p. 61)

goal the speaker's purpose for giving a speech (p. 84)

goals aims that a person hopes to achieve or accomplish through communication (p. 123)

goodwill an audience's respect or positive feeling for a speaker as a person (p. 271)

graduation speech a formal address made at a commencement ceremony in honor of the occasion (p. 427)

grammar the rules and conventions for speaking and writing a language, such as English (p. 331)

group discussion a face-to-face communication of a small number of people who meet for a specific purpose, such as to arrive at a decision, to brainstorm ideas, to share information, or to solve a problem (p. 449; *also,* p. 10)

H

halo effect based on observing a person's behavior in a single situation; judgment of a person's other characteristics without further investigation (p. 128)

hand-held microphone a microphone that is meant to be held in the hand (p. 334)

harshness a quality of voice characterized by an unpleasant, grating sound that may also be hard or metallic (p. 68)

hasty generalizations conclusions or opinions that are drawn from very few observations or that ignore exceptions (p. 90)

hearing the ability to detect sounds (p. 81)

heckler a person who tries purposely to disturb a speaker (p. 343)

hierarchy of needs developed by Abraham Maslow, a ranking of five general categories of needs: physiological, safety, love, esteem, and self-actualization (p. 118)

high-definition television (HDTV) a video technology that creates a sharper image due to its higher resolution (p. 634)

hoarseness a quality of voice characterized by a thickness of sound or by a muffled or rasping sound (p. 69)

hostile audience an audience in which the majority of the listeners oppose the speaker's thesis (p. 400)

house manager the person in charge of the theater ushers, house lighting, air conditioning, heating, and ventilation (p. 612)

hyperbole (See *exaggeration.*)

I

illustration a detailed example (p. 230)

"I" message a statement that begins with "I" and that expresses honestly how a person feels as a result of another person's behavior (p. 178)

impromptu speech a speech given on the spur of the moment with no preparation (p. 318; *also,* p. 436)

improvisation a form of drama that is spontaneous rather than planned (p. 616)

incidental motions in a parliamentary meeting, proposals that relate to questions of procedure arising out of the discussion (p. 529)

individual characteristics a person's personality, interests, and aspirations (p. 14)

inductive approach a method for organizing information that begins with the speaker's reasons and leads up to the thesis (p. 403)

inflection the upward or downward glide of pitch as a person speaks (p. 63)

informal communication giving and receiving messages in casual, person-to-person interactions (p. 159)

informal settings the casual, unstructured situations in which most communication occurs (p. 9)

informal theater a type of drama in which the actors rely on their imaginations to generate the story, dialogue, and movement (p. 589)

information network a single machine in the home connected by fiber-optic cables to a nationwide or worldwide information network (p. 634)

informative interview an interview in which the interviewer gathers information about a topic from a knowledgeable, experienced person (p. 187)

informative speech a speech that provides information to an audience (p. 355)

insight important ideas or new perceptions of life (p. 556)

intensity the depth of feeling a performer has for a part (p. 603)

interactive television a device allowing a viewer to interact with and respond to what is seen on the television screen (p. 634)

interest the involvement or concern an audience shows about a topic (p. 271)

interference anything that gets in the way of clear communication (p. 17)

interlibrary loan services the use of computers to access other libraries' on-line catalogs in order to locate and request specific reference materials (p. 254)

interpersonal communication the communication that occurs between two or more people (p. 3; *also,* p. 139)

interpretation the process of explaining the information that has been selected and organized (p. 111)

interview a formal meeting, usually face to face, in which people obtain information by asking questions (p. 187; *also,* p. 10, p. 244)

interviewee the person who responds to the interviewer's questions (p. 187)

interviewer the person who conducts an interview by asking questions (p. 187)

intimate space the distance, usually about eighteen inches, at which people feel comfortable communicating with family members and close friends (p. 42)

intrapersonal communication self-talk (p. 109)

introduction the beginning of a speech (p. 270); the presentation of one person to another or to a group (p. 170)

introverted describes withdrawn individuals who may prefer to keep to themselves rather than to seek involvement with others through social interaction (p. 122)

irony the use of words to imply something different from, perhaps even the opposite of, what is actually meant (p. 299)

irrelevant evidence information that has nothing to do with the argument being made (p. 92)

jargon language that is used by people within a particular group or field, but is not necessarily understood by those outside the group (p. 307; *also,* p. 33)

job interview an interview in which a person responsible for hiring employees reviews an applicant's qualifications for a job (p. 187)

key the average pitch at which a person speaks (p. 62)

key issues the points of disagreement in a debate (p. 488)

laissez-faire leadership a style of leadership in which responsibilities are shared by all members of the group; also called *nondirective* (p. 459)

larynx the voice box (p. 54)

lavaliere or clip-on microphone a small portable microphone that hangs on a cord around the neck or that is clipped to an article of clothing (p. 334)

lay on the table a subsidiary motion that calls for a temporary postponement of action until someone makes a motion to remove the original motion from the table (p. 528)

leadership the ability to guide a group toward its goal (p. 459)

leading question a question that suggests the answer that is expected or desired (p. 202)

lectern (See *speaker's stand.*)

levels of usage the different kinds of language used for various audiences and purposes (p. 289)

limit or extend debate a subsidiary motion that calls for setting a time limit on individual speeches or for extending the debate to allow more complete discussion of the issue (p. 528)

Lincoln-Douglas debate a form of debate in which only one affirmative and one negative speaker argue a proposition of value (p. 486)

listening getting meaning from sounds that are heard (p. 81)

literal comparison a statement that shows the real similarities between things that are essentially alike (p. 232)

literature writing as an art form that expresses ideas of permanent or universal interest and that is characterized by excellence of form and expression (p. 554)

live television programming that is transmitted as it occurs (p. 633)

loaded words words that evoke very strong positive or negative attitudes toward a person, group, or idea (p. 95)

logical reasoning the use of reasons supported by evidence to build an argument (p. 387)

loudness (See *volume.*)

M

main ideas the speaker's most important points (p. 84)

main motions in a parliamentary meeting, proposals that set forth new items of business to be considered (p. 527)

main points the major ideas of a speech under which the supporting information is organized (p. 266)

majority in voting, the side that wins because over half of the voters support that position (p. 469)

makeup artist the person in a dramatic production responsible for using the special techniques needed for theatrical makeup (p. 612)

manipulation the shrewd or devious management of facts for one's own purposes (p. 396)

manuscript speech a speech that is written out completely and read to an audience (p. 318)

masking adopting facial expressions normally associated with one feeling to disguise other, true feelings (p. 36)

mass media practical methods for communicating with a mass, or large group, of people, including newspapers, magazines, films, billboards, radio, and television (p. 630)

media center a term for today's library, so called because it holds such a wide variety of information sources (p. 248)

melody the variations in pitch that help to give expression to a person's voice (p. 63)

memorized speech a speech that is written out completely and recited word for word from memory (p. 319)

message ideas and feelings that make up the content of communication (p. 4; *also,* p. 27)

metaphor a comparison between essentially unlike things without using the words *like* or *as* (p. 297)

microfiche a sheet of film that bears the reduced-scale record of printed or graphic material (p. 254)

microfilm a roll or reel of film that bears the reduced-scale record of printed or graphic material (p. 254)

microform catalog a microfilm or microfiche machine that contains the library's entire listing of books (p. 249)

microforms various types of photographic film bearing the reduced-scale record of printed or graphic material (p. 254)

microphone an electronic device for broadcasting sound (p. 333)

minutes the written and official record of a meeting's proceedings (p. 521)

miracle plays medieval plays that dramatized events from the Bible (p. 591)

misunderstanding a lack of clear communication (p. 144)

mnemonic devices rhymes, acronyms, or other wordplay that are used to help people remember information (p. 88; *also,* p. 368)

moderated free-form format a type of private group discussion in which a moderator, or leader, introduces the discussion topic and recognizes individuals to speak (p. 452)

modern drama the period of drama, beginning late in the nineteenth century, noted for its use of realism (p. 593)

monologue an extended speech by one character (p. 617)

monotone a melody pattern that consists of only one tone (p. 63)

Monroe motivated sequence an inductive method for presenting information that includes five steps: drawing attention to a problem, showing a need for action, outlining a plan to satisfy that need, visualizing benefits, and suggesting a specific action (p. 404)

mood the emotional tone that a piece of literature exhibits (p. 562)

morality plays medieval plays that presented allegorical stories in which characters personified religious or moral abstractions (p. 591)

motion a proposal for action made by a member of a parliamentary organization (p. 527)

motives the sources of behavior (p. 118)

mystery plays medieval plays that presented events from saints' lives (p. 591)

N

name-calling labeling intended to arouse powerful negative feelings (p. 94)

narration an account of the details of a story or an event; the words spoken by a narrator or announcer (p. 642)

narrator in a radio drama, an announcer who introduces the scenes, provides transitions, and concludes the program (p. 642)

nasal cavity the nose (p. 58)

nasality a quality of voice characterized by too much nasal resonance of all vocal sounds (p. 67)

nasals sounds resonated in the nasal cavity (p. 61)

negative case in debate, the reasons and evidence that refute the affirmative case, defend the status quo, or present a counterplan (p. 496)

negative method an inductive method for organizing information in which the speaker shows that no option other than the one the speaker proposes is acceptable (p. 404)

neutral audience an audience in which the majority of the listeners have not reached a decision about a speaker's thesis (p. 399)

neutral question a question that promotes objectivity by giving no hint of what particular answer a person wants (p. 202)

nonfiction prose that tells about real people and real events (p. 554)

nonverbal clues indicators of the social meaning of communication, such as eye contact, posture, and facial expression (p. 86)

nonverbal language communication without words (p. 28)

nonverbal symbols any means used to communicate without words, including gestures, sounds, facial expressions, and body movements (p. 4)

note cards cards used to record information (or a summary of it) and its source (p. 256)

O

object to consideration an incidental motion that allows the group to dismiss a main motion that is irrelevant, inappropriate, or otherwise undesirable (p. 529)

occasion the time, the place, and all of the other conditions that define the setting in which a person delivers a speech (p. 226)

on-line catalog a computerized card catalog (p. 249)

open questions questions that must be answered with explanations (p. 174; *also,* p. 202)

opinion a personal belief or attitude (p. 229)

optimum pitch the pitch at which a person speaks with the least strain and with the best resonance (p. 62)

oral cavity the mouth (p. 58)

oral interpretation the presentation of a work of literature to a group of listeners in order to express the meaning contained in the literary work (p. 554)

oral reading a performing art in which literature is read aloud and interpreted for an audience (p. 11)

order of names the order in which people are presented to each other (p. 171)

order of precedence in parliamentary meeting, the order in which motions must be voted or acted upon (p. 531)

P

panel format a type of public group discussion in which a group of experts discusses a topic to provide information and opinions that another group can use to reach a decision or to find a solution (p. 451)

pantomime dramatic communication performed entirely without words (p. 613)

paralanguage a type of nonverbal communication that uses voice variation and non-word sounds to accompany a verbal message (p. 40)

parallelism the repetition of words, phrases, or sentences to emphasize an idea or a series of ideas (p. 301)

paraphrasing using one's own words to restate what another person has said (p. 145; *also,* p. 175, p. 203)

parliamentary inquiry an incidental motion made to request information about whether making a motion would be in order (p. 529)

parliamentary procedure a set of rules for conducting orderly meetings (p. 519; *also,* p. 11)

partial demonstration a demonstration in which either some of the parts are already completed or the size of items is exaggerated so the audience can see them clearly (p. 369)

pastoral plays Renaissance plays that presented love stories in idealized woodland settings (p. 592)

pay-cable television a regular subscription service that brings a variety of programs into the home on one channel in exchange for a monthly fee (p. 633)

pay television a type of cable television in which people pay a fee to watch a particular program (p. 633)

perception an active process of giving meaning to information a person receives from the senses (p. 110)

perception check a verbal response stating one person's understanding of someone else's nonverbal behavior (p. 36; *also,* p. 130)

personal reference a speech introduction in which the speaker relates the speech topic directly to the audience's experience (p. 272)

personal space the distance, from eighteen inches to four feet, at which conversations occur between acquaintances (p. 43)

persuasion the attempt to convince others to do something or to change a belief of their own free will (p. 92)

persuasive speech a speech that establishes a fact, changes a belief, or moves an audience to act on a policy (p. 383)

pharyngeal cavity the throat (p. 58)

physical noise any sound that prevents a person from being heard (p. 17)

pitch the highness or lowness of a sound (p. 62)

plagiarism the presentation of another person's words or ideas as if they were the speaker's own (p. 256)

plosives the consonant sounds that form a small explosion when spoken (p. 61)

poetry compressed, highly charged language that appeals to emotions and the imagination, usually arranged in lines with a regular rhythm and often with a definite rhyme scheme (p. 571)

point of order an incidental motion that calls attention to a violation of parliamentary procedure (p. 530)

point of view refers to who is telling the story (p. 568)

poise the quality of looking confident and prepared to handle any problem (p. 194)

postpone indefinitely a subsidiary motion that calls for postponement of discussion for that session and thus prevents the main motion from coming to a vote (p. 528)

postpone to a definite time a subsidiary motion that calls for a postponement of action until a particular time set by the person making the motion (p. 528)

practical communication a type of informal communication which is useful, direct, and goal oriented (p. 159)

precise words words that express a person's thoughts or feelings accurately or exactly (p. 293)

prejudice a prejudgment or bias; a belief that may not be grounded in facts (p. 83)

premise in an argument, a stated or implied starting point that is assumed to be true (p. 91)

prerecorded describes television programming that is recorded earlier for later broadcast (p. 633)

previous question a subsidiary motion that calls for a vote to stop discussion on a motion (p. 528)

***prima facie* case** a case that contains enough reasons and evidence to win a debate if the other side presented no argument (p. 494)

primary amendment an amendment of a main motion (p. 537)

primary source someone who provides information from direct experience (p. 200)

private self the aspects of a person that are most true to his or her self-concept (p. 124; *also,* p. 146)

privileged motions in a parliamentary meeting, proposals that concern the running of the meeting itself (p. 528)

problem-solution method a deductive approach for presenting information in which the speaker first presents the problem and then offers at least one possible solution for that problem (p. 402)

problem-solution pattern in debate, a pattern for organizing information to prove that a significant problem exists, that adopting the proposal will help solve the problem, and that adopting the proposal is the best way to solve the problem; also called *need-plan pattern* (p. 495)

problem-solving method a four-part method that involves identifying the problem, determining its nature and causes, talking about possible ways to solve the problem, and selecting the best way (p. 177)

process speech an informative speech that explains how to do something, how to make something, or how something works; also called a *how-to speech* (p. 355)

producer the head administrator of a dramatic production, responsible for bringing together the script, the theater, the director, and, in the case of professional theater, the financing for a show (p. 609)

progressive format a type of private group discussion in which a large group of people is divided into smaller groups, each of which discusses a different aspect of the topic (p. 452)

pronunciation the combining of precisely articulated speech sounds into distinct words (p. 59; *also,* p. 328)

proof in debate, the reasons and evidence given to answer the questions in the stock issues (p. 490)

propaganda a form of persuasion that deliberately discourages people from thinking for themselves (p. 92)

property crew head the person responsible for collecting properties (or "props") and making them available during both rehearsals and performances (p. 612)

proposition in debate, a statement that asserts a fact, makes a value judgment, or recommends a policy (p. 480)

propositions of fact in debate, statements about what has happened, is happening, or will happen (p. 482)

propositions of policy in debate, statements that focus on specific plans of action (p. 483)

propositions of value in debate, statements that express judgments about the relative merit of a person, place, or thing (p. 483)

prose the normal form of written or spoken language; any type of speech or writing that is not poetry (p. 568)

protagonist the main character in a play (p. 598)

psychological noise the thoughts and feelings that distract people from listening to what is said (p. 17)

public self the aspects of a person that the person chooses to share with everyone (p. 124; *also,* p. 146)

public service announcement (PSA) a brief persuasive or informative message presented on radio and television (p. 647)

public space the distance, beyond twelve feet between speaker and audience, at which such types of communication as public speeches or oral readings take place (p. 44)

public speaking a formal speaking situation in which one person addresses an audience of many individuals to entertain, inform, or persuade them (p. 11)

purpose what a speaker intends to achieve in a speech (p. 220)

Q

quality the tone of a person's voice (p. 67)

question of belief in persuasion, a statement that focuses on what is right or wrong, good or bad, best or worst, moral or immoral (p. 384)

question of fact in persuasion, a statement that focuses on what is either true or false (p. 384); a discussion question that asks for evidence that can be gathered from observation, experimentation, or authoritative sources to determine what is true (p. 455)

question of policy in persuasion, a statement that focuses on a particular action (p. 384); a discussion question that asks what action, if any, should be taken (p. 455)

question of privilege a privileged motion that calls for immediate action on such things as ventilation, heating, lighting, and disturbances (p. 528)

question of value a discussion question that asks for an evaluation of one or more persons, places, things, or ideas (p. 455)

quorum the minimum number of members that must be present for a group to conduct business (p. 522)

quotation a statement of someone's exact words (p. 233)

R

radio drama a radio presentation in which actors present an oral performance of a play or radio script (p. 629)

radio talk show a radio presentation in which a moderator and one or more guests discuss a topic (p. 629)

random sample a sample in which, in theory, every member of a group has an equal chance of being selected (p. 245)

range the spread between the lowest and the highest notes that a person can speak comfortably (p. 63)

rate the speed at which a person talks (p. 66) or reads a selection aloud (p. 567)

reader's theater a form of oral interpretation in which a group of people read and interpret a play (p. 580)

reason a statement that explains or justifies a speaker's thesis or proposition (p. 387; *also* p. 491)

rebuttal in debate, rebuilding an argument after it has been attacked (p. 498)

rebuttal speech in debate, the speech that rebuilds an argument (p. 481)

receiver the person who receives a message (p. 4)

recess a privileged motion that calls for a short break during a meeting (p. 528)

recommendation a short statement that tells an audience the specific behavior the speaker wants them to follow (p. 274)

reconsider a renewal motion that calls for discussion of a motion that has already been passed (p. 530)

recorder (See *secretary.*)

reference works publications containing useful facts and information (p. 250)

refer to a committee a subsidiary motion that calls for shifting discussion of the matter at hand to a smaller group meeting at some other time (p. 528)

refutation in debate, an attack on the argument of the opposition (p. 498)

rehearsals practice sessions (p. 607; *also,* p. 279)

reliable source a person who can be depended on to give accurate information (p. 200)

renewal motions in a parliamentary meeting, proposals that get discussion reopened on decisions that have already been made (p. 530)

reopen nominations an incidental motion made to allow more nominations to be made after nominations have been closed (p. 530)

repetition the use of the same word, phrase, or sentence each time a new point is raised (p. 84); for emphasis, saying something more than once (p. 300); the repeating of a sentence or a phrase that runs like a refrain throughout a speech (p. 422); repeated sounds (p. 573)

request letter a letter that asks for information about a topic (p. 246)

rescind a renewal motion that calls for the cancellation of action taken on a previous motion (p. 530)

resolution the sharpness of a video image, due to the number of picture cells, or pixels (p. 634)

resonance the reinforcement of sound produced by vibration (p. 56)

resonators the bones of the chest, neck, and head and the cavities of the throat, nose, and mouth, which reinforce sound (p. 56)

respect a feeling of high regard, honor, or esteem that a person has for others (p. 143)

restatement the repetition of an idea using different words (p. 300)

résumé a brief account of an applicant's educational background and employment experience (p. 189)

rhetorical question a question that is not meant to be answered but that is asked only for effect (p. 305)

rhythm a rise and fall of the voice created by the flow of stressed and unstressed syllables (p. 571)

role a pattern of behavior that characterizes a person in a given context or situation (p. 124)

roll-call vote a vote in which the secretary calls out each member's name and records his or her response (p. 540)

round-table format a type of private group discussion in which each member of a group discussion gives a brief report on some aspect of a topic and then the group as a whole discusses the separate reports (p. 452)

S

sarcasm cutting or bitter irony (p. 299)

school interview an interview in which an admissions officer interviews an applicant for schooling after high school graduation (p. 187)

second an indication that a person other than the person making a motion is willing to have the group consider the motion (p. 532)

secondary amendment an amendment of a primary amendment (p. 537)

secondary source someone or something that provides information that originated with other people (p. 200)

secretary also called a *recorder,* a member of a discussion group who records what happened in the discussion (p. 462); the major recording officer and keeper of records in a parliamentary organization (p. 525)

self-actualization the drive a person has to take full advantage of his or her talents and abilities (p. 119)

self-concept a collection of perceptions about every aspect of a person's being (p. 114)

semantic noise interference caused by words that trigger strong negative feelings against the speaker or the content of the speech (p. 18)

sender the person who sends a message (p. 4)

sensory images words and phrases that evoke mental pictures by appealing to the senses—sight, hearing, smell, taste, or touch (p. 574)

sensory words words that appeal to one or more of the five senses (p. 296)

set designer the person responsible for designing all visual elements, including stage sets and lighting, that will be used in a production (p. 610)

signal words words that indicate that a list, contrast, or connection is about to be made (p. 85)

sign argument an argument that draws a conclusion based on certain signs or indicators (p. 502)

simile a comparison of two essentially unlike things using the words *like* or *as* (p. 297)

simple majority a majority that consists of at least one more than half the number of people voting (p. 520)

simple words familiar words, usually of one or two syllables (p. 292)

sincerity the quality of being genuine (p. 394)

slang highly informal language that is formed by creating new words or giving common words new meanings (p. 308; *also,* p. 33)

social call a telephone call made for personal reasons (p. 162)

social communication a type of informal communication which is friendly, cordial, and enjoyable (p. 159)

social space the distance, from four to twelve feet, at which interviews and formal conversations occur (p. 43)

sociological characteristics a person's affiliations, educational background, and occupation (p. 14)

sound bites one- or two-second statements in broadcast news (p. 636)

spatial order a pattern of organization in which items are arranged according to their position in space (p. 268; *also,* p. 362)

speaker in fiction, the voice of a character or a role the author has assumed (p. 560)

speaker's stand a piece of furniture designed to hold a speaker's notes or manuscript (p. 332)

special-occasion speech a speech in which the occasion itself sets the tone and determines the content of the speech (p. 417)

specific purpose the specific goal of a speech, stated in a complete sentence (p. 221)

specific words words that identify items within a category (p. 294)

speech of acceptance a speech in which the recipient of an honor, award, or gift expresses appreciation for the honor (p. 430)

speech of introduction a formal speech for the purpose of gaining the audience's attention and setting the stage for the speaker or program that follows (p. 428)

speech of presentation a speech given to present an honor, award, or gift and to honor the person being recognized (p. 429)

stage fright the nervousness that speakers feel before and during the presentation of their speeches (p. 321)

stage manager the person who is in charge of the entire backstage and attempts to ensure that the performance follows the exact pattern the director has set in rehearsals (p. 610)

standard American English language that follows the rules and guidelines found in grammar and composition books (p. 33; *also,* p. 289)

standing committee format a type of private group discussion in which a small group of people is asked to study problems that fall within their scope of duties or functions and then to make recommendations to the organization of which they are a part (p. 452)

standing microphone a microphone attached to a stand or lectern (p. 333)

startling statement in a speech introduction, a brief statement that surprises the audience and thus catches their attention (p. 272)

statement-of-reasons method the classic deductive method for presenting information in which the thesis is stated directly, followed by reasons supporting it (p. 401)

statistics numerical facts (p. 231)

status quo the existing state of affairs (p. 481)

step an abrupt change in pitch (p. 64)

stereotype a biased belief about a whole group of people based on insufficient or irrelevant evidence (p. 94)

stereotyping assigning characteristics to a person solely on the basis of the person's membership in a certain group (p. 129)

stirring ending a speech conclusion that helps intensify the emotion, or feeling, that the speaker wants the audience to experience (p. 274)

stock issues in debate, a formula of set questions that are adapted to a particular debate topic (p. 488)

storyboard a layout that identifies the pictures, video, and audio cues that accompany the written script for a video production (p. 648)

straight refutation in debate, a type of organization in which the entire negative case is a denial of each affirmative argument stated (p. 496)

subject area a general category (p. 216)

sublanguage a subsystem of an established language (p. 33)

subsidiary motions in a parliamentary meeting, proposals that allow members to change or dispose of a main motion being discussed (p. 528)

summary a short restatement of key information (p. 274)

supporting details the examples, facts, statistics, reasons, anecdotes, or expert testimony that a speaker uses to back up main ideas (p. 85)

survey a method of gathering information by questioning people selected at random or from a predetermined list (p. 244)

suspend the rules an incidental motion that calls for suspension, during the current meeting, of any standing rule that the organization may have (p. 530)

symbol something that stands for something else (p. 29)

symposium format a type of public discussion in which several people present short, prepared speeches on the same topic and then discuss among themselves the ideas presented in the speeches (p. 451)

system a group of elements that work together (p. 29)

take from the table a renewal motion that calls for reopening discussion of a motion that had earlier been laid on the table by a subsidiary motion (p. 530)

talent the television performers who appear on camera (p. 646)

technical director the person in charge of constructing sets, positioning and operating lights, managing the curtain, and striking the set when the production is over (p. 610)

technical quality in literature, refers to being well constructed (p. 558)

telemarketing a sales method that uses telephone calls to sell services or products (p. 165)

teleprompter a mechanical device that scrolls the script for a television performer to read (p. 646)

television news story a television presentation in which a reporter or newscaster uses videotape to illustrate a current news event (p. 629)

testimonials statements attesting to the worth of someone or something (p. 389)

testimonial speech a commemorative speech that honors a living person (p. 432)

theater of the absurd a contemporary style of drama in which life is viewed as meaningless and people's strivings as absurd (p. 593)

thesis statement a complete sentence that expresses the speaker's most important idea, or key point, about a topic (p. 223)

thespian an actor (p. 590)

timing the controlled pacing of a speech (p. 341)

tone the speaker's attitude or feeling toward a subject and an audience (p. 302; *also,* p. 419)

topic a specific category within a subject area (p. 216)

topicality in an extemporaneous speech competition, relating everything directly to the topic the speaker has chosen (p. 435)

topical order a pattern of organization in which a topic is broken down into parts that are then arranged in an order determined by the speaker (p. 268; *also,* p. 362)

trachea the windpipe (p. 54)

traditional debate a debate format that involves two affirmative speakers and two negative speakers who argue a proposition of policy; also called *formal debate* (p. 485)

tragedy drama that usually has a sad or disastrous ending and that tells a story of serious and important events in which the main character comes to an unhappy end (p. 593)

transfer a propaganda method that builds a connection between things that are not logically connected (p. 93)

transitional devices bridges between ideas (p. 275)

trust a feeling that a person can rely on someone else (p. 142)

understatement the opposite of exaggeration; the statement of an idea, an event, or a thing in terms that intentionally diminish or lessen its importance (p. 299)

unity the organization of a speech so that all its parts fit together to make a whole and all of the information relates to the specific purpose (p. 270)

universal appeal relevance, or relationship, to the experience of all human beings (p. 555)

verbal language a system of spoken and written words (p. 28)

verbal symbols words (p. 4)

vertical file a collection of pamphlets, photographs, and clippings kept in vertical filing cabinets in some libraries (p. 255)

vice-chairperson an officer of a parliamentary organization who assumes the duties of the chair when the chair is unable to do so (p. 525)

video the section of a television script that describes the video footage and sound effects (p. 644)

visual resources materials that an audience can see, such as slides, pictures, transparencies, videotapes, or films (p. 336)

vividness the quality of being vigorous, exciting, or full of life (p. 296)

vocal folds the muscles of the larynx; also called *vocal cords* (p. 54)

vocalized pauses the meaningless speech sounds that speakers use to fill time (p. 327)

voiced describes sounds made by vibrations of the vocal folds (p. 61)

voiceless describes sounds made when the vocal folds are open so that air breathed out does not vibrate them (p. 61)

voice mail an electronic system that provides the caller with a number of options from which to select, usually by using numbers on a touch-tone telephone pad (p. 166)

voice-over a voice played without an accompanying picture of the speaker, usually over a film of some scene (p. 644)

volume the intensity of sound (p. 65)

vote a method for reaching a group decision in which the opinion held by the majority of the members of a group is adopted as the decision of the entire group (p. 468)

withdraw a motion an incidental motion that gives the person who made the motion permission to remove it from consideration (p. 530)

"you" message a statement that expresses a judgment of another person's actions (p. 178)

INDEX

D

Q

R

S

ACKNOWLEDGMENTS

For permission to reprint copyrighted material, grateful acknowledgment is made to the following sources:

Elizabeth Barnett, Literary Executor: From "Recuerdo" by Edna St. Vincent Millay from *Collected Poems,* HarperCollins. Copyright 1922, 1950 by Edna St. Vincent Millay.

Cambridge University Press: From "The Little Dog" from *Mountains and Molehills* by Frances Cornford. Published by Cambridge University Press, 1934.

Joan Daves Agency as representative of the Heirs of the Estate of Martin Luther King, Jr.: Speech and excerpt from speech "I Have a Dream" by Dr. Martin Luther King, Jr. Copyright © 1963 by Dr. Martin Luther King, Jr.; copyright renewed © 1991 by Coretta Scott King.

Delacorte Press, a division of Bantam Doubleday Dell Publishing Group, Inc.: "The Jacket" from *Small Faces* by Gary Soto. Copyright © 1986 by Gary Soto.

Ronald L. Dodson, Theater/Forensic Director, Westlake High School, Austin, Texas: "The Green Mountain Boys" speech by W. Benson Chiles.

Monica L. Haakonsen: "The Half-Time Show" by Monica Seebohm.

Harcourt Brace & Company: From "The Jilting of Granny Weatherall" from *Flowering Judas and Other Stories* by Katherine Anne Porter. Copyright 1930, renewed 1958 by Katherine Anne Porter.

Harvard University Press and the Trustees of Amherst College: "I Never Saw a Moor" from *The Poems of Emily Dickinson,* edited by Thomas H. Johnson, Cambridge, Massachusetts: The Belknap Press of Harvard University Press. Copyright 1951, © 1955, 1979, 1983 by the President and Fellows of Harvard College.

Henry Holt and Co., Inc.: "Blue-Butterfly Day" from *The Poetry of Robert Frost,* edited by Edward Connery Lathem. Copyright 1923, © 1969 by Holt, Rinehart and Winston; copyright 1951 by Robert Frost.

Alfred A. Knopf, Inc.: From "Dreams" from *The Dream Keeper and Other Poems* by Langston Hughes. Copyright 1932 by Alfred A. Knopf, Inc.; copyright renewed © 1960 by Langston Hughes.

Melodie Lancaster: "The Future We Predict Isn't Inevitable: Reframing Our Success in the Modern World" by Melodie Lancaster, delivered to the Symposium for the Houston Council, American Business Womens' Association, Houston, Texas, February 29, 1992.

National Forensics League: "Fat Chance" by Jennifer Cober, Barbe High School, Louisiana. "With Rest, You Get Noise" by Brian Eanes, Churchill High School, San Antonio, Texas.

The Nobel Foundation: "Nobel Peace Prize Acceptance Speech" by Elie Wiesel. Copyright © 1986 by The Nobel Foundation.

Random House, Inc.: From "Woman Work" from *And Still I Rise* by Maya Angelou. Copyright © 1978 by Maya Angelou. From *Antigone* by Jean Anouilh, translated by Lewis Galantiere. Copyright 1946 by Random House, Inc.; copyright renewed © 1974 by Lewis Galantiere. From *The Diary of Anne Frank* by Albert Hackett and Frances Goodrich. Copyright 1954, 1956 as an unpublished work. Copyright © 1956 by Albert Hackett, Frances Goodrich Hackett and Otto Frank.

Third Woman Press: "Abuelito Who" from *My Wicked, Wicked Ways* by Sandra Cisneros. Copyright © 1987 by Third Woman Press.

U. S. News & World Report, Inc.: From "The First Defect Is Among the Judges Themselves," Interview with William G. Long, Superior Court Judge, King County (Seattle), Washington from "How Much Crime Can America Take?", Interviews with Law-Enforcement Officials from *U. S. News & World Report,* April 20, 1964. Copyright © 1964 by U. S. News & World Report, Inc.

The H. W. Wilson Company: "Introduction of Gertrude Lawrence to the New York Advertising Club" by G. Lynn Sumner from *I Am Happy to Present: A Book of Introductions,* compiled by Guy R. Lyle and Kevin Guingah. Copyright © 1953, 1968 by The H. W. Wilson Company. Entries from "Moize, Elizabeth A." through "Moldings (Architecture)" from *Readers' Guide to Periodical Literature,* 1990, p. 1238. Copyright © 1990 by The H. W. Wilson Company.

Wylie, Aitken & Stone, Inc.: "The Time We Climbed Snake Mountain" by Leslie M. Silko.

PHOTO CREDITS

Abbreviations used: (t) top, (c) center, (b) bottom, (l) left, (r) right, (bkgrd) background, (frgrd) foreground.

COVER: HRW Photo by Michelle Bridwell.

TABLE OF CONTENTS: Page iv (r), Bob Daemmrich/Image Works; v(t), Steve Satushek/The Image Bank; vi(t), David E. Kennedy/TexaStock; vi(b) HRW Photo by Michelle Bridwell; vii(t), James Sugar/Black Star; viii(t), David Young-Wolff/PhotoEdit; viii(b), HRW Photo by Michelle Bridwell; ix(b), Jeffrey Sylvester/FPG International; x(b), David R. Frazier Photolibrary; xi(b), David Young-Wolff/PhotoEdit; xii(l), mga/Photri, Inc.; xii(r), Ellis Herwig/Picture Cube, xiii, Robert Daemmrich/Stock Boston; xiv(t), HRW Photo by Eric Beggs; xiv(b), HRW Photo by Michelle Bridwell; xv, Bob Daemmrich/Stock Boston; xvi(b), Mike Wilson/FPG International; xvii, Comstock; xviii(b), David E. Kennedy/TexaStock; xviv, mga/Photri, Inc.; xxi(l), Garry Gay/The Image Bank; xxii(t), HRW Photo by Michelle Bridwell; xxii(b), Paul Light/Lightwave.

UNIT 1 OPENER: Page xxii(tl), T. Rosenthal/Superstock; xxii(tr), Sullivan/TexaStock; xxii(bkgrd), Craig Tuttle/Stock Market; xxii-l(frgrd), Anthony Edgeworth/The Stock Market; l(t), Elizabeth Crews/Stock Boston; l(cr), Oscar Palmquist/Lightwave.

CHAPTER 1: Page 2(c), HRW Photo by Michelle Bridwell; 2(bl), Daemmrich/The Image Works; (3), David Young-Wolff/PhotoEdit; 5(t), HRW Photo by Daniel Schaefer; 7(b), Tony Freeman/PhotoEdit; 10(t), Winter/Image Works; 10(b), Tony Freeman/PhotoEdit; 11(tr), Bob Daemmrich/Image Works; 11(b), Bob Daemmrich/Image Works; 12(t), Will & Deni McIntyre/Allstock; 12(b), Martin Miller/Positive Images; 15(t), 15(b), Lisa Law/Image Works; 16(bl), David Young-Wolff/PhotoEdit; 16(br), Robert Kristofik/Image Bank; 20(br), David Young-Wolff/PhotoEdit; 21(b), Robert E. Daemmrich/Tony Stone Worldwide; 23(c), ©Michael Sullivan/TexaStock; 23(tr), David Young-Wolff/PhotoEdit; 23(br), Stock Boston; 25(l), Richard Hutchings/PhotoEdit; 25(r), Williamson-Edwards Concepts/Image Bank.

CHAPTER 2: Page 26(tl), Steve Satushek/The Image Bank; 26(tr), HRW Photo by Michelle Bridwell; 26(c) Mary Kate Denny/PhotoEdit; 26(bl), HRW Photo by Stock Editions; 29(t), North Wind Picture Archives; 31(t), HRW Photo by Kevin Vandivier; 35(tr), Richard Hutchings/PhotoEdit; 38(b), Janeart Ltd/The Image Bank; 39(b), W.B. Spunbarg/PhotoEdit; 40(t), The Image Works; 41(br), Arthur Grace/Stock Boston; 42(bl), Rich Vogel/Leo de Wys Inc.; 43(t), 43(b), David R. Frazier Photolibrary; 45 (tl), Lawrence Migdale/Stock Boston; 45 (tr), Richard Hutchings/Photo Researchers; 46(br), HRW Photo by Daniel Schaefer; 47(b), Spencer Grant/Stock Boston; 49(tr), ©Ralph Barrera/TexaStock; 49(c), Laima Druskis/Stock Boston; 49(br), Jim Pickerell/Stock Boston; 50(tr), Mitzi Trumbo/Shooting Star; 50(cr), Kobal Collection/SuperStock; 50(br), Warner Bros./Shooting Star; 51(l), Richard Hutchings/PhotoEdit; 51(r), HRW Photo by Kevin Vandivier.

CHAPTER 3: Page 52(c), HBJ Photo by Sam Joosten; 52(bl), HRW Photo by Russel Dian; 55, Gregg Mancuso/Tony Stone Worldwide, Ltd.; 57(l), HRW Photo by Lee Boltin; 57(c), 57(r), HRW Photo by Ken Karp; 57(b), HRW Photo by Russell Dian; 63, Nathan Benn/Stock Boston; 65, Barbara Davis/University of Texas Speech Dept.; 66, Michael Beasley/Tony Stone Worldwide; 67, Charles Gupton/Stock Boston; 68, Shooting Star; 69, Gerald Brimacombe/The Image Bank; 73(tl), ©David Kennedy/TexaStock; 73(tr), Colin Molyneaux/The Image Bank; 73(b), Alvis Upitis/The Image Bank; 74, HRW Photo by Daniel Schaefer; 75, Richard Hutchings/Photo Researchers, Inc.; 77(l), HRW Photo by Daniel Schaefer; 79(l), HRW Photo by Daniel Schaefer; 79(r), Owen Franken/Stock Boston; 80(tr), HRW Photo by William Hubbell;

CHAPTER 4: Page 80(tr), HRW Photo by William Hubbell; 80(c), ©Michael D. Sullivan/TexaStock; 80(bl), HRW Photo by Russell Dian; 80(br), HRW Photo by Michelle Bridwell; 82, Michael Newman/PhotoEdit; 83, Michael Weisbrot & Family/Stock Boston; 86, Loren Santon/Stony Stone Worldwide; 89(t), Tony Freeman/PhotoEdit; 90, James Sugar/Black Star; 93(t), Brian Vikander/West Light; 94, Bettmann Archives; 97, Jeffry Myers/FPG International; 99, ©David Kennedy/TexaStock; 100, HRW Photo by Britt Runion; 101, Ron Sherman/Stock Boston; 105(l), Mary Kate Kennedy/PhotoEdit; 105(r), Daemmrich/Stock Boston.

UNIT 2 OPENER: Page 106(tl), Ulfike Welsch; 106(tr), HRW Photo by B. Hamill; 106·107(bkgrd), Donald Johnson/Stock Market; 106–107(frgrd), Joseph Nettis/Photo Researchers; 107(t), Tom Campbell/FPG International; 107(c), Daemmrich/The Image Works.

CHAPTER 5: Page 108(bl), HBJ Photo by Rodney Jones; 108(c) HRW Photo by Daniel Schaefer; 108(tr) HRW Photo by Michelle Bridwell; 108(br), George Obremski/The Image Bank; 109, HRW Photo by Daniel Schaefer; 110, Richard Hutchings/PhotoEdit; 112, Rhoda Sidney/PhotoEdit; 114, Daemmrich/Stock Boston; 116, Tony Freeman/PhotoEdit; 122, Tony Freeman/PhotoEdit; 125, Bob Daemmrich/Tony Stone Worldwide; 128, Matt Meadows; 129, David Young-Wolff/PhotoEdit; 131, Michael Newman/PhotoEdit; 132, HRW Photo by Daniel Schaefer; 133, L.O.L./FPG International; 137(l), Rick Friedman/Black Star; 137(r), Charles Gupton/Stock Boston.

CHAPTER 6: Page 138(c), Richard Hutchings/PhotoEdit; 138(r), HRW Photo by Michelle Bridwell; 138(b), Chris Michaels/FPG International; 140, Tony Stone Worldwide; 142, Bob Daemmrich/Stock Boston; 144, Richard Hutchings/PhotoEdit; 146, Brent Jones/Stock Boston; 152, HRW Photo by Daniel Schaefer; 153, Mary Kate Denny/PhotoEdit; 155(t), Richard Hutchings/PhotoEdit; (b), Rhoda Sidney/PhotoEdit; 157(l), Blair Seitz/Photo Researchers; 157(r), Frank Siteman/Stock Boston.

CHAPTER 7: Page 158(bl), HRW Photo by Eric Beggs; 158(b), FPG International; 161, Mark Antman/The Image Works Archives; 163, David R. Frazier Photolibrary; 165, Mark Antman/Image Works; 166, Margot Granitsas/Image Works; 170, John Elk III/Stock Boston; 171, Ken Lax; 173, Comstock; 175, HRW Photo by Russell Dian; 180, HRW Photo by Daniel Schaefer; 181, Jeff Isaac Greenberg/Photo Researchers; 184(tl) Doug Wilson/The Stock Solution; 184(bl) Spencer Grant/Photo Researchers; 185(l), HRW Photo by Daniel Schaefer; 185(r), HRW Photo by Michelle Bridwell.

CHAPTER 8: Page 186(tl), HRW Photo; 186(c), HRW Photo by Michelle Bridwell; 190, Tony Freeman/PhotoEdit; 191, Richard Pasley/Stock Boston; 192, Jeffrey Sylvester/FPG International; 194, Elizabeth Crews/The Image Bank; 198, P.R. Production/Superstock; 200, Tony Freeman/PhotoEdit; 205, Bonnie Kamin/Comstock; 206, HBJ Photo by Britt Runion; 207(l), Daemmrich/Stock Boston; 207(r), Robert E. Daemmrich/Tony Stone Worldwide; 209 (t), Daemmrich/Stock Boston; 209(b), Al Satterwhite/Image Bank; 211(l), Elena Roorid/PhotoEdit; 211(r), Jim Pickerell/Stock Boston.

UNIT 3 OPENER: Page 212–213(frgrd), Gabe Palmer/The Stock Market; 212(t), Richard Hutchings/PhotoEdit; 212(b), Richard Hutchings/PhotoEdit; 213(t), David R. Frazier Photolibrary; 213(b), ©Sullivan/TexaStock.

CHAPTER 9: Page 214(tl), HRW Photo by Lisa Davis; 214(c), HRW Photo by Richard Hutchings; 214(bl), Telegraph Colour Library/FPG International; 216, Rivera Collection/Superstock; 220(tl), Gallery/Stock Boston; 220(tr), ©Smiley/TexaStock; 220(b), David Young-Wolff/PhotoEdit; 227, Bob Daemmrich/Stock Boston; 228(b), Kobal Collection/Superstock.; 229, HRW Photo by Michelle Bridwell; 230, Rick Stewart/Allsport USA; 231, Albe Normandin/The Image Bank; 234, HBJ Photo by Jerry White; 235, David R. Frazier Photolibrary; 237(t), David Young-Wolff/PhotoEdit; 237(c), Tony Freeman/PhotoEdit; 237(b) Daemmrich/The Image Works; 239(r), Rhoda Sidney/Stock Boston; 239(l), Comstock;

CHAPTER 10: Page 240(cl), HRW Photo by Russell Dian; 240(c), Charles Gupton/Tony Stone Worldwide; 240(bl), HRW Photo by Eric Beggs; 240(br), HRW Photo by Rodney Jones; 241, HRW Photo by Russell Dian; 242, Tony Freeman/PhotoEdit; 246, Marc Pokempner/Tony Stone Worldwide; 248, Richard Pasley/Stock Boston; 250(t), Elena Rooraid/PhotoEdit; 252(t), David Young-Wolff/PhotoEdit; 252(b), HRW Photo by Daniel Schaefer; 254, Derek Smith Photo/The Image Bank; 255(l), Dave Schaefer/PhotoEdit; 255(r), Daemmrich/Image Works; 258, HRW Photo by Britt Runion; 259, Michael Melford/Image Bank; 263(l), Tony Freeman/PhotoEdit; 263(r), David R. Frazier Photolibrary.

CHAPTER 11: Page 264(br), mga/Photri Inc.; 264(c), Ken Lax; 270, Steve Kirwan; 271, Tony Freeman/PhotoEdit; 273(l), Thomas R. Fletcher/Stock Boston; 273(c), 273(r), HRW Photo by Daniel Schaefer; 279, Rhoda Sidney/Stock Boston; 282, HRW Photo by Daniel Schaefer; 283(l), Dion Ogust/The Image Works; 283(r), Steve Kirwan; 285(tl), Robert Brenner/PhotoEdit; 285(tr), Superstock; 285(bl), Jack Fields/Photo Researchers; 287(l), Tony Freeman/PhotoEdit; 287(r), Ron Chapple/FPG International.

CHAPTER 12: Page 288(tl), HRW Photo by Russell Dian; 288(c), Ken Lax; 288(br), HRW Photo by Robert Fishman; 288(bkgrd l), M.C. Escher's work METAMORPHOSE III/Cordon Art; 290, Photo Edit; 298, David R. Frazier Photolibrary; 302, Dorothy Littell/Image Works; 304(l), David Pratt/Positive Images; 304(c), Ellis Herwig/Picture Cube; 304(r), Joseph Nettis/Photo Researchers; 306, Dennis Purse/Photo Researchers; 310, HRW Photo by Daniel Schaefer; 311, Alan Oddie/PhotoEdit; 313, HRW Photo; 315(l), HBJ Photo by Sam Joosten; 315(r), Will McIntyre/Photo Researchers.

CHAPTER 13: Page 316(tl), HRW Photo by Russell Dian; 316(bl), HRW Photo by Eric Beggs; 316(c) HRW Photo by Michelle Bridwell; 318(t), Brian Seed/Tony Stone Worldwide; 318(b), Larry Kolvoord/TexaStock; 319(t), HRW Photo by Michelle Bridwell, 319(b), Frank Pedrick/The Image Works, 320, Bob Daemmrich/Stock Boston, 326, HRW Photo by Jeff Rowe, 327, Superstock, 329. Skip Barron/Comstock, 332, Ron Sherman/Stock Boston; 333, Candace Cochrane/Positive Images; 334(t) ©Smiley/TexaStock; 334(b), Robert Daemmrich/The Image Works; 336, HRW Photo by Yoav Levy; 337, David R. Frazier Photolibrary; 341, HRW Photo by Michelle Bridwell; 342, Jeffry Myers/FPG International; 343(l), Culver Pictures, Inc.; 343(r), UPI/Bettman; 346, HRW Photo by Michelle Bridwell; 347, HRW Photo by Michelle Bridwell; 349(t), Robert Houser/Comstock; 349(c) Terry Farmer/Tony Stone Worldwide; 349(b), ©Boroff/TexaStock; 351(r), Robert Daemmrich/Stock Boston; 351(r), Rivera Collection/Superstock.

UNIT 4 OPENER: Page 352(tr), Sarah Putman/The Picture Cube; 352(c), Aneal Vohra/Unicorn Stock Photos; 352(b), HRW Photo by Russell Dian; 352·353(bkgrd), ©Jane Stader/TexaStock; 353(frgrd), Don Carl Steffen/Photo Researchers; 353(t), Jonathan A. Meyers.

CHAPTER 14: Page 354(t), HRW Photo; 354(c), Rhoda Sidney/PhotoEdit; 354(br), HRW Photo by Richard Haynes; 357, The Telegraph Colour Library/FPG International; 358, HRW Photos by John Langford; 360, HRW Photo by Michelle Bridwell; 361(b), Iooss Jr. Inc./The Image Bank; 365, Jay Brousseau/The Image Bank; 370, Rivera Collection/Superstock; 373, John Turner/FPG International; 376, Michael Lyon; 377, Billy E. Barnes/FPG International; 379(tr), John Terence Turner/FPG International; 379(c), HRW Photo by Kevin Vandivier; 379(bl), Stuart Cohen/Comstock; 381(l), HRW Photo by Kevin Vandivier; 381(r), Bob Daemmrich/The Image Works.

CHAPTER 15: Page 382(c), Robert E. Daemmrich/Tony Stone Worldwide; 383, HRW Photo by Russell Dian; 391, Ken Lax; 392, Bob Daemmrich/Stock Boston; 393, R. Llewellyn/J. Barnell/Superstock; 394, Superstock; 395, Bettye Lane/Photo Researchers; 397, Daemmrich/Stock Boston; 398, HRW Photo by Michelle Bridwell; 399, David Pratt/Positive Images; 402, Bob Daemmrich/Stock Boston; 404, Richard Pasley/Stock Boston; 406, Frank Siteman/Stock Boston; 407, Michael Krasowitz/FPG International; 408, Shelley Boyd/Yellow Dog Photo; 410, HBJ Photo by Britt Runion; 411, Bob Daemmrich/Stock Boston; 413, Texas Department of Transportation; 415(l), Richard Hutchings/Photo Researchers; 415(r), P.R. Production/Superstock.

CHAPTER 16: Page 416(tl), Hank Delespinasse/The Image Bank; 416(c), Tony Freeman/PhotoEdit; 416(bl), Stock Editions/HRW Photo; 416(br), Mike Wilson/FPG International; 417, Terry Farmer/Tony Stone Worldwide; 419, Rhoda Sidney/The Image Works; 421, Bob Daemmrich/Stock Boston; 423(t), Tom Owen Edmunds/The Image Bank; 423(c), Cameramann Int'l., Ltd.; 423(l), David Young-Wolff/PhotoEdit; 423(b), HRW Photo by Mark Antman; 427, Rene Sheret/Tony Stone Worldwide; 428, Kennedy/TexaStock; 430, HRW Photo by Stephanie Maze; 431, Joaquin Villegas/Black Star; 432, Halstead/Gamma Liaison; 433, Michael Newman/PhotoEdit; 436, Bob Daemmrich/Stock Boston; 438, Bob Daemmrich/Tony Stone Worldwide; 440, HRW Photo by Daniel Schaefer; 441, Tony Freeman/PhotoEdit; 443, B. King/Gamma Liaison; 444, Michael Grecco/Stock Boston; 445(l); Bob Daemmrich/Stock Boston; 445(r), Gilles Peress/Magnum Photo.

UNIT 5 OPENER: Page 446·447(bkgrd), Cameron Davidson/Comstock; 446(tr), Charles Gupton/Tony Stone Worldwide; 446(c), Stephan Whalen/Zephyr Pictures; 446(frgrd), Robert E. Daemmrich/Tony Stone Worldwide; 447(tr), Daemmrich/Tony Stone Worldwide; 447(frgrd), Robert E. Daemmrich/Tony Stone Worldwide.

CHAPTER 17: Page 448(tr), Farrell Grehau/FPG International; 448(c), Robert E. Daemmrich; 448(bl), Telegraph Colour Library/FPG International; 448(br), Gary Buss/FPG International; 449, Comstock; 450, Daemmrich/The Image Works; 451, ©Larry Kolvoord/TexaStock; 456, Daemmrich/The Image Works; 458, Mike Maas/The Image Bank; 459, Spencer Grant/FPG International; 461, Sven Martson/Comstock; 462, Daemmrich/The Image Works; 464, Ron Chapple/FPG International; 466, Ron Rovtar/FPG International; 469(t), ©Kennedy/TexaStock; 472, HBJ Photo by Britt Runion; 473, Richard Pasley/Stock Boston; 475(r), Terry Farmer/TSW-Click Chicago; 477(l), Robert E. Daemmrich/Tony Stone Worldwide; 477(r), Jeffry Myers/FPG International.

CHAPTER 18: Page 478(t), Ron Rovtar/FPG International; 478(c), HRW Photo by Michelle Bridwell; 478(b), Comstock; 480, Daemmrich/The Image Works; 483, Billy E. Barnes/Stock Boston; 485, Rick Friedman/Black Star; 486, Myron Davis/Nawrocki Stock Photo; 488, Barrera/TexaStock; 494, Richard Hutchings/PhotoEdit; 496, Tony Freeman/PhotoEdit; 500, Ken Lax; 504, Rick Friedman/Black Star; 511, ©David E. Kennedy/TexaStock; 512, David Koelsch; 513, Mary Kate Denny/PhotoEdit; 515(t), UPI/Bettmann; 515(b), Reuters/Bettmann; 517(l), ©Kennedy/TexaStock; 517(r), ©Michael Lyon TexaStock.

CHAPTER 19: Page 518(tl), Comstock; 518(cl), D. Hallinan/FPG International; 518(c), United Nations/FPG International; 518(br), Photri, Inc.; 519, mga/PHOTRI; 521, The Bridgeman Art Library; 524, Billy E. Barnes/Stock Boston; 525, Kenneth Garrett/FPG International; 527, Jim Pickrell/Stock Boston; 529, Bob Daemmrich/Stock Boston; 531, David R. Frazier Photolibrary; 536, Ellis Helmes/Picture Cube; 539, P.R. Production/Superstock; 541(b), Jack Spratt/The Image Bank; 542, ©Mike Boroff/TexaStock; 544, HRW Photo Daniel Schaefer; 545, Bob Daemmrich; 547, The Bettmann Archive; 549(l), Robert E. Daemmrich/Tony Stone Worldwide; 549(r), ©Larry Kolvoord/TexaStock.

UNIT 6 OPENER: Page 550(tr), Bachmann/The Stock Solution; 550(b), HRW Photo by Richard Haynes; 550(l), HRW Photo by Russell Dian; 551(tr), HRW Photo by Henry Friedman; 551(b), HRW Photo by Daniel Schaefer.

CHAPTER 20: Page 552(c), Paul Merideth/Tony Stone Worldwide; 552(bl), HRW Photo by Russell Dian; 561, ©Jane Stader/TexaStock; 564, Steve Kirwan; 567(t), HRW Photo by Michelle Bridwell; 570, Myrleen Ferguson/PhotoEdit; 574, Robert Shafer/Tony Stone Worldwide, Ltd.; 575, Martha Swope Photography; 577, Michael Newman/PhotoEdit; 580, Terry Eiler/Stock Boston; 582, Paul Conklin; 583, Deni Mcintyre/Photo Researchers; 585(t), HRW Photo by Daniel Schaefer; 585(b), David R. Frazier Photolibrary; 587(l), Richard Hutchings/PhotoEdit; 587(r), Tom Carroll/FPG International.

CHAPTER 21: Page 588(t), HRW Photo by Daniel Schaefer; 588(cl), Gregory Heisler/The Image Bank; 588(bl), HRW Photo by Russell Dian; 588(c), HBJ Photo by Earl Kogler; 589, Garry Gay/The Image Bank; 590, S. Violer/Superstock; 591, Tony Freeman/PhotoEdit; 592, Globe Playhouse (c. 1599·1613). C. Walter Hodges; 593, Martha Swope; 594, Catherine Ursillo/Photo Researchers; 596, Lewis & Clark CC. IL/Stock Boston; 597, Richard Termine/Cleveland Play House/Actors: Carmen Thomas, Howard Taylor, Sarah Burke, Helen Gresser, Douglas Simes, Dudley Swetland, Sharon Bicknell, and Tom Lile; 598, Visual Images West; 605(all), Museum of The City of New York, The Theater Collection; 606, Bob Daemmrich/Stock Boston; 608(l), HRW Photo by Russell Dian; 608(r), Richard Hutchings/Photo Researchers; 610, Bachmann/PhotoEdit; 612, Will McIntyre/Photo Researchers; 614,(all), Photo World/FPG International; 616(all), HRW Photo by Richard Haynes; 617, Catherine Noren; 618, Laura Elliott/Comstock; 619, Freeman/Grishaber/PhotoEdit; 620, Jerry Howard/Positive Images; 622, HRW Photo by Daniel Schaefer; 623, Tony Freeman/PhotoEdit; 625(t), Blair Seitz/Photo Researchers; 625(c), Echlin/Image Bank; 625(b), Robert Daemmrich/Tony Stone Worldwide; 627(l), Donnie Beauchamp/Fiesta Texas; 627(r), Robert E. Daemmrich/TSW-Click Chicago.

CHAPTER 22: Page 628(tl), Stock Editions/HRW Photo; 628(c), Elizabeth Crews/The Image Works; 628(bl), HRW Photo by Michelle Bridwell; 628(br), Hans Wolf/The Image Bank; 629, ©Sullivan/TexaStock; 631, Mark Segal/Tony Stone Worldwide; 632, Paul Light/Lightwave; 633, David Joe/Tony Stone Worldwide; 634, Hank Morgan/Science Source/Photo Researchers; 635, UPI/Bettmann Newsphotos; 638, ©Sullivan/TexaStock; 640, The Bettmann Archive; 642, The Bettmann Archive; 646, Robert Brenner/PhotoEdit; 648, Lucas Films, Ltd.; 652, HRW Photo by Lueders Studio; 653, Ken Lax; 657(l), Michael Lyon; 657(r), Kay Chernush/The Image Bank.

ILLUSTRATION CREDITS

Brent Buford: 225, 340b

Holly Coooper: 127, 197, 385, 532, 556, 557, 559, 562, 563, 571, 572, 594

Susan Kenmitz: 33

Precision Graphics: 183

Joan Rivers: 4, 24, 31, 54, 56, 62, 68, 77, 91, 119, 124, 148, 167, 168, 203, 217, 222, 228, 232, 243, 247, 249, 256, 261, 226, 268, 269, 275, 280, 295, 322, 338tl, 338tr, 339, 367, 387, 388, 389, 401, 425, 435, 438, 455, 475, 476, 492, 493, 502, 523, 538, 540, 601, 602, 604, 609, 611, 630, 649

Jane Thurmond: Unit Opener, Chapter Opener and Special Feature design and illustrations; also illustrations on iv, v, ix, x, xi, xii, xvi, xviii, ixx, xx, 53, 81, 159, 187, 215, 265, 289, 293, 317, 338b, 340t, 355, 361, 417, 479, 553, 629

DATE DUE

NOV 18 1998			
DEC 30 1998			
DEC 03 1999			
OCT 25 2004			